BR-BX

Christianity. Bible

Library of Congress Classification
2008

Prepared by the Cataloging Policy and Support Office
Library Services

LIBRARY OF CONGRESS
Cataloging Distribution Service
Washington, D.C.

This edition cumulates all additions and changes to subclasses BR-BX through Weekly List 2008/21, dated May 21, 2008. Additions and changes made subsequent to that date are published in weekly lists posted on the World Wide Web at

<http://www.loc.gov/aba/cataloging/classification/weeklylists/>

and are also available in *Classification Web*, the online Web-based edition of the Library of Congress Classification.

Library of Congress Cataloging-in-Publication Data

Library of Congress.
Library of Congress classification. BR-BX. Christianity. Bible / prepared by the Cataloging Policy and Support Office, Library Services. — 2008 ed.
p. cm.
"This edition cumulates all additions and changes to subclasses BR-BX through Weekly List 2008/21, dated May 21, 2008. Additions and changes made subsequent to that date are published in weekly lists posted on the World Wide Web at <http://www.loc.gov/aba/cataloging/classification/weeklylists/> and are also available in *Classification Web*, the online Web-based edition of the Library of Congress classification." — T.p. verso.
Includes index.
ISBN-13: 978-0-8444-1219-1
ISBN-10: 0-8444-1219-8
1. Classification, Library of Congress. 2. Classification—Books—Christianity. 3. Classification—Books—Bible. I. Library of Congress. Cataloging Policy and Support Office. II. Title. III. Title: Christianity. IV. Title: Bible.
Z696.U5B7 2008 025.4'623—dc22 2008025432

For sale by the Library of Congress Cataloging Distribution Service,
101 Independence Avenue, S.E., Washington, DC 20541-4912.
Product catalog available on the Web at **www.loc.gov/cds**.

PREFACE

The first edition of subclasses BR-BX, *Christianity. Bible*, was published in 1927 in a volume that also included subclasses BL-BQ. The second edition was published in 1962 in the same configuration. Third editions of subclasses BR-BV and subclass BX were published in two separate volumes in 1987 and 1985, respectively. For the 2000 edition, BR-BV and BX were reunited in a single volume. This 2008 edition cumulates additions and changes made since the publication of the 2000 edition.

In the Library of Congress Classification schedules, classification numbers or spans of numbers that appear in parentheses are formerly valid numbers that are now obsolete. Numbers or spans that appear in angle brackets are optional numbers that have never been used at the Library of Congress but are provided for other libraries that wish to use them. In most cases, a parenthesized or angle-bracketed number is accompanied by a "see" reference directing the user to the actual number that the Library of Congress currently uses, or a note explaining Library of Congress practice.

Access to the online version of the full Library of Congress Classification is available on the World Wide Web by subscription to *Classification Web*. Details about ordering and pricing may be obtained from the Cataloging Distribution Service at:

<http://www.loc.gov/cds/>

New or revised numbers and captions are added to the L.C. Classification schedules as a result of development proposals made by the cataloging staff of the Library of Congress and cooperating institutions. Upon approval of these proposals by the weekly editorial meeting of the Cataloging Policy and Support Office, new classification records are created or existing records are revised in the master classification database. Weekly lists of newly approved or revised classification numbers and captions are posted on the World Wide Web at:

<http://www.loc.gov/aba/cataloging/classification/weeklylists/>

Milicent Wewerka, senior subject cataloging policy specialist in the Cataloging Policy and Support Office, is responsible for coordinating the overall intellectual and editorial content of subclasses BR-BX. Kent Griffiths, assistant editor of classification schedules, is responsible for creating new classification records, maintaining the master database, and creating index terms for the captions.

Barbara B. Tillett, Chief
Cataloging Policy and Support Office

June 2008

OUTLINE

BR1-1725	Christianity
BR60-67	Early Christian literature. Fathers of the Church, etc.
BR115	Christianity in relation to special subjects
BR130-133.5	Christian antiquities. Archaeology. Museums
BR140-1510	History
BR160-481	By period
BR160-275	Early and medieval
BR280	Renaissance. Renaissance and Reformation
BR290-481	Modern period
BR323.5-334.2	Luther, Martin
BR500-1510	By region or country
BR1600-1609	Persecution. Martyrs
BR1609.5	Dissent
BR1610	Tolerance and toleration
BR1615-1617	Liberalism
BR1620	Sacrilege (History)
BR1690-1725	Biography
BS1-2970	The Bible
BS11-115	Early versions
BS125-355	Modern texts and versions
BS125-198	English
BS199-313	Other European languages
BS315-355	Non-European languages
BS315	Asian languages
BS325	African languages
BS335	Languages of Oceania and Australasia
BS345	American Indian languages
BS350	Mixed languages
BS355	Artificial languages
BS410-680	Works about the Bible
BS500-534.8	Criticism and interpretation
BS535-537	The Bible as literature
BS546-558	Bible stories. Paraphrases of Bible stories. The Bible story
BS569-580	Men, women, and children of the Bible
BS580	Individual Old Testament characters
BS585-613	Study and teaching
BS647-649	Prophecy
BS650-667	Bible and science
BS670-672	Bible and social sciences
BS701-1830	Old Testament
BS705-815	Early versions

OUTLINE

	The Bible
	Old Testament - Continued
BS825-1013	Modern texts and versions
BS1091-1099	Selections. Quotations
BS1110-1199	Works about the Old Testament
BS1160-1191.5	Criticism and interpretation
BS1200-1830	Special parts of the Old Testament
BS1901-2970	New Testament
BS1937-2020	Early texts and versions
BS2025-2213	Modern texts and versions
BS2260-2269	Selections. Quotations
BS2280-2545	Works about the New Testament
BS2350-2393	Criticism and interpretation
BS2415-2417	The teachings of Jesus
BS2430-2520	Men, women, and children of the New Testament
BS2525-2544	Study and teaching
BS2547-2970	Special parts of the New Testament
BS2640-2765.6	Epistles of Paul
BT10-1480	Doctrinal Theology
BT19-37	Doctrine and dogma
BT93-93.6	Judaism
BT95-97.2	Divine law. Moral government
BT98-180	God
BT109-115	Doctrine of the Trinity
BT117-123	Holy Spirit. The Paraclete
BT126-127.5	Revelation
BT130-153	Divine attributes
BT198-590	Christology
BT296-500	Life of Christ
BT580	Miracles. Apparitions. Shrines, sanctuaries, images, processions, etc.
BT587	Relics
BT595-680	Mary, Mother of Jesus Christ. Mariology
BT650-660	Miracles. Apparitions. Shrines, sanctuaries, images, processions, etc.
BT695-749	Creation
BT750-811	Salvation. Soteriology
BT819-891	Eschatology. Last things
BT899-940	Future state. Future life
BT960-985	Invisible world (saints, demons, etc.)
BT990-1010	Creeds, confessions, covenants, etc.
BT1029-1040	Catechisms

	Doctrinal Theology - Continued
BT1095-1255	Apologetics. Evidences of Christianity
BT1313-1480	History of specific doctrines and movements. Heresies and schisms
BV1-5099	Practical Theology
BV5-530	Worship (Public and private)
BV30-135	Times and seasons. The Church year
BV43-64	Feast days
BV65-70	Saints' days
BV80-105	Fasts
BV107-133	Lord's Day. Sunday. Sabbath
BV150-168	Christian symbols and symbolism
BV169-199	Liturgy and ritual
BV200	Family worship
BV205-287	Prayer
BV301-530	Hymnology
BV360-465	Denominational and special types of hymnbooks in English
BV467-510	Hymns in languages other than English
BV590-1652	Ecclesiastical theology
BV598-603	The Church
BV629-631	Church and state
BV637-637.5	City churches
BV638-638.8	The rural church. The church and country life
BV646-651	Church polity
BV652-652.9	Church management. Efficiency
BV652.95-657	Mass media and telecommunication in religion
BV659-683	Ministry. Clergy. Religious vocations
BV700-707	Parish. Congregation. The local church
BV770-777	Church finance. Church property
BV800-873	Sacraments. Ordinances
BV803-814	Baptism
BV823-828	Holy Communion. Lord's Supper. Eucharist
BV835-838	Marriage
BV840-850	Penance
BV895-896	Shrines. Holy places
BV900-1450	Religious societies, associations, etc.
BV950-1280	Religious societies of men, brotherhoods, etc.
BV1000-1220	Young Men's Christian Associations
BV1300-1395	Religious societies of women
BV1300-1393	Young Women's Christian Associations
BV1460-1615	Religious education (General)

OUTLINE

	Practical Theology
	Ecclesiastical theology - Continued
BV1620-1652	Social life, recreation, etc., in the church
BV2000-3705	Missions
BV2123-2595	Special churches
BV2130-2300	Roman Catholic Church
BV2350-2595	Protestant churches
BV2610-2695	Special types of missions
BV2750-3695	Missions in individual countries
BV3750-3799	Evangelism. Revivals
BV4000-4470	Pastoral theology
BV4019-4180	Education
BV4019-4167	Training for the ordained ministry
BV4168-4180	Training for lay workers
BV4200-4317	Preaching. Homiletics
BV4239-4317	Sermons
BV4390-4399	Personal life of the clergy
BV4400-4470	Practical church work. Social work. Work of the layman
BV4485-5099	Practical religion. The Christian life
BV4520-4526.2	Religious duties
BV4625-4780	Moral theology
BV4625-4627	Sins and vices
BV4630-4647	Virtues
BV4650-4715	Precepts from the Bible
BV4720-4780	Precepts of the Church. Commandments of the Church
BV4800-4897	Works of meditation and devotion
BV4900-4911	Works of consolation and cheer
BV4912-4950	Conversion literature
BV5015-5068	Asceticism
BV5070-5095	Mysticism
BV5099	Quietism
BX1-9999	Christian Denominations
BX1-9.5	Church unity. Ecumenical movement. Interdenominational cooperation
BX100-189	Eastern churches. Oriental churches
BX100-107	General
BX120-129	Armenian Church
BX130-139	Coptic Church
BX140-149	Ethiopic or Abyssinian Church
BX150-159	Nestorian, Chaldean, or East Syrian Church
BX160-169	St. Thomas Christians. Malabar Christians. Mar Thoma Syrian Church

OUTLINE

Christian Denominations
Protestantism
Church of England - Continued

BX5133	Sermons. Tracts. Addresses. Essays
BX5135-5136	Controversial works
BX5137-5139	Creeds and catechisms, etc.
BX5140.5-5147	Liturgy and ritual
BX5148-5149	Sacraments
BX5150-5182.5	Government. Organization. Discipline
BX5183-5187	Religious communities. Conventual life. Religious societies
BX5194-5195	Cathedrals, churches, etc. in England and Wales
BX5197-5199	Biography
BX5200-5207	Dissent and nonconformity
BX5210-5395	Episcopal Church in Scotland
BX5410-5595	Church of Ireland
BX5596-5598	Church in Wales
BX5600-5740	Church of England outside of Great Britain
BX5601-5620	Anglican Church of Canada
BX5800-5995	Protestant Episcopal Church in the United States of America
BX5996-6030	Protestant Episcopal Church outside the United States
BX6051-6093	Reformed Episcopal Church
BX6101-9999	Other Protestant denominations Alphabetical; only larger denominations listed The subarrangement is essentially the same for each sect, the primary features being indicated by way of example under Baptists
BX6101-6193	Adventists. "Millerites"
BX6195-6197	Arminians. Remonstrants
BX6201-6495	Baptists
BX6201-6227	General
BX6231-6328	History. Local divisions
BX6329	Baptists and other churches
BX6330-6331.2	Doctrine
BX6333	Sermons. Tracts
BX6334	Controversial works
BX6335-6336	Creeds. Catechisms
BX6337	Service. Ritual. Liturgy
BX6338-6339	Sacraments
BX6340-6346.3	Government. Discipline
BX6349-6470	Individual branches

OUTLINE

Christian Denominations

Protestantism

Other Protestant denominations - Continued

BX9675	River Brethren. Brethren in Christ
BX9701-9743	Salvation Army
BX9751-9793	Shakers. United Society of Believers. Millennial Church
BX9801-9869	Unitarianism
BX9875-9877.1	United Brethren in Christ. Church of the United Brethren in Christ
BX9881-9882.95	United Church of Canada
BX9884-9886	United Church of Christ
BX9887	United Evangelical Church
BX9889	United Missionary Church
BX9901-9969	Unviersalism. Universalists
BX9975	Volunteers of America
BX9980	Walloon Church
BX9998	Other beliefs and movements akin to Christianity
BX9999	Independent churches, parishes, societies, etc.

Christianity
Periodicals. Serials
1.A1 International or polyglot
1.A2-Z English and American
2 Dutch
3 French
4 German
5 Italian
6 Scandinavian
7 Spanish and Portuguese
9.A-Z Other, A-Z
e.g.
9.F5 Finnish
9.R9 Russian
(10) Yearbooks
see BR1+
Societies
21.A1 International or polyglot
21.A2-Z English and American
22 Dutch
23 French
24 German
25 Italian
26 Scandinavian
27 Spanish and Portuguese
29.A-Z Other, A-Z
e.g.
29.F5 Finnish
29.R9 Russian
33 Institutions. Trusts
e.g. Hibbert Trust (and biography of Robert Hibbert)
Congresses. Conferences
For interdenominational conferences see BX2+
41 General works
43 Organization, methods, etc.
44 Religious writing
Collected works
General
45 Two or more volumes
50 Single volumes. Festschriften
53 Selections (Several authors)
55 Pamphlet collections

Collected works -- Continued

Early Christian literature. Fathers of the Church, etc.

For special subjects see the subject

For linguistic studies of early Greek Fathers, see PA895 or PA3818+

For linguistic studies of early Latin Fathers, see PA2310 or PA6202+

Cf. B630+ Early Christian philosophy

Cf. BR160+ Early church history

Cf. BR1603.A1 Early martyr accounts

Cf. BS2831+ Apocryphal books of the New Testament

60 Collections of several authors

Apostolic Fathers

60.A6 Greek texts. By date

60.A61 Latin translations. By date

60.A62 English translations. By date

60.A63 German translations. By date

60.A64 Other translations (not A-Z). By date

60.A65 History and criticism

62 Minor collections. Letters, papyri, etc.

63 Selections of several authors. Excerpts

65.A-Z Individual authors

Subarrange each author by Table BR1 unless otherwise specified

For biography see BR1720.A+

65.A31-.A316 Ambrose, Saint, Bishop of Milan, d. 397 (Table BR1)

65.A44-.A446 Athanasius, Saint, Patriarch of Alexandria (Table BR1)

Augustine, Saint, Bishop of Hippo

Collected works

65.A5 Latin. By date

65.A5A-.A5Z Other languages, A-Z

Selected works

65.A52 Latin. By date

65.A52A-.A52Z Other languages, A-Z

65.A54-.A88 Separate works. By title

65.A557-.A5572 Adversus Iudaeos (Table BR3)

65.A6-.A62 Confessions (Table BR3)

65.A633-.A634 Contra secundum Iuliani responsionem, operis imperfecti ... (Table BR4)

65.A635-.A636 De beata vita (Table BR4)

65.A6365-.A63652 De bono conjugali (Table BR3)

65.A637-.A638 De catechizandis rudibus (Table BR4)

65.A64-.A65 De civitate Dei (Table BR4)

65.A6544-.A65442 De diversis quaestionibus (Table BR3)

65.A655-.A6552 De doctrina Christiana (Table BR3)

65.A656-.A6562 De excidio urbis Romae (Table BR3)

65.A6567-.A65672 De fide et operibus (Table BR3)

Collected works
Early Christian literature. Fathers of the Church, etc.
Individual authors
Augustine, Saint, Bishop of Hippo
Separate works. By title -- Continued

65.A657-.A658 De fide rerum ... (Table BR4)
65.A659-.A6592 De haeresibus (Table BR3)
65.A66-.A662 De immortalitate animae (Table BR3)
65.A664-.A665 De libero arbitrio (Table BR4)
65.A67-.A672 De magistro (Table BR3)
65.A676-.A6762 De mendacio (Table BR3)
65.A68-.A682 De moralibus ecclesiae Catholicae et Manichaeorum (Table BR3)
65.A685-.A6852 De natura et origine animae (Table BR3)
65.A69-.A692 De ordine (Table BR3)
65.A695-.A696 De praedestinatione sanctorum (Table BR4)
65.A6975-.A69752 De Trinitate (Table BR3)
65.A698-.A6982 De utilitate credendi (Table BR3)
65.A7-.A72 De utilitate ieiunii (Table BR3)
65.A726-.A7262 De vera religione (Table BR3)
65.A728-.A7282 Enarrationes in Psalmos (Table BR3)
65.A73-.A74 Enchiridion (Table BR4)
65.A78-.A79 Epistolae (Letters) (Table BR4)
65.A792-.A7922 Expositio epistulae ad Galatas (Table BR3)
65.A793-.A7932 Expositio quarandam propositionum ex Epistola ad Romanos (Table BR3)
Regula see BX2904.A2
65.A84-.A85 Sermons (Table BR4)
65.A867-.A8672 Societa e ideologie (Table BR3)
65.A87-.A88 Soliloquia (Table BR4)
65.A89A-.A89Z Spurious and doubtful works. By title, A-Z
65.A89S4 Sermons
65.A9 Criticism

Basil, Saint, Bishop of Caesarea, ca. 329-379
Collected works
65.B3 Latin. By date.
65.B3A-.B3Z Other languages, A-Z
Selected works
65.B32 Latin. By date
65.B33A-.B33Z Other languages, A-Z
65.B34A-.B34Z Separate works. By title, A-Z
65.B35A-.B35Z Spurious and doubtful works. By title, A-Z
65.B36 Criticism

John Chrysostom, Saint, d. 407.
Collected works
65.C4 Greek or Latin. By date
65.C4A-.C4Z Other languages, A-Z

Collected works
Early Christian literature. Fathers of the Church, etc.
Individual authors
John Chrysostom, Saint, d. 407 -- Continued
Selected works
65.C42 Greek or Latin. By date
65.C43A-.C43Z Other languages, A-Z
65.C45A-.C45Z Separate works. By title, A-Z
65.C455 Dictionaries, indexes, etc.
65.C46 Criticism
Clement I, Pope (Clemens Romanus)
Collected works
65.C5 Greek. By date
65.C5A-.C5Z Other languages, A-Z
Selected works
65.C52 Greek. By date
65.C53A-.C53Z Other languages, A-Z
65.C54A-.C54Z Separate works. By title, A-Z
65.C55A-.C55Z Spurious and doubtful works. By title, A-Z
65.C55R43 Recognitions
Including versions in Latin, Syriac, etc.
65.C56 Criticism
Clement, of Alexandria, Saint, ca. 150-ca. 215
Collected works
65.C6 Greek or Latin. By date
65.C6A-.C6Z Other languages, A-Z
Selected works
65.C62 Latin. By date
65.C62A-.C62Z Other languages, A-Z
65.C65A-.C65Z Separate works. By title, A-Z
65.C66 Criticism
Cyprian, Saint, Bishop of Carthage
Collected works
65.C8 Latin. By date
65.C8A-.C8Z Other languages, A-Z
Selected works
65.C82 Latin. By date
65.C82A-.C82Z Other languages, A-Z
65.C84A-.C84Z Separate works. By title and date
65.C85A-.C85Z Spurious and doubtful works. By title
65.C86 Criticism
Cyril, Saint, Bishop of Jerusalem, ca. 315-386
Collected works
65.C9 Greek. By date
65.C9A-.C9Z Other languages, A-Z
Selected works
65.C91 Greek. By date

Collected works
Early Christian literature. Fathers of the Church, etc.
Individual authors
Cyril, Saint, Bishop of Jerusalem, ca. 315-386
Selected works -- Continued

65.C92A-.C92Z Other languages, A-Z
65.C934A-.C934Z Spurious and doubtful works. By title
65.C935 Dictionaries, indexes, etc.
65.C936 Criticism
65.C95-.C956 Cyril, Saint, Patriarch of Alexandria, ca. 370-444 (Table BR1)
65.D6-.D66 Pseudo-Dionysius, the Areopagite (Table BR1)
65.E45-.E456 Ennodius, Magnus Felix (Table BR1)
65.E63-.E636 Ephraem, Syrus, Saint, 303-373 (Table BR1)
65.E65-.E656 Epiphanius, Saint, Bishop of Constantia in Cyprus (Table BR1)

Eusebius, of Caesarea, Bishop of Caesarea, ca. 260-ca. 340
Collected works

65.E7 Greek or Latin. By date
65.E72A-.E72Z Other languages, A-Z

Selected works

65.E73 Greek or Latin. By date
65.E74A-.E74Z Other languages, A-Z
65.E75A-.E75Z Separate works. By title, A-Z
65.E76 Criticism
65.E92-.E926 Evagrius, Ponticus, 345?-399 (Table BR1)
65.G2-.G26 Gaudentius, Saint, Bishop of Brescia (Table BR1)
65.G5-.G56 Gregory I, Pope, ca. 540-604 (Table BR1)
65.G6-.G66 Gregory, of Nazianzus, Saint (Table BR1)

Gregory, of Nyssa, Saint, ca. 335-ca. 394
Collected works

65.G7 Greek of Latin. By date
65.G72A-.G72Z Other languages, A-Z

Selected works

65.G73 Greek or Latin. By date
65.G74A-.G74Z Other languages, A-Z
65.G75A-.G75Z Separate works. By title, A-Z
65.G76 Criticism
(65.H4-.H46) Hieronymus, Saint
see BR65.J47+

65.H8-.H86 Hippolytus, Antipope ca. 170-235 or 6 (Table BR1)
65.J47-.J476 Jerome, Saint (Table BR1)
65.J58-.J586 John, of Dalyatha, 8th cent. (Table BR1)
65.J6-.J66 John, of Damascus, Saint (Table BR1)

John, the Solitary, of Apamea see BR65.Y6+
John Chrysostom, Saint, d. 407 see BR65.C4+

Collected works
Early Christian literature. Fathers of the Church, etc.
Individual authors -- Continued

65.L2-.L26	Lactantius, ca. 240-ca.320 (Table BR1)
65.L4-.L46	Leo I, Pope, d. 461 (Table BR1)
65.M33-.M336	Macarius, the Egyptian, Saint, 4th cent. (Table BR1)
65.M383-.M3836	Marius Mercator, fl. 418-449 (Table BR1)
	Maximus, Confessor, Saint, ca. 580-662
	Collected works
65.M4	Greek or Latin. By date
65.M4A-.M4Z	Other languages, A-Z
	Selected works
65.M412	Greek or Latin. By date
65.M412A-.M412Z	Other languages, A-Z
65.M413A-.M413Z	Separate works. By title, A-Z
65.M414A-.M414Z	Spurious and doubtful works. By title, A-Z
65.M415	Dictionaries, indexes, etc.
65.M416	Criticism
65.M42-.M426	Maximus, of Turin, Saint (Table BR1)
65.M45-.M456	Melito, Saint, Bishop of Sardis (Table BR1)
	Origen
	Collected works
65.O5	Greek or Latin. By date
65.O5A-.O5Z	Other languages, A-Z
	Selected works
65.O52	Greek or Latin. By date
65.O53A-.O53Z	Other languages, A-Z
65.O54-.O64	Separate works. By title
	Contra Celsum
65.O55	Original. By date
65.O55A-55.O55Z	Other languages, A-Z
	Criticism
	De principiis
65.O568	Original. By date
65.O568A-.O568Z	Other languages, A-Z
65.O57	Criticism
	Philocalia
65.O6	Original. By date
65.O6A-.O6Z	Other languages, A-Z
65.O62	Criticism
65.O65A-.O65Z	Spurious and doubtful works. By title, A-Z
65.O68	Criticism
65.P46-.P466	Philoponus, John (Table BR1)
65.P47-.P476	Philostorgius (Table BR1)
65.P644-.P6446	Prosper, of Aquitaine, Saint (Table BR1)
	Pseudo-Clementine see BR65.C55A+
	Pseudo-Dionysius see BR65.D6+

Collected works
Early Christian literature. Fathers of the Church, etc.
Individual authors -- Continued
Pseudo-Macarius see BR65.M33+
65.S85-.S856 Šubḥalmaran, Metropolitan of Kirkuk, d. ca. 620 (Table BR1)
Tertullian, ca. 160-ca. 230
Collected works
65.T3 Latin. By date
65.T3A-.T3Z Other languages, A-Z
Selected works
65.T32 Latin. By date
65.T32A-.T32Z Other languages, A-Z
65.T335-.T68 Separate works. By title
65.T3358 Ad martyras
65.T3359 Ad nationes
65.T33593 Ad Scapulam
65.T33595 Ad uxorem
65.T335957 Adversus Hermogenem
65.T336 Adversus Iudaeos
65.T3367 Adversus Praxean
65.T337 Adversus Valentinianos
65.T34 Apologeticum
65.T345 De anima
65.T3465 De baptismo
65.T347 De corona militis
65.T3474 De cultu feminarum
65.T348 De exhortatione castitatis
65.T349 De idololatria
65.T352 De monogamia
65.T354 De oratione
65.T36 De pallio
65.T365 De patientia
65.T366 De praescriptione haereticorum
65.T367 De pudicitia
65.T37 De spectaculis
65.T7 Criticism
65.T75-.T756 Theodoret, Bishop of Cyrrhus (Table BR1)
65.T7574-.T75746 Theodore (Theodoros), Bishop of Mopsuestia, ca. 350-428 or 9 (Table BR1)
65.Y6-.Y66 John, the Solitary, of Apamea (Yohannan Yihidaya) (Table BR1)
History and criticism. Patrology and patristics
Cf. PA6053 Christian poetry in Latin
Cf. Z7791 Bibliography of the Fathers of the Church
66 Periodicals. Societies
66.5 Dictionaries. Indexes. Concordances, etc.

Collected works
Early Christian literature. Fathers of the Church, etc.
History and criticism -- Continued
67 General works
67.2 Publication and distribution
Later writers to 1800
Collections see BR45+
75 Individual authors
e.g. John Bunyan, William Paley, Jeremy Taylor, John Wycliffe
Writers, 19th-20th centuries
Collections see BR45+
Individual authors
Reformation writers are classed in BR330+ Luther; BR336 Melanchthon; BR346 Zwigli; etc.
Writers of particular Christian denominations are classed in BX260 Orthodox Eastern Church; BX890 Catholic Church; BX5037 Church of England; etc.
83 Comprehensive collections
85 Collected addresses, essays, etc.
95 Encyclopedias. Dictionaries
96 Addresses, essays, lectures
For questions and answers on the Bible, see BS612; on the Catholic Church, see BX1754.3; etc.
96.5 Terminology. Abbreviations
Ecclesiastical geography
Cf. BS630+ Biblical geography
97 General works
98 Atlases
99 Dictionaries
99.5 Pictorial works
99.7 Information services
99.74 Computer networks
Including the Internet
Cf. BR115.C65 Christianity and computers
100 Philosophy of Christianity. Philosophy and Christianity
For early works see BR120
Cf. BL51 Philosophy of religion
Cf. BT40+ Philosophical theology
Biography of Christian philosophers
Class here works on the Christian aspects of the life or career of Christian philosophers
For works on the individual aspects of their philosophy, see subclass B
102.A1 Collective
102.A2-Z Individual, A-Z

	Psychology of religious experience. Conversion, etc.
	Cf. BL53+ Religion and psychology
110	General works
111	Liminality
112	Enthusiasm
	Ecstasy, trance states, stigmatization see BV5090+
114	Fanaticism. Religious addiction
115.A-Z	Christianity in relation to special subjects, A-Z
	Cf. BS2415+ Teachings of Jesus
	Cf. BV598+ The Church
	Adoption see HV875.26
	Aesthetics see BR115.A8
115.A35	Agriculture
115.A57	Alchemy
	Amusements see BV4597+
	Animals (Killing of, vivisection, etc.) see BT746+
115.A8	Art. Aesthetics
	Cf. BX1795.A78 Catholic Church and art
	Cf. N7790+ Religious art
	Cf. NA4590+ Religious architecture
	Cf. NB1750+ Religious monuments
	Cf. NB1910+ Religious sculpture
	Cf. ND1430+ Religious painting
	Cf. NE1675 Religious prints, 17th century
	Cf. NE1712 Religious prints, 18th century
	Cf. NE1722 Religious prints, 19th century
	Cf. NE1732 Religious prints, 1875-
	Cf. NE1742 Religious prints, 20th century
115.A82	Astrology. Zodiac
115.A83	Atomic energy
115.A85	Atomic warfare. Nuclear warfare
	Beard see BR115.H34
	Biology see BL224+
115.B55	Birds
115.B57	Blood
	Business see HF5388
115.C3	Capitalism
115.C38	Censorship
	Cemeteries, church burial, etc. see BT826+
	Children
	see BT705 BV639.C4 BV1474+
115.C45	Cities and towns
115.C48	Civil disobedience
115.C5	Civilization
115.C63	Comic, The
	Cf. BR115.H84 Humor, wit
	Colonization see JV321

Christianity in relation to special subjects, A-Z -- Continued

115.C65 Computers

Cf. BR99.74 Computer networks

115.C66 Conservatism

115.C67 Consumption (Economics)

115.C69 Counseling

Cf. BV4012.2 Pastoral counseling

Cf. BV4409 Peer counseling in the Church

115.C8 Culture

Democracy see BR115.P7

Developing countries see BR115.U6

115.D74 Dreams

115.E3 Economics. Labor

For relation to labor alone see HD6338+

Cf. BR115.W4 Wealth

Cf. HD6481+ Catholic labor unionism

Emotions see BV4597.3

Fantasy see BR115.I6

Food see BR115.N87

115.G45 Geography

Cf. BR97+ Ecclesiastical geography

Cf. BS630+ Biblical geography

115.G54 Gifts

115.G58 Global warming

115.G59 Globalization

115.H34 Hair. Haircutting. Beard

Health and healing see BT732+

115.H43 Hedonism

115.H5 History

115.H55 Holocaust, Jewish (1939-1945)

115.H56 Home

115.H6 Homosexuality

115.H8 Humanism

115.H84 Humor. Wit

Cf. BR115.C63 Comic, The

Cf. BS2545.W5 New Testament

Cf. BX4661 Catholic Church

115.H86 Hunger

115.I35 Ideology

115.I6 Imagination. Fantasy

115.I63 Individualism

Cf. B824.A1+ Philosophy

Cf. JC571+ Political theory

115.I68 Interest. Usury

115.I7 International affairs

Cf. BX1793 Catholic Church

Journalism see PN4784.R3

Christianity in relation to special subjects, A-Z -- Continued

115.J8 Justice

Cf. BV4647.J8 Justice (Virtue)

115.K55 Kings and rulers

Labor see BR115.E3

115.L23 Land tenure

115.L25 Language

115.L28 Law

115.L32 Learning and scholarship

Literature see PN49

115.M25 Magic

Marriage see BT706+

Medicine see BT732+

115.N3 Nature

Cf. BT695.5 Doctrinal theology

Cf. GF80 Moral aspects of human ecology

Nuclear warfare see BR115.A85

115.N87 Nutrition. Food

Cf. BR115.H86 Hunger

115.O3 Occult sciences

Peace see BT736.4

Physical education and training see BV4598

115.P7 Politics and government. Democracy

Cf. BX1793 Catholic Church

Polygamy see BT707.5

115.P74 Postmodernism

115.P77 Progress

115.P8 Prophecy

Cf. BS647+ Prophecy in the Bible

Cf. BT235 Messianic prophecies

115.P85 Psychical research

Race see BT734+

115.R4 Reincarnation

115.R55 Rhetoric

Rulers and kings see BR115.K55

115.S26 Satire

Scholarship see BR115.L32

Science see BL239+

Social aspects see BT738+

115.S57 Social sciences

115.S73 Strangers

115.S85 Superstition

115.T42 Technology

115.T73 Tragic, The

115.T76 Transvestism. Transsexualism

115.U6 Underdeveloped areas. Developing countries

115.U73 Urban folklore

Christianity ir relation to special subjects, A-Z
Usury see BR115.I68
Utopias see HX807
115.V55 Virtual reality
115.V64 Voluntarism
War see BT736.2
115.W4 Wealth
Cf. BV772 Church support
Wit see BR115.H84
Women and the Church see BV639.W7
115.W6 World. Church and the world
115.Y43 Year 2000 date conversion (Computer systems)
Zodiac see BR115.A82
Literary history (General): Christian literature
Cf. BR60+ Early Christian literature
Cf. BR138+ Historiography
Cf. BR1609 History of martyr books
Cf. BR1690 Religious biographies and confessions as a subject of study
Cf. BV2369+ Distribution of Christian literature
Cf. BV4818 Devotional literature
Cf. BX4662 Hagiography
117 General works
117.3 Dictionaries
117.5 Christian literature for children
Cf. BS546+ Bible stories
Cf. BV4315 Children's sermons
Cf. BV4560+ Religious works for children
Cf. BV4870+ Devotional works for children
Christian theology
Includes comprehensive treatises descriptive of all fields; introduction to theology; theological methodology; hermeneutics (Biblical hermeneutics, BS476); encyclopedia (not encyclopedias)
118 General works
Study and teaching see BV4019+
General works on Christianity
Cf. BT60 The essence, genius, and nature of Christianity
Treatises
120 Early through 1800
121 1801-1950
121.2 1951-2000
121.3 2001-
123 Addresses, essays, etc. (separates)
For collections see BR45+
For sermons see BV4239+
For special denominations see BX1+

General works on Christianity -- Continued

124 Personal opinions

125 Pamphlets, etc.

125.5 Juvenile works

126 Occult, astrological, symbolic, etc. works

Relation of Christianity to other religious and philosophical systems

Cf. BR135+ Folklore, pagan survivals

127 General works

128.A-Z Special, A-Z

128.A16 African religions

128.A2 Ancient (General)

128.A26 Animism

128.A77 Asian religions

128.A8 Atheism

128.A86 Australian aboriginal religions

Bahai Faith see BP378.6

128.B8 Buddhism

For relation of Christianity to special Buddhist sects see BQ7001+

128.C4 Chinese religions

128.C43 Confucianism

128.D82 Dualism

128.G4 Germanic religions

128.G8 Greek religions and philosophy. Hellenism

Cf. BT1140 Christian apologetics against Greek philosophers

128.H5 Hinduism

Cf. BT1235.H5 Christian apologetics against Hinduism

128.H8 Humanism, Religious

Islam see BP172+

128.J35 Japanese religions

Judaism see BM535

128.M5 Mithraism

128.N48 New Age movement

128.P75 Primitive religion

128.R7 Roman religions, culture, etc.

Cf. BR170 Relation of early Christianity to Roman Empire

Cf. BT1160 Christian apologetics against Roman religions

128.S24 Śaiva Siddhānta

128.S3 Scandinavian religions

128.S5 Shinto

128.S6 Sikhism

128.T34 Taoism

Theosophy see BP567

Relation of Christianity to other religious and philosophical systems
Special, A-Z -- Continued
128.Y63 Yoga
128.Z6 Zoroastrianism
Sources of Christianity. Origins
Cf. BM535 Relation of Judaism to Christianity
129 General works
129.5 Religionsgeschichtliche Schule
Christian antiquities. Archaeology. Museums
130 Periodicals. Societies. Collections
130.5 Dictionaries
131 General works
132 Other
133.A-Z By region or country, A-Z
Under each country (using successive Cutter numbers):
.x1 General works
Local
.x2A-.x2Z By province, etc., A-Z
.x3A-.x3Z By city, A-Z
133.5.A-Z Biography, A-Z
e.g.
133.5.R6 Rossi, Giovanni Battista de
134 Literary discoveries. Papyri, inscriptions, etc.
Cf. BM487.A05+ Dead Sea scrolls
Christian folklore, myths, superstitions, etc.
Including pagan survivals
135 General works
136.A-Z By region or country, A-Z
137 Religious customs and their origins
Historiography. Methodology
Including study of church history, value of, etc.
138 General works
139 Biography of historians
Cf. BR133.5.A+ Biography (Christian antiquities)
139.A1 Collective
139.A7 Arnold, Gottfried
139.B8 Buonaiuti, Ernesto
139.H3 Harnack, Adolf von
139.J6 John, Bishop of Ephesus
139.L4 Lea, Henry Charles
139.M5 Michelet, Jules
139.M6 Mosheim, Johann Lorenz
139.N48 Newman, Albert Henry
Renan, Ernest see PQ2386.R39
139.S4 Schaff, Philip
139.S42 Schleiermacher, Friedrich Ernst Daniel

Historiography. Methodology
Biography of historians -- Continued
139.S9 Strauss, David Friedrich
History
140 Periodicals. Societies
140.5 Congresses. Conferences
Collected works
Including sources
141 Several authors
142 Individual authors
General works
143 Early through 1800
145 1801-1950
145.2 1951-2000
145.3 2001-
Manuals. Compends, etc.
146 General
147 Catholic manuals, etc.
148 General special
149 Outlines, syllabi, tables, etc.
150 Popular works
151 Juvenile works. Works for young people
152 Pictorial works
153 Other
155 Addresses, essays, lectures
156 Historical pageants
157 Christian denominations. Sects (General)
For denominations in a specific region or country see BR500+
For individual denominations see BX1+
158 Jewish Christians
Cf. BR195.J8 Judaistic Christianity
Cf. BV2619+ Missionary work among the Jews
By period
Early and medieval
General works
Early works through 600
Including histories by early Church Fathers and contemporaries
160.A1 Collected works
160.A2 Selections
160.A5-Z Individual authors
Cassiodorus, Senator, ca. 487-ca. 580
160.C2 Original texts
160.C3A-.C3Z Translations, A-Z
160.C35 Criticism

History
By period
Early and medieval
General works
Early works through 600
Individual authors -- Continued
Eusebius, of Caesarea, Bishop of Caesarea, ca. 260-ca.340
160.E4 Original texts
160.E5A-.E5Z Translations, A-Z
160.E55 Criticism
Evagrius, Scholasticus, b. 536?
160.E6 Original texts
160.E7A-.E7Z Translations, A-Z
160.E75 Criticism
Rufinus of Aquileia
160.R7 Original works
160.R8A-.R8Z Translations, A-Z
160.R85 Criticism
Socrates, Scholasticus, ca 379-ca. 440
160.S5 Original works
160.S6A-.S6Z Translations, A-Z
160.S65 Criticism
Sozomen, ca 400-ca. 450
160.S7 Original works
160.S8A-.S8Z Translations, A-Z
160.S85 Criticism
Theodoret, Bishop of Cyrrhus
160.T5 Original works
160.T6A-.T6Z Translations, A-Z
160.T65 Criticism
Theodorus, Anagnostes
160.T7 Original works
160.T8A-.T8Z Translations, A-Z
160.T85 Criticism
160.3 Early writers against Christianity
e.g. Celsus, Platonic philosopher; Julianus Apostata; Porphyrius
601-
For writers against Christianity see BL2700+
161 Medieval and early modern through 1800
162 1801-1950
162.2 1951-2000
162.3 2001-
162.5 Pictorial works
163 General special

History
By period
Early and medieval -- Continued
Apostolic Age to fall of Roman Empire
Cf. BS2407+ New Testament history
Cf. BX2410+ New Testament times

165 General works
166 General special
167 Sources and documents
Cf. BR160+ Early works on the early history of Christianity
168 Study and teaching. Textbooks
Special topics
170 Relation to Roman Empire (including Eastern Empire)
175 Council of Jerusalem (ca. 50)
Persecution see BR1603+
180 Constantine and the Church
182 Early Church in the West
Including Western North Africa and Europe
185 Early Church in Asia
Including general works on the ancient Church in particular areas, places, etc.
190 Early Church in Africa
Including general works on the ancient Church in particular areas, places, etc.
195.A-Z Other special, A-Z
195.A89 Authority in the Church
195.C38 Catechumenate
195.C45 Celibacy. Virginity
195.C46 Children
195.C49 Christian art and symbolism
195.C5 Christian life
195.C53 Church and the world
195.C6 Conversion
195.C64 Councils
195.E9 Evangelistic work
195.F35 Family
195.F37 Fasting
195.F75 Friendship
195.H4 Hellenistic theology
195.J8 Judaistic Christianity
195.L27 Laity
195.L3 Language question
195.L42 Leadership
195.M37 Marriage. Remarriage
195.M43 Medicine

History
By period
Early and medieval
Apostolic Age to fall of Roman Empire
Special topics
Other special, A-Z -- Continued
195.M65 Monasticism. Monastic life
For monasticism and monastic life by place see BR182+
Money see BR195.W4
195.O33 Occultism
195.P36 Pastoral theology
195.P68 Poverty
Property see BR195.W4
195.P74 Prophecy
195.R37 Race
Remarriage see BR195.M37
195.S48 Sex
195.S89 Subintroductae
195.S93 Suffering
195.V44 Vegetarianism
Virginity see BR195.C45
195.W3 War
195.W4 Wealth. Money. Property
195.W6 Women
Period of the ecumenical councils, 325-787
For ecumenical councils after 787 see BX830 0809+
200 General works
203 General special
By century
4th or 4th and 5th centuries
Including Antiochian School
205 General works
207 Bishop Ulfilas and the Gothic Church
210 Council of Nicaea (1st : 325)
213 Council of Saragossa (380)
214 Council of Aquileia (381)
215 Council of Constantinople (1st : 381)
217 Emperor Theodosius I and the Church, 392-395
5th century. Councils of Turin (ca. 400 and 417)
219 General works
220 Council of Ephesus (431)
225 Council of Chalcedon (451)
6th century
227 General works
230 Council of Constantinople (2nd : 553)
7th century

History
By period
Early and medieval
Period of the ecumenical councils, 325-787
By century
7th century -- Continued
232 General works
235 Council of Constantinople (3rd : 681)
8th century. Iconoclasm
238 General works
240 Council of Nicaea (2nd : 787)
242 Council of Frankfurt, 794
Period of the Middle Ages. Charlemagne to Luther.
Cf. BX1068+ Medieval Catholic Church history
250 Periodicals. Societies
251 Collected works
252 General works
253 General special
By period
For early medieval period see BR219+
255 9th-10th centuries
Including period of Charlemagne
Schism between Eastern and Western churches, 1054 see BX303
270 Later medieval period, 1054-
For Hildebrand (Pope Gregory VII) see BX1187
275.A-Z Other special, A-Z
275.J7 Prester John
280 Renaissance. Renaissance and Reformation
Modern period
290 General works
295 Reformation movements before Luther
Cf. BX4800+ Protestantism
Reformation and Counter-Reformation, 1517-1648
300 Periodicals. Societies. Congresses
Collected works
Including sources and documents
301 General
302 Catholic
302.5 Exhibitions
302.8 Dictionaries. Encyclopedias
303 Minor pamphlets of the Reformation period
General works
304 Early through 1800
305 1801-1950
305.2 1951-2000
305.3 2001-

History
By period
Modern period
Reformation and Counter-Reformation, 1517-1648 -- Continued
306 Compends. Manuals
307 General special
308 Juvenile and popular works
309 Addresses, essays, lectures
Biography
Collective
For special countries see BR357.2+
315 General
316 Juvenile works
317 Women of the Reformation
Individual
Calvin, Jean, 1509-1564 see BX9418
Castellion, Sébastien, 1515-1563 see BX9459.C4
Knox, John, ca. 1514-1572 see BX9223
Luther, Martin, 1483-1546
Bibliography see Z8528
323.5 Periodicals. Societies, etc.
323.7 Congresses
324 Dictionaries, indexes, etc.
325 General biography
326 Addresses, essays, lectures
Special periods
326.3 Childhood and youth, 1483-1505
326.4 Monk and professor, 1505-1517
326.5 Breach with Rome to Diet of Worms, 1517-1521. Ninety-five Theses. Indulgence controversy. Leipzig disputation
326.6 Diet of Worms to marriage, 1521-1525. Wartburg. Peasants' War
326.7 Reconstruction of the Church to Religious Peace of Nüremberg, 1525-1532. Disputations with Erasmus and Zwingli. Diet of Augsburg. Coburg
326.8 Religious Peace of Nüremberg to Luther's death, 1532-1546
327 Other
Including anniversaries, celebrations, poetry, drama, portraits, etc.
328 Luther's family
Including biographies of Katharina von Bora, wife of Luther
329 Friends and associates

History
By period
Modern period
Reformation and Counter-Reformation, 1517-1648
Biography
Individual
Luther, Martin, 1483-1546 -- Continued
Works by Luther
Collections
German and Latin
330.A2 Comprehensive. By date
330.A3 Other. Kleinere Schriften, etc. By date
330.A5-Z Translations. By language, A-Z, and date
Selections
German and Latin
331.A2 Comprehensive. By date
331.A3 Other. By date
331.A5-Z Translations. By language, A-Z, and date
e.g.
331.E5 English
331.E6 Selections for daily reading
332.A-Z Individual works, A-Z
If not classed with subject in education, literature, etc.
Catechisms. Larger Catechism. Smaller Catechism see BX8070.L5+
Hauspostille
332.H3 German
332.H4 English
332.H5A-.H5Z Other languages, A-Z
Kirchenpostille
332.K5 German
332.K6 English
332.K7A-.K7Z Other languages, A-Z
Letters
332.L5 German
332.L51 Latin
332.L6 English translations
332.L63 French translations
332.L67 Scandinavian translations
332.L68A-.L68Z Other languages, A-Z
Sermons
Texts
German
332.S3 Collections. Two or more sermons
332.S4 Single sermons
English

History
By period
Modern period
Reformation and Counter-Reformation, 1517-1648
Biography
Individual
Luther, Martin, 1483-1546
Works by Luther
Individual works, A-Z
Sermons
Texts
English -- Continued

332.S5 Collections. Two or more sermons
332.S6 Single sermons
332.S7A-.S7Z Other languages, A-Z
332.S75 Criticism
332.S8 Sprichwörtersammlung
Table talks
Texts
332.T3 German
332.T4 English translations
332.T43 French translations
332.T47 Scandinavian translations
332.T48A-.T48Z Other languages, A-Z
332.T5 Criticism
332.5 Criticism and interpretation
Luther's theology
Criticism of individual works to follow translations
General works
333.A2 Early through 1800
333.A3-Z 1801-1950
333.2 1951-2000
333.3 2001-
333.5.A-Z Special topics, A-Z
333.5.A5 Anthropology
333.5.B3 Baptism
333.5.B5 Bible
333.5.B56 Bishops
333.5.B66 Books
333.5.C37 Children
333.5.C4 Christology
333.5.C5 Church, Doctrine of the
333.5.C55 Conciliar theory
333.5.C6 Confirmation
Conflict see BR333.5.S75
333.5.C68 Creation
333.5.C72 Crosses

History
By period
Modern period
Reformation and Counter-Reformation, 1517-1648
Biography
Individual
Luther, Martin, 1483-1546
Luther's theology
Special topics, A-Z -- Continued

333.5.D4 Devil
Doctrine of the Church see BR333.5.C5
333.5.D73 Drama
333.5.E2 Economics
333.5.E75 Eschatology
333.5.E8 Ethics
333.5.E9 Excommunication
333.5.F33 Faith
333.5.F34 Faith and reason
333.5.F73 Freedom
333.5.H65 Holy Spirit
333.5.H85 Humanism
333.5.I85 Islam
333.5.J4 Jews
333.5.J8 Justification
333.5.L3 Law
333.5.L6 Lord's Supper
333.5.M29 Marriage
333.5.M3 Mary, Virgin
333.5.M43 Meditation
333.5.M57 Missions
333.5.M66 Monastic and religious life
333.5.M9 Mysticism
333.5.O73 Ordination
333.5.P3 Papacy
333.5.P32 Pastoral theology
333.5.P45 Philosophy
333.5.P6 Political science. Two kingdoms doctrine
333.5.P65 Practical theology
333.5.P67 Prayer
333.5.P7 Predestination
Reason and faith see BR333.5.F34
333.5.S33 Sacraments
333.5.S49 Sex
333.5.S6 Sociology. Social ethics
333.5.S65 Spirituality
333.5.S75 Struggle. Conflict
333.5.S85 Suffering of God

History
By period
Modern period
Reformation and Counter-Reformation, 1517-1648
Biography
Individual
Luther, Martin, 1483-1546
Luther's theology
Special topics, A-Z -- Continued

333.5.T74	Trinity
	Two kingdoms doctrine see BR333.5.P6
333.5.W65	Word of God
	Other works on Luther
334.A2	Early through 1800
	e.g.
334.A2C6	Conference du diable avec Luther
334.A3-Z	1801-1950
334.2	1951-2000
334.3	2001-
	Melanchthon, Philipp, 1497-1560
	Bibliography see Z8562.5
335	Biography
	Theological works
	Collected works
336.A2	German and Latin. By date
336.A5-Z	Translations. By language, A-Z, and date
	Selected works
337.A2	German and Latin. By date
337.A5-Z	Translations. By language, A-Z, and date
338.A-Z	Separate works. By title, A-Z, and date
339	Criticism
	Zwingli, Ulrich, 1484-1531
	Bibliography see Z8999
345	Biography
346	Works of Zwingli
350.A-Z	Other, A-Z
	e.g.
	Bucer, Martin see BR350.B93
350.B9	Bullinger, Heinrich
350.B93	Butzer, Martin
	Colet, John see BR754.C6
350.C68	Cousin, Gilbert
350.E55	Enzinas, Francisco de
350.E7	Erasmus and the Reformation
350.F3	Farel, Guillaume
350.F5	Ferdinand I and the Reformation
350.F6	Flacius, Matthias, Illyricus

History
By period
Modern period
Reformation and Counter-Reformation, 1517-1648
Biography
Individual
Other, A-Z -- Continued

350.F7 Franck, Sebastian
350.G7 Grotius and the Reformation
350.H3 Hamilton, Patrick
350.H8 Hutten and the Reformation
350.K2 Karl V and the Reformation
350.K5 Klarenbach, Adolf
350.L28 Lambert, François
350.L3 Łaski, Jan (Iohannes a Lasco)
350.O3 Ochino, Bernardino
350.P3 Paleario, Aonio
350.P4 Petri, Olavus
350.S3 Sarpi, Paolo
350.T8 Tyndale, William
350.V37 Vermigli, Pietro Martire

Special topics
353 Diet of Worms, 1521
355.A-Z Other, A-Z
355.A78 Diet of Augsburg, 1530
355.A8 Peace of Augsburg, 1555
355.B4 Bern Disputation, 1528
Iconoclasm see BR355.I35
355.I35 Idols and images. Iconoclasm
355.J4 Jews
355.L5 Leipzig Disputation, 1519
355.M27 Magdeburg Confession
355.M3 Marburg Conference, 1529
355.P36 Pamphleteering
355.R2 Colloquy of Ratisbon, 1541
355.R3 Colloquy of Ratisbon, 1546
355.S68 Diet of Spires, 1526
355.S7 Diet of Spires, 1529
Council of Trent, 1545-1563 see BX830 1545
355.U5 Union and reform projects
Peace of Westphalia, 1648 see D269

By region or country
Germany
General works see BR300+
358.A-Z By state, province, etc., A-Z
359.A-Z By city, A-Z
Austria

History
By period
Modern period
Reformation and Counter-Reformation, 1517-1648
By region or country
Austria -- Continued

360.A1-.A5	Periodicals. Societies. Collections, etc.
360.A6-Z	General works
360.5.A-Z	Local, A-Z
	Czechoslovakia
365.A1-.A5	Periodicals. Societies. Collections, etc.
365.A6-Z	General works
365.5.A-Z	Local, A-Z
	Hungary
367.A1-.A5	Periodicals. Societies. Collections, etc.
367.A6-Z	General works
367.4.A-Z	Local, A-Z
	Belgium
368.A1-.A5	Periodicals. Societies. Collections, etc.
368.A6-Z	General works
369.A-Z	Local, A-Z
	France
370.A1-.A5	Periodicals. Societies. Collections, etc.
370.A6-Z	General works
372.A-Z	Local, A-Z
	Great Britain. England
375.A1-.A5	Periodicals. Societies. Collections, etc.
375.A6-Z	General works
377	General special
377.5.A-Z	Local, A-Z
378	Collective biography
	Ireland
380.A1-.A5	Periodicals. Societies. Collections, etc.
380.A6-Z	General works
	Scotland
385.A1-.A5	Periodicals. Societies. Collections, etc.
385.A6-Z	General works
	Italy
390.A1-.A5	Periodicals. Societies. Collections, etc.
390.A6-Z	General works
	Netherlands
395.A1-.A5	Periodicals. Societies. Collections, etc.
395.A6-Z	General works
	Scandinavia
400.A1-.A5	Periodicals. Societies. Collections, etc.
400.A6-Z	General works
	Denmark

History
By period
Modern period
Reformation and Counter-Reformation, 1517-1648
By region or country
Scandinavia
Denmark -- Continued
401.A1-.A5 Periodicals. Societies. Collections, etc.
401.A6-Z General works
Iceland
402.A1-.A5 Periodicals. Societies. Collections, etc.
402.A6-Z General works
Norway
403.A1-.A5 Periodicals. Societies. Collections, etc.
403.A6-Z General works
Sweden
404.A1-.A5 Periodicals. Societies. Collections, etc.
404.A6-Z General works
Spain
405.A1-.A5 Periodicals. Societies. Collections, etc.
405.A6-Z General works
Switzerland
410.A1-.A5 Periodicals. Societies. Collections, etc.
410.A6-Z General works
420.A-Z Other regions or countries, A-Z
e.g.
420.P7 Poland
430 Counter-Reformation
For local with history of the Catholic Church by country and period see BX1401+
440 17th (-18th) century
Peace of Westphalia to the present time, 1648-
450 General works
455 Peace of Westphalia to the French Revolution, 1648-1789
470 18th century
475 Period since the French Revolution
477 19th century
20th century
479 General works
481 1945-
By region or country
For the period of the Reformation see BR300+
For the original missionary effort in a country and the continuing effort to gain the unchurched and regain the lapsed see BV2750+
500.A1 Groups of countries not in a particular geographic area

History
By region or country -- Continued
500.A3-Z America
North America
510 General works
512 Historic churches
Prefer denominations in BX and F
United States
513 Periodicals. Societies, etc.
514 Sources. Inventory
515 General works. History
516 Religious freedom. Church and state
516.5 Sects. Relations of religious bodies. Christian union
517 Other
By period
520 Early through 1800
525 1800-1950
526 1950-
By region
For early period see BR520
530 New England
535 South
540 Central. Middle West
545 West
550 Pacific Coast
555.A-.W By state, A-W
Under each:
.x General works
.x2A-.x2Z By county, A-Z
Including rural surveys
560.A-Z By city, A-Z
561.A-Z By university and college, A-Z
Including religious history and works descriptive of religious thought and life
Cf. BV1051.A+ Young Men's Christian Associations
563.A-Z By race or ethnic group, A-Z
African Americans see BR563.N4
563.A82 Asian Americans
563.C45 Chinese Americans
563.C9 Czechs
563.E27 East Indians
563.F54 Finns
563.G3 Germans
563.G73 Greek Americans
563.H57 Hispanic Americans
563.I8 Italians

History
By region or country
America
North America
United States
By race or ethnic group, A-Z -- Continued
563.J35 Japanese Americans
563.K67 Koreans
563.M49 Mexican Americans
563.M68 Mountain whites (Southern states)
563.N4 Negroes. African Americans
Cf. BT82.7 Black theology
563.N67 Norwegian Americans
563.P64 Polish Americans
563.S8 Swedes
563.U45 Ukrainian Americans
565 Historic churches
Prefer denominations in BX and F
569 Biography (Collective)
Prefer denominations in BX
Canada and British America (General)
570 General works
575.A-Z By region, province, etc., A-Z
580.A-Z By city, A-Z
582.A-Z By race or ethnic group, A-Z
582.U57 Ukrainians
600 Latin America
Cf. BX1425+ Catholic Church
Mexico
610 General works
615.A-Z By region, state, city, etc., A-Z
Central America
620 General works
625.A-Z By region or country, A-Z
West Indies
640 General works
645.A-Z By island or group of islands, A-Z
e.g.
645.C9 Cuba
645.H2 Haiti
645.J3 Jamaica
645.P7 Puerto Rico
655 Caribbean Area
South America
660 General works
665 Argentina
670 Bolivia

History
By region or country
America
South America -- Continued
675 Brazil
680 Chile
685 Colombia
690 Ecuador
Guianas
695 General works
700 Guyana
705 Suriname
710 French Guiana
715 Paraguay
720 Peru
725 Uruguay
730 Venezuela
Europe
735 General works
736 Biography (Collective)
737.A-Z By race or ethnic group, A-Z
e.g.
737.C4 Celts
737.S6 Slavs
737.T5 Teutonic race
By region
738 Northern
738.2 Western
738.4 Central
738.6 Eastern
738.8 Southern
Great Britain. England
740 Periodicals. Societies. Collections, etc.
741 Sources and documents (Collected)
General works
742 Early through 1870
742.A2 Documents
743 1871-1950
743.2 1951-2000
743.3 2001-
744 Other
By period
Early and medieval to the Reformation
745 Periodicals. Societies. Collections, etc.
746 General works. History

History
By region or country
Europe
Great Britain. England
By period
Early and medieval to the Reformation -- Continued
747 Other
e.g. The Culdees, parish priests, Anglo-Papal relations, etc.
By period
748 Origins of British Christianity. The Britons. Celtic Church
749 5th-11th centuries. Anglo-Saxons
Including St. Augustine's mission
750 11th-16th centuries
Local history see BR763+
753 By church, abbey, etc., A-Z
For churches in modern use see BX5195.A+
Biography
754.A1 Collective
754.A3-Z Individual, A-Z
754.A33 Aethelwold, Saint, Bishop of Winchester, ca. 904-984
754.A43 Aidan, Saint
754.A56 Anselm, Saint, Archbishop of Canterbury, 1033-1109
754.A8 Augustine, Saint, Archbishop of Canterbury, d.604?
754.A85 Aungerville, Richard, known as Richard de Bury, Bishop of Durham
754.B4 Bek, Antony, Bishop of Durham
754.B45 Benedict Biscop, Saint, 628-690
Bury, Richard de, 1287-1345 see BR754.A85
754.C48 Chichele, Henry, Archbishop of Canterbury, 1362-1443
754.C5 Cobham, Thomas de, Bishop of Worcester
754.C6 Colet, John
754.C66 Courtenay, William, Archbishop of Canterbury
Cranmer, Thomas, Archbishop of Canterbury see DA317.8.C8
754.C7 Crispin, Gilbert
754.D85 Dunstan, Saint
754.E75 Erkenwald, Saint, ca. 630-ca. 693
(754.F6) Foxe, John
see BX5199.F62
754.G8 Gundulf, Bishop of Rochester
754.H83 Hugh, of Lincoln, Saint, 1140-1200

History
By region or country
Europe
Great Britain. England
By period
Early and medieval to the Reformation
Biography
Individual, A-Z -- Continued

754.I5 Islip, John
754.J62 John, Abbot of Ford
754.J63 John, of Beverley, Saint, d.721
754.J64 John, of Wales, 13th cent.
754.K5 Kilwardby, Robert, Cardinal, Archbishop of Canterbury
754.O85 Oswald, Saint, d. 992
754.P4 Peckham, John, Archbishop of Canterbury
754.P43 Pecock, Reginald, 1395-1460?
754.R53 Richard, of Chichester, Saint, 1197 or 8-1253
754.R63 Robert, of Knaresborough, Saint, d. 1218
754.S7 Stretton, Robert de, Bishop of Coventry and Lichfield
Thomas à Becket, Saint, Archbishop of Canterbury see DA209.T4
754.T44 Theodore of Canterbury, 602-690
754.T5 Thomas Wallensis
Tyndale, William see BR350.T8
754.W3 Waynflete, William, 1395?-1486
754.W4 Wenlok, Walter de
754.W84 Wulfstan, Saint, 1012?-1095
Wycliffe see BX4905

Modern
755 General works
By period
16th-17th centuries
Including Elizabethan period and other reigns
For Reformation see BR375+
756 General works
757 Other
e.g. Antinomianism; Conventicle Act, 1670; Corporation Act, 1661; Hampton Court Conference, 1604; Marprelate controversy; Test Act, 1673
For Westminster Assembly see BX9053
758 18th century
Including the Evangelical Revival
759 19th-20th centuries

England (Local)

History
By region or country
Europe
Great Britain. England
England (Local) -- Continued

763.A-Z By region, county, etc., A-Z
764 London
765.A-Z Other cities, A-Z
English biography (Collective)
767 General
768 Women
Wales
770 Periodicals. Societies. Collections, etc.
771 Directories
772 General works
772.A3 Early works
773 Other
By period
774 Early and medieval to Reformation
775 16th-18th centuries
776 1801-1945
776.3 1945-
777.A-Z By region, county, state, etc., A-Z
778.A-Z By city, town, etc., A-Z
779 Biography (Collective)
Scotland
780 Periodicals. Societies. Collections, etc.
781 Directories
782 General works
782.A3 Early works
783 Other
By period
784 Early and medieval to Reformation
785 16th-18th centuries
786 1801-1945
786.3 1945-
787.A-Z By region, county, state, etc., A-Z
788.A-Z By city, town, etc., A-Z
789 Biography (Collective)
Ireland
790 Periodicals. Societies. Collections, etc.
791 Directories
792 General works
792.A3 Early works
793 Other
By period
794 Early and medieval to Reformation

History
By region or country
Europe
Great Britain. England
England (Local)
Ireland
By period -- Continued
795 16th-18th centuries
796 1801-1945
796.3 1945-
797.A-Z By region, county, state, etc., A-Z
798.A-Z By city, town, etc., A-Z
799 Biography (Collective)
Other European countries
810-819 Austria (Table BR2)
820-829 Belgium (Table BR2)
830-839 Bulgaria (Table BR2)
France
840 Periodicals. Societies. Collections, etc.
841 Directories
842 General works
843 Other
By period
844 Early and medieval to the Reformation
845 16th-18th centuries
Including Edict of Nantes, 1598 and its Revocation, 1685
Cf. DC158.2 French Revolution
1789-
Including supression of congregations
Cf. DC192.6 Concordat of 1801
846.A1-.A5 Documents
846.A6-Z General works
846.3 1945-
847.A-Z By region, county, state, etc., A-Z
848.A-Z By city, town, etc., A-Z
849 Biography (Collective)
850-859 Germany (Table BR2 modified)
By period
854 Early and medieval to the Reformation
855 16th-18th centuries
856 1801-1945
856.3-.35 1945-
856.3 Germany and West Germany
856.35 East Germany
860-869 Greece (Table BR2)
Hungary

History
By region or country
Europe
Other European countries
Hungary -- Continued

869.5 Periodicals. Societies. Collections, etc.
869.51 Directories
869.52 General works
869.53 Other
By period
869.54 Early and medieval to Reformation
869.55 16th-18th centuries
869.56 1801-1945
869.563 1945-
869.57.A-Z By region, county, state, etc., A-Z
869.58.A-Z By city, town, etc., A-Z
869.59 Biography (Collective)
870-879 Italy (Table BR2)
880-889 Luxemburg (Table BR2)
900-909 Netherlands (Low Countries). Netherlands (Holland) (Table BR2)
910-919 Portugal (Table BR2)
920-929 Romania (Table BR2)
Russia. Soviet Union
930 Periodicals. Societies. Collections, etc.
931 Directories
932 General works
933 Other
By period
934 Early and medieval Rus'
935 16th-18th centuries
935.5 1801-1917
936 1917-
937.A-Z By region, republic, etc., A-Z
For former Soviet Central Asia see BR1135
938.A-Z By city, town, etc., A-Z
939 Biography (Collective)
940-949 Finland (Table BR2)
950-959 Poland (Table BR2)
960-969 Yugoslavia (Table BR2)
Scandinavia
General
970 Periodicals. Societies. Collections, etc.
971 Directories
972 General works
973 Other
By period

History
  By region or country
    Europe
      Other European countries
        Scandinavia
          General
            By period -- Continued
974 Early and medieval to Reformation
975 16th-18th centuries
976 1801-1945
976.3 1945-
979 Biography (Collective)
980-989 Denmark (Table BR2)
990-999 Iceland (Table BR2)
1000-1009 Norway (Table BR2)
1010-1019 Sweden (Table BR2)
1020-1029 Spain. Spain and Portugal (Table BR2)
  For Portugal alone see BR910+
  By period
1024 Early and medieval to the Reformation
  Including Mozarabs
1030-1039 Switzerland (Table BR2)
  Turkey. Ottoman Empire see BR1080+
1050.A-Z Other, A-Z
  e.g.
1050.B3 Balkan Peninsula
1050.C9 Czechoslovakia
1050.I4 Illyria
1050.M2 Malta
1050.M6 Monaco
1050.U45 Ukraine
  Asia. The Orient
1060 Periodicals. Societies. Collections, etc.
1065 General works
1067.A-Z By race or ethnic group, A-Z
  For groups in specific countries see BR1070+
1067.A7 Arabs
1067.C4 Chinese
  Asia Minor. Southwestern Asia. Near East
1070 General works
  Turkey
1080 General works
1083.A-Z By region, A-Z
1085.A-Z By city, town, etc., A-Z
1090 Arabian Peninsula. Saudi Arabia
1100 Armenia
1102 Georgia

History
By region or country
Asia
Asia Minor. Southwestern Asia. Near East -- Continued

1105 Iraq
1110 Palestine. Israel. Syria. Lebanon
For early period see BR165+
1113.A-Z By city, town, etc., A-Z
e.g.
1113.J5 Jerusalem
1115.A-Z Other, A-Z
e.g.
1115.C9 Cyprus
Central Asia
1120 General works
(1125) Afghanistan
see BR1157+
1135 Former Soviet Central Asia
1140.A-Z Other, A-Z
e.g.
1140.B6 Bokhara (Bukhara)
1140.K5 Khiva (Khorezm)
South Asia
1143 General works
Pakistan
1145 General works
1146.A-Z By region, province, city, etc., A-Z
Bangladesh
1147 General works
1148.A-Z By region, province, city, etc., A-Z
India
1150 Periodicals. Societies. Serials
1155 General works
1156.A-Z By region, province, city, etc., A-Z
Afghanistan
1157 General works
1157.5.A-Z By region, province, city, etc., A-Z
Sri Lanka
1176 General works
1176.5.A-Z By region, province, city, etc., A-Z
Nepal
1177 General works
1177.5.A-Z By region, province, city, etc., A-Z
Southeast Asia
1178 General works
Burma. Myanmar
1179 General works

History
By region or country
Asia. The Orient
Southeast Asia
Burma. Myanmar -- Continued
1179.5.A-Z By region, province, city, etc., A-Z
Cambodia
1185 General works
1185.5.A-Z By region, province, city, etc., A-Z
Laos
1186 General works
1186.5.A-Z By region, province, city, etc., A-Z
Vietnam
1187 General works
1187.5.A-Z By region, province, city, etc., A-Z
Thailand
1195 General works
1196.A-Z By region, province, city, etc., A-Z
Malaysia
1200 General works
1200.5.A-Z By region, province, city, etc., A-Z
1205 Singapore
Indonesia
1220 General works
1221.A-Z By region, province, city, etc., A-Z
Biography
1222 Collective
1223.A-Z Individual, A-Z
Philippines
1260 General works
1261.A-Z By region, province, city, etc., A-Z
Eastern Asia
1275 General works
China
Cf. BV3410+ Missions
1280 Periodicals. Societies. Collections, etc.
1285 General works
By period
1286 16th-17th centuries
1287 18th-19th centuries
1288 20th century
1290.A-Z By region, province, etc., A-Z
e.g.
1290.M3 Manchuria
1295.A-Z By city, town, etc., A-Z
e.g.
1295.S5 Shanghai

History
By region or country
Asia. The Orient
Eastern Asia
China -- Continued
Biography
Class here only native Christians who are not identified with a specific denomination
1296 Collective
1297.A-Z Individual, A-Z
1298 Taiwan
Japan
Cf. BV3440+ Missions
1300 Periodicals. Societies
1302 Collections. Sources
1305 General works
1305.5 General special
By period
1306 Early to 1868
1868-
1306.5 General works
1307 1868-1912
20th century
1308 General works
1309 1945-
1310.A-Z By region, prefecture, county, etc., A-Z
1315.A-Z By city, town, etc., A-Z
Biography
Class here only native Christians who are not identified with a specific denomination
1316 Collective
1317.A-Z Individual, A-Z
Korea
Cf. BV3460+ Missions
1320 Periodicals. Societies. Collections, etc.
1325 General works
By period
1326 16th-17th centuries
1327 18th-19th centuries
1328 20th century
1329 21st century
1330.A-Z By region, province, etc., A-Z
1335.A-Z By city, town, etc., A-Z
Biography
Class here only native Christians who are not identified with a specific denomination
1336 Collective

History
By region or country
Asia. The Orient
Eastern Asia
Korea
Biography -- Continued
1337.A-Z Individual, A-Z
1338 Monogolia
Northern Asia. Siberia
Cf. BV3470+ Missions
1340 Periodicals. Societies. Collections, etc.
1345 General works
By period
1346 16th-17th centuries
1347 18th-19th centuries
1348 20th century
1350.A-Z By region, province, etc., A-Z
1355.A-Z By city, town, etc., A-Z
Biography
Class here only native Christians who are not identified with a specific denomination
1356 Collective
1357.A-Z Individual, A-Z
Africa
1359 Periodicals. Societies. Collections, etc.
1360 General works
Including modern period
By period
Early alone see BR190
1365 Early and medieval
Including together or medieval alone
Modern see BR1360
1367.A-Z By race or ethnic group, A-Z
e.g.
1367.T7 Tswana
1367.Z8 Zulus
North Africa. Northeast Africa
1369 General works
1370 Ethiopia
1380 Egypt
1385 Sudan
1400 Algeria
1405 Morocco
1415 Tunisia
1430 Central Africa. Sub-Saharan Africa
Eastern Africa
1440 General works

History
By region or country
Africa
Eastern Africa -- Continued
1443.A-Z By region, country, etc., A-Z
e.g.
Malawi see BR1446.2+
Nyasaland see BR1446.2+
1443.T3 Tanganyika. Tanzania
Tanzania see BR1443.T3
1443.U33 Uganda
1445.A-Z By city, town, etc., A-Z
Southern Africa
1446 General works
Malawi. Nyasaland
1446.2 General works
1446.4.A-Z By region, province, city, etc., A-Z
Zambia. Northern Rhodesia
1446.6 General works
1446.8.A-Z By region, province, city, etc., A-Z
Zimbabwe
1447 General works
1447.2.A-Z By region, province, city, etc., A-Z
Angola
1447.25 General works
1447.26.A-Z By region, province, city, etc., A-Z
Botswana. Bechuanaland
1447.3 General works
1447.4.A-Z By region, province, city, etc., A-Z
Swaziland
1447.5 General works
1447.6.A-Z By region, province, city, etc., A-Z
Lesotho. Basutoland
1447.7 General works
1447.8.A-Z By region, province, city, etc., A-Z
South Africa
1448 Periodicals. Societies. Serials
1450 General works
1455.A-Z By region, province, city, etc., A-Z
Southwest Africa (Namibia)
1458 General works
1458.2.A-Z By region, province, city, etc., A-Z
West Africa
1460 General works
1463.A-Z By region, country, etc., A-Z

History
By region or country
Africa -- Continued
1470.A-Z Other, A-Z
Including islands
e.g.
1470.M2 Madagascar
1470.M3 Madeira
Atlantic Ocean islands
1475 General works
1476.A-Z By island or group of islands, A-Z
1476.B47 Bermuda Islands
Australia and New Zealand
1480 General works
1483.A-Z By region, state, etc., A-Z
e.g.
1483.N5 New South Wales
1483.Q4 Queensland
1483.T2 Tasmania
1485.A-Z By city, town, etc., A-Z
Oceania. Pacific islands
1490 General works
1495.A-Z By island or group of islands, A-Z
e.g.
1495.F5 Fiji Islands
1495.H3 Hawaiian Islands
1495.M4 Melanesia
1495.N5 New Guinea
1495.N6 New Hebrides
1495.P6 Polynesia
1495.S3 Samoa
1500 Arctic regions. Greenland
1510 Developing countries
Persecution. Martyrs
For persecution of individual sects see BX1+
For the Inquisition see BX1700+
General works
1600 Early through 1800
1601 1801-1950
1601.2 1951-2000
1601.3 2001-
1602 Other
History
General works
Early Christians under the Roman Empire
Early through 1800
1603.A1 Contemporary works (Collected and individual)

Persecution. Martyrs
History
Early Christians under the Roman Empire
General works
Early through 1800 -- Continued
1603.A3-Z Later works through 1800
1604 1801-1950
1604.2 1951-2000
1604.23 2001-
1604.3 Persecutions of pagans by early Christians
1605 Persecutions by Protestants
Cf. BX1492 Persecution of Catholics in England
By region or country
1607 Great Britain
Cf. BX1492 Persecution of Catholics in England
1608.A-Z Other, A-Z
e.g.
1608.B4 Belgium
1608.C7 Communist countries
1608.F8 France
1608.G4 Germany
1608.I7 Ireland
1608.J3 Japan
1608.N4 Netherlands
1608.S8 Spain
Biography
1608.5 Collective
Individual
see BR; BV; BX
1609 Literary and critical history of martyr books
1609.5 Dissent
Tolerance and toleration
1610 General works
By region or country see BR500+
Liberalism
Periodicals, societies see BR1+
Congresses see BR41+
1615 General works
1616 Addresses, essays, lectures
1617 Controversial works against Liberalism
By region or country see BR500+
1620 Sacrilege (History)
Movements transcending geographical and denominational lines and theological disciplines
1625 Anticlericalism
Antinomianism see BT1330
Atheism see BL2747.3

Movements transcending geographical and denominational lines and theological disciplines -- Continued
Deism see BL2747.4
Evangelicalism
For National Association of Evangelicals see BX6.N16
1640.A1 Periodicals. Societies, etc.
1640.A2 Congresses
1640.A25 Collected works (nonserial)
1640.A3-Z General works
By denomination see BX1+
Relations with other religions, denominations, etc.
1641.A1 General works
1641.A3-Z Special, A-Z
1641.C37 Catholic Church
1641.J83 Judaism
1641.M67 Mormon Church
1642.A-Z By region or country, A-Z
Biography
1643.A1 Collective
1643.A3-Z Individual, A-Z
1643.5 Faith Movement (Hagin)
Free Thought see BL2747.5
Fundamentalism see BT82.2
Fundamentalist churches (General) see BX7800.F86+
Liberalism see BR1614.92+
Mysticism see BV5070+
Pentecostalism. Charismatic Movement
Cf. BX9.5.P45 Christian union and Pentecostalism
1644 General works
1644.3 African American and/or Black Pentecostals
By denomination see BX1+
1644.5.A-Z By region or country, A-Z
1644.7 Toronto Blessing
1646 Iconoclasm
Cf. BL485 Idolatry
Cf. BR238+ 8th century
Pietism
1650.A1 Periodicals. Societies, etc.
1650.A13 Congresses
1650.A15 Collected works (nonserial)
General works
1650.A2 Early through 1800
1650.A3-Z 1800-1950
1650.2 1951-2000
1650.3 2001-
By denomination see BX1+
1652.A-Z By country, A-Z

Movements transcending geographical and denominational lines and theological disciplines
Pietism -- Continued
Biography
1653.A1 Collective
1653.A3-Z Individual, A-Z
1661 Primitivism
Quietism see BV5099
Rationalism see BL2747.7
Skepticism see B837.A1+
Biography
Cf. BR315+ Reformation and Counter-Reformation
Cf. BR1608.5+ Persecution. Martyrs
Cf. BX1+ Individual denominations
1690 Religious biographies and confessions as a subject of study
Collective
General
1700.A2 Early through 1800
1700.A3-Z 1801-1950
1700.2 1951-2000
1700.3 2001-
1702 General special
e.g. Last hours
1703 Addresses, essays, lectures
1704 Juvenile works
Including Sunday-school texts, etc.
Cf. BR1711 Lives of the Saints
Lives of the Fathers of the Church (General)
1705.A2 Early through 1800
1705.A3-Z 1801-1950
1706 1951-2000
1706.3 2001-
Lives of the Saints
Including general works on the Saints, their psychology, message, etc.
For Catholic Church and Orthodox Eastern Church, see BX393, BX596, BX4654+, and BX4700
Cf. BT970+ Doctrinal theology
1710 General works
1711 Juvenile works
1712 Pillar saints
Lives of women
1713 General works
Ex-prostitutes
1713.5 Collective
Individual see BR1720.A+
Lives of children

Biography
Collective
Lives of children -- Continued
1714 Collective
1715.A-Z Individual, A-Z
Religious healers
1716.A1 Collective
1716.A3-Z Individual, A-Z
e.g.
1716.B7 Branham, William
1716.S35 Schlatter, Francis
Religious imposters
Cf. BF1783+ Seers and prophets (Occult sciences)
Cf. CT9980+ Biography of charlatans, imposters, rogues, scoundrels, etc., in general
Cf. HV6751+ Offenses against public morals
1718.A1 Collective
1718.A3-Z Individual, A-Z
e.g.
1718.C6 Cohn, Leopold
1718.M3 Matthews, Robert
1718.S4 Schweinfurth, George Jacob
Religious fanatics
For individual sects see BX1+
1719.A1 Collective
1719.A3-Z Individual, A-Z
Individual biography
For biography in relation to a specific topic see the topic, e.g. BR1716 Religious healers; BV3705 Missionaries
For individual denominations see BX1+
Cf. BR1715.A+ Lives of children
1720.A-Z Early Christian biography to ca. 600, A-Z
Including Saints, Fathers of the Church, etc.
For New Testament biography see BS2450+
1720.A3 Aemilianus Cucullatus, Saint
1720.A325 Agatha, Saint
Agnes, Saint see BX4700.A3
1720.A4 Alexis (Alexius), Saint
1720.A5 Ambrose, Saint, Bishop of Milan, d. 397
1720.A6 Anthony, of Egypt, Saint, ca. 250-355 or 6 (Antonius, the Great)
1720.A65 Aphraates, the Persian sage, fl.337-345
1720.A664 Armentarius, Saint
1720.A68 Artemios, Saint, Martyr, d. 363
1720.A69 Asterius, the Sophist
1720.A7 Athanasius, Saint, Patriarch of Alexandria
1720.A8 Athenagoras

Biograph y
Individual biography
Early Christian biography to ca. 600, A-Z -- Continued

1720.A9 Augustine, Saint, Bishop of Hippo
1720.A94 Ausonius, Decimus Magnus
1720.B27 Barbara, Saint
1720.B3 Basil, Saint, Bishop of Caesarea, ca. 329-379
(1720.B44) Benedict Biscop, Saint,
see BR754.B45
1720.B45 Benedict (Benedictus), Saint, Abbot of Monte Cassino
1720.B53 Blaise, Saint
1720.B6 Boethius
1720.B73 Brendan, Saint
1720.B74 Brigid, Saint, of Ireland
1720.C2 Caesarius, of Arles, Saint, 470?-542
1720.C3 Cassianus, Joannes
1720.C4 Cassiodorus, Senator
1720.C44 Cecilia, Saint
1720.C485 Christopher, Saint
1720.C5 John Chrysostom, Saint, d.407 (Chrysostomus, Joannes, Patriarch of Constantinople)
1720.C58 Clément, Saint, Bishop of Metz, 3d cent.
Clement I, Pope (Clemens, Romanus) see BX1004
1720.C6 Clement, of Alexandria, Saint, ca 150-ca. 215
1720.C623 Columba, Saint
1720.C624 Columban, Saint
1720.C79 Cyprian (Cyprianus), of Antioch
1720.C8 Cyprian, Saint, Bishop of Carthage
1720.C88 Cyril, Saint, Bishop of Jerusalem
1720.C9 Cyril, Saint, Patriarch of Alexandria, ca. 370-444.
1720.C94 Cyrus, Saint
1720.D38 David, Saint, of Wales
1720.D45 Demetrius, d. 306?
Denis, Saint, Archbishop of Paris see BX4700.D4
1720.D5 Didymus, of Alexandria, the theologian
1720.D6 Dionysius, of Alexandria, Saint
1720.D7 Dioscurus, Patriarch of Alexandria
1720.E37 Efisio, Saint
1720.E64 Epiphanius, Bishop of Constantia in Cyprus
1720.E65 Epiphanius, Saint, Bishop of Pavia
1720.E7 Erasmus, Saint
1720.E77 Eudocia, Saint
1720.E778 Eugenios, Saint, of Trebizond, 4th cent.
1720.E78 Eugenius, Saint, d. ca. 286
1720.E8 Eusebius, of Caesarea, Bishop of Caesarea
1720.E83 Eustathius, Saint, Bishop of Antioch
1720.E95 Exuperantius, Saint, Bishop of Cingoli

Biography
Individual biography
Early Christian biography to ca. 600, A-Z -- Continued

1720.F4 Felicitas, Saint
1720.F43 Felix, Saint, 3rd cent.
1720.F5 Flavian, Saint, Bishop of Constantinople
1720.F55 Florian, Saint, d. 304
1720.F67 Foy, Saint, ca. 290-303
1720.F73 Front, Saint
1720.G34 Geminianus, Saint, Bishop of Modena
1720.G35 Genesius, of Arles, Saint, d. ca. 303
1720.G37 Geneviève, Saint, ca. 420-ca. 500
1720.G4 George, Saint
1720.G62 Goar, Saint, ca. 495-ca. 570
1720.G66 Gregentios, Saint, Archbishop of Taphar, d. 552
Gregory I (Gregorius I, the Great), Saint, Pope see BX1076
Gregorius, Saint, Bp. of Tours see DC69.8.G7
1720.G7 Gregory of Nazianzus (Gregorius Nazianzenus), Saint, Patriarch of Constantinople
1720.G8 Gregory of Nyssa (Gregorius), Saint, Bishop of Nyssa
Hieronymous, Saint see BR1720.J5
1720.H6 Hilary (Hilarius), Saint, Archbishop of Arles
1720.H7 Hilary (Hilarius), Saint, Bishop of Poitiers
1720.H8 Hippolytus, Saint
1720.H83 Hosius, Bishop of Cordoba
1720.H9 Hypatius
1720.I4 Ignatius, Saint, Bishop of Antioch
1720.I7 Irenaeus, Saint, Bishop of Lyons
1720.J23 Jacob of Serug, 451-521
1720.J3 Januarius, Saint, Bishop of Benevento
1720.J5 Jerome (Hieronymus), Saint
1720.J57 Joachim, Saint
1720.J58 Joannes, Archbishop of Ravenna
John Chrysostom, Saint, d 407. see BR1720.C5
1720.J59 John of Damascus, Saint
1720.J6 John the Presbyter
1720.J78 Justa, Saint, d. ca. 287
1720.J8 Justin, Martyr, Saint
1720.K47 Kerrill, Saint
1720.K52 Kieran, Saint, of Ireland
1720.K54 Kilian, Saint
1720.L2 Lactantius, Lucius Caecilius Firmianus
Leo I, the Great, Saint, Pope see BX1047
1720.L4 Leocadia, of Toledo, Saint
1720.L54 Liborius, Saint, d. 397?
1720.L75 Lucianus, Saint

Biography
Individual biography
Early Christian biography to ca. 600, A-Z -- Continued

1720.L8 Lucy, Saint
1720.M213 Macarius, Saint, the Elder, of Egypt, 4th cent.
1720.M23 Macrina, the Elder, Saint, d. ca. 340
1720.M27 Malchus, monachus, Saint
1720.M274 Mamas
1720.M2815 Marcella, Saint, 330-410
1720.M2822 Marcellina, Saint
1720.M2824 Marcellus, Bishop of Ancyra
1720.M283 Marcian of Syracuse, Saint, d. ca. 255
1720.M295 Martial, Saint, Bishop of Limoges, 3rd cent.
1720.M3 Martin, Saint, Bishop of Tours
1720.M33 Mary, Saint, of Egypt
1720.M35 Mauritius, Saint
1720.M365 Maximus the Confessor
1720.M368 Medicus, Saint, d. ca. 172
1720.M37 Melania, the Younger, Saint, 385?-439
1720.M375 Menas, Saint, of Mareotis, d. 303?
1720.M4 Mercurius, of Caesarea, Saint
1720.M5 Methodius, Saint, Bishop of Olympus
1720.M65 Mitrius, Saint
1720.N45 Niceta (Nicetas), Saint, Bishop of Remesiana
1720.N458 Nicholas, of Sion, Saint, d. 564
1720.N46 Nicholas, Saint, Bishop of Myra
1720.N49 Nilus, the Elder, Saint, d. ca. 430
1720.N5 Ninian, Saint
1720.N53 Nino (Nina), Saint
1720.N55 Niphon, Saint, Bishop of Constantia, fl. 4th cent.
1720.N8 Novatian (Novatianus)
1720.O65 Optatus, Saint
1720.O7 Origin (Origenes)
1720.P23 Pachomius, Saint
1720.P25 Pacianus, Saint, Bishop of Barcelona
1720.P256 Pantaleon, Saint
1720.P257 Papias, Saint, Bishop of Hierapolis, d. ca. 120
1720.P2575 Pardus, Saint
1720.P26 Patrick, Saint
1720.P27 Paul of Samosata (Paulus, of Samosata), Patriarch of Antioch
1720.P28 Paul of Thebes (Paulus Thebaeus), Saint
1720.P29 Paula, Saint
1720.P3 Paulinus, Saint, Bishop of Nola
1720.P42 Perpetua, Saint
1720.P427 Peter, of Alexandria, Saint
1720.P429 Petroc, Saint, 504?-594

Biography
Individual biography
Early Christian biography to ca. 600, A-Z -- Continued

1720.P43 Petrus Iberus, Bishop of Majuma, 411?-491?
1720.P465 Phileas, Saint, Bishop of Thmuis, d. 306
1720.P477 Philomena
1720.P5 Pionius, Saint, d. 251
1720.P53 Pisentius, Saint
1720.P7 Polycarp (Polycarpus), Saint, Bishop of Smyrna
1720.P766 Procopius, Megalomartyr, Saint, d. 303
1720.P77 Prosper, Saint, Bishop of Tarragona
1720.P8 Prosper of Aquitaine (Prosper, Tiro, Aquitanus), Saint
1720.Q5 Quirinus, Saint
1720.R3 Rabbula, Bishop of Edessa
1720.R6 Romain de Blaye, Saint
1720.R8 Rufinus, d. 395
1720.S175 Sabinus, Saint, d. 566
1720.S2 Salvian of Marseilles (Salvianus)
1720.S23 Sargis, Saint, 4th cent.
1720.S25 Satiro, Saint, d. 378
1720.S27 Scholastica, Saint, 6th cent.
1720.S3 Sebastian, Saint
1720.S36 Servatius, Saint
1720.S4 Severinus, Saint
1720.S48 Shenute, ca. 348-466
1720.S5 Sidonius Apollinaris (Sidonius, C. Sollius Modestus Apollinaris)
1720.S518 Simeon Salus
1720.S52 Simeon Stylites, d. 459
1720.S54 Sinaitēs, Anastasios, d. ca. 609 A.D.
1720.S7 Socrates Scholasticus
1720.S73 Sophronius, Saint
1720.S8 Sozomen
1720.S85 Spyridon, Saint, Bishop of Trimithus
1720.S9 Synesius Cyrenaeus, Bishop of Ptolemais
1720.T2 Tarsicius, Saint, Martyr
1720.T25 Tatian (Tatianus), 2d cent.
1720.T3 Tertullian (Tertullianus, Quintus Septimius Florens)
1720.T33 Thecla (Thekla), Saint
1720.T35 Theodore of Mopsuestia (Theodorus, Bishop of Mopsuestia)
1720.T36 Theodoret, Bishop of Cyrrhus
1720.T38 Theodorus Studita, Saint
1720.T4 Theodotus, Saint
1720.T45 Theophilus, Patriarch, Archbishop of Alexandria
1720.T47 Theophilus, Saint, Bishop of Antioch
1720.T5 Ticonius (Tichonius), 4th cent.

Biography
Individual biography
Early Christian biography to ca. 600, A-Z -- Continued

1720.U75 Ursula, Saint
1720.V26 Valentin de Griselles, Saint
1720.V28 Valentine, Saint
1720.V37 Venantius, Saint
1720.V4 Verena (Verena of Zurzach), Saint
1720.V43 Veronica, Saint, 1st cent.
Including her veil
1720.V47 Victorinus, C. Marius
1720.V5 Vigilantius, fl. 394-406
1720.V53 Vincent (Vincentius), of Agen, Saint
1720.V6 Vincent of Lerins (Vincentius Lerinensis), Saint
1720.V64 Vincent, of Saragossa, Saint
1720.V66 Vitalis, Saint
1725.A-Z Other, A-Z

The Bible
General
Texts and versions
1 Polyglot Bibles. By date
3 Minor
For polyglot texts of special parts, see the special part. For specimens of Bible texts in several languages, e.g. John III, 16, see P351-352
3.5 Hebrew-Greek Bibles. By date
Hebrew Old Testament and Greek New Testament
4 Collections
Miscellaneous general collections in print or facsimile

4.5 Works on Biblical manuscripts in general
Early versions
For early versions of special parts of the Bible, see the special part
For bibliographies of Bible manuscripts see Z7771.M3
Syriac. Peshitta
11 Printed texts. By date
Manuscripts. Codices
11.3 General works
Individual manuscripts
11.5.A-Z By name, A-Z
For criticism use subarrangement by author, A-Z
11.7 By number
For criticism use subarrangement by author, A-Z
Translations
12 English
13.A-Z Other European languages, A-Z
Modern non-European languages see BS315+
14 History and criticism
Palestinian Syriac
14.3 Printed texts. By date
Manuscripts. Codices
14.313 General works
Individual manuscripts
14.315.A-Z By name, A-Z
For criticism use subarrangement by author, A-Z
14.317 By number
For criticism use subarrangement by author, A-Z
Translations
14.32 English
14.33.A-Z Other European languages, A-Z
Modern non-European languages see BS315+
14.34 History and criticism
Modern Syriac see BS315.S9

General
Texts and versions
Early versions -- Continued
15 Hebrew
The printed text of the Hebrew Old Testament and the New Testament translated into Hebrew
Samaritan Pentateuch see BM920+
Arabic see BS315.A6+
Ethiopic
31 Printed texts. By date
Manuscripts. Codices
31.3 General works
Individual mansucripts
31.5.A-Z By name, A-Z
For criticism use subarrangement by author, A-Z
31.7 By number
For criticism use subarrangement by author, A-Z
Translations
32 English
33.A-Z Other European languages, A-Z
Modern non-European languages see BS315+
34 History and criticism
Ancient Greek versions
37 Collections
Works in which several texts are published
37.5 Comparative texts of Greek Bibles
38 History and criticism
Manuscripts. Codices
39 General works
Individual manuscripts
Including manuscripts of the whole Bible and fragments of manuscripts containing portions of each Testament
64.A-Z By name, A-Z
Codex alexandrinus
64.A5 Facsimiles
64.A6 Printed editions. By date
64.A7 History and criticism
Beatty papyri
64.B3 Facsimiles
64.B4 Printed editions. By date
64.B5 History and criticism
Codex sinaiticus
64.S3 Facsimiles
64.S4 Printed editions. By date
64.S5 History and criticism
Codex vaticanus

General
Texts and versions
Early versions
Ancient Greek versions
Manuscripts. Codices
Individual manuscripts
By name, A-Z
Codex vaticanus -- Continued
64.V2 Facsimiles
64.V3 Printed editions. By date
64.V4 History and criticism
64.5 By number, A-Z
According to the numbering by Rahlfs
65 Modern printed editions By date
Selections from the Greek Bible see BS399.G7
Latin versions
67 Collections
Works in which several texts are published
67.5 Comparative texts of Latin Bibles
68 History and criticism
Manuscripts. Codices
69 General works
70.A-Z Individual manuscripts (regardless of version), A-Z
By name or other distinctive word
For criticism use subarrangement by author, A-Z
Special versions
Greek-Latin parallel editions are classed with Greek texts
Old Latin. Italic versions. Itala
72 Collections. By title or editor
73 Texts. By date
74 History and criticism
Vulgate
75 Texts. By date
85 History and criticism
89.A-Z Other early and medieval Latin versions, A-Z
90 Modern versions. By date
Selections from the Latin Bible see BS399.L3
Other early versions
Armenian
For modern Armenian see BS315.A73
95 Printed texts. By date
Manuscripts. Codices
95.3 General works
95.5.A-Z Individual manuscripts (regardless of version), A-Z
By name or other distinctive word
For criticism use subarrangement by author, A-Z
96 History and criticism

General
Texts and versions
Early versions
Other early versions -- Continued
Coptic (all dialects)
100 Printed texts. By date
Manuscripts. Codices
100.3 General works
100.5.A-Z Individual manuscripts (regardless of version), A-Z
By name or other distinctive word
For criticism use subarrangement by author, A-Z
101 History and criticism
Gothic
Including fragments of Old and New Testaments
105 Printed texts. By date
Manuscripts. Codices
105.3 General works
105.5.A-Z Individual manuscripts (regardless of version), A-Z
By name or other distinctive word
For criticism use subarrangement by author, A-Z
106 History and criticism
Church Slavic
110 Printed texts. By date
Manuscripts. Codices
110.3 General works
110.5.A-Z Individual manuscripts (regardless of version), A-Z
By name or other distinctive word
For criticism use subarrangement by author, A-Z
111 History and criticism
115.A-Z Other, A-Z
Modern texts and versions
For general works about the Bible in each language see BS455+
Polyglot see BS1
English
Class here the whole Bible only unless otherwise noted
125 Comparative texts of English Bibles. By date
Cf. BS188.A3 Authorized and Revised versions
Cf. BS190.A3 Authorized and American Revision versions
Cf. BS191.A3 Revised Standard and Confraternity of Christian Doctrine versions
Cf. BS1421 Comparative texts of the Psalms

General
Texts and versions
Modern texts and versions
English -- Continued
130 Anglo-Saxon
Class here Bibles and special parts of the Bible in Anglo-Saxon, except works attributed to King Alfred, Caedmon, etc., which are classed in PR, English literature
131 Selections
132 History and criticism, etc.
English versions
Arranged chronologically
135-136 Wycliffe's (1380) (Table BS1)
138.A-Z Other Middle English versions, A-Z
e.g.
138.P8 Purvey's
140-141 Tyndale's (1525-1531) (Table BS1)
All of Tyndale's translation: New Testament and parts of Old Testament
For life of Tyndale see BR350.T8
145-146 Coverdale's (1535) (Table BS1)
150-151 Matthew's (1537) (Table BS1)
152-153 Taverner's (1539) (Table BS1)
Revision of Matthew's
The Great Bible
155-156 Cromwell's edition, 1539 (Table BS1)
160-161 Cranmer's edition, 1540 (Table BS1)
165-166 Cranmer's edition, 1541 (Table BS1)
167 Other editions. By date
170-171 Geneva Bible (1560), "Breeches Bible" (Table BS1)
For Geneva New Testament alone see BS2070+
175-176 Bishop's Bible (1568) (Table BS1)
180-181 Douai (Old Testament, 1609-1610; Rheims New Testament, 1582) (Table BS1)
Including revisions such as the Challoner revision and the Confraternity of Christian Doctrine version.
For other modern Catholic versions in English see BS195.A+
For New Testament alone see BS2080+
King James, Authorized version (1611)
185 Texts
Arrange by date and subarrange by place of publication, A-Z
186 History and criticism, etc.
Revised version (1881-1885)

General
Texts and versions
Modern texts and versions
English
English versions
Revised version (1881-1885) -- Continued

188.A1 Texts. By date
Subarrange by place of publication, A-Z

188.A2 Texts, American version. By date

188.A3 Authorized and Revised versions paralleled
Subdivided by date and place of publication

188.A5-Z History and criticism, etc.

American Revision (1901)

190.A1 Texts. By date.
Subarrange by place of publication, A-Z

190.A3 Authorized and American Revision versions paralleled
Subarrange by date and place of publication

190.A5-Z History and criticism, etc.

Revised Standard version (1946-1952)

191.A1 Texts. By date
Subarrange by place of publication, A-Z

191.A3 Revised Standard and Confraternity of Christian Doctrine versions paralleled

191.A5-Z History and criticism, etc.

New Revised Standard version (1990)

191.5.A1 Texts. By date
Subarrange by place of publication, A-Z

191.5.A5-Z History and criticism, etc.

New English Bible (1961-)

192.A1 Texts. By date
Subarrange by place of publication, A-Z

192.A5-Z History and criticism, etc.

Revised English Bible (1989-)

192.16.A1 Texts. By date
Subarrange by place of publication, A-Z

192.16.A5-Z History and criticism, etc.

Anchor Bible

192.2.A1 Texts. By date
Subarrange by place of publication, A-Z

192.2.A5-Z History and criticism, etc.

New American Bible

192.3.A1 Texts. By date
Subarrange by place of publication, A-Z

192.3.A5-Z History and criticism, etc.

195.A-Z Other versions and revisions. By version, A-Z

195.A53-.A532 Amplified (Table BS2)

General
Texts and versions
Modern texts and versions
English
English versions
Other versions and revisions, A-Z -- Continued

195.B38-.B382 Berkeley version (Table BS2)
195.C6-.C62 Confraternity version (Table BS2)
195.C66-.C662 Contemporary English (Table BS2)
195.D35-.D352 Dolen (Table BS2)
195.E64-.E642 English Standard (Table BS2)
195.E87-.E872 Esposito (Table BS2)
195.G55-.G552 Goble (Table BS2)
195.G57-.G572 God's Word (Table BS2)
195.G58-.G582 Gold (Table BS2)
195.G59-.G592 Golden Bridge version (Table BS2)
Good News Translation see BS195.T63+
195.G84-.G842 Green (Table BS2)
195.H32-.H322 Haak (Table BS2)
195.H64-.H642 House of Yahweh (Table BS2)
195.I56-.I562 International Standard (Table BS2)
195.J4-.J42 Jerusalem (Table BS2)
195.K53-.K532 KJ21 (Table BS2)
195.L32-.L322 Lacey (Table BS2)
195.L35-.L352 Lamsa (Table BS2)
195.L54-.L542 Life messengers (Table BS2)
195.L58-.L582 Living Bible (Table BS2)
195.M47-.M472 The Message (Table BS2)
195.N32-.N322 NET Bible (Table BS2)
195.N35-.N352 New American Standard (Table BS2)
195.N3524-.N35242 New Authorized (Table BS2)
195.N353-.N3532 New Century (Table BS2)
195.N37-.N372 New International (Table BS2)
195.N373-.N3732 New International Readers Version (Table BS2)
195.N375-.N3752 New Jerusalem Bible (Table BS2)
195.N38-.N382 New King James (Table BS2)
195.N394-.N3942 New Living Translation (Table BS2)
195.N4-.N42 New World (Table BS2)
195.P75-.P752 Priests for Equality (Table BS2)
195.S5-.S52 Simplified Living Bible (Table BS2)
195.S75-.S752 Stern (Table BS2)
195.T63-.T632 Today's English. Good News Translation (Table BS2)

Basic English versions
196.A1 Texts. By date
Subarrange by place of publication, A-Z
196.A5-Z History and criticism, etc.

General
Texts and versions
Modern texts and versions
English -- Continued
196.5 Reference editions
Editions for special classes
197 Young people's Bibles. Children's Bibles. By editor or publisher.
Class here relatively complete Bibles omitting portions unsuitable for children.
For less complete selections see BS389+
For Bible stories see BS551+
198.A-Z Other, A-Z
Subarrange by publisher and date
e.g.
198.E3 Eastern Star
198.F8 Freemasons
Mormons see BX8630+
198.O3 Oddfellows
199-313 Other European languages (Table BS10)
Add number in table to BS0
Each language to include its dialects unless otherwise provided for
Non-European languages
Including dialects unless otherwise provided for
315.A-Z Asian languages, A-Z
For languages of the Philippines and the island of New Guinea see BS335.A+
315.A1 General
315.A33 Abor (Table BS5)
315.A35 Afghan. Pushto (Table BS5)
315.A38 Ainu (Table BS5)
315.A47 Angami (Table BS5)
315.A53 Ao (Table BS5)
315.A6-.A69 Arabic (Table BS4)
Arabic (Judeo-Arabic) see BS315.J83+
315.A73 Armenian (Modern) (Table BS5)
For ancient Armenian see BS95+
315.A83 Assamese (Table BS5)
(315.B33) Balangingi
see BS335.B27
315.B34 Balinese (Table BS5)
315.B345 Banggai (Table BS5)
315.B35 Bara (Table BS5)
315.B38 Batak (Table BS5)
(315.B385) Batan
see BS335.B37

General
Texts and versions
Modern texts and versions
Non-European languages
Asian languages, A-Z -- Continued

315.B4-.B49 Bengali (Table BS4)
(315.B52) Berik
see BS335.B47
315.B57 Bikaneri (Table BS5)
(315.B69) Botolan Sambal
see BS335.S24
315.B77 Buginese (Bugi) (Table BS5)
(315.B78) Bukidnon
see BS335.M24
315.B79 Bunak (Table BS5)
315.B8-.B89 Burmese (Table BS4)
315.C37 Car Nicobarese (Table BS5)
315.C5-.C59 Chinese (Table BS4)
Including Canton, Mandarin, Shanghai
315.D32 Daa (Table BS5)
Dayak see BS315.D8+
315.D7 Dusun (Table BS5)
315.D8-.D89 Dyak. Dayak (Table BS4)
315.E83 Even (Table BS5)
315.G3 Garo (Garrow) (Table BS5)
315.G44 Georgian (Table BS5)
315.G48 Ghale (Table BS5)
315.G6 Gond (Gondi) (Table BS5)
315.G85 Gujarati (Gujara) (Table BS5)
315.G88 Gurung (Table BS5)
315.G88 Gurung (Table BS5)
315.H25 Harauti (Table BS5)
315.H4-.H49 Hindi (Table BS4)
315.H73 Hmar (Table BS5)
315.H76 Hmong (Table BS5)
315.I23 Iban (Table BS5)
315.I5-.I59 Indonesian (Table BS4)
(315.J27) Jama Mapun
see BS335.J25
315.J3-.J39 Japanese (Table BS4)
315.J4-.J49 Javanese (Table BS4)
315.J55 Jirel (Table BS5)
315.J83-.J839 Judeo-Arabic (Table BS4)
(315.K25) Kagayanen
see BS335.K15
315.K28 Kannada (Table BS5)

General
Texts and versions
Modern texts and versions
Non-European languages
Asian languages, A-Z -- Continued

315.K3	Karen (Table BS5) Including Pwo Karen, Sgaw Karen
315.K32	Karo-Batak (Table BS5)
315.K35	Kashmiri (Table BS5)
315.K37	Kaw (Table BS5)
315.K39	Kazakh (Table BS5)
315.K46	Ketengban (Table BS5)
315.K5	Khasi (Table BS5)
315.K75	Konkani (Table BS5)
315.K8-.K89	Korean (Table BS4)
315.K915	Kuki (Table BS5)
315.K93	Kului (Table BS5)
315.K95	Kurdish (Table BS5)
315.L33	Lahndā (Table BS5)
315.L35	Lakher (Table BS5)
315.L36	Lambadi (Table BS5)
315.L38	Lao (Table BS5)
315.L46	Lhota (Table BS5)
315.L57	Lisu (Table BS5)
315.L85	Lushai (Table BS5)
315.M13	Maanyan (Table BS5)
315.M14	Madurese (Table BS5)
315.M15	Magar (Table BS5)
315.M17	Makasar (Table BS5)
315.M2-.M29	Malay (Table BS4)
315.M295	Malayalam (Table BS5)
315.M297	Maltese (Table BS5)
315.M298	Mandailing (Table BS5)
315.M3-.M39	Maraṭhi (Table BS4)
315.M48	Mentawai (Table BS5)
315.M66	Mongolian (Table BS5)
315.M86	Mundari (Table BS5)
315.N2	Nagpuria (Table BS5)
315.N27	Nepali (Table BS5)
315.N47	Newari (Table BS5)
315.N53	Nias (Table BS5)
	Numfor see BS335.N8
315.O7	Oriya (Table BS5)
(315.O75)	Orya see BS335.O77
315.P25	Paite (Table BS5)
315.P3	Panjabi (Table BS5)

General
Texts and versions
Modern texts and versions
Non-European languages
Asian languages, A-Z -- Continued

315.P4	Persian (Table BS5)
315.P42	Persian (Judeo-Persian) (Table BS5)
	Pushto see BS315.A35
315.R39	Rawang (Table BS5)
315.R6	Rong (Table BS5)
315.S26	Sangtam (Table BS5)
315.S3-.S39	Sanskrit (Table BS4)
315.S4	Santali (Table BS5)
315.S45	Shan (Table BS5)
315.S5	Siamese. Thai (Table BS5)
315.S53	Simelungun (Table BS5)
(315.S54)	Sindangan Subanun see BS335.S8
315.S55	Sinhalese (Table BS5)
315.S67	Sora (Table BS5)
315.S83	Sumba (Table BS5)
315.S85	Sundanese (Table BS5)
315.S87	Sunwar (Table BS5)
315.S9	Syriac (Modern) (Table BS5) For ancient Syriac see BS11+
315.T23	Talaud (Table BS5)
315.T25	Tamang (Table BS5)
315.T3-.T39	Tamil (Table BS4)
315.T42	Tangkhul (Table BS5)
315.T45	Telugu (Table BS5)
	Thai see BS315.S5
315.T5	Tibetan (Table BS5)
315.T53	Tiddim Chin (Table BS5)
315.T55	Timorese (Table BS5)
(315.T57)	Tiruray see BS335.T5
315.T6	Toba-Batak (Table BS5)
315.T63	Tobelo (Table BS5)
315.T66	Tondano (Table BS5)
315.T68	Toraja (Table BS5)
315.T8	Tulu (Table BS5)
315.U4	Uma (Table BS5)
315.U7	Urdu (Table BS5)
315.V34	Vaiphe (Table BS5)
315.V53	Vietnamese (Table BS5)
(315.Y25)	Yakan see BS335.Y26

General
Texts and versions
Modern texts and versions
Non-European languages
Asian languages, A-Z -- Continued

315.Y3	Yakut (Table BS5)
315.Y32	Yamdena (Table BS5)
325.A-Z	African languages, A-Z
325.A1	General
325.A22	Abe (Table BS5)
325.A25	Acoli (Table BS5)
325.A33	Adangme (Table BS5)
325.A44	Aladian (Table BS5)
325.A5	Alur (Table BS5)
325.A6-.A69	Amharic (Table BS4)
325.A74	Anuak (Table BS5)
325.A8	Asu (Table BS5)
325.B2	Bafia (Table BS5)
325.B26	Bambara (Table BS5)
325.B3	Bangala (Table BS5)
325.B395	Basa (Table BS5)
325.B396	Bassa (Liberia) (Table BS5)
325.B397	Bati (Table BS5)
325.B3973	Baule (Table BS5)
325.B398	Bemba (Table BS5)
325.B4-.B49	Benga (Table BS4)
325.B52	Berber (Table BS5)
325.B6	Bobangi (Table BS5)
325.B7	Bobo (Table BS5)
325.B74	Bor (Table BS5)
325.B77	Boran (Table BS5)
325.B8	Bullon (Bulom) (Table BS5)
325.B83	Bulu (Table BS5)
325.B93	Bwamu (Table BS5)
325.C47	Chewa (Table BS5)
325.C55	Chokwe (Table BS5)
325.C6	Congo (Table BS5)
325.C64	Coptic (Table BS5)
325.D23	Dabida (Table BS5)
325.D3	Dan (Table BS5)
325.D8	Duala (Table BS5)
325.D9	Dyur (Table BS5)
325.E35	Efik (Table BS5)
325.E45	Ekajuk (Table BS5)
325.E5	Engenni (Table BS5)
325.E92	Ewe (Table BS5)
325.F3	Fang (Table BS5)

General
Texts and versions
Modern texts and versions
Non-European languages
African languages, A-Z -- Continued

325.F8	Fulah (Table BS5)
325.G3	Gã (Table BS5)
325.G34	Galla (Table BS5)
325.G392	Gambai (Table BS5)
325.G393	Ganda (Table BS5)
325.G7-.G79	Grebo (Table BS4)
325.G797	Gude (Table BS5)
325.G8	Gusii (Table BS5)
325.G86	Guyuk (Table BS5)
325.H23	Hadiya (Table BS5)
325.H27	Hanga (Ghana) (Table BS5)
325.H3-.H39	Hausa (Table BS4)
325.H395	Haya (Table BS5)
325.I3	Ibo (Table BS5)
325.I4	Igede (Table BS5)
325.I7	Iraqw (Table BS5)
325.J5	Jita (Table BS5)
325.J8	Jukun (Table BS5)
325.K27	Kabyle (Table BS5)
(325.K3-.K39)	Kafir see BS325.X46
325.K394	Kakwa (Table BS5)
325.K395	Kalenjin (Table BS5)
325.K396	Kamba (Table BS5)
325.K397	Kambata (Table BS5)
325.K45	Kaonde (Table BS5)
325.K49	Karamojong (Table BS5)
325.K4912	Karré (Table BS5)
325.K49124	Kasem (Table BS5)
325.K49125	Kasena (Table BS5)
325.K4913	Kavirondo (Table BS5)
325.K4916	Kikuyu (Table BS5)
325.K4924	Kilega (Table BS5)
325.K55	Kimbundu (Mbundu) (Table BS5)
325.K595	Kingwana (Table BS5)
325.K597	Kissi (Table BS5)
325.K598	Kituba (Table BS5)
325.K67	Kongo (Table BS5)
325.K68	Konkomba (Table BS5)
325.K7	Kpelle (Table BS5)
325.K8	Kuanyama (Table BS5)
325.K82	Kulango (Table BS5)

General
Texts and versions
Modern texts and versions
Non-European languages
African languages, A-Z -- Continued

325.K84 Kuo (Table BS5)
325.K85 Kuria (Table BS5)
325.K88 Kussassi (Table BS5)
325.K93 Kweni (Table BS5)
Lango see BS325.K82
325.L36 Latuka (Table BS5)
325.L6 Logbara (Table BS5)
325.L63 Loma (Table BS5)
325.L8 Luba (Table BS5)
325.L85 Lunda (Table BS5)
325.L87 Luragoli (Table BS5)
325.L9 Luyia (Table BS5)
Malagasy see BS335.M2
325.M3 Mandingo (Table BS5)
325.M34 Mano (Table BS5)
325.M38 Masai (Table BS5)
325.M394 Mbunda (Zambia) (Table BS5)
Mbundu see BS325.K55
325.M47 Mende (Table BS5)
325.M48 Meru (Table BS5)
325.M54 Moru (Table BS5)
325.M6 Mossi (Table BS5)
325.M7-.M79 Mpongwe (Table BS4)
325.M84 Murle (Table BS5)
325.N33 Nafaanra (Table BS5)
325.N35 Nama (Table BS5)
325.N392 Nandi (Table BS5)
325.N395 Nankanse (Table BS5)
325.N43 Ndonga (Table BS5)
325.N45 Ngonde (Table BS5)
325.N5 Nika (Table BS5)
325.N55 Nilamba (Table BS5)
325.N8 Nubian (Table BS5)
325.N83 Nuer (Table BS5)
325.N9 Nyamwezi (Table BS5)
325.N914 Nyanja (Table BS5)
325.N92 Nyankole (Table BS5)
325.N93 Nyankore-Kiga (Table BS5)
325.N95 Nyiha (Table BS5)
325.N96 Nyore (Table BS5)
325.O75 Oromo (Table BS5)
325.P3 Padang (Table BS5)

General
Texts and versions
Modern texts and versions
Non-European languages
African languages, A-Z -- Continued

325.R3 Ragoli (Table BS5)
325.R75 Ruanda (Table BS5)
325.R8 Rundi (Table BS5)
325.R85 Ruund (Table BS5)
325.S3 Sango (Table BS5)
325.S33 Sara mbai (Table BS5)
325.S45 Sechuana (Table BS5)
325.S495 Sheetswa (Table BS5)
325.S5 Shilluk (Table BS5)
325.S53 Shona (Table BS5)
325.S55 Sisaala (Table BS5)
325.S6-.S69 Sotho (Table BS4)
325.S9-.S99 Swahili (Table BS4)
325.T4 Teso (Table BS5)
325.T45 Tete (Table BS5)
325.T48 Thonga (Table BS5)
325.T488 Tigré (Table BS5)
325.T49 Tigrinya (Table BS5)
325.T5 Timne (Table BS5)
325.T58 Tiv (Table BS5)
325.T69 Tonga (Zambesi) (Table BS5)
325.T7 Tonga of Inhambane (Table BS5)
325.T87 Tumbuka (Table BS5)
325.T89 Turkana (Table BS5)
325.U3 Uduk (Table BS5)
325.U5 Umbundu (Table BS5)
325.W35 Walamo (Table BS5)
325.W63 Wobe (Table BS5)
325.X46-.X469 Xhosa (Table BS4)
325.Y2-.Y29 Yao (Table BS4)
325.Y6-.Y69 Yoruba (Table BS4)
325.Z3 Zarma (Table BS5)
325.Z5 Ziba (Table BS5)
325.Z8-.Z89 Zulu (Table BS4)
335.A-Z Languages of Oceania and Australasia (Austronesian, Papuan, and Australian), A-Z

For languages of Malaysia and Indonesia (except the island of New Guinea) see BS315.A+

335.A1 General
335.A14 Abaknon (Table BS5)
335.A16 Abau (Table BS5)
335.A2 Abulas (Table BS5)

General
Texts and versions
Modern texts and versions
Non-European languages
Languages of Oceania and Australasia (Austronesian, Papuan, and Australian), A-Z -- Continued

335.A33	Aekyom (Table BS5)
335.A37	Agarabe (Table BS5)
335.A38	Agta (Table BS5)
335.A39	Agutaynon (Table BS5)
335.A44	Alamblak (Table BS5)
335.A46	Ama (Papua New Guinea) (Table BS5)
335.A464	Amanab (Table BS5)
335.A47	Ampale (Table BS5)
335.A5	Angal Heneng (Table BS5)
335.A82	Arop-Lokep (Table BS5)
335.A86	Asaro (Table BS5)
335.A88	Atta (Table BS5)
335.A9	Aulua (Table BS5)
335.A95	Awa (Table BS5)
335.B27	Balangingi (Table BS5)
(335.B3)	Balinese see BS315.B34
335.B33	Bambatana (Table BS5)
335.B35	Bamu River (Table BS5)
335.B36	Barai (Table BS5)
335.B362	Bariai (Table BS5)
335.B366	Baruya (Table BS5)
335.B37	Batan (Table BS5)
335.B43	Bena-Bena (Table BS5)
335.B47	Berik (Table BS5)
335.B5	Bikol (Table BS5)
335.B52	Bimin (Table BS5)
335.B53	Binandere (Table BS5)
	Binukid Manobo see BS335.M24
335.B534	Bine (Table BS5)
335.B54	Binumarien (Table BS5)
(335.B57)	Bisaya see BS335.H5
335.B65	Bontoc (Table BS5) Including Central, Eastern, and Southern Bontoc
	Botolan Sambal see BS335.S24
335.B8	Buang (Table BS5)
335.B85	Bwaidoga (Table BS5)
335.C4	Cebú (Cebuano) (Table BS5)
335.C43	Chabacano (Table BS5)
335.C45	Chamorro (Table BS5)

General
Texts and versions
Modern texts and versions
Non-European languages
Languages of Oceania and Australasia (Austronesian, Papuan, and Australian), A-Z -- Continued

335.C56	Chuave (Table BS5)
	Cotabato Manobo see BS335.M24
335.D35	Daga (Table BS5)
335.D43	Dedua (Table BS5)
(335.D54)	Dimuga see BS335.D35
335.D62	Dobu (Table BS5)
335.E37	Edolo (Table BS5)
335.E93	Ewage (Table BS5)
335.F35	Fasu (Table BS5)
335.F5	Fijian (Table BS5)
335.F6	Florida (Table BS5)
335.G23	Gaddang (Table BS5)
335.G25	Gadsup (Table BS5)
335.G3	Gahuku (Table BS5)
335.G34	Gawigl (Table BS5)
335.G46	Gidra (Table BS5)
335.G5	Gilbertese (Table BS5)
335.G53	Gimi (Table BS5)
335.G6	Gogodala (Table BS5)
335.G62	Golin (Table BS5)
335.G8	Guhu-Samane (Table BS5)
335.G82	Gumasi (Table BS5)
335.G83	Gwahatike (Table BS5)
335.G85	Gwedena (Table BS5)
335.H22	Halia (Table BS5)
335.H25	Hanunóo (Table BS5)
335.H28	Hatam (Table BS5)
335.H3-.H39	Hawaiian (Table BS4)
335.H5	Hiligaynon (Table BS5)
335.H68	Hote (Table BS5)
335.H8	Hula (Table BS5)
335.I2	Iai (Table BS5)
335.I26	Iamalele (Table BS5)
335.I27	Iatmul (Table BS5)
335.I3	Ibanag (Table BS5)
335.I34	Iduna (Table BS5)
335.I36	Ifugao (Table BS5) Including individual Ifugao dialects
335.I4	Iloko (Iloco, Ilocano) (Table BS5)
335.I45	Inoke (Table BS5)

General
Texts and versions
Modern texts and versions
Non-European languages
Languages of Oceania and Australasia (Austronesian, Papuan, and Australian), A-Z -- Continued

335.I83	Itawis (Table BS5)
335.I93	Iwam (Table BS5)
335.J2	Jabim (Table BS5)
335.J25	Jama Mapun (Table BS5)
335.K15	Kagayanen (Table BS5)
335.K16	Kalagan (Table BS5)
335.K17	Kalam (Table BS5)
335.K18	Kamano (Table BS5)
335.K183	Kamasau (Table BS5)
335.K187	Kamula (Table BS5)
335.K195	Kanite (Table BS5)
335.K2	Kankanay (Table BS5) Including Northern Kankanay
335.K3	Kate (Table BS5)
335.K4	Kewa (Table BS5)
335.K5	Kiriwanian (Table BS5)
335.K62	Kobon (Table BS5)
335.K63	Kongara (Table BS5)
335.K65	Koriki (Table BS5)
335.K67	Koronadal Blaan (Table BS5)
335.K7	Kovai (Table BS5)
335.K75	Kuni (Table BS5)
335.K755	Kunimaipa (Table BS5)
335.K77	Kurti (Table BS5)
335.K8-.K89	Kusaie (Table BS4)
335.L6	Lonwolwol (Table BS5)
335.L64	Lote (Table BS5)
335.L66	Lower Tanudan Kalinga (Table BS5)
335.M126	Mabuiag (Table BS5)
335.M14	Magindanao (Table BS5)
335.M16	Mailu (Table BS5)
335.M2	Malagasy (Table BS5)
335.M22	Malu (Solomon Islands) (Table BS5)
335.M237	Mangulasi (Table BS5)
335.M24	Manobo (Table BS5) Including individual Manobo languages and dialects
335.M27	Maori (Table BS5)
335.M295	Maranao (Table BS5)
335.M297	Maring (Table BS5)
335.M3-.M39	Marshall (Table BS4)
	MatigSalug see BS335.M24

General
Texts and versions
Modern texts and versions
Non-European languages
Languages of Oceania and Australasia (Austronesian, Papuan, and Australian), A-Z

335.M43 Meax (Table BS5)
335.M45 Medlpa (Table BS5)
335.M5 Mende (Papua New Guinea) (Table BS5)
335.M53 Minaveha (Table BS5)
335.M55 Misima-Panayati (Table BS5)
335.M6 Molima (Table BS5)
335.M65 Mortlock (Table BS5)
335.M69 Motu (Table BS5)
335.M695 Motuna (Table BS5)
335.M72 Mouk (Table BS5)
335.M77 Mountain Arapesh (Table BS5)
335.M82 Mugil (Table BS5)
335.M85 Murut (Table BS5)
335.M88 Muyuw (Table BS5)
335.N24 Nahu (Table BS5)
335.N26 Narak (Table BS5)
335.N27 Nasioi (Table BS5)
335.N37 Nauru (Table BS5)
Neo-Melanesian see BS335.T64
335.N498 New Caledonia (Table BS5)
(335.N5) Nias
see BS315.N53
335.N54 Nii (Table BS5)
335.N6 Nogugu (Table BS5)
335.N65 Notsi (Table BS5)
335.N67 Notu (Table BS5)
335.N8 Nufor. Numfor (Table BS5)
335.N894 Nukuoro (Table BS5)
335.N896 Nunggubuyu (Table BS5)
335.O35 Oksapmin (Table BS5)
335.O54 Omie (Table BS5)
335.O66 Ono (Table BS5)
335.O75 Orokolo (Table BS5)
335.O77 Orya (Table BS5)
335.P26 Palawano (Table BS5)
335.P3 Pampanga (Table BS5)
335.P33 Pangutaran Sama (Table BS5)
335.P5 Pitjandjara (Table BS5)
335.P6-.P69 Ponape (Table BS4)
335.P87 Purari (Table BS5)
335.R38 Rawa (Table BS5)

General
Texts and versions
Modern texts and versions
Non-European languages
Languages of Oceania and Australasia (Austronesian, Papuan, and Australian), A-Z -- Continued

335.R4 Rennellese (Table BS5)
335.R58 Roro (New Guinea) (Table BS5)
335.R59 Rotokas (Table BS5)
335.R6 Roviana (Table BS5)
335.S24 Sambali (Table BS5)
Including Botolan Sambal and Tina Sambal
335.S3-.S39 Samoan (Table BS4)
335.S43 Sangir (Table BS5)
335.S46 Sawi (Table BS5)
335.S62 Siane (Table BS5)
Sindangan Subanun see BS335.S8
335.S68 Southern Arapesh (Table BS5)
Southern Subanen see BS335.S8
335.S79 Suau (Table BS5)
335.S8 Subanun (Table BS5)
Including Sindangan Subanun, Southern Subanen and Western Subanon
335.T18 Tagabili (Table BS5)
335.T2-.T29 Tagalog (Tagalo) (Table BS4)
335.T293 Tagbanua (Table BS5)
335.T3-.T39 Tahitian (Table BS4)
335.T395 Tairora (Table BS5)
335.T397 Tami (Table BS5)
335.T398 Tausug (Table BS5)
335.T4 Telefol (Table BS5)
335.T45 Teop (Table BS5)
335.T48 Tifal (Table BS5)
Tina Sambal see BS335.S24
335.T5 Tiruray (Table BS5)
335.T6 Toaripi (Table BS5)
335.T64 Tok Pisin. Neo-Melanesian (Table BS5)
335.T643 Tokelauan (Table BS5)
335.T645 Tolai (Table BS5)
335.T65 Tonga of Tonga Islands (Table BS5)
335.T7 Truk (Table BS5)
335.T8 Tubetube (Table BS5)
335.U15 Uare (Table BS5)
335.U2 Ubir (Table BS5)
335.U7 Urii (Table BS5)
335.U73 Urim (Table BS5)
335.U75 Uripiv (Table BS5)

General
Texts and versions
Modern texts and versions
Non-European languages
Languages of Oceania and Australasia (Austronesian, Papuan, and Australian), A-Z -- Continued

335.U86 Usurufa (Table BS5)
335.V37 Vaturanga (Table BS5)
335.W3 Wahgi (Table BS5)
335.W34 Waray (Table BS5)
335.W35 Waris (Table BS5)
335.W37 Washkuk (Table BS5)
335.W4 Wedau (Table BS5)
Western Subanon see BS335.S8
335.W55 Wiru (Table BS5)
335.W63 Wojokeso (Table BS5)
335.Y26 Yakan (Table BS5)
335.Y28 Yale (Table BS5)
335.Y3 Yangoru (Table BS5)
335.Y35 Yanyuwa (Table BS5)
335.Y37 Yareba (Table BS5)
335.Y45 Yele (Table BS5)
335.Y47 Yessan-Mayo (Table BS5)
335.Y65 Yopno (Table BS5)
335.Y87 Yuri (Table BS5)
345.A-Z American Indian languages, A-Z
345.A1 General
345.A2 Early works (to the Revolution)
e.g. Eliot's translation into Massachuset
345.A26 Achuale (Table BS5)
345.A3 Aguaruna (Table BS5)
345.A47 Aleut (Aleutian) (Table BS5)
345.A49 Amahuaca (Table BS5)
345.A58 Apache (Table BS5)
345.A6 Apinayé (Table BS5)
345.A7 Arapaho (Table BS5)
345.A73 Arawakan (Table BS5)
345.A75 Arikara (Table BS5)
345.A87 Aymara (Table BS5)
345.A97 Aztec (Table BS5)
345.B35 Bauré (Table BS5)
345.B65 Bororo (Brazil) (Table BS5)
345.C3 Cakchikel (Table BS5)
345.C4-.C49 Cherokee (Table BS4)
345.C494 Cheyenne (Table BS5)
345.C497 Chinantec (Table BS5)
345.C498 Chipaya (Table BS5)

General
Texts and versions
Modern texts and versions
Non-European languages
American Indian languages, A-Z -- Continued

345.C5-.C59 Chippewa (Table BS4)
345.C6-.C69 Choctaw (Table BS4)
345.C692 Cholti (Table BS5)
345.C693 Chontal (Table BS5)
345.C695 Chulupi (Table BS5)
345.C697 Cocopa (Table BS5)
345.C698 Colorado (Table BS5)
345.C699 Correguaje (Table BS5)
345.C7-.C79 Cree (Table BS4)
345.C8-.C89 Creek (Table BS4)
345.D2-.D29 Dakota (Table BS4)
345.D4 Delaware (Table BS5)
345.E73 Epena Saija (Table BS5)
345.E8-.E89 Eskimo (Table BS4)
Including Inuit and its dialects
345.G8 Guarani (Table BS5)
345.H3 Haida (Table BS5)
345.H66 Hopi (Table BS5)
345.H79 Huao (Table BS5)
345.H83 Huichol (Table BS5)
Inuit see BS345.E8+
345.I7 Iroquois (Table BS5)
345.J29 Jacalteca (Table BS5)
345.J34 Jaminaua (Table BS5)
345.K3 Kaingangue (Table BS5)
345.K35 Kashinaua (Table BS5)
345.K47 Keres (Table BS5)
345.M33 Malecite (Table BS5)
345.M38 Maya (Table BS5)
345.M39 Mazateco (Table BS5)
345.M5-.M59 Micmac (Table BS4)
345.M65 Miskito (Table BS5)
345.M67 Mixe (Table BS5)
345.M68 Mixtec (Table BS5)
345.M7-.M79 Mohawk (Table BS4)
345.M83 Moro (Table BS5)
(345.M85) Mosquito
see BS345.M65
345.M87 Movima (Table BS5)
345.M93 Mundurucu (Table BS5)
345.M96 Muskhogean (Table BS5)
345.N37 Navaho (Table BS5)

General
Texts and versions
Modern texts and versions
Non-European languages
American Indian languages, A-Z -- Continued

345.N49 Nez Percé (Table BS5)
345.O77 Otomi (Table BS5)
345.O87 Ottawa (Table BS5)
345.P3 Patamona (Table BS5)
345.P48 Piratapuyo (Table BS5)
345.P55 Popoloca (Popolaca) (Table BS5)
345.P56 Popoluca (Table BS5)
345.P67 Potawatomi (Table BS5)
345.Q4 Quechua (Table BS5)
345.S4 Seneca (Table BS5)
345.S47 Shawnee (Table BS5)
345.S55 Slave (Table BS5)
345.T27 Tacanan (Table BS5)
345.T3 Tarahumare (Table BS5)
345.T4 Tereno (Table BS5)
345.T45 Tlingit (Table BS5)
345.T65 Totonac (Table BS5)
345.T75 Tsattine (Table BS5)
345.T77 Tsimshian (Table BS5)
345.T8-.T89 Tukkuthkutchin (Tukudh) (Table BS4)
345.T92 Tuneba (Table BS5)
345.T95 Tzeltal (Table BS5)
345.T97 Tzotzil (Table BS5)
345.W3 Warrau (Table BS5)
345.W53 Winnebago (Table BS5)
345.Y28 Yagua (Table BS5)
345.Y3 Yahgan (Table BS5)
345.Z3-.Z39 Zapotec (Table BS4)
345.Z6 Zogue (Table BS5)

350.A-Z Mixed languages, A-Z
350.D8-.D89 Dutch Creole (Table BS4)
350.F7-.F79 French Creole (Table BS4)
350.N4-.N49 Negro English (Table BS4)
350.P3-.P39 Papiamento (Table BS4)
350.P5-.P59 Pidgin English (Table BS4)
350.S43-.S439 Sea Islands Creole (Table BS4)
350.S7-.S79 Spanish Creole (Table BS4)
Tok Pisin see BS335.T64

355.A-Z Artificial languages, A-Z
355.E7-.E79 Esperanto (Table BS4)
355.I3-.I39 Ido (Table BS4)
355.V7-.V79 Volapük (Table BS4)

General -- Continued
Liturgical lessons
see Selections, BS390+, unless otherwise provided for
Selections. Quotations
Subarrange under each language by compiler or date
For selections and quotations in a topical arrangement see BS432
389 Polyglot
English
390 For daily reading
General works
391.A2 Early through 1800
391.A3-Z 1801-1950
391.2 1951-2000
391.3 2001-
392 Dutch
393 French
394 German
395 Italian
396 Scandinavian
397 Spanish and Portuguese
399.A-Z Other languages, A-Z
e.g.
399.G7 Greek
399.L3 Latin
Abridgments
405 English
406.A-Z Other languages, A-Z
408 Thumb Bibles
409 Parodies, imitations, etc.
Works about the Bible
Cf. BS584.82+ Bible study
410 Periodicals. Serials
411 Societies. Conventions, etc.
Cf. BV2369+ Bible societies
Collected works
413 Several authors. Festschriften
Including series of monographs
415 Individual authors
415.3 Databases
415.5 Prefaces
416 Excerpts and sayings about the Bible
417 Reference handbooks. Manuals, helps
418 Epitomes. Summaries
419 Tables, etc.

General
Works about the Bible -- Continued
Concordances
Cf. BS1121+ Old Testament
Cf. BS1434 Psalms
Cf. BS2301+ New Testament
420 Polyglot
421 Hebrew
422 Greek
423 Latin
425 English
426 French
427 German
428.A-Z Other languages, A-Z
e.g.
428.N8 Norwegian
428.S65 Spanish
428.S8 Swedish
428.W4 Welsh
429 Other
e.g. Cruttwell's Concordance of parallels (for any language)
430 Cross references
432 Topical indexes, analyses, digests
435 Biblical names
e.g. Onomastica sacra
440 Dictionaries. Glossaries. Encyclopedias
For New Testament dictionaries, etc. see BS2312
443 Polyglot
Biographical dictionaries see BS570
Dictionaries of antiquities see BS622
Introductory works
History of the Bible
445 General works
447 General special
447.5.A-Z By region or country, A-Z
448 Other. Pageants, etc.
Translations of the Bible
449 Theory and principles of translation
450 History
Including history of translating the Bible
For history of early versions see BS11+
Cf. BV2369+ Bible societies
453 Catholic Bible translation (General and modern)
For history see BS450
For controversial works see BS470

General
Works about the Bible
Introductory works
History of the Bible
Translations of the Bible
History -- Continued

454 Protestant Bible translation (General)
For controversial works see BS470
Cf. BS450 History of translations

455 The English Bible
For works on specific editions and versions see BS125+

460.A-Z Other modern European languages, A-Z
For works on specific editions and versions under each see BS199+

Non-European languages see BS315+

Specimens of Bible texts in several languages see P351+

History of commentaries see BS482

History of Biblical criticism see BS500

History of the study and teaching of the Bible see BS584.82+

465 Canon of the Bible

470 Protestant and Catholic Bibles compared

471 Textual criticism
Cf. BS4.5 Works on Biblical manuscripts

Influence of the Bible see BS538.7

General works. Introductions (both general and special). Isagogics
Class here both general and special introductions. Special introductions treat the origin, authorship, authenticity, general characteristics, contents, and aim of the different books of the Bible. General introductions, in addition, treat textual criticism, the versions, and the canon.

474 Early through 1800

475 1801-1950

475.2 1951-2000

475.3 2001-

Juvenile works see BS539

476 Hermeneutics. Exegetics. Principles of interpretation

477 Symbolism
For mythological, allegorical, numerical, astronomical interpretations of the Bible see BS534

478 Typology
Cf. BT225 Christology

General
Works about the Bible
Introductory works -- Continued
480 Inspiration. Authority. Credibility
Including Old Testament treated singly
Cf. BS533 Rationalistic works
Cf. BS1180 Historical criticism (O.T.)
Cf. BS2375 Historical criticism (New estament)
Cf. BT89 Authority of the Scriptures
Cf. BT1255 Ancient monuments, tablets, etc.
481 Harmony of the Bible
Including Harmony of the Old Testament
Commentaries
482 History and general works on commentaries
By language
Greek
483 Early through 1950
483.2 1951-2000
483.3 2001-
483.5 Sermons. Meditations. Devotions
Latin
485 Early through 1950
485.2 1951-2000
485.3 2001-
485.5 Sermons. Meditations. Devotions
English
490 Early through 1800
491 1801-1950
491.2 1951-2000
491.3 2001-
491.5 Sermons. Meditations. Devotions
Dutch
492 Early through 1950
492.2 1951-2000
492.3 2001-
492.5 Sermons. Meditations. Devotions
French
493 Early through 1950
493.2 1951-2000
493.3 2001-
493.5 Sermons. Meditations. Devotions
German
494 Early through 1950
494.2 1951-2000
494.3 2001-
494.5 Sermons. Meditations. Devotions
Italian

General
Works about the Bible
Commentaries
By language
Italian -- Continued
495 Early through 1950
495.2 1951-2000
495.3 2001-
495.5 Sermons. Meditations. Devotions
Scandinavian
496 Early through 1950
496.2 1951-2000
496.3 2001-
496.5 Sermons. Meditations. Devotions
Spanish and Portuguese
497 Early through 1950
497.2 1951-2000
497.3 2001-
497.5 Sermons. Meditations. Devotions
498.A-Z Other languages, A-Z
e.g.
498.C3 Catalan
498.W4 Welsh
Criticism and interpretation
500 History of Biblical criticism
Biography
501.A1 Collective
501.A3-Z Individual, A-Z
General works. The higher criticism
503 Greek
505 Latin
English
510 Early through 1800
511 1801-1950
511.2 1951-2000
511.3 2001-
Dutch
512 Early through 1950
512.2 1951-2000
512.3 2001-
French
513 Early through 1950
513.2 1951-2000
513.3 2001-
German
514 Early through 1950
514.2 1951-2000

General
Works about the Bible
Criticism and interpretation
General works. The higher criticism
German -- Continued
514.3 2001-
Italian
515 Early through 1950
515.2 1951-2000
515.3 2001-
Scandinavian
516 Early through 1950
516.2 1951-2000
516.3 2001-
Spanish and Portuguese
517 Early through 1950
517.2 1951-2000
517.3 2001-
518.A-Z Other languages, A-Z
519 Authorship
520 Historical criticism
520.5 Myth in the bible
521 Demythologization
521.2 Black interpretations
521.4 Feminist criticism
521.5 Form criticism
521.7 Narrative criticism
521.8 Canonical criticism
521.88 Social scientific criticism
521.9 Socio-rhetorical criticism
522 Tradition
Lower criticism see BS471
525 Word studies (General and individual)
530 Pamphlets, etc.
531 Addresses, essays, lectures on Biblical criticism
Cf. BS540 Bible in general
533 Rationalistic criticism
534 Mythological, allegorical, numerical, astronomical interpretations of the Bible
Cf. BS1191 Old Testament
Cf. BS2391 New Testament
534.5 Homiletical use
534.8 Data processing
The Bible as literature
535 General works
536 Poetry of the Bible
Cf. BS1401+ Poetry of the Old Testament

General
Works about the Bible
The Bible as literature -- Continued
Parables of the Bible see BS680.P3
Parables of Jesus see BT373+
Proverbs of the Bible see BS680.P7
537 Rhetoric of the Bible. Language, style. Metaphors, parallelism, etc.
Popular works about the Bible
538 General works
538.3 Use of the Bible
Cf. BS619 Bible in public addresses
538.5 Appreciation of the Bible
538.7 Influence of the Bible. Bible and civilization
539 Juvenile works about the Bible
Class here general works, not textbooks or Bible stories
Including juvenile works about the Old Testament
540 Addresses, essays, lectures on the Bible (General)
Cf. BS531 Biblical criticism
Theology of the Bible
For the theology of special topics see BS680.A+
543.A1 Collections, etc.
543.A2-Z General works
544 God in the Bible
For God in the Old Testament see BS1192.6
For God in the New Testament see BS2398
Ethics of the Bible see BS680.E84
Bible stories. Paraphrases of Bible stories. The Bible story
Class here stories from the whole Bible and the Old Testament alone
546 General methods
Including how to tell Bible stories to children, etc.
Texts by language
Class translations with the language into which translated
For texts for Jewish use see BM107
Polyglot
547 Early through 1950
547.2 1951-2000
547.3 2001-
Latin
548 Early through 1950
548.2 1951-2000
548.3 2001-
English
549 Early through 1800
550 1801-1950
550.2 1951-2000

General
Works about the Bible
Bible stories. Paraphrases of Bible stories. The Bible story
Texts by language
English -- Continued
550.3 2001-
Juvenile
551.A2 Early through 1800
551.A3-Z 1801-1950
551.2 1951-2000
551.3 2001-
Dutch
552 Early through 1950
552.2 1951-2000
552.3 2001-
French
553 Early through 1950
553.2 1951-2000
553.3 2001-
German
For poetical paraphrases in Middle High German see PT1505
554 Early through 1950
554.2 1951-2000
554.3 2001-
Italian
555 Early through 1950
555.2 1951-2000
555.3 2001-
Scandinavian
556 Early through 1950
556.2 1951-2000
556.3 2001-
Spanish and Portuguese
557 Early through 1950
557.2 1951-2000
557.3 2001-
558.A-Z Other languages, A-Z
559 Bible and Bible stories in verse (English)
For other languages, especially rimed versions and metrical paraphrases by a single author, see PA-PT
560 Bible pictures for children. "Hieroglyphic" Bibles
Subarrange by date
For Biblical subjects in art see N8020+
For block books see Z240+
For Biblia pauperum see Z241.B6

General
Works about the Bible -- Continued
Men, women, and children of the Bible
For New Testament see BS2429.2+
569 Genealogy (General)
For special groups in general or in the Old Testament see BS573+
For individual Old Testament characters see BS580.A+
For special groups in the New Testament see BS2440+
For individual New Testament characters see BS2450+
For genealogy of Jesus see BT314
Biography
Including whole Bible and Old Testament
Collective
570 Dictionaries
571 General works
571.A1 Compilations of Biblical texts
Juvenile works (Whole Bible and Old Testament) see BS547+
Juvenile works (New Testament) see BS2400+
Study and teaching (Whole Bible) see BS604+
Study and teaching (Old Testament) see BS1193
Study and teaching (New Testament) see BS2534+
571.5 Sermons on Bible characters
572 Pamphlets, etc.
Special groups of Bible characters
573 Patriarchs
Prophets
see BS1505+
574 Sons of Jacob. Twelve tribes of Israel
574.3 Ushpizin
574.5 Men and boys in the Bible
575 Women and girls in the Bible
For girls alone see BS578
Cf. BS680.W7 Attitude toward women
Children in the Bible
576 General works
577 Boys
578 Girls
579.A-Z Other, A-Z
579.B3 Backsliders
579.B5 Blind
579.B7 Brothers
579.F3 Fathers

General
Works about the Bible
Men, women, and children of the Bible
Biography
Collective
Special groups of Bible characters
Other, A-Z -- Continued

579.H4 Heroes
579.H8 Husbands and wives. Parents
579.J83 Judges
579.K5 Kings
Married people see BS579.H8
579.M65 Mothers
579.O87 Outsiders
Parents see BS579.H8
579.R6 Rogues
579.S55 Single people
Wives and husbands see BS579.H8

580.A-Z Individual Old Testament characters, A-Z
Including stories, meditations, juvenile works, etc.
Whenever Biblical books bear the names of these characters, classify purely biographical material in BS580, all other material with the book in question

580.A23 Aaron
580.A25 Abel
580.A27 Abishag, the Shunammite
580.A3 Abraham, the patriarch
Cf. BS1238.S24 Sacrifice of Isaac
580.A35 Absalom, son of David
580.A4 Adam
580.A5 Ahab, King of Israel
580.A55 Ahaz, King of Judah
580.A6 Amos, the prophet
580.B3 Balaam, the prophet
580.B36 Baruch ben Neriah
580.B46 Benjamin
580.C3 Cain
580.C33 Caleb
580.D2 Daniel, the prophet
580.D3 David, King of Israel
580.D4 Deborah, Judge of Israel
580.D55 Dinah
580.E3 Ehud, Judge of Israel
580.E4 Elijah, the prophet
580.E5 Elisha, the prophet
580.E6 Enoch

General
Works about the Bible
Men, women, and children of the Bible
Biography
Individual Old Testament characters, A-Z -- Continued

580.E65 Esau
Cf. BS1199.E37 Edom. Edomites
580.E8 Esther, Queen of Persia
580.E85 Eve
580.E88 Ezekiel, the prophet
580.E9 Ezra
580.G5 Gideon, Judge of Israel
580.G6 Gog and Magog
580.H24 Hagar
580.H27 Ham
580.H3 Hannah
580.H4 Hezekiah, King of Israel
580.H6 Hosea, the prophet
580.I67 Isaac, the patriarch
Cf. BS1238.S24 Sacrifice of Isaac
580.I7 Isaiah, the prophet
580.I74 Ishmael
580.J3 Jacob, the patriarch
580.J35 Jehoshaphat, King of Judah
580.J36 Jephthah's daughter
580.J4 Jeremiah, the prophet
580.J44 Jeroboam I, King of Israel
580.J446 Jethro
580.J45 Jezebel, Queen consort of Ahab, King of Israel
580.J47 Joab
580.J48 Joash, King of Judah
580.J5 Job, the patriarch
580.J53 Joel, the prophet
580.J55 Jonah, the prophet
580.J57 Jonathan, son of Saul
580.J6 Joseph, the patriarch
580.J7 Joshua, son of Nun
580.J75 Josiah, King of Judah
580.J8 Judith
580.K67 Korah
580.L6 Lot
580.M3 Manasseh, King of Judah
580.M4 Melchizedek, King of Salem
580.M5 Methuselah
580.M53 Michal
580.M54 Miriam
580.M57 Mordecai, cousin of Esther, Queen of Persia

General
Works about the Bible
Men, women, and children of the Bible
Biography
Individual Old Testament characters, A-Z -- Continued

580.M6 Moses
580.N2 Naaman
580.N3 Nathan, the prophet
580.N4 Nebuchadnezzar II, King of Babylonia
580.N45 Nehemiah, the prophet
580.N6 Noah
580.R3 Rahab
580.R4 Rebekah
580.R8 Ruth
580.S15 Samson, Judge of Israel
580.S2 Samuel, Judge of Israel
580.S25 Sarah
580.S3 Saul, King of Israel
580.S37 Serah
580.S42 Seth
580.S45 Shadrach, Meshach, and Abednego
580.S48 Sheba, Queen of
580.S55 Simeon, the Just
580.S6 Solomon, King of Israel
580.T47 Terah
580.T63 Tobias
580.W58 Wisdom (Biblical character)
580.Z55 Zipporah
580.Z6 Zorobabel

Study and teaching
Cf. BS546 How to tell Bible stories
Cf. BS632 Biblical geography
Cf. BS636 Biblical history
Periodicals see BS410
Collections see BS413+

585 History
586.A-Z By region or country, A-Z
587 Catholic Church and Bible study
Cf. BS453 Catholic Bible translation
Cf. BS470 Protestant and Catholic Bibles compared
Cf. BS606+ Catholic textbooks
Cf. BS617.5 Bible reading in the vernacular
588.A-Z Protestant churches and Bible study. By denomination, A-Z
588.B35 Baptists
588.R44 Reformed Church
588.U54 United Methodist Church (U.S.)

General
Works about the Bible
Study and teaching -- Continued
Outlines, syllabi, etc.
590 Early through 1800
591 1801-1950
592 1951-2000
593 2001-
General works
600.A2 Early through 1800
600.A3-Z 1801-1950
600.2 1951-2000
600.3 2001-
601 College students and the Bible
602 Secular schools and the Bible
Cf. LC107+ Public school question, secularization, religious instruction in the public schools
Cf. LC401+ The Bible and religious instruction in the public schools
603 Bible schools. Bible classes. Bible institutes
Class here works for lay instruction
Cf. BV1505 Sunday School conferences and institutes
Cf. BV4019+ Bible institutes for the training of clergymen
Vacation Bible schools see BV1585
Textbooks
For translations, see the language into which translated
Cf. BS547+ Bible stories
Cf. BS1194 Old Testament textbooks
Cf. BS2400+ New Testament stories
Cf. BS2534+ New Testament textbooks
English
604 Early through 1800
605 1801-1950
605.2 1951-2000
605.3 2001-
605.5 Textbooks for foreigners
Catholic textbooks
606 Early through 1950
606.2 1951-2000
606.3 2001-
French
607 Early through 1950
607.2 1951-2000
607.3 2001-
German

General
Works about the Bible
Study and teaching
Textbooks
German -- Continued
608 Early through 1950
608.2 1951-2000
608.3 2001-
Italian
609 Early through 1950
609.2 1951-2000
609.3 2001-
610.A-Z Other languages, A-Z
612 Questions and answers. Bible quizzes
For works in the form of textbooks see BS604+
613 Other
e.g. Books of the Bible in rhyme
Bible-centered games see GV1507.B5
Bible crossword puzzles see GV1507.C7
615 Curiosities of the Bible
Class here information that is rare, quaint, curious, obscure, or little known in relation to Biblical subjects
Bible reading and marking
Cf. BS587 Catholic Church and Bible study
617 General works
617.5 Bible reading in the vernacular
617.7 Bible memorization
617.8 Devotional use
618 The bible and the child
619 The Bible in public addresses
Auxiliary topics
Cf. BS1196+ Old Testament
Cf. BS2406.5+ New Testament
Antiquities. Biblical archaeology, manners and customs
Class here works on antiquities, geography, and natural history
Cf. BS1180 Historical criticism (Old Testament)
Cf. BS2375 Historical criticism (New Testament)
Cf. DS109+ Jerusalem
Cf. DS111+ Palestine
620.A1 Periodicals. Societies
General works
620.A2 Early through 1800
620.A3-Z 1801-1947
621 1948-
Cf. BM175.Q6 Qumran community
Cf. BM487.A05+ Dead Sea scrolls

General
Works about the Bible
Auxiliary topics
Antiquities. Biblical archaeology, manners and customs -- Continued
622 Dictionaries
Musical instruments and music in the Bible see ML166
625 Biblical folklore and legends
Cf. BS1196 Old Testament legends
Biblical geography. Mountains, rivers, etc.
Cf. DS101+ Palestine
630 General works
Atlases see G2230+
632 Study and teaching. Textbooks
633 Juvenile works
Biblical history. Bible and history
Including works on Biblical history and geography
For paraphrases, the Bible story, etc. see BS546+
General works
635.A2 Early works through 1800
635.A5-Z 1801-1950
635.2 1951-2000
635.3 2001-
636 Study and teaching. Outlines, etc.
For Sunday-school textbooks see BS604+
Garden of Eden see BS1237
Deluge see BS658
Biblical chronology
Including Old Testament chronology
General works
637.A2 Early through 1800
637.A5-Z 1801-1950
637.2 1951-2000
637.3 2001-
New Testament chronology see BS2409
Chronology of the Gospels see BS2559
Chronology of the kings of Israel and Judah see BS1331+
Chronology of the life of Jesus Christ see BT303.8
Medical and sanitary knowledge see R135.5
Miracles
General works see BT97+
Old Testament miracles see BS1199.M5
New Testament miracles see BS2545.M5
Miracles of Christ see BT363+
645 Philosophy. Psychology
Cf. BS648 Prophecy

General
Works about the Bible
Auxiliary topics -- Continued

646 Revelation. Apocalyptic literature
Cf. BS1705 Old Testament apocryphal literature
Cf. BS2910+ New Testament apocryphal literature
Cf. BT126+ Revelation (Doctrinal theology)

Prophecy
Class here prophecy in the sense of the prediction of future events. For prophecy in the sense of the proclamation of the divine message, see BS1198, BS1505, BS1560
Cf. BR115.P8 Prophecy in the history of Christianity
Cf. BS1198 Old Testament prophecy
Cf. BS1501+ The Prophetic books
Cf. BS1556 Prophecy of the Book of Daniel
Cf. BS1560 The Minor Prophets
Cf. BS2820+ The Book of Revelation
Cf. BT235 Messianic prophecy
Cf. BT370 Jesus Christ's prophecies

647.A1 Periodicals. Serials
General works
647.A2 Early through 1800
647.A5-Z 1800-1950
647.2 1951-2000
647.3 2001-
647.5 Chronology of the prophecies
648 Psychology. Inspiration, etc.
649.A-Z Prophecy of special future events, A-Z
649.A35 Africa
649.A68 Armageddon
649.A7 Assyria
649.B3 Babylon
649.B33 Bahai Faith
649.B56 Blacks
649.C58 Church
649.C8 Communism
649.C83 Computers
649.D3 Dark Day
649.D42 Depressions. Economic collapse
649.E3 Eastern question
Economic collapse see BS649.D42
649.E4 Edomites
649.E5 Egypt
649.E63 End of the world
649.E8 Europe
649.F3 Fascism
649.F8 France

General
Works about the Bible
Auxiliary topics
Prophecy
Prophecy of special future events, A-Z -- Continued

649.G6 Gold
649.G7 Great Britain
649.H5 Hitler, Adolf
649.I56 International organization. New World Order
649.I73 Iran
649.J3 Japan
649.J38 Jerusalem
649.J4 Jerusalem Temple
649.J5 Jews
Cf. DS149+ Zionism
649.K45 Kennedy, John F. (John Fitzgerald), 1917-1963
649.L3 Latin Confederation
649.L4 League of Nations
Middle East see BS649.N45
649.M77 Muḥammad, Prophet, d. 632
649.M8 Mussolini, Benito
649.N3 Napoleon III
649.N45 Near East
Negroes see BS649.B56
New World Order see BS649.I56
649.N55 New York
649.P3 Palestine
649.P4 Peace
649.R7 Rome
649.R9 Russia
649.S4 Sebastião, King of Portugal
649.S43 Second Advent
649.S7 Socialism
649.S8 Steam engines
Temple of Jerusalem see BS649.J4
649.T8 Turkey
649.T87 Twelve Tribes of Israel
649.U6 United States
649.W67 World War III

Bible and science
650 General works
Genesis and science. Creation. Cosmogony
For geology see BS657
Cf. BL224+ Natural theology
651 General works
652 Other
Rationalistic works see BS533

General
Works about the Bible
Auxiliary topics
Bible and science -- Continued
Special topics
655 Astronomy
Meteorology
656 General works
656.5 Storms
657 Geology
658 The Deluge
Including Noah's ark
For discussion of Noah's ark as a Biblical antiquity and expeditions to find it see DS51.A66
Cf. BL325.D4 The Deluge in comparative mythology
659 Evolution
Cf. BL263 Religion and the science of evolution
Natural history. Nature
Cf. BL262+ Religion and science
Cf. BS1199.N34 Nature in the Old Testament
660 General works
661 Man. Ethnology
663 Animals
Cf. BS680.A5 Treatment of animals in the Bible
664 Birds
665 Plants. Trees. Flowers. Herbs
667 Minerals. Precious stones
Bible and social sciences
670 Social teachings of the Bible. Bible and economics
671 Bible and labor
672 Bible and civil government
680.A-Z Topics (not otherwise provided for), A-Z
Cf. BS1199.A+ Topics (not otherwise provided for) in the Old Testament
Cf. BS1237+ Topics in Genesis
Cf. BS2417.A+ Topics in the teachings of Jesus
Cf. BS2545.A+ Topics (not otherwise provided for) in the New Testament
Cf. BS2655.A+ Topics in the teachings of Paul
Achievement see BS680.P44
680.A33 Aesthetics
680.A34 Aged. Older people. Old age
680.A48 Angels
680.A5 Animals, Treatment of
680.A58 Anxiety

General
Works about the Bible
Topics (not otherwise provided for), A-Z -- Continued

680.A7 Arabs
680.A77 Art. The arts
680.A8 Asceticism
680.A86 Assurance
680.A93 Authority
680.B48 Blacks
680.B5 Blessing and cursing
680.B52 Blindness
680.B53 Blood
680.B6 Body, Human
680.B8 Business
680.C3 Capital punishment
680.C37 Caring
680.C45 Child sacrifice
680.C46 Childbirth
680.C47 Christian life
680.C48 Church renewal
680.C5 Cities and towns
Coins see CJ255
680.C55 Colors
680.C6 Commerce
Community see BS680.P43
680.C63 Conflict management
680.C64 Contentment
680.C65 Costume (Religious aspects, symbolism, etc.)
680.C66 Courage
680.C67 Covenants
680.C69 Creation
680.C7 Crimes
Cursing see BS680.B5
Darkness see BS680.L53
680.D39 Day of Jehovah
Death see BS680.L5
680.D5 Demoniac possession. Demonology
Demonology see BS680.D5
680.D56 Devil
Diakonia see BS680.S47
Disabilities, People with see BS680.P435
680.D58 Discipline
680.D62 Divorce
680.D76 Drugs
680.E3 Education
680.E38 Emigration and immigration
680.E4 Emotions

General
Works about the Bible
Topics (not otherwise provided for), A-Z -- Continued

680.E8 Eschatology
680.E84 Ethics
680.E85 Ethnicity
680.E86 Evangelistic work
Evil and good see BS680.G6
680.E88 Excommunication. Expulsion
680.E9 Exodus, The
Cf. BS1199.E93 The Exodus as a topic in the Old Testament
680.F27 Faith
680.F3 Family
680.F32 Famines
680.F35 Farewells
680.F36 Fasting
680.F37 Fasts and feasts
680.F38 Fatherhood
680.F4 Fear
680.F43 Feet
680.F45 Fellowship
Feminism see BS680.W7
680.F53 Fire
680.F55 First fruits
680.F6 Food
680.F64 Forgiveness of sin. Forgiveness
Fragrances see BS680.O34
680.F7 Freedom
680.F74 Friendship
680.F8 Future
680.F83 Future life
680.G37 Gardening
680.G5 Gifts, Spiritual
680.G57 Gods
680.G6 Good and evil
680.G7 Grace
680.G74 Gratitude
680.H35 Handicraft
680.H4 Healing
680.H413 Health
680.H416 Heart
680.H42 Heaven
680.H43 Hell
680.H45 Hides and skins
680.H47 History
680.H54 Holiness

General
Works about the Bible
Topics (not otherwise provided for), A-Z -- Continued

680.H56 Holy Spirit. Spirit of God
680.H58 Homeland
680.H59 Homelessness
680.H6 Homes
680.H67 Homosexuality
680.H7 Hope
Human body see BS680.B6
680.H85 Human rights
Humor see BS680.W63
680.H94 Hymns
Immigration see BS680.E38
680.I65 Iran
680.I7 Irony
680.J37 Jerusalem
680.J4 Jews
680.J6 Joy and sorrow
680.J76 Judgment of God
680.J8 Justice. Social justice
680.K52 Kingdom of God
680.K55 Knowledge
680.K85 Kurds
680.L25 Land use
680.L3 Laughter
680.L33 Law
680.L4 Leadership
680.L5 Life and death
680.L53 Light and darkness
680.L57 Listening
680.L6 Lot (Choice by)
680.L64 Love
680.L65 Loyalty
680.L87 Lust
680.M3 Magic
Cf. BF1623.B53 Magic and the Bible (Occultism)
680.M35 Marriage
680.M38 Meditation
680.M39 Meekness
680.M4 Messiah
Cf. BM615+ Messiah in Jewish theology
680.M5 Miracles
680.M53 Miscegenation
680.M57 Money
Cf. BS680.W38 Wealth
680.M6 Monsters

General
Works about the Bible
Topics (not otherwise provided for), A-Z -- Continued

680.M63 Motherhood
Names see BS435
680.N6 Nonviolence
680.N8 Numbers
680.O22 Oaths
680.O26 Occult sciences
680.O3 Occupations
680.O34 Odors. Fragrances
680.O5 Oils
Old age see BS680.A34
680.O6 Ophir
680.O64 Oppression
680.P3 Parables
680.P32 Parapsychology
680.P33 Passover
680.P35 Pastoral life (i.e. country life)
680.P36 Patriarchy
680.P37 Patriotism
680.P4 Peace
680.P43 People of God. Community
680.P435 People with disabilities
680.P44 Performance. Achievement
680.P45 Political science
Possession, Demoniac see BS680.D5
680.P47 Poverty
680.P5 Power
680.P63 Praise
680.P64 Prayer. Prayers
680.P65 Predestination
Priesthood see BS680.P66
680.P66 Priests. Priesthood
680.P68 Promises
680.P7 Proverbs
680.P78 Punishment
680.P8 Purity, Ritual
680.Q4 Questions in the Bible
680.R2 Race
680.R28 Reconciliation
680.R3 Recreation
680.R36 Repentance
680.R365 Restoration of the Jews
680.R37 Resurrection
680.R39 Revivals
680.R4 Reward

General
Works about the Bible
Topics (not otherwise provided for), A-Z -- Continued

	Ritual purity see BS680.P8
680.S17	Sabbath. Sunday
680.S2	Sacrifice
680.S24	Salt
680.S25	Salvation
680.S35	Sea
680.S4	Self-sacrifice
680.S47	Service. Diakonia
680.S5	Sex
680.S53	Sex role
	Shepherds see BS680.P35
680.S57	Sin
	Skins see BS680.H45
	Slavery see HT915
	Social justice see BS680.J8
680.S63	Social problems
680.S64	Solitude
680.S66	Son of God
	Sorrow see BS680.J6
	Spirit of God see BS680.H56
	Spiritual gifts see BS680.G5
	Spiritual healing see BS680.H4
680.S7	Spiritual life
680.S73	Spiritual warfare
	Spiritualism and the Bible see BF1275.B5
	Spiritualist messages, Biblical see BF1311.B5
680.S76	Stealing
680.S78	Stewardship
	Storms see BS656.5
680.S79	Stress (Psychology)
680.S85	Suddenness
680.S854	Suffering
680.S855	Suicide
680.S86	Supernatural phenomena
680.T32	Tabernacle (Typology)
680.T4	Temple of God (Symbolism)
680.T43	Temptation
680.T45	Theophanies
680.T47	Theosophy
680.T5	Threats
680.T54	Time
680.T56	Tithes
680.U55	Universalism
680.V4	Vegetarianism

General
Works about the Bible
Topics (not otherwise provided for), A-Z -- Continued
680.V55 Violence
680.V56 Virtues
680.V57 Visions
680.V6 Vocation
680.W17 Walls
680.W2 War
680.W26 Water
680.W38 Wealth
Cf. BS680.M57 Money
680.W4 Weights and measures
680.W5 Wells
680.W53 Wilderness
680.W55 Wine
680.W6 Wisdom
680.W63 Wit and humor
680.W64 Witchcraft
680.W7 Women (Attitude toward). Feminism
680.W75 Work
680.W78 Worship
680.Y68 Youth
Old Testament
BS701-BS1830 covers the Old Testament, except for certain topics, e.g. biography, that by exception are classed under the whole Bible in BS1-BS680.
Texts and versions
Polyglot Old Testaments
701 General
703 Minor
For polyglot texts of special parts, see the special part, e.g. BS1419 Polyglot Psalms
704 Collections
Class here miscellaneous general collections in print or facsimile
704.5 Works on Old Testament manuscripts in general
Early versions
Aramaic
For passages in Daniel and Ezra combined, written originally in Aramaic see BS1550
705 Printed texts. By date
Manuscripts. Codices
705.3 General works
Individual manuscripts
705.5.A-Z By name, A-Z
For criticism use subarrangement by author, A-Z

Old Testament
Texts and versions
Early versions
Aramaic
Manuscripts. Codices
Individual manuscripts -- Continued
705.7 By number
For criticism use subarrangement by author, A-Z
Translations
706 English
707.A-Z Other European languages, A-Z
Modern non-European languages see BS315+
708 History and criticism
The Targumin
Class individual Targumin with the Biblical book that they render into Aramaic
709 Printed texts. By date
Manuscripts. Codices
709.13 General works
Individual manuscripts
709.15.A-Z By name, A-Z
For criticism use subarrangement by author, A-Z
709.17 By number
For criticism use subarrangement by author, A-Z
Translations
709.2 English
709.3.A-Z Other European languages, A-Z
Modern non-European languages see BS315+
709.4 History and criticism
Syriac. Peshitta
711 Printed texts. By date
Manuscripts. Codices
711.3 General works
Individual manuscripts
711.5.A-Z By name, A-Z
For criticism use subarrangement by author, A-Z
711.7 By number
For criticism use subarrangement by author, A-Z
Translations
712 English
713.A-Z Other European languages, A-Z
Modern non-European languages see BS315+
714 History and criticism
Palestinian Syriac
714.3 Printed texts. By date
Manuscripts. Codices
714.33 General works

Old Testament
Texts and versions
Early versions
Syriac. Peshitta
Palestinian Syriac
Manuscripts. Codices -- Continued
Individual manuscripts
714.35.A-Z By name, A-Z
For criticism use subarrangement by author, A-Z
714.37 By number
For criticism use subarrangement by author, A-Z
Translations
714.4 English
714.5.A-Z Other European languages, A-Z
Modern non-European languages see BS315+
714.6 History and criticism
Modern Syriac see BS315.S9
Hebrew
715 Printed editions. By date
Manuscripts. Codices
715.3 General works
Individual manuscripts
715.5.A-Z By name, A-Z
For criticism use subarrangement by author, A-Z
715.7 By number
For criticism use subarrangement by author, A-Z
Translations
English see BS825+
Other languages
Early see BS705+
Modern European languages see BS899+
Modern non-European languages see BS315+
718 History and criticism. Masorah.
Samaritan Pentateuch see BM920+
Arabic
725 Printed texts. By date
Manuscripts. Codices
725.3 General works
Individual manuscripts
725.5.A-Z By name, A-Z
For criticism use subarrangment by author, A-Z
725.7 By number
For criticism use subarrangment by author, A-Z
Translations
726 English
727.A-Z Other European languages, A-Z
Modern non-European languages see BS315+

Old Testament
Texts and versions
Early versions
Arabic -- Continued
728 History and criticism
Ethiopic
731 Printed texts. By date
Manuscripts. Codices
731.3 General works
Individual manuscripts
731.5.A-Z By name, A-Z
For criticism use subarrangement by author, A-Z
731.7 By number
For criticism use subarrangement by author, A-Z
Translations
732 English
733.A-Z Other European languages, A-Z
Modern non-European languages see BS315+
734 History and criticism
Ancient Greek versions
737 Collected works
Including works in which various texts are published
737.5 Comparative texts of Greek Old Testaments
Cf. BS760+ Hexapla
738 History and criticism
Manuscripts. Codices
739 General works
Individual manuscripts see BS764.A+
Special versions
Those with Latin parallels are to be classed with original texts
Septuagint
741 Special editions. By editor or date
Translations
742.A-Z English. By translator, A-Z
743.A-Z Other modern European languages, A-Z
744 History and criticism
744.A7 Aristeas' epistle
Aquila
745 Special editions. By editor or date
Translations
746.A-Z English. By translator, A-Z
747.A-Z Other modern European languages, A-Z
748 History and criticism
Symmachus
751 Special editions. By editor or date
Translations

Old Testament
Texts and versions
Early versions
Ancient Greek versions
Special versions
Symmachus
Translations -- Continued
752.A-Z English. By translator, A-Z
753.A-Z Other modern European languages, A-Z
754 History and criticism
Theodotion
755 Special editions. By editor or date
Translations
756.A-Z English. By translator, A-Z
757.A-Z Other modern European languages, A-Z
758 History and criticism
Hexapla
760 Special editions. By editor or date
Translations
761.A-Z English. By translator, A-Z
762.A-Z Other modern European languages, A-Z
763 History and criticism
Individual manuscripts
Class here manuscripts of the whole Old Testament, fragments of manuscripts, and manuscripts of parts of the Old Testament, e.g. the Pentateuch, including the Old Testament portion of manuscripts of the whole Greek Bible
764.A-Z By name, A-Z
e.g.
Washington manuscript
764.W29 Facsimiles
764.W3 Printed editions
764.W4 History and criticism
764.5 By number
According to the numbering by Rahlfs
765 Modern editions. By date.
For editions of the Septuagint see BS741+
767-790 Latin versions
767 Collections
Works in which several texts are published
767.5 Comparative texts of Latin Bibles
768 History and criticism
Manuscripts. Codices
769 General works

Old Testament
Texts and versions
Early versions
Latin versions
Manuscripts. Codices -- Continued
770.A-Z Individual manuscripts (regardless of version), A-Z
By name or other distinctive word
For criticism use subarrangement by author, A-Z
Special versions
Greek-Latin parallel editions are classed with Greek texts
Old Latin. Italic versions. Itala
772 Collections. By title or editor
773 Texts. By date
774 History and criticism
Vulgate
775 Texts. By date
785 History and criticism
789.A-Z Other early and medieval Latin versions, A-Z
790 Modern versions. By date
Other early versions
Armenian
795 Printed texts. By date
Manuscripts. Codices
795.3 General works
795.5.A-Z Individual manuscripts (regardless of version), A-Z
By name or other distinctive word
For criticism use subarrangement by author, A-Z
796 History and criticism
Coptic (all dialects)
800 Printed texts. By date
Manuscripts. Codices
800.3 General works
800.5.A-Z Individual manuscripts (regardless of version), A-Z
By name or other distinctive word
For criticism use subarrangement by author, A-Z
801 History and criticism
Gothic see BS105+
Church Slavic
810 Printed texts. By date
Manuscripts. Codices
810.3 General works
810.5.A-Z Individual manuscripts (regardless of version), A-Z
By name or other distinctive word
For criticism use subarrangement by author, A-Z
811 History and criticism
815.A-Z Other, A-Z

Old Testament
Texts and versions -- Continued
Modern texts and versions of the Old Testament
For general works about the Old Testament in each language see BS1131+
Polyglot see BS701+
English

825	Comparative texts of English Bibles. By date Cf. BS888.A3 Authorized and Revised versions Cf. BS890.A3 Authorized and American Revision versions Cf. BS891.A3 Revised Standard and Confraternity of Christian Doctrine versions Cf. BS1421 Comparative texts of the Psalms
	Anglo-Saxon see BS130
	English versions Arranged chronologically
835-836	Wycliffe's (1380) (Table BS1)
838.A-Z	Other Middle English versions, A-Z e.g.
838.P8	Purvey's
	Tyndale's (1525-1531) see BS140+
845-846	Coverdale's (1535) (Table BS1)
850-851	Matthew's (1537) (Table BS1)
852-853	Taverner's (1539) (Table BS1) Revision of Matthew's
	The Great Bible
855-856	Cromwell's edition, 1539 (Table BS1)
860-861	Cranmer's edition, 1540 (Table BS1)
865-866	Cranmer's edition, 1541 (Table BS1)
867	Other editions. By date
870-871	Geneva Bible (1560), "Breeches Bible" (Table BS1)
875-876	Bishop's Bible (1568) (Table BS1)
880-881	Douai (1609-1610) (Table BS1) Including revisions such as the Challoner revision and the Confraternity of Christian Doctrine version. For other modern Catholic versions in English see BS895.A+
	King James, Authorized version (1611)
885	Texts Arrange by date and subarrange by place of publication, A-Z
886	History and criticism, etc.
	Revised version (1881-1885)
888.A1	Texts. By date Subarrange by place of publication, A-Z
888.A2	Texts, American version. By date

Old Testament
Texts and versions
Modern texts and versions of the Old Testament
English
English versions
Revised version (1881-1885) -- Continued

888.A3 Authorized and Revised versions paralleled
Subdivided by date and place of publication
888.A5-Z History and criticism, etc.
American Revision (1901)
890.A1 Texts. By date.
Subarrange by place of publication, A-Z
890.A3 Authorized and American Revision versions paralleled
Subarrange by date and place of publication
890.A5-Z History and criticism, etc.
Revised Standard version (1946-1952)
891.A1 Texts. By date
Subarranged by date of publication, A-Z
891.A3 Revised Standard and Confraternity of Christian Doctrine versions paralleled
891.A5-Z History and criticism, etc.
New Revised Standard version (1990)
891.5.A1 Texts. By date
Subarrange by place of publication, A-Z
891.5.A5-Z History and criticism, etc.
New English Bible (1961-)
892.A1 Texts. By date
Subarrange by place of publication, A-Z
892.A5-Z History and criticism, etc.
Revised English Bible (1989-)
892.16.A1 Texts. By date
Subarranged by place of publication, A-Z
892.16.A5-Z History and criticism, etc.
Anchor Bible
892.2.A1 Texts. By date
Subarrange by place of publication, A-Z
892.2.A5-Z History and criticism, etc.
New American Bible
892.3.A1 Texts. By date
Subarrange by place of publication, A-Z
892.3.A5-Z History and criticism, etc.
895.A-Z Other versions and revisions. By version, A-Z
895.A53-.A532 Amplified (Table BS2)
895.B38-.B382 Berkeley version (Table BS2)
895.C6-.C62 Confraternity version (Table BS2)
895.C66-.C662 Contemporary English (Table BS2)

Old Testament
Texts and versions
Modern texts and versions of the Old Testament
English
English versions
Other versions and revisions, A-Z -- Continued

895.D35-.D352 Dolen (Table BS2)
895.E64-.E642 English Standard (Table BS2)
895.G55-.G552 Goble (Table BS2)
895.G57-.G572 God's Word (Table BS2)
895.G58-.G582 Gold (Table BS2)
895.G59-.G592 Golden Bridge version (Table BS2)
Good News Translation see BS895.T63+
895.G84-.G842 Green (Table BS2)
895.H64-.H642 House of Yahweh (Table BS2)
895.I56-.I562 International Standard (Table BS2)
895.J4-.J42 Jerusalem (Table BS2)
895.K53-.K532 KJ21 (Table BS2)
895.L35-.L352 Lamsa (Table BS2)
895.L54-.L542 Life messengers (Table BS2)
895.L58-.L582 Living Bible (Table BS2)
895.M47-.M472 The Message (Table BS2)
895.N32-.N322 NET Bible (Table BS2)
895.N35-.N352 New American Standard (Table BS2)
895.N3524-.N35242 New Authorized (Table BS2)
895.N353-.N3532 New Century (Table BS2)
895.N37-.N372 New International (Table BS2)
895.N373-.N3732 New International Readers Version (Table BS2)
895.N375-.N3752 New Jerusalem Bible (Table BS2)
895.N38-.N382 New King James (Table BS2)
895.N394-.N3942 New Living Translation (Table BS2)
895.N4-.N42 New World (Table BS2)
895.P74-.P742 Priests for Equality (Table BS2)
895.S5-.S52 Simplified Living Bible (Table BS2)
895.S75-.S752 Stern (Table BS2)
895.T63-.T632 Today's English. Good News Translation (Table BS2)

Basic English versions
896.A1 Texts. By date
Subarrange by place of publication, A-Z
896.A5-Z History and criticism, etc.
896.5 Reference editions
Editions for special classes
897 Young people's Bibles. Children's Bibles. By editor or publisher.
Class here relatively complete Bibles omitting portions unsuitable for children.

Old Testament
Texts and versions
Modern texts and versions of the Old Testament
English
Editions for special classes -- Continued
898.A-Z Other, A-Z
Subarrange by publisher and date
e.g.
898.E3 Eastern Star
898.F8 Freemasons
Mormons see BX8630+
898.O3 Oddfellows
899-1013 Other modern European languages (Table BS10)
Add number in table to BS700
Each language to include its dialects unless otherwise provided for
Modern non-European languages see BS315+
Selections. Quotations
Subarrange each language by editor or compiler
For selections and quotations in any topical arrangement see BS432
1091 English
1092 Dutch
1093 French
1094 German
1095 Italian
1096 Scandinavian
1097 Spanish and Portuguese
1099.A-Z Other languages, A-Z
1104 Harmonies. Parallel Old Testament passages
Subarrange each language by editor or compiler
1104.A2 Hebrew
1104.A3 Greek
1104.A4 Latin
1104.A5 English
1104.A6-Z Other languages, A-Z
Works about the Old Testament
Periodicals see BS410
Societies see BS411
Collections of monographs, studies, etc.
1110 Several authors
1115 Individual authors
Concordances
1121 Hebrew
1122 Greek
1123 Latin
1125 English

Old Testament
Works about the Old Testament
Concordances -- Continued
1126 French
1127 German
1128.A-Z Other languages, A-Z
Dictionaries see BS440
Introductory works
History of the Old Testament
1130 General works
History of translations of the Old Testament
Including history of translating the Old Testament
1131 General works
1132 Jewish Bible translation
1133 The English Old Testament
For works on specific editions and versions see BS825+
1134.A-Z The Old Testament in other modern European languages, A-Z
For works on specific editions and versions see BS899+
The Old Testament in non-European languages see BS315+
The Old Testament in ancient languages see BS705+
History of Old Testament criticism and interpretation see BS1160
1135 Canon of the Old Testament
1136 Textual criticism
Cf. BS704.5 Works on Old Testament manuscripts
General works. Introductions
Class here both general and special introductions. Special introductions treat the origin, authorship, authenticity, general characteristics, contents, and aim of the different books of the Bible. General introductions, in addition, treat textual criticism, the versions, and the canon
1139 Early through 1800
1140 1801-1950
1140.2 1951-2000
1140.3 2001-
Hermeneutics, exegetics see BS476
Symbolism see BS477
Typology see BS478
Inspiration, authority, credibility see BS480
Harmony of the Old Testament see BS481
Outlines, compends, etc. see BS1193
Philosophy of the Old Testament see BS645

Old Testament
Works about the Old Testament -- Continued
Commentaries
Greek
1143 Early through 1950
1951-2000
1143.2 General works
1143.5 Sermons. Meditations. Devotions
2001-
1143.52 General works
1143.55 Sermons. Meditations. Devotions
Latin
1145 Early through 1950
1951-2000
1145.2 General works
1145.5 Sermons. Meditations. Devotions
2001-
1145.52 General works
1145.55 Sermons. Meditations. Devotions
English
1150 Early through 1800
1151 1801-1950
1951-2000
1151.2 General works
1151.5 Sermons. Meditations. Devotions
2001-
1151.52 General works
1151.55 Sermons. Meditations. Devotions
Dutch
1152 Early through 1950
1951-2000
1152.2 General works
1152.5 Sermons. Meditations. Devotions
2001-
1152.52 General works
1152.55 Sermons. Meditations. Devotions
French
1153 Early through 1950
1951-2000
1153.2 General works
1153.5 Sermons. Meditations. Devotions
2001-
1153.52 General works
1153.55 Sermons. Meditations. Devotions
German
1154 Early through 1950
1951-2000

Old Testament
Works about the Old Testament
Commentaries
German
1951-2000 -- Continued
1154.2 General works
1154.5 Sermons. Meditations. Devotions
2001-
1154.52 General works
1154.55 Sermons. Meditations. Devotions
Italian
1155 Early through 1950
1951-2000
1155.2 General works
1155.5 Sermons. Meditations. Devotions
2001-
1155.52 General works
1155.55 Sermons. Meditations. Devotions
Scandinavian
1156 Early through 1950
1951-2000
1156.2 General works
1156.5 Sermons. Meditations. Devotions
2001-
1156.52 General works
1156.55 Sermons. Meditations. Devotions
Spanish and Portuguese
1157 Early through 1950
1951-2000
1157.2 General works
1157.5 Sermons. Meditations. Devotions
2001-
1157.52 General works
1157.55 Sermons. Meditations. Devotions
1158.A-Z Other languages, A-Z
Criticism and interpretation
1160 History of Old Testament criticism and interpretation
Biography
Including criticism
1161.A1 Collective
1161.A3-Z Individual, A-Z
e.g.
1161.P5 Philo Judaeus (Philo of Alexandria)
1161.S58 Solomon ben Isaac, called RaSHI
1161.S6 Spinoza, Benedictus de
General works
Including the Higher criticism

Old Testament
Works about the Old Testament
Criticism and interpretation
General works -- Continued

1163 Greek
1165 Latin
English
1170 Early through 1800
1171 1801-1950
1171.2 1951-2000
1171.3 2001-
Dutch
1172 Early through 1950
1172.2 1951-2000
1172.3 2001-
French
1173 Early through 1950
1173.2 1951-2000
1173.3 2001-
German
1174 Early through 1950
1174.2 1951-2000
1174.3 2001-
Italian
1175 Early through 1950
1175.2 1951-2000
1175.3 2001-
Scandinavian
1176 Early through 1950
1176.2 1951-2000
1176.3 2001-
Spanish and Portuguese
1177 Early through 1950
1177.2 1951-2000
1177.3 2001-
1178.A-Z Other languages, A-Z
1179 Rationalistic works
1180 Historical criticism
Including evidences of monuments, etc.
Cf. BS1236 Comparative theology of Genesis
1181 Documentary hypothesis
1181.17 D Document
1181.2 E Document
1181.4 J Document
1181.6 P Document
1181.8 Feminist criticism
1182 Form criticism

Old Testament
Works about the Old Testament
Criticism and interpretation -- Continued

1182.3 Narrative criticism
1182.5 Socio-rhetorical criticism
1182.6 Social scientific criticism
1182.7 Structuralist criticism
1183 Myth in the Old Testament
1184 Relation of Middle Eastern literature to the Old Testament
Including specific literatures, e.g. Assyro-Babylonian
Lower criticism see BS1136
Language of the Old Testament see PJ4543+
1185 Word studies (General and individual)
1186 Jewish criticism of the Old Testament
1186.5 Gay interpretations
1187 Minor works
1188 Addresses, essays, lectures (on Old Testament criticism)
1191 Mythological, allegorical, numerical, astronomical interpretation of the Old Testament
1191.5 Homiletical use
Juvenile works about the Old Testament see BS539
1192 Addresses, essays, lectures on the Old Testament (General)
1192.5 Theology of the Old Testament
For the theology of special parts and books of the Old Testament, see the number for theology or criticism under each part and book
For the theology of special topics see BS1199.A+
Cf. BM165+ History of Judaism
Cf. BM603 History of Jewish doctrine
1192.5.A1 Collected works
1192.5.A3-Z General works
1192.6 God in the Old Testament
Ethics of the Old Testament see BS1199.E8
Bible stories from the Old Testament see BS546+
Men, women, and children of the Old Testament see BS569+
Study and teaching
For the study and teaching of special parts and books of the Old Testament, see the number for study and teaching or criticism under each part and book
Periodicals see BS410
Societies see BS411
1193 General works. Outlines, tables, etc.
1194 Textbooks
1195 Questions and answers

Old Testament
Works about the Old Testament -- Continued
Auxiliary topics
1196 Old Testament legends
Including post-Biblical legends about Old Testament characters, events, etc.
Old Testament geography see BS630+
1197 Old Testament history
For study and teaching see BS1193
Cf. BM150+ History of Judaism
Cf. BS1130+ History of the Old Testament
Cf. BS1180 Historical criticism
Old Testament chronology see BS637+
1198 Old Testament prophecy
Cf. BS1501+ Prophetic books
1199.A-Z Topics (not otherwise provided for), A-Z
1199.A25 Abnormalities, Human. People with disabilities
1199.A3 Admonition
1199.A34 Aesthetics. Human beauty
1199.A35 Aging
1199.A37 Altars
1199.A44 Amalekites
1199.A47 Ancestor worship
1199.A5 Angels
1199.A53 Anger
1199.A57 Animals, Treatment of
1199.A65 Arabia
1199.A66 Arabs
1199.A7 Armenia
1199.A77 Asherah (Semitic deity)
1199.A8 Right of asylum
1199.A85 Atonement
1199.B3 Babylonian captivity. Babylonian exile
Cf. BS649.B3 Babylon in prophecy
Beauty, Human see BS1199.A34
1199.B43 Bedouins
1199.B48 Blacks
1199.B5 Blessing and cursing
1199.B54 Blood
1199.B62 Body, Human
1199.B65 Books mentioned
1199.C36 Cannibalism
1199.C43 Christian life
1199.C45 Church renewal
Coins see CJ255
1199.C57 Colors
1199.C58 Communication

Old Testament
Works about the Old Testament
Topics (not otherwise provided for), A-Z -- Continued

Community see BS1199.P45
1199.C6 Covenants
1199.C73 Creation
Cf. BS651+ Genesis and Science. Creation. Cosmogony
1199.D3 Day of Jehovah
1199.D34 Death
1199.D4 Devil
1199.D5 Dialogue
Dining see BS1199.D55
1199.D55 Dinners and dining
Divine messengers see BS1199.A5
1199.D73 Dragons
1199.D75 Drinking cups
1199.E27 Earth
1199.E35 Economics
1199.E37 Edom. Edomites
Cf. BS580.E65 Esau
1199.E38 Education
1199.E59 Egypt
1199.E63 Election (Theology)
1199.E72 Equality
1199.E73 Erotica
1199.E75 Eschatology
1199.E8 Ethics
1199.E84 Ethnicity
1199.E9 Euphemism
Evil see BS1199.G65
Exile, Babylonian see BS1199.B3
1199.E93 Exodus, The
Face of God see BS1192.6
1199.F3 Faith
Falsehood see BS1199.T7
1199.F32 Family
1199.F35 Fasts and feasts
1199.F39 Fear
1199.F4 Fear of God
Feasts see BS1199.F35
1199.F6 Flesh
1199.F65 Folly. Fools
1199.F73 Friendship
1199.F75 Funeral dirges
1199.F8 Future life
Gentiles see BS1199.N6

Old Testament
Works about the Old Testament
Topics (not otherwise provided for), A-Z -- Continued

1199.G5	Giants
1199.G58	Gibeonites
	God see BS1192.6
1199.G63	Gods
1199.G65	Good and evil
1199.G68	Grace
1199.G7	Greek philosophy
1199.H37	Happiness
1199.H39	Healing
1199.H4	Heart
1199.H5	History
1199.H6	Holiness
1199.H65	Hope
	Human abnormalities see BS1199.A25
	Human beauty see BS1199.A34
	Humor see BS1199.W58
1199.I34	Idols and images
1199.I48	Image of God
1199.I52	Incense
1199.I53	Interest and usury
1199.I55	Interpersonal relations
1199.I64	Iran
1199.I7	Irony. Satire
1199.J38	Jerusalem
1199.J4	Jews
1199.J6	Joy
1199.J77	Jubilee
1199.J8	Justice. Social justice
	Justice, Administration of see BS1199.L3
1199.J83	Justification
1199.K48	Kingdom of God
1199.K5	Kings and rulers
1199.L27	Laments
1199.L28	Land tenure. Land use
	Land use see BS1199.L28
1199.L3	Law
1199.L4	Leadership
1199.L43	Lebanon
1199.L57	Lists
1199.L67	Love and worship of God
1199.M2	Man
1199.M3	Marriage
1199.M35	Mediator
1199.M4	Memory

Old Testament
Works about the Old Testament
Topics (not otherwise provided for), A-Z -- Continued

1199.M43 Menstruation
1199.M44 Messiah
Cf. BT230+ Messiahship
1199.M45 Metaphor
1199.M47 Military art and science
1199.M5 Miracles
1199.M53 Missions
1199.M6 Monsters
1199.N2 Names
1199.N3 Nationalism
1199.N34 Nature
1199.N38 Naval art and science
Negroes see BS1199.B48
1199.N53 Night
1199.N6 Non-Jews. Gentiles
1199.N85 Numbers
1199.O27 Oaths
1199.O33 Obedience
1199.P26 Palestine
1199.P3 Parables
1199.P32 Paradox
1199.P34 Particularism. Universalism
1199.P37 Passover
1199.P4 Peace
1199.P45 People of God. Community
People with disabilities see BS1199.A25
1199.P5 Piety
1199.P54 Pilgrims and pilgrimages
1199.P57 Polemics
1199.P6 Politics
Including treaties
1199.P64 Poverty
1199.P67 Praise
1199.P68 Prayer. Prayers
1199.P69 Preaching
1199.P695 Presence of God
1199.P7 Priests. Priesthood
Providence and government of God see BS1192.6
1199.P9 Psychology
1199.P93 Public worship
1199.P95 Purity, Ritual
1199.Q43 Queens
1199.R27 Rape
1199.R35 Reconciliation

Old Testament
Works about the Old Testament
Topics (not otherwise provided for), A-Z -- Continued

1199.R37	Remnant
1199.R4	Revelation
1199.R43	Reward
1199.R5	Rhetoric
1199.R53	Riddles
	Ritual purity see BS1199.P95
1199.R55	Roads
1199.R57	Rocks
1199.R6	Rosh ha-shanah
	Rulers see BS1199.K5
1199.R85	Running
1199.S18	Sabbath
1199.S2	Sacrifice
1199.S25	Salvation
	Satire see BS1199.I7
1199.S37	Serpents
1199.S4	Servant of Jehovah
1199.S45	Sex
1199.S5	Shame
1199.S54	Sin
	Social justice see BS1199.J8
1199.S59	Social stratification
1199.S6	Social teachings
1199.S63	Soil fertility
1199.S64	Solitude
1199.S66	Son of God
1199.S67	Son of Man
1199.S68	Space perception
1199.S69	Spirit
1199.S7	Spiritual life
1199.S75	Stewardship
1199.S78	Success
1199.S8	Suffering
1199.S82	Suffering of God
1199.S9	Sun worship
1199.S94	Supernatural phenomena
1199.T3	Taboo
1199.T4	Temptation
1199.T42	Tents
1199.T43	Theocracy
1199.T44	Theodicy
1199.T447	Theomachy
1199.T45	Theophanies
1199.T46	Thought and thinking

Old Testament
Works about the Old Testament
Topics (not otherwise provided for), A-Z -- Continued

1199.T47	Throne of God
1199.T5	Time
1199.T55	Tithes
1199.T68	Tradition
1199.T69	Tragic, The
	Treaties see BS1199.P6
1199.T7	Truthfulness and falsehood
	Universalism see BS1199.P34
	Usury see BS1199.I53
1199.V45	Vendetta
1199.V5	Victory
1199.V56	Violence
1199.V58	Visions
1199.V67	Vows
1199.W2	War
1199.W22	Water
1199.W35	Wealth
1199.W56	Wilderness
1199.W58	Wit and humor
1199.W7	Women (Attitude toward)
1199.W73	Word of God
1199.W735	Work
1199.W74	World
1199.W76	Worship
	Worship, Public see BS1199.P93
	Worship of God see BS1199.L67
1199.W85	Written communication
1199.Y6	Youth

Old Testament -- Continued

Special parts of the Old Testament

The names of the Biblical books and the order of their arrangement is that of the Authorized Version of the English Bible. Variations in the form of names as they occur in the Douai Bible are enclosed in parentheses after the Authorized Version name. Names of books that the Authorized Version includes with the Apocrypha--in editions containing the Apocrypha--are inserted in the Authorized Version order of the books at the most suitable place and reference is made to BS1691-1825.5. However, if a book like the History of Susannah is part of the book of Daniel in the Douai Version, no account is taken of the fact.

Other libraries using this classification must decide in advance which edition they will follow (Authorized Version, Douai, Hebrew Bible). If the Douai Version is followed, brackets around numbers so enclosed are canceled and numbers BS1691-1825.5 are instead enclosed in brackets.

Inserted into the order of the books are the names of groups, e.g. Pentateuch, the most comprehensive always preceding. This applies also to group names, as they occur in the Hebrew Bible, e.g. Five Scrolls. Similar arrangement is provided for frequent combinations that have no particular name of their own, e.g. Psalms, Proverbs, Job. Liturgical lessons are likewise included, not from a liturgical point of view but from that of Biblical studies.

1200 Miscellaneous groups (Table BS6)

Three books or more that do not fit into any known combination of books, e.g. Song of Solomon, Genesis, Job

1201-1205.6 Historical books (Table BS7)

Cf. BS1286.5 Former Prophets of the Hebrew Bible

1208 Harmonies and parallels (Table BS6)

e.g. Samuel, Kings, and Chronicles

1209 Octateuch (Table BS6)

1210 Heptateuch (Table BS6)

1211-1215.6 Hexateuch (Table BS7)

1216 Paraphrases

Including such medieval works as Sefer ha-yashar

1221-1225.6 Pentateuch (Torah) (Table BS7 modified)

For Samaritan Pentateuch see BM920+

Texts

1224.A-Z Other early languages and European languages, A-Z

e.g.

1224.A7-.A77 Aramaic

Targum Onkelos

1224.A7 Texts. By date

Old Testament
  Special parts of the Old Testament
    Historical books
      Pentateuch (Torah)
        Texts
          Other early languages and European languages, A-Z
            Aramaic
              Targum Onkelos -- Continued
1224.A73 Criticism
1224.A735 Palestinian Targumim
                Jonathan. Pseudo-Jonathan
1224.A74 Texts. By date
1224.A75 Criticism
                Targum Yerushalmi
                  Including Fragment Targum and Neofiti Targum
1224.A76 Texts. By date
1224.A77 Criticism
        Criticism, commentaries, etc.
1225 Early through 1950
            Rashi, 1040-1105. Perush Rashi 'al ha-Torah see BS1225.S6
1225.S6 Solomon ben Isaac, called RaSHI, 1040-1105. Perush 'al ha -Torah
1226 Paraphrases
1227 Study and teaching
1231-1235.6 Genesis. Genesis and Exodus (Table BS7 modified)
          Criticism, commentaries, etc.
(1235.6.A-Z) Special topics, A-Z
              see BS1237+
1235.7 Paraphrases
1236 Comparative theology of Genesis
            e.g. Sumerian and Assyrian cosmogony
          Special topics
1237 Garden of Eden
1238.A-Z Other special, A-Z
1238.B2 Babel, Tower of
              Creation see BS651+
1238.D42 Deception
              The Deluge see BS658
1238.E84 Ethics
1238.F34 Family
1238.H66 Homosexuality
1238.J87 Justice
1238.K56 Kinship
1238.M37 Marriage
1238.N35 Names
              Negro in Biblical ethnology see HT1589

Old Testament
Special parts of the Old Testament
Historical books
Pentateuch (Torah)
Genesis. Genesis and Exodus
Special topics
Other special, A-Z -- Continued
Noah's ark see BS658
1238.P53 Place
1238.P7 Prophecies
1238.S24 Sacrifice of Isaac. Akedah
Tower of Babel see BS1238.B2
1239 Study and teaching
Including textbooks
1241-1245.6 Exodus (Table BS7)
Including Israel's wanderings
For The Exodus as an event see BS680.E9; BS1199.E93
For Decalog see BS1281+
1251-1255.6 Leviticus (Table BS7)
1261-1265.6 Numbers (Table BS7)
1271-1275.6 Deuteronomy (Table BS7)
1281-1285.6 Decalog. The Ten Commandments (Table BS7)
Cf. BM520+ Jewish law
Cf. BM520.75 Precepts of the Ten commandments in Judaism
Cf. BV4655+ Moral theology
1286 Prophets (Nevi'im). Prophets of the Hebrew Bible (Table BS6)
In the Hebrew Bible the "Prophets" embrace Joshua, Judges, Samuel, Kings, Isaiah, Jeremiah, Ezekiel, and the Minor Prophets. Of these, Joshua, Judges, Samuel, and Kings are known as the "Former Prophets," the others as the "Latter Prophets"
1286.5 Former Prophets (Table BS6)
Latter prophets see BS1501+
Haftaroth see BM670.H3
1291-1295.6 Joshua (Josue) (Table BS7)
1301-1305.6 Judges (Table BS7)
1308 The Writings (Hebrew Bible). Hagiographa. The Kethubim (Table BS6)
The Writings (Hagiographa) are Psalms, Proverbs, Job, Song of Songs, Ruth, Lamentations, Ecclesiastes, Esther, Daniel, Ezra, Nehemiah, 1 Chronicles, 2 Chronicles

Old Testament
Special parts of the Old Testament
Historical books -- Continued
The Five Scrolls (Hebrew Bible)
The Five Scrolls are the Song of Songs, Ruth, Lamentations, Ecclesiastes, Esther
1309 General works (Table BS6)
1310 Paraphrases
1311-1315.6 Ruth (Table BS7)
1321-1325.6 Samuel (1 and 2 Kings, Douai Bible) (Table BS7)
The first book, the second book, and both together in one arrangement
1326 Paraphrases
1331-1335.6 Kings (3 and 4 Kings, Douai Bible) (Table BS7)
1336 Paraphrases
1341-1345.6 Chronicles (1 and 2 Paralipomenon, Douai Bible) (Table BS7)
1351-1355.6 Ezra (1 Esdras of the Vulgate) (Table BS7)
Not to be confused with 1 Esdras of the Apocrypha
1361-1365.6 Nehemiah (2 Esdras of the Vulgate) (Table BS7)
Not to be confused with 2 Esdras of the Apocrypha
<1368> Tobit (Tobias) (Table BS6a)
see BS1721+
<1369> Judith (Table BS6a)
see BS1731+
1371-1375.6 Esther (Table BS7)
1376 Paraphrases
1401-1405.6 Poetical books. Old Testament lyrics. Songs, hymns, etc. (Table BS7)
The Poetical Books are Job, Psalms, Proverbs, Ecclesiastes, and Song of Solomon
Class here also works containing the poetry of the Old Testament and works on this poetry
1410 Psalms, Proverbs, Job (in combination) (Table BS6)
1411-1415.6 Job (Table BS7)
1416 Paraphrases
1417 Dramatic versions
Psalms
Texts
1419 Polyglot. By date
Hebrew
1420.A-Z Printed texts. By editor, A-Z, or date
Manuscripts
1420.3 General works
Individual manuscripts
1420.5.A-Z By name, A-Z
1420.7 By number

Old Testament
Special parts of the Old Testament
Poetical books. Old Testament lyrics. Songs, hymns, etc.
Psalms
Texts -- Continued
English
1421 Comparative texts
1422 Standard versions. By date
1423 Selections. By editor
Cf. BS1436 Selections for church services
1424 Private versions. By translator, editor, or name
1425.A-Z Other early languages and modern European languages, A-Z
e.g.
1425.F7 Old French. By date
1425.F8 Modern French. By date
Modern non-European languages see BS315+
History and criticism
General works. Commentaries
1429 Early through 1800
1430 1801-1950
1951-2000
1430.2 Criticism
1430.3 Commentaries
1430.4 Sermons. Meditations. Devotions
1430.5 Other
2001-
1430.52 Criticism
1430.53 Commentaries
1430.54 Sermons. Meditations. Devotions
1430.55 Other
1430.6.A-Z Special topics, A-Z
Use Cutter numbers at BS1199
1433 Addresses, essays, lectures
1434 Concordances. Indexes, etc.
1435 Use in Christian liturgy
1436 Selections for church services. By editor or date
Cf. BV199.R5 Responsive services (General)
Cf. BX2033 Catholic Church
Cf. BX5146 Church of England
Cf. BX5946.A+ Protestant Episcopal Church in the United States of America
Metrical versions. Paraphrases
Cf. BX5146 Psalters (Church of England)
1440 English
e.g.
1440.A1 History and criticism

Old Testament
Special parts of the Old Testament
Poetical books. Old Testament lyrics. Songs, hymns, etc.
Psalms
Metrical versions. Paraphrases
English -- Continued

1440.B7 Brady and Tate

Watts: Psalms and hymns

1440.W3 Editions. By date

1440.W35 Selections

1440.W4 Editions. By editor (Barlow, Dwight, Worchester, etc.)

1441 Greek. Greek and Latin. By editor or date

1442 Latin. By editor or date

1443.A-Z Other languages, A-Z
Subarrange by editor or date

1445.A-Z Special groups, A-Z

1445.D4 Deliverance

1445.I46 Imprecatory

1445.L3 Lamentation

1445.M4 Messianic. Regal. Royal

1445.P4 Penitential

1445.S6 Songs of degrees. Songs of the return. Songs of ascents. Pilgrim Psalms (120-134)

1445.S66 Songs of the sons of Korah (42-49, 84-85, 87-88)

1445.T35 Tamid

1450 Special Psalms. By number
Subarrange by editor or date
Classify according to the numbering of the Hebrew (and Protestant) Bible, e.g. BS1450 23rd, for Psalm XXIII. Convert the numbering found in certain Greek and Latin versions as follows:
Greek-Latin 1-8 is Hebrew 1-8
Greek-Latin 9 is Hebrew 9-10
Greek-Latin 10-112 is Hebrew 11-113
Greek-Latin 113 is Hebrew 114-115
Greek-Latin 114-115 is Hebrew 116
Greek-Latin 116-145 is Hebrew 117-146
Greek-Latin 146-147 is Hebrew 147
Greek-Latin 148-150 is Hebrew 148-150

1451 Study and teaching of the Psalms

Proverbs see BS1461+

Song of Solomon see BS1481+

1455 Wisdom literature. Gnomic literature (Table BS6)
Wisdom literature comprises the Book of Proverbs, Job, Ecclesiastes, the Song of Solomon, the Wisdom of Solomon, and Ecclesiasticus

	Old Testament
	Special parts of the Old Testament
	Poetical books. Old Testament lyrics. Songs, hymns, etc.
	Wisdom literature. Gnomic literature -- Continued
1456	Study and teaching
1461-1465.6	Book of Proverbs (Table BS7)
1466	Paraphrases
1467	Study and teaching
	Job see BS1411+
1471-1475.6	Ecclesiastes. The Preacher. Koheleth (Table BS7)
1476	Paraphrases
1481-1485.6	Song of Solomon. Song of Songs. Canticle of Canticles (Table BS7)
1486	Paraphrases
	Metrical versions
1487	English
1489.A-Z	Other languages, A-Z
1490	Dramatic versions
<1491>	Wisdom of Solomon (Table BS6a) see BS1751+
<1496>	Ecclesiasticus. Sirach. The Wisdom of Jesus the Son of Sirach. Ben Sira. (Table BS6a) see BS1761+
1501-1505.6	Prophetic books. The Prophets (Table BS7) Including the lives of the prophets in BS1505+ Cf. BS647+ Prophecy Cf. BS1198 Old Testament prophecy Cf. BS1286 Prophets (Hebrew Bible) Cf. BS1286.5 Former Prophets (Hebrew Bible) Cf. BS1560 Minor Prophets Cf. BT235 Messianic prophecy
1505.7	Paraphrases
1506	Study and teaching Including textbooks
(1508)	Major Prophets see BS1501+
	Minor Prophets see BS1560
	Former Prophets of the Hebrew Bible see BS1286.5
(1509)	Latter Prophets (Isaiah, Jeremiah, Ezekiel and the twelve Minor Prophets) see BS1501+
1511-1515.6	Isaiah (Isaias) (Table BS7) The whole book or chapters 1-39 only
1516	Paraphrases
	Metrical versions
1517	English
1519.A-Z	Other languages, A-Z

Old Testament
Special parts of the Old Testament
Prophetic books. The Prophets
Isaiah (Isaias) -- Continued

1520 Deutero-Isaiah. Trito-Isaiah (Table BS6)
Chapters 40-66 or 40-55 alone
1520.5 Trito-Isaiah (Table BS6)
Chapters 56-66 alone
1521-1525.6 Jeremiah (Jeremias) (Table BS7)
1531-1535.6 Lamentations (Table BS7)
1536 Paraphrases
Metrical versions
1537 English
1539.A-Z Other languages, A-Z
<1540> Baruch (Table BS6a)
see BS1771+
1541-1545.6 Ezekiel (Ezechiel) (Table BS7)
1550 Daniel, Ezra, Nehemiah (in combination) (Table BS6)
Including editions and studies of those passages originally in Aramaic
1551-1555.6 Daniel (Table BS7)
1556 Prophecies and visions of Daniel
Including Daniel and Revelation
Cf. BS649.A+ Special topics in prophecy, e.g. Turkey, Great Britain, the Jews, etc.
Apocalypses see BS646
1560 The Minor Prophets (Table BS6)
1561-1565.6 Hosea (Osee) (Table BS7)
1571-1575.6 Joel (Table BS7)
1581-1585.6 Amos (Table BS7)
1586 Paraphrases
1591-1595.6 Obadiah (Abdias) (Table BS7)
1601-1605.6 Jonah (Jonas) (Table BS7)
1606 Paraphrases
1611-1615.6 Micah (Micheas) (Table BS7)
1621-1625.6 Nahum (Table BS7)
1625 Criticism, commentaries, etc.
1625.N26-.N3 Pesher Nahum (Dead Sea scrolls)
1625.N26 Text in original language
1625.N27 Facsimiles
Translations
1625.N28 English
1625.N29A-.N29Z Other languages, A-Z
Subarrange by date
1631-1635.6 Habakkuk (Habacuc) (Table BS7)
1635 Criticism, commentaries, etc.
1635.H26-.H3 Habakkuk commentary (Dead Sea Scrolls)

Old Testament
Special parts of the Old Testament
Prophetic books. The Prophets
The Minor Prophets
Habakkuk (Habacuc)
Criticism, commentaries, etc.
Habakkuk commentary (Dead Sea Scrolls) -- Continued

1635.H26 Text in original language
1635.H27 Facsimiles
Translations
1635.H28 English
1635.H29A-.H29Z Other languages, A-Z
Subarrange by date
1635.H3 History and criticism
1641-1645.6 Zephaniah (Sophonias) (Table BS7)
1651-1655.6 Haggai (Aggeus) (Table BS7)
1661-1665.6 Zechariah (Zacharias) (Table BS7)
1671-1675.6 Malachi (Malachias) (Table BS7)
<1685> Maccabees, 1st (Machabees, 1st) (Table BS6a)
see BS1821+
<1686> Maccabees, 2nd (Machabees, 2nd) (Table BS6a)
see BS1821+
Apocrypha and apocryphal books
Including works covering both Old and New Testament apocryphal books
Including the Pseudepigrapha
Texts
1691 Polyglot. Texts in Hebrew, Aramaic, or Greek. By date
1692 English. By date
1693.A-Z Other languages. By language, A-Z, and date
Selections
1695 English
1696.A-Z Other languages, A-Z
1700 History and criticism. Commentaries
1705 Apocalypses
Cf. BL501 Apocalypticism, apocalyptic literature
Cf. BS646 Apocalypses in canonical books
Cf. BS2820+ Book of Revelation
Cf. BS2910+ New Testament apocalypses
Cf. BT235 Messianic prophecy
Special books of the Apocrypha
Texts in Greek are classified as translations
For an alternative classification of the books of the Apocrypha according to the arrangement of the Douai version see instructions above BS1200

Old Testament
Special parts of the Old Testament
Apocrypha and apocryphal books
Special books of the Apocrypha -- Continued

1711-1715.6 Esdras I and II (Table BS7)
Not to be confused with the books of Ezra and Nehemiah that are called First and Second Esdras in the Vulgate.
1721-1725.6 Tobit (Tobias) (Table BS7)
1731-1735.6 Judith (Table BS7)
1741-1745.6 Rest of Esther (Additions to Esther) (Table BS7)
1751-1755.6 Wisdom of Solomon (Table BS7)
1761-1765.6 Ecclesiasticus. Sirach. Wisdom of Jesus the Son of Sirach (Table BS7)
1771-1775.6 Baruch (Table BS7)
Including the Letter of Jeremiah, sometimes included as chapter 6 of Baruch
Cf. BS1830.B3+ Apocalypse of Baruch
1781-1785.6 Song of the Three Children. Prayer of Azariah and the Song of the Three Young Men. (Table BS7)
1791-1795.6 History of Susanna (Table BS7)
1801-1805.6 Bel and the Dragon (Table BS7)
1811-1815.6 Prayer of Manasses (Table BS7)
1821-1825.6 Maccabees I-IV. Scroll of Antiochus (Table BS7)
1830.A-Z Special apocryphal books (The Pseudepigrapha), A-Z
1830.A25-.A252 Adam and Eve, Life of (Table BS8)
1830.A26-.A262 Adam books (Table BS8)
Cf. BS1830.A25+ Life of Adam and Eve
Cf. BS1830.C65+ Conflict of Adam and Eve with Satan
1830.A6-.A62 Apocalypse of Abraham (Table BS8)
1830.A63-.A64 Ascension of Isaiah (Table BS8)
1830.A7-.A8 Assumption of Moses (Table BS8)
1830.B3-.B4 Apocalypse of Baruch (Syriac) (2 Baruch) (Table BS8)
1830.B45-.B46 Apocalypse of Baruch (Greek) (3 Baruch) (Table BS8)
1830.C65-.C652 Conflict of Adam and Eve with Satan (Table BS8)
1830.D35-.D36 Daniel-Diegese (Table BS8)
1830.D38-.D382 Syriac Apocalypse of Daniel (Table BS8)
1830.E45-.E46 Apocalypse of Elijah (Table BS8)
Book of Enoch
1830.E6-.E7 1 Enoch. Ethiopic Book of Enoch (Table BS8)
1830.E8-.E81 2 Enoch. Slavonic Book of Enoch (Table BS8)
1830.E82-.E83 3 Enoch. Hebrew Book of Enoch (Table BS8)
1830.E86-.E862 Apocalypse of Esdras (Table BS8)
1830.E92-.E93 Ezekiel (Apocryphal book) (Table BS8)
1830.G4-.G5 Genesis Apocryphon (Table BS8)
1830.J6-.J62 Joseph and Asenath (Table BS8)

Old Testament
Special parts of the Old Testament
Apocrypha and apocryphal books
Special apocryphal books (The Pseudepigrapha), A-Z -- Continued

1830.J7-.J8 Book of Jubilees (Table BS8)
1830.L58-.L582 Lives of the Prophets (Table BS8)
1830.N37-.N372 Narrative of Zosimus (Table BS8)
1830.O3-.O4 Odes of Solomon (Table BS8)
1830.P22-.P23 Paralipomena Jeremiae (Table BS8)
Psalms of Solomon
Texts
1830.P7A1 Polyglot. By date
1830.P7A3 English. By date
1830.P7A5-.P7Z Other languages, A-Z
Subarrange each language by date
1830.P73 History, criticism, etc.
Including works on manuscripts
1830.T14-.T142 Testament of Adam (Table BS8)
1830.T16-.T17 Testament of Job (Table BS8)
1830.T18-.T182 Testament of Solomon (Table BS8)
1830.T2-.T3 Testament of the Three Patriarchs (Table BS8)
1830.T31-.T32 Testament of Abraham (Table BS8)
1830.T33-.T34 Testament of Isaac (Table BS8)
1830.T35-.T36 Testament of Jacob (Table BS8)
1830.T4-.T5 Testament of the Twelve Patriarchs (Table BS8)
1830.T51-.T52 Testament of Reuben (Table BS8)
1830.T53-.T54 Testament of Simeon (Table BS8)
1830.T55-.T56 Testament of Levi (Table BS8)
1830.T57-.T58 Testament of Judah (Table BS8)
1830.T59-.T592 Testament of Issachar (Table BS8)
1830.T61-.T62 Testament of Zebulun (Table BS8)
1830.T63-.T64 Testament of Dan (Table BS8)
1830.T65-.T66 Testament of Naphtali (Table BS8)
1830.T67-.T68 Testament of Gad (Table BS8)
1830.T69-.T692 Testament of Asher (Table BS8)
1830.T71-.T72 Testament of Joseph (Table BS8)
1830.T73-.T74 Testament of Benjamin (Table BS8)

New Testament
Texts and versions
1901 Polyglot New Testaments
Subarrange by date
For polyglot texts of special parts, see the special part, e.g. BS2549, Polyglot Gospels
For Specimens of Bible texts in several languages, e.g. John III, 16 see P351+

New Testament
Texts and versions -- Continued
1904 Collected works
Class here miscellaneous general collected works in print or facsimile
1904.5 Works on New Testament manuscripts in general
Early texts and versions
The Greek New Testament
1937 Collected works
Class here works in which various texts are published
1937.5 Comparative texts of Greek New Testaments
1938 History and criticism
Cf. BS2325 Textual criticism of the New Testament
Manuscripts. Codices
Class here manuscripts of the whole New Testament and fragments of manuscripts, including the New Testament portion of manuscripts of the whole Greek Bible
1939 General works
Individual manuscripts
Including criticism
1964.A-Z By name, A-Z
1964.5 By number
According to the numbering by Gregory
1965 Modern printed editions. By date
1965.2 Translation helps
1965.5 Interlinear translations
1966 Selections from the Greek New Testament
1967-1990 Latin versions
1967 Collections
Works in which several texts are published
1967.5 Comparative texts of Latin Bibles
1968 History and criticism
Manuscripts. Codices
1969 General works
1970.A-Z Individual manuscripts (regardless of version), A-Z
By name or other distinctive word
For criticism use subarrangement by author, A-Z
Special versions
Greek-Latin parallel editions are classed with Greek texts
Old Latin. Italic versions. Itala
1972 Collections. By title or editor
1973 Texts. By date
1974 History and criticism
Vulgate
1975 Texts. By date
1985 History and criticism

New Testament
Texts and versions
Early texts and versions
Latin versions
Special versions -- Continued
1989.A-Z Other early and medieval Latin versions, A-Z
1990 Modern Latin versions
Syriac versions
1992 Texts. By date
Manuscripts. Codices
1992.3 General works
1992.5.A-Z Individual manuscripts (regardless of version), A-Z
By name or other distinctive word
1993.A-Z Special versions. By name, A-Z
e.g.
Peshitta
1993.P4 Texts. By date
Translations
1993.P5 English
1993.P6A-.P6Z Other, A-Z
Palestinian Syriac
1993.2 Texts. By date
Manuscripts. Codices
1993.3 General works
1993.5.A-Z Individual manuscripts (regardless of version), A-Z
By name or other distinctive word
Modern Syriac see BS315.S9
1994 History and criticism
Other early versions
Including modern versions in these languages
Armenian
1995 Printed texts. By date
Manuscripts. Codices
1995.3 General works
1995.5.A-Z Individual manuscripts (regardless of version), A-Z
By name or other distinctive word
1996 History and criticism
Coptic
2000 Printed texts. By date
Manuscripts. Codices
2000.3 General works
2000.5.A-Z Individual manuscripts (regardless of version), A-Z
By name or other distinctive word
2001 History and criticism
Ethiopic
2005 Printed texts. By date
Manuscripts. Codices

New Testament
Texts and versions
Early texts and versions
Other early versions
Ethiopic
Manuscripts. Codices -- Continued
2005.3 General works
2005.5.A-Z Individual manuscripts (regradless of version), A-Z
By name or other distinctive word
2006 History and criticism
Gothic see BS105+
Hebrew
2010 Printed texts. By date
Manuscripts. Codices
2010.3 General works
2010.5.A-Z Individual manuscripts (regardless of version), A-Z
By name or other distinctive word
2011 History and criticism
Church Slavic
2015 Printed texts. By date
Manuscripts. Codices
2015.3 General works
2015.5.A-Z Individual manuscripts (regardless of version), A-Z
By name or other distinctive word
2016 History and criticism
2020.A-Z Other, A-Z
Arabic see BS315.A6+
Modern texts and versions of the New Testament
English
2025 Comparative texts of English Bibles. By date
Cf. BS2088.A3 Autorized and Revised versions
Cf. BS2090.A3 Authorized and American Revision versions
Cf. BS2091.A3 Revised Standard and Confraternity of Christian Doctrine versions
Anglo-Saxon see BS130
English versions
Arranged chronologically
2035-2036 Wycliffe's (1380) (Table BS1)
2038.A-Z Other Middle English versions, A-Z
e.g.
2038.P8 Purvey's
(2040-2041) Tyndale's (1525-1531)
see BS140+
2045-2046 Coverdale's (1535) (Table BS1)
2050-2051 Matthew's (1537) (Table BS1)

New Testament
Texts and versions
Modern texts and versions of the New Testament
English
English versions -- Continued

2052-2053 Taverner's (1539) (Table BS1)
Revision of Matthew's
The Great Bible
2055-2056 Cromwell's edition, 1539 (Table BS1)
2060-2061 Cranmer's edition, 1540 (Table BS1)
2065-2066 Cranmer's edition, 1541 (Table BS1)
2067 Other editions. By date
2070-2071 Geneva, 1557 (Table BS1)
2075-2076 Bishop's Bible (1568) (Table BS1)
2080-2081 Rheims, 1582 (Table BS1)
Including revisions such as the Challoner revision, the Confraternity version
For texts published with Douai Old Testament see BS180+
King James, Authorized version (1611)
2085 Texts
Arrange by date and subarrange by place of publication, A-Z
2086 History and criticism, etc.
Revised version (1881-1885)
2088.A1 Texts. By date
Subarrange by place of publication, A-Z
2088.A2 Texts, American version. By date
2088.A3 Authorized and Revised versions paralleled
Subdivided by date and place of publication
2088.A5-Z History and criticism, etc.
American Revision (1901)
2090.A1 Texts. By date.
Subarrange by place of publication, A-Z
2090.A3 Authorized and American Revision versions paralleled
Subarrange by date and place of publication
2090.A5-Z History and criticism, etc.
Revised Standard version (1946-1952)
2091.A1 Texts. By date
Subarrange by place of publication, A-Z
2091.A3 Revised Standard and Confraternity of Christian Doctrine versions paralleled
2091.A5-Z History and criticism, etc.
New Revised Standard version (1990)
2091.5.A1 Texts. By date
Subarrange by place of publication, A-Z

New Testament
Texts and versions
Modern texts and versions of the New Testament
English
English versions
New Revised Standard version (1990) -- Continued
2091.5.A5-Z History and criticism, etc.
New English Bible (1961-)
2092.A1 Texts. By date
Subarrange by place of publication, A-Z
2092.A5-Z History and criticism, etc.
Revised English Bible (1989-)
2092.16.A1 Texts. By date
Subarrange by place of publication, A-Z
2092.16.A5-Z History and criticism, etc.
Anchor Bible
2092.2.A1 Texts. By date
Subarrange by place of publication, A-Z
2092.2.A5-Z History and criticism, etc.
New American Bible
2092.3.A1 Texts. By date
Subarrange by place of publication, A-Z
2092.3.A5-Z History and criticism, etc.
2095.A-Z Other versions and revisions. By version, A-Z
2095.A53-.A532 Amplified (Table BS2)
2095.B38-.B382 Berkeley version (Table BS2)
2095.B53-.B532 Blair (Table BS2)
2095.C6-.C62 Confraternity version (Table BS2)
2095.C66-.C662 Contemporary English (Table BS2)
2095.D35-.D352 Dolen (Table BS2)
2095.E64-.E642 English Standard (Table BS2)
2095.G55-.G552 Goble (Table BS2)
2095.G57-.G572 God's Word (Table BS2)
2095.G58-.G582 Gold (Table BS2)
2095.G59-.G592 Golden Bridge version (Table BS2)
Good News Translation see BS2095.T63+
2095.G84-.G842 Green (Table BS2)
2095.H59-.H592 Holman Christian Standard (Table BS2)
2095.H64-.H642 House of Yahweh (Table BS2)
2095.I56-.I562 International Standard (Table BS2)
2095.J4-.J42 Jerusalem (Table BS2)
2095.K53-.K532 KJ21 (Table BS2)
2095.L35-.L352 Lamsa (Table BS2)
2095.L54-.L542 Life messengers (Table BS2)
2095.L58-.L582 Living Bible (Table BS2)
2095.M47-.M472 The Message (Table BS2)
2095.M79-.M792 Morford (Table BS2)

New Testament
Texts and versions
Modern texts and versions of the New Testament
English
English versions
Other versions and revisions, A-Z -- Continued
2095.N32-.N322 NET Bible (Table BS2)
2095.N35-.N352 New American Standard (Table BS2)
2095.N3524-.N35242 New Authorized (Table BS2)
2095.N353-.N3532 New Century (Table BS2)
2095.N37-.N372 New International (Table BS2)
2095.N373-.N3732 New International Readers Version (Table BS2)
2095.N375-.N3752 New Jerusalem Bible (Table BS2)
2095.N38-.N382 New King James (Table BS2)
2095.N394-.N3942 New Living Translation (Table BS2)
2095.N4-.N42 New World (Table BS2)
2095.S5-.S52 Simplified Living Bible (Table BS2)
2095.S75-.S752 Stern (Table BS2)
2095.T63-.T632 Today's English. Good News Translation (Table BS2)
2095.W67-.W672 World English Bible (Table BS2)
Basic English versions
2096.A1 Texts. By date
Subarrange by place of publication, A-Z
2096.A5-Z History and criticism, etc.
2096.5 Reference editions
Editions for special classes
2097 Young people's Bibles. Children's Bibles. By editor or publisher.
Class here relatively complete Bibles omitting portions unsuitable for children.
2098.A-Z Other, A-Z
Subarrange by publisher and date
e.g.
2098.E3 Eastern Star
2098.F8 Freemasons
Mormons see BX8630+
2098.O3 Oddfellows
2099-2213 Other modern European languages (Table BS10)
Add number in table to BS1900
Each language to include its dialects unless otherwise provided for
Modern non-European languages see BS315+

New Testament -- Continued
Selections. Quotations
Subarrange under each language by compiler or date
For New Testament quotations in early Christian literature see BR66+
For selections and quotations in any topical arrangement see BS2310
For Old Testament quotations in the New Testament see BS2387
2260 Polyglot
2261 English
2262 Dutch
2263 French
2264 German
2265 Italian
2266 Scandinavian
2267 Spanish and Portuguese
2269.A-Z Other languages, A-Z
Works about the New Testament
Periodicals see BS410
Societies see BS411
Collections of monographs, studies, etc.
2280 Several authors
2290 Individual authors
Concordances
2301 Hebrew
2302 Greek
2303 Latin
2305 English
2306 French
2307 German
2308.A-Z Other languages, A-Z
2310 Topical indexes, references, tables, etc.
2312 Dictionaries
Introductory works
History of the New Testament
2315 General works
2315.5 Date of authorship
2316 History of translations of the New Testament
Including history of translating the New Testament
2317 The English New Testament
For works on specific editions and versions see BS2025+
2318.A-Z The New Testament in other modern European languages, A-Z
For works on specific editions and versions see BS2099+

New Testament
Works about the New Testament
Introductory works
History of the New Testament
History of translations of the New Testament -- Continued
The New Testament in non-European languages see BS315+
The New Testament in ancient languages see BS1937+
History of New Testament criticism and interpretation see BS2350
2320 Canon
2325 Textual criticism
Cf. BS1904.5 Works on New Testament manuscripts in general
General works. Introductions
Class here both general and special introductions. Special introductions treat the origin, authorship, authenticity, general characteristics, contents, and aim of the different books of the Bible. General introductions, in addition, treat textual criticism, the versions, and the canon
2329 Early through 1800
2330 1801-1950
2330.2 1951-2000
2330.3 2001-
2331 Hermeneutics. Exegetics. Principles of interpretation
Symbolism see BS477
Typology see BS478
2332 Inspiration. Authenticity
Commentaries
Greek
2333 Early through 1950
1951-2000
2333.2 General works
2333.5 Sermons. Meditations. Devotions
2001-
2333.52 General works
2333.55 Sermons. Meditations. Devotions
Latin
2335 Early through 1950
1951-2000
2335.2 General works
2335.5 Sermons. Meditations. Devotions
2001-
2335.52 General works

New Testament
Works about the New Testament
Commentaries
Latin
2001- -- Continued
2335.55 Sermons. Meditations. Devotions
English
2340 Early through 1800
2341 1801-1950
1951-2000
2341.2 General works
2341.3 Sermons. Meditations. Devotions
2001-
2341.52 General works
2341.55 Sermons. Meditations. Devotions
Dutch
2342 Early through 1950
1951-2000
2342.2 General works
2342.5 Sermons. Meditations. Devotions
2001-
2342.52 General works
2342.55 Sermons. Meditations. Devotions
French
2343 Early through 1950
1951-2000
2343.2 General works
2343.5 Sermons. Meditations. Devotions
2001-
2343.52 General works
2343.55 Sermons. Meditations. Devotions
German
2344 Early through 1950
1951-2000
2344.2 General works
2344.5 Sermons. Meditations. Devotions
2001-
2344.52 General works
2344.55 Sermons. Meditations. Devotions
Italian
2345 Early through 1950
1951-2000
2345.2 General works
2345.5 Sermons. Meditations. Devotions
2001-
2345.52 General works
2345.55 Sermons. Meditations. Devotions

New Testament
Works about the New Testament
Commentaries -- Continued
Scandinavian
2346 Early through 1950
1951-2000
2346.2 General works
2346.5 Sermons. Meditations. Devotions
2001-
2346.52 General works
2346.55 Sermons. Meditations. Devotions
Spanish and Portuguese
2347 Early through 1950
1951-2000
2347.2 General works
2347.5 Sermons. Meditations. Devotions
2001-
2347.52 General works
2347.55 Sermons. Meditations. Devotions
2348.A-Z Other languages, A-Z
Criticism and interpretation
2350 History of New Testament criticism and interpretation
2351.A-Z Biography, A-Z
Including criticism
e.g.
2351.A1 Collective
2351.B3 Bauer, Bruno
2351.W4 Wetzstein, Johann Jakob
General works. The Higher criticism
2353 Greek
2355 Latin
Early through 1800
English
2361 1801-1950
2361.2 1951-2000
2361.3 2001-
Dutch
2362 Early through 1950
2362.2 1951-2000
2362.3 2001-
French
2363 Early through 1950
2363.2 1951-2000
2363.3 2001-
German
2364 Early through 1950
2364.2 1951-2000

New Testament
Works about the New Testament
Criticism and interpretation
General works. The Higher criticism
German -- Continued
2364.3 2001-
Italian
2365 Early through 1950
2365.2 1951-2000
2365.3 2001-
Scandinavian
2366 Early through 1950
2366.2 1951-2000
2366.3 2001-
Spanish and Portuguese
2367 Early through 1950
2367.2 1951-2000
2367.3 2001-
2368.A-Z Other languages, A-Z
2370 General special
2372 Rationalistic works
2375 Historical criticism
Cf. BS2410 History of Christianity in New Testament times
2376 Eschatological school of criticism
2377 Form criticism
For works limited to the Gospels see BS2555.A2+
2377.3 Narrative criticism
2377.5 Structuralism
2377.6 Deconstruction
2378 Demythologization
2379 Feminist criticism
2380 Socio-rhetorical criticism
Comparative religion of the New Testament see BR127+
Lower criticism see BS2325
Language of the New Testament see PA800+
2385 Word studies (General and individual)
2387 Relations of Old and New Testaments
Including Old Testament quotations and references
Cf. BS478 Typology
2390 Other works
Including minor works
2391 Mythological, allegorical, numerical, astronomical interpretations of the New Testament
2392 Homiletical use
2393 Addresses, essays, etc. on New Testament criticism
2395 Addresses, essays, etc. on the New Testament in general

New Testament
Works about the New Testament -- Continued
Theology of the New Testament
For the theology of special parts and books of the New Testament, see the number for theology or criticism under each part and book
For the theology of special topics see BS2545.A+
Cf. BS2415+ Teachings of Jesus
Cf. BS2651+ Pauline theology
2397.A1 Collections
2397.A3-Z General works
2398 God in the New Testament
Including teachings of Jesus and of Paul about God
Ethics of the New Testament see BS2545.E8
Bible stories from the New Testament
Cf. BT302 Juvenile lives of Christ
English
2400 General works
2401 Juvenile
2403 French
2404 German
2405.A-Z Other languages, A-Z
2406 New Testament pictures for children
Auxiliary topics
2406.5 Antiquities. Archaeology
Cf. BR130+ Christian antiquities
New Testament history
Cf. BR165+ Apostolic Age
Cf. BS2375 Historical criticism
Cf. BS2410 History of Christianity in New Testament times
2407 General works
2408 Study and teaching
For Sunday-school textbooks see BS2534+
2409 New Testament chronology
2410 History of Christianity in New Testament times
Class here works on history in its contemporary setting and background
The teachings of Jesus
Including the belief of Jesus
2415.A2 Selections from Scripture
Cf. BT306 Words of Jesus
2415.A3 Other collections
2415.A4-Z General works
Cf. BT198+ Christology
2416 Juvenile works
2417.A-Z Topics (not otherwise provided for), A-Z

New Testament
Works about the New Testament
The teachings of Jesus
Topics (not otherwise provided for), A-Z -- Continued

2417.A4 Aggression
2417.C4 Children
2417.C45 Children of God
2417.C5 Christian life
2417.C53 Church
2417.C55 Church and state
2417.C69 Covenants
2417.D6 Divorce
2417.E3 Economics. Labor
2417.E7 Eschatology
2417.E8 Ethics
2417.F7 Future life
2417.H34 Hate
2417.H37 Healing
2417.H4 Heaven
2417.J4 Jews
2417.J83 Judgment
2417.K5 Kingdom of God
Labor see BS2417.E3
2417.L3 Law
2417.L7 Love
2417.M25 Man
2417.M3 Marriage
2417.M4 Mental hygiene
Money see BS2417.W4
2417.N37 Naturalism
2417.P2 Pacifism
2417.P25 Parent and child
2417.P36 Persecution
2417.P6 Political teachings
2417.P68 Poverty
2417.R3 Race problems
2417.R4 Reward
2417.S4 Service
2417.S52 Sin
2417.S7 Social teachings
2417.T7 Truth
2417.V56 Violence
2417.W2 War
2417.W4 Wealth. Money
2417.W57 Wisdom
2417.W6 Women (Attitude toward)
2417.W65 Worship

New Testament
Works about the New Testament -- Continued
Men, women, and children of the New Testament
Genealogy see BS569
Biography
Cf. BS570+ Biography (Bible as a whole and Old Testament alone)
Collective
2430 General works
2431 Sermons
2433 Juvenile works
Textbooks see BS2534+
Special groups
2440 Lives of the Apostles and disciples
Cf. BS2618 Work and teaching of the Apostles
2441 Lives of the Evangelists
2445 Women in the New Testament
2446 Children in the New Testament
2447 Men in the New Testament
2448.A-Z Other special, A-Z
2448.R63 Rogues and vagabonds
2448.S6 Soldiers
2450-2520 Individual New Testament characters
Including stories, meditations, etc.
Whenever Biblical books bear the names of these characters, classify purely biographical material in BS2450+, all other material with the book in question
For life of Jesus Christ see BT296+
2450 A - Andrew
2450.A6 Ananias and Sapphira
2451 Andrew, Apostle, Saint
2452 Andrew - James
2452.A5 Anna, the Prophetess
2452.B2 Barabbas
2452.B28 Barnabas, Apostle, Saint
2452.B29 Bartholomew, Apostle, Saint
2452.B3 Bartimaeus
2452.B36 Beloved Disciple
2452.B4 Berenice
2452.C34 Caiaphas
2452.C6 Cornelius, the Centurion
2452.D5 Dismas, Saint
2452.D67 Dorcas
2452.H47 Herodias
2453 James, Apostle, Saint (James, the son of Zebedee)
Cf. BT685.5 Cult
2454 James - John

New Testament
Works about the New Testament
Men, women, and children of the New Testament
Biography
Individual New Testament characters
James - John -- Continued

2454.J3 James, Brother of the Lord
2455 John, Apostle, Saint
2456 John the Baptist
Cf. BT691 Cult
2458 Joseph, Saint
Cf. BT690+ Cult
Cf. BX2164 Prayers and devotions
2460 Joseph - Luke
2460.J8 Judas Iscariot
2460.J85 Jude, Saint
Cf. BT693 Cult
2460.J88 Junia
2460.L3 Lazarus, Saint
2465 Luke, Saint
2470 Luke - Mark
2475 Mark, Saint
2480 Mark - Mary
2480.M3 Martha, Saint
Mary, Mother of Jesus Christ see BT595+
2485 Mary Magdalene, Saint
2490 Mary - Matthew
2490.M2 Mary of Bethany
2495 Matthew, Apostle, Saint
2500 Matthew - Paul
2500.N5 Nicodemus
Paul, Apostle, Saint
2505.A3 Compilations from Scripture
General works
2505.A5-Z Early through 1950
2506 1951-2000
2506.3 2001-
2506.5 Juvenile works
2507 Study and teaching. Textbooks
2510 Paul - Peter
2515 Peter, the Apostle, Saint
2520 Peter - Z
2520.P5 Philip, the evangelist
2520.P55 Pilate, Pontius
2520.S6 Salome
2520.S7 Simon of Cyrene
2520.S8 Stephen, Saint

New Testament
Works about the New Testament
Men, women, and children of the New Testament
Biography
Individual New Testament characters
Peter - Z -- Continued
2520.S9 Sychar, Woman of
2520.T45 Thomas, Apostle, Saint
2520.T5 Timothy
2520.Z3 Zacchaeus
Study and teaching
see also Study and teaching under individual books of the New Testament
Cf. BS2408 New Testament history
Cf. BS2505+ Life of Paul
Cf. BT296+ Life of Jesus
2525 Outlines, syllabi, etc.
2530 General works
Including the life and teachings of Jesus Christ
Textbooks
Under each language, class translations with the language into which translated
Cf. BS2400+ New Testament stories
English
2534 Early through 1800
2535 1801-1950
2535.2 1951-2000
2535.3 2001-
2536 Catholic textbooks
2537 French
2538 German
2539 Italian
2540 Scandinavian
2541 Spanish and Portuguese
2542.A-Z Other languages, A-Z
2543 Addresses, essays, lectures
2544 Questions and answers
2545.A-Z Topics (not otherwise provided for), A-Z
For the teachings of Jesus see BS2415+
2545.A25 Acceptance
2545.A37 Africa
2545.A66 Apostasy
2545.A67 Apostolate
2545.A73 Ark of the Covenant

New Testament
Works about the New Testament
Topics (not otherwise provided for), A-Z -- Continued

(2545.A75) Astronomy
Use this Cutter number only when applying Table BS9 for parts of the New Testament
For general works on New Testament astronomy see BS2391

2545.A8 Atonement
2545.A92 Avarice
2545.B36 Baptism
2545.B5 Blessing and cursing
2545.B63 Body, Human
2545.B7 Brotherliness
2545.C43 Character
2545.C44 Chastity. Virginity
2545.C45 Children of God
2545.C48 Christian life
2545.C5 Church
2545.C55 Church and state
2545.C553 Church and the world
2545.C554 Church fund raising
2545.C555 Church officers
2545.C56 Clergy. Ministry (ordained)
Cf. BS2545.P69 Priests, priesthood
Coins see CJ255
2545.C567 Compassion
2545.C57 Concord
2545.C573 Conflict management
2545.C58 Conscience
2545.C584 Consolation
2545.C59 Conversion
2545.C6 Cosmology
2545.C63 Covenants
2545.C74 Creeds
2545.C76 Crowds
2545.C84 Culture conflict
2545.C95 Cyprus
Darkness see BS2545.L54
2545.D4 Deacons
2545.D45 Death
2545.D5 Demonic possession. Demonology. Devil
Devil see BS2545.D5
2545.D56 Dinners and dining. Meals
2545.D58 Divorce
Eating see BS2545.D56
2545.E4 Education

New Testament
Works about the New Testament
Topics (not otherwise provided for), A-Z -- Continued

2545.E46 Emperor worship
2545.E67 Ephesus
2545.E7 Eschatology
2545.E8 Ethics
Cf. BJ1188.5+ Christian ethics
2545.E815 Ethnicity
2545.E82 Evangelistic work
2545.F3 Faith
2545.F33 Family
2545.F35 Farewells
2545.F36 Fasting
2545.F38 Fear
2545.F4 Fellowship
2545.F5 Fishing
2545.F55 Flesh. Flesh and spirit
2545.F6 Forgiveness of sin. Forgiveness
2545.F7 Freedom
2545.F75 Friendship
2545.F88 Future life
2545.G34 Galilee (Israel)
2545.G4 Gentiles
2545.G47 Gifts, Spiritual
2545.G55 Glory
2545.G63 Glossolalia
2545.G65 Good and evil
2545.G73 Grace
2545.H27 Hairdressing
2545.H3 Hardness of heart
2545.H4 Healing
2545.H55 History. Historiography
2545.H6 Holiness
2545.H62 Holy Spirit. Spirit
2545.H627 Home. Households
2545.H63 Homosexuality
2545.H634 Honor
2545.H64 Hope
2545.H66 Hospitality
Households see BS2545.H627
Human body see BS2545.B63
2545.H94 Hymns
2545.I35 Idols and images
2545.I53 Incarnation
Irony see BS2545.W5
2545.I75 Israel (Christian theology)

New Testament
Works about the New Testament
Topics (not otherwise provided for), A-Z -- Continued

2545.J35	Jealousy
2545.J4	Jerusalem
2545.J44	Jews. Judaism
2545.J6	Joy
	Judaism see BS2545.J44
2545.J8	Justice
2545.J82	Justification
2545.K43	Kerygma
2545.K5	Kings and rulers
2545.L3	Language
2545.L34	Law
2545.L42	Leadership
2545.L47	Lesbianism
2545.L54	Light and darkness
2545.L58	Lord's Supper
2545.L6	Love
	Lust see BS2545.S36
2545.M25	Magic
2545.M27	Man
2545.M3	Marriage
	Meals see BS2545.D56
2545.M39	Men, Attitude toward
	Ministry (ordained) see BS2545.C56
2545.M5	Miracles
2545.M54	Mission of the Church
2545.M87	Mystery
2545.M9	Mysticism
2545.N3	Names
	Name of God see BS2398
2545.N48	New and old
	Nonviolence see BS2545.P4
2545.O25	Oaths
2545.O26	Obedience
2545.O3	Occultism
2545.O4	Offense
	Old and new see BS2545.N48
2545.P4	Pacifism. Nonviolence
2545.P43	Palestine
2545.P45	Pastoral theology
2545.P47	Pauline churches
2545.P5	Peace
2545.P55	Perfection
2545.P57	Perserverance
2545.P6	Political science

New Testament
Works about the New Testament
Topics (not otherwise provided for), A-Z -- Continued

2545.P65 Poverty
2545.P66 Power
2545.P663 Powers, principalities, etc.
2545.P67 Prayer. Prayers
Prayers of Jesus see BV229+
2545.P68 Preaching
2545.P684 Preexistence
2545.P687 Presence of God
2545.P69 Priests. Priesthood
Cf. BS2545.C56 Clergy. Ministry (ordained)
Principalities see BS2545.P663
2545.P696 Property
2545.P7 Prophecies
2545.P72 Prophecy
2545.P9 Psychology
2545.P95 Purity, Ritual
2545.R34 Reconciliation
2545.R36 Redemption
2545.R38 Regeneration
2545.R4 Reincarnation
2545.R43 Religious tolerance
2545.R45 Repentance
2545.R46 Rest
2545.R47 Resurrection
2545.R49 Revelation
2545.R54 Rhetoric
2545.R65 Rome
2545.S22 Sabbath
2545.S23 Sacraments
2545.S24 Sacrifice
2545.S25 Salvation
2545.S27 Sanctification
2545.S33 Self-deception
2545.S35 Service
2545.S36 Sex. Lust
2545.S37 Sex role
2545.S42 Ships
2545.S45 Sin
2545.S55 Sociology
2545.S57 Son of Man
2545.S6 Speeches
Spirit, Holy see BS2545.H62
Spirit and flesh see BS2545.F55
2545.S64 Spiritual formation

New Testament
Works about the New Testament
Topics (not otherwise provided for), A-Z -- Continued
Spiritual gifts see BS2545.G47
2545.S65 Spiritual life
2545.S67 Spiritual warfare
2545.S77 Stewardship
2545.S8 Strangers
2545.S9 Suffering
(2545.S97) Symbolism. Symbols
Use this Cutter number only when applying Table BS9 for parts of the New Testament
For general works on New Testament symbolism see BS477
2545.T33 Taxation
2545.T45 Temple of God
2545.T47 Theodicy
2545.T5 Time
2545.T55 Tithes
2545.T7 Tradition
2545.T73 Trials
2545.T78 Truth
2545.V55 Violence
2545.V57 Visions
Virginity see BS2545.C44
2545.W3 War
2545.W33 Water
2545.W37 Wealth
2545.W43 Widows
2545.W45 Wisdom
2545.W5 Wit and humor. Irony
2545.W54 Witness bearing. Testimony
2545.W65 Women, Attitude toward
2545.W67 Work
World and the Church see BS2545.C553
Special parts of the New Testament
2547 Epistles and Gospels, Liturgical (Table BS6)
Class here historical and other series of lessons from the Liturgical Epistles and Gospels, including texts and commentaries
For sermons see BV4240+ or the denomination in subclass BX
Cf. BS2565 Gospels, Liturgical
Cf. BS2638 Epistles, Liturgical
2548 Gospels and Acts of the Apostles (Table BS6)
Gospels
2549 Polyglot texts

New Testament
Special parts of the New Testament
Gospels
Polyglot texts -- Continued
(2549.J3-.J5) Jefferson Bible
see BT304.95.J44
Syriac versions
2550 West Syriac. Jacobite. Estrangelo
2550.A2 Texts. By date
Translations
2550.A3 English. By date
2550.A4-.A49 Other languages (alphabetically)
2550.A5 History and criticism
2550.T2 Tatian's Diatessaron
2550.T2A2 Texts. By date
Translations
2550.T2A3 English. By date
2550.T2A4-.T2A49 Other languages (alphabetically)
2550.T2A5-.T2Z History and criticism
2550.5 East Syriac. Nestorian
Texts in other languages
2551 Greek
2551.A2 Printed texts. By date
2551.A2A-.A2Z Works on the Greek text
Patristic witnesses to the Greek text
2551.A25 General works
2551.A26A-.A26Z By Greek Father, A-Z
Manuscripts
2551.A3 General works
Individual manuscripts
2551.A4 By number
Subarrange by editor or date
2551.A5-Z By name
Subarrange by editor or date
2552 Latin
2552.A2 Printed texts. By date
2552.A2A-.A2Z Works on the Latin text
Manuscripts
2552.A3 General works
Individual manuscripts
2552.A4 By number
Subarrange by editor or date
2552.A5-Z By name
Subarrange by editor or date
English
2553.A3 Authorized version. By date
2553.A5-.Z6 Other versions. By version and date

New Testament
Special parts of the New Testament
Gospels
Texts in other languages
English -- Continued

2553.Z7 Unidentified versions

2554.A-Z Other European languages, A-Z
Subarrange by translator or date

Non-European languages see BS315+

Criticism. Commentaries, etc.
Including "form criticism"

2555.A2 Early through 1800

2555.A21-Z 1801-1950

1951-2000

2555.2 Criticism

2555.3 Commentaries

2555.4 Sermons. Meditations. Devotions

2555.5 Other

2001-

2555.52 Criticism

2555.53 Commentaries

2555.54 Sermons. Meditations. Devotions

2555.55 Other

2555.6.A-Z Special topics, A-Z
For list of Cutter numbers see BS2545.A+
Cf. BS2417.A+ Teachings of Jesus

2556 Study and teaching
Including textbooks

Paraphrases

2557 English

Other languages see BS2551+

Biography of the Gospels see BS2430+

2559 Chronology of the Gospels

Harmonies of the Gospels. Parallel texts
Cf. BS2550.T2 Tatian's Diatessaron

Elementary textbooks see BS2556

2560.A2 Greek
Subarrange by editor or date

2560.A3 Latin
Subarrange by editor or date

2560.A5-Z English. By editor, A-Z, or date
Cf. BT298+ Harmonized Gospels in English in one narrative

Medieval European languages
see PA-PT

2561.A-Z Other European languages, A-Z
e.g.

New Testament
Special parts of the New Testament
Gospels
Harmonies of the Gospels. Parallel texts
Other European languages, A-Z -- Continued
2561.G3 German
2561.S8 Swedish
Non-European languages see BS315+
2562 History and criticism
2565 Gospels, Liturgical (Table BS6)
Class here historical and other series of lessons from the Liturgical Gospels, including texts and commentaries
For sermons see BV4240+ or the denomination in subclass BX
2570-2575.6 Matthew (Table BS9)
2576 Study and teaching
2577 Paraphrases
2580-2585.6 Mark (Table BS9)
2586 Study and teaching
2587 Paraphrases
2589 Luke and Acts. Lucan writings (Table BS6)
2589.6.A-Z Special topics, A-Z
For list of Cutter numbers see BS2545.A+
2590-2595.6 Luke (Table BS9)
2596 Study and teaching
2597 Paraphrases
2601 Johannine writings. Johannine theology (Table BS6)
2610-2615.6 John (Table BS9)
2616 Study and teaching
2617 Paraphrases
2617.5 Acts of the Apostles and the Epistles (Table BS6)
2617.8 Acts of the Apostles, the Epistles, and Revelation (Table BS6)
2618 Work and teaching of the Apostles
2619 Study and teaching
Including textbooks
2620-2625.6 Acts of the Apostles (Table BS9)
2626 Study and teaching
Including textbooks
2627 Paraphrases
2628 Juvenile works
2629 Epistles and Revelation (Table BS6)
2630-2635.6 Epistles (Table BS9)
2636 Study and teaching
Including textbooks
2637 Paraphrases

New Testament
Special parts of the New Testament
Epistles -- Continued
2638 Epistles, Liturgical (Table BS6)
Class here historical and other series of lessons from the Liturgical Epistles, including texts and commentaries.
For sermons see BV4240+ or the denomination in subclass BX
Epistles of Paul
Texts
2640 Polyglot
2641 Greek
2642 Latin
2643 English
Subarrange by translator or date
2644.A-Z Other early languages and modern European languages. By language, A-Z
Subarrange by translator or date
Modern non-European languages see BS315+
Criticism. Commentaries, etc.
2649 Early through 1800
2650 1801-1950
1951-2000
2650.2 Criticism
2650.3 Commentaries
2650.4 Sermons. Meditations. Devotions
2650.5 Other
2001-
2650.52 Criticism
2650.53 Commentaries
2650.54 Sermons. Meditations. Devotions
2650.55 Other
Pauline theology
2651 General works
Including relation of Paul to Christianity
2652 Other
Including minor works
2653 Paul or Jesus?
2655.A-Z Topics (not otherwise provided for), A-Z
For individual epistles use Cutter numbers at BS2545
2655.A35 Adoption
2655.A5 Analogy
2655.A6 Apostles
2655.A65 Asceticism
2655.A67 Asthenia
2655.A7 Atonement
2655.A8 Authority

New Testament
Special parts of the New Testament
Epistles
Epistles of Paul
Topics (not otherwise provided for), A-Z -- Continued

2655.B34 Baptism
2655.B5 Bible and tradition
2655.B55 Blessing and cursing
2655.C36 Canon
2655.C38 Celibacy
2655.C4 Christian life
2655.C5 Church
2655.C52 Church discipline
2655.C53 Church finance
2655.C57 City churches
2655.C7 Conscience
2655.C74 Covenants
2655.C8 Creation
2655.C95 Cynics (Greek philosophy)
2655.D34 Death
2655.D4 Demoniac possession
Dietary laws see BS2655.F66
2655.E3 Education
2655.E7 Eschatology
2655.E8 Ethics
2655.E93 Example
2655.F2 Faith
2655.F3 Family
2655.F5 Flesh
2655.F66 Food. Dietary laws
Freedom see BS2655.L5
2655.G54 Gifts, Spiritual
Glory of God see BS2398
God see BS2398
2655.G6 Government (Resistance to)
2655.G65 Grace
2655.G7 Greek literature
2655.H34 Heaven
2655.H5 History
2655.H6 Holiness
2655.H67 Holy Spirit. Spirit
2655.H69 Hope
2655.H72 House churches
2655.I33 Identification (Religion)
2655.I63 Inheritance
2655.I65 Intermediate state
2655.J38 Jerusalem

BS

New Testament
Special parts of the New Testament
Epistles
Epistles of Paul
Topics (not otherwise provided for), A-Z -- Continued

2655.J4	Jews and Judaism
2655.J6	Joy
2655.J73	Judgment Day
2655.J74	Judgment of God
2655.J8	Justification
2655.K5	Kingdom of God
2655.L3	Language. Philology
2655.L35	Law
2655.L42	Leadership
2655.L47	Letter and spirit antithesis
2655.L5	Liberty. Freedom
2655.L53	Life
2655.L57	Lord's Supper
2655.L6	Love
2655.M3	Man
2655.M34	Marriage
2655.M47	Metaphor
2655.M56	Miracles
2655.M57	Mission of the Church
2655.M8	Mysteries (Religious)
2655.M82	Mystery
2655.M85	Mystical union
2655.M9	Mysticism
2655.N3	Natural theology
2655.P28	Paradox
2655.P3	Pastoral teaching
2655.P5	Perfection
2655.P53	Perseverance
	Philology see BS2655.L3
2655.P6	Piety
2655.P64	Politics
2655.P66	Powers, principalities, etc.
2655.P73	Prayer
2655.P8	Preaching
2655.P83	Predestination
2655.P87	Prophecy
2655.P88	Psychology
2655.P89	Public worship
2655.R29	Reconciliation
2655.R3	Redemption
2655.R32	Relation to the Old Testament
2655.R33	Religious tolerance

New Testament
Special parts of the New Testament
Epistles
Epistles of Paul
Topics (not otherwise provided for), A-Z -- Continued

2655.R35 Resurrection
2655.R37 Revelation
2655.R4 Reward
Righteousness of God see BS2398
2655.R6 Roman law
2655.S23 Sacrifice
2655.S25 Salvation
Scripture and tradition see BS2655.B5
2655.S49 Sex
2655.S54 Sin
2655.S55 Slaves. Slavery
2655.S57 Small groups
2655.S6 Social teachings
Spirit see BS2655.H67
Spirit and letter antithesis see BS2655.L47
Spiritual gifts see BS2655.G54
2655.S62 Spiritual life
2655.S65 Stewardship
2655.S8 Suffering
2655.T4 Teaching methods
2655.T5 Thanksgivings
2655.T54 Theomachy
Tolerance, Religious see BS2655.R33
2655.T75 Trinity
2655.V6 Vocation
Weakness see BS2655.A67
2655.W5 Women (Attitude toward)
2657 Study and teaching
Including textbooks, outlines, etc.
Life of Paul see BS2505+
2658 Paraphrases
2660-2665.6 Romans (Table BS9)
2667 Paraphrases
2670-2675.6 Corinthians, 1st and 2nd (Table BS9)
The first or second epistle treated separately, or the two together
2677 Paraphrases
2680-2685.6 Galatians (Table BS9)
2687 Paraphrases
2690-2695.6 Ephesians (Table BS9)
2700-2705.6 Philippians (Table BS9)
2710-2715.6 Colossians (Table BS9)

New Testament
Special parts of the New Testament
Epistles
Epistles of Paul
Colossians -- Continued
2717 Paraphrases
2720-2725.6 Thessalonians, 1st and 2nd (Table BS9)
The first or second epistle treated separately, or the two together
2730-2735.6 Pastoral Epistles (Table BS9)
2740-2745.6 Timothy, 1st and 2nd (Table BS9)
The first or second epistle treated separately, or the two together
2750-2755.6 Titus (Table BS9)
2760-2765.6 Philemon (Table BS9)
2770-2775.6 Hebrews (Table BS9)
2777 General Epistles. Catholic Epistles (Table BS6)
2780-2785.6 James (Table BS9)
2790-2795.6 Peter, 1st and 2nd (Table BS9)
The first or second epistle treated separately, or the two together
2800-2805.6 Epistles of John, 1st, 2nd, and 3rd (Table BS9)
The first, second, or third epistle treated separately, or the three together
2810-2815.6 Jude (Table BS9)
2820-2825.6 Revelation. Apocalypse (Table BS9)
Cf. BS1556 Prophecies and visions of Daniel and Revelation
2826 Pamphlets
2827 Revelation and history
New Testament apocryphal books
Cf. BS1691+ Old and New Testament apocryphal books combined
Texts
2831 Polyglot
Subarrange by editor or date
2832 English
Subarrange by editor or date
2833.A-Z Other languages, A-Z
Subarrange by date
2840 History and criticism
Special parts of the apocryphal books
Gospels
Collections
2850.A1 Polyglot
2850.A3 English
2850.A5-Z Other languages, A-Z

New Testament
Special parts of the New Testament
New Testament apocryphal books
Special parts of the apocryphal books
Gospels -- Continued

2851 History and criticism
2860.A-Z Individual gospels, A-Z
Cf. BT441 Records of the trial of Jesus
2860.A7-.A72 Arabic Gospel of the Infancy (Table BS8)
2860.A76-.A762 Armenian Infancy Gospel (Table BS8)
2860.B4-.B42 Gospel of Barnabas (Table BS8)
2860.G3-.G32 Gamaliel (Table BS8)
2860.H5-.H6 Hebrews (Table BS8)
2860.J2-.J3 Book of James (Protoevangelium Jacobi) (Table BS8)
2860.J6-.J62 John (Table BS8)
2860.J83-.J832 Gospel of Judas (Table BS8)
2860.N5-.N6 Nicodemus (Table BS8)
2860.P5-.P6 Peter (Table BS8)
2860.P62-.P63 Gospel of the Infancy according to St. Peter (Table BS8)
2860.P66-.P67 Philip (Coptic gospel) (Table BS8)
2860.P7-.P8 Pseudo-Matthew (Table BS8)
2860.S4-.S42 Secret Gospel According to Mark (Table BS8)
2860.T4-.T42 Thomas (Infancy gospel) (Table BS8)
2860.T5-.T52 Thomas (Coptic gospel) (Table BS8)
2860.T7-.T8 Transitus Mariae (Table BS8)
2860.T9-.T92 Twelve Apostles (Table BS8)
2860.Z8 Unidentified gospel fragments

Acts
Collections
2870.A1 Polyglot
2870.A3 English
2870.A5-Z Other languages, A-Z
2871 History and criticism
2880.A-Z Individual acts, A-Z
2880.A37-.A372 Acts of Andrew (Table BS8)
2880.A6-.A7 Acts of Andrew and Matthew (Table BS8)
2880.A87-.A872 Ascents of James (Table BS8)
2880.J2-.J3 Acts of James (Table BS8)
2880.J6-.J62 Acts of John (Table BS8)
2880.M35-.M352 Acts of Mar Mari (Table BS8)
2880.P3-.P4 Acts of Paul. Acts of Paul of Thecla (Table BS8)
2880.P47-.P472 Acts of Peter (Table BS8)
2880.P55-.P552 Acts of Philip (Table BS8)
Recognitions (Pseudo-Clementine) see BR65.C55R43

New Testament
Special parts of the New Testament
New Testament apocryphal books
Special parts of the apocryphal books
Acts
Individual acts, A-Z -- Continued
2880.T4-.T5 Acts of Thomas (Table BS8)
Epistles
Collections
2890.A1 Polyglot
2890.A3 English
2890.A5-Z Other languages, A-Z
2891 History and criticism
2900.A-Z Individual epistles, A-Z
2900.A2-.A3 Abgar Epistles (and Teaching of Addai) (Table BS8)
2900.A6-.A7 Epistle of the Apostles (Epistola Apostolorum) (Table BS8)
2900.B2-.B3 Epistle of Barnabas (Table BS8)
2900.H4-.H5 Hermas, 2nd cent. Shepherd. Shepherd of Hermas (Table BS8)
2900.J4-.J5 Epistle of Jesus Christ (Table BS8)
2900.L35-.L36 Epistle to the Laodiceans (Table BS8)
2900.L47-.L472 Letter of Paul to the Corinthians (Table BS8)
Sunday letter see BS2900.J4+
Apocalypses
Collections
2910.A1 Polyglot
2910.A3 English
2910.A5-Z Other languages, A-Z
2911 History and criticism
2920.A-Z Individual Apocalypses, A-Z
2920.M3-.M4 Apocalypse of Mary (Table BS8)
2920.P3-.P4 Apocalypse of Paul (Table BS8)
For the Coptic work called Apocalypse of Paul see BT1392.A637+
2920.P5-.P6 Apocalypse of Peter (Table BS8)
Didactic works
Collections
2930.A1 Polyglot
2930.A3 English
2930.A5-Z Other languages, A-Z
2931 History and criticism
2940.A-Z Individual didactic works, A-Z
2940.T4-.T5 Teaching of the Twelve Apostles. Didache (Table BS8)
Cf. KBR196 Canon law

New Testament
Special parts of the New Testament
New Testament apocryphal books
Special parts of the apocryphal books -- Continued
Doctrinal works
Collections
2950.A1 Polyglot
2950.A3 English
2950.A5-Z Other languages, A-Z
2951 History and criticism
2960.A-Z Individual doctrinal works, A-Z
2960.P5-.P6 Preaching of Peter (Table BS8)
2960.T5-.T6 Testament of Our Lord (Table BS8)
Cf. KBR197.33 Canan law
2970 Apocryphal writings and sayings of Jesus. Agrapha. Logia

Doctrinal theology
Periodicals. Serials see BR1+
Collected works
10 Several authors
15 Individual authors
Dictionaries see BR95
Doctrine and dogma
19 Theory
History
Including history of theological controversies
General works
20 Early through 1800
21 1801-1950
21.2 1951-2000
21.3 2001-
22 General special
By period
Pre-Reformation period
Cf. BT1319+ Pre-Reformation heresies and schisms
23 General works
24 Apostolic period
25 Post-Apostolic period to 590 A.D.
26 590-1517. Scholastic period
1517- (Reformation and later periods)
27 General works
28 19th-20th centuries
30.A-Z By region or country, A-Z
e.g.
30.G3 Germany
30.N5 Netherlands
By theologian
see the theologian for general works on his theology; for special doctrines in his or her theology, see the doctrine
Attitudes toward doctrine and dogma
32 Adiaphora. Things neutral
33 Latitudinarianism. Indifference
Cf. BR755+ Church history of England
37 Secrecy. Discipline of the secret. Disciplina arcani
Philosophy. Philosophical theology
40 General works
45 Necessity, value, etc. of doctrinal systems
50 Criterion of truth. Faith and reason
55 Other
60 The essence, genius, and nature of Christianity
Doctrinal, dogmatic, systematic theology
65 Introductions. Prolegomena, etc.
Formal treatises

Doctrinal, dogmatic, systematic theology
Formal treatises -- Continued
70 Early through 1800
75 1801-1950
75.2 1951-2000
75.3 2001-
77 Popular works
77.3 Compends. Outlines, etc.
78 General special
79 Law and gospel
Cf. BT95+ Divine law
80 Addresses, essays, sermons, etc.
For collections see BT10+
Schools of thought affecting doctrine and dogma (19th-20th centuries)
82 Modernism
82.2 Fundamentalism
For individual Fundamentalist denominations see subclass BX
For Fundamentalist churches in general see BX7800.F86+
82.25 Dominion theology
82.3 Modernist-Fundamentalist controversy
82.7 Black theology
Cf. BR563.N4 African Americans and Christianity
Cf. BT83.9 Womanism
Dialectical theology
83 General works
83.2 Neo-orthodoxy
83.5 Death of God theology
83.53 Empirical theology
83.55 Feminist theology
Cf. BT83.9 Womanism
Cf. BT704 Doctrinal anthropology
83.57 Liberation theology
83.575 Hispanic American theology
83.58 Minjung theology
83.583 Mujerista theology
83.585 Negative theology
83.587 Open theism
83.59 Political theology
83.595 Postliberal theology
83.597 Postmodern theology
83.6 Process theology
83.67 Romanticism
83.7 Secularization
83.78 Storytelling. Narrative theology

Doctrinal, dogmatic, systematic theology
Schools of thought affecting doctrine and dogma (19th-20th centuries) -- Continued
83.8 Deconstruction
Dispensationalism see BT157
Solidarity see BT738.45
83.85 Theology of religions
83.9 Womanism
84 Existentialism
85 Critical theory
Authority
88 General works
88.5 Rule of faith
89 Scriptures
Cf. BS480 Inspiration of the Bible
90 Tradition
Cf. BS522 Tradition and Biblical criticism
91 Church. Teaching office of the Church
Cf. BV740+ Freedom and authority
92 Private judgment. Experience as authority
Judaism
Cf. BM535 Relation of Christianity to Judaism
Cf. BT1120 Apologetic works against Jewish opponents of Christianity
93 General works
93.5 Jerusalem in Christianity
93.55 Jewish festivals in Christianity
Including individual festivals
93.6 Jewish-Arab relations and Christianity
93.8 Palestine in Christianity. Palestinian liberation and Christianity
94 Kingdom of God. Kingdom of Christ
Cf. BT890+ Eschatology
Divine law. Moral government
General works
95 Early through 1800
96 1801-1950
96.2 1951-2000
96.3 2001-
General works

Divine law. Moral government -- Continued
Miracles
For individual biography, see BR1720; BX4700+, e.g. BR1720.J3, Januarius, Saint, Bp. of Benevento
Cf. BS1199.M5 Miracles of the Old Testament
Cf. BS2545.M5 Miracles of the New Testament
Cf. BT363+ Miracles of Christ (New Testament)
Cf. BT580 Other miracles and apparitions of Christ
Cf. BT650+ Miracles and apparitions of Mary
Cf. BV5090+ Mystic phenomena. Stigmata, etc.
Cf. BX2225 Miracles associated with the Eucharist
97.A2 Early through 1800
97.A3-Z 1801-1950
97.2 1951-2000
97.3 2001-
God
Cf. BL200 Theism (Natural theology)
98 History of doctrines concerning God
For Biblical teaching about God or God in the Bible see BS544, BS1192.6, BS2398
For works by individual theologians concerning God and critical works about the theologian's doctrine of God see BT100+
General works
For critical works about a theologian's doctrine of God, assign two Cutter numbers, the first for the theologian and the second for the author of the work, e.g. BT100.T4S8 Thomas Aquinas, Saint / Stufler, Johann
Including works by individual theologians concerning God and critical works about the theologian's doctrine of God, classed according to the period in which the theologian lived
100 Early through 1800
101 1801-1950
101.A1 Collected works
102 1951-2000
102.A1 Collected works
103 2001-
107 Juvenile works
108 Study and teaching
Doctrine of the Trinity
Cf. BL474 Trinities (Religious doctrines in general)
Cf. BT220 Incarnation
109 History of doctrines concerning the Trinity
General works
110 Early works through 1800
111 1801-1950

God
Doctrine of the Trinity
General works -- Continued
111.2 1951-2000
111.3 2001-
112 Sources in Scripture
113 Addresses, essays, sermons, etc.
114 Procession of the Son from the Father and of the Holy Spirit from the Father and Son
115 Anti-Trinitarian works
Cf. BT1350 Arianism
Cf. BT1474 Tritheism
Cf. BT1480 Socinianism
Cf. BX9801+ Unitarianism
Holy Spirit. The Paraclete
117 Congresses
118 Collected works
119 History of doctrines concerning the Holy Spirit
For Biblical teaching about the Holy Spirit or the Holy Spirit in the Bible see BS680.H56
General works
120 Early through 1800
121 1801-1950
121.2 1951-2000
121.3 2001-
122 Addresses, essays, sermons, etc.
122.5 Glossolalia. Gift of tongues
Cf. BL54 Glossolalia as a phenomenon in non-Christian religions
123 Other
e.g. Baptism with the Holy Spirit, Baptism with fire
124 Divine immanence
124.5 Transcendence
125 Inspiration
Cf. BS480 Inspiration of the Bible
Revelation
126 Biblical teaching
126.5 History of doctrines
General works
127.A2 Early through 1800
127.A3-Z 1801-1950
127.2 1951-2000
127.3 2001-
127.5 Mystery
127.7 Theonomy
128 Theophanies. Divine manifestations
Divine attributes

God
Divine attributes -- Continued
130 General works
Individual attributes
131 Omniscience
132 Omnipresence
133 Omnipotence
135 Providence. Divine intervention
137 Goodness
140 Love
Cf. BV4817 Man's adoration and love of God
145 Righteousness
147 Holiness
148 Simplicity. Unicity. Unity. Oneness
150 Wisdom
153.A-Z Other attributes, A-Z
Anger see BT153.W7
153.B4 Beauty
Eternity see BT153.I47
Fairness see BT153.I49
153.F3 Fatherhood. Masculinity
Femininity see BT153.M6
153.I47 Immutability. Eternity. Timelessness
153.I49 Impartiality. Fairness
Impassibility see BT153.S8
153.I6 Incomparability
153.J4 Jealousy
Masculinity see BT153.F3
153.M4 Mercy
153.M6 Motherhood. Femininity
Cf. BL215.5 Comparative religions
Passibility see BT153.S8
153.P36 Patience
153.S8 Suffering of God. Passibility. Impassibility
Timelessness see BT153.I47
153.W7 Wrath. Anger
155 Covenants. Covenant theology. Federal theology. Covenants of works and grace
157 Dispensational theology. Dispensationalism
Cf. BT885+ Premillennialism
Theodicy. Vindication of the justice of God
160 General works
God in relation to disasters
161 General works
162.A-Z Individual disasters or types of disasters, A-Z
e.g.
162.E2 Earthquakes

God -- Continued
165 God and man. The Divine Union, adoption, etc.
175 Addresses, essays, lectures, etc.
180.A-Z Other special, A-Z
Absence of God see BT180.H54
180.C6 Consciousness of God
180.G6 Glory of God
180.H54 Hidden God. Absence of God
180.J8 Judgment of God
180.N2 Names of God
180.P6 Presence of God. Shekinah
180.P7 Promises of God
180.W67 Word of God
Cf. BT210 Christology
Christology
For devotional literature see BT306.28+, if of a biographical nature, otherwise BV
Cf. BS2415+ Teachings of Jesus
Cf. BS2530 New Testament study and teaching
198 History of Christological doctrines and study
Cf. BT1313+ Heresies inclusive of those of a Christological nature
199 Collected works. Quotations
199.5 Dictionaries. Encyclopedias
General works. The person of Jesus
200 Early through 1800
201 1801-1950
202 1951-2000
203 2001-
205 General special
207 Study and teaching
Including outlines, textbooks, etc.
210 Logos. The Word of God
Natures of Christ
212 General works
213 Hypostatic union
Divinity of Christ
General works
214 Early through 1800
215 1801-1950
216 1951-2000
216.3 2001-
216.5 Christ's knowledge of his own divinity
Humanity
218 General works
220 Incarnation. Kenosis
Cf. BT317 Virgin birth

Christology
Natures of Christ
Humanity -- Continued
221 Sinlessness
222 States of Christ
For individual steps in either state, see the special step, e.g. Birth, see BT315; Descent into Hell, see BT470
223 State of humiliation
224 State of exaltation
225 Typology. Old Testament types of Christ
Messiahship
230 General works
232 Son of Man
Servant of Jehovah see BS1199.S4
235 Messianic prophecy
For individual books of the Old Testament, see the book
Cf. BS1199.M44 Messiah in the Old Testament
240 Messianic expectation
For individual Christian sects, see the sect
For Second Coming of Christ see BT885+
Cf. BM615+ Messianic concept in Judaism
245 Messianic secret
Offices of Christ
250 General works
252 Prophetic office
Cf. BS2415+ Teachings of Jesus
Cf. BT370 Prophecies
Cf. BT373+ Parables
Cf. BT380+ Sermon on the Mount
Cf. BT590.E8 Jesus' evangelistic methods
Cf. BT590.P7 Jesus' preaching methods
Cf. BT590.T5 Jesus' teaching methods
Priestly office
254 General works
255 Mediation. Intercession
257 Servanthood. Slavery
260 Priesthood and the believer
Sacrifice. Atonement. Reconciliation. Satisfaction
For Biblical teaching, see numbers for special topics in the Bible, e.g. BS2545.S24 Sacrifice in the New Testament
Cf. BT430+ Passion of Jesus
263 History of doctrines
General works
264 Early through 1800
265 1801-1950
265.2 1951-2000
265.3 2001-

Christology
Offices of Christ
Priestly office
Sacrifice. Atonement. Reconciliation. Satisfaction -- Continued
267 Extent of the Atonement
Cf. BT809+ Predestination, election
268 Sermons. Meditations. Devotional works
Cf. BR129+ Sources of Christianity
Cf. BT453 The Cross, its lessons, and significance
270 Royal office
Cf. BT94 Kingdom of Christ
295 Other
Life of Christ
296 Background studies
297 Sources of biography
Compilations of Biblical texts
English
For harmonies see BS2560+
298 Early through 1800
Subarrange by editor or compiler
299 1801-1950
Subarrange by editor or compiler
299.2 1951-2000
Subarrange by editor or compiler
299.3 2001-
Subarrange by editor or compiler
Other languages see BS2560+
Biographies
General works
300 Early through 1800
301 1801-1950
301.2 1951-2000
301.3 2001-
301.9 History and criticism
302 Juvenile works
Including verse
For special topics see BT310+
303 General special
303.2 Historicity of Christ
303.8 Chronology of the life of Christ
Cf. BS2559 Chronology of the Gospels
303.9 Geography of the life of Christ. Journeys of Christ
Cf. BS630+ Biblical geography
Cf. DS101+ The Holy Land
Character and personality
304 General works

Christology
Life of Christ
Character and personality -- Continued
304.2 Example
304.3 Influence
304.5 Appreciation
304.7 Significance
Special interpretations of Jesus
304.9 General works
304.912 African American
304.914 Buddhist
Anthroposophical see BP596.J4
Islamic see BP172+
Jewish see BM620
Mormon see BX8643.J4
Mythical see BT303.2
304.92 New Thought
304.93 Occult, astrological, etc.
304.94 Oriental
304.95 Rationalist
304.95.J44 Jefferson Bible (Life and morals of Jesus of Nazareth)
Subarrange by date
Rosicrucian see BF1623.R7
304.96 Spiritualist
Cf. BF1275.C5 Christianity and spiritualism
Cf. BF1311.J5 Spirit messages of Jesus Christ (Mediumship)
304.97 Theosophical
306 Words of Christ. Sayings
Cf. BS2415+ Teachings of Jesus
Cf. BS2970 Agrapha
Cf. BT455+ Last words
Devotional works on the life of Christ
Class here devotional material that progresses event by event from the birth to death of Christ, the whole being a systematic presentation of the life of Christ
Sermons
306.28 Early through 1800
306.29 1801-1950
306.3 1951-2000
306.33 2001-
Meditations
306.38 Early through 1800
306.39 1801-1950
306.4 1951-2000
306.43 2001-

Christology
Life of Christ
Devotional works on the life of Christ -- Continued
Other devotional works
306.48 Early through 1800
306.49 1801-1950
306.5 1951-2000
306.53 2001-
307 Study and teaching
Including outlines, textbooks, etc.
308 Addresses essays, lectures, etc.
Occult, astrological interpretations see BT304.93
Fictional lives of Christ. Stories of the life of Christ
see P-PZ
Special topics
Early life
310 General works
313 The Holy Family
314 Genealogy
Birth. Nativity. The Magi. Epiphany. Flight into Egypt, etc.
Bible texts
315.A3 English
315.A32A-.A32Z Other languages, A-Z
Subarrange by date
General works
315.A33-Z Early through 1950
315.2 1951-2000
315.3 2001-
317 Virgin birth
318 Date of birth
318.5 Circumcision
319 Presentation
320 Childhood
330 Education
Public life
340 General works
350 Baptism
355 Temptation
360 Calling of and relations with the Apostles
361 Adversaries
Miracles
363.A-Z Bible texts. By language, A-Z
Subarrange by date
General works
364 Early through 1800
365 1801-1950

Christology
Life of Christ
Special topics
Public life
Miracles
General works -- Continued
366 1951-2000
366.3 2001-
367.A-Z Special, A-Z
367.F4 Feeding of the five thousand
367.H38 Healing of the Gerasene demoniac
367.H4 Healing of the man born blind
(367.H42) Healing of the man sick of the palsy
see BT367.H45
367.H43 Healing of the nobleman's son
367.H45 Healing of the paralytic
367.H47 Healing of the ten lepers
367.H48 Healing of the woman with the flow of blood
367.M37 Marriage in Cana
367.M57 Miraculous draught of fishes
367.O64 Opening the eyes of one blind at Bethsaida
367.R34 Raising of Jairus' daughter
367.R36 Raising of Lazarus
367.S74 Stilling of the storm
367.W34 Walking on the water
370 Prophecies
Parables
373.A-Z Bible texts. By language, A-Z
Subarrange by date
General works
374 Early through 1800
375 1801-1950
375.2 1951-2000
375.3 2001-
376 Juvenile works
377 Study and teaching
Including textbooks
378.A-Z Special, A-Z
378.B2 Barren fig tree
378.D5 Dives and Lazarus
378.G6 Good Samaritan
378.G7 Great supper
378.H54 Hidden treasure
378.H68 House built upon a rock
Importunate widow see BT378.U4
378.L3 Laborers in the vineyard
378.L43 Leaven

Christology
Life of Christ
Special topics
Public life
Parables
Special, A-Z -- Continued

378.L56	Lost coin
378.L6	Lost sheep
	Marriage of the king's son see BT378.G7
378.M8	Mustard seed
378.N48	New wine into old wineskins
378.P4	Pearl of great price
378.P5	Pharisee and publican
378.P8	Prodigal son
378.R5	Rich fool
	Rich man and Lazarus see BT378.D5
378.S7	Sower
378.T3	Talents
378.T34	Tares
378.T4	Ten virgins
	Treasure see BT378.H54
378.T85	Two sons
378.U37	Unforgiving servant
378.U4	Unjust judge. Importunate widow
378.U5	Unjust steward
378.W5	Wicked husbandmen
	Sermon on the Mount
	Bible texts
380.A3	English. By date
380.A32A-.A32Z	Other languages, A-Z Subarrange by date
	General works
380.A33-Z	Early through 1950
380.2	1951-2000
380.3	2001-
382	The Beatitudes
	Prayers see BV229+
	The Lord's Prayer see BV230+
	Final stage. Transfiguration to Ascension
400	General works
410	Transfiguration
414	Holy Week For Ceremonial see BV90+
415	Entry into Jerusalem Cf. BV91 Palm Sunday
416	Cleansing of the Temple
420	Last Supper

Christology
Life of Christ
Special topics
Public life
Final stage. Transfiguration to Ascension -- Continued
Passion
Bible texts
430.A3 English. By date
430.A32A-.A32Z Other languages, A-Z
Subarrange by date
General works
430.A33-Z Early through 1950
431 1951-2000
431.3 2001-
431.5 Role of Jews
431.6 Role of Romans
435 Gethsemane. Betrayal
Trial
440 General works
441 Archaeological records
e.g. Mahan's compilations, Acta Pilati, etc.
Cf. BS2860.N5+ Gospel of Nicodemus
445 Condemnation
Crucifixion
450 General works
453 The Cross, its lessons, and significance
Cf. BT263+ Atonement
Cf. BV160 Symbolism
Seven last words
General works
455 Early through 1950
456 1951-2000
457 2001-
460 Descent from the Cross. Entombment
465 Relics of the Passion, Cross, etc.
Cf. BT587.A+ Individual relics
468 Three days in the tomb
470 Descent into Hell
Resurrection
Bible texts
480.A3 English. By date
480.A32A-.A32Z Other languages, A-Z
Subarrange by date
General works
480.A33-Z Early through 1950
481 1951-2000
482 2001-

Christology
Life of Christ
Special topics
Public life
Final stage. Transfiguration to Ascension
Resurrection -- Continued
485 The forty days from resurrection to Ascension
490 Appearance to disciples and others
Great Commission see BV2074
500 Ascension
Agrapha (Words of Christ not in the New Testament) see BS2970
520 Legendary and apocryphal narratives
Including legends of the Virgin and Christ
Cf. BS2831+ Apocryphal books of the New Testament
Jesus Christ in literature
see P-PZ
Jesus Christ in art see N8050+
575 Jesus Christ in the liturgy
Miracles. Apparitions. Shrines, sanctuaries, images, processions, etc
580.A1 General works
580.A2A-.A2Z By region or country, A-Z
580.A3-Z Special. By place, A-Z
580.A48 Alicante (Spain)
580.A73 Arés (France)
580.A74 Arles (France)
580.A86 Atlacomulca (Mexico)
580.B8 Burgos (Spain)
580.C28 Cachuy (Peru)
580.C4 Chalma (Mexico)
580.D34 Damascus (Syria)
580.D68 Dozulé (France)
580.E75 Esquípulas (Guatemala)
580.H83 Huarás (Peru) Province
580.L55 Lima (Peru)
580.M37 Matosinhos (Portugal)
580.M5 Mexico (City)
580.O72 Otatitlán (Mexico)
580.O8 Ourique (Portugal)
580.P5 Piedad (Mexico)
580.P54 Pieve di Cento (Italy)
580.P67 Portalegre (Portugal)
580.P8 Prague (Czechoslovakia)
580.S34 Scicli (Sicily)
580.S36 Scottsdale (Arizona)
580.S48 Seville (Spain)

Christology
Miracles. Apparitions. Shrines, sanctuaries, images, processions, etc
Special. By place, A-Z -- Continued
580.S67 Sotaquí (Chile)
580.X63 Xochimilco (Distrito Federal, Mexico)
Roman Catholic cults
see BX2157+
Relics
General works see BT465
587.A-Z Special, A-Z
587.C6 Holy Coat of Argenteuil
587.C64 Holy Coat of Mcʻxetʻa, Georgia
587.C65 Holy Coat of Palma, Majorca
587.C7 Holy Coat of Treves
Cross, etc. see BT465
587.C8 Crown of thorns
587.M3 Mandylion of Edessa
Cf. BR1720.V43 Veil of Veronica
587.S4 Holy Shroud of Turin
587.S83 Sudarium of Oviedo
587.V3 Valencia chalice
Veil of Veronica see BR1720.V43
590.A-Z Topics (not otherwise provided for), A-Z
590.A55 Anniversaries
Appearance see BT590.P45
Art see N8050+
590.B5 Blood of Christ
590.C48 Children, Attitude toward
590.C5 Citizenship of Christ
590.C74 Controversies of Christ
590.C78 Counseling methods
590.C8 Courage of Christ
590.C85 Cult
Cf. BX2157+ Roman Catholic cults
590.E8 Evangelistic methods
Face see BT590.P45
590.F3 Fasting
590.F7 Friends and associates
Homiletics see BT590.P7
590.H8 Humor
590.I3 Iconography
590.J28 Jesus prayer
590.J3 Jewish dietary laws, Attitude toward
590.J34 Jewish law, Attitude toward
590.J36 Jewish sacrifice, Attitude toward
590.J8 Judaism, Relation to. Jewishness

Christology
Topics (not otherwise provided for), A-Z -- Continued
590.K6 Knowledge
Knowledge of his own divinity see BT216.5
590.L3 Language
590.N2 Names and titles
590.O4 Old Testament, Attitude toward
590.P3 Paradoxes
590.P45 Physical appearance
590.P57 Power
590.P7 Preaching methods. Homiletics
590.P75 Presence
590.P9 Psychology
590.R57 Ritual purity, Attitude toward
590.S4 Science. Christ and science
590.S48 Silence
590.S5 Similitudes
590.S65 Spiritual life
590.T5 Teaching methods
Teachings of Jesus see BS2415+
590.T6 Tears
Wit and humor see BT590.H8
590.W6 Women, Attitude toward
Mary, Mother of Jesus Christ. Mariology
595 Periodicals. Societies. Congresses
(596) Yearbooks
see BT595
Collected works
597 Several authors
598 Individual authors
599 Dictionaries
General works
600 Early through 1800
601 1801-1950
602 1951-2000
603 2001-
Biography
604 Early through 1800
605 1801-1950
605.2 1951-2000
605.3 2001-
605.4.A-Z Special interpretations of the Virgin Mary, A-Z
605.4.H45 Hermetic
Jewish see BM621
Mormon see BX8643.M37
605.5 Words
Magnificat see BV199.C32M3+

Mary, Mother of Jesus Christ. Mariology -- Continued
606 Study and teaching. Textbooks. Catechisms
607 Juvenile works
Legends see BT675
Sermons
608.A1 Several authors
608.A5-Z Individual authors
Including single sermons
608.5 Meditations
Cf. BX2160+ Catholic prayers and devotions to the Virgin Mary
608.7 The Virgin Mary and education
608.732 The Virgin Mary in literature. Literary collections see P-PZ
The Virgin Mary in art see N8070
Theology
History of doctrines
610 General works
611 In Scripture
612 In the early Church
613 General works
614 Controversial literature
615 Annunciation
For Feast of the Annunciation see BV50.A6
620 Immaculate Conception
Including the Bull "Ineffabilis"
For Feast of the Immaculate Conception see BV50.I6
622 Sinlessness. Debitum peccati
625 Perpetual virginity
Death and Assumption
For Feast of the Assumption see BV50.A7
630 General works
635 Tomb at Jerusalem
638 Offices of the Virgin Mary
640 Intercession. Mediation. Coredemption
Cultus of the Virgin Mary. Hyperdulia
Cf. BX809+ Sodalities
Cf. BX2055.A+ Prayers for sodalities
Cf. BX2160+ Prayers and devotions
645 General works
By region or country see BT652.A+
Special cults, appearances, etc. see BT653+
645.3 The Virgin Mary in the Liturgy
Cf. BX2024+ Liturgy
645.5 Feasts
For special feasts see BV50.A+
646 Marian Year

Mary, Mother of Jesus Christ. Mariology -- Continued
Miracles. Apparitions. Shrines, sanctuaries, images, processions, etc.

650 General works
652.A-Z By region or country, A-Z
Special
Under each are included all works for which there exists a special name, whether it be that of an appearance, cult, devotion, title, or other designation of the Virgin Mary
Lourdes
653 General works
654.A-Z Shrines and sanctuaries named after Lourdes, A-Z
e.g.
654.O6 Ostakker (Belgium). Notre Dame de Lourdes en Flandre (Basilica)
660.A-Z Other, A-Z
África, Virgen de see BT660.C46
660.A32 Agony, Our Lady of the
660.A35 Alicante (Spain). Virgen del Remedio
660.A42 Altagracia, Nuestra Señora de la
660.A43 Altavilla Silentina (Italy). Maria Santissima della Neve
660.A45 Altino Mountain (Italy)
660.A46 Andacollo, Virgen de
660.A5 Angeles, Nuestra Señora de los
660.A52 Antipolo (Philippines)
660.A53 Aokpe, Our Lady of
660.A67 Aránzazu, Nuestra Señora de
660.A675 Arboló, Nuestra Señora de
660.A68 Arco, Madonna dell'
660.A82 Asunción, Virgen de la
660.A85 Atocha, Nuestra Señora de
660.A94 Aušros Vartai (Vilnius, Lithuania)
660.B24 Bahia (Brazil)
660.B26 Balestrino (Italy)
660.B27 Banahao, Mount (Philippines)
660.B28 Banneux, Onze-Lieve-Vrouw van
660.B33 Batim (India)
660.B35 Bayside (New York)
660.B4 Beauraing, Notre-Dame de
660.B46 Belém, Nossa Senhora de
660.B52 Berga (Spain). Santuari de la Mare de Déu de Queralt
660.B54 Bilbao (Spain)
660.B55 Blanca, Nuestra Señora de la
660.B6 Bordeaux. Notre-Dame des Pleurs
660.B752 Boulogne, Our Lady of
660.B76 Bulacan, Luzon (Province)
660.C3 Cabo, Nossa Senhora do

Mary, Mother of Jesus Christ. Mariology
Miracles. Apparitions. Shrines, sanctuaries, images, processions, etc.
Special
Other, A-Z -- Continued

660.C312 Cabra Island (Philippines)
660.C315 Cairo
660.C318 Campania (Italy)
660.C32 Candelaria, Nuestra Señora de la
660.C33A-.C33Z Special and local, A-Z
660.C33C3 Candelaria de Caima
660.C33C6 Candelaria de Copiapó
660.C34 Cap-de-la-Madeleine (Québec). National Shrine of Our Lady of the Cape
660.C344 Capilla, Virgen de la
660.C347 Capodigiano, Madonna di
660.C349 Caridad, Virgen de la
660.C35 Carmel
660.C36A-.C36Z Special and local, A-Z
660.C36C8 Carmen de Cuyo
660.C37 Castellaro (Italy). Santuario di Nostra Signora Di Lampedusa
660.C374 Castelmonte (Italy). Santuario
660.C38 Catalão
660.C45 Český Krumlov (Czechoslovakia)
660.C46 Ceuta. Virgen de África
660.C5 Chiquinquirá, Nuestra Señora del Rosario de
660.C64 Colere (Italy)
Conquistadora (Statue) see BT660.S45
660.C65 Copacabana (Bolivia). Santuario de la Virgen
660.C67 Corella (Spain)
660.C68 Coromoto, Nuestra Señora de
660.C79 Cuapa (Nicaragua)
660.C83 Cuenca (Ecuador)
660.C9 Częstochowa, Our Lady of (Icon)
660.D3 Damascus (Syria)
660.D35 Debowiec
660.D4 Desamparados, Nuestra Señora de los
660.D57 Divina Pastora
660.E42 Ellwangen (Germany). Wallfahrtskirche Unsere Liebe Frau auf dem Schönenberg
660.E43 El Palmar de Troya (Spain)
660.E45 El Rocio (Spain)
660.E8 Espino, Nuestra Señora del
660.F3 Fatima, Nossa Senhora da
660.F46 Florânia (Brazil). Santuário de Nossa Senhora das Graças

Mary, Mother of Jesus Christ. Mariology
Miracles. Apparitions. Shrines, sanctuaries, images, processions, etc.
Special
Other, A-Z -- Continued

660.F58 Föching (Germany)
660.F585 Foggia, Vergine Incoronata di
660.F68 Fuencisla, Nuestra Señora de la
660.F7 Fuensanta, Santuario de Nuestra Señora de la
Garabandal (Spain) see BT660.S343
660.G5 Genazzano (Italy). Madonna del Buon Consiglio
660.G75 Granada (City). Virgen de las Angustias
660.G755 Grazie (Italy). Santa Maria Vergine delle Grazie
660.G8 Guadalupe. Virgen del Tepeyac
660.G82A-.G82Z Special and local, A-Z
660.G82N5 Nicoya (Costa Rica)
660.G83 Guaditoca, Nuestra Señora de
660.G835 Guanajuato, Nuestra Señora de
660.H34 Heede (Emsland, Germany)
660.H4 Henar, Nuestra Señora del
660.H44 Heroldsbach (Germany)
660.H45 's-Hertogenbosch (Netherlands)
660.H67 Hoshiv (Ukraine)
660.H8 Huelva (Spain). Nuestra Señora de la Cinta
660.I93 Izamal, Our Lady of
660.J4 Jerez de la Frontera (Spain)
660.K4 Kérizien
660.K52 Kibeho (Rwanda)
660.K7 Knock, Our Lady of
660.K75 Kraków (Poland)
Lampedusa, Nostra Signora di see BT660.C37
660.L3 Lavasina, Notre-Dame-des-Graces de
660.L5 Liesse, Notre-Dame de
660.L58 Lipa City (Philippines)
660.L6 Lirios, Virgen de los
660.L7 Loreto, Madonna di
660.L78 Lubbock (Texas)
660.L82 Luján, Nuestra Señora de
660.M34 Malpartida de Plascencia (Spain). Virgen de la Luz
660.M3594 Máriapócs (Hungary)
660.M3595 Mariastein (Austria)
660.M3597 Mariazell (Austria)
660.M37 Marpingen (Germany)
660.M38 Marta (Italy)
660.M44 Međugorje (Bosnia and Hercegovina)
660.M47 Mercy, Our Lady of
660.M63 Milici, Madonna dei

Mary, Mother of Jesus Christ. Mariology
Miracles. Apparitions. Shrines, sanctuaries, images, processions, etc.
Special
Other, A-Z -- Continued

660.M64 Molfetta (Italy)
660.M653 Mondim de Basto (Portugal). Capela da Nossa Senhora de Graça
Montaigu (Belgium) see BT660.S5
660.M654 Montefalco (Italy). Madonna della Stella (Sanctuary)
660.M655 Montenero, Madonna di
660.M67 Montserrat, Nuestra Señora de
660.M675 Monzón (Spain). Santuario de Nuestra Señora de la Alegría
660.M88 Muto Mountain (Italy)
660.M93 Myans (France)
660.N37 Natividade do Carangola (Brazil)
660.N4 Necedah (Wisconsin)
660.N43 Neukirchen beim Heiligen Blut (Germany)
660.N44 New York (New York). Madonna of 115th Street (Harlem)
660.N47 Nieves de Chinchilla, Virgen de las
660.N67 Novellara (Italy). Santuario della Madonna della Fossetta
660.N69 Novyy Sverzhen (Byelorussian S.S.R.)
660.N84 Nuria, Nuestra Señora de
660.O44 Oliveto Citra (Italy)
660.O5 Onteniente (Spain)
660.O83 Osor (Spain). Santuari del Coll
Palmar de Troya, El (Spain) see BT660.E43
660.P35 Peinière, Notre-Dame de la
660.P38 Pellevoisin (France)
660.P39 Peña de Francia (Peñafrancia), Nuestra Señora de la
660.P393 Peñablanca (Chile)
660.P395 Peñarroya, Nuestra Señora de
660.P44 Perpetual Help, Our Lady of
660.P48 Pfaffenhofen a.d. Roth (Germany)
660.P53 Pilar, Nuestra Señora del
660.P535 Pino, Virgen del
660.P536 Piombino (Italy)
660.P54 Pitié, Notre-Dame de
660.P58 Pochaev (Ukraine)
660.P65 Pompeii. Santissima Vergine del Rosario (Basilica)
660.P7 Pontmain (France)
660.P75 Porreras, Balearic Islands. Santuario de Montesión
660.P8 Prompt Succor, Our Lady of
660.P95 Pueblito, Our Lady of

BT

Mary, Mother of Jesus Christ. Mariology
Miracles. Apparitions. Shrines, sanctuaries, images, processions, etc.
Special
Other, A-Z -- Continued

660.P97	Puianello (Italy). Santuario della Madonna della Salute
660.Q5	Quito, Nuestra Señora de la Merced de
660.R28	Raffadali (Italy). Madonna degli Infermi
660.R3	Remedios, Nuestra Señora de los
660.R36	Remonot, Grotte chàpelle de Notre Dame de
660.R38	Reus (Spain). Nuestra Señora de la Misericordia
660.R54	Rocamadour
	Rocío, El (Spain) see BT660.E45
660.R6	Rome (Italy)
	Romeria del Rocío see BT660.E45
660.R63	Romigier, Notre Dame de
660.R67	Rosary, Our Lady of the
660.R87	Ruvo de Puglia (Italy). Santuario di Santa Maria di Calentano
660.S2	Sabadell, Santuari de la Mare de Déu de la Salut
660.S25	Saint-Bauzille-de-la-Sylve (France)
660.S28	Salamanca (Spain). Nuestra Señora de Valdejimena (Shrine)
660.S33	Salette, Notre-Dame de la
660.S335	San Damiano (Italy)
660.S338	San Juan de los Lagos, Nuestra Señora de
660.S34	San Lorenzo de Morunys (Spain). Santuari de Lord
660.S342	San Nicolás de los Arroyos (Argentina)
660.S343	San Sebastián de Garabandal (Spain)
660.S43	Santa Cruz de La Palma, Canary Islands. Santuario de Nuestra Señora de las Nieves
660.S45	Santa Fe, N.M. Cathedral of San Francisco de Asia. La Conquistadora (Statue)
660.S47	Santander (Spain)
660.S49	Savona (Italy). Madonna di Misericordia
660.S5	Scherpenheuvel (Belgium)
660.S58	Šiluva (Lithuania)
660.S65	Socavón, Virgen del
660.S84	Suyapa, Nuestra Señora de
660.S9	Syracuse (Sicily). La Madonna della lacrime
660.T3	Talpa, Nuestra Señora del Rosario de
(660.T42)	Tepeyac, Virgen del see BT660.G8
660.T44	Terlizzi (Italy). Madonna di Sovereto
660.T47	Tilly-sur-Suelles, Notre-Dame de
660.T48	Tinos Island (Greece). Proskynēma stēn Megalocharē tēs Tēnou

Mary, Mother of Jesus Christ. Mariology
Miracles. Apparitions. Shrines, sanctuaries, images, processions, etc.
Special
Other, A-Z -- Continued

660.T57 Todi (Italy). La Madonna del Campione
660.T62 Torreciudad, Virgen de la
660.T64 Tossignano, Madonna di
660.T7 Treviso (Italy). Santuario della Madonna delle Grazie
660.T73 Tuticorin (Italy). Lady of Snows
660.U37 Ujarrás (Costa Rica)
660.U53 Umbe Spring (Spain)
660.V33 Valls (Spain). Santa Maria de la Candela
660.V35 Valverde de la Virgen (Spain). Santuario de la Virgen del Camino
660.V37 Varese. Santa Maria del Monte
660.V39 Vēḷāṅkaṇṇi (India). Puṉita Ārōkkiya Aṉṉaiyiṉ Pērālayam
660.V47 Vich (Spain)
660.V57 Virtudes, Nuestra Señora de las
660.W3 Walsingham, Our Lady of
660.W35 Washington (D.C.). National Shrine of the Immaculate Conception
660.W352C93 Czech National Chapel
660.W352O72 Oratory of Our Lady of Peace and Good Voyage
660.W352.A-Z Individual chapels and oratories, A-Z
660.W45 Werl (Germany). Madonna von Werl
660.Z34 Zarvanyt͡sia (Ukraine)
660.Z6 Zorita (Spain). Nuestra Señora de la Fuenta Santa
670.A-Z Other special topics, A-Z
670.B55 Black Virgins
670.J68 Journeys
670.P75 Psychology of Mary
670.P8 Purification
670.R4 Relics. Girdle, etc.
670.S8 Suffering
670.S85 Symbolism
670.T5 Titles
675 Legendary and apocryphal narratives
Cf. BT520 Christology
680 Controversial works against Catholic doctrines, cults, etc., in regard to the Virgin Mary

Cults of Saints Anne and Joachim, parents of the Virgin Mary
683 General works
685 Cult of Saint Anne

Saint James
Biography see BS2453

Saint James -- Continued
685.5 Cultus
Saint Joseph
690 General works. Theology. Cultus
Biography see BS2458
Prayers and devotions see BX2164
Saint John the Baptist
Biography see BS2456
691 Cultus
Saint Jude
Biography see BS2460.J85
693 Cultus
Saint Peter
Biography see BS2515
694 Cultus
Creation
Cf. BL239+ Religion and science
Cf. BS650+ Bible and science
Cf. BS651+ Creationism
695 General works
695.5 Nature. Ecological theology
696 Life. Reverence for life
Divine law, moral government, miracles see BT95+
Providence of God see BT135
Kingdom of God see BT94
Man. Doctrinal anthropology
General works
700 Early through 1800
701 1801-1950
701.2 1951-2000
701.3 2001-
702 General special
703 Pamphlets, essays, etc.
703.5 Men
704 Woman
Cf. BT83.55 Feminist theology
Cf. BV639.W7 The Church and women
705 Children
Cf. BT758 Infant salvation
Cf. BV639.C4 Children in the Church
705.5 Youth
Cf. BV639.Y7 Youth in the Church
705.8 Man-woman relationships
705.9 Unmarried couples
Marriage
706 General works
707 Divorce

Creation
Man. Doctrinal anthropology
Marriage -- Continued
707.3 Interracial marriage
707.5 Polygamy
707.6 Same-sex marriage
707.7 Family
Sex
708 General works
708.3 Androgyny
708.4 Erotica
708.5 Masturbation
708.6 Sodomy
709 Play. Laughter
709.5 Creativity
710 Fall of man
712 Evolution
713 Self
714 Shame
Sin
715 General works
720 Original sin. Depravity
721 Sin against the Holy Spirit. Unpardonable sin
722 Guilt
Probation see BT927
725 Temptation
730 Accountability. Moral responsibility. Moral agency
730.5 Failure
731 Alienation
Freedom see BT809+
731.5 Anxiety
Man in health and sickness
732 General works
732.2 Use of Medicine
Mental health
732.4 General works
732.45 Recovery movement
Spiritual healing
732.5 General works
Biography and memoirs of healers
732.55 Collective
732.56A-.56Z Individual, A-Z
732.7 Suffering. Affliction. Pain
Cf. BJ1409 Ethics
Cf. BV4900+ Works of consolation and cheer
732.8 Suffering of children
Man and race

Creation
Man. Doctrinal anthropology
Man and race -- Continued
734 General works
734.2 Race problem
For material dealing with a particular country, see D-F
734.3 Segregation
Man and state
Cf. BV629+ Church and state
736 General works
736.15 The Christian and violence
736.2 The Christian and war
Including the arms race and arms trade
736.4 The Christian and peace
736.6 The Christian and nonviolence. Passive resistance
Man and society. Christian sociology
738 General works
Cf. BV625 Church and society
Cf. HN31 Church and social problems
738.15 Theology of civil rights
738.17 Theology of education
738.25 Theology of power
738.27 Theology of reconciliation
738.3 Theology of revolution
738.4 Theology of service
738.45 Theology of solidarity
738.48 Theology of welfare
738.5 Theology of work
Natural and spiritual body. The soul
Cf. BD419+ Ontology
Cf. BF1001+ Psychic research
Cf. BL290 Comparative religion
General works
740 Early through 1800
741 1801-1950
741.2 1951-2000
741.3 2001-
743 Pamphlets, addresses, essays, etc.
745 Other
Animals
746 General works
747 Killing of animals. Vivisection
748 Use of meat
749 Vegetarianism
Salvation. Soteriology
Cf. BT155 Covenants
Cf. BT263+ Atonement

Salvation. Soteriology -- Continued
General works
750 Early through 1800
751 1801-1950
751.2 1951-2000
751.3 2001-
752 General special
753 Pamphlets, addresses, essays, sermons, etc.
755 Catholic Church and salvation
Including salvation outside the Catholic Church
758 Infant salvation
759 Salvation outside the Church
Cf. BT755 Catholic Church and salvation
Cf. BT850+ Limbo
Grace
General works
760 Early through 1800
761 1801-1950
761.2 1951-2000
761.3 2001-
762 Molinism
General works
Justification. Imputation. Righteousness
763 Early through 1800
764 1801-1950
764.2 1951-2000
764.3 2001-
765 Sanctification
766 Perfection. Perfect love. Entire sanctification. Second blessing
Cf. BX2350.5+ Catholic Church
767 Holiness. Purity
767.3 Spiritual gifts
767.5 Universal priesthood
767.7 Mystical union
Cf. BT165 God and man
767.8 Deification. Theosis
768 Perseverance of the saints
769 Other
Faith. Faith and works
General works
770 Early through 1800
771 1801-1950
771.2 1951-2000
771.3 2001-
772 Addresses, essays, lectures
773 Works as a means of grace. Good works. Merit

Salvation. Soteriology -- Continued
774 Religious doubt
774.5 Despair
775 Redemption
Cf. BT263+ Atonement
780 Conversion
Cf. BR110+ Psychology of conversion
Cf. BV4912+ Conversion literature
Cf. BV4912+ Conversion literature
783 Apostasy
785 Assurance
790 Regeneration
795 Forgiveness. Remission of sins
800 Repentance. Contrition. Attrition
805 Crying. Gift of tears. Compunction
Freedom. Autonomy. Predestination and Free will. Election. Effectual calling. Reprobation
Cf. BJ1460+ Ethics
Cf. BT267 Extent of the Atonement
809 History
General works
810 Early through 1950
810.2 1951-2000
810.3 2001-
811 Eternal security of the believer
The Church see BV598+
Communion of saints see BT972
Ministry see BV659+
Scripture see BS480
Law and Gospel see BT79
Sacraments see BV800+
Eschatology. Last things
819 Collected works
819.5 History
General works
820 Early through 1800
821 1801-1950
821.2 1951-2000
821.3 2001-
823 Addresses, essays, lectures, sermons, etc.
824 Anti-eschatological literature
Class here works on life on earth, not in the hereafter
Cf. BT925 Undesirability of immortality
824.5 Realized eschatology
Death
825 General works

Eschatology. Last things
Death -- Continued
Disposal of the body
Cf. RA619+ Public health
826 General works
826.2 Burial. Cemeteries
826.4 Cremation
826.6 Particular judgment
827 Translation to Heaven
830 Intermediate state
Heaven and Hell
832 General works
833 Other
e.g. Dreams and visions
Hades. Sheol. Hell. Future punishment
834 Collected works
Including selections from several authors
General works
835 Early through 1800
836 1801-1950
836.2 1951-2000
836.3 2001-
837 Works against the doctrine of endless punishment
838 Other
General works
Purgatory
840 Early through 1800
841 1801-1950
842 1951-2000
843 2001-
Heaven. Paradise
For children in Heaven see BV4907
844 Collected works
Including selections from several authors
General works
845 Early through 1800
846 1801-1950
846.2 1951-2000
846.3 2001-
847 Heavenly recognition
848 Other
e.g. Dreams and visions
849 Juvenile works
Limbo
850 General works
855 Limbus patrum
860 Limbus infantium

Eschatology. Last things -- Continued
Resurrection
Cf. BT480+ Christ's Resurrection
General works
870 Early through 1800
871 1801-1950
872 1951-2000
873 2001-
End of the age. End of the world
Including precursory signs
875.A1-.A5 Periodicals. Collected works
General works
875.A6-Z Early through 1950
876 1951-2000
877 2001-
Judgment
General works
880 Early through 1800
881 1801-1950
882 1951-2000
883 2001-
Second Coming of Christ. Second Advent. Parousia
Cf. BS649.S43 Bible prophecy
Cf. BX6101+ Adventists
General works
885 Early through 1950
886 1951-2000
886.3 2001-
Antichrist see BT985
887 Rapture
888 Tribulation
Millennium. Chiliasm. Premillennialism. Postmillennialism
Cf. BT94 Kingdom of God. Kingdom of Christ
890.A1-.A5 Periodicals. Collected works
General works
890.A6-Z Early through 1950
891 1951-2000
892 2001-
By region or country see BR500+
Future state. Future life
Cf. BL735 Classical mythology
899 Collected works
Including selections from several authors
General works
900 Early through 1800
901 1801-1950
902 1951-2000

Future state. Future life
General works -- Continued
903 2001-
904 Addresses, essays, lectures, sermons, etc.
Eternity
General works
910 Early through 1800
911 1801-1950
912 1951-2000
913 2001-
Immortality
Cf. BD419+ Ontology
Cf. BF1001+ Psychic research
Cf. BL530 Comparative religion
919 Collected works
Including selections from several authors
General works
920 Early through 1800
921 1801-1950
921.2 1951-2000
921.3 2001-
923 Addresses, essays, lectures, sermons, etc.
925 Other
e.g. Physical immortality, undesirability of immortality
927 Probation
930 Annihilation
Reward and punishment
940 General works
Eternal punishment see BT834+
Invisible world
Including spirits, angels, saints, demons, etc.
General works
960 Early through 1800
961 1801-1951
962 1951-2000
963 2001-
Angels
General works
965 Early through 1800
966 1801-1950
966.2 1951-2000
966.3 2001-
968.A-Z Individual angels, A-Z
968.G2 Gabriel, archangel
968.M5 Michael, archangel
968.R34 Raguel, archangel
968.U75 Uriel, archangel

Invisible world -- Continued
Saints
Cf. BR1710+ Biography
Cf. BS2430+ Biography (New Testament)
Cf. BX380+ Orthodox Eastern Church (General)
Cf. BX393 Biography (Orthodox Eastern Church)
Cf. BX575+ Russian Orthodox Eastern Church (General)
Cf. BX596 Biography (Russian Orthodox Eastern Church)
Cf. BX2325+ Canonization and cultus (Catholic Church)
Cf. BX4654+ Biography (Catholic Church)
970 General works
972 Communion of saints
Demons. Evil spirits
Cf. BF1501+ Demonology
975 General works
The Devil. Satan
General works
980 Early through 1950
981 1951-2000
982 2001-
985 Antichrist
Creeds, confessions, covenants, etc.
For creeds, catechisms, etc. of individual churches and denominations, see the individual church or denomination
990 General works
Apostles' Creed
General works
992 Early through 1800
993 1801-1950
993.2 1951-2000
993.3 2001-
995 Athanasian Creed
999 Nicene Creed. Niceno-Constantinopolitan Creed
1003.A-Z Other early creeds, A-Z
1010 Covenants
Catechisms
For individual denominations see subclass BX
1029 Latin
English
1030 Early through 1800
1031 1801-1950
1031.2 1951-2000
1031.3 2001-
1033 French
1034 German
1035 Italian

Catechisms -- Continued
1036 Scandinavian
1037 Spanish and Portuguese
1039.A-Z Other languages, A-Z
e.g.
1039.D8 Dutch
1039.P7 Polish
1039.W4 Welsh
1040 Picture catechisms
Apologetics. Evidences of Christianity
For works on the early Church, ca. 30-600 see BR60+
1095 Collections
General works
1100 601 through 1800
1101 1801-1950
1102 1951-2000
1103 2001-
1105 Addresses, essays, lectures, sermons, etc.
Study and teaching
Including outlines, etc.
1107 General works
1108 Elementary textbooks
History
1109 General works
By period
1110 Apostolic. Apologetics in the the New Testament
Early Church, ca 30-600
Cf. BT1140 Controversial works against the Greek philosophers
Cf. BT1160 Controversial works against the Romans
1115 General works
(1116) Individual authors of the early Church
see BR65
1117 601-
Against opponents of Christianity
1120 Jews
Cf. BM585+ Controversial works against Judaism
1130 Heathen
1140 Greek philosophers
1150 Neo-Platonists
1160 Romans
1170 Muslims
Cf. BP172+ Relation to Christianity
Cf. BV2625+ Missions to Muslims
1180 Deists
1185 Pantheists
1190 French encyclopedists

	Apologetics. Evidences of Christianity
	Against opponents of Christianity -- Continued
1200	Modern philosophers
	Rationalists, agnostics, and skeptics
	General works
1209	Early through 1800
1210	1801-1950
1211	1951-2000
1212	2001-
1213	Existentialists
1215	Socialists and communists
1220	Scientists
	Adherents of modern non-Christian religions
1230	General works
1235.A-Z	Individual religions, A-Z
	e.g.
	Brahmanism see BT1235.H5
1235.H5	Hinduism. Brahmanism
	Islam see BT1170
	Judaism see BT1120
	Theosophy see BP575
1240	Other (not A-Z)
	e.g. Spiritualists
	Evidence from history
1250	General works
1255	Ancient monuments, tablets, etc.
	History of specific doctrines and movements. Heresies and schisms
	Including texts, liturgies, etc.
	General works
1313	Early through 1800
1315	1801-1950
1315.2	1951-2000
1315.3	2001-
1317	General special
1318	Addresses, essays, lectures
	By period
	Early to the Reformation, 1517
1319	General works
1320	Adoptionism
	Albigenses see BX4890+
1323	Alogi
1325	Amalricians
	Anomaeans see BT1350
1330	Antinomianism
1336	Apellianists
1340	Apollinarianism

History of specific doctrines and movements. Heresies and schisms
By period
Early to the Reformation, 1517 -- Continued
Apostolic Brethren see BX1257
1350 Arianism
1355 Bogomiles
1358 Brethren of the Free Spirit
1360 Cathari
Cf. BX4890+ Albigenses
1365 Circumcellions
1368 Docetism
1370 Donatists
1375 Ebionism (Ebionites)
1377 Elkesaites
1378 Encratites
Euchites see BT1417
1380 Eutychians
Gnosticism (Christian)
Cf. BT1415 Marcionites
Cf. BT1437 Naassenes
Cf. BT1475 Valentinians
1390 General works
Nag Hammadi Codices
Texts
1391.A05 Facsimiles. By date
1391.A1 Original language. By date
Translations
1391.A3 English. By date
1391.A4 French. By date
1391.A5 German. By date
1391.A6A-.A6Z Other languages. By language, A-Z, and date
1391.A62 Periodicals
1391.A7-Z History and criticism
1392.A-Z Individual tractates, A-Z
1392.A37-.A372 Acts of Peter and the Twelve Apostles (Table BS8)
1392.A44-.A442 Allogenes (Table BS8)
1392.A63-.A632 Apocalypse of Adam (Table BS8)
1392.A637-.A6372 Apocalypse of Paul (Table BS8)
1392.A64-.A642 Apocalypse of Peter (Table BS8)
1392.A65-.A652 Apocryphon of James (Table BS8)
1392.A75-.A752 Apocryphon of John (Table BS8)
1392.B65-.B652 Book of Thomas the Contender (Table BS8)
1392.C65-.C652 Concept of our Great Power (Table BS8)
1392.D52-.D522 Dialogue of the Savior (Table BS8)
1392.E92-.E922 Eugnostos the Blessed (Table BS8)
1392.E93-.E932 Exegesis on the soul (Table BS8)

History of specific doctrines and movements. Heresies and schisms
By period
Early to the Reformation, 1517
Gnosticism (Christian)
Nag Hammadi Codices
Individual tractates, A-Z -- Continued

1392.F57-.F572 First Apocalypse of James (Table BS8)
1392.G65-.G652 Gospel according to Mary (Table BS8)
1392.G67-.G672 Gospel of the Egyptians (Table BS8)
Gospel of Thomas see BS2860.T5+
1392.G68-.G682 Gospel of Truth (Table BS8)
1392.H94-.H942 Hypostasis of the Archons (Table BS8)
1392.I58-.I582 Interpretation of Knowledge (Table BS8)
1392.L47-.L472 Letter of Peter to Philip (Table BS8)
1392.M37-.M372 Marsanes (Table BS8)
1392.P35-.P352 Paraphrase of Shem (Table BS8)
1392.S42-.S422 Second Apocalypse of James (Table BS8)
1392.S45-.S452 Sentences of Sextus (Table BS8)
1392.T43-.T432 Teachings of Silvanus (Table BS8)
1392.T47-.T472 Testimony of truth (Table BS8)
1392.T74-.T742 Treatise on resurrection (Table BS8)
1392.T76-.T762 Treatise on the origin of the world (Table BS8)
1392.T79-.T792 Trimorphic Protennoia (Table BS8)
1392.V35-.V352 Valentinian exposition (Table BS8)
1392.Z65-.Z652 Zostrianos (Table BS8)
Hesychasm see BX384.5
1395 Jovinianists
Macedonians see BT1464
1405 Mandaeans. Sabians. St. John's Christians
1410 Manichaeism
1415 Marcionites
1417 Messalians. Euchites
1420 Monarchians
Cf. BT1320 Adoptionists
Cf. BT1470 Sabellians
1425 Monophysites
Cf. BT1380 Eutychians
1430 Monothelitism (Monothelites)
1435 Montanism
1437 Naassenes
1440 Nestorians
1442 Nihilianism
1445 Paulicians
Pelagianism
1450 General works
1460 Semi-Pelagianism

History of specific doctrines and movements. Heresies and schisms
By period
Early to the Reformation, 1517 -- Continued
1463 Petrobrusians
1464 Pneumatomachi
1465 Priscillianism
Quartodecimanism see BV55+
1470 Sabellianism (Sabellians)
Sabians see BT1405
1472 Speronists
St. John's Christians see BT1405
1473 Subordinationism
1474 Tritheism
1475 Valentinians
Modern, 1517-
Cf. BX1+ Individual denominations
1476 General works
Antinomianism see BT1330
Arminianism see BX6195+
Hesychasm see BX384.5
Mandaeans see BT1405
Socinianism
Including biographies of founders
Cf. BX9801+ Unitarianism
1480.A1-.A2 Collected works
1480.A3A-.A3Z Works of Fausto Soccino. By title, A-Z
1480.A5 Racovian catechism
1480.A6-Z General works

Practical theology
  General
1 Periodicals. Societies
2 Collected works
2.5 Dictionaries
3 General works
4 Other
  Worship (Public and private)
    History
5 General works
      By period
6 Primitive and early church
7 Medieval
8 Modern
    General works
9 Early through 1800
10 1801-1950
10.2 1951-2000
10.3 2001-
    Public worship (General)
15 Spirit and manner of public worship
16 Interfaith worship
20 Duty and claims of public worship
  Cf. BV4523 Duty of churchgoing
25 Manuals for the conduct of religious services
  For individual denominations see BX1+
26 Worship in school and college
  Worship in the church school see BV1522
26.2 Children in public worship
  Cf. BV199.C4 Children's liturgies
  Cf. BV1522 Worship in the church school
26.7 Women in public worship
  Cf. BV199.W6 Women's services
27 Sunday services at special times
  Including evening services, aftermeetings, etc.
  For individual denominations see BX1+
    Weekday services. Noon services
  For individual denominations see BX1+
28 General works
  Prayer meetings see BV285.A1+
29 Youth services

Worship (Public and private) -- Continued
Times and seasons. The Church year
Including devotional materials except Catholic for which see BX2170.A4 Advent devotions; BX2170.C55 Church year devotions; etc.
For liturgy and ritual of individual sects see BX1+
Cf. BV4254.2+ Sermons for special occasions, days, festivals, etc.
30 General works
35 Other
e.g. Origins of feasts and fasts
40 Advent
Feast days
43 General works
Christmas. Feast of the Nativity
Cf. BV1572.C5 Sunday-school services
Cf. PN4305.C5 Recitations
Cf. PN6071.C6 Literary selections
Cf. PN6110.C5 Poetry
Cf. PN6120.C5 Plays
45 General works
47 St. Nicholas (Nicholas, Saint, Bp. of Myra) legend
50.A-Z Other immovable feasts, A-Z
50.A4 All Souls' Day
50.A6 Annunciation
50.A7 Assumption of the Blessed Virgin Mary
50.C3 Candlemas
50.E7 Epiphany. Epiphany season
50.E93 Exaltation of the Cross. Holy Cross Day
50.H6 Holy Innocents' Day
50.I6 Immaculate Conception
50.N48 New Year's Eve. Watch Night
Presentation of Jesus Christ see BV50.C3
50.P7 Presentation of the Blessed Virgin Mary
50.T8 Transfiguration
50.V5 Visitation
Watch Night see BV50.N48
The movable feasts
55 Easter
Including the Quartodeciman controversy
Cf. BT480+ The Resurrection of Christ
57 Ascension Day
60 Pentecost. Whitsunday
Cf. GT4995.P45 Manners and customs
Pentecost season
61 General works
62 Trinity Sunday

Worship (Public and private)
Times and seasons. The Church year
Feast days
The movable feasts
Pentecost season -- Continued
63 Corpus Christi. Fête-Dieu
64.A-Z Other movable feasts, A-Z
e.g.
64.J4-Z Jesus Christ, the King
64.S3 Sacred Heart of Jesus
Saints' days
65 General works
Special
67 All Saints
70.A-Z Other, A-Z
e.g.
70.A6 Saint Andrew's Day
70.J6 John the Baptist's Day
75 Thanksgiving Day
Fasts
Cf. BV4727 Fasting on appointed days
80 General works
Pre-Lent. Septuagesima
82 General works
83 Sexagesima
84 Quinquagesima
Lent
85 General works
Passiontide
88 General works
89 Passion Sunday
Holy Week
For events of Holy Week see BT414
90 General works
91 Palm Sunday
Cf. BT415 Christ's entry into Jerusalem
94 Maundy Thursday
95 Good Friday
Fast Day
United States
100 General works
101.A-.W By state, A-W
102.A-Z Other countries, A-Z
105.A-Z Other fasts, A-Z
e.g.
105.E6 Ember days
105.F7 Fridays

Worship (Public and private)
Times and seasons. The Church year
Fasts
Other fasts, A-Z -- Continued
105.R7 Rogation days
Lord's Day. Sunday. Sabbath
107 Periodicals. Societies
General works
109 Early through 1800
110 1801-1950
111 1951-2000
111.3 2001-
113 Addresses, essays, lectures
Hebrew Sabbath see BM685
Christian Sabbath see BV107+
125 Seventh day
Sunday observance
Cf. BV4723 Precepts of the Church
130.A1 Periodicals. Congresses
130.A2-Z General works
133 Sunday legislation
135.A-Z Other special days and seasons, A-Z
e.g.
135.N5 New Year's Day
Christian symbols and symbolism
Cf. BR133.A+ Antiquities of individual countries
Cf. N7810+ Christian art, Christian symbolism in art
150 General works
153.A-Z By region or country, A-Z
155 Early Christian emblems
160 The Cross. Crosses. Crucifixes
Class here works on the symbolism of the cross and on crosses and crucifixes located in churches, religious institutions, etc. For works on outdoor crosses, see CC300+. For works on crosses as religious art, see N8053
165 Liturgical symbolism: Colors, lights, etc.
167 Vestments, altar cloths, etc.
Cf. BX1925 Catholic Church
Cf. BX5180 Church of England
Cf. NK4850 Costume (Art)
Cf. NK9310+ Ecclesiastical embroidery
168.A-Z Other special, A-Z
168.A3 Adzes
168.A5 Animals
168.C4 Chi Rho
168.D6 Dove

Worship (Public and private)
Christian symbols and symbolism
Other special, A-Z -- Continued
168.F4 Fish
168.F5 Flags. Pennants
168.F56 Flowers
168.G45 Gems
168.G7 Grain
168.L55 Lions
Pennants see BV168.F5
168.P58 Plants
168.S5 Ship
168.S7 Pastoral staff
Temple of God see BS680.T4
168.T7 Tree of life
Liturgy and ritual
For individual churches see BX1+
Cf. NA4605 Liturgy and architecture
169 Periodicals. Serials
169.5 Congress. Conferences
170 Collected works
173 Dictionaries
General works
174 Early through 1800
175 1801-1950
176 1951-2000
176.3 2001-
178 General special
180 Ritualism (General)
181 Controversial works
182 Liturgical movement
Special
185 Early Christian liturgy and ritual
185.2 Stational liturgy
186 Eastern
For Oriental churches see BX107
For Orthodox Eastern Church see BX350+
For Catholic Oriental churches see BX4710.1+
186.5 Western
For Catholic Church see BX1970+
For Church of England see BX5140.5+
186.7 Ecumenical
193.A-Z By region or country, A-Z
e.g.
193.G7 Great Britain
Cf. BX5142+ Early British rites

Worshiр (Public and private)
Liturgy and ritual
Special -- Continued
194.A-Z Parts of the service, A-Z
e.g.
194.C6 Commemoration of the saints and the faithful departed
194.C7 Confession
194.O34 Offertories. Offering
194.R5 Reading of Scripture
Cf. BV199.A2 Bible selections for public reading
The altar, liturgical objects, etc.
Including altar guilds
Cf. BV150+ Christian symbols and symbolism
Cf. NA5050+ Ecclesiastical furniture
195 General works
195.5 Acolytes. Altar servers
For works limited to individual sects see BX1+
196.A-Z Special objects, etc., A-Z
196.C3 Candles
Holy oils see BV196.H7
196.H7 Holy Sepulcher in liturgy
196.O5 Oils. Holy oils
196.P3 Pax (Osculatory)
197.A-Z Special liturgical functions, A-Z
e.g.
197.B5 Benediction
197.G5 Genuflexion. Prostration
197.I6 Use of incense
197.P65 Posture
197.P7 Procession
Prostration see BV197.G5
197.S5 Sign of the Cross, etc.
197.S55 Sitting
Service books. Liturgies
198 General works
199.A1-.A4 Bible selections for public reading
199.A2 General
Cf. BV199.R5 Responsive readings
199.A3 Old Testament
199.A4 New Testament
199.A5-Z Other special, A-Z
199.A64 Aged, older people, retired, etc., Services for
199.B4 Benedictions
199.C3 Canticles
Cf. BX5946.A+ Episcopal Church. Protestant
Episcopal Church

Worship (Public and private)
Liturgy and ritual
Service books. Liturgies
Other special, A-Z
Canticles -- Continued

199.C32A-.C32Z Individual canticles, A-Z
For works emphasizing the Biblical text see BS1+
Magnificat
199.C32M3 Texts in Hebrew, Greek, or Latin. By date
199.C32M32-.C32M349 Other translations
199.C32M35-.C32M399 History and criticism
Nunc dimittis
199.C32N8 Texts in Hebrew, Greek, or Latin. By date
199.C32N82-.C32N829 Other translations
199.C32N83-.C32N839 History and criticism
Te Deum laudamus see BV469.T4+
199.C4 Children's services
199.C45 Christmas services
199.C6 Communion services
199.D3 Daily offices. Divine office
199.D37 Dedication of infants
199.D4 Dedication services
Divine office see BV199.D3
199.F8 Funeral services
199.G39 Gays, Services for
199.I5 Installation services
199.L42 Lectionaries
199.L58 Litanies
199.M3 Marriage services
199.M4 Memorial services
199.M43 Men's services
199.M5 Military services (for the army and navy)
199.N3 Naval services
199.O3 Occasional services
Older people, Services for see BV199.A64
199.P25 Passover services (Christian observance)
199.P3 Patriotic services
199.P7 Procession services
199.R5 Responsive readings
199.S3 School services
199.S5 Seamen's services
199.W3 Wartime services

Worship (Public and private)
Liturgy and ritual
Service books. Liturgies
Other special, A-Z -- Continued
199.W6 Women's services
Cf. BV26.7 Women in public worship
200 Family worship
Cf. BV255+ Family prayers and devotions
Cf. BV4526+ Religion of the family
Cf. BX2170.F3 Catholic Church
Prayer
205 Collected works
By two or more authors
207 History
General works. Nature, obligation, etc.
209 Early through 1800
210 1801-1950
210.2 1951-2000
210.3 2001-
212 Juvenile works
213 Addresses, essays, lectures
214 Study and teaching
215 Instructions and helps in regard to prayer
220 Efficacy of prayer. Answers to prayer
225 Psychology of prayer
226 Public prayer
227 Other
e.g. Invocation of the dead, prayer for the dead
Prayers
Bible prayers
see BS680.P64 BS1199.P68 BS2545.P67
Prayers of Jesus
Including Jesus' teaching on prayer, and works on the prayers of Jesus
229 General works
The Lord's Prayer
230 General works
Special parts
231 Introduction
231.1 First petition
231.2 Second petition
231.3 Third petition
231.4 Fourth petition
231.5 Fifth petition
231.6 Sixth petition
231.7 Seventh petition
231.8 Conclusion

Worship (Public and private)
Prayer
Prayers
Prayers of Jesus
The Lord's Prayer -- Continued
232 Juvenile works
233 Other
Polyglot editions see P351
234 Other prayers of Jesus
236 Early Christian prayers
237 Medieval prayers
General collections of prayers of one or more persons
Class translations with the language of the translation and not with the language of the original text
245 English
246 French
247 German
248 Spanish and Portuguese
249.A-Z Other languages, A-Z
Pulpit prayers
Class translations with the language of the translation and not with the language of the original text
Including prayers for all church meetings
250 English
251 French
252 German
253 Spanish and Portuguese
254.A-Z Other languages, A-Z
Family prayers and devotions
Class translations with the language of the translation and not with the language of the original text
255 English
256 French
257 German
258 Spanish and Portuguese
259.A-Z Other languages, A-Z
Private prayers and devotions
Class translations with the language of the translation and not with the language of the original text
Cf. BV4800+ Works of devotion and meditation
260 English
261 French
262 German
263 Spanish and Portuguese
264.A-Z Other languages, A-Z

Worship (Public and private)
Prayer
Prayers -- Continued
Children's prayers
Class translations with the language of the translation and not with the language of the original text
Cf. BV283.C5 Prayers concerning children
265 English
266 French
267 German
268 Spanish and Portuguese
269.A-Z Other languages, A-Z
Prayers for special times, seasons, and days see BV30+
Prayers for special classes
270 Sick
273 Soldiers and sailors
Including the armed forces in general
275 Prisoners
280 Legislative bodies
283.A-Z Other special prayers, A-Z
283.A4 Air pilots' prayers
283.A63 Animals, Prayers for
283.B43 Bedtime prayers
283.B7 Boys' prayers
283.C44 Christian union, Prayers for
283.C47 Clergy, Prayers for
283.C5 Concerning children
Cf. BV265+ Children's prayers
283.C7 Prayers in colleges
283.D3 Daughters of the American Revolution
283.F3 Farmers' prayers
283.F67 Forgiveness, Prayers for
283.G5 Girls' prayers
283.G7 Grace before and after meals
283.H8 Husbands' prayers
283.J6 Journalists' prayers
283.M7 Mothers' prayers
283.P4 Peace prayers
283.P45 Physicians' prayers
283.P7 Polar expedition prayers
283.S3 School prayers
283.S84 Suffering, Prayers for the
283.S9 Sunday school prayers
283.T42 Teachers' prayers
283.T7 Travelers' prayers
283.V64 Volunteers' prayers
283.W3 Wartime prayers

Worshiр (Public and private)
Prayer
Prayers
Other special prayers, A-Z -- Continued
283.W6 Women's prayers
283.Y6 Young people's prayers
284.A-Z Prayers (Individual), A-Z
e.g.
Cf. BX2175.A+ Catholic Church
284.A5 Anima Christi
Prayer meetings
285.A1 Periodicals. Societies
285.A2-Z General works
287 Prayer groups
288 Audio-visual aids in public worship
289 Drama in public worship
290 Music in divine worship. Church choirs
Cf. BV340+ Use of hymns
Cf. BX9187 Use of instrumental music in Presbyterian churches
Cf. ML3001 Music
Hymnology
Class here books with words only even though tunes are indicated and books discussing hymn writers or the origin and meaning of hymns
For books with words and music or music only see subclass M
For books discussing composers of hymns or the tunes themselves see subclass ML
301 Periodicals. Societies
303 Collected works
305 Dictionaries. Indexes. Concordances, etc.
For works dealing with an individual hymnal, see the hymnal
History and criticism
310 General works
311 Addresses, essays, lectures
312 English hymns
313 American hymns
314.A-Z Other hymns. By country, A-Z
For individual languages see BV467+
Famous hymns and their story
315 General works
Individual hymns
317.A-Z English, A-Z
e.g.
317.A2 Abide with me
317.J4 Jerusalem, my happy home
317.S5 Shall we meet beyond the river

Worship (Public and private)
Hymnology
History and criticism
Famous hymns and their story
Individual hymns
English, A-Z -- Continued
317.T5 Thou everywhere
Other see BV467+
320 Early and medieval hymns
Biography of hymn writers
For literature, see PR, PS, etc.
325 Collective
330.A-Z Individual, A-Z
e.g.
330.G4 Gerhardt, Paulus
Cf. PT1729.G5 German literature
Grundtvig, Nicolai Frederik S. see PT8130
330.H4 Heermann, Johann
Luther, Martin see BR325
330.S4 Sankey, Ira David
330.W3 Wallin, Johan Olof
Watts, Isaac see BX5207.W3
Wesley, Charles see BX8495.W4
335 Hymn writing. Metrics. Analysis
Use of hymns
For singing in divine worship see BV290
Cf. BV4235.H94 Use of hymn texts in sermons
340 Devotional use
341 Hymn festivals
Hymns. Hymnbooks
Cf. BV520 Sunday school and school hymns
Cf. M2115+ Hymns with tunes
Polyglot
Class here hymns in more than one language
343.A-Z By denomination, A-Z
e.g.
343.A6 Anabaptists
349 Nondenominational
English
350 Best, famous, etc., hymns
353 Children's hymns
Cf. BV520 Sunday school songs and hymns
354 Youth hymns
Translations of Greek and Latin hymns see BV467+
355.A-Z Translations from other languages. By language from which translated, A-Z
e.g.

BV

Worship (Public and private)
Hymnology
Hymns. Hymnbooks
English
Translations from other languages. By language from which translated, A-Z -- Continued
355.G3 German
Denominational hymnbooks in English
Unless individual branches are specified, class all branches with the family
360 Catholic Church
360.A1 History
Anglican. Church of England
370 General works
370.A1 History
372 Episcopal Church
372.A1 History
373 Reformed Episcopal
373.A1 History
375 Adventist
375.A1 History
377.A-.B Adventist - Baptist
Baptist
380 General works
380.A1 History
381.A-Z Individual branches, A-Z
381.F6 Original Freewill
381.F7 Freewill
381.O6 Old School
381.S4 Seventh-Day
383.B-.C Baptist - Christian Church
385 Christian Church (General Convention of the Christian Church)
385.A1 History
387.C-.C Christian Church - Christian Science
387.C45 Christian Congregation in the United States
390 Christian Science
390.A1 History
391.C-.C Christian Science - Church
391.C5 Christian Union
392 Church ...
392.C4 Church of God (Anderson, Ind.)
Church of the Brethren, Dunkards see BV403.G4
393.C-.C Churches - Congregational
393.C5 Churches of God in North America
395 Congregational
395.A1 History

Worship (Public and private)
Hymnology
Hymns. Hymnbooks
English
Denominational hymnbooks in English -- Continued
396.C-.D Congregational - Disciples of Christ
397 Disciples of Christ
397.A1 History
399.D-.F Disciples of Christ - Friends
399.E77 Evangelical Association
399.E8 Evangelical Synod of North America
400 Friends
400.A1 History
403.F-.L Friends - Lutheran
403.G4 German Baptist Brethren (Church of the Brethren, Dunkards)
403.J45 Jehovah's Witnesses
403.L5 Liberal Catholic Church
410 Lutheran
410.A1 History
411.L-.M Lutheran - Mennonite
412 Mennonite
412.A1 History
413.M-.M Mennonite - Methodist
Methodist
Methodist Episcopal Church
After May 10, 1939, Methodist Church (United States)
415 General works
415.A1 History and criticism
415.A3 Official collections. By date
415.A5-Z Other collections. By compiler, A-Z
416.A-Z Other Methodist churches, A-Z
416.M2 Methodist Episcopal Church, South (Table BV9)
416.M25 Congregational Methodist Church (Table BV9)
416.M3 Free Methodist Church (Table BV9)
416.M35 Methodist Church (Canada) (Table BV9)
416.M4 Methodist Protestant Church (Table BV9)
416.M5 Primitive Methodist Church (Table BV9)
416.M6 Wesleyan Methodist Church (Table BV9)
Colored Methodist
416.M7 African Methodist Episcopal Church (Table BV9)
416.M75 African Methodist Episcopal Zion Church (Table BV9)
416.M8 Christian Methodist Episcopal Church (Table BV9)

Worshi p (Public and private)
Hymnology
Hymns. Hymnbooks
English
Denominational hymnbooks in English -- Continued

416.5.M-.M Methodist - Moravian
417 Moravian (United Brethren)
417.A1 History
418.M-.M Moravian - Mormon
420 Mormon (Church of Jesus Christ of Latter-Day Saints)
420.A1 History
423.M-.N Mormon - New Jerusalem Church
423.M8 Muggletonians
425 New Jerusalem Church (Swedenborgianism)
425.A1 History
427.N-.P New Jerusalem Church - Presbyterian
Orthodox Eastern Church, Greek see BV467+
427.P5 Pillar of Fire Church
Presbyterian
430 General works
430.A1 History
431 Scottish
431.A1 History
432.P-.R Presbyterian - Reformed
Reformed
433 General works
433.A1 History
434 Reformed Church in America (Dutch Reformed)
434.A1 History
435 Reformed Church in the United States (German Reformed)
435.A1 History
437.R-.S Reformed - Salvation Army
437.R56 Reorganized Church of Jesus Christ of Latter Day Saints. Community of Christ
440 Salvation Army
440.A1 History
441.S-.S Salvation Army - Shakers
442 Shakers
442.A1 History
443.S-.U Shakers - Unitarian
443.S57 Smith's Friends
443.S6 Spiritualists (as religious sect)
445 Unitarian
445.A1 History
447.U-.U Unitarian - Universalist

Worship (Public and private)
Hymnology
Hymns. Hymnbooks
English
Denominational hymnbooks in English
Unitarian - Universalist -- Continued
447.U3 United Brethren in Christ
447.U38 United Church of Canada
447.U4 United Evangelical Church
450 Universalist
450.A1 History
453.U-.Y Universalist - Young Men's Christian Association
455 Young Men's Christian Association
455.A1 History
457.Y-Z Young Men's Christian Association - Z
459 Nondenominational hymnbooks in English
For Brady and Tate's Psalms and hymns see BS1440.B7
For Watt's Psalms and hymns see BS1440.W3+
Hymnbooks in English. Special types or services
460 Revivals. Camp meetings
461 Spirituals
463 Soldiers and sailors
465.A-Z Other, A-Z
465.B2 Baptism
465.C4 Christian Endeavor
College hymns see BV525
465.C5 Communion
465.M5 Missionary services
School hymns see BV525
Sunday school hymns see BV520
465.W3 Wartime
Hymns in languages other than English
Greek
Including translations from Greek
467 General works
467.5.A-Z Hymns of individual authors and individual hymns of unknown authors, A-Z
e.g.
467.5.C6-.C64 Saint Cosmas, of Jerusalem, Bp. of Majuna (Table BV1)
467.5.R6-.R64 Saint Romanus Melodus (Table BV1)
467.5.S9-.S94 Synesius Cyrenaeus, Bp. of Ptolemais (Table BV1)
Latin
Cf. BX2043 Tropers
468 General works

Worshi (Public and private)
Hymnology
Hymns. Hymnbooks
Hymns in languages other than English
Latin -- Continued

469.A-Z Hymns of individual authors and individual hymns of unknown authors, A-Z
e.g.
469.A4-.A44 Adam de Saint Victor (Table BV1)
469.A6-.A64 Ambrose, Saint (Table BV1)
Ave Maria Stella
469.A8 Text. By date
469.A82 History and criticism
Dies irae
469.D5 Text. By date
469.D52 History and criticism
Francis, Saint see BV489.F7+
Gloria in excelsis
469.G5 Text. By date
469.G52 History and criticism
469.H5-.H54 Hilary of Poitiers, Saint (Table BV1)
Magnificat see BV199.C32M3+
469.P5-.P54 Pietro Damiani, Saint (Table BV1)
Salve Regina
469.S3 Text. By date
469.S32 History and criticism
Stabat Mater
469.S7 Text. By date
469.S72 History and criticism
Te Deum laudamus
469.T4 Text. By date
469.T42 History and criticism
Veni Creator Spiritus
469.V46 Text. By date
469.V462 History and criticism
Other languages
470-474 Dutch (Table BV2 modified)
473.A-Z By country, A-Z
For Netherlands see BV470
475-479 French (Table BV2 modified)
478.A-Z By country, A-Z
For France see BV475
480-484 German (High and Low) (Table BV2 modified)
481.A-Z By denomination, A-Z
481.L6-.L9 Lutheran hymnals
481.L6 Published in Germany

Worship (Public and private)
Hymnology
Hymns. Hymnbooks
Hymns in languages other than English
Other languages
German (High and Low)
By denomination, A-Z
Lutheran hymnals -- Continued
481.L7A-.L7Z Published in other European countries. By country, A-Z
481.L8 Published in the United States
481.L9A-.L9Z Other hymnals. By compiler or title, A-Z
Including hymnals not used for congregational purposes
483.A-Z By country, A-Z
For Germany see BV480
485-489 Italian (Table BV2 modified)
488.A-Z By country, A-Z
For Italy see BV485
489.A-Z Hymns of individual authors and individual hymns of unknown authors, A-Z
e.g.
Francis of Assisi, Saint
489.F7 Collected works. By date
489.F73 History and criticism (General)
489.F74A-.F74Z Individual hymns. By title, A-Z
Cantico di frate sole
489.F74C36 Text. By date
489.F74C37-.F74C379 History and criticism
489.5 Scandinavian
490-494 Dano-Norwegian (Table BV2 modified)
493.A-Z By country, A-Z
For Denmark or Norway see BV490
495-499 Icelandic (Table BV2 modified)
498.A-Z By country, A-Z
For Iceland see BV495
500-504 Swedish (Table BV2 modified)
503.A-Z By country, A-Z
For Sweden see BV500
505-509 Spanish and Portuguese (Table BV2 modified)
508.A-Z By country, A-Z
For Spain or Portugal see BV505
510.A-Z Other languages, A-Z
e.g.
510.C9 Czech
510.F5 Finnish

Worship (Public and private)
Hymnology
Hymns. Hymnbooks
Hymns in languages other than English
Other languages
Other languages, A-Z -- Continued
510.H8 Hungarian
510.P6 Polish
510.R9 Russian
510.S9 Syriac
510.W4 Welsh
520 Sunday school songs and hymns
For hymns under individual denominations, see the language
525 School and college hymns
530 Carols
Ecclesiastical theology
Church institutions, societies, etc., and their work
590 Collected works
593 General works
595 Sermons, addresses, essays, etc.
The Church
For the teachings of Jesus concerning the Church see BS2417.C53
For the teaching of the New Testament concerning the Church see BS2545.C5
For the teaching of the Epistles of Paul concerning the Church see BS2655.C5
598 History of doctrines concerning the Church
599 Congresses
600.A1 Collected works
General works
Cf. BT91 Authority of the Church; teaching office of the Church
Cf. BX1746 The nature of the Church in Catholic theology
600.A2 Early through 1800
600.A5-Z 1800-1950
600.2 1951-2000
600.3 2001-
Church as the "Mystical Body of Christ"
Cf. BT767.7 Mystical union
600.4 History of the doctrine
600.5 General works
600.8 Foundation of the Church
Cf. BR129+ Sources of Christianity
Cf. BS2653 Paul or Jesus?

Ecclesiastical theology
The Church -- Continued
"Marks" of the Church. "Notes" of the Church. Characteristics
601 General works
601.2 Apostolicity
601.3 Catholicity
601.4 Holiness
Unity
Cf. BX1+ Christian unity; Ecumenical movement
601.5 General works
601.57 Petrine office
Cf. BX1805+ Papal primacy
601.6.A-Z Other characteristics, A-Z
601.6.C7 Credibility
601.6.I5 Infallibility
Cf. BX1806 Papal infallibility
601.6.N4 Necessity
601.6.V5 Visibility
601.7 The local church and its place in the universal Church
601.8 Mission of the Church
601.85 House churches
601.9 Non-institutional churches
602 Study and teaching. Textbooks
602.5 Juvenile works
603 Sermons, addresses, essays, etc.
Special aspects of Church institutions (General)
Cf. BR115.A+ Christianity in its special aspects
604 Building and equipment
Cf. BV652.7 Church maintenance and housekeeping
Cf. NA4790+ Architecture
610 Church and morals
615 Church and intellectual development. Church and modern thought
Cf. BX1395 Catholic Church and modern thought
Church and civilization see BR115.C5
625 Church and society. Church and community
Including the social function of the Church, cooperative church work, etc.
Cf. BT738+ Man and society (Doctrinal theology)
Cf. BV4325 Pastor's relations to the community
Cf. HN30+ Church and social problems
626 Church federations. Church councils
For national (except United States) and all local organizations see BR500+
For international and United States national organizations see BX6.A+

Ecclesiastical theology
Special aspects of Church institutions (General) -- Continued
Church and economics. Church and labor see BR115.E3
628 Church and industry
Church and state
Including Church and civil government. Passive obedience
Cf. BX1790+ Catholic Church and the state
General works
629 Early through 1800
Late modern, 1801-
630.A1 Collected works. Serials
630.A3-Z 1801-1950
630.2 1951-2000
630.3 2001-
631 Addresses, essays, lectures
By region or country see BR500+
Catholic Church by region or country see BX1401+
Church of England and the state see BX5157
633 National churches
634 The cathedral
For individual denominations see BX1+
636 The community church. The federated church. Interdenominational use of churches
City churches
637 General works
637.5 City clergy
637.7 The suburban church
Cf. BX1407.S8 Catholic suburban churches
637.8 Small churches (Small congregations)
637.9 Big churches (Big congregations)
The rural church. The Church and country life
For local descriptive works other than the United States see subclass BR
Cf. BV1210 Young Men's Christian Associations and rural communities
Cf. BV1524 Rural Sunday schools
Cf. BX1407.R8 Rural churches of the Catholic Church
638 General works
638.4 The larger parish
638.7 Rural clergy
638.8 Popular works. Stories, anecdotes, etc.
639.A-Z The Church and special classes, A-Z
For local see BR500+
Cf. BV4440+ Church work with special classes, A-Z
639.B7 Boys
639.C4 Children. The junior church
Including church membership

Ecclesiastical theology
Special aspects of Church institutions (General)
The Church and special classes, A-Z
639.C6 College students
639.E45 Emigrants
Foreign populations see BV639.I4
639.I4 Immigrants. Foreign populations
The junior church see BV639.C4
639.M4 Men
639.M56 Minorities
639.P6 Poor
639.S5 Single people
639.W7 Women
Cf. BR195.W6 Women in the early Church
Working men see BR115.E3
639.Y7 Young men and women
640 Other
e.g. Lack of spirituality in the modern Church
For church fellowship see BV820
Church polity
Class here works on church government and organization
Cf. BX1+ Church polity of individual denominations
History
General works
646 Early through 1800
647 1801-1950
647.2 1951-2000
647.3 2001-
By period
648 Early. Origins to Reformation
Modern
General works
649 Early through 1800
e.g. Hooker's Ecclesiastical polity
650 1801-1950
650.2 1951-2000
650.3 2001-
651 Church manuals, guides, etc.
Church management. Efficiency
652.A1 Periodicals. Societies. Serials
652.A3-Z General works
652.1 Church leadership
652.13 Personnel management
652.15 Church meetings
652.2 Group work
652.23 Church marketing
652.24 New church development. Starting new churches

Ecclesiastical theology
Church management. Efficiency -- Continued
Church growth
652.25 General works
By region or country see BR500+
652.3 Canvassing
652.35 Church consultation. Outside consultants
652.4 Church surveys (General)
For individual surveys see BR500+
Cf. BX1407.S6 Social surveys (Catholic Church)
Cf. HN1+ Social survey
652.5 Church attendance
Cf. BV4523 Duty of church going
652.6 Busing in church work
652.7 Church maintenance and housekeeping
652.75 Church purchasing
652.77 Electronic data processing
Audiovisual aids
652.8 General works
652.82 Motion pictures
652.83 Phonorecords. Phonotapes
652.9 Other
Mass media and telecommunication in religion
Cf. BV2082.M3 Mass media in missionary work
652.95 General works
652.97.A-Z By region or country, A-Z
653 Advertising. Publicity. Public relations
653.2 Direct-mail
653.3 Church bulletins. Church newsletters
Including clip art and cartoons
653.7 Church signs
Religious broadcasting
655 General works
655.2.A-Z By region or country, A-Z
Radio broadcasting
656 General works
656.2 Citizens band radio
656.3 Television broadcasting
656.4 Telephone in church work
657 The religious press
Ministry. Clergy. Religious vocations
For pastoral theology, including personal life of the clergy see BV4000+
For individual denominations see BX1+
General works
659 Early through 1800
660 1801-1950

Ecclesiastical theology
Ministry. Clergy. Religious vocations
General works -- Continued
660.2 1951-2000
660.3 2001-
By region or country see BR500+
662 Sermons, addresses, essays
For early works through 1800 see BV659
663 Addresses, essays, lectures
Including satire
664 Election. Selection, appointment, etc.
For ecclesiastical patronage see BR500+
Cf. BV4011.4 Vocation, internal call, etc.
Holy orders. Ordination
For sacrament of Ordination see BV830
664.5 General works
665 Apostolic succession
Episcopacy. Prelacy
General works
669 Early through 1800
670 1800-1950
670.2 1951-2000
670.3 2001-
671 Validity of non-episcopal ordination
671.3 Major orders
671.5 Minor orders
672 Parity
672.3 Per saltum
672.5 Ex-clergy
Kinds of ministries
For individual denominations see BX1+
Parish priests, presbyters, ministers, pastors see BV659+
673 Canons (Cathedral, collegiate, etc.). Minor canons
674 Associate ministers. Assistant ministers
675 Group ministry
675.5 Cooperative ministry
675.7 Clergy couples
Ministers of education see BV1531
Ministers of music see MT88
Itinerant ministers (Methodist) see BX8345
Chaplains see BV4375+
Coffee house ministry see BV4377
Missionaries see BV2059+
Evangelists see BV3750+
676 Women ministers. Ordination of women
676.3 Interim ministers
676.5 Part-time ministers

Ecclesiastical theology
Ministry. Clergy. Religious vocations
Kinds of ministries -- Continued
677 Lay ministry. Lay preachers
680 Elder. Deacon. Deaconess
Including ordained or installed local church officials
For "Elder" as title of clergyman see BV659+
For modern deacon and deaconess movement see BV4423+
683 Religious occupations. Church work as a profession
687 The layman in church organization. Rights, etc.
Cf. BV4400+ Church work for the layman
Cf. BV4525 Duties of laymen
Cf. BX1920 Catholic Church
690 See. Diocese
Parish. Congregation. The local church
700 General works
705 Church officers, trustees, ushers, etc.
707 Church records. Forms, etc.
Cf. BV773 Accounts, records, forms, etc.
Cf. BX1945 Catholic Church
710 Council. Synod. Presbytery
Including general policy only
For individual denominations see BX1+
720 General or ecumenical council. Conciliar theory
Sources of authority see BT88+
Freedom and authority. Discipline. Schism
740 General works
741 Religious liberty
Including history and principles, liberty of conscience, etc.
For church history in individual countries see BR500+
Church law. Discipline. Courts. Trials
see class K
Church finance
Cf. BV652.75 Church purchasing
Cf. BV705 Church officers, trustees, etc.
Cf. BV707 Church records, etc.
770 General works
771 Taxes for support of churches
772 Stewardship. Systematic giving. Christian giving. Tithing
Cf. BV4729 Precepts of the Church
772.5 Fund raising
773 Accounts, records, forms, etc.
Cf. BX1947 Catholic Church
773.5 Pew rents
774 Free sittings. Free churches
Cleric support see BV4380+

Ecclesiastical theology
Church finance -- Continued
774.5 Other
Church property. Benefices
Including gifts, bequests, etc.
Cf. HD101+ Land, including church lands
775 General works
777 Taxation of church property
779 Simony
Sacraments. Ordinances
For individual denominations see BX1+
800 General works
Baptism
For individual denominations see BX1+
Cf. GT2460+ Manners and customs
Cf. GT5080 Official ceremonies of royalty
803 History
Biblical sources see BS1+
807 Doctrinal sources in the early Church
Including liturgies
808 Archaeological works
809 Study and teaching. Catechisms
General works
810 Early through 1800
811 1801-1950
811.2 1951-2000
811.3 2001-
811.45 Element: Water
811.5 Mode of baptism. Immersion
811.6 Formula of baptism
811.7 Baptismal regeneration. Forgiveness of sin
811.8 Lay baptism
811.9 Heretical and schismatic baptism
812 Addresses, essays, lectures
Infant baptism. Pedobaptism
Including baptized children in the Church
General works
813.A2 Early through 1800
813.A3-Z 1801-1950
813.2 1951-2000
813.3 2001-
813.5 Baptism for the dead
Cf. BX8655.3 Mormonism
Water baptism vs. Spirit baptism (Society of Friends) see BX7748.B2
Baptism with the Holy Spirit see BT123
814 Other (not A-Z)

Ecclesiastical theology
Sacraments. Ordinances -- Continued
815 Confirmation
For individual denominations see BX1+
820 Church fellowship. Church membership
Including relation of the sacraments to membership
Holy Communion. Lord's Supper. Eucharist
For individual denominations see BX1+
Cf. BT420 Last Supper (Life of Christ)
823 History. Agape
Including the teaching of individual theologians
Cf. BV873.L6 Love feasts
General works
824 Early through 1800
825 1801-1950
825.2 1951-2000
825.3 2001-
Celebration. Liturgy
825.5 General works
825.52 Elements: Bread and wine
825.54 Consecration. Eucharistic prayers
Cf. BX2015.6 Catholic Church
825.56 Reservation
Terms of admission
825.58 Admission age
825.6 Fasting communion
825.7 Restricted communion. Close and open communion
825.8 Frequency of communion
825.85 First communion
Cf. BX2237 Catholic Church
825.9 World Communion Sunday
Communion sermons see BV4257.5
826.5 Devotional works for use by the communicant
827 Pamphlets
828 Other works. Stories, etc.
For communion tokens see CJ5407+
830 Holy Orders. Ordination
For individual denominations see BX1+
Marriage
For individual denominations see BX1+
835 General works
837 Sermons on marriage
Cf. BV4278 Marriage sermons (i.e. at a marriage service)
838 Remarriage
Penance
840 General works

Ecclesiastical theology
Sacraments. Ordinances
Penance -- Continued
Confession. Confession and absolution
For individual denominations see BX1+
845 General works
847 Controversial works against the confessional
Cf. BX2267 Catholic Church
850 Absolution
Unction
859 General works
860 Unction of the sick
Cf. BX2290 Catholic Church
873.A-Z Other, A-Z
873.E8 Exorcism
873.F7 Foot washing
Imposition of hands see BV873.L3
873.I54 Initiation rites
873.L3 Laying on of hands. Imposition of hands
873.L6 Love feasts
Cf. BV823+ Agape
Sacramentals
Cf. BX2295+ Catholic Church
875 General works
880 Consecration. Dedication of churches
Cf. BV199.D4 Liturgy and ritual of dedication
885 Holy water
890 Relics
Cf. BX2315 Catholic Church
Shrines. Holy places
Cf. BT580 Jesus Christ
Cf. BT650+ Mary, Virgin
Cf. BX2320+ Catholic Church
895 General works
896.A-Z By region or country, A-Z
Religious societies, associations, etc.
For individual religious denominations see BX1+
900 General works
International Order of the King's Daughters and Sons
910.A1 Periodicals. Societies
910.A3-Z General works
Salvation Army see BX9701+
930 United States Christian Commission
935.A-Z Other societies for both men and women, A-Z
e.g.
935.C5 Christian World Brotherhood
940 Religious societies for young people (General)

Ecclesiastical theology
Religious societies, associations, etc. -- Continued
Religious societies of men, brotherhoods, etc.
Cf. BV4410 Practical church work
950 General works
By period
955 Early through 1800
19th-20th centuries
960 General works
School and college societies, movements, etc.
Including associations for both young men and women
For societies for women alone see BV1300+
970.A1 General works
970.A3-Z Individual societies, movements, etc., A-Z
e.g.
970.I6 Inter-Varsity Christian Fellowship
970.N3 National Intercollegiate Christian Council
970.S6 Student Christian Movement of Great Britain and Ireland
970.W8 World's Student Christian Federation
Young Men's Christian Associations
1000 Periodicals
(1005) Yearbooks
see BV1000
1010 Congresses. Conferences
1020 Collected works
History
1030 General works
1032 World Alliance of Y.M.C.A.'s
1035 International Committee
1037 World's Committee, 1926-
United States
1040 General works
1045.A-.W By state, A-W
1050.A-Z By city, A-Z
1051.A-Z Associations in individual colleges, seminaries, etc., A-Z
e.g.
1051.B7 Brown University
1051.D6 Drew Theological Seminary
1051.Y3 Yale University
1060.A-Z Other countries, A-Z
1065.A-Z Other cities, A-Z
1070 Directories
Biography
1080 Collective

Ecclesiastical theology
Religious societies, associations, etc.
Religious societies of men, brotherhoods, etc.
By period
19th-20th centuries
Young Men's Christian Associations
Biography -- Continued
1085.A-Z Individual, A-Z
e.g.
1085.E3 Eddy, George Sherwood
1085.M3 McBurney, Robert Ross
1085.M4 Messer, Loring Wilbur
1085.M75 Mott, John Raleigh
1085.W4 Williams, Sir George
1090 General works
1095 Addresses, essays, lectures
1100 Organization and management
Including secretaryship, finance, advertising, etc.
1110 Buildings and equipment
Special branches of Y.M.C.A. work
County work see BV1210
1115 Religious work
1120 Social service
1125 Work in foreign countries
Educational work
Including the Y.M.C.A. colleges
1130 General works
1133.A-Z By city, A-Z
1140 Social life. Amusements, etc.
1145 Physical education
1150 Relief, etc.
Work with special classes
1160 Youth, especially boys
1165 Young adults (22-24)
1166 Adults (25+)
1170 College and school students
Cf. BV1051.A+ Y.M.C.A. in colleges, seminaries, etc.
1172 Families
1175 Commercial travelers
1180 Immigrants
1185 Industrial workers
1190 Blacks. African Americans
1200 Railroad employees
1210 Rural communities. "Country life"
Cf. BV638+ The rural church

Ecclesiastical theology
Religious societies, associations, etc.
Religious societies of men, brotherhoods, etc.
By period
19th-20th centuries
Young Men's Christian Associations
Work with special classes -- Continued
1220 Soldiers and sailors
For World War I, 1914-1918 see D639.Y7
For World War II, 1939-1945 see D810.Y7
Young Men's Christian Union
1250 Serials, reports, etc.
1260 General works
Biography
1265.A1 Collective
1265.A2-Z Individual, A-Z
e.g.
1265.B3 Baldwin, William Henry
1280.A-Z Other societies of men, A-Z
Religious societies of women
Cf. BV4420 Practical church work
Young Women's Christian Associations
1300 Periodicals
1310 Congresses
1320 Collected works
1330 Directories. Yearbooks
For individual cities see BV1355.A+
History
1340 General works
United States
1350 General works
1353.A-.W By state, A-W
1355.A-Z By city, A-Z
1356.A-Z Associations in individual schools and colleges, A-Z
1360.A-Z Other countries, A-Z
Biography
1365 Collective
1370.A-Z Individual, A-Z
e.g.
1370.C7 Cratty, Mabel
1370.D6 Dodge, Grace Hoadley
1370.G3 Gage, Frances Cousens
1370.S5 Simms, Florence
1375 General works
1377 Organization and management
Including secretaryship, finance, etc.
Education and training

Ecclesiastical theology
Religious societies, associations, etc.
Religious societies of women
Young Women's Christian Associations
Education and training -- Continued
1380 General works
1383 Textbooks
1385 Pageants, plays, etc.
1390 Addresses, essays, lectures
1392.A-Z Special branches of Y.W.C.A. work, A-Z
1393.A-Z Work with special classes, A-Z
African Americans see BV1393.B58
1393.B58 Blacks. African Americans
1393.B8 Business and professional women
1393.G5 Girls
Negroes see BV1393.B58
Professional women see BV1393.B8
1393.S4 Servants
King's Daughters see BV910.A1+
1395.A-Z Other, A-Z
For the individual denominations see BX1+
Other societies of young people
For the individual denominations see BX1+
Cf. BV4427+ Practical church work
1410 Lend a Hand Society
Young People's Society of Christian Endeavor, International Society of Christian Endeavor, etc.
1420 Periodicals
Conventions
1421.A1-.A5 International
1421.A1-.A4 Serials
1421.A5 Special. By date
1421.A6-Z Other
Biography
1423.A1 Collective
1423.A2-Z Individual, A-Z
e.g.
1423.C6 Clark, Francis Edward
1424 History
1425 General works
1426 Manual of methods, etc.
1427 Addresses, essays, lectures
1428.A-Z Special branches, A-Z
e.g.
1428.F6 Floating Society
1428.K5 Keystone League
1428.S4 Senior Society

Ecclesiastical theology
Religious societies, associations, etc.
Other societies of young people
Young People's Society of Christian Endeavor, International Society of Christian Endeavor, etc. -- Continued
1429 Junior Society
1430.A-Z Other, A-Z
e.g.
1430.A6 American Youth Foundation
Epworth League see BX8205
Westminster Fellowship see BX8905
Young People's Religious Union see BX9803
Societies for boys
1440.A1 General works
1440.A2-Z Individual societies, A-Z
Societies for girls
1450.A1 General works
1450.A2-Z Individual societies, A-Z
Religious education (General)
For religious education under individual denominations see BX1+
Cf. BS603 Bible schools and classes
Cf. BV4019+ Education for the ministry (General)
Cf. BX900+ Education for Catholic priesthood
Cf. LC321+ General education under church control
1460 Periodicals. Serials
1461 Dictionaries
1462 Collected works
1463 Conventions, conferences, etc.
1464 Theory, philosophy, etc.
History
1465 General works
United States
1467 General works
1468.A-.W By state, A-W
1469.A-Z By city, A-Z
1470.A-Z Other countries, A-Z
Biography
1470.2 Collective
1470.3.A-Z Individual, A-Z
General works
1471 Early through 1950
1471.2 1951-2000
1471.3 2001-
1473 Sermons, addresses, essays, etc.
By age group

Ecclesiastical theology
Religious education (General)
By age group -- Continued
Children (2-14)
Including the religious life of the child
Cf. BV1590 Religious training in the home
General works
1474 Early through 1800
1475 1801-1950
1475.2 1951-2000
1475.3 2001-
By age
1475.7 Two and three (Nursery children)
1475.8 Four and five (Kindergarten children)
Six to eleven see BV1474+
1475.9 Twelve to fourteen (Adolescents)
1477 Sermons, addresses, essays, etc.
1478 Sponsorship. Duties of godparents
1485 Young people (15-21)
1486 Young adults (22-24)
Adults
1488 General works
1489 Older people
Special kinds of school for religious education
Sunday schools (Church schools)
For Sunday-school extension in the United States see BV1516.A1+
For individual denominations see BX1+
1500 Periodicals. Serials
1503 Societies
1505 Congresses. Conventions. Institutes. Workshops
1505.A1 General works on organization, utility, etc.
1507 Collected works
1510 Dictionaries. Encyclopedias
History
1515 General works
By region or country
United States
1516.A1 General works
1516.A2A-.A2W By state, A-W
1516.A5-Z By city, A-Z
1517.A-Z Other regions or countries, A-Z
Biography
1518.A1 Collective
1518.A2-Z Individual, A-Z
General works
Including organization, management, etc.

Ecclesiastical theology
Religious education (General)
Special kinds of schools for religious education
Sunday schools (Church schools)
General works -- Continued

1519 Early through 1800
1520 1801-1950
1521 1951-2000
1521.3 2001-
1521.5 Juvenile works
1522 Worship in the church school
1523.A-Z Special topics, A-Z
1523.A37 African American Sunday schools
1523.A7 Attendance
1523.C6 Counseling, guidance, etc.
Cf. BV4409 Peer counseling in the church
1523.E9 Evangelism in the church school
Cf. BV2615+ Missionary work for and among children
1523.G75 Growth
1523.R2 Racial attitudes
1523.V5 Visitation
1523.5 Extension work
Cf. BV1516.A1+ Extension work in the United States
1524 Rural Sunday schools
1525 Sermons, addresses, essays, etc.
1526 Pocketbooks, calendars, etc.
For superintendents see BV1531
For teachers see BV1534+
1527 Records, forms, etc.
1528 Building and equipment
Cf. BV652.75 Church purchasing
Officers and teachers
1530 General works
Teachers and teaching see BV1534+
1531 Superintendent. Director of religious education. Minister of education
1532 Other officers. Secretary, treasurer, etc.
Cf. BV1527 Records, etc.
Teacher training. Leadership training
1533 General works
1533.5 Mentoring
Methods of teaching. Aids and devices
Cf. BV1579 Intergenerational Christian education
Cf. BV1587 Outdoor Christian education
1534 General works

Ecclesiastical theology
Religious education (General)
Special kinds of schools for religious education
Sunday schools (Church schools)
Methods of teaching. Aids and devices -- Continued

1534.2 Catechetics
Cf. BX1968 Catholic catechetics
Cf. BX8070.L8 Lutheran catechetics

1534.3 Storytelling
Cf. BS546 How to tell Bible stories to children

Illustrative stories, parables, phrases, anecdotes, etc. see BV4224+

Sermons and talks to children, Sunday school talks see BV4315

1534.4 The drama, pageants, etc., as method

1534.45 Biography as a teaching method

1534.5 Goup discussion

1534.7 Memory work

1534.75 Arts

1534.8 Music

Audiovisual aids

1535 General works

1535.Z9 Catalogs

1535.2 Pictures

1535.23 Maps

1535.25 Bulletin boards

1535.27 Blackboards

1535.3 Filmstrips

1535.4 Motion pictures
Including sound films

1535.5 Phonographs

1535.6 Tape recorders

1535.7 Radio

1535.8 Television

1535.9.A-Z Other, A-Z

1535.9.D73 Drawing

Origami see BV1535.9.P34

1535.9.P34 Paper work. Origami

1535.9.P8 Puppets. Puppet plays

1536 Manual methods for children. Occupations, busy work, etc.

1536.3 Games

1536.4 Electronic data processing

1536.5 Other
For Sunday school libraries see Z675.S9

BV

Ecclesiastical theology
Religious education (General)
Special kinds of schools for religious education
Sunday schools (Church schools) -- Continued
Special departments of the Sunday school

Except for pre-school children, the arrangement of the special departments is based on a three-year cycle. For two-year, four-year, and other cycles, see BV1549.5-BV1549.99.

Under each special department, include problems and textbooks; also include special departments of the weekday school, the vacation Bible school, etc.

1537 Cradle roll
Elementary
1538 General works
1539 Nursery (Ages 2 and 3)
1540 Kindergarten. Beginners (Ages 4 and 5). Pre-Reading group
1545 Primary (Ages 6 to 8)
1546 Junior (Ages 9 to 11)
Secondary
1547 General works
1548 Intermediate (Ages 12 to 14)
1549 Senior (Ages 15 to 17)
1549.2 Young people (Ages 18 to 21)
1549.3 Young adults (Ages 22 to 24)
1549.4 Young married people
Two-year, four-year, and other cycles

Classification numbers for the three-year cycle are provided in BV1537-BV1549.3. Because of the difficulty of intercalating two-year or four-year cycles, as well as works for public and private schools, special arrangements are provided for these other cycles in the numbers that follow

2-year cycles
1549.5 Elementary
1549.52 Primary (Ages 6 and 7)
1549.53 Junior (Ages 8 and 9)
1549.54 Secondary
1549.55 Intermediate (Ages 10 and 11)
1549.56 Senior (Ages 12 and 13)
1549.57 Young people (Ages 14 to 21)
4-year cycles
1549.6 Elementary
1549.62 Primary (Ages 6 to 9)
1549.63 Junior (Ages 10 to 13)
1549.64 Secondary

Ecclesiastical theology
Religious education (General)
Special kinds of schools for religious education
Sunday schools (Church schools)
Special departments of the Sunday school
Two-year, four-year, and other cycles
4-year cycles
Secondary -- Continued

1549.65 Intermediate (Ages 14 to 17)
1549.66 Senior (Ages 18 to 21)
6-3-3-4 cycle
1549.7 Elementary
1549.71 Grade 1
1549.72 Grade 2
1549.73 Grade 3
1549.74 Grade 4
1549.75 Grade 5
1549.76 Grade 6
1549.77 Junior High
1549.771 Grade 7
1549.772 Grade 8
1549.773 Grade 9
1549.78 Senior High
1549.781 Grade 10
1549.782 Grade 11
1549.783 Grade 12
(1549.785) College
Works for college are classified by subject
(1549.786) Year 1
(1549.787) Year 2
(1549.788) Year 3
(1549.789) Year 4
8-4-4 cycle
1549.8 Elementary
1549.81 Grade 1
1549.82 Grade 2
1549.83 Grade 3
1549.84 Grade 4
1549.85 Grade 5
1549.86 Grade 6
1549.87 Grade 7
1549.88 Grade 8
1549.9 High school
1549.91 Grade 9
1549.92 Grade 10
1549.93 Grade 11
1549.94 Grade 12

Ecclesiastical theology
Religious education (General)
Special kinds of schools for religious education
Sunday schools (Church schools)
Special departments of the Sunday school
Two-year, four-year, and other cycles
8-4-4 cycle -- Continued
(1549.95) College
Works for college are classified by subject
(1549.96) Year 1
(1549.97) Year 2
(1549.98) Year 3
(1549.99) Year 4
Adults. The men's class (Ages 25 and over)
1550 General works
1552 The women's class (Ages 25 and over)
Lesson materials
Cf. BS546+ Bible stories
Cf. BS2400+ New Testament stories
Cf. BT1029+ Catechisms
Cf. BX1+ Individual denominations
1558 General works
1559 Curricula. Outlines of courses, syllabi, etc.
Textbooks, lesson helps, etc.
International Sunday-school lessons
1560.A1-.A4 Official reports, etc.
1560.A5 History
1560.A6-Z Notes, commentaries, etc., on the lessons (Nonofficial)
1561 Other works
1565.A-Z Textbooks on special topics (not otherwise provided for in BR-BV). By subject, A-Z
e.g.
1565.C5 Citizenship
Service materials
For individual denominations see BX1+
Cf. BV283.S9 Sunday school prayers
Cf. BV520 Sunday school hymns
1570 General works
Special days
1572.A1 General works
1572.A2-Z Individual days, A-Z
e.g.
1572.C45 Children's Day
1572.C5 Christmas
1572.E2 Easter
1572.G6 Golden Rule Sunday

Ecclesiastical theology
Religious education (General)
Special kinds of schools for religious education
Sunday schools (Church schools)
Service materials -- Continued

1573 Other
Class here materials for entertainments, concerts, exercises, etc.

The church school in special relations

1576 With boys

1577 With girls

1578 With the home
Including church school parent-teachers associations, home departments, etc.

1579 Intergenerational

Other part-time agencies of religious education
Weekday schools. Released time. Saturday schools

1580 General works

1583 Textbooks and manuals

1585 Vacation schools. Summer camps
Including textbooks and manuals

1587 Outdoor religious education

1590 Religious education of children in the home

Religious education in public and private schools
Public schools see LC401+

1607 Parochial schools

1609 Preparatory schools

Colleges and universities

1610 General works

1612.A-Z Special departments and schools of religion, A-Z
Cf. BV4019+ Theological education
Cf. BX900+ Catholic theological education

1615.A-Z Special classes, groups, etc., A-Z
For special age groups see BV1474+

Children with mental disabilities see BV1615.M4

Children with social disabilities see BV1615.S6

1615.D4 Deaf

1615.D48 Developmentally disabled children

1615.H35 Handicapped. People with disabilities

1615.M37 Mental disabilities, People with

1615.M4 Mental disabilities, Children with. Slow learning children

People with disabilities see BV1615.H35

People with mental disabilities see BV1615.M37

Slow learning children see BV1615.M4

1615.S6 Social disabilities, Children with

Social life, recreation, etc., in the Church
Cf. BV4597+ Amusements and Christian life

Ecclesiastical theology
Social life, recreation, etc., in the Church -- Continued
1620 General works
1630 Parish houses
1635 Church dinners
1640 Recreation and physical culture for the young
Cf. BV4598 Physical education and Christianity
Cf. GV443 Physical training for children
1643 Motion pictures in the Church
Cf. BV1535.4 Religious education
Cf. PN1995.5 Relation to ethics, etc.
1645 Gymnasiums
Cf. GV403+ Gymnasiums (General)
1650 Camps. Work camps
Cf. BV1585 Summer camps (Religious education)
Cf. GV191.68+ Camping (General)
1651 Rest homes
1652 Church conference centers
Missions
Cf. BX9.5.M5 Missions and Christian union
General and foreign
2000 Periodicals. Serials
2010 Societies
2020 Congresses. Conferences
2025 Museums. Exhibitions
Collected works
2030 Several authors
2035 Individual authors
2040 Dictionaries. Encyclopedias
2045 Atlases
2050 Directories. Yearbooks, etc.
General works
2059 Early through 1800
2060 1801-1950
2061 1951-2000
2061.3 2001-
2063 General special
Missionary apologetics, etc.
2064 Popular works
e.g. Romance of missions
2065 Juvenile works
2067 Minor works. Pamphlets, etc.
2070 Addresses, essays, lectures, etc.
For collected works see BV2030+
Biography see BV3700+
Missiologists
2072 Collective biography

Missions
General and foreign
Missiologists -- Continued
2072.2.A-Z Individual biography, A-Z
Bible and missions
For the mission idea in the Old Testament see BS1199.M53
2073 General works
2074 Great Commission
2075 Sermons on missionary topics
2080 Criticisms of missions
2081 Mission finance
2082.A-Z Special problems and methods on the mission field, A-Z
Agricultural work see S532
2082.A8 Audiovisual aids
Including films, phonorecords, etc.
For radio see BV2082.R3
2082.A9 Aviation in missionary work
Bible publication and distribution see BV2369+
2082.B63 Boats in missionary work
Christian literature distribution see BV2369+
2082.D38 Data processing in missionary work
Education work see BV2630
2082.I45 Illiteracy
2082.I5 Indigenous church administration
2082.I57 Intercultural communication
2082.I6 Interdenominational cooperation
2082.L3 Language
2082.M3 Mass media in missionary work
Medical missions see R722+
Mission presses see BV2369+
Music see ML2999+
Polygamy see HQ992
2082.R3 Radio in missionary work
2082.S56 Short-term missions
Social problems and service see HN32
Tract distribution see BV2374+
2085 Readers. Speakers. Selections
2086 Missionary plays, pageants, etc.
2087 Missionary stories
Study and teaching about missions
Including textbooks
2090 General works
2090.5 Works for children and adolescents
Education and training of missionaries
2091 General works
2092.A-Z By region or country, A-Z

Missions
General and foreign
Education and training of missionaries -- Continued
2093.A-Z By institution, A-Z
2094 Leaves and furloughs
Personal life of missionaries
Missionaries' wives see BV2611
2094.5 Missionaries' children
2094.6 Psychology
2095 Missionary meetings. Programs, outlines, etc.
History and statistics
Cf. BV2050 Directories, yearbooks, etc.
2100 General works
2105 General special
e.g. Contributions to knowledge from missions
By period
2110 Early and medieval
For early history of Christianity see BR165+
2120 Modern
2121.A-Z Missionary activities of individual countries, A-Z
For Catholic missions see BV2190+
For Protestant missions see BV2410+; BV2410+
Special churches
2123 Orthodox Eastern Church
2127 Oriental churches
Catholic Church
Cf. BX1837 Congregation of the Propaganda
2130 Periodicals. Serials
2155 Societies. Institutions
2160 Congresses. Conferences
2165 Exhibitions
Collected works
2170 Several authors
2175 Individual authors
2178 Directories. Yearbooks
2180 General works
2183 Addresses, essays, lectures
2184 Catholic and Protestant missions compared
History
2185 General works
Missionary activities of individual countries
2190 United States
2195 Canada
2200 Great Britain
2210 France
2220 Italy
2230 Spain and Portugal

Missions
Special churches
Catholic Church
History
Missionary activities of individual countries -- Continued
2235 Developing countries
2240.A-Z Other, A-Z
e.g.
2240.B4 Belgium
Missions of individual monastic orders and societies of laymen
For activities limited to a specific region or country see BV2750+
For history of the order, in case of doubt see BX2400+
2245 Augustinians
2250 Benedictines
2255 Capuchins
2260 Cistercians
2270 Dominicans
Franciscans
2280.A1 Periodicals. Serials
2280.A2-Z General works
Jesuits
For Jesuit missions in New France see F1030.7+
Letters. Lettres edifiantes, etc.
For letters relating to New France see F1030.7+
Collected works. By first date
2290.A2 French
2290.A25-.A3 Translations (alphabetically)
e.g.
2290.A25 English
2290.A27 German
2290.A28 Italian
2290.A3 Spanish
2290.A5A-.A5Z Single volumes of collections. By language, A-Z
2290.A6-Z Works about Jesuit missions
2300.A-Z Other, A-Z
2300.C3 Carmelites
2300.C35 Catholic Foreign Mission Society of America. Maryknoll Fathers
Foreign Mission Sisters of St. Dominic see BV2300.M4
2300.G4 Gemeinschaft von den heiligen Engeln
2300.H64 Holy Spirit Missionary Sisters
2300.M3 Mariannhill Fathers
2300.M34 Marist Brothers

Missions
Special churches
Catholic Church
History
Missions of individual monastic orders and societies of laymen
Other, A-Z -- Continued
Maryknoll Fathers see BV2300.C35
2300.M4 Maryknoll Sisters
2300.M5 Missionary Canonesses of St. Augustine
2300.M53 Missionary Sisters of St. Columban
2300.O2 Oblates of Mary Immaculate
2300.P3 Papal Volunteers for Latin America
2300.P35 Passionists
(2300.P5) Pia società di San Francesco Saverio per le missioni estere
see BV2300.X84
2300.P54 Pii operai catechisti rurali
2300.S24 Salesians
2300.S5 Society of African Missions
2300.S53 Society of Catholic Medical Missionaries
2300.S6 Society of the Divine Word
2300.V56 Vincentians
2300.W5 White Fathers
2300.W6 White Sisters
2300.X84 Xaverian Missionary Fathers
Protestant churches
Periodicals
2350 American
2351 English
2352 Dutch
2353 French
2354 German
2355.A-Z Other, A-Z
e.g.
2355.S9 Swedish
Societies
For individual religious bodies see BV2495+
For societies relating to an individual country see BV2750+
For United States cities see BV2805.A+
2360 American
2361 English
2362 French
2363 German
2365.A-Z Other, A-Z
e.g.

Missions
Special churches
Protestant churches
Societies
Other, A-Z -- Continued
2365.S9 Swiss
Bible societies. Distribution of the Bible and other Christian literature
Including publication of the Bible
2369 General works
2369.5.A-Z By region or country, A-Z
2370.A-Z Individual societies, A-Z
e.g. American Bible Society, British and Foreign Bible Society
Biography
2372.A1 Collective
2372.A3-Z Individual, A-Z
Tract societies
2374 General works. History, etc.
2375.A-Z Individual societies, A-Z
e.g. American Tract Society, Boston; North China Tract Society
Tracts see BV4510.A1+
Biography of colporteurs
2380.A1 Collective
2380.A3-Z Individual, A-Z
e.g.
2380.P4 Perkins, George Augustus
2380.V3 Vassar, John Ellison
2390 Congresses
2395 Criticism of Protestant missions
Protestant and Catholic missions compared see BV2184
Collected works see BV2030+
General works see BV2059+
History
2400 General works
Missionary activities of individual countries
United States
2410 General works
2414.A-.W By state, A-W
2415.A-Z By city, A-Z
2416.A-Z By institution, A-Z
e.g.
2416.M6 Mount Holyoke College
2416.W5 Williams College
2417.A-Z By ethnic group, A-Z
e.g.

Missions
Special churches
Protestant churches
History
Missionary activities of individual countries
United States
By ethnic group, A-Z -- Continued

2417.S4 Scandinavian
2418 Canada
2420 Great Britain
2430 France
2440 Germany
2450 Netherlands
2458 Scandinavian countries
2460 Switzerland
2470.A-Z Other, A-Z

By denomination
Cf. BV2750+ Missions to individual countries (including home missions)

2495 Adventist (Table BV3)
2498 Anabaptist (Table BV3)
Cf. BV2545 Mennonite
2500 Anglican (Church of England) (Table BV3)
Baptist
2520 General works (Table BV3)
2521 African American Baptist (Table BV3)
2525 Christian Church (Table BV3)
2525.2 Christian Churches and Churches of Christ (Table BV3)
2526 Christian Reformed Church (Table BV3)
2528 Churches of Christ (Table BV3)
2530 Congregational (Table BV3)
2532 Disciples of Christ (Table BV3)
Episcopal Church see BV2575
2533 Evangelical and Reformed Church (Table BV3)
2535 Friends (Table BV3)
Cf. BX7748.I65 International activities
2540 Lutheran (Table BV3)
2545 Mennonite (Table BV3)
Cf. BV2498 Anabaptist
Methodist
2550 General works (Table BV3)
2551 African American Methodist (Table BV3)
2560 Moravian (Table BV3)
2565 Pentecostal churches (Table BV3)
Mormons see BX8661
2570 Presbyterian (Table BV3)

Missions
Special churches
Protestant churches
History
By denomination -- Continued
2575 Protestant Episcopal Church in the United States of America. Episcopal Church (Table BV3)
2580 Reformed Church in America (Dutch) (Table BV3)
2585 Reformed Church in the United States (German) (Table BV3)
Shakers see BX9779+
2590 United Brethren in Christ (Table BV3)
2592 United Church of Christ (Table BV3)
2595.A-Z Other, A-Z
Subarrange each denomination using .A1-5 for periodicals and societies
e.g.
2595.A8 Assemblies of God, General Council
2595.C47 Christian and Missionary Alliance
2595.C48 Church of God (Cleveland, Tenn.)
2595.C5 Church of the Brethren
2595.C6 Church of the Nazarene
2595.E8 Evangelical Church
2595.P4 Pentecostal Assemblies of the World
2595.S3 Salvation Army
2595.U5 Unitarian
2595.U53 United Church of Canada
2595.U55 United Evangelical Church
2595.U6 Universalist
Special types of missions
Work of women
For periodicals and societies, see general missions, home missions, etc.
2610 General works
2611 Missionaries' wives
Work among women
2612 Periodicals. Societies
2613 General works
Work for and among children
Cf. BV2065 Juvenile works on missions
2615 Periodicals. Societies
2616 General works
2617 Work of youth
Work among special classes. By religion
Class here works about the United States; class works about other countries with the country
Buddhists

Missions
Special types of missions
Work among special classes. By religion
Buddhists -- Continued
2618.A1 Periodicals. Societies
2618.A5-Z General works
2618.15.A-Z Individual missions, A-Z
2618.2.A-Z Biography of missionaries, A-Z
Biography of converted Buddhists
2618.3 Collective
2618.4.A-Z Individual, A-Z
e.g.
2618.4.M5 Miao-Chi
2618.4.Z9 Anonymous persons
Jews
2619 Periodicals. Societies
2620 General works
2621.A-Z Individual missions, A-Z
2622.A-Z Biography of missionaries, A-Z
Biography of converted Jews
2623.A1 Collective
2623.A2-Z Individual, A-Z
e.g.
2623.C3 Capadose, Abraham
2623.L4 Leila Ada
2623.Z9 Anonymous persons
Muslims
2625 General works
2626.A-Z Biography of missionaries, A-Z
Biography of converted Muslims
2626.3 Collective
2626.4.A-Z Individual, A-Z
2627 Mormons
2628.A-Z Other, A-Z
2628.A7 Armenians
2628.C65 Confucianists
Nestorians
2628.N4 General works
2628.N5A-.N5Z Biography, A-Z
2628.N5F5 Fiske, Fidelia
2628.N5S8 Stoddard, David Tappan
2630 Educational work of missionaries
Class here individual countries
Social service of missionaries see HN32
Agricultural missions see S532
Medical missions see R722+

Missions
Special types of missions
Medical missions -- Continued
Religious work of medical missionaries in individual countries see BV2750+

2637 Missions to leprosy patients
2650 Home missions (General)
Including Inner missions
For other than general works see BV2750+
2653 City missions (General)
Including biography
Cf. BV2750+ Missions in individual countries
Rescue missions
2655 General works
2656.A-Z Individual missions. By place, A-Z
e.g.
2656.C4P3 Pacific Garden Mission (Chicago)
2656.G7H3 Haven of Rest Rescue Mission (Grand Rapids)
2656.G7W4 West Fulton Street Gospel Mission (Grand Rapids)
2656.N4B67 Bowery Mission and Young Men's Home (New York)
2656.N4G65 God's Lighthouse Mission (New York)
Biography
2657.A1 Collective
2657.A2-Z Individual, A-Z
e.g.
2657.C7 Crittenton, Charles Nelson
2657.H3 Hadley, Samuel Hopkins
2657.M3 McAuley, Jeremiah
2657.R3 Ranney, David James
Work among special classes. By occupation
Sailors
Cf. HV3025+ Assistance and relief
Cf. VB290+ Sailors' homes
2660 Periodicals. Serials
2665 Societies
2670 General works
2672.A-Z By denomination, A-Z
2675.A-Z Individual churches, chapels, bethels. By place, A-Z
2678.A-Z Biography, A-Z
e.g.
2678.M3 Malmberg, Carl Axel
2678.T3 Taylor, Edward Thompson
2678.W3 Watson, Sydney
Soldiers
Including all branches of the defense establishments
Cf. UB380+ Soldiers' homes
2680 Periodicals. Societies

Missions
Special types of missions
Work among special classes. By occupation
Soldiers -- Continued
2685 General works
2690.A-Z By region or country, A-Z
For individual wars, see D-F, e.g. E635 for the United States Christian Commission in the Civil War
2692.A-Z Individual missions, A-Z
e.g.
2692.W5 Winchester, England. Soldiers' Home and Evangelistic Mission
2695.A-Z Other classes, A-Z
2695.B5 Blind
2695.E4 Emigrants
2695.F3 Farmers
2695.M5 Migrant labor
Prisoners see BV4465
2695.R3 Railroad men
2695.U64 Unemployed
2695.W6 Workingmen
Missions in individual countries
Class here the original missionary effort in a country and the continuing missionary effort. For the history of Christianity as established in a particular country, see BR500+. For biographies of native Christians, see BR500+ or BX
Unless otherwise specified .A3 is used under each for Periodicals, societies, etc.
2750 Groups of countries not in a particular geographical area
America
2755 General works
2757 Early through 1800
For sources of American history, see E-F
North America
2759 Societies. Congresses, etc.
2760 General works
United States
2762 Periodicals (General)
Cf. BV2766.A+ Individual denominations
2763 Societies (General)
Cf. BV2766.A+ Individual denominations
2765 General works
Biography
2765.5.A1 Collective
2765.5.A2-Z Individual, A-Z

Missions
Missions in individual countries
America
North America
United States -- Continued

2766.A-Z Individual denominations, A-Z

Under each (using successive Cutter numbers):

(1) Periodicals

(2) Societies

(3) General works

By period

2770 17th-18th centuries

2775 19th-20th centuries

2777 Juvenile works

2778 Study and teaching. Textbooks

By ethnic group

American Indians see E98.M6

Individual tribes see E99.A+

2783 African Americans

2784 Migrants

Immigrants and foreign elements in the United States

2785 General works

2787 Chinese

2788.A-Z Other, A-Z

2788.C3 Catholic immigrants

2788.F5 Filipino

2788.F7 French-Canadians

2788.G3 German

2788.H56 Hispanic

2788.I73 Iranian

2788.I8 Italian

2788.J3 Japanese

2788.L3 Latin-American

2788.M4 Mexican

2788.P64 Polish

2788.S68 Slavic

2788.S8 Swedish

2788.V53 Vietnamese

By region

2790 New England

2791 Northeastern states. Old Northwest

2793 Southern States

2796 Central States

2799 Western States

2800 Southwest. Spanish United States

Missions
Missions in individual countries
America
North America
United States
By region -- Continued
2801 Pacific Coast
Including the Canadian coast
2803.A-.W By state, A-W
2805.A-Z By city, A-Z
Including home missions, city missions, etc.
2806.A-Z Institutions. By place, A-Z
For rescue missions see BV2656.A+
2807.A-Z Biography of city missionaries, A-Z
e.g.
2807.E6 Emery, Joseph
2807.W5 Whittemore, Emma (Mott)
2808 American possessions
Canada and British America (General)
2810 General works
Biography
For works on early Jesuit missionaries see F1030.7+
2813.A1 Collective
2813.A2-Z Individual, A-Z
e.g.
2813.B7 Breynat, Gabriel Joseph Elie, Abp.
2813.F4 Feller, Henrietta (Odin)
2815.A-Z By region, province, territory, A-Z
e.g.
2815.L2 Labrador
2815.M6 Montreal
2815.N6 Northwest, Canadian
2815.Q3 Quebec
2815.R8 Rupert's Land
2815.Y8 Yukon
2820.A-Z By city, A-Z
Latin America
General works
2829 Early through 1800
2830 1801-1950
2831 1951-2000
2831.3 2001-
Biography
2832 Collective
2832.2.A-Z Individual, A-Z
Mexico

Missions
Missions in individual countries
America
Latin America
Mexico -- Continued
General works
2833 Early through 1800
2835 1801-1950
2835.2 1951-2000
2835.3 2001-
Biography
2836.A1 Collective
2836.A2-Z Individual, A-Z
2837.A-Z By region, state, etc., A-Z
Central America
2840 General works
2842 Biography
For individual countries see BV2843.A+
2843.A-Z By country, A-Z
2843.B8-.B9 Belize (Table BV4)
2843.C6-.C7 Costa Rica (Table BV4)
2843.G8-.G9 Guatemala (Table BV4)
2843.H6-.H7 Honduras (Table BV4)
2843.N5-.N6 Nicaragua (Table BV4)
2843.P3-.P4 Panama (Table BV4)
2843.S3-.S4 El Salvador (Table BV4)
West Indies
General works
2844 Early through 1800
2845 1801-1950
2845.2 1951-2000
2845.3 2001-
2846.A-Z Biography, A-Z
For individual islands or group of islands see BV2848.A+
2848.A-Z By island or group of islands, A-Z
e.g.
2848.C9-.C92 Cuba (Table BV4)
Danish Virgin Islands see BV2848.V5+
2848.D6-.D7 Dominican Republic (Table BV4)
2848.H3-.H4 Haiti (Republic) (Table BV4)
2848.J2-.J3 Jamaica (Table BV4)
2848.P7-.P8 Puerto Rico (Table BV4)
2848.V5-.V6 Virgin Islands of the United States (Table BV4)
2849 Bermudas
South America
For works before 1800 see BV2829

Missions
Missions in individual countries
America
Latin America
South America -- Continued

2850 Periodicals. Societies
2851 General works
Missions to Indians see F2230.1.M5
Biography
For individual countries see BV2853.A+
2851.8 Collective
2852.A-Z Individual, A-Z
2853.A-Z By country, A-Z
2853.A7-.A8 Argentina (Table BV4)
Cf. BV2853.P4+ Patagonia
2853.B4-.B5 Bolivia (Table BV4)
2853.B6-.B7 Brazil (Table BV4)
2853.B8-.B9 British Guiana. Guyana (Table BV4)
2853.C5-.C6 Chile (Table BV4)
2853.C7-.C8 Colombia (Table BV4)
2853.D8-.D9 Dutch Guiana. Netherlands Guiana. Suriname (Table BV4)
2853.E15-.E16 Easter Island (Table BV4)
2853.E2-.E3 Ecuador (Table BV4)
2853.F8-.F9 French Guiana (Table BV4)
Netherlands Guiana see BV2853.D8+
2853.P2-.P3 Paraguay (Table BV4)
2853.P4-.P5 Patagonia (Table BV4)
2853.P6-.P7 Peru (Table BV4)
Suriname see BV2853.D8+
2853.U8-.U9 Uruguay (Table BV4)
2853.V4-.V5 Venezuela (Table BV4)
Europe
2855 General works
Biography
2855.5 Collective
2855.6.A-Z Individual, A-Z
2857.A-Z By race or ethnic group, A-Z
e.g.
2857.S7 Slovenes
Great Britain
2860 General works
England
2863 General works
2864.A-Z By county, region, A-Z
2865 London
2867.A-Z Other cities, A-Z

Missions
Missions in individual countries
Europe
Great Britain -- Continued
Scotland
2870 General works
2873.A-Z By county, region, A-Z
2875.A-Z By city, A-Z
Ireland
2880 General works
2883.A-Z By county, region, A-Z
2885.A-Z By city, A-Z
2890.A-Z Other special, A-Z
2895 British colonies (General)
Continental Europe
2900 General works
Austria
2910 General works
2913.A-Z By province, region, etc., A-Z
e.g.
Bohemia see BV3145.C9
2915.A-Z By city, A-Z
Belgium
2920 General works
2923.A-Z By province, region, etc., A-Z
2925.A-Z By city, A-Z
Bulgaria
2930 General works
2933.A-Z By province, region, etc., A-Z
2935.A-Z By city, A-Z
France
2940 General works
2943.A-Z By region, department, etc., A-Z
2945.A-Z By city, A-Z
Germany
Including Innere Mission
2950 General works
2953.A-Z By province, region, etc., A-Z
2955.A-Z By city, A-Z
2957.A-Z Biography, A-Z
e.g.
2957.W5 Wichern, Johann Hinrich
Greece
2960 General works
2963.A-Z By province, region, etc., A-Z
2965.A-Z By city, A-Z
2967.A-Z Biography, A-Z

Missions
Missions in individual countries
Europe
Continental Europe -- Continued
Italy
2970 General works
2973.A-Z By province, region, etc., A-Z
2975.A-Z By city, A-Z
Luxemburg
2980 General works
2983.A-Z By region, etc., A-Z
2985.A-Z By city, A-Z
Netherlands (Holland)
3000 General works
3003.A-Z By province, region, etc., A-Z
3005.A-Z By city, A-Z
Portugal
3010 General works
3013.A-Z By district, region, etc., A-Z
3015.A-Z By city, A-Z
Romania
3020 General works
3023.A-Z By county, region, etc., A-Z
3025.A-Z By city, A-Z
Russia. Soviet Union. Russia (Federation)
3030 General works
3033.A-Z By republic, region, etc., A-Z
3035.A-Z By city, A-Z
3037.A-Z Biography, A-Z
3040 Finland
3050 Poland
Scandinavia
3060 General works
Denmark
3070 General works
3073.A-Z By province, region, etc., A-Z
3075.A-Z By city, A-Z
3077.A-Z Biography, A-Z
Greenland see BV3690+
3085 Iceland
Norway
3090 General works
3093.A-Z By province, region, etc., A-Z
3095.A-Z By city, A-Z
3097.A-Z Biography, A-Z
Sweden
3100 General works

Missions
Missions in individual countries
Europe
Continental Europe
Scandinavia
Sweden -- Continued
3103.A-Z By province, region, etc., A-Z
3105.A-Z By city, A-Z
3107.A-Z Biography, A-Z
Yugoslavia
3110 General works
3113.A-Z By province, region, etc., A-Z
3115.A-Z By city, A-Z
Spain
3120 General works
3123.A-Z By province, region, etc., A-Z
3125.A-Z By city, A-Z
3127.A-Z Biography, A-Z
Switzerland
3130 General works
3133.A-Z By canton, region, etc., A-Z
3135.A-Z By city, A-Z
Turkey see BV3170+
3145.A-Z Other, A-Z
e.g.
3145.C9 Czechoslovakia
3147 Mediterranean Region. The Levant
Asia. The Orient. The East
General works
3149 Early through 1800
3150 1801-1950
3151 1951-2000
3151.3 2001-
Biography
3152.4 Collective
3152.5.A-Z Individual, A-Z
Asia Minor. Southwestern Asia. The Middle East
3160 General works
Turkey
3170 General works
3173.A-Z By vilayet, region, A-Z
3175.A-Z By city, A-Z
3177.A-Z Biography, A-Z
Arabia
3180 General works
3182.A-Z Biography, A-Z
Armenia

BV

Missions
Missions in individual countries
Asia. The Orient. The East
Asia Minor. Southwestern Asia. The Middle East
Armenia -- Continued
3190 General works
3192.A-Z Biography, A-Z
Palestine. Syria. Israel
3200 General works
3202.A-Z Biography, A-Z
3210.A-Z Other, A-Z
e.g.
3210.C9 Cyprus
3210.I7 Iraq
3210.J6 Jordan
3210.L4 Lebanon
Persia. Iran
3215 General works
3217.A-Z Biography, A-Z
Central Asia
3220 General works
3225 Afghanistan
3230 Mongolia. Outer Mongolia
Cf. BV3420.M7 China
Former Soviet Central Asia. West Turkestan
3235 General works
3240.A-Z By region, republic, province, etc., A-Z
e.g.
3240.B6 Bokhara
3240.K3 Kazakhstan
3240.K4 Khiva. Khorezm
Khorezm see BV3240.K4
3240.K5 Kirghizistan
3240.S3 Samarkand
3240.T3 Tajikistan
3240.T8 Turkmenistan
3240.U9 Uzbekistan
Southern Asia
3250 General works
3255.A-Z By race, A-Z
e.g.
3255.L2 Laos
Pakistan
3256 General works
3258.A-Z Biography, A-Z
Bangladesh
3259 General works

Missions
Missions in individual countries
Asia. The Orient. The East
Southern Asia
Bangladesh -- Continued
3259.5.A-Z Biography, A-Z
India. East Indies (General)
3260 Periodicals. Societies
General works
3263 Early through 1800
3265 1801-1950
3265.2 1951-2000
3265.3 2001-
By period
3267 Before 1800 (modern works)
19th-20th centuries
see BV3265+
Biography
3269.A1 Collective
3269.A2 Women
3269.A3-Z Individual, A-Z
e.g.
3269.A65 Andrews, Charles Freer
3269.C3 Carey, William
3269.C4 Chundra Lee
3269.C5 Clark, Robert
3269.D8 Duff, Alexander
3269.L5 Lievens, Constant
3269.S6 Skrefsrud, Lars Olsen
By kingdom, state, region, etc.
Burma. The Karens
3270 General works
Biography
3271.A1 Collective
3271.A2-Z Individual, A-Z
e.g.
3271.J7 Judson, Adoniram
3271.J8 The Mrs. Judsons
3271.J81 Ann Hasseltine
3271.J82 Sarah (Hall) Boardman
3271.J83 Emily Chubbuck
Sri Lanka
3275 General works
3277.A-Z Biography, A-Z
3280.A-Z Other, A-Z
e.g.
3280.A8 Assam

Missions
Missions in individual countries
Asia. The Orient. The East
Southern Asia
India. East Indies (General)
By kingdom, state, region, etc.
Other, A-Z -- Continued
3280.K3 Kashmir
3280.M25 Madras
3280.N6 North-West Frontier Province
3280.O7 Orissa
3280.P8 Punjab
3280.S3 Santals
3280.T3 Tamils
3280.T4 Telugus
3290.A-Z By city, A-Z
Southeast Asia
3298 General works
Biography
3299 Collective
3299.5.A-Z Individual, A-Z
For biographies of individuals associated with one country, see the country
Indochina. Malay Peninsula
3300 General works
Cambodia
3305 General works
Biography
3306 Collective
3306.2.A-Z Individual, A-Z
Vietnam
3310 General works
Biography
3311 Collective
3311.2.A-Z Individual, A-Z
3312.A-Z By region, state, etc., A-Z
e.g.
Annam
3312.A55 General works
Biography
3312.A552 Collective
3312.A553A-.A553Z Individual, A-Z
Cochin China
3312.C63 General works
Biography
3312.C632 Collective
3312.C633A-.C633Z Individual, A-Z

Missions
Missions in individual countries
Asia. The Orient. The East
Southeast Asia
Indochina. Malay Peninsula
Vietnam
By region, state, etc., A-Z -- Continued
Tongking (Tonkin)
3312.T65 General works
Biography
3312.T652 Collective
3312.T653A-.T653Z Individual, A-Z
Thailand
3315 General works
Biography
3316 Collective
3317.A-Z Individual, A-Z
3320 Malaysia. Malaya
Including Sabah and Sarawak
3324 Singapore
3325.A-Z Other, A-Z
e.g.
Annam. Vietnam see BV3310+
3325.L3 Laos
Tongking (Tonkin) see BV3312.T65+
Vietnam see BV3310+
Malay Archipelago
3330 General works
Indonesia
3340 General works
Biography
3342.A1 Collective
3342.A2-Z Individual, A-Z
3345 Borneo
For Sabah and Sarawak see BV3320
For Brunei see BV3378
3350 Celebes
3355 Java
3360 Moluccas
3365 Sumatra
3370.A-Z Other, A-Z
3370.B3 Bali (Island)
3370.F66 Flores (Island)
3370.H3 Halmahera

Missions
Missions in individual countries
Asia. The Orient. The East
Southeast Asia
Malay Archipelago
Indonesia
Other, A-Z -- Continued

3370.I7 Irian Barat. Irian Jaya. Papua
Class here works on the Indonesian province of Papua, formerly called Irian Barat and Irian Jaya
For works on the island of New Guinea as a whole and for works on the country of Papua New Guinea see BV3680.N5+

3370.N5 Nias Island

(3370.N6) North Borneo, Sabah
see BV3320

3370.N87 Nusa Tenggara

Portuguese Timor see BV3370.T56

Pulaupulau Riouw see BV3370.R5

3370.R5 Rhio Archipelago

3370.S3 Sangir Islands

3370.S6 Soemba

3370.S78 Sumba Island

3370.S8 Sunda Islands

3370.T56 Timor. Timur

Timur see BV3370.T56

3373.A-Z By ethnic group, A-Z

3373.C54 Chinese

3373.J35 Jalé

3373.M67 Mori

3373.S3 Sawi

3373.T67 Toraja

3373.U35 Uhunduni

3378 Brunei

Philippines

3380 General works

Biography

3382.A1 Collective

3382.A2-Z Individual, A-Z

3390.A-Z Other, A-Z
e.g.

3390.A5 Amboyna

Eastern Asia

3400 General works

Biography

3403 Collective

Missions
Missions in individual countries
Asia. The Orient. The East
Eastern Asia
Biography -- Continued
3405.A-Z Individual, A-Z
For biographies of individuals associated with one country, see the country
China
3410 Periodicals. Societies. Congresses
General works
3413 Early through 1800
3415 1800-1949
3415.2 1950-
By period
3417 Before 1800 (Modern works)
19th-20th centuries
see BV3415+
3420.A-Z By province, region, etc., A-Z
e.g.
3420.A5 Anhwei
3420.C5 Chekiang
3420.H6 Honan
3420.K8 Kwangsi
3420.M2 Manchuria
3420.M7 Mongolia
3420.S45 Shantung
3420.S6 Shensi
3420.S85 Szechwan
3420.T5 Tibet
3420.Y8 Yunnan
3423.A-Z By tribe, A-Z
e.g.
3423.L5 Lisu
3423.L6 Lolos
3425.A-Z By city, A-Z
Biography
3427.A1 Collective
3427.A2-Z Individual, A-Z
e.g.
3427.G5 Gilmour, James
3427.M6 Morrison, Robert
3427.R5 Richard, Timothy
3427.S8 Stam, John Cornelius
3427.T3 Taylor, James Hudson
Taiwan
3430 General works

Missions
Missions in individual countries
Asia. The Orient. The East
Eastern Asia
Taiwan -- Continued
Biography
3431 Collective
3431.2.A-Z Individual, A-Z
Japan
3440 Periodicals. Societies. Congresses
General works
3443 Early through 1800
3445 1801-1950
3445.2 1951-2000
3445.3 2001-
By period
3447 Before 1800 (Modern works)
19th-20th centuries
see BV3445+
3450.A-Z By province, island, region, etc., A-Z
Under each:
.x General works
Biography
.x2A2 Collective
.x2A3-.x2Z Individual, A-Z
3455.A-Z By city, A-Z
Biography
3457.A1 Collective
3457.A2-Z Individual, A-Z
e.g.
3457.K3 Kagawa, Toyohiko
3457.N4 Neesima, Joseph Hardy
Niijima, Jō see BV3457.N4
Korea
3460 General works
Biography
3462.A1 Collective
3462.A2-Z Individual, A-Z
e.g.
3462.B7 Brelenieres, Just de
Northern Asia. Siberia
3470 Periodicals. Societies. Congresses
General works
3473 Early through 1800
3475 1801-1950
3475.2 1951-2000
3475.3 2001-

Missions
Missions in individual countries
Asia. The Orient. The East
Northern Asia. Siberia -- Continued
By period
3477 Before 1800 (Modern works)
19th-20th centuries
see BV3475+
3480.A-Z By province, region, etc., A-Z
3485.A-Z By city, A-Z
Biography
3487.A1 Collective
3487.A2-Z Individual, A-Z
Africa
3500.A1-.A7 Periodicals. Societies. Congresses
3500.A71-Z General works
Biography
3503 Collective
3505.A-Z Individual, A-Z
For the individual country or region see BV3560+
3510 North Africa
For the individual country or region see BV3560+
Central Africa. Sub-Saharan Africa
3520 General works
3522.A-Z Biography, A-Z
For the individual country see BV3625.A+
East Africa
3530 General works
3532.A-Z Biography, A-Z
For the individual country see BV3625.A+
West Africa
3540 General works
3542.A-Z Biography, A-Z
For the individual country see BV3625.A+
Southern Africa
For the individual country see BV3625.A+
3550 Periodicals. Societies, etc.
3555 General works
Biography, A-Z
e.g.
Livingstone, David see DT1110.L58
3557.M7 Moffat, Robert
3557.T5 Tiyo Soga
Southwest Africa see BV3625.N42+
By region or country
Ethiopia (Abyssinia)
3560 General works

Missions
Missions in individual countries
Africa
By region or country
Ethiopia (Abyssinia) -- Continued
Biography
3562.A2 Collective
3562.A3-Z Individual, A-Z
Egypt
3570 General works
Biography
3572.A2 Collective
3572.A3-Z Individual, A-Z
Barbary States
3580 General works
Algeria
3585 General works
Biography
3587.A2 Collective
3587.A3-Z Individual, A-Z
Morocco
3590 General works
Biography
3592.A2 Collective
3592.A3-Z Individual, A-Z
Libya (Tripoli)
3595 General works
Biography
3597.A2 Collective
3597.A3-Z Individual, A-Z
Tunisia (Tunis)
3600 General works
Biography
3602.A2 Collective
3602.A3-Z Individual, A-Z
3605.A-Z Other, A-Z
3625.A-Z Other regions or countries, A-Z
3625.A6-.A62 Angola (Table BV5)
3625.A7-.A72 Ashanti (Table BV5)
3625.B35-.B352 Barotseland (Table BV5)
3625.B4-.B5 Basutoland. Lesotho (Table BV5)
3625.B54-.B55 Bechuanaland. Botswana (Table BV5)
Benin see BV3625.D3+
Burkina Faso see BV3625.U7+
3625.B8-.B82 Burundi (Table BV5)
3625.C27-.C272 Calabar (Table BV5)
3625.C29-.C3 Cameroons (Table BV5)

Missions
Missions in individual countries
Africa
By region or country
Other regions or countries, A-Z
Cameroons -- Continued

3625.C32-.C33	British Cameroons (Table BV5)
3625.C34-.C35	French Cameroons (Table BV5)
3625.C37-.C372	Cape Verde (Table BV5)
3625.C4-.C42	Central African Republic (Table BV5)
3625.C47-.C48	Chad (Table BV5)
3625.C58-.C582	Comoros (Table BV5)
	Congo region. Zaire
3625.C6	General works
	Biography
3625.C62	Collective
3625.C63A-.C63Z	Individual, A-Z
3625.C7-.C72	Corisco (Table BV5)
	Côte d'Ivoire see BV3625.I8+
3625.D3-.D32	Dahomey. Benin (Table BV5)
	Equatorial Guinea see BV3625.G82+
3625.E7-.E72	Eritrea (Table BV5)
(3625.F4-.F5)	Fingoland see BV3630.F55
3625.F7-.F72	French West Africa (Table BV5)
3625.G2-.G3	Gabon (Table BV5 modified)
3625.G3A-.G3Z	Individual biography, A-Z e.g. Schweitzer, Albert see R722.32.S35
	Ghana see BV3625.G6+
3625.G6-.G62	Gold Coast. Ghana (Table BV5)
3625.G8-.G812	Guinea (Table BV5)
3625.G814-.G815	French Guinea. Guinea (Table BV5)
3625.G817-.G818	Portuguese Guinea. Guinea-Bissau (Table BV5)
3625.G82-.G822	Spanish Guinea. Equatorial Guinea (Table BV5)
3625.I5-.I52	Ijebus (Table BV5)
3625.I8-.I82	Ivory Coast. Côte d'Ivoire (Table BV5)
	Kaffraria see BV3625.S67+
3625.K4-.K42	Kenya (Table BV5)
	Kongo see BV3625.C6+
	Lesotho see BV3625.B4+
3625.L5-.L6	Liberia (Table BV5)
3625.M2-.M22	Madagascar (Table BV5)
	Malawi see BV3625.N8+
3625.M24-.M242	Mali (Table BV5)
3625.M29-.M3	Mashonaland (Table BV5)
3625.M32-.M33	Matabeleland (Table BV5)

Missions
Missions in individual countries
Africa
By region or country
Other regions or countries, A-Z -- Continued

3625.M343-.M344 Mauritius (Table BV5)
Mossiland see BV3625.U7+
3625.M65-.M66 Mozambique (Table BV5)
3625.N42-.N43 Namibia. Southwest Africa (Table BV5)
3625.N48-.N49 Niger region (Table BV5)
3625.N5-.N6 Nigeria (Table BV5)
3625.N78-.N782 Nyanza (Table BV5)
3625.N8-.N82 Nyasaland. Malawi (Table BV5)
3625.O9-.O92 Ovamboland (Table BV5)
3625.P6-.P62 Pondoland (Table BV5)
3625.R5-.R512 Rhodesia (Table BV5)
3625.R52-.R522 Northern Rhodesia. Zambia (Table BV5)
3625.R53-.R532 Southern Rhodesia. Zimbabwe (Table BV5)
3625.R8-.R82 Ruanda-Urundi. Ruanda. Rwanda (Table BV5)
Rwanda see BV3625.R8+
3625.S3-.S32 Saint Helena (Table BV5)
3625.S35-.S352 Senegal (Table BV5)
3625.S4-.S5 Sierra Leone (Table BV5)
3625.S56-.S562 Somalia (Table BV5)
3625.S67-.S672 South Africa (Table BV5)
Southwest Africa see BV3625.N42+
3625.S8-.S812 Sudan (Region) (Table BV5)
3625.S82-.S83 Sudan (Republic). Egyptian Sudan. Anglo-Egyptian Sudan (Table BV5)
3625.S9-.S92 Swaziland (Table BV5)
Tanganyika Territory see BV3625.T4+
3625.T4-.T42 Tanzania (Table BV5)
3625.T6-.T62 Togo (Table BV5)
Transvaal see BV3625.S67+
(3625.U2-.U22) Ubangi Chari
see BV3625.C4+
3625.U3-.U4 Uganda (Table BV5)
3625.U6-.U62 Upper Nile (Table BV5)
3625.U7-.U72 Upper Volta. Mossiland. Burkina Faso (Table BV5)
3625.U8-.U82 Urundi (Table BV5)
Zaire see BV3625.C6+
Zambia see BV3625.R52+
3625.Z3-.Z32 Zanzibar (Table BV5)
Zimbabwe see BV3625.R53+
Zululand see BV3625.S67+

Missions
Missions in individual countries
Africa -- Continued

3630.A-Z By ethnic group, A-Z
Where name of ethnic group and country or region are basically alike, see the country or region
3630.A4 Akans
3630.B23 Bacama
3630.B24 Bakongo
3630.B25 Bamangwato
3630.B3 Bantus
3630.B39 Bayaka
3630.B46 Bemba
3630.B8 Bulu
3630.F55 Fingos
3630.G3 Gallas
3630.H3 Haya
Hottentots see BV3630.K47
Ibos see BV3630.I2
3630.I2 Igbo
3630.K3 Kagoro
3630.K32 Kaguru
3630.K35 Kamwe
3630.K45 Kgatla
3630.K47 Khoikhoi
3630.K5 Kikuyu
3630.K63 Koma (Nigerian and Cameroon people)
3630.L6 Lozi
3630.M25 Makua
3630.M3 Masai
3630.M32 Mashona
3630.M35 Mbata
3630.M64 Mongo
3630.N9 Nyanja
3630.R64 Rolong
3630.T58 Tiv
3630.X65 Xosa
3630.Y6 Yoruba

Oceania
3640 General works
Australia (and New Zealand)
3650 General works
3660.A-Z By state, territory, A-Z
e.g.
3660.N6 New South Wales
3660.T2 Tasmania

Missions
Missions in individual countries
Oceania
Australia (and New Zealand) -- Continued
3665 New Zealand
Including missions to Maori
Biography
3667.A1 Collective
3667.A2-Z Individual, A-Z
e.g.
3667.F5 Flynn, John
3667.M3 Marsden, Samuel
3667.S8 Stack, James West
Pacific islands. South Sea islands
3670 General works
3672.A-Z Biography, A-Z
For the individual islands see BV3680.A+
By group of islands
Melanesia
3675 General works
Biography
3676.A1 Collective
3676.A2-Z Individual, A-Z
e.g.
3676.P3 Patteson, John Coleridge, Bp.
Micronesia
3677 General works
Biography
3678.A1 Collective
3678.A2-Z Individual, A-Z
e.g.
3678.W5 Wilson, Eleanor
Polynesia
3678.5 General works
Biography
3678.6.A1 Collective
3678.6.A2-Z Individual, A-Z
3680.A-Z By individual island, A-Z
Including groups of islands other than those classed in BV3675-BV3678.6
3680.B3-.B32 Bachian (Island) (Table BV5)
3680.B5-.B52 Bismarck Archipelago (Table BV5)
3680.C3-.C32 Caroline Islands (Table BV5)
3680.C45-.C452 Chuuk. Truk (Table BV5)
3680.C66-.C662 Cook Islands (Table BV5)
Easter Island see BV2853.E15+
3680.F5-.F6 Fiji Islands (Table BV5 modified)

Missions
Missions in individual countries
Oceania
Pacific islands. South Sea islands
By individual island, A-Z
Fiji Islands -- Continued

3680.F6A-.F6Z Individual biography, A-Z
e.g.
3680.F6C3 Calvert, James
3680.F6H77 Hunt, John
3680.F8-.F82 French Polynesia (Table BV5)
3680.G5-.G52 Gilbert Islands (Table BV5)
3680.G8-.G82 Guam (Table BV5)
Hawaiian Islands. Sandwich Islands
3680.H2 Periodicals. Societies
3680.H3 General works
Biography
3680.H4A1 Collective
3680.H4A2-.H4Z Individual, A-Z
e.g.
3680.H4A4 Alexander, William Patterson
3680.H4C6 Coan, Titus
3680.H4P68 Puaaiki, Batimea
3680.H4T4 Thurston, Lucy (Goodale)
3680.L5-.L52 Likiep Atoll (Table BV5)
3680.M28-.M282 Mariana Islands (Table BV5)
3680.M3-.M32 Marquesas Islands (Table BV5)
3680.M35-.M352 Marshall Islands (Table BV5)
3680.M6-.M62 Molokai (Table BV5)
3680.N4-.N42 New Caledonia (Table BV5)
3680.N5-.N52 New Guinea (Table BV5)
Including Papua New Guinea
For the Indonesian province of Papua see BV3370.I7
For life of James Chalmers see DU746.C4
3680.N59-.N6 New Hebrides (Table BV5 modified)
3680.N6A-.N6Z Individual biography, A-Z
e.g.
3680.N6P37 Paton, John Gibson
3680.P5-.P52 Pitcairn (Table BV5)
3680.R3-.R32 Rarotonga (Table BV5)
3680.S3-.S32 Samoa (Table BV5)
3680.S6-.S62 Solomon Islands (Table BV5)
3680.T2-.T3 Tahiti (Table BV5)
3680.T6-.T62 Tonga (Table BV5)
Truk see BV3680.C45+

Missions
Missions in individual countries -- Continued
Arctic regions
Cf. BV2810+ Canada
3690 General works
3695.A-Z Individual biography, A-Z
e.g.
3695.E4 Egede (Hans and Poul)
3697 Missions to Romanies (Gypsies)
Biography
3700 Collective
For works concerned with: missionaries from a single country to several countries, see BV2190+, BV2410+; missionaries from a single country to a single country, see BV2807; BV2813; BV2836; etc.; collective biography of missionaries from a specific denomination or religious order to several countries, see BV2123; BV2185; BV2245; BV2495; etc.; missionaries from a specific denomination or religious order to a single country, see BV2807; BV2813; BV2842; etc.
3703 Women
3705.A-Z Individual, A-Z
For missionaries to special classes, types, etc., see BV2618.4; BV2657; etc.
For persons active in a single country, see BV2807; BV2813; etc.
Class here persons active in more than one country regardless of their religious affiliation, e.g.
3705.F7 Franson, Fredrik
3705.M3 Martyn, Henry
3705.M5 Miles, Samuel John
Evangelism. Revivals
3750 Periodicals. Serials
3752 Societies
3755 Congresses. Conferences. Councils
3760 Collected works
History of revivals and evangelistic work
For individual evangelists see BV3785.A+
Cf. BR195.E9 Evangelism in the early Church
3770 General works
America. United States
For early history in the United States see BR513+
3773 General works
3774.A-Z By region or state, A-Z
3775.A-Z By city, A-Z
3777.A-Z Other regions or countries, A-Z

Evangelism. Revivals -- Continued
Biography and memoirs of evangelists
Including stories from personal experience
3780 Collective
3785.A-Z Individual, A-Z
e.g.
3785.A4 Alexander, Charles McCallon
3785.C3 Caughey, James
3785.G69 Graham, William Franklin
3785.M7 Moody, Dwight Lyman
3785.O7 Orr, James Edwin
3785.S6 Smith, Rodney (Gipsy Smith)
3785.S8 Sunday, William Ashley
3790 General works
3793 General special
3795 Addresses, essays, lectures
3796 Study and teaching. Textbooks
Works by evangelists. Sermons, etc.
3797.A1 Several authors
3797.A3-Z Individual authors, A-Z
Evangelistic work with special classes
see BV2612+ Missionary work among special classes; BV4440+ Church work with special classes; BV4922+ Works for the conversion of special classes; BX2347.5 Parish missions
Camp meetings
Cf. BV1585 Summer camps for children
Cf. BV1650 Camps, summer camps
Cf. BX8475+ Methodist Church
3798 General works
3799.A-Z Individual meetings, A-Z
Pastoral theology
Cf. BX9.5.P3 Christian union and pastoral theology
4000 Periodicals. Societies
4002 Congresses. Conventions
4005 Collected works
4005.5 Dictionaries
4006 History
For early Church see BR195.P36
General works
4009 Early through 1800
4010 1801-1950
4011 1951-2000
4011.3 2001-
Special
Office see BV659+
4011.4 Vocation, internal call, etc.

Pastoral theology
Special -- Continued
4011.5 Ethics and etiquette
4011.6 Spiritual development. Prayer. Religious life
Group ministry see BV675
4011.7 Professional development. Study of the Bible
4011.8 Sabbatical leave
Pastoral psychology and psychiatry
4012 General works
4012.2 Pastoral counseling
Cf. BV4409 Peer counseling in the Church
4012.25 Counseling centers: organization, etc.
Counseling of special groups, etc. see BV4435+
4012.27 Marriage counseling. Divorce mediation
4012.3 Pastoral work in mental institutions
Pastoral work in cities see BV637.5
Pastoral work in rural areas see BV638.7
Other pastoral offices see BV4320+
4013 Other aspects of the ministry
4014 Pastoral life. Scenes and incidents
4015 Popular works. Anecdotes, etc.
Cf. BV638.8 Popular works, stories, etc. on the rural church
Cf. PN6231.C5 Wit and humor (Clerical)
4016 Handbooks. Manuals, etc.
4017 Addresses, essays, lectures
Education
Training for the ordained ministry
Including theological seminaries, theological departments or schools in universities, and Bible institutes
4019 Periodicals. Societies, etc.
4020 General works
4022 Addresses, essays, lectures
4023 History of the study of theology
For general history of theological education in individual denominations see BX1+
By region or country
United States
4025 Periodicals. Serials
4030 General works
4033 New England
4035 Central
4037 South
4039 West
4040.A-.W By state, A-W

Pastoral theology
Education
Training for the ordained ministry
By region or country
United States -- Continued
4070.A-Z By institution, A-Z
Subarrange individual institutions by Table BV7 unless Table BV6 has already been applied to a specific institution. Where Table BV6 has already been applied for a specific institution, continue to apply that table for the institution
The Cutter number span for the institution listed below is provided as an example
For Orthodox Eastern Church institutions see BX483 BX612.8 etc.; for Roman Catholic institutions see BX915+
4070.A51-.A589 Andover Newton Theological School (Table BV6)
Education of African American ministers
4080 General works
4085.A-Z By institution, A-Z
4140.A-Z Other regions or countries, A-Z
American institutions abroad
4150.A2 General works
4150.A3-Z By institution, A-Z
4160.A-Z Other institutions, A-Z
Subarrange each institution by Table BV7
4163 Pretheological (Preseminary) education
4163.5 Cooperative ventures among theological seminaries
4164 Seminary extension
4164.5 Fieldwork. Theological field education
4165 Post-ordination training
4166 Administration and trusteeship of theological schools
4166.5 Theological seminary presidents, deans, rectors
4167 Finance
Training for lay workers
Cf. BV4401 Training for practical church work
4168 Periodicals. Societies. Collections, etc.
4170 General works
4171 History
By region or country
United States
4172 Periodicals. Societies
4173 General works
4175.A-.W By state, A-W
4176.A-Z By institution, A-Z
Subarrange each institution by Table BV7
Other regions or countries, A-Z

Pastoral theology
Education
Training for lay workers
By region or country
Other regions or countries, A-Z -- Continued
4178 General works
American institutions abroad
4179.A2 General works
4179.A3-Z By institution, A-Z
4180.A-Z Other institutions, A-Z
Subarrange each institution by Table BV7
Preaching. Homiletics
4200 Periodicals. Serials
4202 Congresses. Conferences
4205 Collected works
4206 Dictionaries. Encyclopedias
History
Including studies of great preachers
4207 General works
4208.A-Z By region or country, A-Z
General works. Treatises
4209 Latin
English and American
4210 Early through 1800
4211 1801-1950
4211.2 1951-2000
4211.3 2001-
4212 Dutch
4213 French
4214 German
4215 Italian
4216 Scandinavian
4217 Spanish and Portuguese
4219.A-Z Other languages, A-Z
4221 Other works
4222 Sermons, addresses, essays, etc. on preaching
4223 Outlines, texts, etc.
For Catholic sermon outlines see BX1756.A1
Illustrations for sermons
Including catechetical illustrations
Cf. BV4307.S7 Story sermons
4224 Early through 1800
4225 1801-1950
4225.2 1951-2000
4225.3 2001-
4226 Use of illustrations
4227 Audio-visual aids, object lessons, etc.

Pastoral theology
Preaching. Homiletics -- Continued
4230 Memoranda. Pocketbooks, etc.
4235.A-Z Special topics, A-Z
4235.A44 Aged, Preaching to. Older people, Preaching to
Cf. BV4316.A4 Sermons for older people
4235.A83 Asian Americans, Preaching to
4235.A87 Autobiographical preaching
4235.B56 Biographical preaching
Book review sermons see BV4235.B6
4235.B6 Books. Book review sermons
4235.C4 Children, Preaching to
Cf. BV4315 Sermons for children
4235.C47 Clown ministry
4235.C64 Collaborative preaching
4235.D4 Devotional exercises, Leading of
4235.D63 Doctrinal preaching
Doctrinal sermons see BV4235.T43
4235.D7 Dramatized sermons
4235.E75 Ethics of preaching
4235.E8 Extemporaneous preaching. Preaching without notes
4235.F44 Feminism
4235.H85 Humor
4235.H94 Hymn texts in sermons
4235.L3 Lay preaching
4235.L43 Lectionary preaching
4235.L57 Listening to sermons, preaching
4235.L58 Liturgical preaching
4235.M68 Motion pictures
4235.N65 Non church-affiliated people, Preaching to
Older people, Preaching to see BV4235.A44
4235.O7 Open-air preaching
4235.P7 Politics and the pulpit
Preaching without notes see BV4235.E8
4235.P79 Psychology of preaching
Public speaking see PN4173
4235.S6 Social problems
4235.S76 Storytelling
Cf. BV4307.S7 Story sermons
4235.T43 Teaching sermons. Doctrinal sermons
4235.T65 Topical preaching
4235.W65 Women, Preaching to
4235.Y6 Youth, Preaching to

Pastoral theology
Preaching. Homiletics -- Continued
Sermons
Sermons on the Bible if arranged in the order of the Bible and forming a substantial contribution to the study of the Bible or part of it are classified with the whole Bible or its parts
Sermons on any special subject are classified with the subject, e.g. BT753, Salvation; E188.5, U.S. Colonial history; E297, U.S. Revolution; D743.9, World War II
Sermons on an individual person are classed with the person, e.g. BT608, the Virgin Mary; E312.62+, George Washington
Sermons on a special topic relating to Jesus Christ are classed with the special topic; general sermons on Jesus Christ are classed here
For individual denominations see BX1+
Collections of sermons
Several authors from two or more denominations
4239 Polyglot
Individual languages (Original or translated)
Individual languages (Original or translated)
4240 Latin
4241 English
4241.A2 Middle English
4241.5 African American sermons. Black sermons
4242 Pamphlet collections
4243 French
4244 German
4245 Italian
4246 Scandinavian
4247 Spanish and Portuguese
4249.A-Z Other languages, A-Z
Individual authors
Including single sermons, also anonymous sermons, by title
For single sermons prefer the special kind or topic
For the individual denomination, whenever known, except in cases of transfer from one to another denomination see BX1+
4253 English
4254.A-Z Other languages, A-Z
Sermons for special occasions, days, festivals, etc., regardless of language or denomination
4254.2 Collections of occasional sermons for more than one occasion
4254.3 Collections of festival-day sermons for more than one festival

Pastoral theology
Preaching. Homiletics
Sermons
Sermons for special occasions, days, festivals, etc., regardless of language or denomination -- Continued
Individual occasions, days, festivals, etc.
Including single sermons
4254.5 Advent sermons
4254.7 All Saints' Day sermons
4254.75 American Revolution Bicentennial sermons
4255 Baccalaureate and commencement sermons. Graduation sermons
4255.2 Baptismal sermons
4257 Christmas sermons
Commencement sermons see BV4255
4257.5 Communion sermons
4257.7 Confirmation sermons
4258 Dedication sermons
4259 Easter sermons
4260 Election sermons
4260.A1 General collections
4260.A2-.W United States. By state
Under each state (unless otherwise specified):
.x Collections of sermons
.x2 Individual sermons. By date
Connecticut
4260.C8 Collections of sermons
4260.C9 Individual sermons. By date
Massachusetts
4260.M4 Collections of sermons
4260.M5 Individual sermons. By date
New Hampshire
4260.N4 Collections of sermons
4260.N45 Individual sermons. By date
Vermont
4260.V5 Collections of sermons
4260.V6 Individual sermons. By date
4261 Other than United States. By author
4262 Execution sermons
Class here sermons on the execution of criminals
4270 Fast-day sermons
4275 Funeral sermons
For sermons containing information about the deceased, see biography
4276 Good Friday sermons
Graduation sermons see BV4255
Holy Week sermons see BV4298

Pastoral theology
Preaching. Homiletics
Sermons
Sermons for special occasions, days, festivals, etc., regardless of language or denomination
Individual occasions, days, festivals, etc. -- Continued
4277 Lenten sermons
4278 Marriage sermons
Masonic sermons see HS397
4279 Memorial day sermons. Remembrance day sermons
Missionary sermons see BV2075
4281 Mother's Day sermons
4282 New Year's sermons
Ordination sermons
For individual denominations see BX1+
4285 General works
4290 Installation
4295 Consecration
4298 Passion Week sermons. Holy Week sermons
4300 Pastoral charges. Episcopal charges
4300.5 Pentecost sermons
4301 Radio and television sermons
For individual denominations see BX1+
Temperance sermons see HV5072
4305 Thanksgiving sermons
4306 Visitation sermons
4307.A-Z Sermons in special forms, A-Z
e.g.
4307.D5 Dialogue sermons
4307.S7 Story sermons
Cf. BV4235.S76 Storytelling in preaching
4308 Sermons for family devotions
Sermons and talks to special classes of persons
4309 Women
Cf. BV4313 Sermons and talks to young women
Young people (Students, etc.)
Cf. BV4255 Baccalaureate and commencement sermons
Cf. BX1756.Z8 Catholic sermons
4310 General works
4313 Young women
4315 Children
Including Sunday-school talks
For Catholic sermons see BX1756.Z9
Cf. BV4235.C4 Preaching to children
4316.A-Z Other, A-Z
4316.A37 Addicts

Pastoral theology
Preaching. Homiletics
Sermons
Sermons and talks to special classes of persons
Other, A-Z -- Continued
4316.A4 Aged. Older people
Cf. BV4235.A44 Preaching to older people
4316.C7 Court and courtiers
Courtiers see BV4316.C7
4316.F7 Farmers
4316.G6 Governors and governing bodies
4316.I7 Ironworkers
4316.J3 Judges
Magistrates (Governors, administrators, etc.) see BV4316.G6
4316.M5 Medical students
Older people see BV4316.A4
4316.P7 Prisoners
4316.R3 Railroad workers
4316.S3 Sailors
4316.S4 Servants
4316.S6 Slaves
4316.S7 Soldiers
4316.T4 Teachers
4316.T5 Theological students
4317 Selections for clergymen
4319 Communication
Other pastoral offices
For liturgy, prayers, etc. see BV169+
4320 The minister and his people. Pastoral visiting
Including lay visiting
Cf. BV652.3 Canvassing
Cf. BV1523.V5 Church school visitation
4325 Relations to the community
Cf. BV625 Church and community
4327 Relations to the state
4330 Service to the afflicted. Care of the bereaved
Service to the sick, suffering, and people with disabilities
4335 General works
4337 Healing of the sick
Cf. BT732.5+ Healing (Doctrinal theology)
Cf. RT120.P37 Parish nursing
Cf. RZ400+ Mental healing
4338 Terminally ill. Dying
4339 Service to the victims of crimes
4340 Service to prisoners
4341 Service to ex-convicts

Pastoral theology
Other pastoral offices -- Continued
4345 Counsels to communicants
4350 Confirmation lessons
4355 Relations to the young
4360 Relations to religious education and the church school
4365 The pastor emeritus
4370 Relations to missions
Evangelism see BV3750+
Chaplains
Cf. HV8867 Prison chaplains
Cf. UH20+ Military chaplains
Cf. VG20+ Naval chaplains
4375 General works
4375.5 Police chaplains
4376 School and college chaplains. Campus ministry
4377 Coffee house ministry
4379 Office organization. Filing systems
Cf. Z675.C5 Church libraries
4379.5 Time management
Cleric support
4380 General works
4381 Parsonages. Deaneries. Rectories. Vicarages
4382 Provision for old age
Cf. BV4365 The pastor emeritus
Homes for retired clergymen
4383.A1 General works
4383.A3-Z Special. By place, A-Z
e.g.
4383.D3 Daytona Beach, Fla. Olds Hall
4385 Relief of widows and orphans of clergymen
Personal life of the clergy
4390 Celibacy
Cf. BX1912.85 Catholic Church
Sexual behavior
4392 General works
4392.5 Sexual misconduct
4393 Marriage
4395 Wife
4395.5 Divorce
4396 Home and family
Including achievements of children
4397 Personal finance
Health and hygiene
4397.5 General works
Mental health
4398 General works

Pastoral theology
Personal life of the clergy
Health and hygiene
Mental health -- Continued
4398.5 Counseling centers
4399 Alcoholism
Cf. HV5186+ Alcoholism and Christianity
Practical church work. Social work. Work of the layman
Cf. BV598+ The Church and its influence
Cf. BV3750+ Evangelism
Cf. BV4320 Lay visiting
Cf. HN30+ The Church and social problems
Cf. HV530 Philanthropy
4400 General works
4401 Study and teaching. Training
Including textbooks
Cf. BV4168+ Training lay workers
Church work as a profession see BV683
By region or country
4403 United States
4404.A-Z Other regions and countries, A-Z
Communities and institutions, confraternities, brotherhoods, etc.
Including Protestant monasticism
For Catholic communities see BX2347.7+
4405 General works
4406.A-Z By region or country, A-Z
Individual communities, etc.
4406.8 L'Abri (Table BV8)
4406.9 American Colony (Jerusalem) (Table BV8)
4407 Bose (Table BV8)
4407.3 Christ Communal Organization (Table BV8)
4407.4 Community of Reconciliation (Bulawayo, Zimbabwe) (Table BV8)
4407.5 Corrymeela (Table BV8)
4407.6 Gamonal Community (Gamonal, Burgos, Spain) (Table BV8)
4407.63 Habitat for Humanity (Table BV8)
4407.65 Juhonkylä (Table BV8)
4407.67 Koinonia Partners (Americus, Ga.) (Table BV8)
Formerly Koinonia Community, then Koinonia Farm
4407.7 Michaelsbruderschaft (Table BV8)
4407.8 Reba Place Fellowship (Table BV8)
4408 Taize (Table BV8)
4408.5 Mentoring
4409 Peer counseling
4409.5 Respite care

Pastoral theology
Practical church work. Social work. Work of the layman -- Continued
By special classes of persons
Men
General works see BV4400+
4410 Men's clubs, brotherhood, etc.
Cf. BV950+ Religious societies, etc.
Women
4415 General works
4420 Societies, guilds, etc.
Cf. BV1300+ Religious societies, etc.
4422 Sisterhoods (Protestant)
For individual denominations see BX1+
4422.5 Married people
Deacons and deaconesses
4423 General works
(4424.A-Z) By denomination, A-Z
see BX1+
4425.A-Z Biography, A-Z
Young people
4427 General works
4430 Societies (General)
Cf. BV1410+ Religious societies
Church work with special classes
Cf. BX2347.8.A+ Catholic Church
Older people
4435 General works
4435.3 Older women
4435.5 Nursing home patients
4437 Single people
4437.3 Unmarried couples
4437.5 Gays. Lesbians. Homosexuals
4438 Families
4438.5 Problem families
4438.6 Divorced people
4438.7 Single parents
People preparing for marriage see BV4012.27
4439 Remarried people
4439.5 Stepfamilies
Men
4440 General works
4441 Men and Religion Forward Movement
4445 Women
Including employed women
4445.3 Mothers
4445.5 Abused women. Battered women

Pastoral theology
Practical church work. Social work. Work of the layman
Church work with special classes -- Continued

4445.6 Pregnant women
4445.7 Pregnant teenagers
4446 Young adults. Young married couples
4447 Young men and women
Cf. BV4377 Coffee house ministry
4450 Young men and boys
4455 Young women and girls
Children
Religious education see BV1474+
Problem children see BV4464
Sexually abused children see BV4464.3
4456 Homeless persons
4457 Soldiers and sailors
4458 Sailors
4459 Veterans
4459.5 Prisoners of war
People with disabilities, sick, etc.
Cf. BV4335+ Pastoral services to the sick, etc.
Cf. RT120.P37 Parish nursing
4460 General works
4460.3 Substance abuse patients. Narcotic addicts
4460.4 Medication abusers
4460.5 Alcoholics
4460.6 Terminally ill. Dying
Cf. BV4338 Pastoral services to the terminally ill
4460.7 AIDS patients
4460.8 Sexual disorder patients. Sex addicts
4461 People with mental disabilities, mentally ill, etc.
Cf. BV4012.3 Pastoral work in mental institutions
4461.3 Developmentally disabled
4461.5 Narcissists
4461.6 Obsessive-compulsive disorder patients
4462 Blind
4463 Deaf
4463.3 Ex-cultists
4463.5 Adult child abuse victims
4463.6 Adult children of alcoholics
4463.65 Adult children of divorced parents
4463.7 Children of alcoholics
4464 Problem children
4464.2 Children of prisoners
4464.3 Sexually abused children
4464.5 Juvenile delinquents
Criminals

Pastoral theology
Practical church work. Social work. Work of the layman
Church work with special classes
Criminals -- Continued

4464.7 General works
4465 Prisoners
Cf. HV8865+ Administrative aspects
4465.5 Victims of crimes
4466 Refugees
4466.5 Nomads
4467 Tourists, travelers, etc.
4468 Minorities. Special ethnic groups
4468.2.A-Z By ethnic group, A-Z
4468.2.A34 African Americans
4468.2.A74 Asian Americans
4468.2.B55 Blacks (outside the U.S.)
4468.2.H57 Hispanic Americans
4468.2.K6 Korean Americans
4468.2.M48 Mexican Americans
4469 Apartment dwellers
4470 Other
For parish libraries see Z675.C5

Practical religion. The Christian life
Class here works on the spiritual life of specific denominations unless special provision has been made under the denomination, e.g. BX2349+, Catholic Church; BX7738, Society of Friends

4485 Periodicals
4485.5 Congresses. Conventions
4486 Societies
4487.A-Z Movements to promote the Christian life, A-Z
4487.A32 L'Abri (Organization)
4487.A45 All Night Vigil Movement
4487.A5 Andaktsbokselskapet
(4487.C5) Children of God
see BP605.C38
4487.D4 Deutsche Christentumsgesellschaft
4487.D57 Disciplined Order of Christ
4487.E9 Evangelical academies
4487.G38 Gen Movement
4487.G4 Gerhard-Tersteegen-Konferenz
4487.K5 Keswick Movement
4487.L54 Lighthouse movement
Moral Re-Armament see BJ10.M6+
4487.N48 Neuwerk movement
4487.O9 Oxford Group
Founded by Frank N. D. Buchman in 1928

Practical religion. The Christian life
Movements to promote the Christian life, A-Z -- Continued
4487.Y6 Young Life Campaign
4488 Dictionaries
4490 History
For special time periods, places or churches, see the time period, place, or church
4495 Collections
General works
4499 Polyglot
English
4500 Early through 1800
4501 1801-1950
4501.2 1951-2000
4501.3 2001-
4502 French
4503 German
4504 Italian
4505 Scandinavian
4506 Spanish and Portuguese
4509.A-Z Other languages, A-Z
e.g.
4509.C8 Czech
4509.D8 Dutch
4509.5 General special
e.g. Identification with Christ
Addresses, essays, lectures
4510.A1 Collected works
4510.A2 Early through 1800
4510.A3-Z 1801-1950
4510.2 1951-2000
4510.3 2001-
Tract societies see BV2374+
4511 Study and teaching. Textbooks
4513 Keepsakes, tokens, etc.
Stories, allegories, emblems, etc.
Cf. BV638.8 Popular works, stories, etc. on the rural church
4515 Early through 1950
4515.2 1951-2000
4515.3 2001-
4517 Anecdotes, etc.
4517.5 Fellowship. Community. Koinonia

Practical religion. The Christian life -- Continued
4518 Monastic and religious life
Early Church before the foundation of orders
Cf. BX385+ Orthodox Eastern Church
Cf. BX580+ Russian Church
Cf. BX2400+ Catholic Church
Cf. BX5183+ Church of England
Cf. BX5970+ Protestant Episcopal Church
Cf. BX8071.5 Lutheran churches
Religious duties
Including witnessing, counsel to converts, etc.
4520 General works
4521 Religious leadership
Cf. BV659+ Ministry
4523 Church attendance
Cf. BV20 Duty and claims of public worship
Cf. BV652.5 Church administration
Cf. GT485 Church going customs
4525 Duties of church members. The layman
Cf. BV687 The layman in church organization
Religion of the family. The Christian home
Cf. BV1590 Religious training of children in the home
General works
4526 Early through 1950
4526.2 1951-2000
4526.3 2001-
Religious works for special classes of persons
Cf. BV4843+ Works of meditation and devotion
Women
For works for mothers see BV4529.18
Cf. BV4550+ Young women and girls
4527 General works
4527.4 Empty nesters
4528 Widows
4528.15 Wives
Men
For works for fathers see BV4529.17
4528.2 General works
4528.3 Husbands
4528.5 Grandparents
Parents
For parents of children with special problems or conditions see BV4596.P33
4529 General works
4529.15 Adoptive parents
4529.17 Fathers

Practical religion. The Christian life
Religious works for special classes of persons
Parents -- Continued
4529.18 Mothers
Including single mothers
4529.2 Young adults. Young married couples
Youth
Including students
English
4530 Early through 1800
4530.A1 Periodicals
4531 1801-1950
4531.A1 Periodicals
4531.2 1951-2000
4531.2.A1 Periodicals
4531.3 2001-
4532 French
4533 German
4534 Italian
4535 Scandinavian
4536 Spanish and Portuguese
4539.A-Z Other languages, A-Z
Young men and boys
e.g. College men in doubt
English
4540 Early through 1800
4541 1801-1950
4541.2 1951-2000
4541.3 2001-
4542 French
4543 German
4544 Italian
4545 Scandinavian
4546 Spanish and Portuguese
4549.A-Z Other languages, A-Z
Young women and girls
English
4550 Early through 1800
4551 1801-1950
4551.2 1951-2000
4551.3 2001-
4552 French
4553 German
4554 Italian
4555 Scandinavian
4556 Spanish and Portuguese
4559.A-Z Other languages, A-Z

Practical religion. The Christian life
Religious works for special classes of persons
Youth -- Continued
Children
For Bible stories see BS546+
Cf. BV4910.5 Works for sick children
4560 Periodicals. Serials
4565 Collected works
For multiple authors in one volume see BV4570+
General works
English
4570 Early through 1800
4571 1801-1950
4571.2 1951-2000
4571.3 2001-
4572 French
4573 German
4574 Italian
4575 Scandinavian
4576 Spanish and Portuguese
4579.A-Z Other languages, A-Z
4579.5 Middle age
Older people
Cf. BJ1691 Ethics for older people
Cf. HQ1060+ Social groups
4580.A1 Periodicals
4580.A2-Z General works
The afflicted and suffering see BV4909
The sick and crippled see BV4910+
The lonely see BV4911
Soldiers. Soldiers and sailors
4588 General works
4589 Religious experiences among soldiers
Cf. BV2680+ Missions
Sailors
4590 General works
4591 Religious experiences among sailors
Cf. BV2660+ Missions
4593 Employees. Workers
4595 Prisoners
4596.A-Z Other, A-Z
4596.A2 Abused wives. Abused women
Abused women see BV4596.A2
4596.A23 Acquaintance rape victims
4596.A25 Adult child abuse victims
Including adult child sexual abuse victims
4596.A27 Adult children of alcoholics

Practical religion. The Christian life
Religious works for special classes of persons
Other, A-Z -- Continued

4596.A274	Adult children of dysfunctional families
4596.A28	Adult children of narcotic addicts
4596.A48	Alcoholics
4596.A54	Animal lovers
4596.A78	Artists
4596.A8	Athletes
4596.A85	Authors
4596.A87	Automobile drivers
4596.B37	Baseball players
4596.B57	Bird watchers
4596.B8	Businessmen. Businesswomen
	Businesswomen see BV4596.B8
4596.C3	Campers
4596.C48	Choirs
	Christian educators see BV4596.E38
4596.C49	Church committee members
	Church school teachers see BV4596.S9
4596.C54	Clerks
4596.C57	Codependents
4596.C58	Compulsive eaters
4596.C6	Country musicians
4596.C65	Cowboys
4596.D53	Dieters
4596.D58	Divorced people
4596.E38	Educators, Christian
4596.E6	Emigrants and immigrants
4596.E67	Entertainers
4596.E93	Executives
4596.F3	Farmers
4596.F4	Feminists
4596.F5	Fishermen
4596.F6	Football players
4596.G36	Gardeners
4596.G38	Gays
4596.G64	Golfers
4596.H5	Hippies
	Immigrants see BV4596.E6
4596.I57	Internet addicts
4596.K39	Kayakers
4596.L3	Lawyers
4596.L52	Librarians
4596.M3	Married people. Spouses
4596.M5	Miners
4596.M67	Motorcyclists

Practical religion. The Christian life
Religious works for special classes of persons
Other, A-Z -- Continued

4596.M87 Musicians
4596.N37 Narcotic addicts
4596.N44 Needleworkers
4596.N48 New church members
4596.N8 Nurses
Office workers see BV4596.C54
4596.P3 Parents of bereaved children
4596.P33 Parents of chronically ill children
4596.P35 Parents of children with disabilities
4596.P37 Parents of sexually abused children
4596.P38 Pastoral search committees
4596.P4 Peasants
4596.P5 Physicians
4596.P7 Police
4596.P75 Princes and princesses
Princesses see BV4596.P75
4596.P8 Professional men (General)
4596.R43 Relationship addicts
4596.R45 Remarried people
4596.R47 Retirees
4596.S35 Scientists
4596.S39 Separated people
4596.S42 Sex addicts
4596.S48 Single parents
For single mothers see BV4529.18
4596.S5 Single people
Spouses see BV4596.M3
4596.S9 Sunday-school teachers
4596.S93 Surfers
4596.T43 Teachers
4596.T45 Television actors and actresses
4596.T88 Twelve-step program participants
4596.U53 Unemployed
4596.W37 War criminals
4596.W66 Woodworkers
4596.W67 Workaholics
4596.Y68 Youth leaders

Christian life in relation to special topics
Amusements
Cf. BV1620+ Social life, amusements, etc. in the Church

4597 General works
Dance see GV1740+
Motion pictures see PN1995.5

Practical religion. The Christian life
Christian life in relation to special topics
Amusements -- Continued
Radio broadcasts see PN1991.6
Television broadcasts see PN1992.6
Theater see PN2047+

4597.2 Attitude change
4597.3 Emotions
4597.4 Hunting
4597.5 Immoral books. Prohibited books
Cf. BV4730 Commandments of the Church
Cf. Z1019+ Bibliography
4597.52 Interpersonal relations
4597.53.A-Z Special topics, A-Z
4597.53.C56 Commitment
4597.53.C58 Conflict management
4597.53.C62 Control
4597.53.C64 Conversation. Oral communication
4597.53.I52 Influence
4597.53.I55 Intimacy
4597.53.L43 Leadership
Oral communication see BV4597.53.C64
4597.53.P73 Praise
4597.53.S44 Self-disclosure
4597.53.T78 Trust
4597.54 Judgment
4597.55 Leisure
4597.555 Life cycle, Human
4597.56 Masculinity
4597.565 Memory
Personality
4597.57 General works
4597.58.A-Z Special topics, A-Z
4597.58.B37 Bashfulness
4597.58.P47 Perfectionism
4597.58.R47 Resilience
4597.59 Pleasure
4597.6 Pornography
4598 Physical education. Physical fitness
Cf. BV1640 Church recreation and physical culture
4598.15 Risk taking
4598.2 Self-actualization
4598.23 Self-confidence
4598.236 Self-efficacy
4598.24 Self-esteem
4598.25 Self-perception
4598.3 Success

BV

Practical religion. The Christian life
Christian life in relation to special topics -- Continued
4598.4 Thought and thinking
4598.5 Time management
4598.7 Habits
4599 Vacations
4599.5.A-Z Other special topics, A-Z
4599.5.B67 Boredom
4599.5.C45 Character
4599.5.C65 Coincidence
4599.5.H67 Hobbies
4599.5.I53 Individual differences
4599.5.M66 Motivation
4599.5.P75 Problem solving
Moral theology
Cf. BJ1188.5+ Christian ethics
General works see BJ1240+
Conscience see BJ1278.C66
Scruples see BJ1278.S37
Human acts see BJ1240+
Divine law see BT95+
Human law
see class K
Natural law see K400+
Sins and vices
Cf. BJ1534 Ethics
4625 General works
4625.2 Distinction of sins
Original sin see BT720
Actual sin see BT715+
Unpardonable sin see BT721
4625.5 Mortal sin
Venial sin
4625.6 General works
4625.7 Imperfections
Deadly sins. Capital sins
Including pride, covetousness, lust, anger, gluttony, envy, sloth
4626 General works
Individual deadly sins see BV4627.A+
4627.A-Z Individual sins, A-Z
4627.A3 Adultery
4627.A5 Anger
4627.A8 Avarice. Covetousness
4627.B6 Blasphemy
Covetousness see BV4627.A8
Detraction see BV4627.S6

Practical religion. The Christian life
Moral theology
Sins and vices
Individual sins, A-Z
4627.E36 Egoism
4627.E5 Envy
4627.E9 Extortion
4627.F3 Falsehood
4627.F7 Frivolity
4627.G5 Gluttony
4627.H38 Hate
4627.H8 Hypocrisy
4627.I34 Idolatry
4627.J43 Jealousy
Lewdness see BV4627.L5
4627.L5 Licentiousness. Lewdness
4627.L8 Lust
Including sexual sins in general
4627.M8 Murder
4627.N4 Negligence
4627.P3 Partisanship
4627.P7 Pride
Profanity see BV4627.S9
4627.Q3 Quarreling
4627.R37 Resentment
4627.R4 Revenge
4627.S2 Sacrilege
Sexual sins (General) see BV4627.L8
4627.S6 Slander. Detraction
4627.S65 Sloth
4627.S9 Swearing. Profanity
4627.T4 Temper
4627.W67 Worldliness
Virtues
Cf. BJ1518+ Ethics
4630 General works
4633 General special
e.g. Virtues of unbelievers (Theological works)
Theological virtues (Faith, hope, charity)
4635 General works
4637 Faith. Trust in God
4638 Hope
4639 Charity. Love
4645 Cardinal virtues
Including fortitude, justice, prudence, temperance
Individual cardinal virtues see BV4647.A+
4647.A-Z Other individual virtues, A-Z

Practical religion. The Christian life
Moral theology
Virtues
Other individual virtues, A-Z -- Continued

4647.A25 Acquiescence. Agreement. Submissiveness
Agreement see BV4647.A25
4647.A78 Assertiveness
4647.B7 Brotherliness
Caring see BV4647.S9
4647.C5 Chastity. Virginity
Compassion see BV4647.S9
4647.C6 Concord
4647.C63 Confidence
4647.C7 Contentment
4647.C75 Courage. Heroism
4647.D5 Dignity
4647.D58 Discipline
4647.D6 Discretion
4647.E53 Encouragement
4647.E93 Expectation. Waiting
4647.F55 Forgiveness
4647.F6 Fortitude
4647.F7 Friendship
4647.G45 Generosity
4647.G8 Gratitude. Thankfulness
Happiness see BV4647.J68
4647.H4 Helping behavior. Helpfulness
Heroism see BV4647.C75
4647.H6 Honor
4647.H67 Hospitality
4647.H8 Humility
4647.I5 Innocence
4647.I55 Integrity
4647.J68 Joy. Happiness
4647.J8 Justice
Cf. BR115.J8 Christianity and justice
4647.K5 Kindness
4647.L56 Listening
4647.L6 Loyalty
4647.M2 Magnanimity
4647.M3 Meekness
4647.M4 Mercy
4647.M63 Modesty
4647.N6 Nonresistance
4647.O2 Obedience
4647.P3 Patience
4647.P33 Patriotism

Practical religion. The Christian life
Moral theology
Virtues
Other individual virtues, A-Z -- Continued

4647.P35 Peace (Theology)
4647.P45 Perseverance
4647.P5 Piety
4647.P6 Poverty
4647.P8 Prudence
4647.R4 Resignation
4647.S39 Self-control
4647.S4 Self-denial
4647.S43 Self-respect
4647.S48 Simplicity
4647.S5 Sincerity
Submissiveness see BV4647.A25
4647.S9 Sympathy. Compassion. Caring
4647.T4 Temperance
Thankfulness see BV4647.G8
4647.T5 Thrift
4647.T7 Truthfulness
Virginity see BV4647.C5
Waiting see BV4647.E93
4647.W7 Wrath

Precepts from the Bible
4650 General works
Precepts from the Decalogue. Ten Commandments
For Jewish works see BM520+
Cf. BS1281+ Texts and textual criticism
4655 General works
4656 Juvenile works
By commandment
4657 First Commandment
Catholic and Lutheran First Commandment includes the usual Protestant First and Second Commandment
4659 Second Commandment
4664 Third Commandment
Catholic and Lutheran Second Commandment
4670 Fourth Commandment
Catholic and Lutheran Third Commandment
4675 Fifth Commandment
Catholic and Lutheran Fourth Commandment

Practical religion. The Christian life
Moral theology
Precepts from the Bible
Precepts from the Decalogue. Ten Commandments
By commandment -- Continued
4680 Sixth Commandment
Catholic and Lutheran Fifth Commandment
Cf. BT736.2 The Christian and war
Cf. CR4571+ Dueling
Cf. HQ767+ Abortion
Cf. HV6499+ Homicide, murder, etc.
Cf. HV6543+ Suicide
Cf. JZ5581 Peace literature
4695 Seventh Commandment
Catholic and Lutheran Sixth Commandment
4700 Eighth Commandment
Catholic and Lutheran Seventh Commandment
4705 Ninth Commandment
Catholic and Lutheran Eighth Commandment
4710 Tenth Commandment
Catholic and Lutheran Ninth and Tenth Commandment
Precepts from the New Testament
4713 General works
4714 Christ's Summary of the Law
4715 The Golden Rule
Precepts of the Church. Commandments of the Church
4720 General works
4723 Sunday and holy day observance
Cf. BV130+ Sunday observance
4725 Confession once a year
Cf. BX2266.F7 Frequency of confession
4726 Communion at Easter time. Easter duty
4727 Fasting on appointed days
Cf. BV80+ Fasts
Marriage rules (General) see HQ1051+
Marriage rules (Catholic Church) see BX2250+
4729 Church support
Cf. BV772 Christian giving
4730 Prohibited books
Cf. Z1019+ Bibliography
4740 Vocation. Calling
4780.A-Z Other, A-Z
e.g.
4780.O2 Oaths (in law)
Cf. BX7748.O2 Society of Friends

Practical religion. The Christian life -- Continued
Works of meditation and devotion
Cf. BM724 Jewish works
Cf. BX2177+ Catholic works
Collections by two or more authors
4800 Devotional series
4801 General collections
4805 Minor collections. Pamphlets, etc.
Selections for daily reading
For the civil year. Devotional calendars
For Catholic authors, one or more see BX2170.C56
Cf. BS390+ Selections in English for daily reading from the Bible
4810 Two or more authors
4811 Individual authors
For the Church year
4812.A1 Two or more authors
For Catholic authors, one or more see BX2170.C55
4812.A3-Z Individual authors
General works
4813 Art of meditation
4815 Nature of devotion
4817 Adoration and love of God
4818 History and criticism of devotional literature
Devotional works of individual authors
Imitatio Christi
Medieval translations are classed in literature, e.g., PT4846.I5, Low German
Editions. By language
Subarrange under each language by translator, editor or date
4819 Polyglot
4820 Latin
4821 English
4823 French
e.g.
4823.C7 Corneille, Pierre, 1606-1684. Imitation de Jésus-Christ
4824 German
4825 Italian
4828.A-Z Other languages, A-Z
4829 History and criticism
Other works. By language
4830 Greek and Latin
English
4831 Early through 1800
4832 1801-1950

Practical religion. The Christian life
Works of meditation and devotion
Devotional works of individual authors
Other works. By language
English -- Continued
4832.2 1951-2000
4832.3 2001-
4833 French
4834 German
4835 Italian
4836 Scandinavian
4837 Spanish and Portuguese
4839.A-Z Other, A-Z
e.g.
Afrikaans see BV4839.D8
4839.C9 Czech
4839.D8 Dutch. Afrikaans
4839.R8 Russian
Works for special times, seasons, and days of the Church year see BV30+
Works for special classes of readers
For special classes not listed below see BV4527+
4843 Men
4844 Women
4845 Parents. Grandparents
4846 Fathers. Grandfathers
4847 Mothers. Grandmothers
Young men and women
4850 General works
4855 Young men and boys
4860 Young women and girls
Children
4870 General works
Sick children see BV4910.5
Older people see BV4580.A1+
Workingmen see BV4593
Soldiers and sailors see BV4588+
Prisoners see BV4595
4897.A-Z For special occasions and times (other than of the Church year), A-Z
e.g.
4897.A1 General
Prefer BV4830+ in case of doubt
4897.D7 Drought
Old age see BV4580.A1+
4897.P4 Pestilence
Sickness see BV4910+

Practical religion. The Christian life
Works of meditation and devotion
For special occasions and times (other than of the Church year), A-Z -- Continued
4897.W2 Wartime
Cf. BV4588+ Religious works for soldiers and sailors
Works of consolation and cheer
Cf. BR1702 Last hours
4900 Collected works
4901 Selections from the Bible
General works
4904 Early through 1800
4905 1801-1950
4905.2 1951-2000
4905.3 2001-
Works for special classes of persons
4906 Bereaved children
4907 Bereaved parents
Including the death of children, children in Heaven
4908 Widows
4908.5 The anxious. Those seeking peace of mind
4909 The afflicted and suffering
Cf. BV283.S84 Prayers
Cf. BX384.S5 Orthodox Eastern Church
Cf. BX2170.S5 Catholic Church
The sick and crippled
4910 General works
4910.3 AIDS patients
4910.33 Cancer patients
4910.335 Chronic fatigue syndrome patients
4910.337 Chronic pain patients
4910.34 Depressed persons
4910.35 Eating disorders patients
4910.4 Insomniacs
4910.45 Post-traumatic stress disorder patients
4910.5 Sick children
4910.6.A-Z Other, A-Z
4910.6.A55 Alzheimer's disease patients
4910.6.C76 Crohn's disease patients
4910.6.H44 Hepatitis patients
4910.9 Families or caregivers of the sick and older people
4911 The lonely
Conversion literature

Practical religion. The Christian life
Conversion literature -- Continued
Religious experience. Conversion
Cf. BR110+ Psychology of religious experience
Cf. BR195.C6 Apostolic Age to Fall of Roman Empire
Cf. BT780 Doctrinal theology
Cf. BV3750+ Evangelism
4912 Collected works
General works
4914 Early through 1800
4915 1801-1950
4916 1951-2000
4916.3 2001-
Appeals to the unconverted, backsliders, doubters, etc.
4920 Early to 1800
e.g. Baxter's Call to the unconverted
4921 1801-1950
4921.2 1951-2000
4921.3 2001-
Works for the conversion of special classes
Children see BV4925+
4922 Jews
4923.A-Z Other, A-Z
e.g.
4923.J3 Japanese
Conversion of children
4925 General works
Biography
4926 Collective
Individual see BV4935.A+
Biography of converts
For converted Jews see BV2623.A1+
For Catholic converts see BX4668+
4930 Collective
4932 New Testament conversions
4935.A-Z Individual, A-Z
4935.Z9 Anonymous persons
4936 "Fearful examples." Fate of atheists, etc.
Arranged by author or title, not by subject
Works for the recently converted see BV4520+
4950 Other
Asceticism
Including works on asceticism and mysticism
Cf. BV4800+ Works of meditation and devotion
Cf. BV5070+ Mysticism
Cf. BX2435 Monastic life
Cf. BX4210+ Guides for nuns, sisters, etc.

Practical religion. The Christian life
Asceticism -- Continued
5015 Periodicals
5017 Collected works
History
5021 General works
By period
5023 Ancient
5025 Medieval
5027 Modern
5029.A-Z By region or country, A-Z
General works
English
5030 Early to 1800
5031 1801-1950
5031.2 1951-2000
5031.3 2001-
5032 French
5033 German
5034 Italian
5035 Scandinavian
5036 Spanish and Portuguese
5039.A-Z Other languages, A-Z
e.g.
5039.C8 Czech
5039.D8 Dutch
5043 Obstacles to perfection
5045 Internal aids
e.g. Desire for perfection, examination of conscience, self-examination
For prayer see BV205+
Cf. BX2377 Catholic Church
External aids
5050 General works
5053 Spiritual direction
5055 Austerities. Fasting, etc.
5058 Reading
Confession see BV845+
Communion see BV823+
5067 Pilgrimages
Cf. BX2323+ Catholic Church
5068.A-Z Other, A-Z
e.g.
Flagellation see HV8613+
5068.R4 Retreats
Cf. BX2375+ Catholic Church
Biography see BV5095.A1+

Practical religion. The Christian life -- Continued
Mysticism
Cf. B828.A1+ Modern philosophy
Cf. BR110+ Psychology of religion
Cf. BV5083 Psychology of mysticism
5070 Periodicals. Societies
5072 Collected works
History
5075 General works
5077.A-Z By region or country, A-Z
General works
5080 Early through 1800
1801-1950
5081 Comprehensive works
5082 General works
5082.2 1951-2000
5082.3 2001-
5083 General special. Psychology. etc.
5085 Addresses, essays, lectures
Mystic phenomena
5090 General works
5091.A-Z Special, A-Z
Prefer Biography for individual cases, e.g. BX4700
e.g.
5091.C7 Contemplation
5091.E3 Ecstasy
5091.R4 Revelation and prophecies (Personal)
5091.S7 Stigmatization
5091.V6 Visions
Biography
5095.A1 Collective
5095.A2-Z Individual, A-Z
Cf. PA-PT, Literature
e.g.
(5095.A8) Avila, Juan de
see BX4700.J5686
Bernard de Clairvaux, Saint see BX4700.B5
5095.B7 Bohme, Jakob
5095.E3 Eckhart, meister
5095.J3 Jan van Ruysbroeck
John of the Cross, Saint see BX4700.J7
5095.L3 Law, William
Saint-Martin, Louis Claude de see B2145
Seuse, Heinrich see BV5095.S85
5095.S5 Singh, Sundar
5095.S85 Suso, Heinrich
5095.T3 Tauler, Johannes

Practical religion. The Christian life
Mysticism
Biography
Individual, A-Z -- Continued
Teresa, of Avila, Saint, 1515-1582 see BX4700.T4
5095.T4 Tersteegen, Gerhard
5099 Quietism
For Molinos, Fénelon, Mme. Gugon, etc., see BX4705

Christian denominations

Cf. BR157 Christian denominations (General)

Cf. BT1313+ History of specific doctrines and movements. Heresies and schisms

Church unity. Ecumenical movement. Interdenominational cooperation

For the relationship of one denomination to another, see the denomination in BX100+

Cf. BV625 Church and society, Church and community, cooperative church work, etc.

Cf. BV626 Church federations, Church councils (General)

1 Periodicals

Societies. Associations, conferences, etc.

2 General works

Evangelical Alliance. World's Evangelical Alliance

3.A2 General conferences. By date

3.A5-Z General works. Histories

National branches

United States

4.A1 Annual reports

4.A4 Conferences. By date

4.A5-Z General works

5.A-Z Other countries, A-Z

6.A-Z Other, A-Z

Subarrange by date

Including international and United States national organizations; for other national and all local organizations, see BR555+

e.g.

6.F4 Federal Council of the Churches of Christ in America

6.G8 Gustav-Adolf-Verein

6.N16 National Association of Evangelicals

6.N2 National Council of the Churches of Christ in the United States of America

6.W55 World Conference of Christian Youth

World Conference on Faith and Order

6.W7 General collections. Serials

6.W75 Individual. By date

World Council of Churches

6.W77 Assembly. By date

Subarrange each assembly like BX6.W77 1975

5th Assembly, Nairobi, 1975

6.W77 1975 .A2 Preparatory studies. By title

6.W77 1975 .A3 Reports. By title

6.W77 1975 .A4 Biography (Collective)

6.W77 1975 .A5-Z Works about the assembly

6.W773 Central Committee

Church unity. Ecumenical movement. Interdenominational cooperation
Societies. Associations, conferences, etc.
Other, A-Z
World Council of Churches -- Continued
Commission on Faith and Order
6.W775A2 Minutes, reports. By date
6.W775A4-.W775A49 Special commissions. By key word
6.W775A5-.W775Z Works about the Commission on Faith and Order
6.W776A-.W776Z Other commissions, departments, etc. By key word
6.W78 Works about the World Council of Churches as a whole
6.3 Dictionaries. Encyclopedias
History
6.5 General works
By country
see BR516.5; BR744; BR813; BR853; etc.
Biography
6.7 Collective
6.8.A-Z Individual, A-Z
General works
6.9 Collections
7 Early through 1800
8 1801-1950
8.A1 Collections
8.2 1951-2000
8.2.A1 Collections
8.3 2001-
9 Addresses, essays, sermons
9.5.A-Z Special topics, A-Z
9.5.A37 African influences
9.5.B34 Baptism in the Holy Spirit
9.5.B5 Bible
Christian saints, Veneration of see BX9.5.V45
9.5.C5 Church polity
Close and open communion see BV825.7
9.5.C6 Communicatio in sacris
Community churches see BV636
9.5.C65 Councils and synods
9.5.E64 Episcopacy
9.5.E94 Evangelicalism
9.5.E97 Excommunication
Federated churches see BV636
Icons, Veneration of see BX9.5.V44
9.5.I5 Intercommunion
Interdenominational cooperation see BV625
9.5.L43 Lectionaries
9.5.L55 Liturgics

Church unity. Ecumenical movement. Interdenominational cooperation
Special topics, A-Z -- Continued
9.5.M37 Mary, Blessed Virgin, Saint
9.5.M5 Missions
9.5.P29 Papacy
9.5.P3 Pastoral theology
9.5.P45 Pentecostalism
9.5.R35 Reception
9.5.R38 Recognition
9.5.R4 Religious education
9.5.S2 Sacraments
9.5.S5 Simultaneum
Synods see BX9.5.C65
9.5.U5 Unionism
9.5.U53 United churches
9.5.V44 Veneration of icons
9.5.V45 Veneration of saints
9.5.W65 Women
9.5.Y68 Youth
Eastern churches. Oriental churches
Class here general works, or works without the Orthodox Eastern Church
Cf. BX4710.1+ Eastern churches in communion with Rome; Uniats
100 Periodicals
100.2 Societies
100.5 Congresses
100.6 Documents
100.7 Dictionaries
100.8 Directories
101 Collections
Patrology see BR60+
Historical works
102 Early through 1800
103 1801-1950
103.2 1951-2000
103.3 2001-
General works. Doctrines, etc.
105 Early through 1800
106 1801-1950
106.2 1951-2000
106.23 2001-

Eastern churches. Oriental churches -- Continued
Eastern churches (except the Orthodox Eastern Church) and other churches
For Orthodox Eastern Church (alone or with other Eastern churches) in relation to other churches see BX324+
106.3 Relation to the Catholic Church
107 Liturgy and ritual
Individual church divisions
Armenian Church
120 Periodicals. Societies
120.5 Dictionaries. Encyclopedias
121 Documents. Councils, etc.
History
General works
122 Early through 1800
123 1801-1950
123.2 1951-2000
123.3 2001-
124.A-Z By country, A-Z
For Armenia see BX122+
124.5.A-Z By city, town, etc., A-Z
e.g.
124.5.J4 Jerusalem
General works. Doctrine, etc.
125 Early through 1800
126 1801-1950
126.2 1951-2000
126.3 2001-
126.6 Sermons
Liturgy and ritual
127.A1 Polyglot. By date
127.A2 Original language. By date
127.A3 English. By date
127.A5A-.A5Z Other languages, A-Z
127.A6-Z History, treatises, etc.
Church year
127.13 General works
127.14 Fasts and feasts
127.15 Christian life. Spiritual life
127.2 Monasticism
127.3 Monasticism for women
128.A-Z Individual churches, monasteries, etc. By place and name, A-Z, or by name, A-Z
Biography
129.A1 Collective

Eastern churches. Oriental churches
Individual church divisions
Armenian Church
Biography -- Continued
129.A3-Z Individual
e.g.
129.V3 Varden, of Armenia, Saint
130-139 Coptic Church (Table BX31)
140-149 Ethiopic or Abyssinian Church. Ya'Ityoṗyā 'ortodoks tawā hedo béta kerestiyān (Table BX31)
150-159 Nestorian, Chaldean, or East Syrian Church (Table BX31)
160-169 St. Thomas Christians. Malabar Christians. Mar Thoma Syrian Church (Table BX31)
Founded by Nestorian Christians; later some united with the Catholic Church, others with the Jacobite Church
170-179 Syrian or Jacobite Church (Table BX31)
Cf. BX120+ Armenian Church
Cf. BX130+ Coptic Church
Cf. BX140+ Ethiopic Church
180-189 Maronite Church (Table BX31 modified)
History
General works
182 Early to 1182
(183) 1182-1917
see BX4713.522
(183.2) 1918-
see BX4713.523
Orthodox Eastern Church
Popularly known as the Orthodox Church, formerly as the Greek Church
200 Periodicals
210 Societies
215 Congresses
220 Documents
230 Dictionaries. Encyclopedias
240 Directories. Yearbooks
Collected works
250 Several authors
260 Individual authors
Study and teaching
271.A-Z Individual schools, A-Z
271.C5 Hiera Theologike Schole tes Chalkes
Canonical collections of councils and synods
272 General (Collected)
Pan-orthodox (general) councils
272.2 General works
Individual councils

Orthodox Eastern Church
Canonical collections of councils and synods
Pan-orthodox (general) councils
Individual councils -- Continued
274 Council of Haghia Sophia, 1341
275 Council of Constantinople, 1583
276 Council of Constantinople, 1587
278 Council of Constantinople, 1593
279 Council of Moscow, 1666-1667
280 Council of Jerusalem, 1672
282 Council of Constantinople, 1755-1756
284 Council of Constantinople, 1848
285 Council of Constantinople, 1872
286 Council of Constantinople, 1902-1904
287 Council of Constantinople, 1923
288.A-Z Other councils. By place, A-Z
History
290 General works
By period
Early and medieval
300 General works
301 Acacian Schism, 484-519
303 Great Schism, 1054
305 Arsenite Schism, 1261-1310
310 Modern
General works. Doctrine, etc.
For Fathers of the Church see BR60+
Cf. BX345 Creeds and catechisms
320 Early through 1950
320.2 1951-2000
320.3 2001-
323 General special
Special movements
323.5 Charismatic movement
The Orthodox Eastern Church and other churches
324 General works
Relation to the Anglican Communion see BX5004.3
324.3 Relation to the Roman Catholic Church
324.4 Relation to the Eastern Catholic Churches in communion with the Roman Catholic Church
324.43 Relation to the Old Catholic Church
324.45 Relation to Oriental Orthodox Churches
324.5 Relation to Protestant churches
324.52 Relation to Lutheran churches
324.53 Relation to Methodist Church
324.54 Relation to Pentecostal churches
324.55 Relation to Reformed churches

Orthodox Eastern Church
The Orthodox Eastern Church and other churches -- Continued
324.6 Relation to the Unification Church
325 Addresses, essays, lectures
330 Sermons
335 Church and state
337 Orthodox social teachings, Christian sociology
337.5 Human ecology
340 Government and organization
341 Liturgical objects. Vestments
341.5 Priests
341.52 Women clergy. Ordination of women
341.6 Work of the priest. Pastoral theology
342 Laymen
342.5 Women
342.6 Youth
Church law. Nomocanon
343 General works
344.A-Z Special topics, A-Z
344.C5 Church discipline
344.E9 Excommunication
345 Creeds and catechisms
Liturgy and ritual
Texts
350.A1 Polyglot
350.A2 Greek
350.A3A-.A3Z Other ancient texts. By language, A-Z and date
e.g.
350.A3L3 Latin
350.A3S8 Syriac
350.A4 Russian. By date
350.A5 English. By translator (or editor), A-Z, or by date
350.A6 Other languages, A-Z, and date
e.g.
350.A6C45 Church Slavic
350.A6G4 German
350.A7-Z History, treatises, etc.
355 Divine Liturgy. Divine (Eucharistic) Liturgy. Liturgy of St. John Chrysostom (by itself or with other Eucharistic Liturgies) (Table BX34)
356 Liturgy of St. Basil the Great (Table BX34)
357 Liturgy of St. James (Table BX34)
358 Preparatory prayers before the Liturgy (Table BX34)
Liturgy of the Pre-Sanctified. Liturgy of St. Gregory Dialogos see BX375.P7
360 Prayer books. Euchologion, etc. (Table BX34)

Orthodox Eastern Church
Liturgy and ritual -- Continued
370 Psalters and hymnals (Table BX34)
For hymns see BV467+
375.A-Z Other special liturgical works, A-Z
375.A55 Akathistoi (Table BX5)
375.A6 Andreas, Saint, Great Canon (Table BX5)
375.A65 Apostolos (Table BX5)
375.A7 Archieratikon (Table BX5)
375.A84 Asmatikē akolouthia tēs hyperagias Theotokou tēs Apokalypseōs (Table BX5)
375.C43 Chin Koronovanīi͡a (Table BX5)
375.E75 Euchologion (Table BX5)
375.E8 Evangeliaries (Table BX5)
375.H35 Hai hierai akolouthiai tēs M. Hevdomados kai tou Pascha (Table BX5)
Hesperinon see BX375.V4
375.H6 Horologion (Table BX5)
375.K6 Kontakarion (Table BX5)
375.L37 Lectionaries (Table BX5)
375.L4 Leitourgikon (Table BX5)
375.M27 Marriage service (Table BX5)
Matins see BX375.O77
Mattins see BX375.O77
375.M37 Menaion (Table BX5)
375.M4 Menologion (Table BX5)
375.M43 Mesi͡atseslov (Table BX5)
375.M53 Mikros paraklētikos kanōn. Small paraklesis (Table BX5)
Morning prayer service see BX375.O77
375.N44 Nekrosimes akolouthies (Table BX5)
375.O3 Oktoechos (Table BX5)
375.O77 Orthros. Matins or Mattins. Morning prayer service (Table BX5)
375.P4 Pentekostarion (Table BX5)
375.P7 Leitourgia proēgiasmenōn (Table BX5)
375.S87 Synaptai (Table BX5)
375.S9 Synaxarion (Table BX5)
375.S94 Synodicon (Table BX5)
(375.T73) Trebnik
see BX375.E75
375.T75 Triodion (Table BX5)
375.T76 Trithektē (Table BX5)
375.T9 Typikon (Table BX5)
375.V4 Vespers (Table BX5)
376.A-Z Prayer books for the laity. By language, A-Z
e.g.
376.E5 English

Orthodox Eastern Church
Liturgy and ritual
Prayer books for the laity. By language, A-Z -- Continued

376.R8 Russian
376.S4 Serbian
Church year
376.3 General works
376.35.A-Z Seasons, A-Z
376.35.H64 Holy Week and Pascha
376.35.L47 Lent
Fasts and feast days
376.4 General works
376.5.A-Z Special days, A-Z
376.5.E4 Elijah the Prophet's Day
376.5.F4 Feast of the Three Hierarchs
376.5.N5 Saint Nicholas' Day
376.5.P45 Saint Philip the Apostle's Day
Sacraments
377 General works
378.A-Z Special, A-Z
378.B3 Baptism
378.C5 Communion
378.C6 Confession
378.C63 Confirmation
Divorce see BX378.M2
378.M2 Matrimony. Divorce
378.O7 Ordination
378.5 Icons (not A-Z)
Saints. Hagiology
Cf. BX393 Lives of the Greek saints
380 General works
380.5 Canonization
381 Church work. Social service
Christian life. Spiritual life
382 General works
382.2 Family religious life. The Orthodox family
382.5 Spiritual direction
Devotional literature
383 General works
384.A-Z Works descriptive of the Christian life and devotional readings for special classes of persons, A-Z
e.g.
384.S5 Sick and sorrowing
384.Y68 Youth
384.5 Mysticism. Hesychasm

Orthodox Eastern Church -- Continued
Monasticism
Cf. BX384.5 Mysticism. Hesychasm
Cf. BX580+ Monasticism in the Russian Church
385.A1 General works
385.A2-Z By place, A-Z
Including one or more monasteries in an established group
e.g.
Athos
385.A8 General works
385.A82A-.A82Z Individual monasteries, A-Z
Rules, discipline, etc.
386 General works
386.2 Rule of St. Basil
386.2.A2 Greek texts. By date
386.2.A4-.Z4 Other languages, A-Z
Subarrange by date
386.2.Z5A-.Z5Z Commentaries. By author, A-Z
Individual monasteries (except in established group)
387 Sinai. St. Catharine
388.A-Z Other monasteries, A-Z
389.A-Z Other special topics, A-Z
389.H64 Holiness
389.M35 Man
389.P45 Philosophy
Biography
Cf. BR1705+ Fathers of the Church
390 Collective
393 Saints
Cf. BX596 Russian saints
394 History and criticism. Historiography. Hagiography
395.A-Z Individual, A-Z
For particular divisions of the church, see the division, e.g. BX597, Russian Church; BX619, Church of the Kingdom of Greece; etc.
e.g.
395.A756 Arsenios, Abp. of Elassona, 1550-1626
395.G48 Germanos, Exarch of the Ecumenical Patriarchate in Central Europe
395.G72 Gregorios V, Patriarch of Constantinople, 1745-1821
395.K9 Kyrillos Loukaris, Patriarch of Constantinople, 1572-1638
395.L46 Leo, Metropolitan of Synada, 937-ca.1003
395.M3 Macarius III, patriarch of Antioch
395.M35 Matthaios, Metropolitan of Ephesus, 1271 or 2-ca. 1355
395.M354 Mauropous, Ioannes, Metropolitan of Euchaita

Orthodox Eastern Church
Biography
Individual, A-Z -- Continued
395.M37 Maximus, the Greek, d. 1556
Cf. B785.M298+ Maximus as a philosopher
Cf. PG3305.M3 Russian literature
395.P5 Photius I, Saint, patriarch of Constantinople
Divisions of the Church
400 Patriarchates of the East. Melchites
410 Constantinople (Ecumenical patriarchate)
420 Alexandria (Orthodox patriarchate)
430 Antioch (Orthodox patriarchate)
440 Jerusalem (Orthodox patriarchate)
Cyprus (Archdiocese). Autokephalos Ekklēsia tēs Kyprou
450 General works
Biography
450.9 Collective
450.92 Cypriot saints (Collective)
450.93.A-Z Individual, A-Z
Church of Mt. Sinai see BX387
Russian Orthodox Church. Russkaı͡a pravoslavnaı͡a t͡serkov′
Since 2007, in canonical communication with the Russkaı͡a pravoslavnaı͡a t͡serkov′ zagranit͡seĭ
For the church to 2007 see BX598
460 Periodicals
463 Societies
465 Documents. Councils, etc.
470 Dictionaries
475 Directories. Yearbooks
Collected works
478 Several authors
480 Individual authors
482 Study and teaching
483.A-Z Individual schools, A-Z
e.g.
483.K5 Kiev. Dukhovnaı͡a akademii͡a
483.M6 Moscow. Dukhovnaı͡a akademii͡a
483.P3 Paris. Institute de théologie orthodoxe
483.T7 Troı͡tskaı͡a Sergieva lavra. Seminarii͡a
History
485 General works
By period
Beginnings of Christianity in Russia see BR934+
487 980-1237. Vladimir the Great, 980-1015
488 1237-1461. Mongolian period

Orthodox Eastern Church
Divisions of the Church
Russian Orthodox Church. Russkaia pravoslavnaia tserkov'
History
By period -- Continued

489 1461-1589. Period of the two metropolitanates (Moscow and Kiev)
490 1589-1720. Patriarchate of Moscow
491 1720-1917 (World War I). Synodal period
492 1917-1991. Soviet period
493 1991- Post-Soviet period

By region or country
Russian Empire. Former Soviet Union
Including Russian Federation
General works see BX485+

494.A-Z Local (other than city), A-Z
Including ecclesiastical jurisdictions (ecclesiastical provinces, archdioceses, dioceses, vicariates apostolic, prefectures apostolic, missions, and archdeaconates). In assigning Cutter numbers, various jurisdictions named after the same city or area should be differentiated
e.g.

494.B3 Baltic Provinces
494.P6 Polotsk
495.A-Z By city, A-Z
e.g.

495.K6 Kostroma
495.M55 Moscow
495.N6 Novgorod
495.R6 Rostov
495.5 Outside of the former Soviet Union
For Russkaia pravoslavnaia tserkov' zagranitsei (Synodal Church) see BX598

United States
496.A1 Periodicals
496.A3 Documents
(496.A5) Yearbooks
see BX496.A1
496.A6 Collections
496.A7 Study and teaching
496.A8-Z General works
497.A-.W By state, A-W
498.A-Z By city, A-Z
500.A-Z Other regions or countries, A-Z
e.g.

Orthodox Eastern Church
Divisions of the Church
Russian Orthodox Church. Russkaia pravoslavnaia t͡serkov′
By region or country
Outside of the Soviet Union
Other regions or countries, A-Z -- Continued

500.C9 Czechoslovakia. Czech Republic. Slovakia
510 General works
511 Pamphlets, etc.
512 Addresses, essays, lectures
513 Sermons
515 Polemical works against the Russian Church

Government and organization
520 General works
522 Patriarchate
523 Holy Synod (Sinod)
525 Metropolitanates
e.g. Leningrad, Moscow, Kiev
530 Eparchies or Dioceses
533 Vicariates
535 Deaneries
537 Parishes

Clergy
540 General works
545 White or secular clergy
e.g. Priests ("Popes"), deacons, etc.
550 Black or regular clergy (Monks of St. Basil)
Cf. BX580+ Monasticism
555 Archbishops and bishops
557 Laity
558 Church membership

Worship
Cf. BX575+ Saints. Hagiology
560 General works
563 Creeds and catechisms
(565) Liturgy and ritual
see BX350

Special liturgical works
(568) Evangelistaria
see BX375.E8
(569) Ostromirovo evangelio
see BX375.E8
(570) Apostoli
see BX375.A65
(571) Psalteria
see BX370

Orthodox Eastern Church
Divisions of the Church
Russian Orthodox Church. Russkai͡a pravoslavnai͡a t͡serkov′
Worship
Liturgy and ritual
Special liturgical works -- Continued

(573) Other, A-Z
see BX375

Saints. Hagiology
575 General works
576 Canonization
Worship. Relics, etc.
577 General works
577.5 Icons (not A-Z)
Lives of the saints
General see BX393
Russian saints see BX596
578 Devotional literature
Monasticism
580 Documentary sources
581 General works
582 Rules, discipline, etc.
For Rule of St. Basil see BX386.2
583.A-Z Individual monasteries, A-Z
e.g.
583.K5 Kiev. Pecherskai͡a lavra
Individual churches
590.A-Z Russia. By place, A-Z
Including the Russian Empire, former Soviet Union, and the Russian Federation
591.A-Z United States. By place, A-Z
592.A-Z Other countries, A-Z
Each country subarranged by place, A-Z
Biography
595 Collective
596 Lives of the Russian saints
For the lives of Russian and other saints treated together see BX393
597.A-Z Individual, A-Z
e.g.
597.I55 Innokentii, Metropolitan of Moscow
John, of Kronstadt, Saint, 1829-1909 see BX597.S4
597.K5 Khomiakov, Aleksei Stepanovich
597.N5 Nikon, Patriarch of Moscow
597.S37 Serafim, Saint
597.S4 Sergiev, Ioann. Il'ich

Orthodox Eastern Church
Divisions of the Church
Russian Orthodox Church. Russkai͡a pravoslavnai͡a t͡serkov′
Biography
Individual, A-Z -- Continued
597.S43 Sergii, Patriarch of Russia
597.S45 Sergii Radonezhskii, Saint
597.Z9 Anonymous persons
598 Russkai͡a pravoslavnai͡a t͡serkov' zagranit͡seĭ. (Karlowitsky) Synod of Bishops of the Russian Orthodox Church outside Russia (or, abroad, or in exile) (to 2007) (Table BX3)
Cf. BX460+ Russian Orthodox Church
Dissent
599 General works
601 Raskolniks. Old Believers
Other sects
see BT1319+ ; BX800+
605.A-Z Biography, A-Z
e.g.
605.A8 Avvakum, Protopope
605.N5 Nikita, called Pustosviat
610-619 Greek Orthodox Church. Orthodoxos Ekklēsia tēs Hellados (Table BX6)
Biography
619.A1 Collective
619.A3-Z Individual, A-Z
e.g.
619.M28 Makrakes, Apostolos
619.P45 Pharmakides Theokletos
620 Old Calendarists
630-639 Orthodox Church in Austria and Hungary (Table BX6 modified)
Including the Austro-Hungarian Empire
History
General works see BX633.A1
633.A1 General works
633.A5-Z By country, A-Z
e.g.
Bohemia see BX750.C9
633.B8 Bukowina
Czechoslovakia see BX750.C9
633.G3 Galicia
633.H8 Hungary
Class here works on Hungary before and after 1918

Orthodox Eastern Church
Divisions of the Church -- Continued
640-649 Albanian Autocephalous Orthodox Church. Kisha Ortodokse Autoqefale Shqiptare (Table BX6)
650-659 Bulgarian Orthodox Church. Bŭlgarska pravoslavna t︠s︡ŭrkva (Table BX6)
660-669 Georgian Apostolic Church. Sak'art'velos avtokep'aluri mart'lmadidebeli eklesia (Table BX6)
670-679 Montenegrin Church (Table BX6)
690-699 Romanian Orthodox Church. Biserica Ortodoxă Română (Table BX6)
710-719 Serbian Orthodox Church. Srpska pravoslavna crkva (Table BX6)
Cf. BX670+ Montenegrin Church
720-729 Macedonian Orthodox Church. Makedonska pravoslavna crkva (Table BX6)
729.5 Orthodox Eastern Church, Ukrainian (Table BX3 modified)
History
729.5.A4 General and Ukraine
729.5.A45A-.A45Z Other countries, A-Z
Canada see BX743+
United States see BX738.U4+
Orthodox Church in other regions or countries
Class here works in which the Church is either indigenous to a country or a result of immigration
For all Orthodox bodies, see other countries except the Russian Church, BX496+
North America
729.9 General works
United States
730 Periodicals. Societies
731 Directories. Yearbooks
732 Documents
Study and teaching
732.5 General works
Education of the clergy and religious men and women
732.6 General works
732.7.A-Z By country, A-Z
732.8.A-Z Seminaries, colleges, etc. By place, A-Z
History
733 General works
734.A-Z Local, A-Z
Including individual dioceses, monasteries, and churches
735.A1-.A5 Collected works

Orthodox Eastern Church
Divisions of the Church
Orthodox Church in other regions or countries
North America
United States -- Continued

735.A6-Z General works
Including catechisms

736 Sermons. Tracts. Addresses. Essays
For collections see BX735.A1+

(737) Ritual and liturgy
see BX350.A1+

738.A-Z Individual bodies, A-Z
Subarrange each body by Table BX7
e.g.

738.A5-.A59 Albanian Orthodox Church of America (Table BX7)

738.A6-.A69 American Carpatho-Russian Orthodox Greek Catholic Diocese in the U. S. A. (Table BX7)

738.A75-.A759 Antiochian Orthodox Christian Archdiocese of North America (Table BX7)

738.G7-.G79 Greek Orthodox Archdiocese of America. Hellēnikē Orthodoxos Archiepiskopē Amerikēs (Table BX7)

738.O77-.O779 Orthodox Church in America (Table BX7)

738.R6-.R69 Romanian Orthodox Episcopate of America. Episcopia Ortodoxă Română din America (Table BX7)

738.U4-.U49 Ukrainian Orthodox Church of the U.S.A. (Table BX7)

Biography

739.A1 Collective

739.A3-Z Individual, A-Z

Canada
For Independent Greek Church see BX7990.I55

743 Periodicals. Societies

743.1 Directories. Yearbooks

743.2 Documents

Study and teaching

743.25 General works

Education of the clergy and of religious men and women

743.26 General works

743.28.A-Z Seminaries, colleges, etc. By place, A-Z

History

743.3 General works

743.4.A-Z Local, A-Z
Including individual dioceses, monasteries, and churches

Orthodox Eastern Church
Divisions of the Church
Orthodox Church in other regions or countries
North America
Canada -- Continued

743.5 General works
Including catechisms
743.6 Sermons. Tracts. Addresses. Essays
(743.7) Ritual and liturgy
see BX350.A1+
743.8 Other topics (not A-Z)
Biography
743.9.A1 Collective
743.9.A3-Z Individual, A-Z
South America
745 Brazil
746.A-Z Other regions or countries, A-Z
Europe
Great Britain
747 Periodicals. Societies
747.1 Directories. Yearbooks
747.2 Documents
Study and teaching
747.25 General works
Education of the clergy and of religious men and women
747.26 General works
747.28.A-Z Seminaries, colleges, etc. By place, A-Z
History
747.3 General works
747.4.A-Z Local, A-Z
Including individual dioceses, monasteries, and churches
747.5 General works
Including catechisms
747.6 Sermons. Tracts. Addresses. Essays
(747.7) Ritual and liturgy
see BX350.A1+
747.8 Other topics (not A-Z)
Biography
747.9.A1 Collective
747.9.A3-Z Individual, A-Z
750.A-Z Other regions and countries, A-Z
Cf. BX460+ Principal Orthodox Churches
750.B3 Balkan Peninsula
750.B67 Bosnia and Hercegovina
750.C76 Croatia

Orthodox Eastern Church
Divisions of the Church
Orthodox Church in other regions or countries
Europe
Other regions and countries, A-Z -- Continued
750.C9 Czechoslovakia. Czech Republic. Slovakia
750.E8 Estonia
750.F56 Finland
750.L38 Latvia
750.M65 Moldova
750.P6 Poland
750.S56 Slovenia
Ukraine see BX729.5
750.W5 White Russia
750.Y8 Yugoslavia
For Bosnia and Hercegovina see BX750.B67
For Croatia see BX750.C76
For Slovenia see BX750.S56
For the Macedonian Orthodox Church see BX720+
For the Serbian Orthodox Church see BX710+
Asia
751 General works
752.A-Z By region or country, A-Z
Africa
753 General works
754.A-Z By region or country, A-Z
755 Australia
756 Western rites
Catholic Church
Periodicals
800.A1 Polyglot
800.A2-Z Latin
801 English
802 French
803 German
804 Italian
805 Spanish and Portuguese
806.A-Z Other. By language, A-Z
e.g.
806.C3 Catalan
806.P6 Polish
Societies. Confraternities, etc.
808 General works
808.5.A-Z By region or country, A-Z
For individual local societies see BX810+
Individual societies, sodalities, etc.

Catholic Church
Societies. Confraternities, etc.
Individual societies, sodalities, etc. -- Continued

809.A-Z	Other than local, A-Z
	e.g.
809.A6	Apostleship of Prayer
	Catholic action societies see BX2348.Z6+
809.F6	Focolare Movement
809.H7	Holy Name Society
	Knights of Columbus see HS1538.A+
	Ladies of Charity of St. Vincent de Paul
809.L3	Periodicals
809.L32	General works
	United States
809.L33A1-.L33A5	General works
809.L33A6-.L33Z	Local, A-Z
809.L34A-.L34Z	Other countries, A-Z
809.L35	Legion of Mary
(809.O6)	Opus Dei
	see BX819.3.O68
809.S4	St. John Berchman's Sanctuary Society
809.S462	Sankt Knuds gilde
	Society of St. Vincent de Paul
809.S5	Periodicals
809.S6	General works
	United States
809.S7A1-.S7A5	General works
809.S7A6-.S7Z	Local, A-Z
809.S8A-.S8Z	Other countries, A-Z
809.V6	Sodality of the Blessed Virgin Mary
809.Y6-.Y64	Young Christian Workers
809.Y6	Periodicals
809.Y62	General works
	United States
809.Y63A1-.Y63A5	General works
809.Y63A6-.Y63Z	Local, A-Z
809.Y64A-.Y64Z	Other countries, A-Z
	Local societies. By name, A-Z
810	United States
811	English
812	French
813	German
814	Italian
815	Spanish and Portuguese
816.A-Z	Other, A-Z
	e.g.
816.C3	Canadian

Catholic Church
Societies. Confraternities, etc.
Individual societies, sodalities, etc.
Local societies. By name, A-Z
Other, A-Z -- Continued
816.Y8 Yugoslav
Gesellenvereine
817.A1 General works
817.A5-Z Individual societies, A-Z
Secular institutes
818.A1 General works
818.A5-Z Individual institutes, A-Z
818.5.A-Z By region or country, A-Z
Personal prelatures
819 General works
819.3.A-Z Individual prelatures, A-Z
e.g.
819.3.O68 Opus Dei
Councils
General works
820 Early through 1800
821 1801-1950
822 1951-2000
823 2001-
Western (post-schismatic) councils
For councils up to 1054 see BR200+ ; BR250+
Collective
(825.A1-.A29) Acts, decrees, canons, etc.
see KBR830
(825.A1901) Mansi, J.D., ed. Sacrorum conciliorum nova et amplissima collectio ... Paris, 1901-
see KBR200.M36
825.A3-Z Histories, etc.
826.A-Z Special topics, A-Z
e.g.
826.E5 Enthronement of Gospels
Individual. By date of opening
830 0809 Council of Aachen (Table BX8)
830 0869 4th Council of Constantinople (Table BX8)
830 0879 Council of Union (Table BX8)
830 1064 Council of Mantua (Table BX8)
830 1123 1st Lateran Council (Table BX8)
830 1139 2nd Lateran Council (Table BX8)
830 1179 3rd Lateran Council (Table BX8)
830 1215 4th Lateran Council (Table BX8)
830 1245 1st Council of Lyons (Table BX8)
830 1274 2nd Council of Lyons (Table BX8)

Catholic Church
Councils
Western (post-schismatic) councils
Individual. By date of opening -- Continued

830 1311 Council of Vienne (Table BX8)
830 1409 Council of Pisa (Table BX8)
830 1414 Council of Constance (Table BX8)
830 1423 Council of Pavia-Siena (Table BX8)
830 1431 Council of Basel (Table BX8)
830 1438 Council of Ferrara-Florence (Table BX8)
830 1511 2nd Council of Pisa (Table BX8)
830 1512 5th Lateran Council (Table BX8)
830 1545 Council of Trent (Table BX8)
830 1596 Council of Brest-Litovsk (Table BX8)
830 1869 1st Vatican Council (Table BX8)
830 1962 2nd Vatican Council (Table BX8)
830.5 Episcopal synods
831 Special. By date of opening
Subarrange each synod by Table BX8
Plenary councils. National councils
Under each country include the diocesan and provincial councils that are in a straight line of succession legislating for the whole area; for all others, see BX1401+
Latin America
831.5 General works
832 Special. By date of opening
Subarrange each council by Table BX8
United States
833 General works
835 Special. By date of opening
e.g.
835 1852 1st Plenary Council of Baltimore
835 1866 2nd Plenary Council of Baltimore
835 1884 3rd Plenary Council of Baltimore
837.A-Z Other countries, A-Z
e.g.
837.C2 Canada
837.C2 1909 1st Plenary Council, Quebec
837.5 Episcopal conferences
838 Diocesan synods
Including diocesan pastoral councils
For senates of priests see BX1914.5
839.A-Z Congresses, conferences, etc. By place, A-Z
For local congresses see BX1401+
Cf. BT595 Marian congresses
Cf. BX2215.A1 Eucharistic congresses

Catholic Church -- Continued
Museums. Exhibitions
840.A1-.A4 General works
840.A5-Z Special and local, A-Z
841 Dictionaries. Encyclopedias
842 Handbooks, manuals, etc.
842.5 Computer network resources
843 Pictorial works
Cf. BX956 History of the Papacy
845 Directories. Yearbooks
Class here general directories and yearbooks of the United States (General); for other countries, see BX1419-BX1692; for United States local, see BX1408-BX1692
847 Atlases
Documents
Collections
850 General works
Bulls
855 General works
857 Works about bulls
860 Encyclicals
863 Epistolae. Letters
Cf. BX860 Encyclicals
865 Other (not A-Z)
870 Documents of individual popes. Bullaria, Regesta, etc. By date of accession of pope
e.g.
870 1963 Paul VI
870 1978 Aug. John Paul I
870 1978 Oct. John Paul II
873 Special documents. By date of issue, including month and day
For documents on special subjects, see the subject in classes A-Z, e.g. BX4725, Bull "Unigenitus," on the Jansenists
Commentaries on documents may be arranged by author or main entry, e.g. Chevrot's work on Pius XII's encyclical of October 20, 1939: BX873 1939 Oct.20.C5
Works about papal documents
873.5 General works
873.7 Dictionaries. Indexes
Episcopal charges. Pastoral letters
874.A2 Collections
874.A3-Z Individual charges and letters. By bishop and title, A-Z
Forgeries of documents
General works
875.A2 Early through 1800
875.A3 1801-1950

Catholic Church
Documents
Forgeries of documents
General works -- Continued
875.A4 1951-2000
875.A43 2001-
875.A5-Z Special, A-Z
e.g.
Donation of Constantine
875.D6 Texts. By date
875.D6A-.D6Z Translations. By language, A-Z, and date
875.D7 History and criticism
Pseudo-Isidorian Decretals
875.P7 Texts
875.P8 History and criticism
General collected works
Several authors
Including series of monographs
880 General works
885 Minor collections
Individual authors
890 Early through 1950
Including single works of medieval writers
For early Christian literature, Fathers of the Church see BR65.A+
For the medieval summa theologica see BX1749+
891 1951-2000
891.3 2001-
Study and teaching
Cf. LC461+ Education
895 General works
Education of the clergy and of religious men and women
900 General works
903 General special
e.g. Seminary life
904 Outlines, syllabi, tables, etc. Manuals
904.8 History of the study of theology
For individual countries see BX905+
By region or country
United States
905 General works
908.A-.W By state, A-W
909.A-Z By city, A-Z
910.A-Z Other regions or countries, A-Z
Seminaries, colleges, etc.

Catholic Church
Study and teaching
Education of the clergy and of religious men and women
Seminaries, colleges, etc. -- Continued
915.A-Z United States. By city, A-Z
Under each:
.xA1-.xA59 Official publications
.xA1-.xA39 Serial publications
.xA4-.xA59 Monographs
.xA6-.xZ Nonofficial publications
920.A-Z Other regions or countries. By city, A-Z
Under each:
.xA1-.xA59 Official publications
.xA1-.xA39 Serial publications
.xA4-.xA59 Monographs
.xA6-.xZ Nonofficial publications
Education of the laity
921 General works
922 College and university education
Juvenile education. Elementary schools, high schools, Sunday schools
Including organization and methods
Cf. BX2373.T4 Meditations for teachers
923 Periodicals. Societies, etc.
General works
925.A2 Early through 1800
925.A3-Z 1801-1950
926 1951-2000
926.3 2001-
929 Curricula, outlines, etc.
Textbooks, etc.
Cf. BX1958+ Catechisms
930 General works
930.5 History and criticism
By region or country
932 United States
933.A-Z Other regions or countries, A-Z
935 Inquirers, catechumens, neophytes, etc.
Study and teaching of Church history
Includes outlines of courses
938 General works
939.A-Z Individual historians, A-Z
e.g.
939.A4 Alegre, Francisco Javier
939.B3 Bargellini, Piero
939.C6 Courcy de Laroche-Héron, Henri de
939.G33 Gasquet, Francis Aidan, cardinal

Catholic Church
Study and teaching of Church history
Individual historians, A-Z -- Continued
939.L3 Lasserre, Henri de Monzie de
939.P3 Pastor, Ludwig, freiherr von
History
940 Periodicals. Societies
Collected works
941 General
942 Sources
Cf. BX850+ Documents
General works
944 Early to 1800
945 1801-1950
945.2 1951-2000
945.3 2001-
946 General special
948 Textbooks. Juvenile works
949 Addresses, essays, lectures
History of the Papacy
Including lives of the popes
For individual popes see BX965+
For the position of the pope in church government, etc. see BX1805+
General works
Early through 1800
Liber pontificalis
950.A2 Latin texts. By date
950.A5-.Z4 Other. By language
950.Z5 History and criticism
953 Other works
955 1801-1950
955.2 1951-2000
955.3 2001-
956 Pictorial works
Cf. BX843 Catholic Church
957 General special
958.A-Z Special topics, A-Z
958.A23 Abdication
958.C4 Chair of St. Peter
Christian union and Catholic Church see BX9.5.P29
958.C7 Criminal history
958.E55 Enthronement
958.F2 Fables concerning popes
e.g.Pope Joan
958.H64 Holy years
958.L5 Liberty

Catholic Church
History
History of the Papacy
Special topics, A-Z -- Continued
958.M6 Monuments
958.N35 Names
958.P6 Portraits
958.P75 Prophecies
958.R4 Residence
958.T7 Tombs
958.V7 Voyages
960 Pamphlets, etc.
By period
Under each:
.A2-.A3 Documents
.A2 Collections
.A3 Individual. By date
For special topics, see the topic
To the Council of Trent, 1545
965 General works
To 590 A.D.
970 General works
980 Origins
Individual popes
Saint Peter, d. 64 or 67 see BS2515
1002 Saint Linus, 67-76
1003 Saint Anacletus I, 76-88
1004 Saint Clement I (Clemens, Romanus), 88-97
1005 Saint Evaristus, 97-105
1006 Saint Alexander I, 105-115
1007 Saint Sixtus (Xystus) I, 115-125
1008 Saint Telesphorus, 125-136
1009 Saint Hyginus, 136-140
1010 Saint Pius I, 140-155
1011 Saint Anicetus, 155-166
1012 Saint Soter, 166-175
1013 Saint Eleutherius, 175-189
1014 Saint Victor I, 189-199
1015 Saint Zephyrinus, 199-217
1016 Saint Callistus I, 217-222
1016.5 Saint Hippolytus, 217-235 (Antipope)
1017 Saint Urban I, 222-230
1018 Saint Pontian, 230-235
1019 Saint Anterus, 235-236
1020 Saint Fabian, 236-250
1021 Saint Cornelius, 251-253

Catholic Church
History
By period
To the Council of Trent
To 590 A.D.
Individual popes
Saint Cornelius, 251-253
Novatianus, 251 (Antipope) see BR1720.N8
1023 Saint Lucius I, 253-254
1024 Saint Stephen I, 254-257
1025 Saint Sixtus (Xystus) II, 257-258
1026 Saint Dionysius, 259-268
1027 Saint Felix I, 269-274
1028 Saint Eutychian, 275-283
1029 Saint Caius, 283-296
1030 Saint Marcellinus, 296-304
1031 Saint Marcellus I, 308-309
1032 Saint Eusebius, 309 (310)
1033 Saint Melchiades (Miltiades), 311-314
1034 Saint Sylvester I, 314-335
1035 Saint Marcus, 336
1036 Saint Julius I, 337-352
1037 Liberius, 352-366
1038 Felix II, 355-365 (Antipope)
1039 Damasus I, 366-384
1039.5 Ursinus, 366-367 (Antipope)
1040 Saint Siricius, 384-399
1041 Saint Anastasius I, 399-401
1042 Saint Innocent I, 401-417
1043 Saint Zosimus, 417-418
1044 Saint Boniface I, 418-422
1044.5 Eulalius, 418-419 (Antipope)
1045 Saint Celestine I, 422-432
1046 Saint Sixtus (Xystus) III, 432-440
1047 Saint Leo I, The Great, 440-461
1048 Saint Hilarius, 461-468
1049 Saint Simplicius, 468-483
1050 Saint Felix III (II), 483-492
1051 Saint Gelasius I, 492-496
1052 Anastasius II, 496-498
1053 Saint Symmachus, 498-514
1053.5 Laurentius, 498, 501-505 (Antipope)
1054 Saint Hormisdas, 514-523
1055 Saint John I, 523-526
1056 Saint Felix IV (III), 526-530
1057 Boniface II, 530-532
1057.5 Dioscorus, 530 (Antipope)

Catholic Church
History
By period
To the Council of Trent, 1545
To 590 A.D.
Individual popes -- Continued
1058 John II, 533-535
1059 Saint Agapetus I, 535-536
1060 Saint Silverius, 536-537 (Exiled)
1061 Vigilius, 537-555
1062 Pelagius I, 556-561
1063 John III, 561-574
1064 Benedict I, 575-579
1065 Pelagius II, 579-590
1066 Special topics (not A-Z)
e.g. The Papacy and the primitive Church
Medieval Church
1068 General works
1069 The German popes
1069.5 Special topics (not A-Z)
590-1049
1070 General works
Individual popes
1076 Saint Gregory I, The Great, 590-604
1077 Sabinianus, 604-606
1078 Boniface III, 607
1079 Saint Boniface IV, 608-615
1080 Saint Deusdedit (Adeodatus I), 615-618
1081 Boniface V, 619-625
1082 Honorius I, 625-638
1083 Severinus, 640
1084 John IV, 640-642
1085 Theodore I, 642-649
1086 Saint Martin I, 649-655 (Exiled)
1087 Saint Eugenius I, 654-657
1088 Saint Vitalian, 657-672
1089 Adeodatus II, 672-676
1090 Donus, 676-678
1091 Saint Agatho, 678-681
1092 Saint Leo II, 682-683
1093 Saint Benedict II, 684-685
1094 John V, 685-686
1095 Conon, 686-687
1095.3 Theodore, 687 (Antipope)
1095.5 Paschal, 687 (Antipope)
1096 Saint Sergius I, 687-701
1097 John VI, 701-705

Catholic Church
History
By period
To the Council of Trent, 1545
590-1049
Individual popes -- Continued

1098 John VII, 705-707
1099 Sisinnius, 708
1100 Constantine, 708-715
1101 Saint Gregory II, 715-731
1102 Saint Gregory III, 731-741
1103 Saint Zacharias, 741-752
1104 Stephen II, 752
1105 Stephen III, 752-757
1106 Saint Paul I, 757-767
1107 Constantine, 767-769 (Antipope)
1108 Stephen IV, 768-772
1109 Adrian I, 772-795
1110 Saint Leo III, 795-816
1111 Stephen V, 816-817
1112 Saint Paschal I, 817-824
1113 Eugenius II, 824-827
1114 Valentine, 827
1115 Gregory IV, 827-844
1115.5 John, 844 (Antipope)
1116 Sergius II, 844-847
1117 Saint Leo IV, 847-855
1118 Benedict III, 855-858
1119 Anastasius, 855 (Antipope)
1120 Saint Nicholas I, 858-867
1121 Adrian II, 867-872
1122 John VIII, 872-882
1123 Marinus I (Martin II), 882-884
1124 Saint Adrian III, 884-885
1125 Stephen VI, 885-891
1126 Formosus, 891-896
1127 Boniface VI, 896
1128 Stephen VII, 896-897
1129 Romanus, 897
1130 Theodore II, 897
1131 John IX, 898-900
1132 Benedict IV, 900-903
1133 Leo V, 903
1134 Christopher, 903-904 (Antipope)
1135 Sergius III, 904-911
1136 Anastasius III, 911-913
1137 Lando, 913-914

Catholic Church
History
By period
To the Council of Trent, 1545
590-1049
Individual popes -- Continued

1138 John X, 914-928
1139 Leo VI, 928
1140 Stephen VIII, 928-931
1141 John XI, 931-935
1142 Leo VII, 936-939
1143 Stephen IX, 939-942
1144 Marinus II (Martin III), 942-946
1145 Agapetus II, 946-955
1146 John XII, 955-964 (Deposed)
1147 Leo VIII, 963-965
1148 Benedict V, 964-966
1149 John XIII, 965-972
1150 Benedict VI, 973-974
1151 Boniface VII, 974 (Antipope)
Cf. BX1154 Antipope second time
1152 Benedict VII, 974-983
1153 John XIV, 983-984
1154 Boniface VII, 984-985 (Antipope)
Cf. BX1151 Antipope first time
1155 John XV, 985-996
1156 Gregory V, 996-999
1157 John XVI, 997-998 (Antipope)
1158 Sylvester II, 999-1003
1159 John XVII, 1003
1160 John XVIII, 1004-1009
1161 Sergius IV, 1009-1012
1162 Benedict VIII, 1012-1024
1162.5 Gregory, 1012 (Antipope)
1163 John XIX, 1024-1032
1164 Benedict IX, 1032-1044
Cf. BX1165.5 Pope second time
Cf. BX1168 Pope third time
1165 Sylvester III, 1045
1165.5 Benedict IX, 1045
Cf. BX1164 Pope first time
Cf. BX1168 Pope third time
1166 Gregory VI, 1045-1046
1167 Clement II, 1046-1047
1168 Benedict IX, 1047-1048
Cf. BX1164 Pope first time
Cf. BX1165.5 Pope second time

Catholic Church
History
By period
To the Council of Trent, 1545
590-1049
Individual popes -- Continued
1169 Damasus II, 1048
Special topics
1171 Roman Church and the Byzantine Empire
1173 Church and Charlemagne
1175 Church and the Holy Roman Empire
Cf. BX1210+ Popes and Hohenstaufen
1176 Other special (not A-Z)
1049-1122
Including works on the 11th century
1178 General works
Individual popes
1180 Saint Leo IX, 1049-1054
1181 Victor II, 1055-1057
1182 Stephen X, 1057-1058
1183 Benedict X, 1058-1059 (Antipope)
1184 Nicholas II, 1059-1061
1185 Alexander II, 1061-1073
1186 Honorius II, 1061-1072 (Antipope)
1187 Saint Gregory VII, 1073-1085
1188 Clement III, 1084-1100 (Antipope)
1189 Victor III, 1086-1087
1190 Urban II, 1088-1099
1191 Paschal II, 1099-1118
1191.3 Theodoric, 1100 (Antipope)
1191.5 Albertus, 1102 (Antipope)
1192 Sylvester IV, 1105-1111 (Antipope)
1193 Gelasius II, 1118-1119
1194 Gregory VIII, 1118-1121 (Antipope)
1195 Callistus II, 1119-1124
Special topics
German Papacy see BX1069
1197 Papacy and the Normans
1198 Investiture struggle
1199 Concordat of Worms, 1122
1200 Other special (not A-Z)
1122-1305. Popes and Hohenstaufen
Including works on the 12th and 13th centuries
1210 General works
Individual popes
1216 Honorius II, 1124-1130
1217 Celestine II, 1124 (Antipope)

Catholic Church
History
By period
To the Council of Trent, 1545
1122-1305. Popes and Hohenstaufen
Individual popes -- Continued

1218 Innocent II, 1130-1143
1219 Anacletus II, 1130-1138 (Antipope)
1220 Victor IV, 1138 (Antipope)
1221 Celestine II, 1143-1144
1222 Lucius II, 1144-1145
1223 Eugenius III, 1145-1153
1224 Anastasius IV, 1153-1154
1225 Adrian IV, 1154-1159
1226 Alexander III, 1159-1181
1227 Victor IV, 1159-1164 (Antipope)
1228 Paschal III, 1164-1168 (Antipope)
1229 Callistus III, 1168-1178 (Antipope)
1230 Innocent III, 1179-1180 (Antipope)
1231 Lucius III, 1181-1185
1232 Urban III, 1185-1187
1233 Gregory VIII, 1187
1234 Clement III, 1187-1191
1235 Celestine III, 1191-1198
1236 Innocent III, 1198-1216
1237 Honorius III, 1216-1227
1238 Gregory IX, 1227-1241
1239 Celestine IV, 1241
1240 Innocent IV, 1243-1254
1241 Alexander IV, 1254-1261
1242 Urban IV, 1261-1264
1243 Clement IV, 1265-1268
1244 Gregory X, 1271-1276
1245 Innocent V, 1276
1246 Adrian V, 1276
1247 John XXI, 1276-1277
1248 Nicholas III, 1277-1280
1249 Martin IV, 1281-1285
1250 Honorius IV, 1285-1287
1251 Nicholas IV, 1288-1292
1252 Saint Celestine V, 1294
1253 Boniface VIII, 1294-1303
1254 Benedict XI, 1303-1304

Special topics

1256 Arnaldo da Brescia and the Arnoldists
1257 Apostolic Brethren. Segarelli, Dolcino, etc.
1260 Papacy and Barbarossa

Catholic Church
History
By period
To the Council of Trent, 1545
1122-1305. Popes and Hohenstaufen
Special topics -- Continued
1261 Papacy and Frederick II
1262 Papacy and Philip IV
1263 Other special (not A-Z)
1305-1447. Schisms and councils
Including 14th century
1270 General works
Individual popes
1275 Clement V, 1305-1314
1276 John XXII, 1316-1334
1277 Nicolas V, 1328-1330 (Antipope)
1278 Benedict XII, 1334-1342
1279 Clement VI, 1342-1352
1280 Innocent VI, 1352-1362
1281 Urban V, 1362-1370
1282 Gregory XI, 1371-1378
1283 Urban VI, 1378-1389
1284 Clement VII, 1378-1394 (Antipope)
1285 Boniface IX, 1389-1404
1286 Benedict XIII, 1394-1423 (Antipope)
1287 Innocent VII, 1404-1406
1288 Gregory XII, 1406-1415
1289 Alexander V, 1409-1410 (Antipope)
1290 John XXIII, 1410-1415 (Antipope)
1291 Martin V, 1417-1431
1292 Clement VIII, 1424-1429 (Antipope)
1293 Benedict XIV, 1425-1430 (Antipope)
1294 Eugenius IV, 1431-1447
1295 Felix V, 1439-1449 (Antipope)
Special topics
1300 The French Papacy. Babylonian Captivity
Including the return from Avignon
1301 The Great Western Schism, 1378-1417
1302 Other special topics
1447- . Modern history
1304 General works
1447-1572. Renaissance and Reformation
Including works on the 15th and 16th centuries
1305 General works
Individual popes
1306 Nicholas V, 1447-1455
1307 Callistus III, 1445-1458

Catholic Church
History
By period
1447- . Modern history
1447-1572. Renaissance and Reformation
Individual popes -- Continued
1308 Pius II, 1458-1464
1309 Paul II, 1464-1471
1310 Sixtus IV, 1471-1484
1311 Innocent VIII, 1484-1492
1312 Alexander VI, 1492-1503
1313 Pius III, 1503
1314 Julius II, 1503-1513
1315 Leo X, 1513-1521
1316 Adrian VI, 1522-1523
1317 Clement VII, 1523-1534
1318 Paul III, 1534-1549
1319 Julius III, 1550-1555
1320 Marcellus II, 1555
1321 Paul IV, 1555-1559
1322 Pius IV, 1559-1565
1323 Saint Pius V, 1566-1572
Special topics
1325 Papacy and the Renaissance
1326 Papacy and the Reformation
Counter Reformation see BR430
1328 Philip II and the Papacy
1329 Other special topics
1572-1789
1330 General works
Individual popes
1334 Gregory XIII, 1572-1585
1335 Sixtus V, 1585-1590
1336 Urban VII, 1590
1337 Gregory XIV, 1590-1591
1338 Innocent IX, 1591
1339 Clement VIII, 1592-1605
1340 Leo XI, 1605
1341 Paul V, 1605-1621
1342 Gregory XV, 1621-1623
1343 Urban VIII, 1623-1644
1344 Innocent X, 1644-1655
1345 Alexander VII, 1655-1667
1346 Clement IX, 1667-1669
1347 Clement X, 1670-1676
1348 Innocent XI, 1676-1689
1349 Alexander VIII, 1689-1691

Catholic Church
History
By period
1447- . Modern history
1572-1789
Individual popes -- Continued
1350 Innocent XII, 1691-1700
1351 Clement XI, 1700-1721
1352 Innocent XIII, 1721-1724
1353 Benedict XIII, 1724-1730
1354 Clement XII, 1730-1740
1355 Benedict XIV, 1740-1758
1356 Clement XIII, 1758-1769
1357 Clement XIV, 1769-1774
1360 1572-1700
1361 18th century
1789-
1365 General works
Individual popes
1368 Pius VI, 1775-1799
1369 Pius VII, 1800-1823
1370 Leo XII, 1823-1829
1371 Pius VIII, 1829-1830
1372 Gregory XVI, 1831-1846
1373 Pius IX, 1846-1878
1374 Leo XIII, 1878-1903
1375 Saint Pius X, 1903-1914
1376 Benedict XV, 1914-1922
1377 Pius XI, 1922-1939
1378 Pius XII, 1939-1958
1378.2 John XXIII, 1958-1963
1378.3 Paul VI, 1963-1978
1378.4 John Paul I, 1978
1378.5 John Paul II, 1978-2005
1378.6 Benedict XVI, 2005-
Special topics
1385 Papacy and French Revolution
Cf. DC158.2 Religious history during the French Revolution
Other topics see BX1395+
19th century
1386 General works
Individual popes see BX1368+
Special topics
1387 Papacy and Holy Alliance
1388 Loss of temporal power
Cf. DG798.7 Papal States

Catholic Church
History
By period
1447- . Modern history
1789-
19th century
Special topics -- Continued
Other topics see BX1395+
20th century
1389 General works
Individual popes see BX1368+
Special topics
Papacy and World War I see D622
Papacy and World War II see D810.C6
Other topics see BX1395+
1390 1965-
Catholic Church and modernism, liberalism, etc., since 1789
1395 Catholic Church and modern thought
1396 Modernism
1396.2 Liberalism
1396.3 Socialism
Cf. HX54 Catholic socialism
1396.4 Communism
1396.6 Nationalism
1396.7 Internationalism
1397 Other (not A-Z)
By region or country
Including diplomatic relations with special countries
For periods before the Reformation unless treating specifically of the Catholic Church see BR1+
1401.A1 Groups of countries not in a particular geographical area
e.g. Communist countries
1401.A3-Z America
North America
General works
1402 Early through 1800
1403 1801-1950
1403.2 1951-2000
1403.3 2001-
United States
1404 Periodicals. Societies. Congresses
Cf. BX810 Local societies
Cf. BX1407.A+ Special topics
Directories, yearbooks see BX845
1405 Documents
General works

Catholic Church
History
By region or country
North America
United States
General works -- Continued

1406 Early through 1950
For early works of North America see BX1402

1406.2 1951-2000

1406.3 2001-

1407.A-Z Special topics, A-Z

African Americans see BX1407.N4

1407.A5 Americanism

1407.A58 Anglican use churches

1407.A9 Austrians

1407.B4 Belgians

1407.B57 Bishops. Hierarchy

Bohemians see BX1407.C9

1407.C2 Cahenslyism
Including cases

1407.C27 Catholic traditionalist movement

1407.C48 City churches

1407.C6 Clergy

1407.C7 Communism

1407.C76 Conservatism. Conservative movements

Conservative movements see BX1407.C76

1407.C83 Cubans

1407.C9 Czechs

1407.D45 Democracy

1407.D54 Diocesan government

1407.E22 East Europeans

1407.E45 Employees

1407.F7 French

1407.F75 French Canadians

1407.G4 Germans

Hierarchy see BX1407.B57

1407.H55 Hispanic Americans

1407.I45 Immigrants

1407.I5 Intellectual life

1407.I7 Irish

1407.I8 Italians

1407.L5 Lithuanians

1407.M48 Mexican Americans

1407.M68 Motion pictures

1407.M84 Multiculturalism. Religious pluralism

1407.N4 Negroes. African Americans

1407.P24 Pacifism

Catholic Church
History
By region or country
North America
United States
Special topics, A-Z -- Continued

1407.P3 Parishes
1407.P46 Pensions
1407.P6 Poles
1407.P63 Political activity
1407.P67 Portuguese
1407.P8 Property
1407.P83 Puerto Ricans
Religious pluralism see BX1407.M84
Retirement systems see BX1407.P46
1407.R7 Rumanians
1407.R8 Rural churches. Rural church work
1407.S24 Salaries
1407.S55 Slovaks
1407.S56 Slovenes
1407.S6 Social conditions and social surveys
1407.S66 Spirituality
1407.S8 Suburban churches
1407.S9 Swiss
1407.T4 Teaching office
1407.T77 Trusteeism
1407.U6 Uniats
Cf. BX4711.72+ Ruthenians in the United States
1407.V54 Vietnamese
1407.W65 Women

By region
1408 New England
1410 South
1411 Central States
1412 West
1413 Pacific Coast

States, cities, etc.
1415.A-.W By state, A-W
1417.A-Z Ecclesiastical jurisdictions. By place, A-Z
1418.A-Z By city, A-Z

Canada
1419 Periodicals. Societies, etc.
General works
1420 Early through 1800
1421 1801-1950
1421.2 1951-2000

Catholic Church
History
By region or country
North America
Canada
General works -- Continued
1421.3 2001-
1422.A-Z By province, A-Z
1423.A-Z Ecclesiastical jurisdictions. By place, A-Z
1424.A-Z By city, A-Z
Latin America
1425.A1 Periodicals. Societies. Congresses
1425.A2 Collected works
Documents
1425.A3 Collections
1425.A35 Special. By date
1425.A4 Directories
General works
1425.A5-Z Early through 1800
1426 1801-1950
1426.2 1951-2000
1426.3 2001-
Mexico
1427.A1 Periodicals. Societies. Congresses
1427.A2 Collected works
Documents
1427.A3 Collections
1427.A35 Special. By date
1427.A4 Directories
General works
1427.A5-Z Early through 1800
1428 1801-1950
1428.2 1951-2000
1428.3 2001-
1429.A-Z By state, A-Z
1430.A-Z Ecclesiastical jurisdictions. By place, A-Z
1431.A-Z By city, A-Z
Central America
1432 General works
1434-1435 Belize (Table BX9)
1436-1437 Costa Rica (Table BX9)
1438-1439 Guatemala (Table BX9)
1440-1441 Honduras (Table BX9)
1442-1443 Nicaragua (Table BX9)
1444-1445 Panama (Table BX9)
1446-1447 El Salvador (Salvador) (Table BX9)
West Indies

Catholic Church
History
By region or country
Latin America
West Indies -- Continued
1448 General works
1449-1450 Bahamas (Table BX9)
1451-1452 Cuba (Table BX9)
1453-1454 Haiti (Table BX9)
1455-1456 Jamaica (Table BX9)
1457-1458 Puerto Rico (Table BX9)
1459.A-Z Other, A-Z
South America
General works
1460 Early to 1800
1461 1801-1950
1461.2 1951-2000
1461.3 2001-
Individual countries
1462-1463 Argentina (Table BX9)
1464-1465 Bolivia (Table BX9)
1466-1467 Brazil (Table BX9)
1468-1469 Chile (Table BX9)
1470-1471 Colombia (Table BX9)
1472-1473 Ecuador (Table BX9)
Guiana
1474 General works
1476-1477 Guyana (Table BX9)
1478-1479 Suriname (Table BX9)
1480-1481 French Guiana (Table BX9)
1482-1483 Paraguay (Table BX9)
1484-1485 Peru (Table BX9)
1486-1487 Uruguay (Table BX9)
1488-1489 Venezuela (Table BX9)
Europe
1490 General (Table BX10)
By region
1490.4 Central
1490.5 Eastern
1490.6 Northern
1490.7 German-speaking
Great Britain. England
1491 General (Table BX10)
By period
Pre-Reformation period see BR745+
1492 Reformation to Catholic Emancipation Act, 1517-1829. Protestant persecution of Catholics

Catholic Church
History
By region or country
Europe
By region
Great Britain. England
By period -- Continued
1493 1801-1945
1493.2 1945-
Local (England)
1494.A-Z Counties, etc., A-Z
1495.A-Z Ecclesiastical jurisdictions. By place, A-Z
1496.A-Z Cities, A-Z
1497-1502 Scotland (Table BX32)
1503-1508 Ireland (Table BX32)
1509-1514 Wales (Table BX32)
Austria
1515 General (Table BX10)
By period
1516 Through 1800
1517 1801-1945
1517.2 1945-
Local
1520.A-Z Country divisions, A-Z
1521.A-Z Ecclesiastical jurisdictions. By place, A-Z
1522.A-Z Cities, A-Z
Belgium
1523 General (Table BX10)
By period
1524 Through 1789
1525 1789-1945
1525.2 1945-
Local
1526.A-Z Country divisions, A-Z
Including ecclesiastical jurisdictions, by place, A-Z
1527.A-Z Cities, A-Z
Czechoslovakia
1527.3 General (Table BX10)
Local
1527.4.A-Z Country divisions, A-Z
Including ecclesiastical jurisdictions, by place, A-Z
For Slovak Republic see BX1582.4+
1527.5.A-Z Cities, A-Z
France
1528 General (Table BX10)
By period
1529 Through 1789

Catholic Church
History
By region or country
Europe
France
By period -- Continued
1530 1789-1945
Cf. DC192.6 Concordat of 1801
1530.2 1945-
Local
1531.A-Z Country divisions, A-Z
1532.A-Z Ecclesiastical jurisdictions. By place, A-Z
1533.A-Z Cities, A-Z
Germany
1534 General (Table BX10)
By period
1535 Through 1789
1536 1789-1945
Including Concordat of 1933
1536.2 1945-
Local
1537.A-Z Country divisions, A-Z
1538.A-Z Ecclesiastical jurisdictions. By place, A-Z
1539.A-Z Cities, A-Z
1540-1542 Greece (Table BX33)
Hungary
1542.3 General (Table BX10)
Local
1542.4.A-Z Country divisions, A-Z
Including ecclesiastical jurisdictions, by place, A-Z
1542.5.A-Z Cities, A-Z
Italy
1543 General (Table BX10)
By period
1544 Through 1789
1545 1789-1945
Including Concordat of 1929
1545.2 1945-
Local
1546.A-Z Country divisions, A-Z
1547.A-Z Ecclesiastical jurisdictions. By place, A-Z
1548.A-Z Cities, A-Z
Netherlands (Holland)
1549 General (Table BX10)
By period
1550 Through 1789
1551 1789-1945

Catalogue entries:

Catholic Church
History
By region or country
Europe
Netherlands (Holland)
By period -- Continued
1551.2 1945-
Local
1552.A-Z Country divisions, A-Z
1553.A-Z Ecclesiastical jurisdictions. By place, A-Z
1554.A-Z Cities, A-Z
1555-1557 Portugal (Table BX33)
Soviet Union
For Soviet Union in Central Asia see BX1637+
For Soviet Union in Northern Asia see BX1671+
1558 General (Table BX10)
By period
1558.2 Through 1917
1558.3 1917-
Local
1559.A-Z Country divisions, A-Z
Including ecclesiastical jurisdictions, by place, A-Z
1560.A-Z Cities, A-Z
1561-1563 Finland (Table BX33)
Poland
1564 General (Table BX10)
By period
1565 Through 1795
1566 1795-1945
1566.2 1945-
Local
1567.A-Z Country divisions, A-Z
1568.A-Z Ecclesiastical jurisdictions. By place, A-Z
1569.A-Z Cities, A-Z
Lithuania
1569.2 General (Table BX10)
By period
1569.3 Through 1795
1569.4 1795-1945
1569.5 1945-1991
1569.6 1991-
Local
1569.7.A-Z Country divisions, A-Z
1569.8.A-Z Ecclesiastical jurisdictions. By place, A-Z
1569.9.A-Z Cities, A-Z
Scandinavia
1570 General (Table BX10)

Catholic Church
History
By region or country
Europe
Scandinavia -- Continued
1571-1573 Denmark (Table BX33)
1574-1576 Iceland (Table BX33)
1577-1579 Norway (Table BX33)
1580-1582 Sweden (Table BX33)
Slovakia. Slovak Republic
1582.4 General (Table BX10)
Local
1582.5.A-Z Country divisions, A-Z
Including ecclesiastical jurisdictions, by place, A-Z
1582.6.A-Z Cities, A-Z
Spain
1583 General (Table BX10)
By period
1584 To 1789
1585 1789-1945
1585.2 1945-
Local
1586.A-Z Country divisions, A-Z
1587.A-Z Ecclesiastical jurisdictions. By place, A-Z
1588.A-Z Cities, A-Z
Switzerland
1589 General (Table BX10)
By period
1590 To 1789
1591 1789-1945
1591.2 1945-
Local
1592.A-Z Country divisions, A-Z
1593.A-Z Ecclesiastical jurisdictions. By place, A-Z
1594.A-Z Cities, A-Z
Balkan states
1598 General (Table BX10)
1599-1601 Bulgaria (Table BX33)
1605-1607 Romania (Table BX33)
1608-1610 Yugoslavia (Table BX33)
1612.A-Z Other European regions or countries, A-Z
e.g.
1612.C76 Croatia
Czechoslovakia see BX1527.3+
1612.L8 Luxemburg
1612.M3 Malta
1612.M6 Monaco

Catholic Church
History
By region or country -- Continued
Asia
1615 General (Table BX10)
Southwestern Asia
1617 General (Table BX10)
1619-1621 Turkey (Table BX11)
Cyprus
1621.3 General (Table BX10)
1621.4.A-Z Country divisions, A-Z
Including ecclesiastical jurisdictions, by place, A-Z
1621.5.A-Z Cities, A-Z
1622-1624 Armenia (Table BX11)
Georgia (Republic)
1624.3 General (Table BX10)
1624.4.A-Z Country divisions, A-Z
Including ecclesiastical jurisdictions, by place, A-Z
1624.5.A-Z Cities, A-Z
1625-1627 Iraq (Table BX11)
Syria
1627.3 General (Table BX10)
1627.4.A-Z Country divisions, A-Z
Including ecclesiastical jurisdictions, by place, A-Z
1627.5.A-Z Cities, A-Z
1628-1630 Israel (Table BX11)
Lebanon
1630.3 General (Table BX10)
1630.4.A-Z Country divisions, A-Z
Including ecclesiastical jurisdictions, by place, A-Z
1630.5.A-Z Cities, A-Z
Jordan
1630.7 General (Table BX10)
1630.8.A-Z Country divisions, A-Z
Including ecclesiastical jurisdictions, by place, A-Z
1630.9.A-Z Cities, A-Z
1631-1633 Saudi Arabia (Table BX11)
1634-1636 Iran (Table BX11)
Central Asia. Soviet Central Asia
1637 General (Table BX10)
1638 Afghanistan
1640 Bokhara (Bukhara)
1641 Khiva. Khorezm
1642.A-Z Other, A-Z
South Asia. Southeast Asia
1643 General
India

Catholic Church
History
By region or country
Asia
South Asia. Southeast Asia
India -- Continued
1644 General works
1644.2.A-Z By region, state, etc., A-Z
Including ecclesiastical jurisdictions, by place, A-Z
1644.3.A-Z Cities, A-Z
1644.4 Pakistan
1644.5 Bangladesh
1645 Burma. Myanmar
1646 Sri Lanka
Indochina. Malay Peninsula
1649 General (Table BX10)
1650.A-Z Country divisions, A-Z
Including ecclesiastical jurisdictions, by place, A-Z
e.g.
1650.A7 Annam. Vietnam
1650.C3 Cambodia. Kampuchea
1650.C7 Cochin China
Kampuchea see BX1650.C3
1650.L2 Laos
1650.M3 Malaya. Straits Settlements
1650.S56 Singapore
1650.T5 Thailand
1650.T7 Tongking (Tonkin)
Vietnam see BX1650.A7
Indonesia (Malay Archipelago)
1652 General (Table BX10)
Indonesia (Republic). Dutch East Indies
1653 General (Table BX10)
1654.A-Z Country divisions, A-Z
Including ecclesiastical jurisdictions, by place, A-Z
e.g.
1654.B6 Borneo
1654.C4 Celebes
1654.J3 Java
1654.S8 Sumatra
1655.A-Z Cities, A-Z
1655.5 Timor
Philippine Islands
1656 General (Table BX10)
By period
1657 Through 1789
1658 1789-1945

Catholic Church
History
By region or country
Asia
South Asia. Southeast Asia
Indonesia (Malay Archipelago)
Philippine Islands
By period -- Continued
1658.2 1945-
Local
1659.A-Z Country divisions, A-Z
e.g.
1659.L8 Luzon
1660.A-Z Ecclesiastical jurisdictions. By place, A-Z
1661.A-Z Cities, A-Z
Eastern Asia. The Far East
1662 General (Table BX10)
1665-1667 China (Table BX11)
Taiwan
1667.5 General (Table BX10)
1667.6.A-Z Country divisions, A-Z
Including ecclesiastical jurisdictions, by place, A-Z
1667.7.A-Z Cities, A-Z
1668-1670 Japan (Table BX11)
Korea
1670.5 General (Table BX10)
1670.6.A-Z Country divisions, A-Z
Including ecclesiastical jurisdictions, by place, A-Z
1670.7.A-Z Cities, A-Z
1671-1673 Northern Asia. Siberia (Table BX11)
Africa
1675 General (Table BX10)
1677-1679 Egypt (Table BX11)
1680 North Africa
1680.3 Central Africa. Sub-Saharan Africa
1680.5 East Africa
1680.7 West Africa
1681 Southern Africa
1682.A-Z By region or country, A-Z
e.g.
1682.A5 Angola
1682.C6 Congo. Zaire
1682.E8 Ethiopia
1682.M3 Madagascar
1682.M6 Morocco
1682.P6 Portuguese possessions (Former)
Zaire see BX1682.C6

Catholic Church
History
By region or country -- Continued
Australia and New Zealand
Class here works on Australia and New Zealand either alone or together
1685 General (Table BX10)
1686.A-Z Country divisions, A-Z
1687.A-Z Ecclesiastical jurisdictions. By place, A-Z
1688.A-Z Cities, A-Z
Pacific Islands
1690 General (Table BX10)
1691.A-Z Groups of islands, individual islands, cities, etc., A-Z
e.g.
1691.H3 Hawaiian Islands
1692.A-Z Ecclesiastical jurisdictions. By place, A-Z
1695.A-Z By national and ethnic group outside its native country, A-Z
For works for or on such groups in an individual country, see the country
e.g.
1695.C7-Z Croatians
1695.L5 Letts
History of the Inquisition
Cf. BX1822 Congregation of the Holy Office
1700 Documents
1705 Collections
General works
1710 Early through 1800
1711 1801-1950
1712 1951-2000
1713 2001-
1715 Addresses, essays, lectures
By region or country
1720 France
1723 Italy
1725 Netherlands
Portugal
1730 General works
1731 Auto-da-fé sermons
1733.A-Z Portuguese colonies, A-Z
e.g.
1733.B6 Brazil
1733.G7 Goa
Spain and its dependencies
Including works on Spain and Portugal
1735 General works
Spanish colonies and dependencies

Catholic Church
History
History of the Inquisition
By region or country
Spain and its dependencies
Spanish colonies and dependencies -- Continued
Spanish America
1739 General works
1740.A-Z Individual colonies, A-Z
e.g.
1740.A7 Argentina
1740.C2 Cartagena
1740.C5 Chile
1740.C9 Cuba
1740.G8 Guatemala
La Plata see BX1740.A7
Lima see BX1740.P5
1740.M6 Mexico. Yucatan
1740.P5 Peru
Including Lima
Yucatan see BX1740.M6
1743.A-Z Other, A-Z
e.g.
1743.C2 Canary Islands
1743.M2 Majorca
1743.P4 Philippine Islands
1745.A-Z Other regions or countries, A-Z
e.g.
1745.B4 Belgium
Theology. Doctrine. Dogmatics
For special doctrines see BT, e.g. BT620, Immaculate Conception; BT755, Salvation and the Catholic Church; BT840+, Purgatory; but BX2157+, Cult of the Sacred Heart; BX2159.P7, Cult of the Precious Blood
1745.5 Dictionaries. Encyclopedias
1746 The nature of the Church in Catholic theology
1747 History of Catholic doctrines
1747.5 Collections of doctrinal decisions, opinions, sources, etc.
General works
Early through 1800
The great medieval theologians to the Council of Trent or circa 1550
Including the medieval summa theologica
Cf. B734 Medieval Scholasticism
1749.A1 Collected works
1749.A2-Z Individual theologians, A-Z
e. g.

Catholic Church
Theology. Doctrine. Dogmatics
General works
Early through 1800
The great medieval theologians to the Council of Trent or circa 1550
Individual theologians, A-Z -- Continued
Thomas, Aquinas, Saint
Summa contra gentiles
Texts
1749.T38 Latin
1749.T39-.T449 Translations (by language alphabetically)
1749.T45 Criticism
Summa theologica
Texts
1749.T48 Latin
1749.T484-.T59 Translations (by language alphabetically)
1749.T6 Criticism
1551-1800
1750.A1 Collected works
1750.A2-Z Individual theologians, A-Z
1801-1950
Cf. B839.A1+ Modern Scholasticism, Neo-Scholasticism, Neo-Thomism
1751.A1 Collected works
1751.A2-Z Individual theologians, A-Z
1951-2000
1751.2.A1 Collected works
1751.2.A2-Z Individual theologians, A-Z
1751.3 2001-
1752 Apologetic works
Cf. BT1120+ Apologetics against opponents of Christianity
1753 General special
Pictorial works see BX843
1754 Popular works
1754.3 Questions and answers
1754.5 Juvenile works
Cf. BX930+ Textbooks
1755 Pamphlets, tracts, etc.
Sermons
For sermons on special topics, see the subject
For sermons by Fathers of the Church see BR60+
For sermons by medieval saints see BX890
Cf. BX880+ Collected works
Cf. BX2375+ Retreat addresses, conferences, meditations

Catholic Church
Sermons -- Continued
1756.A1 Outlines, plans, etc.
1756.A2 Sermons by several authors
1756.A3-.Z7 Sermons by individual authors. By author and title, A-Z
1756.Z8 Sermons for young people
1756.Z9 Sermons for children
Moral theology. Casuistry. Cases of conscience, etc.
(1757.A1) Periodicals. Societies
see BJ1188.5
(1757.A2) Dictionaries
see BJ1199
General works
(1757.A3-Z) Early to 1800
see BJ1240+
(1758) 1801-1950
see BJ1249
(1758.A2) 1951-
see BJ1249
(1759) Other
see BJ1249
(1759.5.A-Z) Special topics, A-Z
(1759.5.A7) Artificial insemination
see HQ761
Atomic warfare
see BR115.A85
(1759.5.B5) Birth control
see HQ766.3
(1759.5.B7) Brain surgery
see RD594
(1759.5.E6) Epikeia
see BJ1278.E64
(1759.5.H8) Hypnotism
see BF1152
(1759.5.H9) Hysterectomy
see RG391
(1759.5.M4) Medicine
see R724+
(1759.5.M5) Miscegenation
see E185.62; GN254; HD1031
(1759.5.N3) Narcoanalysis
see K5478
(1759.5.P75) Probabilism
see BJ1278.P76
(1759.5.S4) Scruples
see BJ1278.S37

BX

Catholic Church
Moral theology. Casuistry. Cases of conscience, etc.
Special topics, A-Z -- Continued
(1759.5.T7) Transplantation (Physiology)
see RD120.7+
Controversial works against the Catholic Church
Including history
For controversial works against individual religious orders, see BX2905; BX3005; etc.
For controversial works against Catholic monasticism in general see BX2439+
1760 Periodicals. Societies
1762 Collected works
General works
1763 Early through 1800
1765 1801-1950
1765.2 1951-2000
1765.3 2001-
1766 Anti-Catholicism. Anti-Papism
1767 Addresses, essays, sermons
By region or country
For defenses of the Catholic Church see BX1781+
1770 United States
1773 Latin America
1775.A-Z Other regions or countries, A-Z
Biography (Anti-Catholic works) see BX4650+
Autobiography see BX1760+
Nun's autobiography see BX4215
1779 Joint debates and discussions on Catholicism
1779.5 Controversial works by Catholics against the Catholic Church
Catholic Church and other churches
Including the problem of Christian union and reunion, etc.
Cf. BX9.5.P29 Papacy and Christian union
1781 Periodicals
1782 Societies
1783 Congresses, conferences, etc.
1784 General works
1785 Attitude toward the ecumenical movement
1786 Special aspects of the subject as a whole
1787 Participation in inter-faith movements
1788 Participation in interdenominational movements

Catholic Church
Catholic Church and other churches -- Continued
Relation to other churches
see the broader confessional or denominational family of churches (e.g. Protestant churches, see BX4818.3; Anglican Communion, see BX5004.2; Orthodox and Oriental, see BX324.3; Oriental alone, see BX106.3; Lutheran, see BX8063.7.C3; Methodists, see BX8329.C3; Pentecostals, see BX8764.2; Presbyterians, see BX9171.C38) or for United or Uniting churches and/ or those without broader confessional or denominational affiliation see the individual church in BX.
Catholic Church and the Jews see BM535
1789.5 Catholic Church and occult sciences
Catholic Church and the state
General works
1790 Early through 1950
1791 1951-2000
1791.3 2001-
1793 Catholic viewpoint on political theory, world politics, international relations, etc.
By country (general) see BR500+
By country (Church history) see BX1401+
Diplomatic relations with special countries see BX1401+
1795.A-Z Other special topics, A-Z
1795.A54 Animals
1795.A78 Art. Arts
1795.A82 Astrology
1795.A85 Atomic warfare. Nuclear warfare
1795.B63 Body, Human
1795.B84 Bullying
1795.C35 Capitalism
1795.C48 Childbirth
1795.C58 Civil rights
Cf. BX1795.H85 Human rights
1795.C64 Cohabitation
1795.C67 Communication
1795.C68 Compulsive behavior
1795.C69 Controversies
1795.C85 Culture
1795.D53 Dialogue
1795.D55 Dignity
1795.D57 Disarmament
1795.D59 Distributive justice
1795.E27 Economics
1795.E44 Emigration and immigration
1795.E74 Ethnicity

Catholic Church
Other special topics, A-Z -- Continued

1795.E85 Evolution
1795.F44 Feminism
Gay rights see BX1795.H66
1795.G66 Globalization
1795.H4 Health
1795.H64 Holocaust, Jewish (1939-1945)
1795.H66 Homosexuality. Gay rights
1795.H69 Hope
1795.H82 Human ecology
1795.H84 Human reproduction
1795.H85 Human rights
Cf. BX1795.C58 Civil rights
Immigration see BX1795.E44
1795.I57 Intellectual life. Learning and scholarship
1795.J87 Justice
1795.J88 Justifiable homicide
Learning see BX1795.I57
1795.M34 Man-woman relationships
1795.M38 Materialism
1795.N36 Nature
1795.N66 Nonviolence
Nuclear warfare see BX1795.A85
1795.P37 Parapsychology
1795.P43 Peace
1795.P47 Philosophy
1795.P72 Preaching
1795.P75 Property
1795.P79 Psychology
1795.P83 Public welfare
1795.R33 Race relations
Scholarship see BX1795.I57
1795.S35 Science
1795.S48 Sex
1795.S62 Social justice
1795.S63 Socialism
For modern period (1789-) see BX1396.3
1795.T42 Technology
1795.U54 Unemployment
1795.V56 Violence
1795.W37 War
1795.W4 Wealth
Welfare, Public see BX1795.P83
Woman-man relationships see BX1795.M34
1795.W67 Work

Catholic Church -- Continued
Government and organization of the Catholic Church
For Councils see BX820+
General works
1800 Early through 1800
1801 1801-1950
1802 1951-2000
1803 2001-
The Pope
Including duties, election, etc.
Cf. BV601.57 Petrine office
1805 General works
1806 Teaching office. Infallibility
1808 Nepotism
1810 Temporal power
1815 College of Cardinals
Curia Romana
1818 General works
Congregations
1820 General works
Individual congregations
1822 Congregation of the Holy Office. Congregatio Sancti Officii
1825 Congregation of the Consistory. Congregatio Consistorialis
1827 Congregation for the Oriental Church. Congregatio pro Ecclesia Orientali
Cf. BX4710.1+ Eastern churches in communion with Rome
1828 Congregation of the Sacraments. Congregatio de Disciplina Sacramentorum
1831 Congregation of the Council. Congregatio Concilii
1834 Congregation of Religious. Congregatio de Sodalibus Religiosis
1837 Congregation of the Propaganda. Congregatio de Propaganda Fide
Congregation of the Index. Congregatio Indicis see BX1855.I5
1843 Congregation of Rites. Congregatio Sacrarum Rituum
1846 Congregation of Ceremonies. Congregatio Ceremonialis
1849 Congregation For Extraordinary Affairs. Congregatio pro Negotiis Ecclesiasticis Extraordinariis
1852 Congregation of Studies. Congregatio Studiorum
1855.A-Z Other Congregations now obsolete, A-Z
e.g.
1855.I5 Congregation of the Index

Catholic Church
Government and organization of the Catholic Church
Curia Romana
Congregations
Individual congregations
Other congregations now obsolete, A-Z -- Continued
1855.L7 Congregation of the Loreto
1855.S3 Congregation of the Fabric of Saint Peter's
Tribunals and offices
1860 General works
1862 Sacred Penitentiaria. Sacra Paenitentiaria Apostolica
1865 Sacred Roman Rota. Sacra Rota Romana
1868 Apostolic Signatura. Signatura Apostolica
Offices
1870 General works
1872 Apostolic Chancery. Cancellaria Apostolica
1875 Apostolic Dataria. Dataria Apostolica
1878 Apostolic Chamber. Reverenda Camera Apostolica
1881 Secretariate of State
1884 Secretariate of Briefs to Princes
1887 Secretariate of Latin Letters
Commissions of Cardinals
1890 General works
1895.A-Z Individual commissions, A-Z
e.g.
1895.A3 Commission for the Administration of the Funds of the Holy See
1895.B5 Commission for Biblical Studies
1895.C6 Commission for the Codification of the Canon Law
1895.C7 Commission for the Conservation of the Faith in Rome
1895.H5 Commission for Historical Studies
1897 Pontifical family (Palatine Prelates, etc.)
1899 College of Apostolic Prothonotaries
1905 Prelates. Patriarchs. Metropolitans. Archbishops. Bishops
For episcopal conferences see BX837.5
For diocesan pastoral councils see BX838
1908 Legates. Nuncios
1910 Vicars. Vicars and prefects apostolic
1911 Archdeacons. Rural deans. Vicars forane. Chorepiscopi, etc.
Priests. Deacons. Spiritual directors
1912 General works
1912.2 Women clergy. Ordination of women
1912.5 Spiritual life of the priest
Including retreat addresses, conferences, meditations
Personal life of the priest

Catholic Church
Government and organization of the Catholic Church
Priests. Deacons. Spiritual directors
Personal life of the priest -- Continued
1912.7 General works
1912.8 Alcoholism
1912.85 Celibacy
1912.9 Sexual behavior
1912.95 Retirement
1913 Work of the priest. Pastoral theology
1914 The priest in special services (not A-Z)
e.g. Administrative, teaching, chaplain, etc., services
1914.5 Senates of priests
1915 Minor orders: Subdeacons, acolytes, readers, exorcists, doorkeepers
1916 Parish ministries
Cf. BX2347.2 Parish social ministry organizations
1918 Catechists
1919 Employees
Including wages, salaries
1920 Laymen. Parish councils
1925 Costume. Vestments. Liturgical objects
Cf. BX2790 Monastic costume
Cf. NK4850 Art
1927 Tonsure. Hair. Beard
Rules and ordinances for the clergy
Cf. BV4390 Celibacy of the clergy
1930 General works
By place, A-Z
e.g.
1932.D8 Dublin
1932.F7 France
1933 The cathedral
1934 The church. Sanctity, etc.
Canon law
see KBR, KBU
1945 Manuals and forms for secretaries, etc.
1947 Parish records, accounts, etc.
1950 Finances, subsidies, etc.
1955 Benefices
1956 Chantries
Creeds and catechisms
Catechismus romanus. Catechism of the Council of Trent
1958.A2 Latin editions. By date
1958.A3-Z Other languages, A-Z
Subarrange by date
1959 History and criticism

Catholic Church
Creeds and catechisms -- Continued
Catechismus Ecclesiae Catholicae (1992)
1959.2 Latin editions. By date
1959.3.A-Z Other languages, A-Z
Subarrange by date
1959.5 History and criticism
Other catechisms
Class translations with the language into which they are translated.
1960.A1 Collections
1960.A2 Polyglot
1960.A3-Z Latin
1961 English
1962 French
1963 German
1964 Italian
1965 Spanish and Portuguese
1966.A-Z Other languages, A-Z
1968 Works about the catechisms. Catechetics and catechization
For catechumens see BX935
For works about the catechisms of individual authors see BX1960+
1969 Forms of worship. Catholic practice
Liturgy and ritual
Cf. BX1843 Congregation of Rites
Cf. BX1925 Liturgical objects
1970.A1 Periodicals. Societies. Congresses
1970.A25-.A6 Documents
Class here documents by the pope or the Congregation of Rites
Dictionaries see BV173
1970.A7-Z General works
1970.15 Christian assembly. Religious gatherings. Congregation at worship
Including Sunday religious gatherings
1970.2 Children in public worship
1970.23 Youth in public worship
1970.25 Women in public worship
1970.3 Liturgical environment. Church buildings as liturgical spaces
Cf. NA4828 Architecture
1970.5 Liturgy committees
Ceremonies of the Church. Rubrics
1971.A2 Caeremoniale romanum (Ceremonies of the Pope). By date

Catholic Church
Liturgy and ritual
Ceremonies of the Church. Rubrics -- Continued

1971.A25 Ceremonial of bishops. By date
Ceremonial (Ceremonies of priests)
1971.A3 General works, and United States. By date
1971.A4-.A49 Other countries
Arrange alphabetically by country and date
1971.A5-Z Works on the ceremonies
1972 Manuals for sacristans, servers, alter servers, etc.
By period
1973 Early and medieval
1975 Modern
1977.A-Z By region or country, A-Z
Including the liturgical texts of one country or one locality
e.g.
For individual texts see BX1999.8+
1977.F8 France
1977.G3 Germany
1977.G7 Great Britain
Cf. BX5142+ Early British rites
1977.S8 Sweden
Biography of liturgical authors
1979.A1 Collective
1979.A3-Z Individual, A-Z
Lay service books
For the lay service books of a particular city, see the city
Cf. BX2016 Missals for lay use
Cf. BX2079+ Prayer books for the laity
1980 Latin
1980.A2 Texts. By date
1980.A3A-.A3Z Texts for individual churches, academies, etc., A-Z
1981 English
1981.A2 Texts. By date
1981.A3A-.A3Z Texts for individual churches, academies, etc., A-Z
1982 French
1982.A2 Texts. By date
1982.A3A-.A3Z Texts for individual churches, academies, etc., A-Z
1983 German
1983.A2 Texts. By date
1983.A3A-.A3Z Texts for individual churches, academies, etc., A-Z
1984 Italian
1984.A2 Texts. By date
1984.A3A-.A3Z Texts for individual churches, academies, etc., A-Z
1985 Spanish and Portuguese
1985.A2 Texts. By date
1985.A3A-.A3Z Texts for individual churches, academies, etc., A-Z

Catholic Church
Liturgy and ritual
Lay service books -- Continued
1990.A-Z Other languages, A-Z
Collections of liturgical texts see BV170
1995 Early non-Roman western rites
Including rites still in use in cities named
1995.A1 General
1995.A5 Ambrosian. Milan (Table BX12)
1995.C4 Celtic
For individual Celtic rites see BX1999.8+
1995.G3 Gallican. Lyons (Table BX12)
1995.M7 Mozarabic, Spanish, Visigothic. Toledo (Table BX12)
1996.A-Z Western (or Roman) rites in liturgical languages other than Latin, A-Z
e.g.
1996.C5 Church Slavic (Roman-Slavonic rite)
Local rites and usages see BX1977.A+
Uniat rites see BX4710.1+
Guides for the recitation of offices. Ordo divini officii recitandi. Directorium
1999.A1 General works. History and criticism
1999.A15 Ordo perpetuus
1999.A25 Ordo universalis. By date
1999.A3A-.A3Z Local. By country, province, diocese, or city, A-Z, and date
1999.A4A-.A4Z By religious order, A-Z
Cf. BX2049.A1+ Liturgy and ritual of special orders
1999.A5-.Z6 By editor
If place or order is unknown
1999.Z7A-.Z7Z Editions for lay use
Special liturgical books
By conventional English name if known
Including in one alphabet pre-Tridentine and post-Tridentine texts, and also some "extra-liturgical" texts
For official vernacular editions issued in accordance with the Second Vatican Council's Constitutio de sacra liturgia, see the class for the vernacular editions if the greater part of the text is in the vernacular; for editions predominantly in Latin, see the class for Latin
For musical forms (Graduals, antiphonaries, etc.), see Class M
For books with famous illustrations, illuminations, etc., see Class N
1999.8 Agenda (Table BX13)
1999.85 Antiphonaries (Table BX13)

Catholic Church
Liturgy and ritual
Special liturgical books -- Continued
2000 Breviaries. The divine office. Liturgia horarum. Liturgy of the hours (Table BX13)
Cf. BX2080 Book of hours
Cf. BX2090 Primers
Special canonical hours
2000.6 Matins (Table BX13)
2000.62 Lauds (Table BX13)
2000.63 Prime (Table BX13)
2000.64 Terce (Table BX13)
2000.65 Sext (Table BX13)
2000.66 None (Table BX13)
2000.67 Vespers (Table BX13)
2000.68 Compline (Table BX13)
Ceremonials
Caeremoniale romanum see BX1971.A2
Ceremonial of bishops see BX1971.A25
Ceremonial see BX1971.A3
2002 Collectars (Table BX13)
2003 Epistles and Gospels. Lectionaries. Epistolaries (Table BX13)
For studies of the texts for homiletic purposes see BS2547+; BS2638
For sermons, i.e. Church year sermons see BX1756.A1+
For meditations see BX2170.C55
2005 Evangeliaria. Evangelistaries. Gospels (Table BX13)
For studies of the texts for homiletic purposes see BS2547+; BS2565
For sermons, i.e. Church year sermons see BX1756.A1+
For meditations see BX2170.C55
Exorcisms see BF1559
Forty hours' devotions see BX2169
2010 Holy Week Offices (Table BX13)
Excerpted from Breviary and Missal, or Breviary alone
For Holy Week masses see BX2015.8.H6+
Cf. BX2045.H6+ Holy Saturday rite
Cf. BX2045.H7+ Holy Week rite
Lectionaries see BX2003
2013 Litanies (Table BX13)
2013.5 Manuals (Table BX13)
Including medieval forms for the administration of the sacraments

Catholic Church
Liturgy and ritual
Special liturgical books -- Continued
2014 Martyrologies. The Roman Martyrology (Table BX13)
Cf. BX4660+ Martyrologies (Historical and popular)
Missals
2015 General (Table BX13)
2015.2 History
2015.25 Language
2015.3 Rubrics
For servers' manuals see BX1972
2015.4 Dialog mass
Elements see BX2231
Altar and liturgical objects see BV195+
Vestments see BV167
Parts. Selections. Excerpts
Acclamations see BX2045.A3+
2015.55 Ordinary (Table BX13)
2015.6 Canons of the mass. Eucharistic prayers. Anaphorae (Table BX13)
2015.62 Prayers of the faithful. General intercessions (Table BX13)
Proper prayers
2015.68 General works (Table BX13)
2015.7 Collects. Orations (Table BX13)
2015.72 Secret prayers (Table BX13)
2015.74 Post-Communion prayers (Table BX13)
2015.77 Prefaces (Table BX13)
2015.78 Common of saints (Table BX13)
Epistles see BX2003
Gospels see BX2005
Masses of seasons of the Church Year
2015.782 Advent (Table BX13)
2015.783 Christmas (Table BX13)
2015.7835 Epiphany (Table BX13)
2015.784 Lent (Table BX13)
2015.785 Holy Week. Paschal triduum (Table BX13)
2015.786 Easter (Table BX13)
2015.789 Ordinary time (Table BX13)
2015.8.A-Z Individual masses, A-Z
2015.8.H6-.H63 Holy Week masses (Table BX14)
Masses for the dead see BX2015.8.R4+
2015.8.N8-.N83 Nuptial masses (Table BX14)
2015.8.R4-.R43 Requiem masses (Table BX14)
2015.9.A-Z Masses of individual feasts and saints, A-Z
e.g.
Dog masses see BX2015.9.H8

Catholic Church
Liturgy and ritual
Special liturgical books
Missals
Masses of individual feasts and saints, A-Z -- Continued

2015.9.H8 Hubert, Saint
2015.9.J6 Joseph, Saint
Labor Day see BX2015.9.J6
2015.9.M3 Mary, Blessed Virgin, Saint
2016 Missals for lay use (Table BX13)
Cf. BX1980+ Lay service books
Cf. BX2079+ Prayer books for the laity
2017 Ordines Romani. Ordinarium. Ordinals (Table BX13)
Ordo divini officii recitandi see BX1999.A1+
2020 Offices for the Dead (Table BX13)
Cf. BX2015.8.R4+ Requiem masses
Offices of the Virgin Mary
2024 General works (Table BX13)
2025 Little Office of the Blessed Virgin Mary (Table BX13)
2027 Little Office of the Immaculate Conception (Table BX13)
2029 Passionarium (Table BX13)
Pontificals
2030 General (Table BX13)
2031.A-Z Excerpts, A-Z
e.g.
2031.D2-.D23 De benedictione et impositione primarii lapidis pro ecclesia aedificanda (Table BX14)
2031.D4-.D43 De ecclesiae benedictione (Table BX14)
2031.R5-.R53 Ritus ordinum (Table BX14)
2032 Processionals (Table BX13)
2033 Psalters (Table BX13)
2035 Rituals (Table BX13)
Early forms are entered under their own names, e. g. Agenda, Manual, Sacerdotal
2035.A25 Excerpts in Latin. By date
Class here excerpts primarily for the administration of the sacraments
For non-Latin excerpts, see the number for the whole Ritual
2035.5 Memoriale rituum (Table BX13)
2035.6.A-Z Special parts, A-Z
2035.6.A55-.A553 Anointing. Unction. Viaticum (Table BX14)
2035.6.B3-.B33 Baptism (Table BX14)
Cf. BX2045.R38+ Reception of baptized Christians

Catholic Church
Liturgy and ritual
Special liturgical books
Rituals
Special parts, A-Z -- Continued

2035.6.B54-.B543	Blessings and consecrations (Table BX14) For blessing and consecrations excerpted from one or more liturgical books see BX2046+
2035.6.F85-.F853	Funerals (Table BX14)
2035.6.M37-.M373	Marriage (Table BX14)
	Unction see BX2035.6.A55+
	Viaticum see BX2035.6.A55+
2036	Sacerdotals (Table BX13)
	Sacramentaries
2037.A2	Latin texts. By date
2037.A3A-.A3Z	Latin texts. By name
2037.A3B4-.A3B439	Bergomense sacramentary (Table BX15)
2037.A3B7-.A3B739	Brescian sacramentary (Table BX15)
2037.A3D73-.A3D7339	Drogo sacramentary (Table BX15)
2037.A3G3-.A3G339	Gallican sacramentary. Missale Gothicum. Missale Gallicanum vetus. Bobbio Missal (Table BX15)
2037.A3G4-.A3G439	Gelasian sacramentary. Liber sacramentorum Romanae Ecclesiae. Gallone sacramentary. Angoulême sacramentary (Table BX15)
2037.A3G7-.A3G739	Gregorian sacramentary (Table BX15)
2037.A3L4-.A3L439	Leonine sacramentary (Table BX15)
2037.A3R6-.A3R639	Sacramentarium Rossianum (Table BX15)
2037.A6-Z	General works
2040	Stations of the Cross (Table BX13)
2043	Tropers. Graduals. Sequences. Proses. Tracts (Table BX13)
2045.A-Z	Other special, A-Z
2045.A3-.A33	Acclamations (Table BX14)
2045.A4-.A43	Christus vincit (Table BX14)
2045.C34-.C343	Calendar (Table BX14)
2045.C55-.C553	Children's liturgies (Table BX14)
2045.C59-.C593	Commissioning of lay sacramentalists, acolytes, lectors, etc. (Table BX14)
2045.C595-.C5953	Confession (Communal) (Table BX14)
2045.C6-.C63	Corpus Christi rite (Table BX14)
2045.C76-.C763	Crowning of an image of the Blessed Virgin Mary (Table BX14)
2045.C87-.C873	Cursing, Liturgical. Malediction (Table BX14)
2045.E86-.E863	Experimental liturgies (Table BX14)
2045.E89-.E893	Exultets (Table BX14)
2045.G38-.G383	Gathering rites. Opening rites (Table BX14)

Catholic Church
Liturgy and ritual
Special liturgical books
Other special, A-Z -- Continued

2045.H55-.H553	Holy Communion outside Mass (Table BX14)
2045.H6-.H63	Holy Saturday rite (Table BX14)
2045.H65-.H653	Holy Thursday rite (Table BX14)
2045.H7-.H73	Holy Week rite (Table BX14)
2045.I55-.I553	Initiation of adults (Table BX14)
2045.I56-.I563	Initiation of children (Table BX14)
2045.L39-.L393	Lay-led Sunday worship services (Table BX14)
	Malediction see BX2045.C87+
	Maudy Thursday see BX2045.H65+
2045.O3-.O33	Office of the Nativity (Table BX14)
2045.O35-.O353	Officia propria (Local) (Table BX14)
	Officia propria (Monastic) see BX2049.A1+
	Opening rites see BX2045.G38+
2045.P75-.P753	Profession of vows (Table BX14) Cf. BX2049.A1+ Rituals of individual orders
2045.R38-.R383	Reception of baptized Christians (Table BX14)
2045.R4-.R43	Responses (Table BX14)
2045.R5-.R53	Rimed offices (Table BX14)
2045.T44-.T443	Teenagers' services (Table BX14)
2045.V5-.V53	Vigil services (Table BX14)
2045.W34-.W343	Wake services (Table BX14)
2045.W65-.W653	Women, Worship services for (Table BX14)
	Excerpts from one or more liturgical books, by purpose
	Administration of the sacraments see BX2035
	Blessings and consecrations Cf. BX2295+ Sacramentals
2046.A-Z	Persons, A-Z e.g.
2046.A1	General works
2046.A2	Abbots (Blessing of)
2046.B5	Bishops (Consecration of)
2046.R8	Rulers (Coronation of)
2046.V7	Vows (Blessing of)
2046.W6	Women (Churching of)
2047.A-Z	Things, A-Z e.g.
2047.A1	General works
2047.A5	Altar vessels
2047.A6	Altars
	Baptismal water see BX2047.H6
2047.C5	Chrism and holy oils
2047.C6	Churches
2047.H6	Holy water. Baptismal water

Catholic Church
Liturgy and ritual -- Continued
Special liturgical actions, e.g. genuflexion, Sign of the Cross, etc. see BV197.A+
"Extra-liturgical" functions. Popular devotions
Stations of the Cross see BX2040
Devotions to Jesus, the Virgin Mary, angels, and saints see BX2159.A+
Eucharistic devotions see BX2169
Other special devotions see BX2170.A+
2048 Texts for the use of priests
e.g. Altar prayers
Liturgy and ritual of individual religious orders
2049.A1 General
2049.A2-Z Individual orders, A-Z
Subarrange each order by Table BX12
e.g.
2049.B4 Benedictines (Table BX12)
2049.C2 Carmelites (Table BX12)
2049.C3 Carthusians (Table BX12)
2049.D6 Dominicans (Table BX12)
2049.F7 Franciscans (Table BX12)
2049.S5 Sisters of Charity of St. Vincent de Paul of New York (Table BX12)
Prayer books for individual religious orders
2050.A1 General
2050.A2-Z Individual orders, A-Z
e.g.
2050.D7 Dominicans
2050.F7 Franciscans
2055.A-Z Prayer books for sodalities, etc., A-Z
e.g.
2055.A6 Apostleship of Prayer
2055.C4 Children of Mary
2055.G8 Archconfraternity of the Guard of Honor of the Sacred Heart of Jesus
2055.H7 Holy Name Society
2055.S2 Sodality of the Sacred Heart of Jesus
2055.V5 Sodality of the Blessed Virgin Mary
Prayer books for Sisters. By order
2060.A1 General
2060.A2-Z Individual orders, A-Z
e.g.
2060.D6 Dominican Sisters
2060.F7 Franciscan Sisters of St. Kunegunda
2060.M5 Sisters of Mercy
2060.P7 Sisters of the Presentation of the Blessed Virgin Mary

Catholic Church
Liturgy and ritual
Prayer books for Sisters. By order
Individual orders, A-Z -- Continued
2060.V5 Sisters of the Visitation
2063 Prayer books for the clergy
2064 Prayer books for seminarians
Prayer books for the laity
Cf. BX1980+ Lay service books
Cf. BX2016 Missals for lay use
Early through 1800
2079 Collections
2080 Books of hours
2085 Hortulus animae
2090 Primers
2095 Other prayer books
1801-1950
For translations, see the language into which translated
2109 Polyglot
2110 English
2113 French
2116 German
2119 Italian
2122 Spanish and Portuguese
2125.A-Z Russian and other Slavic, A-Z
2128.A-Z Other languages, A-Z
e.g.
2128.D8 Dutch
2128.L5 Lithuanian
1951-2000
For translations, see the language into which translated
2129 Polyglot
2130 English
2133 French
2136 German
2139 Italian
2142 Spanish and Portuguese
2145.A-Z Russian and other Slavic, A-Z
2148.A-Z Other languages, A-Z
e.g.
2148.D8 Dutch
2148.L5 Lithuanian
2001-
For translations, see the language into which translated
2149 Polyglot
2149.2 English
2149.3 French

Catholic Church
Liturgy and ritual
Prayer books for the laity
20001- -- Continued
2149.4 German
2149.5 Italian
2149.6 Spanish and Portuguese
2149.7.A-Z Russian and other Slavic, A-Z
2149.8.A-Z Other languages, A-Z
Prayer books for youth
Class here First Communion prayer books, etc.
2150 English
2151 French
2152 German
2153 Italian
2154 Spanish and Portuguese
2155.A-Z Other languages, A-Z
Devotion to the Sacred Heart (or Hearts)
For sodality manuals see BX2055.A+
Cf. BX2160.3+ Devotion to the Sacred Heart of Mary
2157 General
2158 Prayers and devotions
2159.A-Z Other special devotions to Jesus, A-Z
e.g.
For Eucharistic prayers and devotions see BX2169
2159.C4 Child Jesus. Holy Infancy. Holy Childhood
Holy Childhood see BX2159.C4
2159.H6 Holy Face
2159.H7 Holy Hour
Holy Infancy see BX2159.C4
2159.H75 Holy Name
2159.M9 Mystical Body
2159.P3 Passion of Christ
2159.P7 Precious Blood
2159.S37 Scourging of Christ
Prayers and devotions to the Virgin Mary
Including meditations on the Virgin Mary
For sodality manuals see BX2055.A+
Cf. BT608.5 Non-Catholic meditations and devotions to the Virgin Mary
General
2160.A2 Early through 1800
2160.A3-Z 1801-1950
2160.2 1951-2000
2160.23 2001-
Special
Devotion to the Sacred Heart of Mary

Catholic Church
Liturgy and ritual
Prayers and devotions to the Virgin Mary
Special
Devotion to the Sacred Heart of Mary -- Continued

2160.3 General
2160.4 Prayers and devotions
2161 Month of Mary. May devotions
2161.5.A-Z Other, A-Z
e.g.
2161.5.S6 Sorrows of the Blessed Virgin Mary
2162.A-Z Prayers and devotions for special shrines, A-Z
e.g.
2162.E4 Einsiedeln
2162.G8 Guadalupe
2163 The Rosary
Cf. BX2310.R7 Sacramentals
2163.5 Miraculous Medal
Special prayers see BX2175.A+
2164 Prayers and devotions to St. Joseph
Other special devotions
2165 Prayers and devotions to the angels
Prayers and devotions to the saints and martyrs
2166 General
2167.A-Z Individual saints and martyrs, A-Z
e.g.
2167.A5 Anne, Saint
2167.A6 Antonio da Padova, Saint
2167.F73 Francisco de Paula, Saint
Joseph, Saint see BX2164
2167.L7 Loyola, Ignatius, Saint
2167.R5 Rita da Cascia, Saint
2167.T4 Teresa, of Avila, Saint, 1515-1582
2167.T5 Thérèse, de Lisieux, Saint, 1873-1897
2167.T6 Thomas Aquinas, Saint
2167.U4 Ulrich, Bp. of Augsburg, Saint
2167.V45 Vincent de Paul, Saint
2169 Prayers and devotions for communicants at mass
Class here prayers and devotions in connection with the Sacrament, Communion, or Mass, including the Forty hours devotions
For Eucharistic prayers see BX2015.6
For sodality manuals see BX2055.A+
2170.A-Z Other prayers and devotions, A-Z
e.g.
2170.A4 Advent devotions
2170.A5 Aged. Older people (Prayers for)

Catalic Church
Liturgy and ritual
Other special devotions
Other prayers and devotions, A-Z -- Continued
Care of souls in purgatory see BX2170.D5
Church meetings see BX2170.P32
2170.C55 Church year devotions
2170.C56 Civil year devotions
2170.D5 Dead (Prayers for). Care of souls in purgatory. November devotions
2170.D9 Dying (Prayers for)
2170.F3 Family devotions
2170.H4 Holy Family (Devotions to)
2170.H5 Holy Spirit (Devotions to)
2170.H6 Holy Week devotions
2170.I6 Indulgenced prayers
2170.K55 Kings and rulers
2170.L4 Lenten devotions
2170.M3 Married people (Prayers for). Spouses (Prayers for)
2170.M4 Men (Prayers for)
2170.M6 Monthly devotions (General)
November devotions see BX2170.D5
2170.N7 Novenas (General)
2170.N9 Nurses (Prayers for)
Older people (Prayers for) see BX2170.A5
2170.P32 Parish meetings
2170.P4 Pentecost devotions
2170.R4 Refugees (Prayers for)
Rulers see BX2170.K55
2170.S3 Schools and colleges
Seminarians see BX2064
2170.S5 Sick and sorrowing (Prayers for)
2170.S6 Soldiers and sailors (Prayers for)
Including the Armed Forces in general
Spouses see BX2170.M3
2170.T43 Teachers (Prayers for)
2170.T5 Three hours' devotions
2170.V5 Virgins (Prayers for)
2170.W2 Wartime prayers
2170.W7 Women and girls (Prayers for)
2175.A-Z Special prayers, A-Z
2175.A3 Adoro te
2175.A48 Angelus
2175.A5 Anima Christi
Cf. BV284.A5 General
2175.A8 Ave Maria
2175.M5 Memorare

Catholic Church
Liturgy and ritual
Special prayers, A-Z -- Continued
2175.R6 Rorate coeli
Meditations. Devotional readings. Spiritual exercises, etc.
For meditations on the Virgin Mary see BX2160+
Cf. BV4800+ Works of meditation and devotion (General)
Cf. BX2169 Eucharistic prayers and devotions, etc.
Cf. BX2349+ Christian life
2177 Collections (General)
2177.5 History and criticism of devotional literature
Meditations by the saints
Including selections
2178 General
2179.A-Z Individual saints, A-Z
Under each (unless otherwise specified):

.x	*Collections or selections*
.x2A-.x2Z	*Separate works, A-Z*
.x3	*History, commentaries, etc.*

e.g.
Loyola, Ignacio de. Exercitia spiritualia
2179.L7A-.L7Z By language, A-Z
2179.L8 History, commentaries, etc.
Teresa, of Avila, Saint, 1515-1582
2179.T3A-.T3Z Selections. By language, A-Z
2179.T4A-.T4Z Separate works, A-Z
e.g.
2179.T4C3 Camino de perfección
Other spiritual authors. By language
2180 Latin
English
2181 Early through 1800
2182 1801-1950
2182.2 1951-2000
2182.3 2001-
2183 French
2184 German
2185 Italian
2186 Spanish and Portuguese
2187.A-Z Other languages, A-Z
2188.A-Z For individual religious orders and fraternities, A-Z
e.g.
2188.F7 Franciscans
2188.S52 Sisters of Charity of St. Vincent de Paul of New York
For the young
2198 English
Other languages see BX2180+

Catholic Church -- Continued
Hymns (English) see BV360+
Hymns (Other languages) see BV467+
Sacraments of the Catholic Church
Class here works on the liturgy of the sacraments
For the liturgical texts see BX1970+
Cf. BV800+ Christian sacraments in general
Cf. BX1828 Congregation of the Sacraments
2200 General works
2203 General special
e.g. Death and the sacraments, neuroses and the sacraments
Special sacraments
2205 Baptism
2210 Confirmation
Eucharist. Communion. Holy Sacrament
Cf. BX2169 Eucharistic prayers and devotions
2215.A1 Societies. Conferences. Collections
Including local, national, and international Eucharistic conferences
General works
2215.A3-Z Early through 1950
2215.2 1951-2000
2215.3 2001-
History see BV823
2218 Sacrificial character
2220 Real presence. Transubstantiation
2225 Miracles. Legends, etc.
Mass
For missals see BX2015+
General works
2230 Early to 1950
2230.2 1951-2000
2230.3 2001-
2230.5 History
2231 Elements: Bread and wine
2231.4 Celebration outside the Church
2231.5 Concelebration
2231.7 Private celebration
2232 Consecration
2233 Adoration
2233.3 Exposition
2233.6 Reservation
2234 Application. Intention
Communion. Reception of the Eucharist
2235 General works
2235.5 Under one or both species

Catholic Church
Sacraments of the Catholic Church
Special sacraments
Eucharist. Communion. Holy Sacrament
Communion. Reception of the Eucharist -- Continued

2236 Requirements for communion
Including age (Early Communion); preparation (Confession); etc.
Cf. BX2169 advice to communicants, devotional manuals
2236.2 Participation by children and youth
2236.3 Fasting communion
Including dispensations
2236.6 Frequency of Communion
Cf. BV4726 Easter duty
2237 First Communion
Cf. BV825.85 Ecclesiastical theology
2237.5 Viaticum
2237.7 Lay administration
2238 Study and teaching
2238.3 Pictures, illustrations, etc.
2238.4 Puppet plays at children's mass
2239 Sermons
Other devotional literature: Meditations, prayers, etc. see BX2169
2240 Holy Orders. Ordination
Marriage
2250 General works
2254 Divorce
2255 Remarriage
Penance
2260 General works
Confession
2261 Penitentials. Manuals for confessors
2262 History
2263.A-Z By country, A-Z
General works
2264 Early to 1800
2265 1801-1950
2265.2 1951-2000
2265.3 2001-
2266.A-Z Special topics, A-Z
2266.C5 Children's confession
Examination of conscience see BX2377
2266.F7 Frequency of confession
Cf. BV4725 Confession once a year
2266.M3 Marriage and the confessional

BX

Catholic Church
Sacraments of the Catholic Church
Special sacraments
Penance
Confession
Special topics, A-Z -- Continued
2266.P7 Prisoners' confessions
2267 Controversial works against the confessional
2270 Absolution
2275 Excommunication
Indulgences
Cf. BX2170.I6 Indulgenced prayers
2279 Collections
General works
2280 Early to 1800
2281 1801-1950
2281.2 1951-2000
2281.3 2001-
2282 Special indulgences (not A-Z)
2283 Abuses. Sale, etc.
2290 Extreme Unction
2292 Last sacraments. Ministry to the sick and dying
Sacramentals
2295 General works
Consecrations. Dedications
2300 General works
2302 Consecration of churches, cemeteries, etc.
2304 Consecration of bishops, etc.
2305 Consecration of virgins, etc.
Holy water
2307 General works
2307.3 Baptismal water
2307.5 Easter water
2307.7 Gregorian water
2308 Candles and lamps
2310.A-Z Other, A-Z
2310.C7 Crosses. Crucifixes
Crucifixes see BX2310.C7
2310.H6 Holy cards
2310.M5 Medals
Cf. CJ5793.R34 Catalogs of religious medals
2310.R7 Rosaries
Cf. BX2163 Prayers and devotions to the Virgin Mary
2310.S3 Scapulars
2312 Images

Catholic Church -- Continued

2315 Relics. Veneration, etc.

For relics of the saints see BX2333

Cf. BT587.S4 Holy Shroud of Turin

Shrines. Holy Places

2320 General works

2320.5.A-Z By region or country, A-Z

2321.A-Z Individual, A-Z

e.g.

For shrines of the Blessed Virgin Mary (unless purely descriptive) see BT650+

Cf. BT580 Christology

2321.A5 Aix-la-Chapelle

2321.A8 Assisi

2321.B6 Bom Jesus do monte

2321.D4 Derg, Lough. St. Patrick's Purgatory (Cave), Ireland

2321.L7 Loreto

2321.P4 Peña de Francia

2321.S3 Santiago de Compostela

Pilgrimages

2323 General works

Individual shrines see BX2321.A+

By region or country see BX2320.5.A+

Procesions

2324.A1 General works

2324.A5-Z By country, A-Z

Individual shrines see BX2321.A+

Saints. Hagiology

Cf. BX4662 Hagiography

2325 General works

2330 Canonization. Beatification

2333 Cultus. Relics

Lives of the saints (General) see BX4654+

Individual saints see BX4700.A+

2340 Exorcisms

Cf. BF1559 Demonology

2345 Votive offerings

Missions see BV2130+

Practical religion

Church work. Social service

Cf. RA975.C37 Catholic hospitals and health facilities

2347 General works

2347.2 Parish social ministry organizations

Cf. BX1916 Parish ministries

2347.4 Evangelistic work. Convert making

2347.5 Parish missions

For sermons see BX1756.A1+

Catholic Church
Practical religion
Church work. Social service -- Continued
Christian communities. Base (Basic) communities
Cf. BV4405+ General and Protestant communities

2347.7 General works
2347.72.A-Z By region or country, A-Z
2347.8.A-Z Work with, and attitude towards, special groups, classes, etc., A-Z
2347.8.A4 Aged. Older people
2347.8.A52 AIDS patients
2347.8.A55 Alcoholics
2347.8.B32 Baby boom generation
2347.8.B47 Bereaved
2347.8.B7 Boys
2347.8.C5 Children
2347.8.E82 Ex-church members
2347.8.E84 Ex-concentration camp inmates
2347.8.F3 Families
Foreign populations see BX2347.8.I46
Gays see BX2347.8.H65
2347.8.H34 Handicapped. People with disabilities
2347.8.H63 Homeless persons
2347.8.H65 Homosexuals
2347.8.I46 Immigrants. Foreign populations
2347.8.I49 Indians
2347.8.J89 Juvenile delinquents
2347.8.L3 Laboring classes
2347.8.M35 Married people
2347.8.M4 Mental disabilities, People with
2347.8.M42 Mentally ill
2347.8.N87 Nursing home patients
Older people see BX2347.8.A4
People with disabilities see BX2347.8.H34
People with mental disabilities see BX2347.8.M4
2347.8.P66 Poor
2347.8.P74 Prisoners
2347.8.P75 Prostitutes
2347.8.R44 Refugees
2347.8.S5 Sick
2347.8.S6 Soldiers and sailors
2347.8.S8 Students
2347.8.T69 Tourists, travelers, etc.
2347.8.W6 Women
2347.8.Y64 Young adults
2347.8.Y65 Young men
2347.8.Y66 Young women

Catholic Church
Practical religion
Church work. Social service
Work with, and attitude towards, special groups, classes, etc., A-Z -- Continued

2347.8.Y7 Youth

Catholic Action

2348.A1 Periodicals

Societies see BX2348.Z6+

2348.A2 Congresses

2348.A3 Collections. Collected works

2348.A4 Study and teaching

2348.A5 History and description

2348.A8-.Z4 General works. Theory. Principles

2348.Z5 Pamphlets, addresses, essays, etc.

By country

Including under each: local history, description, and local societies and organizations

2348.Z6 United States

2348.Z7A-.Z7Z Local, A-Z

2348.Z8A-.Z8Z Other countries, A-Z

Christian life

General works

2349 Early to 1800

2350 1800-1950

2350.A1 Periodicals. Societies. Collections

2350.2 1951-2000

2350.3 2001-

Perfection

2350.5 General works

Ways to perfection

2350.52 Purgative way

2350.53 Illuminative way

2350.54 Unitive way

2350.57 Charismatic movement

2350.6 Recollection

2350.65 Spirituality

By region or country see BX1401+

2350.7 Spiritual direction

2350.75 Journaling

2350.8 Married people

2350.9 Single people

2351 The Catholic family

Religious works for special classes of persons

2352 Parents

2352.5 Men. Fathers

2353 Women. Mothers

Catholic Church
Christian life
Religious works for special classes of persons
Women. Mothers -- Continued

2354 Widows
2355 Young men and women
2360 Young men and boys
Young women and girls
2365.A1 Periodicals
2365.A3-Z General works
Children
2370 Periodicals
2371 General works
2372 Older people
2373.A-Z Other classes, A-Z
2373.B47 Bereaved
2373.D42 Deaf
2373.L46 Lesbians
2373.N8 Nurses
2373.P7 Policemen
2373.S5 Sick. Afflicted
2373.S55 Single people
2373.S7 Soldiers and sailors
2373.S8 Students
2373.T4 Teachers
Retreats
Including Cursillo movement
2375.A1 Periodicals
2375.A2 Societies
2375.A3 General works. Organization and management
2375.A4 Retreat houses
2375.A5-Z Retreat addresses, conferences, meditations
Cf. BX2179.L7+ Spiritual exercises of Loyola
For special classes of persons
Clergy see BX1912.5
Religious
General see BX2385
Men see BX2435
Women see BX4214
Individual religious orders
see BX2903, BX3003, etc., Monastic life of each order
2376.A-Z Other, A-Z
2376.C5 Children
2376.M4 Men
2376.M5 Missionaries
2376.N8 Nurses
2376.S7 Students

Catholic Church
Christian life
Retreats
Retreat addresses, conferences, meditations
For special classes of persons
Other, A-Z -- Continued

2376.T44 Teenage girls
2376.W6 Women
2376.Y6 Young men
2376.Y7 Young women
2376.Y73 Youth
2376.5 Devotional literature for retreatants
2377 Examination of conscience
Cf. BX2261+ Confession

Religious life. Religious state
Cf. BX903 Seminary life
Cf. BX1912.5 Spiritual life of the priest
Cf. BX2435 Monastic life
Cf. BX4210+ Convent life

2380 Vocation for the religious life
Including vocation for all forms of church service, e.g. Secular clergy
For the vocation of women for the religious life see BX4210+

2385 General works
Including retreat addresses, conferences, meditations

2386 Evangelical counsels
Perfection see BX2350.5+

Monasticism. Religious orders
Cf. BX1834 Congregation of Religious
Cf. LC490+ Education under religious orders

2400 Periodicals. Serials
2405 Congresses
Collected works
2410 Several authors
2415 Individual authors
2420 Dictionaries. Encyclopedias
2425 Directories
2427 Religious in church law
General works
2430 Early through 1800
2431 1801-1950
2432 1951-2000
2432.3 2001-
Government and administration
2433 General works
2433.2 General chapters

Catholic Church
Monasticism. Religious orders
Government and administration -- Continued
2433.4 Visitations
2433.6 Local chapters, councils, etc.
2433.8 Relations with Rome, bishops, etc.
Superiors
2434 General works
2434.2 Major superiors. Abbots, provincials, etc.
2434.4 Lesser officials. Novice-masters, procurators, etc.
2434.6 Local superiors
2434.8 Consultors, etc.
2435 Monastic life. Vows. Discipline, etc.
Including retreat addresses, conferences, meditations
Cf. BX2049.A1+ Liturgy and ritual
Cf. BX2350.5+ Perfection
Cf. BX2438.5 Houses of prayer
Monastic rules
Cf. BX386.2 Rule of St. Basil
Cf. BX2904.A2 Rule of St. Augustine
Cf. BX3004.A2+ Rule of St. Benedict
2436 General works
2436.5.A-Z Special rules not associated with one order, A-Z
Class rules associated with one order with the order
Regula Chrodegangi
2436.5.C4 Latin text. By date
2436.5.C4A-.C4Z Other languages. By language and date
2436.5.C42A-.C42Z Commentaries. By author
Regula Magistri
2436.5.M3 Latin text. By date
2436.5.M3A-.M3Z Other languages. By language and date
2436.5.M32A-.M32Z Commentaries. By author
2437 Manuals, catechisms, etc.
2437.5 Provision for old age
2438 Spiritual direction. Manuals for superiors, etc.
2438.5 Houses of prayer
Controversial literature
2439.A1 Collections
General works
2439.A2 Early through 1800
2439.A3-Z 1801-1950
2439.2 1951-2000
2439.3 2001-
2440 General special
2445 Addresses, essays, sermons
2455 Origins
Including pre-Christian monasticism

Catholic Church
Monasticism. Religious orders -- Continued
History
General works
2460 Early through 1800
2461 1801-1950
2461.2 1951-2000
2461.3 2001-
2462 General special
By period
(2465) Before the foundation of orders
see BR195.M65
2470 Medieval
2475 Modern
By region or country
Including individual monasteries of men
For individual convents of women, see the order
2501 America
North America
2503 General works
United States
2505 General works
By region
2508 New England
2511 South
2514 Central
2518 West
2521 Pacific Coast
2523.A-.W By state, A-W
2524.A-Z Ecclesiastical jurisdictions. By place, A-Z
2525.A-Z By city, monastery, abbey, etc., A-Z
Canada
2527 General works
2528.A-Z By province, A-Z
2529.A-Z By city, monastery, etc., A-Z
2529.5 Latin America
Mexico
2530 General works
2531.A-Z By state, A-Z
2532.A-Z By city, monastery, etc., A-Z
Central America
2533 General works
2534-2535 Belize (Table BX9)
2536-2537 Costa Rica (Table BX9)
2538-2539 Guatemala (Table BX9)
2540-2541 Honduras (Table BX9)
2542-2543 Nicaragua (Table BX9)

Catholic Church
Monasticism. Religious orders
History
By region or country
Central America -- Continued
2544-2545 Panama (Table BX9)
2546-2547 El Salvador (Table BX9)
West Indies
2548 General works
2550-2551 Bahamas (Table BX9)
2552-2553 Cuba (Table BX9)
2554-2555 Haiti (Table BX9)
2556-2557 Jamaica (Table BX9)
2558-2559 Puerto Rico (Table BX9)
2560.A-Z Other, A-Z
South America
2561 General works
2562-2563 Argentina (Table BX9)
2564-2565 Bolivia (Table BX9)
2566-2567 Brazil (Table BX9)
2568-2569 Chile (Table BX9)
2570-2571 Colombia (Table BX9)
2572-2573 Ecuador (Table BX9)
Guiana
2574 General works
2576-2577 Guyana (Table BX9)
2578-2579 Suriname (Table BX9)
2580-2581 French Guiana (Table BX9)
2582-2583 Paraguay (Table BX9)
2584-2585 Peru (Table BX9)
2586-2587 Uruguay (Table BX9)
2588-2589 Venezuela (Table BX9)
Europe
2590 General works
Great Britain. England
2592 General works
2594.A-2695.Z By English county, A-Z
By English city, monastery, abbey, etc.
London
2595.A1 General works
2595.A3-Z By monastery, abbey, etc., A-Z
e.g.
2595.C5 Charterhouse
2595.O7 Oratory of St. Philip Neri
2596.A-Z Other, A-Z
2597-2599 Scotland (Table BX11)
2600-2602 Ireland (Table BX11)

Catholic Church
Monasticism. Religious orders
History
By region or country
Europe
Great Britain -- Continued

2603-2605 Wales (Table BX11)
2607-2609 Austria (Table BX11)
2610-2612 Belgium (Table BX11)
2613-2615 France (Table BX11)
2616-2618 Germany (Table BX11)
2619-2621 Greece (Table BX11)
2622-2624 Italy (Table BX11)
2625-2627 Netherlands (Table BX11)
2628-2630 Portugal (Table BX11)
2631-2633 Russia. Soviet Union (Table BX11)
For Soviet Central Asia see BX2699+
For Siberia see BX2729+
Cf. BX580+ Russian Orthodox Eastern Church
2634-2636 Finland (Table BX11)
2637-2639 Poland (Table BX11)
Scandinavia
2640 General works
2642-2644 Denmark (Table BX11)
2645-2647 Iceland (Table BX11)
2648-2650 Norway (Table BX11)
2651-2653 Sweden (Table BX11)
2654-2656 Spain (Table BX11)
2657-2659 Switzerland (Table BX11)
2660-2662 Turkey (Table BX11)
For Turkey in Asia see BX2681+
Other Balkan states
2663 General works
2664-2666 Bulgaria (Table BX11)
2670-2672 Romania (Table BX11)
2673-2675 Yugoslavia (Table BX11)
2676.A-Z Other European regions or countries, A-Z
e.g.
2676.C9 Czechoslovakia
2676.L8 Luxembourg
Asia
2677 General works
2679 Southwestern Asia
Turkey in Asia
Cf. BX2660+ Turkey in Europe
2681 General works
2682.A-Z By vilayet, region, etc., A-Z

BX

Catholic Church
Monasticism. Religious orders
History
By region or country
Asia
Southwestern Asia
Turkey in Asia -- Continued
2683.A-Z By city, monastery, abbey, etc., A-Z
2684-2686 Armenia (Table BX11)
2687-2689 Iraq (Table BX11)
Syria
2689.3 General works
2689.4.A-Z By political division or ecclesiastical jurisdiction, A-Z
2689.5.A-Z By city, A-Z
Including individual monasteries and abbeys by city, A-Z, or by name if nonurban
2690-2692 Israel (Table BX11)
Lebanon
2692.3 General works
2692.4.A-Z By political division or ecclesiastical jurisdiction, A-Z
2692.5.A-Z By city, A-Z
Including individual monasteries and abbeys by city, A-Z, or by name if nonurban
Jordan
2692.7 General works
2692.8.A-Z By political division or ecclesiastical jurisdiction, A-Z
2692.9.A-Z By city, A-Z
Including individual monasteries and abbeys by city, A-Z, or by name if nonurban
2693-2695 Saudi Arabia (Table BX11)
2696-2698 Iran (Table BX11)
Central Asia. Soviet Central Asia
2699 General works
2700 Afghanistan
2702 Bokhara (Bukhara)
2703 Khiva. Khorezm
2704.A-Z Other, A-Z
Southern Asia. Southeast Asia
2705 General works
2706 India
2707 Burma. Myanmar
2708 Sri Lanka
2711-2713 Indochina. Malay Peninsula (Table BX11)
Class here works on Kampuchea, Cochin China, Laos, Malaya, Thailand, Tongking, Vietnam
Indonesia (Malay Archipelago)
2714 General works

Catholic Church
Monasticism. Religious orders
History
By region or country
Asia
Southern Asia. Southeast Asia
Indonesia (Malay Archipelago) -- Continued
2715-2717 Indonesia (Republic). Dutch East Indies (Table BX11)
Class here works on Borneo, Celebes, Java, Sumatra, etc.
2718-2720 Philippines (Table BX11)
Eastern Asia. The Far East
2722 General works
2723-2725 China (Table BX11)
2726-2728 Japan (Table BX11)
2729-2731 Northern Asia. Siberia (Table BX11)
Africa
2732 General works
Egypt
2734 General works
2735.A-Z By political division or ecclesiastical jurisdiction, A-Z
2736.A-Z By city, A-Z
Including individual monasteries and abbeys by city, A-Z, or by name if nonurban
2737 South Africa
2740.A-Z Other country divisions, A-Z
Australia and New Zealand
2743 General works
2744.A-Z By country division, A-Z
2745.A-Z By city, monastery, abbey, etc., A-Z
Pacific islands
2747 General works
2749.A-Z By island or group of islands, A-Z
2790 Costume. Habit
Cf. BX4223 Religious orders of women
Cf. GT1950 Religious and military orders
Biography
2800 Collective
For individual orders, see the order
Individual see BX4700+
Special classes of religious orders
Orders for men see BX2430+
Orders for women see BX4200+
2810 Contemplative
Teaching see LC490+
2815 Preaching

Catholic Church
Monasticism. Religious orders
Special classes of religious orders -- Continued
2818 Military
2820 Mendicant. Friars
2825 Hospitalers
2830 Canons regular
2832 Clerks regular
2835 Brothers. Lay brothers
2840 Tertiary. Third orders
Hermits. Anchorites
Cf. BR1712 Pillar saints
2845 General works
2847.A-Z By region or country, A-Z
e.g.
2847.G7 Great Britain
2847.M3 Majorca
Individual orders of men
2890 Alexian Brothers (Table BX18)
2892 Antoinine Canons (Table BX18)
2896 Assumptionists (Table BX18)
Atonement Friars see BX3664
2900 Augustinian Canons (Table BX18 modified)
2900.Z6A-.Z6Z By branch, congregation, etc., A-Z
Premonstratensians see BX3901+
2900.Z6S5 Generaal Kapittel van Sion
2900.Z6W5 Windesheim Congregation
2901-2956 Augustinians. Augustinian Eremites (Table BX16 modified)
Rules. Instruction. Constitution, etc.
2904.A2 Rule of St. Augustine. Latin texts. By date
History
2954.A-Z Other branches (not otherwise provided for), A-Z
2954.A92 Augustinian Recollets
2960 Barnabites (Table BX18)
2962 Bartholomites (Table BX18)
2970 Basilians (Table BX18)
For Basilians of the Oriental rites see BX4710.76
For Basilians of the Orthodox Eastern Church see BX385+
Cf. BX386.2 Rule of St. Basil
2974 Beghards (Table BX18)
3001-3056 Benedictines (Table BX16 modified)
See also Celestines, Camaldolites, Cistercians, Cluniacs, Olivetans, Trappists, Vallombrosans, Williamites (Benedictine)
Rules. Instructions. Constitution, etc.

Catholic Church
Monasticism. Religious orders
Individual orders of men
Benedictines
Rules. Instructions. Constitution, etc. -- Continued
Rule of St. Benedict
3004.A2 Latin texts. By date
3004.A4-.Z4 Other languages, A-Z
Subarrange by date
3004.Z5 Commentaries. By author
History
3050.A-Z By congregation or province, A-Z
3050.B8 Bursfelder Kongregation
3050.M3 Congregation de Saint Maur. Maurists
3050.S6 Congregation de France (Solesmes)
Bernardines (Cistercians) see BX3401+
3057 Bernardines (Franciscans) (Table BX18)
3058 Bethlehemites (Table BX18)
3058.3 Brothers Hospitallers of St. John of God (Table BX18)
3058.5 Brothers of Charity (Table BX18)
3058.7 Brothers of Christian Instruction of Ploermel (Table BX18)
3058.8 Brothers of Christian Instruction of Saint Gabriel (Table BX18)
3059 Brothers of Holy Cross (Table BX18)
3059.2 Brothers of Mercy of Trier (Table BX18)
Brothers of St. Francis Xavier see BX4192
3059.5 Brothers of Saint Hippolytus (Table BX18)
3059.7 Brothers of St. Joseph (Table BX18)
3060 Brothers of the Christian Schools (Table BX18)
3065 Brothers of the Christian Schools of Ireland (Table BX18)
3070 Brothers of the Common Life (Table BX18)
3080 Brothers of the Sacred Heart (Table BX18)
3085 Camaldolites (Table BX18)
3090 Camillians (Table BX18)
3095 Canons of the Holy Sepulcher (Table BX18)
Canons Regular of St. Augustine see BX2900
Canons Regular of the Holy Cross see BX3493
3101-3156 Capuchins (Table BX16)
3201-3256 Carmelites. White Friars (Table BX16)
3260 Carmelites of Mary Immaculate (Table BX18)
3301-3356 Carthusians (Table BX16)
Catholic Apostolate see BX3866
3375 Celestines (Table BX18)
Christian Brothers see BX3060
Christian Brothers of Ireland see BX3065
Christian Instruction Brothers of Ploermel see BX3058.7

Catholic Church
Monasticism. Religious orders
Individual orders of men -- Continued
Christian Instruction Brothers of Saint Gabriel see BX3058.8
3401-3456 Cistercians. Bernardines (Table BX16)
Cistercians of the Strict Observance see BX4101+
3458 Claretian Missionaries (Table BX18)
Clerics of St. Viator see BX4178
Clerks Regular for the Care of the Sick see BX3090
Clerks Regular, Minor see BX3814
Clerks Regular of St. Paul see BX2960
3459 Clerks Regular of Somaschi (Table BX18)
Clerks Regular of the Pious Schools see BX3888
Cluniacs
3460 General works
3467 In France
3470.A-Z In other countries, A-Z
3472 Comboni Missionaries (Table BX18)
3474 Communità dei Figli di Dio (Table BX18)
3475 Congregation of Holy Cross (Table BX18)
Cf. BX3059 Brothers of Holy Cross
Congregation of Priests of the Mission see BX3770
3480 Congregation of the Holy Ghost (Table BX18)
Cf. BX3682 Holy Ghost Fathers
Congregation of the Holy Ghost and of the Immaculate Heart of Mary see BX3682
3482 Congregation of the Immaculate Heart of Mary (Table BX18)
3484 Congregation of the Priests of the Sacred Heart (Table BX18)
3486 Congregation of the Sacred Hearts of Jesus and Mary (Table BX18)
3487 Congregazione di San Giuseppe (Table BX18)
3488 Congregazione religiosa Figli di Maria Immacolata (Table BX18)
3490 Conventuals. Conventual Franciscan Fathers (Table BX18)
3493 Crosier Fathers (Table BX18)
3494 Discalced Mercedarians (Table BX18)
3495 Doctrinarians (Table BX18)
3501-3556 Dominicans. Friars Preachers. Black Friars (Table BX16)
3565 Eudists (Table BX18)
3570 Family of the Sacred Heart of Jesus (Table BX18)
3573 Fathers of Mercy (Table BX18)
3577 Fathers of the Blessed Sacrament (Table BX18)
3585 Florians (Table BX18)

Catholic Church
Monasticism. Religious orders
Individual orders of men -- Continued
3590 Franciscan Brothers (Table BX18)
Franciscans. Minorites. Friars Minor. Gray Friars
3601 Periodicals. Societies. Serials
3601.3 Collected works (nonserial)
3601.5 Congresses
3602.A1 Dictionaries. Encyclopedias
3602.A15 Directories
General works
3602.A2 Early through 1800
3602.A3-Z 1801-1950
3602.2 1951-2000
3602.3 2001-
3603 Monastic life. Vows. Discipline, etc.
3603.3 Lay brothers
Rules. Instructions. Constitution, etc.
3604.A2 Latin texts. By date
3604.A4-.Z4 Other languages. By language, A-Z, and date
3604.Z5 Commentaries
Liturgy and ritual see BX2049.A1+
Prayer books and devotions see BX2050.A1+
Government and administration
3604.4 General works
3604.42 General chapters. Visitations
3604.44 Local government
3604.5 Relations with Rome, bishops, etc.
3604.6 Superiors
Controversial works against the order
3605.A2 Early through 1800
3605.A3-Z 1801-1950
3605.2 1951-2000
3605.3 2001-
Missions see BV2280.A1+
History
For individual monasteries, abbeys, etc., see BX2525.A+ BX2529.A+ etc.
General works
3606.A2 Early through 1800
3606.A3-Z 1801-1950
3606.2 1951-2000
3606.3 2001-
By region or country
America. North America
3607 General works
United States

Catholic Church
Monasticism. Religious orders
Individual orders of men
Franciscans. Minorites. Friars Minor. Gray Friars
History
By region or country
America. North America
United States -- Continued

3608 General works
3609.A-.W By state, A-W
3610.A-Z By city, etc., A-Z
Canada
3611.A1 General works
3611.A5-Z Local, A-Z
Mexico
3612.A1 General works
3612.A5-Z Local, A-Z
Central America
3612.4 General works
3612.5.A-Z By country, A-Z
West Indies
3612.6 General works
3612.7.A-Z By country, A-Z
3613.5 Latin America
South America
3614.A1 General works
3614.A5-Z By country, A-Z
Europe
3615 General works
Great Britain. England
3616 General works
3617.A-Z By English county, A-Z
3618.A-Z By city, A-Z
By monastery see BX2595+
Ireland
3619 General works
3620.A-Z By Irish county, A-Z
3621.A-Z By city, A-Z
By monastery see BX2600+
Scotland
3622 General works
3623.A-Z By Scottish region, A-Z
3624.A-Z By city, A-Z
By monastery see BX2597+
Wales
3625 General works
3626.A-Z By Welsh county, A-Z

Catholic Church
Monasticism. Religious orders
Individual orders of men
Franciscans. Minorites. Friars Minor. Gray Friars
History
By region or country
Europe
Wales -- Continued

3627.A-Z	By city, A-Z
	By monastery see BX2603+
	Austria
3628	General works
3629.A-Z	By country division, A-Z
	For Bohemia and the Czech Republic see BX3645.C9
3630.A-Z	By city, A-Z
	France
3631	General works
3632.A-Z	By country division, A-Z
3633.A-Z	By city, A-Z
	Germany
3634	General works
3635.A-Z	By country division, A-Z
3636.A-Z	By city, A-Z
	Italy
3637	General works
3638.A-Z	By country division, A-Z
3639.A-Z	By city, A-Z
	Netherlands (Low countries). Holland
3640.A1	General works
3640.A5-Z	Local, A-Z
	Belgium
3641.A1	General works
3641.A5-Z	Local, A-Z
	Portugal
3642.A1	General works
3642.A5-Z	Local, A-Z
	Scandinavia
3643.A1	General works
	By country
	Denmark
3643.D4	General works
3643.D5A-.D5Z	Local, A-Z
	Iceland
3643.I2	General works
3643.I3A-.I3Z	Local, A-Z
	Norway

Catholic Church
Monasticism. Religious orders
Individual orders of men
Franciscans. Minorites. Friars Minor. Gray Friars
History
By region or country
Europe
Scandinavia
By country
Norway -- Continued

3643.N8	General works
3643.N9A-.N9Z	Local, A-Z
	Sweden
3643.S8	General works
3643.S9A-.S9Z	Local, A-Z
	Spain
3644.A1	General works
3644.A5-Z	Local, A-Z
3645.A-Z	Other European regions or countries, A-Z
3645.C9	Czech Republic. Bohemia
3645.L5	Lithuania
3645.P6	Poland
3645.R8	Russia. Soviet Union
3645.S9	Switzerland
	Asia
3646.A1	General works
3646.A5-Z	By country, A-Z
	Africa
3647.A1	General works
3647.A5-Z	By country, A-Z
	Australia and New Zealand
3648.A1	General works
3648.A5-Z	By country, A-Z
	Oceania
3649.A1	General works
3649.A5-Z	By country, A-Z
3649.5	Developing countries
3650.A-Z	By congregation, province, custody, commissariat, etc., A-Z
	Tertiaries. Third Order
3651	General works
3652.A-Z	Rules. Manuals and guides. By language, A-Z, and date
3653.A-Z	By region or country, A-Z
3654	Third Order Regular of St. Francis (Table BX18)
	Biography
3655	Collective

Catholic Church
Monasticism. Religious orders
Individual orders of men
Franciscans. Minorites. Friars Minor. Gray Friars
Biography -- Continued

(3656) Individual
see BX4700+

3659 Fraters van Tilburg (Table BX18)
3661 Fraticelli (Table BX18)
3663 Frères de la Vierge des pauvres (Table BX18)
3663.5 Frères de l'instruction Chrétienne (Table BX18)
3664 Friars of the Atonement (Table BX18)
Gemeinschaft von den Heiligen Engeln see BV2300.G4
3670 Gilbertines (Table BX18)
3672 Grandmont, Order of (Table BX18)
3674 Hermanos de la Hospitalidad (Table BX18)
3674.5 Hermits of Bethlehem of the Heart of Jesus (Table BX18)
3675 Hermits of Saint Paul (Table BX18)
3678 Hieronymites (Table BX18)
3680 Holy Family Missionaries (Table BX18)
3682 Holy Ghost Fathers (Table BX18)
3688 Humiliati (Table BX18)
3698 Jesuats (Table BX18)
3701-3756 Jesuits. Society of Jesus (Table BX16)
3765 Krizovnici s cervenou kuezdou (Table BX18)
3770 Lazarists. Vincentians. Congregation of the Mission (Table BX18)
3775 Little Brothers of Jesus (Table BX18)
Little Brothers of Saint Francis see BX3654
3777 Little Brothers of St. John (Table BX18)
3782 Marian Fathers (Table BX18)
3784 Marianists (Table BX18)
Mariannhill Fathers see BV2300.M3
3788 Marist Brothers (Table BX18)
3790 Marist Fathers. Society of Mary (Table BX18)
Maryknoll Fathers see BV2300.C35
Maurists see BX3050.M3
(3796) Mekhitarists. Mechitarists
see BX4715.76
3800 Mercedarians (Table BX18)
Mercedarians, Discalced see BX3494
3810 Minims. Minimites (Table BX18)
3814 Minor Clerks Regular (Table BX18)
3816 Missionaries de l'Immaculée-Conception de Lourdes (Table BX18)
3816.7 Missionaries of St. Francis de Sales of Annecy (Table BX18)

Catholic Church
Monasticism. Religious orders
Individual orders of men -- Continued

(3816.8) Missionaries of St. Francis Xavier
see BV2300.X84
3817 Missionaries of the Consolata (Table BX18)
3821 Oblates of Mary Immaculate (Table BX18)
3825 Oblates of St. Francis de Sales (Table BX18)
3828 Oblates of the Virgin Mary (Table BX18)
3840 Olivetans (Table BX18)
Oratorians
3850 Oratory of St. Philip Neri (Table BX18 modified)
3853.A-Z By country, A-Z
3855 French Congregation of the Oratory (Table BX18)
Order of Grandmont see BX3672
3858 Order of the Knights of Jesus Christ (Table BX18)
3866 Pallottines (Table BX18)
3880 Passionists (Table BX18)
3884 Pauline Fathers (Order of St. Paul the First Hermit) (Table BX18)
3885 Paulist Fathers. Paulists. Congregation of the Missionary Priests of St. Paul, the Apostle (Table BX18)
Pia società di San Francesco Saverio per le missioni estere see BV2300.P5
3888 Piarists. Clerks Regular of the Pious Schools (Table BX18)
3890 Pious Society of St. Paul (Table BX18)
3901-3956 Premonstratensians. Premonstrants. White Canons. Norbertines (Table BX16)
3958 Priests of the Most Precious Blood (Table BX18)
Recollets (Augustinian) see BX2954.A92
3970 Recollets (Bernardine) (Table BX18)
3980 Recollets (Franciscan) (Table BX18)
4020 Redemptorists (Table BX18)
4025 Resurrectionists (Religious order) (Table BX18)
4027 Rosminians (Table BX18)
Sacred Heart Brothers see BX3080
4030 St. Joseph's Society of the Sacred Heart (Table BX18)
4040 Salesian Cooperators (Table BX18)
4045 Salesians (Table BX18)
4050 Salvatorians (Table BX18)
4052 Scalabrianians (Table BX18)
4053 Sei Pauro Shūdōkai (Japan) (Table BX18)
4055 Servites (Table BX18)
Society of African Missions see BV2300.S5
Society of the Divine Word see BV2300.S6
4058 Stigmatine Fathers (Table BX18)

Catholic Church
Monasticism. Religious orders
Individual orders of men -- Continued

4060 Sulpicians (Table BX18)
4075 Sylvestrines (Table BX18)
4085 Theatines (Table BX18)
4101-4156 Trappists (Table BX16)
4158 Trinitarians (Table BX18)
4165 Val des Ecoliers, Congrégation du (Table BX18)
4170 Valliscaulians (Table BX18)
4175 Vallombrosans (Table BX18)
4178 Viatorians (Table BX18)
Vincentians see BX3770
4181 White Fathers (Table BX18)
4183 Williamites (Benedictine) (Table BX18)
4192 Xaverian Brothers (Table BX18)
Religious orders of women. Convents, etc.
4200 General works
4205 General special
4208 Government and administration
4208.2 General chapters
4208.4 Visitations
4208.6 Local chapters, councils, etc.
4208.8 Relations with Rome, bishops, etc.
Superioresses
4209 General works
4209.2 Major superioresses. Mothers general, abbesses, etc.
4209.4 Lesser officials. Novice-mistresses, procuratrixes, etc.
4209.6 Local superioresses
4209.8 Consultors, etc.
Religious life
Including spiritual reading
4210 General works
4210.5 Education
4211 Ceremonies. Consecration, etc.
4212 Laws. Rules, etc.
4213 Manuals
Prayer books see BX2060.A1+
4214 Retreats for sisters
Including addresses, conferences, meditations
4215 Anti-Catholic works. Exposures, etc.
4216.A-Z Individual cases, A-Z
e.g.
4216.M6 Monk, Maria
4220.A-Z By region or country, A-Z
4223 Costume. Habit
4224 Health and hygiene

Catalog Church
Monasticism. Religious orders
Religious orders of women. Convents, etc. -- Continued
4225 Biography (Collective)
Special classes of religious orders
4230 Contemplative
4235 Canonesses
Missionary orders see BV2245+
4237 Social service orders
Works of charity and mercy
4240 Nursing orders
Teaching orders see LC490+
Individual orders of women
4260 Ancille della Santissima Vergine (Table BX18)
4261 Annunciates (Belgium) (Table BX18)
4262 Annunciates of Bourges (Table BX18)
4263 Augustines de Saint-Coeur de Marie (Table BX18)
4264 Augustinian Canonesses (Table BX18)
4265-4268 Augustinian Eremites (Second Order). Augustinian Nuns (Table BX17)
4269 Basilian Nuns (Table BX18)
4272 Beguines (Table BX18)
4275-4278 Benedictine Nuns (Table BX17)
4280 Benedictine Sisters of Perpetual Adoration, Clyde, Mo. (Table BX18)
4281 Benedictine Sisters of the Blessed Sacrament (Table BX18)
4283 Bernardines (Cistercian Nuns) (Table BX18)
4284 Bernardines (Franciscan Nuns) (Table BX18)
4285-4288 Birgittines (Table BX17)
4290 Bon Secours de Troyes (Table BX18)
4291 Brigidines (Table BX18)
4292 Canonesses Regular of the Holy Sepulcher (Table BX18)
4294 Canonesses Regular of Windesheim (Table BX18)
4301-4304 Capuchin Nuns (Table BX17)
4308 Carmelitas de Santa Teresa (Table BX18)
4312 Carmelite Nuns of the Ancient Observance (Table BX18)
4315 Carmelite Sisters for the Aged and Infirm (Table BX18)
4315.5 Carmelite Sisters of Charity (Table BX18)
4316 Carmelite Sisters of Corpus Christi (Table BX18)
4317 Carmelite Sisters of the Divine Heart of Jesus (Table BX18)
4318 Carmelite Sisters of the Most Sacred Heart of Los Angeles (Table BX18)
4319 Carmelite Sisters of the Third Order (Mexico) (Table BX18)

Catholic Church
Monasticism. Religious orders
Individual orders of women -- Continued

4320 Carmelite Sisters of the Third Order (Venezuela) (Table BX18)
4321-4324 Carmelites (Second Order). Carmelite Nuns (Table BX17)
4326 Carthusians (Second Order). Carthusian Nuns (Table BX18)
4326.5 Cenacolo domenicano (Table BX18)
4327 Christian Virgins (Table BX18)
4327.5 Chung-hua shêng mu hui (Sisters of Our Lady of China) (Table BX18)
4328 Cistercians (Second Order). Cistercian Nuns (Table BX18)
4328.5 Colettines (Table BX18)
4328.7 Company of Mary (Table BX18)
4329 Conceptionists (Table BX18)
4330 Congregacão das Irmãs-Auxiliares de Nossa Senhora de piedade (Table BX18)
4330.2 Congregacão das Irmãs Franciscanas de Nossa Senhora Aparecida (Table BX18)
4330.5 Congregación de Hermanas de la Beata Mariana de Jesús (Table BX18)
4330.6 Congregación de Hermanas de la Virgen Maria del Monte Carmelo (Table BX18)
4330.8 Congregación de Nuestra Señora de los Desamparados (Table BX18)
4331 Congrégation de Notre Dame (Table BX18)
4331.2 Congrégation de Notre Dame de Montréal (Table BX18)
4331.4 Congrégation de Notre Dame de Sion (Table BX18)
4331.43 Congrégation de Sainte Clothilde (Table BX18)
4331.47 Congrégation de soeurs de Notre-Dame du Bon-Conseil (Table BX18)
4331.5 Congregation of Antonian Sisters of Mary (Table BX18)
4331.6 Congregation of Our Lady of Covadonga (Table BX18)
4331.8 Congregation of the Dominican Sisters of the Perpetual Rosary (Table BX18)
4332 Congregation of the Holy Union of the Sacred Hearts (Table BX18)
4332.3 Congregation of the Religious of the Virgin Mary (Table BX18)
4332.4 Congregation of the Rosary (Table BX18)
4332.5 Congregazione del Buon Gesù (Table BX18)
4332.6 Congregazione delle Figlie de San Giuseppe (Table BX18)

Catholic Church
Monasticism. Religious orders
Individual orders of women -- Continued

4332.8 Damas Apostólicas del Sagrado Corazón de Jesús (Table BX18)
4332.9 Daughters of Charity of Canossa (Table BX18)
4333 Daughters of Charity of St. Vincent de Paul, Emmitsburg, Md. (Table BX18)
4333.1 Daughters of Divine Charity (Table BX18)
4333.2 Daughters of Jesus (Table BX18)
4333.4 Daughters of Mary, Help of Christians (Table BX18)
4333.6 Daughters of Our Lady of Mercy (Table BX18)
4333.7 Daughters of Our Lady of the Sacred Heart (Table BX18)
4333.8 Daughters of St. Mary of Providence (Table BX18)
4334 Daughters of St. Paul (Table BX18)
4334.15 Daughters of the Church (Table BX18)
4334.2 Daughters of the Cross (Table BX18)
4334.4 Daughters of the Heart of Jesus (Table BX18)
4334.5 Daughters of the Heart of Mary (Table BX18)
4334.6 Daughters of the Holy Ghost (Table BX18)
4334.65 Daughters of the Most Holy Redeemer (Table BX18)
4334.7 Daughters of the Oratory (Table BX18)
4334.8 Daughters of Wisdom (Table BX18)
4335 Devout Virgins of St. Catherine (Table BX18)
4335.5 Discepole de Gesù Eucaristico (Table BX18)
4336 Dominicaines de Béthanie (Table BX18)
4336.2 Dominicaines missionaires de Notre-Dame de la Délivrance (Table BX18)
4336.5 Dominican Nuns of the Annunciation (Table BX18)
4336.7 Dominican Rural Missionaries (Table BX18)
4337 Dominican Sisters. Dominican Nuns (Table BX18 modified)

Variant name: Sisters of the Third Order of St. Dominic. Dominicans (Second Order)

4337.15 American Congregation of the Sacred Heart of Jesus (Caldwell, N.J.) (Table BX18)
4337.23 Congregation of Our Lady of the Rosary (Table BX18)
4337.24 Congregation of Our Lady of the Sacred Heart, Grand Rapids (Table BX18)
4337.25 Congregation of Our Lady of the Sacred Heart, Springfield, Ill. (Table BX18)
4337.26 Congregation of St. Catharine of Sienna, Racine, Wis. (Table BX18)
4337.28 Congregation of St. Catharine of Sienna, Salisbury, Rhodesia (Table BX18)
4337.29 Congregation of St. Catharine of Sienna, Trinidad and Tobago (Table BX18)

Catholic Church
Monasticism. Religious orders
Individual orders of women
Dominican Sisters. Dominican Nuns -- Continued

4337.3 Congregation of St. Mary of the Springs. Motherhouse, Columbus, Ohio (Table BX18)
4337.32 Congregation of the Holy Cross, Brooklyn (Table BX18)
4337.34 Congregation of the Immaculate Conception, Great Bend, Kans. (Table BX18)
4337.36 Congregation of the Most Holy Name of Jesus, San Rafael, Calif. (Table BX18)
4337.38 Congregation of the Most Holy Rosary, Adrian, Mich. (Table BX18)
4337.4 Congregation of the Most Holy Rosary, Sinsinawa, Wis. (Table BX18)
4337.5.A-Z Other congregations. By place, A-Z
4337.7 Dominican Sisters of Bethany (Table BX18)
4338 Dominican Sisters of Charity of the Presentation of the Blessed Virgin Mary (Table BX18)
4339 Dominican Sisters of the Sick Poor (Table BX18)
4340 Dominicas Dueñas de Zamora (Table BX18)
4341 Družba sestara Presvetog Srca Isusova (Table BX18)
4344.5 Esclavas del Corazon de Jesus (Table BX18)
4345 Faithful Companions of Jesus (Table BX18)
4346 Felician Sisters of the Order of St. Francis (Table BX18)
4346.3 Figlie dell'Immacolata Concezione di Sant'Arcangelo (Table BX18)
Filles de Jésus see BX4333.2
4346.5 Filles de la Sainte-Vierge (Table BX18)
4346.7 Filles de Marie (Yaoundé, Cameroon) (Table BX18)
4347 Filles de Notre-Dame des Sept-Douleurs (Table BX18)
4347.5 Filles de Saint-Francois de Sales (Table BX18)
4348 Filles de Sainte-Marie de Torfou (Table BX18)
4348.5 Filles du Providence de Sées (Table BX18)
4349 Filles du Sacré Coeur de Marie (Table BX18)
Foreign Mission Sisters of St. Dominic see BV2300.M4
4350 Franciscaines du Sacré-Coeur (Table BX18)
4351 Franciscan Missionaries of Mary (Table BX18)
4351.3 Franciscan Missionaries of St. Joseph (Table BX18)
4351.5 Franciscan Missionary Poor Clares of the Blessed Sacrament (Table BX18)
4352 Franciscan Missionary Sisters of the Sacred Heart (Table BX18)
4352.5 Franciscan Nuns of the Most Blessed Sacrament (Table BX18)
4352.7 Franciscan sisters (Third Order Regular women in general) (Table BX18)

Catholic Church
Monasticism. Religious orders
Individual orders of women -- Continued

4353 Franciscan Sisters, Daughters of the Sacred Hearts of Jesus and Mary (Table BX18)
4354 Franciscan Sisters of Christian Charity, Manitowoc, Wis. (Table BX18)
4355 Franciscan Sisters of Our Lady of the Angels (Table BX18)
4355.3 Franciscan Sisters of Penance and Christian Charity (Table BX18)
4355.5 Franciscan Sisters of St. Elizabeth (Table BX18)
4356 Franciscan Sisters of St. Kunegunda (Table BX18)
4357 Franciscan Sisters of St. Paul (Table BX18)
4358 Franciscan Sisters of the Atonement (Table BX18)
4358.2 Franciscan Sisters of the Eucharist (Table BX18)
4358.3 Franciscan Sisters of the Immaculate Conception (Table BX18)
4358.5 Franciscan Sisters of the Sacred Heart (Table BX18)
4361-4364 Franciscans (Second Order). Poor Clares (Table BX17)
4366 Grey Nuns (Table BX18)
Grey Nuns of Québec see BX4532.54
4366.3 Grey Nuns of the Cross (Table BX18)
4366.6 Grey Sisters of St. Elizabeth (Table BX18)
4367 Helpers of the Holy Souls (Table BX18)
4368 Hermanas adoratrices del santisimo sacramento (Table BX18)
4368.2 Hermanas de la Cruz (Table BX18)
4368.25 Hermanas de los Pobres de San Pedro Claver (Table BX18)
4368.27 Hermanas Franciscanas de Ntra. Sra. del Buen Consejo (Table BX18)
4368.3 Hermanitas de Ancianos Desamparados (Table BX18)
4369 Hijas de Jesús (Table BX18)
4369.2 Hijas de la Misericordia (Table BX18)
4369.3 Hijas de San José (Table BX18)
4369.5 Hijas del Santisimo Salvador (Table BX18)
4370 Hospitaller Sisters of Santa Maria Nuova (Table BX18)
4371-4374 Institute of the Blessed Virgin Mary "Jesuitesses" (Table BX17)
Cf. BX4435+ Sacred Heart, Society of the
4375 Instituto de Damas Catequistas (Table BX18)
4380 Instituto de las esclavas del corazón de Jesús (Table BX18)
4382 Instituto Hermanas Pobres Bonaerenses de San José (Table BX18)
4383 Josephite Sisters of Charity (Table BX18)

Catholic Church
Monasticism. Religious orders
Individual orders of women -- Continued

4384 Katharinenschwestern (Table BX18)
4385 Ladies of Nazareth (Table BX18)
Ladies of the Sacred Heart see BX4435+
4390 Little Company of Mary (Table BX18)
4392 Little Franciscan Sisters of Mary (Table BX18)
4393 Little Servant Sisters of the Immaculate Conception (Table BX18)
4394 Little Sisters of Divine Providence (Table BX18)
4394.5 Little Sisters of Jesus (Table BX18)
4395 Little Sisters of the Assumption (Table BX18)
4397 Little Sisters of the Immaculate Conception (Table BX18)
4401-4404 Little Sisters of the Poor (Table BX17)
4405.2 Magdalens (Table BX18)
4405.25 Marianist Sisters (Table BX18)
Maryknoll Sisters see BV2300.M4
Medical Mission Sisters see BV2300.S53
4405.3 Mercedarian Sisters of Charity (Table BX18)
4405.4 Minim Sisters of the Sacred Heart (Table BX18)
4405.5 Minim Sisters of the Sorrowful Mother (Table BX18)
4405.6 Misericordia Sisters (Table BX18)
4405.7 Misioneras de María Immaculada y Santa Catalina de Sena (Table BX18)
4406 Mission Helpers of the Sacred Heart (Table BX18)
4406.2 Missionaires de l'Immaculée Conception de Lourdes (Table BX18)
4406.3 Missionarie della Passione di Nostro Signor Gesu Cristo (Table BX18)
4406.5 Missionaries of Charity (Table BX18)
4406.6 Missionary Benedictine Sisters (Table BX18)
Missionary Canonesses of St. Augustine see BV2300.M5
4406.8 Missionary Servants of Saint Joseph (Table BX18)
4406.9 Missionary Servants of the Most Blessed Trinity (Table BX18)
4406.95 Missionary Sisters of Christ the King (Table BX18)
4406.955 Missionary Sisters of Mary Help of Christians (Table BX18)
4407 Missionary Sisters of Mother of God (Table BX18)
Missionary Sisters of St. Columban see BV2300.M53
4407.3 Missionary Sisters of St. Dominic (Table BX18)
4407.4 Missionary Sisters of the Blessed Sacrament and Mary Immaculate (Table BX18)
4407.5 Missionary Sisters of the Consolata (Table BX18)
4408 Missionary Sisters of the Sacred Heart (Table BX18)
4408.5 Missionary Sisters of the Society of Mary (Table BX18)

Catholic Church
Monasticism. Religious orders
Individual orders of women -- Continued

4410	Mothers of the Helpless (Table BX18)
4411	Notre Dame des Missions (Table BX18)
4411.5	Nuns of the Perpetual Adoration of the Blessed Sacrament (Table BX18)
4412	Oblate Sisters of Providence (Table BX18)
4412.5	Oblate Sisters of the Holy Ghost (Table BX18)
4412.6	Oblates de Béthanie (Table BX18)
	Olivetans
4412.7	Olivetan Benedictine Sisters (U.S.) (Table BX18)
4413	Orant Sisters of the Assumption (Table BX18)
4413.3	Orden de Santiago (Table BX18)
4413.5	Order of Fontevraud (Table BX18)
4414	Order of St. Elizabeth of Hungary (Table BX18)
4415	Order of the Incarnate Word and Blessed Sacrament (Table BX18)
	Order of the Visitation see BX4546+
4415.5	Our Lady of Victory Missionary Sisters (Table BX18)
4415.8	Pallottine Missionary Sisters (Table BX18)
4416	Parish Visitors of Mary Immaculate (Table BX18)
4416.2	Passionist Nuns (Table BX18)
4416.5	Petites soeurs de saint Francois d'Assise (Table BX18)
4416.7	Piccole serve del Sacro Cuore (Table BX18)
	Poor Clares see BX4361+
4417	Poor Handmaids of Jesus Christ (Table BX18)
4418	Poor School Sisters of Notre Dame (Table BX18)
4418.5	Poor Servants of the Mother of God (Table BX18)
4418.7	Poor Sisters of Nazareth (Table BX18)
4419	Poor Sisters of St. Francis Seraph of the Perpetual Adoration (Table BX18)
4421-4424	Premonstratensians (Second Order). Premonstratensian Nuns (Table BX17)
	Presentation Sisters see BX4511
4426	Recollets (Augustinian Nuns) (Table BX18)
4427	Recollets (Bernardine) (Table BX18)
4428	Religieuze Penitenten-Recollectinen van de Reforme van Limburg (Franciscan) (Table BX18)
4428.5	Religiosas Angélicas (Table BX18)
4428.67	Religiosas Franciscanas Misioneras de la Immaculada (Table BX18)
4428.8	Religiosas Maltezas da Sagrado Ordem de S. João do Hospital de Jerusalem (Estremoz, Portugal) (Table BX18)
4428.9	Religiosas Reparadoras del Sagrado Corazón (Table BX18)

Catholic Church
Monasticism. Religious orders
Individual orders of women -- Continued

4429 Religious Hospitallers of St. Joseph (Table BX18)
4429.5 Religious Hospitallers of the Misericorde of Jesus (Table BX18)
4431 Religious of Jesus and Mary (Table BX18)
4432 Religious of Our Lady of the Retreat in the Cenacle (Table BX18)
4433 Religious of the Sacred Heart of Mary (Table BX18)
4434 Religious Teachers Filippini (Table BX18)
4435-4438 Sacred Heart, Society of the (Table BX17)
4439 Schonstatter Marienschwestern (Table BX18)
4441-4444 School Sisters of Notre Dame (Table BX17)
4446 School Sisters of St. Francis, Milwaukee, Wis. (Table BX18)
4446.3 Schulschwestern vom Dritten Orden des Heiligen Franziskus, Bressanone (Table BX18)
4446.6 Schulschwestern vom Dritten Orden des Heiligen Franziskus von Assisi, Amstetten (Table BX18)
4446.7 Seishin Jijo Shūdōkai (Table BX18)
4446.75 Servants of Mary, Protectors of Young Women and Working Women (Table BX18)
4446.8 Servants of Relief for Incurable Cancer (Table BX18)
4447 Servants of the Holy Infancy of Jesus (Table BX18)
4447.3 Siervas de la Madre de Dios (Table BX18)
4447.5 Siervas de la Pasión (Table BX18)
4447.8 Sisters Adorers of the Most Precious Blood (Table BX18)
4448 Sisters Adorers of the Precious Blood (Table BX18)
4448.5 Sisters Marianites of Holy Cross (Table BX18)
4449 Sisters of bon secours of Paris (Table BX18)
4450 Sisters of Charitable Instruction of the Child Jesus (Table BX18)
4451 Sisters of Charity, Irish (Table BX18)
4452 Sisters of Charity Federation in the Vincentian-Setonian Tradition (Table BX18)
4453 Sisters of Charity of Cincinnati, Ohio (Table BX18)
4454 Sisters of Charity of Leavenworth, Kansas (Table BX18)
4455 Sisters of Charity of Mother Seton, Greensburg, Pa. (Table BX18)
4456 Sisters of Charity of Nazareth, Nazareth, Ky. (Table BX18)
4457 Sisters of Charity of Providence (Table BX18)
4458 Sisters of Charity of St. Augustine (Table BX18)
4459 Sisters of Charity of St. Elizabeth, Convent Station, N.J. (Table BX18)
4460 Sisters of Charity of St. Paul of Chartres (Table BX18)

Catholic Church
Monasticism. Religious orders
Individual orders of women -- Continued

4461-4464 Sisters of Charity of St. Vincent de Paul (Table BX17 modified)
4463.6.A-Z By congregation, province, etc., A-Z
Sisters of Charity of Cincinnati, Ohio see BX4453
Sisters of Charity of St. Elizabeth, Convent Station, N.J. see BX4459
4463.6.D4 Sisters of Charity of St. Vincent de Paul, Deinze, Belgium
Daughters of Charity of St. Vincent de Paul, Emmitsburg, Md. see BX4333
Sisters of Charity of Mother Seton, Greensburg, Pa. see BX4455
4463.6.M4 Sisters of Charity of St. Vincent de Paul, Mexico
4463.6.N5 Sisters of Charity of St. Vincent de Paul of New York
4467 Sisters of Charity of the Blessed Virgin Mary, Dubuque, Iowa (Table BX18)
4468 Sisters of Charity of the Incarnate Word, Houston, Texas (Table BX18)
4469 Sisters of Charity of the Incarnate Word, San Antonio (Table BX18)
4471 Sisters of Christian Charity (Table BX18)
4473 Sisters of Divine Providence (Table BX18)
4474 Sisters of Divine Providence. Kentucky (Table BX18)
4474.5 Sisters of Divine Providence of San Antonio, Texas (Table BX18)
4476 Sisters of Loretto at the Foot of the Cross (Table BX18)
4477 Sisters of Marie-Auxiliatrice (Table BX18)
4478 Sisters of Mary Immaculate (Table BX18)
4479 Sisters of Mary Reparatrix (Table BX18)
4481-4484 Sisters of Mercy. Sisters of Mercy of the Union in the U.S.A. Institute of the Sisters of Mercy of the Americas (Table BX17 modified)
4483.5.A-Z Independent motherhouses, A-Z
4483.6.A-Z Provinces of the Union, A-Z
4484.7 Sisters of Mercy of St. Charles Borromeo (Table BX18)
4484.8 Sisters of Mercy of the Holy Cross (Table BX18)
4484.9 Sisters of Mount Carmel of Louisiana (Table BX18)
4485.2 Sisters of Notre Dame (Table BX18)
4485.3 Sisters of Notre Dame de Namur (Table BX18)
4485.4 Sisters of Our Lady of Calvary (Table BX18)
4485.5 Sisters of Our Lady of Charity of the Good Shepherd (Table BX18)
4485.6 Sisters of Our Lady of Charity of the Refuge (Table BX18)

Catholic Church
Monasticism. Religious orders
Individual orders of women -- Continued
Sisters of Our Lady of China see BX4327.5

4485.65 Sisters of Our Lady of Compassion (Table BX18)
4485.68 Sisters of Our Lady of the Missions (Table BX18)
4485.7 Sisters of Our Lady of the Sacred Heart (Table BX18)
4485.9 Sisters of Perpetual Adoration (Table BX18)
4486 Sisters of Providence, Saint Mary-of-the-Woods, Ind. (Table BX18)
4486.17 Sisters of Providence of St. Vincent de Paul (Table BX18)
4486.2 Sisters of Reparation of the Congregation of Mary (Table BX18)
4486.3 Sisters of St. Agnes, Fond du Lac (Table BX18)
4486.4 Sisters of St. Ann (Table BX18)
4486.45 Sisters of St. Basil the Great (Table BX18)
4486.5 Sisters of St. Casimir (Table BX18)
4486.6 Sisters of St. Dorothy (Table BX18)
4486.65 Sisters of St. Francis, Maryville, Mo. (Table BX18)
4486.67 Sisters of St. Francis, Rochester, Minn. (Table BX18)
4486.7 Sisters of St. Francis of Penance and Christian Charity (Table BX18)
4486.74 Sisters of St. Francis of Philadelphia (Table BX18)
4486.76 Sisters of Saint Francis of the Immaculate Conception of the Blessed Virgin Mary (Clinton, Iowa) (Table BX18)
4486.8 Sisters of St. John the Baptist (Table BX18)
4487-4490 Sisters of St. Joseph (Table BX17 modified)
Including all branches stemming from the original foundation in France in 1650
4489.5.A-Z Independent motherhouses in France, A-Z
4489.6.A-Z Independent motherhouses in the U.S.A., A-Z
4489.6.B6 Boston
4489.6.B7 Brentwood, N.Y.
4489.6.B8 Buffalo
4489.6.C3 Carondelet
4489.6.C32 Province of Augusta
4489.6.C33 Province of Los Angeles
4489.6.C34 Province of St. Louis
4489.6.C35 Province of St. Paul
4489.6.C36 Province of Troy
4489.6.C5 Concordia, Kans.
4489.6.N3 Nazareth, Mich.
4489.6.P5 Philadelphia
4489.6.S2 St. Augustine, Fla.
4489.6.S65 Springfield, Mass.
4489.6.W5 Wichita

Catholic Church
Monasticism. Religious orders
Individual orders of women
Sisters of St. Joseph -- Continued

4489.7.A-Z Other independent motherhouses, A-Z
4490.3 Sisters of St. Joseph of Cluny (Table BX18)
4490.5 Sisters of St. Joseph of Newark (Table BX18)
4490.7 Sisters of St. Joseph of the Apparition (Table BX18)
4490.75 Sisters of St. Joseph of the Sacred Heart (Table BX18)
4490.8 Sisters of St. Joseph of the Third Order of St. Dominic (Table BX18)
4490.85 Sisters of St. Joseph of the Third Order of St. Francis (Table BX18)
4490.9 Sisters of St. Louis (Table BX18)
4491 Sisters of St. Mary of Namur (Table BX18)
4491.3 Sisters of St. Mary of the Third Order of St. Francis, St. Louis (Table BX18)
4491.6 Sisters of St. Thomas of Villanova (Table BX18)
4491.8 Sisters of Saints Cyril and Methodius (Table BX18)
4491.9 Sisters of Service (Table BX18)
4492 Sisters of the Assumption (Table BX18)
4493 Sisters of the Blessed Sacrament for Indians and Colored People (Table BX18)
4493.3 Sisters of the Common Life (Table BX18)
4493.5 Sisters of the Divine Compassion, White Plains, N.Y. (Table BX18)
4494 Sisters of the Divine Savior (Table BX18)
4495 Sisters of the Good Samaritan (Table BX18)
4495.5 Sisters of the Guardian Angel (Table BX18)
4496 Sisters of the Holy Cross (Table BX18)
4496.5 Sisters of the Holy Faith (Table BX18)
4496.7 Sisters of the Holy Family (Table BX18)
4497 Sisters of the Holy Family of Nazareth (Table BX18)
4498 Sisters of the Holy Family of San Francisco (Table BX18)
4499 Sisters of the Holy Names of Jesus and Mary (Table BX18)
4500 Sisters of the Immaculate Conception of Castres, France (Table BX18)
4500.5 Sisters of the Immaculate Conception of Our Lady of Lourdes (Table BX18)
4500.6 Sisters of the Immaculate Conception of the Blessed Virgin Mary (Table BX18)
4500.8 Sisters of the Incarnate Word and Blessed Sacrament (Table BX18)
4501 Sisters of the Infant Jesus (Table BX18)
4501.5 Sisters of the Most Holy Trinity (Table BX18)
Sisters of the Order of St. Dominic see BX4337

Catholic Church
Monasticism. Religious orders
Individual orders of women -- Continued

4507 Sisters of the Poor Child Jesus (Table BX18)
4507.5 Sisters of the Poor of St. Francis (Table BX18)
4508 Sisters of the Precious Blood (Table BX18)
4509 Sisters of the Presentation of Mary (Table BX18)
Founded at Bourg, France, in 1796
4511 Sisters of the Presentation of the Blessed Virgin Mary (Table BX18)
Founded at Cork, Ireland
4511.5 Sisters of the Resurrection (Table BX18)
4512 Sisters of the Sacred Hearts and of Perpetual Adoration (Table BX18)
4512.5 Sisters of the Sorrowful Mother (Table BX18)
4513 Sisters of the Third Franciscan Order, Minor Conventuals, Syracuse, N.Y. (Table BX18)
4514 Sisters of the Third Order of St. Francis, Glen Riddle, Pa. (Table BX18)
4514.5 Sisters of the Third Order of St. Francis, Kaufbeuren, Ger. (Table BX18)
4514.7 Sisters of the Third Order of St. Francis, Pittsburg (Table BX18)
4515 Sisters of the Third Order of St. Francis of Assisi (Table BX18)
4516 Sisters of the Third Order of St. Francis of Mary Immaculate, Joliet, Ill. (Table BX18)
4517 Sisters of the Third Order of Saint Francis of Penance and of Charity, Tiffin, Ohio (Table BX18)
4517.7 Sisters of the Third Order of St. Francis of the Good Shepherd (Table BX18)
4518 Sisters of the Third Order of St. Francis of the Holy Family (Table BX18)
4519 Sisters of the Third Order of St. Francis of the Perpetual Adoration (Table BX18)
4520 Sisters of the Third Order Regular of St. Francis, Oldenburg, Ind. (Table BX18)
4520.2 Sisters of the Third Order Regular of St. Francis of Allegany, New York (Table BX18)
4520.3 Sisters of the Third Order Regular of St. Francis of the Congregation of Our Lady of Lourdes, Sylvania, Ohio (Table BX18)
Sisters of the Visitation see BX4546+
4520.8 Sisters, Servants of Mary Immaculate (Table BX18)
4520.9 Sisters Servants of the Holy Spirit of Perpetual Adoration (Table BX18)

Catholic Church
Monasticism. Religious orders
Individual orders of women -- Continued

4521-4524 Sisters, Servants of the Immaculate Heart of Mary (Table BX17)
Society of Catholic Medical Missionaries see BV2300.S53
4525 Society of Mary of Paris (Table BX18)
4526 Society of Mary Reparatrix (Table BX18)
4527 Society of the Holy Child Jesus (Table BX18)
Society of the Sacred Heart see BX4435+
4529 Society of the Servants of the Holy Ghost (Table BX18)
Society of the Sisters of the Holy Names of Jesus and Mary see BX4499
4531 Soeurs adoratrices et victimes de la justice de Dieu (Table BX18)
4531.4 Soeurs africaines de l'Immaculée-Conception de Ouagadougou (Table BX18)
4532 Soeurs augustines de Meaux (Table BX18)
4532.5 Soeurs de Charité de Sainte-Marie (Table BX18)
4532.54 Soeurs de Charité de Québec (Table BX18)
4532.55 Soeurs de la Charité de Saint-Hyacinthe (Table BX18)
4532.6 Soeurs de la Croix de Strasbourg (Table BX18)
4532.8 Soeurs de la Présentation de Marie (Table BX18)
4533 Soeurs de l'Immaculée-Conception de Niort (Table BX18)
4534 Soeurs de l'instruction chrétienne (Saint-Gildas-des-Bois) (Table BX18)
4534.3 Soeurs de Notre-Dame du Mont-Carmel (Table BX18)
4535 Soeurs de Saint-Augustin (Table BX18)
4535.2 Soeurs de Sainte Anne de la Providence de Saumur (Table BX18)
4535.5 Soeurs de Sainte-Marie de l'Assomption (Table BX18)
4535.7 Soeurs de Sainte-Marthe de Saint-Hyacinthe (Table BX18)
4536 Soeurs des prisons de la Congrégation de Marie-Joseph (Table BX18)
4537 Soeurs des Sacrés Coeurs de Jésus et de Marie (Table BX18)
4537.13 Soeurs du Tres Saint-Sacrement et de la charité de Bourges (Table BX18)
4537.17 Soeurs gardes-malades de Notre-Dame Auxiliatrice (Table BX18)
4537.2 Soeurs gardes-malades des Saints Noms de Jésus et de Marie (Table BX18)
Soeurs grises see BX4366
4537.26 Suore del Preziosissimo Sangue (Table BX18)

Catholic Church
Monasticism. Religious orders
Individual orders of women -- Continued

4537.3 Suore della divina volontà (Table BX18)
4537.5 Suore di Santa Maria (Table BX18)
4537.55 Suore domenicane del SS. Sacramento (Table BX18)
4537.6 Suore francescane dell'Immacolata Concezione di Lipari (Table BX18)
4537.8 Suore oblate di Santa Chiara (Table BX18)
4537.85 Suore riparatrici de Sacro Cuore (Table BX18)
4537.9 Suore rosarie (Table BX18)
4538 Trappistines (Table BX18)
4539 Trinitarian Nuns (Table BX18)
4541-4544 Ursulines (Table BX17)
4545 Vallombrosan Nuns (Table BX18)
4546-4549 Visitation Order (Table BX17)
White Sisters see BV2300.W6
4550 Yongwonhan Toum ui Songmo Sunyohoe (Korea) (Table BX18)
4551 Zgromadzenie Sióstr Franciszkanek Rodziny Marii (Table BX18)
4551.5 Zgromadzenie Sióstr Niepokalanego Poczecia Najświetszej Marya Panny (Table BX18)
4552 Zgromadzenie Sióstr Pasterek od Opatrzności Boskiej (Table BX18)
4552.5 Zgromadzenie Sióstr Urszulanek Serca Jezusa Konajacego (Table BX18)
4553 Zusters van Barmhartigheid (Table BX18)
4554 Zusters van Liefde van Onze Lieve Vrouw (Table BX18)
4555 Zusters van Sint Vincentius a Paulo (Table BX18)
4556 Zusters van't geloove (Table BX18)
4561 Zwartzusters (Belgium) (Table BX18)
4563 Zwartzusters van de Heilige Philippus Neri te Sint-Niklaas (Table BX18)

Churches, cathedrals, abbeys (as parish churches), etc.
See subclass NA for architecture
See classes D-F for historical sources
For Shrines of the Virgin Mary see BT650+

United States
4600 General works
4601.A-.W By state, A-W
4603.A-Z By city, A-Z
Including individual churches, etc., by city or by name if nonurban
4605 Canada (Table BX19)
4607.A-Z Other British America. By country or island, A-Z
Subarrange each country or island by Table BX20

Catholic Church
Churches, cathedrals, abbeys (as parish churches), etc. -- Continued

4610 Mexico (Table BX19)
4615.A-Z Central America. By country, A-Z
Subarrange each country by Table BX20
4618.A-Z West Indies. By island or group of islands, A-Z
Subarrange each island or group of islands by Table BX20
South America
4620 General works
4621 Argentina (Table BX19)
4622 Brazil (Table BX19)
4623 Chile (Table BX19)
4624 Peru (Table BX19)
4625.A-Z Other countries, A-Z
Subarrange each country by Table BX20
Europe
4627 General works
4627.5 Austria (Table BX19)
4628 Czechoslovakia (Table BX19)
4629 France (Table BX19)
4630 Germany (Table BX19)
4631 Great Britain. England and Wales (Table BX19)
4632 Ireland (Table BX19)
4633 Scotland (Table BX19)
4634 Italy (Table BX19)
4635 Portugal (Table BX19)
4636 Spain (Table BX19)
4636.5 Sweden (Table BX19)
4637 Switzerland (Table BX19)
4638.A-Z Other countries, A-Z
Subarrange each country by Table BX20
4640.A-Z Asia. By country, A-Z
Subarrange each country by Table BX20
e.g.
Japan
4640.J2 General works. Collections
4640.J3A-.J3Z By city, A-Z
Including individual churches, by city, A-Z, or by name if nonurban
Philippines
4640.P5 General works. Collections
4640.P6 Manila
4640.P7A-.P7Z Other local, A-Z
Including individual churches, by city, A-Z, or by name if nonurban

Catholic Church
Churches, cathedrals, abbeys (as parish churches), etc. -- Continued
4642.A-Z Africa. By country, A-Z
Subarrange each country by Table BX20
4644.A-Z Australia and Pacific islands. By country, or island, or group of islands, A-Z
Subarrange each country, island, or group of islands by Table BX20
e.g.
Hawaii
4644.H2 General works. Collections
4644.H3 Honolulu
4644.H4A-.H4Z Other local, A-Z
Including individual churches, by city, A-Z, or by name if nonurban
Biography and portraits
Collective
General
4650 Early through 1800
4651 1801-1950
4651.2 1951-2000
4651.3 2001-
4652 Addresses, essays, lectures
4653 Juvenile works
Lives of the saints and martyrs
General works
4654 Early to 1800
4655 1801-1950
4655.A2 Acta Sanctorum (Bollandiana)
4655.A3 Analecta Bollandiana
Supplement to Acta Sanctorum
4655.A4-Z Other
4655.2 1951-2000
4655.3 2001-
4655.8 Dictionaries
4656 Women saints
4656.2 Child saints
4656.5 Patron saints
4656.8 New saints
4657 Minor works
4658 Juvenile works
4659.A-Z By country, A-Z
Both for saints native to a country as well as for saints whose cultus is observed in a country
e.g.
4659.E4 Egypt

BX

Catholic Church
Biography and portraits
Collective
Lives of the saints and martyrs
By country, A-Z -- Continued

4659.F8 France. Gaul
4659.G3 Germany
4659.G7 Great Britain
4659.I8 Italy
4659.L3 Latin America
4659.N4 Netherlands
4659.P8 Portugal
4659.S8 Spain

Martyrologies (Historical and popular)
Cf. BX2014 Liturgy and ritual
Texts

4660.A1 Latin. By date
4660.A3 English. By date
4660.A4A-.A4Z Other languages. By language, A-Z, and date
4660.A6-Z History and criticism
Cf. BR1609 Literary and critical history of martyr books

4661 Other
Including ecclesiastical geography, married saints, humor of the saints, etc.

4662 History and criticism. Historiography. Hagiography
e.g. The work of the Bollandists

Lives of the popes see BX950+
Lives of the cardinals
General works

4663 Early through 1800
4664 1801-1950
4664.2 1951-2000
4664.3 2001-
4665.A-Z By region or country, A-Z

Bishops and archbishops

4666 General works

By country see BX4669.8+

4667 Lives of women
Cf. BX4656 Women saints

Lives of converts

4668.A1 Collective
4668.A2-Z Individual, A-Z
4668.15 History and criticism

Narratives and lives of former priests or members of monastic orders, etc.

4668.2 Collective

Catholic Church
Biography and portraits
Collective
Narratives and lives of former priests or members of monastic orders, etc. -- Continued

4668.3.A-Z Individual, A-Z
4668.3.Z9 Anonymous persons
4669 Other groups (not A-Z)
e.g. Doctors of the Church
For monastic and religious orders see BX2800+
By region or country
America
4669.8 General works
4670 United States
4671 Canada
4671.5 Latin America
4672 Mexico
4673 Central America
4674 West Indies
South America
4674.5 General works
4675.A-Z Individual regions or countries, A-Z
Europe
4675.5 General works
4676 Great Britain
Cf. BR754.A1+ Early and medieval period
4678 Ireland
4680 Austria
4681 Belgium
4682 France
4683 Germany
4684 Italy
4685 Portugal
4686 Scandinavia
4688 Spain
4689 Switzerland
4690.A-Z Other, A-Z
e.g.
4690.N4 Netherlands
4692 Asia
4694 Africa
4696 Australia
4698 Pacific islands
Individual

Catholic Church
Biography and portraits
Individual -- Continued

4700.A-Z Saints, A-Z
Cutter numbers listed below are provided as examples
For British medieval saints see BR754.A1+
For early Church to ca. 600 see BR1720+
For individual Biblical characters of the Old Testament see BS580.A+
For individual Biblical characters of the New Testament see BS2450+
For individual popes see BX1001+

4700.A3 Agnes
4700.A37 Alacoque, Marguerite Marie
4700.A375 Albertus Magnus, Bishop of Ratisbon
Cf. B765.A4+ Philosophy
Aloysius Gonzaga see BX4700.L75
Ambrose, Bishop of Milan see BR1720.A5
Andrew, Apostle see BS2451
4700.A45 Angela Merici
(4700.A58) Anselm, Archbishop of Canterbury
see BR754.A56
4700.A6 Antonio da Padova
4700.B2 Baylon, Pascual
4700.B25 Bellarmino, Roberto Francesco Romolo
(4700.B3) Benedict, Abbot of Monte Cassino
see BR1720.B45
4700.B4 Berchmans, Jan
Bernadette Soubirous see BX4700.S65
4700.B5 Bernard de Clairvaux
4700.B55 Bernardino da Siena
Birgitta, of Sweden
4700.B6 General works
Individual works
4700.B62 Revelationes
4700.B62A1 Latin texts. By date
4700.B62A2-.B62Z49 Translations. By language and date
4700.B62Z5-.B62Z99 Criticism
4700.B67 Bobola, Andrzej
4700.B68 Bonaventura, Cardinal
4700.B7 Bonifacius, originally Winfried, Abp. of Mainz
Borromeo, Charles see BX4700.C25
4700.B75 Bosco, Giovanni
(4700.B8) Brendan
see BR1720.B73
Bridget, of Sweden see BX4700.B6+
Brigid of Ireland see BR1720.B74

Catholic Church
Biography and portraits
Individual
Saints, A-Z -- Continued

4700.B87	Brito, João de
	Bruno I, Abp. of Cologne and Duke of Lorraine see DD137.9.B8
4700.B95	Bufalo, Gaspare del
4700.C13	Cabrini, Frances Xavier
	Caesarius, of Arles see BR1720.C2
4700.C155	Cafasso, Giuseppe
4700.C17	Calabria, Giovanni
4700.C18	Camillus de Lellis
4700.C19	Campion, Edmund
4700.C2	Canisius, Petrus
4700.C25	Carlo Borromeo
4700.C252	Carlo da Sesse
4700.C255	Catarina Thomasa
4700.C4	Caterina da Siena (Catherine of Siena)
4700.C45	Catharina of Alexandria (Catherine of Alexandria)
(4700.C5)	Cecilia see BR1720.C44
4700.C55	Chanel, Pierre Louis Marie
4700.C56	Chantal, Jeanne Françoise (Frémiot) de Rabutin, baronne de
	Charles Borromeo see BX4700.C25
(4700.C57)	Christopher see BR1720.C485
	Chrysostom, John see BR1720.C5
4700.C6	Clara of Assisi
4700.C62	Claret y Clará, Antonio María, Abp.
4700.C65	Claver, Pedro
4700.C66	Clotilda, Queen, consort of Clovis, King of the Franks Cf. DC67.2 Clotilda as queen
(4700.C7)	Columba see BR1720.C623
(4700.C75)	Columban see BR1720.C624
4700.C783	Cottolengo, Giuseppe
	Cyril (Cyrillus), Bp. of Jerusalem see BR1720.C88
4700.C9	Cyril (Cyrillus) of Thessalonica Including works on Saints Cyril and Methodius treated together
	Cyril (Cyrillus), Patriarch of Alexandria see BR1720.C9
4700.D4	Denis, Archbishop of Paris
4700.D7	Dominic (Domingo de Guzmán)
4700.E4	Elizabeth, of Hungary

Catholic Church
Biography and portraits
Individual
Saints, A-Z -- Continued

4700.E5	Émilie
4700.E78	Eudes, Jean
4700.F33	Filippo Neri
4700.F34	Fisher, John, Bishop of Rochester
	Francis Borgia see BX4700.F75
	Francis de Sales see BX4700.F85
	Francis of Assisi (Francesco d'Assisi)
4700.F6	General works
	Legends
4700.F61	Collections
	Individual works
	Under each:
	.xA1 — *Texts. By date*
	.xA4-.xZ49 — *Translations. By language, A-Z, and date*
	.xZ5-.xZ99 — *Criticism (including concordances)*
4700.F62	Actus
4700.F63	Fioretti
4700.F64	Legenda antiqua
4700.F65	Legenda Bonaventurae
4700.F658	Legenda Perugia
4700.F66	Legenda trium sociorum
4700.F665	Sacrum commercium beati Francisci cum Domina Paupertate
4700.F67	Speculum perfectionis
4700.F68	Vita Thomae Celanensis
4700.F69	Juvenile works: Life and legends
	Francis Solano see BX4700.S6
4700.F75	Francisco de Borja
4700.F8	Francisco Xavier
4700.F85	François de Sales, Bishop of Geneva
4700.G2	Gabriele (Gabriel Possenti)
4700.G22	Galgani, Gemma
4700.G24	Garicoits, Michel
4700.G3	Geneviève, of Paris
	George see BR1720.G4
4700.G47	Gerard Majella
	Gonzaga, Luigi see BX4700.L75
	Gregorius, Bp. of Tours see DC69.8.G7
4700.G83	Grignon de Montfort, Louis Marie
4700.H5	Hildegard (Hildegard von Bingen)
4700.H55	Hofbauer, Klemens Maria
	Hugh de Avalon, Bp. of Lincoln see BR754.H83

Catholic Church
Biography and portraits
Individual
Saints, A-Z -- Continued

	Ignatius Loyola see BX4700.L7
4700.I78	Isidorus, Bishop of Seville
	Januarius, Bishop of Benevento see BR1720.J3
	Jerome see BR1720.J5
	Joachim see BT683+
	Joan of Arc see DC103+
4700.J564	Jogues, Isaac
	John Chrysostom see BR1720.C5
4700.J5686	John of Avila
	John of the Cross see BX4700.J7
4700.J65	Juan de Dios
4700.J7	Juan de la Cruz
4700.K55	Kolbe, Maximilian
4700.K6	Konrad von Parzham
4700.L2	Labouré, Catherine
4700.L25	Labre, Benoît Joseph
4700.L3	La Salle, Jean Baptiste de Cf. LB475.L2+ La Salle as educator
4700.L5	Le Gras, Louise (de Marillac)
4700.L56	Leonardo Murialdo
4700.L6	Liguori, Alfonso Maria de'
	Louise de Marillac see BX4700.L5
4700.L7	Loyola, Ignacio de
4700.L73	Lucia Filippini
4700.L75	Luigi Gonzaga
4700.M2	Madeleine Sophie
4700.M36	Margherita de Cortona
4700.M368	Maria Goretti
4700.M37	Maria Maddalena de' Pazzi
(4700.M39)	Martin, Bishop of Tours see BR1720.M3
4700.M43	Mazzarello, Maria Domenica
4700.M5	Methodius, Archbishop of Moravia Cf. BX4700.C9 Saint Cyril
	More, Thomas see DA334.M8
	Neri, Filippo see BX4700.F33
	Nicholas, Bishop of Myra see BR1720.N46
4700.N66	Nikolaus von de Flue
	Ninian see BR1720.N5
4700.P25	Paolo della Croce (Paul of the Cross)
	Patrick see BR1720.P26
	Saint Patrick's Purgatory (Cave) see BX2321.D4
	Paul of the Cross see BX4700.P25

Catholic Church
Biography and portraits
Individual
Saints, A-Z -- Continued

	Paul of Thebes (Paulus Thebaeus) see BR1720.P28
	Paulinus, Bishop of Nola see BR1720.P3
4700.P38	Pelletier, Marie de Saint Euphrasie
4700.P77	Pietro Damiani
4700.P775	Pignatelli, José María
4700.R36	Realino, Bernardino
4700.R5	Rita da Cascia
4700.R6	Rosa, of Lima
4700.S35	Savio, Domenico
4700.S4	Seton, Elizabeth Ann
4700.S6	Solano, Francisco
4700.S65	Soubirous, Bernadette Cf. BT653+ Lourdes
4700.S7	Stanislaw, Kostka
4700.S77	Strambi, Vincenzo Maria
4700.T4	Teresa, of Avila
	Autobiography
4700.T4A15	Spanish. By date
4700.T4A2	English. By date
4700.T4A23	French. By date
4700.T4A25	German. By date
4700.T4A27	Italian. By date
4700.T4A28-.T4A295	Other languages (alphabetically)
	Letters
4700.T4A3	Spanish. By date
4700.T4A31	English. By date
4700.T4A33	French. By date
4700.T4A35	German. By date
4700.T4A37	Italian. By date
4700.T4A38-.T4A395	Other languages (alphabetically)
4700.T4A4-.T4Z	Other authors
4700.T43	Teresa Margherita del Sacro Cuore de Gesù
4700.T5	Thérèse, de Lisieux
	Thomas à Becket see DA209.T4
4700.T6	Thomas Aquinas
4700.T61	Legends
4700.T72	Thouret, Jeanne Antide
4700.V27	Valdivielso Sáez, Héctor
	Vialar, Emilie de see BX4700.E5
4700.V5	Vianney, Jean Baptiste Marie
4700.V6	Vincent de Paul
4700.V7	Vincentius Ferrerius
	Vladimir see DK75

Catholic Church
Biography and portraits
Individual -- Continued

4705.A-Z Other, A-Z

Cutter numbers listed below are provided as examples
For lives of missionaries see BV3705.A+
For lives of mystics see BV5095.A1+
For lives of popes (To 590) see BX1001+
For lives of popes (590-1049) see BX1076+
For lives of popes (1049-1122) see BX1180+
For lives of popes (1122-1305) see BX1216+
For lives of popes (1305-1447) see BX1275+
For lives of popes (1447-1572) see BX1306+
For lives of popes (1572-1789) see BX1334+
For lives of popes (1789-) see BX1368+
For narratives and lives of former priests or members of monastic orders, etc. see BX4668.3.A+
For lives of the saints see BX4700.A+
For Jansenists see BX4735.A1+

4705.A2 Abailard, Pierre
Albornoz, Gil Alvarez Carrillo de, Cardinal see DG797.55.A5
Beda Venerabilis see PR1578
4705.B7 Bossuet, Jacques Bénigne, Bishop of Meaux
4705.B73 Bourgeoys, Marguerite
4705.C7795 Coughlin, Charles Edward
4705.D25 Damien, Father
4705.F65 Foucauld, Charles Eugène, vicomte de
4705.G4173 Geneviève, soeur, O.P.
4705.G45 Gerson, Joannes
4705.G7464 Guillaume de Saint-Thierry (William, of Saint-Thierry), ca. 1085-1148?
4705.G8 Guyon, Jeanne Marie (Bouvier de la Motte) (Table P-PZ40)
4705.H463 Heloïse
4705.K4936 Kim, Su-hwan, Cardinal
Kolbe, Maximilian, Saint see BX4700.K55
4705.L3 Lateau, Louise
4705.L4 Lavigerie, Charles Martial Allemand, Cardinal
4705.M13 McAuley, Mary Catherine, Mother
4705.M3 Manning, Henry Edward, Cardinal
4705.M36 Marie de l'Incarnation, mère
Monastic name: Marie Guyard
4705.M4124 Martín de Porres
4705.M5 Mercier, Désiré Felician François Joseph, Cardinal
4705.M5565 Mindszenty, József, Cardinal
4705.N47 Neumann, Therese

Catholic Church
Biography and portraits
Individual
Other, A-Z -- Continued
4705.N5 Newman, John Henry, Cardinal
4705.N58 Nicolaus Cusanus, Cardinal
4705.O8 Ozanam, Antoine Frédéric
4705.P3663 Pamphili, Olimpia (Maidalchini)
Paolo, Servita see DG678.317
Peckham, John, Archbishop of Canterbury see BR754.P4
Pole, Reginald, Cardinal see DA317.8.P6
4705.P72 Pro Juárez, Miguel Augustin
Sarpi, Paolo see DG678.317
Savonarola, Girolamo, 1452-1498 see DG737.97
Seton, Elizabeth Ann, Mother see BX4700.S4
4705.S814 Stein, Edith
Cf. B3332.S67+ Stein as philosopher
4705.S82 Steno, Nicolaus, Bishop
Cf. QE22.S77 Steno as a scientist
Suger, Abbot of Saint Denis see DC89.7.S8
4705.S93 Szabó, Ferenc
4705.T27 Talbot, Matt
Teilhard de Chardin, Pierre (as a philosopher) see B2430.T37+
Teilhard de Chardin, Pierre (as a paleontologist) see QE707.T4
4705.T69 Torquemada, Juan de, Cardinal
4705.T7 Torquemada, Tomás de
Cf. BX1735+ Spanish Inquisition
4705.V55 Vieira, António
Cf. F2528 Vieira as historical figure
William, of Saint-Thierry, Abbot of Saint-Thierry, ca. 1085-1148? see BX4705.G7464
Eastern churches in communion with Rome. Catholics of the Oriental rites. Uniats
For individual jurisdictions, churches, monasteries, biographies, see the specific rite
Cf. BX324.4 Relation of the Orthodox Eastern Church to Eastern Catholic churches in communion with the Roman Catholic Church
Cf. BX1827 Congregation for the Oriental Church
4710.1 Periodicals. Societies
4710.12 Congresses. Councils. Synods
4710.125 Directories
4710.13 Documents
Collections

Catholic Church
Eastern churches in communion with Rome. Catholics of the Oriental rites. Uniats
Collections -- Continued
4710.14 Several authors
4710.15 Individual authors
History
4710.2 General works
By period
4710.22 To 1917
4710.23 1918-
4710.25 Outside of native area
General works. Doctrine. Government
4710.32 Early to 1800
4710.33 1801-1950
4710.34 1951-2000
4710.35 2001-
Ecclesiastical jurisdictions; patriarchates, ex-archates, dioceses, etc.
see the specific rite
Canon law
4710.52 Documents
4710.55 Treatises
Liturgy and ritual
4710.62 General collections
4710.63 History and criticism
4710.65.A-Z Special books. By title, A-Z
Under each:
.x *Texts. By date*
.x3A-.x3Z *Criticism*
4710.67 Lay folk's books
4710.68 Hagiography. Icons (not A-Z)
Sermons
4710.69 Several authors
Individual authors
see the specific rite
Christian life. Spiritual life
4710.7 General works
4710.72 Devotional literature
Monasticism
4710.74 General works
4710.75 Collections
4710.76 Orders
4710.77 Orders of the Roman Church adapted to the East. Inter-ritual orders
Individual churches, monasteries, etc.
see the specific rite

Catholic Church
Eastern churches in communion with Rome. Catholics of the Oriental rites. Uniats -- Continued
Biography
Saints
4710.9 Collective
Individual
see the specific rite
Other
4710.94 Collective
Individual
see the specific rite
Churches of the Byzantine rite
4711.1-.195 General works (Table BX21)
4711.21-.2195 Albanian (Table BX21)
4711.22-.2295 Bulgarian (Table BX21)
4711.23-.2395 Greek (Table BX21)
4711.24-.2495 Italo-Greek (Table BX21)
4711.25-.2595 Italo-Albanian (Table BX21)
4711.26-.2695 Yugoslav (Table BX21)
4711.3-.395 Melchite (Table BX21)
4711.4-.495 Romanian (Table BX21)
4711.5-.595 Russian (Table BX21)
4711.6-.695 Ukrainian (Table BX21 modified)
4711.7 Outside native area
United States
4711.72 General works
4711.73.A-Z By diocese, A-Z
Cf. BX1417.A+ Dioceses of the Roman Catholic Church
4711.736.A-Z Individual churches, monasteries, etc. By place and name or by name if nonurban, A-Z
Biography
4711.737 Collective
4711.738.A-Z Individual, A-Z
Canada
4711.74 General works
4711.745.A-Z By province, A-Z
4711.75.A-Z By diocese, A-Z
4711.751.A-Z By city, A-Z
4711.752.A-Z Individual churches, monasteries, etc. By place and name or by name if nonurban, A-Z
4711.76 Brazil
4711.77.A-Z Other countries, A-Z
4711.8-.895 Hungarian (Table BX21)
4711.9-.995 Ruthenian (Table BX21)
Churches of the Alexandrian rite

Catholic Church
Eastern churches in communion with Rome. Catholics of the Oriental rites. Uniats
Churches of the Alexandrian rite -- Continued

4712.1-.195	General works (Table BX21)
4712.2-.295	Coptic (Table BX21)
4712.3-.395	Ethiopian (Table BX21)
	Churches of the Antiochene or West-Syrian rite
4713.1-.195	General works (Table BX21)
4713.3-.395	Malankarese (Table BX21)
4713.5-.595	Maronite (Table BX21)
	By period
	To 1182 see BX182
4713.522	1182-1917
4713.523	1918-
4713.7-.795	Syrian (Table BX21)
	Churches of the Chaldean or East-Syrian rite
4714.1-.195	General works (Table BX21)
4714.3-.395	Chaldean (Table BX21)
4714.5-.595	Syro-Malabarese (Table BX21)
	Church of the Armenian rite
4715.1	Periodicals. Societies
4715.12	Congresses. Councils. Synods
4715.125	Directories
4715.13	Documents
	Collections
4715.14	Several authors
4715.15	Individual authors
	History
4715.2	General works
	By period
4715.22	To 1917
4715.23	1918-
4715.25	Outside of native area
	General works. Doctrine. Government
4715.32	Early to 1800
4715.33	1801-1950
4715.34	1951-2000
4715.35	2001-
4715.4.A-Z	Ecclesiastical jurisdictions; patriarchates, ex-archates, dioceses, etc., A-Z
	Canon law
4715.52	Documents
4715.55	Treatises
	Liturgy and ritual
4715.62	General collections
4715.63	History and criticism

BX

Catholic Church
Eastern churches in communion with Rome. Catholics of the Oriental rites. Uniats
Church of the Armenian rite
Liturgy and ritual -- Continued
4715.65.A-Z Special books. By title, A-Z
Under each:
.x Texts. By date
.x3A-.x3Z Criticism
4715.67 Lay folk's books
4715.68 Hagiography. Icons (not A-Z)
Sermons
4715.69 Several authors
4715.692.A-Z Individual authors. By author and title, A-Z
Christian life. Spiritual life
4715.7 General works
4715.72 Devotional literature
Monasticism
4715.74 General works
4715.75 Collections
4715.76 Orders
4715.77 Orders of the Roman Church adapted to the East. Inter-ritual orders
4715.8.A-Z Individual churches, monasteries, etc., A-Z. By place or by name if nonurban
Biography
Saints
4715.9 Collective
4715.92.A-Z Individual, A-Z
Other
4715.94 Collective
4715.95.A-Z Individual, A-Z
Dissenting sects other than Protestant
Cf. BT1319+ Dissenting sects prior to the Reformation, 1517
4716.4 Directories
4717 General works
For Catholic apologetics and controversial works see BX1781+
Jansenists
Cf. BX1529 Catholic Church in France to 1789
4718.5 Congresses
4719 Collections. Sources
General works
4720 Early through 1800
4721 1801-1950
4722 1951-2000

Catholic Church
Dissenting sects other than Protestant
Jansenists
General works -- Continued
4723 2001-
Documents
4725 Bull "Unigenitus," 1713
4726 Other. By date
By region or country
France
General see BX4720+
Local
4730 Port Royal
4731.A-Z Other, A-Z
e.g.
4731.N3 Nantes
4732 The Convulsionaries
4733 Holland
4734.A-Z Other regions or countries, A-Z
Biography
4735.A1 Collective
4735.A3-Z Individual, A-Z
4735.A5 Ans, Paul Ernest Ruth d'
4735.A55 Arnauld, Agnès (Mother Agnès de Saint-Paul)
4735.A6 Arnauld, Antoine
4735.A7 Arnauld, Henri, Bishop of Angers
4735.A8 Arnauld, Jacqueline Marie Angélique (Mother Angélique)
4735.A82 Arnauld d'Andilly, Angélique de Saint Jean, Mother
4735.D8 Du Vergier de Hauranne, Jean, Abbé de Saint-Cyran
4735.G47 Germain, Claude
4735.J3 Jansenius, Cornelius, Bishop
4735.L4 Le Maistre, Isaac Louis (Le Maistre de Sacy)
4735.P26 Pascal, Blaise
Cf. B1900+ Philosophy
Cf. PQ1876.P3 French literature
4735.P3 Pascal, Jacqueline
4735.Q4 Quesnel, Pasquier
4737 French schisms of the 19th century
Eglise constitutionelle; Louisets (Incommunicants, Petite Eglise); Eglise catholique française (Chatel, Fabré-Palaprat)
4740 German Catholics
Johannes Czerski, Johannes Ronge
Old Catholics
4751 Periodicals. Societies
4755 Conferences. Congresses

Catholic Church
Dissenting sects other than Protestant
Old Catholics -- Continued
4757 Directories. Yearbooks
4758.A-Z Episcopal charges, etc. By bishop, A-Z
4759 Collections
4761 Study and teaching
4763 Seminaries
History
4765 General works
By region or country
4767 Germany
4768 Great Britain
4769 United States
4769.5 Polish National Catholic Church of America (Table BX3)
4770.A-Z Other regions or countries, A-Z
e.g.
4770.N4 Netherlands
4770.S9 Switzerland
4771 General works. Theology. Doctrine, etc.
4773 Liturgy and ritual
Sermons. Tracts. Addresses. Essays
Collected see BX4759
4777 Individual
Individual churches. By place
4781 United States
4783 Other
Biography
4791 Collective
4793.A-Z Individual, A-Z
e.g.
4793.L3 Lasaulx, Amalie von
4793.L7 Loyson, Charles Jean Marie, known as Pere Hyacinthe
Quietism see BV5099
Independent Catholic Churches
4793.5 Directories
4794 General works
4794.15 Bishops. Validity of orders
4794.16 Priesthood. Priests
4794.2.A-Z By region or country, A-Z
Biography
4794.25 Collective
Individual
see individual denominations
4795.A-Z Other dissenting sects, A-Z

Catholic Church
Dissenting sects other than Protestant
Other dissenting sects, A-Z -- Continued

4795.C36 Catholic Apostolic Church (Metropolis of Glastonbury)
4795.C4-.C48 Ceskoslovenská cirkev (Czechoslovak Church) (Table BX4)
4795.E35 Eglise catholique apostolique et gallicane autocéphale
4795.E4 Eglise catholique celtique
4795.G76 Gnostic Orthodox Church of Christ in America
4795.H64 Holy Orthodox Catholic Church (U.S.)
4795.I48 Iglesia Católica Apostólica Ortodoxa Latino America del Patriarcado Intercontinental
4795.I5 Iglesia filipina independiente
4795.I6 Independent (Irish) Catholic Church
4795.K6 Kościól, Polsko-Katolicki
4795.L4-.L48 Liberal Catholic Church (Table BX4)
4795.L5 Lithuanian National Catholic Church of America
4795.M2-.M28 Mariavites (Table BX4)
4795.N67 North American Old Roman Catholic Church
4795.O73 Orden de la Santa Faz
4795.O77 Orthodox Catholic Church of America
Polish National Catholic Church of America see BX4769.5
4795.S37 Servant Catholic Church
4795.S52 Slaves of the Immaculate Heart of Mary
4795.T73 Tridentine Latin Rite
4795.T74 Trois Saints Coeurs
4795.W47 Western Orthodox Church in America

Protestantism
4800 Periodicals. Societies
For general religious publications see BR1+
Cf. BX1760+ Anti-Catholic works
4800.5 Directories
4801 Collections
Including documents
Cf. BR330+ Works of Luther, Melancthon, Zwingli
History
General works
4804 Early through 1800
4805 1801-1950
4805.2 1951-2000
4805.3 2001-
4807 Minor works
General works
4809 Early through 1800
4810 1801-1950
4811 1951-2000

Protestantism
General works -- Continued
4811.3 2001-
4815 Sermons, addresses, essays, etc.
4817 General special
e.g. Protestantism and society
Protestantism in relation to other branches of Christianity
4818 General works
4818.3 Relation to the Roman Catholic Church
Relation to Eastern churches see BX324+
Controversial works against Protestantism
4819 Early through 1800
4820 1801-1950
4821 1951-2000
4821.3 2001-
Biography
4825 Collective
see also individual demonimations
4826 Pre-Reformation biography
Including Huss, Wycliffe, etc.
4827.A-Z Individual, A-Z
This number is to be used only for theologians whose importance is not limited to individual denominations
e.g.
4827.B3 Barth, Karl
4827.B38 Baur, Ferdinand Christian
4827.B67 Brunner, Heinrich Emil
4827.B78 Bultmann, Rudolf Karl
4827.G7 Gregory, Caspar René
4827.H3 Harnack, Adolf von
4827.K5 Kierkegaard, Søren Aabye
Cf. B4370+ Kierkegaard as philosopher
Cf. PT8142 Kierkegaard as author
4827.L2 Lagarde, Paul Anton de
4827.N5 Niebuhr, Reinhold
4827.O3 Oberlin, Johann Friedrich
4827.O8 Overbeck, Franz Camillo
4827.R46 Richardson, Alan
4827.R6 Rothe, Richard
4827.S3 Schleiermacher, Friedrich Ernst Daniel
Cf. B3090+ Schleiermacher as philosopher
4827.S35 Schweitzer, Albert, as theologian
Cf. B2430.S37+ Schweitzer as philosopher
Cf. CT1018.S45+ Schweitzer (General biography)
Cf. ML416.S33 Schweitzer as musician
Cf. R722.32.S35 Schweitzer as medical missionary
4827.S4 Semler, Johann Salomo

Protestantism
Biography
Individual, A-Z -- Continued
4827.S8 Strauss, David Friedrich
Cf. B3340+ Strauss as philosopher
4827.T53 Tillich, Paul
4827.T7 Troeltsch, Ernst
4827.V5 Vinet, Alexandre Rodolphe
Cf. B4651.V5+ Vinet as philosopher
4827.W45 Wieman, Henry Nelson
By region or country
Under each:
.A2 Periodicals. Societies
Cf. BR500+ History of Christianity
(4830) America
see BR500.A3+
(4831) United States
see BR513+
(4832) Canada
see BR570+
4832.5 Latin America
4833 Mexico
Central America
4833.5 General works
4834.A-Z By region or country, A-Z
4835.A-Z West Indies, A-Z
4836.A-Z South America. By region or country, A-Z
Europe
4837 General works
Great Britain
4838 General works
4839 Ireland
4840 Scotland
4841 Austria
4842 Belgium
4843 France
For period before 1789 see BX9450+
Cf. BR370+ Reformation
Germany
Including former West Germany
Including Barmen Theologische Erklarung
4844 General works
4844.5 Germans outside Germany
4844.55 Bekennende Kirche (Table BX3)
4844.6 Evangelische Kirche in Deutschland (Table BX3)
Former East Germany
4844.8 General works (Table BX3)

Protestantism
By region or country
Europe
Former East Germany -- Continued
4844.82 Bund der Evangelischen Kirchen in der DDR (Table BX3)
4845 Greece
4846 Holland (Netherlands)
4847 Italy
4848 Portugal
4849 Soviet Union
4850 Scandinavia
4851 Spain
4852 Switzerland
4853 Turkey
4854.A-Z Other regions or countries, A-Z
e.g.
4854.C9 Czechoslovakia. Czech Republic
4854.E2 Eastern Europe
4854.H8 Hungary
4854.P7 Poland
Asia
4857 Philippines
Other individual countries see BR1060+
Africa see BR1359+
Australia see BR1480+
4861.A-Z Pacific islands, A-Z
Individual sects
Pre-Reformation
Arnoldists see BX1256
Waldenses and Albigenses
4872 Periodicals. Societies
General works
4873 Early through 1800
4875 1801-1950
4876 1951-2000
4876.3 2001-
Waldenses (Vaudois)
4878 Periodicals. Societies. Yearbooks
General works
4880 Early through 1800
4881 1801-1950
4881.2 1951-2000
4881.3 2001-
4881.5.A-Z By country (other than homeland), A-Z
Biography
4882 Collective

Protestantism
Individual sects
Pre-Reformation
Waldenses and Albigenses
Waldenses (Vaudois)
Biography -- Continued
4883.A-Z Individual, A-Z
Albigenses
General works
4890 Early through 1800
4891 1801-1950
4891.2 1951-2000
4891.3 2001-
Biography
4892 Collective
4893.A-Z Individual, A-Z
Lollards. Wycliffites
General works
4900 Early through 1800
For works by Wycliffe see BR75
4901 1801-1950
4901.2 1951-2000
4901.3 2001-
Biography
4903 Collective
Individual
4905 Wycliffe
4906.A-Z Other, A-Z
e.g.
4906.O6 Oldcastle, Sir John, styled Lord Cobham
Hussites
General works
4913 Early through 1800
4915 1801-1950
4915.2 1951-2000
4915.3 2001-
Biography
4916 Collective
Individual
4917 John Huss
4918.A-Z Other, A-Z
e.g.
4918.C45 Chelčický, Petr
Bohemian Brethren
Cf. BX8551+ Moravians
General works
4920 Early through 1800

Protestantism
Individual sects
Pre-Reformation
Hussites
Bohemian Brethren
General works -- Continued
4921 1801-1950
4922 1951-2000
4923 2001-
4924.A-Z Biography, A-Z
4924.A1 Collective
4924.B55 Blahoslav, Jan
4924.C6 Comenius, Johann Amos
Post-Reformation
Anabaptists
Cf. BX6201+ Baptists
Cf. BX8101+ Mennonites
4929 Periodicals. Societies. Collections
4929.5 Congresses
General works
4930 Early through 1800
4931 1801-1950
4931.2 1951-2000
4931.3 2001-
4933.A-Z By region or country, A-Z
e.g.
4933.S9 Switzerland
4935.A-Z Special topics, A-Z
4935.P74 Preaching
Biography
4940 Collective
Individual
4945 John of Leyden (Jan Beukelszoon, Jan van Leyden, Johann von Leiden)
4946.A-Z Other, A-Z
e.g.
4946.D4 Denck, Johannes
4946.G7 Grebel, Konrad
4946.H4 Hetzer, Ludwig
4946.H8 Hubmaier, Balthasar
4946.M8 Münzer, Thomas
Lutheranism see BX8064+
Calvinism
General works see BX9420+
Congregationalism see BX7101+
Presbyterianism see BX8901+
Puritanism see BX9301+

Protestantism
Individual sects
Post-Reformation -- Continued
Plain People
4950 General works
4951.A-Z By region or country, A-Z
Other modern Protestant sects (except Anglican) see BX6101+
Anglican Communion
5001 Periodicals. Serials
5002 Societies. Institutions
Conferences see BX5021+
5003 Collected works
Anglican Communion and other churches
Cf. BX5127+ Church of England and other churches
Cf. BX5926+ Episcopal Church and other churches
5004 General works
5004.2 Relations with the Catholic Church
5004.3 Relations with the Orthodox Eastern Church
5004.4 Relations with the Lutheran Church
Cf. BX8063.7.C5 Church of England and Lutheran churches
5004.5 Relations with the Reformed Church
5005 General works. History
5006 Minor works
5007 Dictionaries. Encyclopedias
Sermons
Cf. BX5133.A+ Church of England
Cf. BX5937.A+ Episcopal Church
5008.A1 Collections
5008.A2-Z Individual authors
Liturgy and ritual see BX5140.5+
5008.5 Government
5008.6 Religious communities. Conventual life
5008.9.A-Z Other special, A-Z
5008.9.H42 Health. Medicine
Medicine see BX5008.9.H42
5008.9.M96 Mystical union
5009 Biography (Collective)
Prefer church of individual countries, BX5197 BX5390 etc.
Church of England
5011 Periodicals. Serials
5013 Societies. Institutions
e.g.
5013.S6 Society for Promoting Christian Knowledge (S.P.C.K.)
(5015) Yearbooks
see BX5011

Church of England -- Continued
5017 Convocations
5018 National Assembly
Conferences. Congresses
5021 General
Including international church congresses
5023 Diocesan and local
Dictionaries, encyclopedias see BX5007
5031 Directories. Clergy lists, etc.
Documents
5033 Collections
5033.5 Special. By date
5034.A-Z Episcopal charges, etc. By bishop, A-Z
Collections of monographs, etc.
5035 Several authors
5037 Individual authors
Study and teaching
5041 General works
Individual seminaries see BV4160.A+
Sunday schools (Church schools)
5046 Societies. Conventions, etc.
5047 General works. Organization, etc.
5049 Textbooks, etc.
5050.A-Z Individual Sunday schools. By place, A-Z
History
Cf. BX1491+ History of Roman Catholic Church in Great Britain
5051 Periodicals. Societies, etc.
5052 Collected works
General works
5053 Early through 1800
5055 1801-1950
5055.2 1951-2000
5055.3 2001-
5056 General special
e.g. Historical continuity of the church
5057 Textbooks, etc.
5059 Addresses, essays, lectures
By period
For laws, ordinances, etc. see BX5151+
To Conquest (Anglo-Saxon Church) see BR748
Medieval period see BR750
5067 1500-1558. Reformation
Cf. BR375+ Reformation in Great Britain
1558-1660
5070 General works
5071 Elizabethan period, 1558-1603

Church of England
History
By period
1558-1660 -- Continued
5072 Period of James I, 1603-1625
5073 Church and Puritanism, 1640-1649
Charles I, 1625-1649. Civil War, 1642-1649
5075 General works
5075.A5 Contemporary works
5075.A6-Z Other works
William Laud, abp. of Canterbury see DA396.L3
Westminster Assembly see BX9053
5077 Commonwealth, 1649-1660
1660-1833
5081 General works
5085 Restoration period
5086 Revolution of 1688
5087 Nonjurors (1689-)
18th century
5088 General works
5089 Church and Methodism (1739-)
Evangelical revival see BX5125
5092 Other special
5092.A5 Contemporary works
1833-
5093 General works
Including works on the 19th century
Oxford or Tractarian Movement. Puseyism
5094 Periodicals. Serials
5095 Documents
5097 Tracts for the times
5098 Histories
General works
5099 Contemporary works
5100 Other
5101 Later history (ca. 1850-)
Local divisions
5103 Wales
Cf. BX5596+ Church in Wales
5103.A1-.A5 Documents
5103.A6-Z General works
5105.A-Z By county or shire, A-Z
By diocese
5106 General works
5107.A-Z Individual, A-Z
5107.B2 Bangor
5107.B3 Bath and Wells

Church of England
Local divisions
By diocese
Individual, A-Z -- Continued

5107.B6 Birmingham
5107.B7 Blackburn
5107.B75 Bradford
5107.B8 Bristol
Canterbury
5107.C1 Province
5107.C2 Diocese
5107.C3 Carlisle
5107.C4 Chelmsford
5107.C5 Chester
5107.C6 Chichester
5107.C7 Coventry
5107.D4 Derby
5107.D8 Durham
5107.E5 Ely
5107.E8 Exeter
5107.G5 Gloucester
5107.G8 Guildford
5107.H5 Hereford
5107.L3 Leicester
5107.L4 Lichfield
5107.L5 Lincoln
5107.L6 Liverpool
5107.L7 Llandaff
5107.L8 London
5107.M4 Manchester
5107.M6 Monmouth
5107.N6 Newcastle
5107.N8 Norwich
5107.O8 Oxford
5107.P4 Peterborough
5107.P6 Portsmouth
5107.R5 Ripon
5107.R6 Rochester
5107.S2 St. Albans
5107.S3 St. Asaph
5107.S4 St. David's
5107.S5 St. Edmundsbury and Ipswich
5107.S6 Salisbury
5107.S7 Sheffield
5107.S8 Sodor and Man
5107.S9 Southwark
5107.S93 Southwell

Church of England
Local divisions
By diocese
Individual, A-Z -- Continued
5107.S97 Swansea and Brecon
5107.T8 Truro
5107.W2 Wakefield
5107.W6 Winchester
5107.W8 Worcester
York
5107.Y5 Province
5107.Y6 Diocese
5108.A-Z By archdeaconry, A-Z
By rural deanery
5109.A3 General works
5109.A4-Z Individual, A-Z
5110.A-Z By town, parish, etc., A-Z
Special parties and movements
Cf. BX5067+ History of the Church of England
5115 General works
5117 Broad Church
5119 Low Church
High Church. Anglo-Catholicism
5121.A1 Periodicals
5121.A3-Z General works
5123 Ritualist movement
5125 Evangelical movement
5125.5 Charismatic movement
5126 Other special movements
Including Modernism, Liberalism, etc.
Church of England and other churches
5127 Relations with the Orthodox Eastern Church
5128 Relations with the Oriental churches
5128.2 Assyrian Church of the East
5129 Relations with the Roman Catholic Church
Including proposals for reunion
Cf. BX5178 Anglican orders
5129.5 Proposed reunion with Catholic and Protestant churches
5129.8.A-5129.Z Relations with other churches, A-Z
5129.8.C45 Church of South India
Lutheran Church see BX8063.7.C5
5129.8.M4 Methodist Church
Protestant Episcopal Church in the U.S.A. see BX5927.8
General works on the Church of England
Including doctrinal works
5130 Early to 1800
5131 1801-1950

Church of England
General works on the Church of England -- Continued
5131.2 1951-2000
5131.3 2001-
5132 Minor works. Pamphlets, etc.
Sermons. Tracts. Addresses. Essays
Sermons on special subjects may be classified with the subject, especially biography and history
For sermons for children, young people, etc. see BV4310+
For individual essays, lectures, etc. on general doctrines or polity see BX5132
Cf. BX5035+ Collected works
Several authors
Homilies of the church
5133.A1A3 Texts. By date
5133.A1A33-.A1A39 Criticism
5133.A1A4 Other
5133.A3-Z Individual authors. By author and title, A-Z
5135 Controversial works against the Church
Including satires, etc.
5136 Controversial works in defense of the Church of England
5137 Articles of religion. The Thirty-nine articles
5139 Creeds and catechisms
5140 Juvenile works on the church and its doctrines
Liturgy and ritual
For church year, festivals, fasts, etc. see BV30+
5140.5 Periodicals. Societies. Serials
5141.A1 Collected works
5141.A3-Z General works
Sources
Cf. BV193.G7 Liturgy and ritual in Great Britain
5142 Sarum use
5143.A-Z Other uses, A-Z
e.g.
5143.D8 Durham
5143.E9 Exeter
5143.Y6 York
5144 Other Pre-Reformation sources (not A-Z)
5145 Prayer books. Book of Common Prayer
5145.A1 Prayer books of Henry VIII
5145.A2 Prayer books of Edward VI
5145.A3 History
Later forms
5145.A4 English editions. By date
5145.A5 English editions (undated)
5145.A55 Adaptations. Selections

Church of England
Liturgy and ritual
Prayer books. Book of Common Prayer -- Continued

5145.A6A-.A6Z Other languages, A-Z
Special parts
5145.A62 Collects
5145.A63 Communion service
5145.A633 General confession
Lectionary see BX5147.L4
5145.A65 Litany
5145.A66 Morning and evening prayer
Cf. BX5147.B74 Breviaries
5145.A67 Ordinal
5145.A7-Z History. Dictionaries. Treatises
For all forms of Anglican prayer books
Alternate Service Book 1980
5145.5.A1 Texts. By date
5145.5.A2 Selections
5145.5.A3-5145.Z Criticism
5146 Psalter
Cf. M2167+ Editions pointed for chanting
5146.A1 English editions. By date
5146.A2 English editions (undated)
5146.A3A-.A3Z Translations. By language, A-Z
5146.A5-Z History, etc.
5147.A-Z Other special, A-Z
Including devotional works for special classes
5147.A25 Accession service
5147.A5 Aged, Devotions for. Older people, Devotions for
5147.B5 Ceremonial of bishops
5147.B74 Breviaries
Cf. BX5145.A66 Prayer books for morning and evening prayer
5147.B9 Burial service
5147.C6 Coronation service
5147.D4 Dead (Prayers for)
5147.E8 Eucharistic prayers
5147.F35 Family devotions
5147.H6 Holy Week offices
Homilies see BX5133.A1A3+
Hymns see BV370+
5147.L37 Lent
5147.L39 Lesser festivals and holidays
5147.L4 Lessons. Lectionaries. Gospels and Epistles
For sermons on the lessons see BX5133.A+
5147.M5 Missionary services
5147.O3 Occasional services

Church of England
Liturgy and ritual
Other special, A-Z -- Continued
Older people, Devotions for see BX5147.A5
5147.P7 Priest's manuals
5147.P8 Processionals
5147.R8 Rural church services
5147.S3 School services
5147.W3 Wartime prayers
5147.W4 Westminster Abbey services
5147.Z9 Services for particular days. By date
Sacraments, etc.
Including theology, liturgy, rite
5148 General works
5149.A-Z Individual, A-Z
e.g.
5149.B2 Baptism
5149.C5 Communion. Eucharist
5149.C6 Confession and absolution
5149.C7 Confirmation
Marriage
5149.M2 General works
5149.M3 Divorce
5149.M4 Remarriage
5149.M5 Same-sex marriage
5149.O7 Ordination
5149.P4 Penance
Government. Organization. Discipline
Including constitutional history
5150 General works
Laws, ordinances, etc.
5151.A3 Collections
5151.A5-Z Histories and commentaries
5153 Individual laws, etc. By date
5153.5.A-Z Special topics, A-Z
e.g.
5153.5.D5 Dispensations
5153.5.P3 Parishes
5154 Courts
Including the High Commission
5155 Trials
5157 Church and state. Establishment and endowment
5165 Estates and revenues
Including maintenance, patronage, benefices, Queen Anne's Bounty, tithes, etc.
5170 Convocations (Constitution, etc.)
5173 The cathedral

Church of England
Government. organization. Discipline -- Continued
Clergy
Directories see BX5031
5175 General works
Bishops. Episcopacy
5176 General works
Episcopal charges see BX5034.A+
5178 Anglican orders
5179 Other church officers (Clerical and lay)
Including rural deans, lay readers, church wardens, parish clerks
5180 Vestments
Including cassock and gown, liturgical symbolism and colors, etc.
5182 Laity
5182.3 Women
5182.5 Children
Including the children's parish
Religious communities. Conventual life
5183 General works
Men
5184.A1 General works
5184.A2-Z Individual communities
Women
5185.A1 General works
5185.A2-Z Individual communities
5186.A-Z Individual communities for men and women. By name, A-Z
5187 Religious societies
5190 Benevolent work. Social work, welfare work, etc.
Cathedrals, churches, etc., in England and Wales
5194 General works
5195.A-Z Individual churches, etc. By place, A-Z, or by name if nonurban
Biography
Cf. BR754.A1+ Early and medieval Britain
5197 Collective
5198 Archbishops of Canterbury
5199.A-Z Individual, A-Z
e.g.
5199.A6 Andrewes, Lancelot, Bp. of Winchester
Arnold, Thomas see LF795.R92
5199.B4 Benson, Edward White, Abp. of Canterbury
Berkeley, George, Bp. of Cloyne see B1303+
5199.B9 Butler, Joseph, Bp. of Durham
5199.C3 Carpenter, William Boyd, Bp. of Ripon
5199.C4 Church, Richard William

	Church of England
	Biography
	Individual, A-Z -- Continued
	Colet, John see BR754.C6
	Cranmer, Thomas, Abp. of Canterbury see DA317.8.C8
5199.D25	Davidson, Randall Thomas, Abp. of Canterbury
	Donne, John see PR2245+
5199.F3	Farrar, Frederic William
5199.F62	Foxe, John
5199.F8	Fuller, Thomas
5199.G64	Gore, Charles
5199.H25	Hall, Joseph
5199.H4	Heber, Reginald, Bp. of Calcutta
5199.H77	Holland, Henry Scott
5199.H8	Hook, Walter Farquhar
5199.I6	Inge, William Ralph
5199.K3	Keble, John
	Kingsley, Charles see PR4840+
	Langton, Stephen, Cardinal, Abp. of Canterbury see DA228.L3
5199.L2	Latimer, Hugh, Bp. of Worcester
5199.L28	Laud, William, Abp. of Canterbury
5199.N55	Newton, John
5199.P3	Parker, Matthew, Abp. of Canterbury
5199.P9	Pusey, Edward Bouverie
5199.R4	Richmond, Legh
5199.R5	Ridley, Nicholas, Bp. of London
5199.R7	Robertson, Frederick William
5199.R7224	Robinson, J. Armitage (Joseph Armitage), 1853-1933
5199.R84	Runcie, Robert A. K., Abp. of Canterbury
5199.S3	Scott, Thomas
5199.S45	Selwyn, George Augustus, Bp. of Lichfield
5199.S5315	Sheppard, Hugh Richard Lawrie
5199.S55	Simeon, Charles
5199.S8	Stanley, Arthur Penrhyn
5199.T4	Temple, Frederick, Abp. of Canterbury
5199.T42	Temple, William, Abp. of Canterbury
5199.T45	Thirlwall, Connop, Bp. of St. David's
	Thomas à Becket, Saint, Abp. of Canterbury see DA209.T4
5199.T6	Tillotson, John, Abp. of Canterbury
	Ussher, James, Abp. of Armagh see BX5595.U8
5199.W35	Warburton, William, Bp. of Gloucester
	Whately, Richard, Abp. of Dublin see BX5595.W5
5199.W535	Whitgift, John, Abp. of Canterbury
5199.W6	Wilberforce, Samuel, Bp. of Winchester
5199.W7	Winnington-Ingram, Arthur Foley, Bp. of London

Church of England
Biography
Individual, A-Z -- Continued
5199.W86 Wordsworth, Christopher, Bp. of Lincoln
Dissent and nonconformity
That is, from the Church of England
Cf. BX9331+ Puritanism in Great Britain
5200 Collected works
e.g., Baxter, Watts, etc.
5201 Sermons. Tracts. Addresses. Essays
5201.A1 Collections
General works. Histories
5202 Early through 1800
5203 1801-1950
5203.2 1951-2000
5203.3 2001-
5203.5 Works against dissenters
By country
5203.7 Ireland
5203.7 Ireland
5204.A-Z By county, A-Z
5205.A-Z By city, etc., A-Z
Biography
5206 Collective
5207.A-Z Individual, A-Z
5207.B3 Baxter, Richard
5207.D7 Doddridge, Philip
5207.H37 Henry, Matthew
5207.H4 Heywood, Oliver
5207.J4 Jay, William
5207.W3 Watts, Isaac
Episcopal Church in Scotland
5210 Periodicals. Serials
5220 Societies
(5225) Yearbooks
see BX5210
Conferences. Councils, etc.
5230 General
5235.A-Z Local, A-Z
5240 Directories
Cf. BX5225 Yearbooks
Documents
5245 Collections
5246 Special. By date
Collected works
5250 Several authors
5255 Individual authors

Church of England
Episcopal Church in Scotland -- Continued
5270 Study and teaching
For individual seminaries see BV4160.A+
History
5300 General works
5303.A-Z By county, etc., A-Z
5305.A-Z By diocese, A-Z
5310.A-Z By city, etc., A-Z
5320 General works. Principles, etc.
Sermons. Tracts. Addresses. Essays
Several authors
Homilies of the church
5330.A1A3 Texts. By date
5330.A1A33-.A1A39 Criticism
5330.A1A4 Other
5330.A3-Z Individual authors. By author and title, A-Z
Liturgy and ritual
5335 General works
5336 Book of common prayer
5336.A4 Editions. By date
5337.A-Z Special parts, A-Z
e.g.
5337.C7 Communion
Government and discipline
5340 General works
5345 Trials
5350 Church and state. Establishment and endowment
5351 Estates and revenues
Including maintenance, patronage, tithes, etc.
5355 Clergy
Cathedrals, churches, etc.
5369 General works
5370.A-Z Individual cathedrals, churches, etc. By place and name of church, A-Z
Biography
5390 Collective
5395.A-Z Individual, A-Z
e.g.
5395.F58 Forbes, Alexander Penrose, Bp. of Brechin
5395.L4 Leighton, Robert, Abp. of Glasgow
Church of Ireland
5410 Periodicals. Serials
5420 Societies
(5425) Yearbooks
see BX5410
Conferences. Councils, etc.

Church of England
Church of Ireland
Conferences. Councils, etc. -- Continued
5430 General
5435.A-Z Local, A-Z
5440 Directories
Cf. BX5425 Yearbooks
Documents
5445 Collections
5446 Special. By date
Collected works
5450 Several authors
5455 Individual authors
5470 Study and teaching
For individual seminaries see BV4160.A+
History
5500 General works
5503.A-Z By county, etc., A-Z
5505.A-Z By diocese or ecclesiastical province, A-Z
5510.A-Z By city, etc., A-Z
5520 General works. Principles, etc.
Sermons. Tracts. Addresses. Essays
Several authors
Homilies of the church
5530.A1A3 Texts. By date
5530.A1A33-.A1A39 Criticism
5530.A1A4 Other
5530.A3-Z Individual authors. By author and title, A-Z
Liturgy and ritual
5535 General works
5536 Book of common prayer
5536.A4 Editions. By date
5537.A-Z Special parts, A-Z
e.g.
5537.C7 Communion
Government and discipline
5540 General works
5545 Trials
5550 Church and state. Establishment and endowment
5551 Estates and revenues
Including maintenance, patronage, tithes, etc.
5555 Clergy
Cathedrals, churches, etc.
5569 General works
5570.A-Z Individual cathedrals, churches, etc. By place and name of church, A-Z
Biography

Church of England
Church of Ireland
Biography -- Continued
5590 Collective
5595.A-Z Individual, A-Z
e.g.
5595.U8 Ussher, James, Abp. of Armagh
5595.W5 Whately, Richard, Abp. of Dublin
5596-5598 Church in Wales (Table BX2)
Since 1920. For earlier material, see Church of England generally and BX5103 particularly
History
5596.A4-.Z3 General
(5596.Z4A-.Z4Z) By diocese, A-Z
see BX5107
(5596.Z5A-.Z5Z) By county, A-Z
see BX5105
(5596.Z6A-.Z6Z) By city, A-Z
see BX5110
Church of England outside of Great Britain
5600 General works
5600.A2-.A5 Periodicals
Protestant Episcopal Church in the United States of America see BX5800+
Anglican Church of Canada
Formerly the Church of England in Canada
5601 Periodicals. Serials
5602 Societies
Conferences, etc.
5603 General
5604.A-Z Local, A-Z
5605 Directories
Documents
5606 Collections
5607 Special. By date
5608 Collected works
5609 Study and teaching
For individual seminaries see BV4160.A+
History
5610 General works
5612.A-Z By ecclesiastical province, diocese, etc., A-Z
5613.A-Z By city, etc., A-Z
5614 General works
Sermons. Tracts. Addresses. Essays
5615.A1 Collections
5615.A2-Z Individual authors. By author and title, A-Z
5616 Liturgy and ritual

Church of England
Church of England outside of Great Britain
Anglican Church of Canada -- Continued
5616.2 Government and discipline
Religious communities. Conventual life
5616.4 General works
Men
5616.5 General works
5616.6.A-Z Individual communities, A-Z
Women
5616.7 General works
5616.8.A-Z Individual communities, A-Z
5617.A-Z Individual churches. By place, A-Z, or by name if nonurban
5618.A-Z Relations with other churches, A-Z
5618.U5 United Church of Canada
Biography
5619 Collective
5620.A-Z Individual, A-Z
e.g.
5620.C7 Cronyn, Benjamin, Bp.
5620.M4 Medley, John, Bp.
5620.M62 Mountain, Jacob, Bp.
5620.S75 Strachan, John, Bp.
Other American
Covers general, and period before self-governing units were established
5621 Periodicals. Serials
5622 Societies
Conferences, etc.
5623 General
5624.A-Z Local, A-Z
5625 Directories
Documents
5626 Collections
5627 Special. By date
5628 Collected works
5629 Study and teaching
For individual seminaries see BV4160.A+
History
5630 General works
5631.A-Z By country, A-Z
5632.A-Z By ecclesiastical province, diocese, etc., A-Z
5633.A-Z By city, etc., A-Z
5634 General works
Sermons. Tracts. Addresses. Essays
5635.A1 Collections

Church of England
Church of England outside of Great Britain
Other American
Sermons. Tracts. Addresses. Essays -- Continued
5635.A2-Z Individual authors. By author and title, A-Z
5636 Liturgy and ritual
5636.2 Government and discipline
Religious communities. Conventual life
5636.4 General works
Men
5636.5 General works
5636.6.A-Z Individual communities, A-Z
Women
5636.7 General works
5636.8.A-Z Individual communities, A-Z
5637.A-Z Individual churches. By place, A-Z, or by name if nonurban
5638.A-Z Relations with other churches, A-Z
Biography
5639 Collective
5640.A-Z Individual, A-Z
5640.4 Church in the Province of the West Indies (Table BX3 modified)
History
5640.4.A4 General
5640.4.A43A-.A43Z States, A-Z
5640.4.A44A-.A44Z Dioceses, archdioceses, and ecclesiastical provinces, A-Z
5640.4.A45A-.A45Z Cities, A-Z
Other European
Covers general, and period before self-governing units were established
5641 Periodicals. Serials
5642 Societies
Conferences, etc.
5643 General
5644.A-Z Local, A-Z
5645 Directories
Documents
5646 Collections
5647 Special. By date
5648 Collected works
5649 Study and teaching
For individual seminaries see BV4160.A+
History
5650 General works
5651.A-Z By country, A-Z

Church of England
Church of England outside of Great Britain
Other European
History -- Continued
5652.A-Z By ecclesiastical province, diocese, etc., A-Z
5653.A-Z By city, etc., A-Z
5654 General works
Sermons. Tracts. Addresses. Essays
5655.A1 Collections
5655.A2-Z Individual authors. By author and title, A-Z
5656 Liturgy and ritual
5656.2 Government and discipline
Religious communities. Conventual life
5656.4 General works
Men
5656.5 General works
5656.6.A-Z Individual communities, A-Z
Women
5656.7 General works
5656.8.A-Z Individual communities, A-Z
5657.A-Z Individual churches. By place, A-Z, or by name if nonurban
5658.A-Z Relations with other churches, A-Z
Biography
5659 Collective
5660.A-Z Individual, A-Z
Asian
Covers general, and period before self-governing units were established
5661 Periodicals. Serials
5662 Societies
Conferences, etc.
5663 General
5664.A-Z Local, A-Z
5665 Directories
Documents
5666 Collections
5667 Special. By date
5668 Collected works
5669 Study and teaching
For individual seminaries see BV4160.A+
History
5670 General works
5671.A-Z By country, A-Z
5672.A-Z By ecclesiastical province, diocese, etc., A-Z
5673.A-Z By city, etc., A-Z
5674 General works

Church of England
Church of England outside of Great Britain
Asian -- Continued
Sermons. Tracts. Addresses. Essays
5675.A1 Collections
5675.A2-Z Individual authors. By author and title, A-Z
5676 Liturgy and ritual
5676.2 Government and discipline
Religious communities. Conventual life
5676.4 General works
Men
5676.5 General works
5676.6.A-Z Individual communities, A-Z
Women
5676.7 General works
5676.8.A-Z Individual communities, A-Z
5677.A-Z Individual churches. By place, A-Z, or by name if nonurban
5678.A-Z Relations with other churches, A-Z
Biography
5679 Collective
5680.A-Z Individual, A-Z
Church of South India see BX7066.5
5680.3 Chung Hua Sheng Kung Hui (Table BX3 modified)
History
5680.3.A4 General
5680.3.A43A-.A43Z States, A-Z
5680.3.A44A-.A44Z Dioceses, archdioceses, and ecclesiastical provinces, A-Z
5680.3.A45A-.A45Z Cities, A-Z
5680.5 Church of India, Pakistan, Burma, and Ceylon (Table BX3 modified)
History
5680.5.A4 General
5680.5.A43A-.A43Z States, A-Z
5680.5.A44A-.A44Z Dioceses, archdioceses, and ecclesiastical provinces, A-Z
5680.5.A45A-.A45Z Cities, A-Z
5680.6 Episcopal Church in Jerusalem and the Middle East (Table BX3 modified)
History
5680.6.A4 General
5680.6.A43A-.A43Z States, A-Z
5680.6.A44A-.A44Z Dioceses, archdioceses, and ecclesiastical provinces, A-Z
5680.6.A45A-.A45Z Cities, A-Z
5680.7 Nippon Sei Ko Kai (Table BX3 modified)

Church of England
Church of England outside of Great Britain
Asian
Nippon Sei Ko Kai -- Continued
History
5680.7.A4 General
5680.7.A43A-.A43Z States, A-Z
5680.7.A44A-.A44Z Dioceses, archdioceses, and ecclesiastical provinces, A-Z
5680.7.A45A-.A45Z Cities, A-Z
5680.9 Anglican Diocese of the Republic of Singapore (Table BX3 modified)
History
5680.9.A4 General
5680.9.A43A-.A43Z States, A-Z
5680.9.A44A-.A44Z Dioceses, archdioceses, and ecclesiastical provinces, A-Z
5680.9.A45A-.A45Z Cities, A-Z
African
Covers general, and period before self-governing units were established
5681 Periodicals. Serials
5682 Societies
Conferences, etc.
5683 General
5684.A-Z Local, A-Z
5685 Directories
Documents
5686 Collections
5687 Special. By date
5688 Collected works
5689 Study and teaching
For individual seminaries see BV4160.A+
History
5690 General works
5691.A-Z By country, A-Z
5692.A-Z By ecclesiastical province, diocese, etc., A-Z
5693.A-Z By city, etc., A-Z
5694 General works
Sermons. Tracts. Addresses. Essays
5695.A1 Collections
5695.A2-Z Individual authors. By author and title, A-Z
5696 Liturgy and ritual
5696.2 Government and discipline
Religious communities. Conventual life
5696.4 General works
Men

Church of England
Church of England outside of Great Britain
African
Religious communities. Conventual life
Men -- Continued
5696.5 General works
5696.6.A-Z Individual communities, A-Z
Women
5696.7 General works
5696.8.A-Z Individual communities, A-Z
5697.A-Z Individual churches. By place, A-Z, or by name if nonurban
5698.A-Z Relations with other churches, A-Z
Biography
5699 Collective
5700.A-Z Individual, A-Z
5700.4 Church of the Province of Central Africa (Table BX3 modified)
History
5700.4.A4 General
5700.4.A43A-.A43Z States, A-Z
5700.4.A44A-.A44Z Dioceses, archdioceses, and ecclesiastical provinces, A-Z
5700.4.A45A-.A45Z Cities, A-Z
5700.5 Church of the Province of East Africa (Table BX3 modified)
History
5700.5.A4 General
5700.5.A43A-.A43Z States, A-Z
5700.5.A44A-.A44Z Dioceses, archdioceses, and ecclesiastical provinces, A-Z
5700.5.A45A-.A45Z Cities, A-Z
5700.54 Church of the Province of the Indian Ocean (Table BX3 modified)
History
5700.54.A4 General
5700.54.A43A-.A43Z States, A-Z
5700.54.A44A-.A44Z Dioceses, archdioceses, and ecclesiastical provinces, A-Z
5700.54.A45A-.A45Z Cities, A-Z
5700.55 Church of the Province of Kenya (Table BX3 modified)
History
5700.55.A4 General
5700.55.A43A-.A43Z States, A-Z
5700.55.A44A-.A44Z Dioceses, archdioceses, and ecclesiastical provinces, A-Z
5700.55.A45A-.A45Z Cities, A-Z

Church of England
Church of England outside of Great Britain
African -- Continued

5700.57 Church of the Province of Nigeria (Table BX3 modified)
History
5700.57.A4 General
5700.57.A43A-.A43Z States, A-Z
5700.57.A44A-.A44Z Dioceses, archdioceses, and ecclesiastical provinces, A-Z
5700.57.A45A-.A45Z Cities, A-Z
5700.6 Church of the Province of Southern Africa (Table BX3 modified)
History
5700.6.A4 General
5700.6.A43A-.A43Z States, A-Z
5700.6.A44A-.A44Z Dioceses, archdioceses, and ecclesiastical provinces, A-Z
5700.6.A45A-.A45Z Cities, A-Z
5700.7 Church of the Province of West Africa (Table BX3 modified)
History
5700.7.A4 General
5700.7.A43A-.A43Z States, A-Z
5700.7.A44A-.A44Z Dioceses, archdioceses, and ecclesiastical provinces, A-Z
5700.7.A45A-.A45Z Cities, A-Z
5700.8 Church of Uganda, Rwanda, and Burundi (Table BX3 modified)
History
5700.8.A4 General
5700.8.A43A-.A43Z States, A-Z
5700.8.A44A-.A44Z Dioceses, archdioceses, and ecclesiastical provinces, A-Z
5700.8.A45A-.A45Z Cities, A-Z
5700.9 Episcopal Church of the Province of the Sudan (Table BX3 modified)
History
5700.9.A4 General
5700.9.A43A-.A43Z States, A-Z
5700.9.A44A-.A44Z Dioceses, archdioceses, and ecclesiastical provinces, A-Z
5700.9.A45A-.A45Z Cities, A-Z

Australian and New Zealand
Church of England in Australia and Tasmania. Anglican Church of Australia
5701 Periodicals. Serials
5702 Societies

Church of England
Church of England outside of Great Britain
Australian and New Zealand
Church of England in Australia and Tasmania. Anglican Church of Australia -- Continued
Conferences, etc.
5703 General
5704.A-Z Local, A-Z
5705 Directories
Documents
5706 Collections
5707 Special. By date
5708 Collected works
5709 Study and teaching
For individual seminaries see BV4160.A+
History
5710 General works
5711.A-Z By civil province, etc., A-Z
5712.A-Z By ecclesiastical province, diocese, etc., A-Z
5713.A-Z By city, etc., A-Z
5714 General works
Sermons. Tracts. Addresses. Essays
5715.A1 Collections
5715.A2-Z Individual authors. By author and title, A-Z
5716 Liturgy and ritual
5716.2 Government and discipline
Religious communities. Conventual life
5716.4 General works
Men
5716.5 General works
5716.6.A-Z Individual communities, A-Z
Women
5716.7 General works
5716.8.A-Z Individual communities, A-Z
5717.A-Z Individual churches. By place, A-Z, or by name if nonurban
5718.A-Z Relations with other churches, A-Z
Biography
5719 Collective
5720.A-Z Individual, A-Z
5720.5 Church of the Province of New Zealand (Table BX3 modified)
History
5720.5.A4 General
5720.5.A43A-.A43Z States, A-Z
5720.5.A44A-.A44Z Dioceses, archdioceses, and ecclesiastical provinces, A-Z

Church of England
Church of England outside of Great Britain
Australian and New Zealand
Church of the Province of New Zealand
History -- Continued
5720.5.A45A-.A45Z Cities, A-Z
5720.8 Province of Papua New Guinea (Table BX3 modified)
History
5720.8.A4 General
5720.8.A43A-.A43Z States, A-Z
5720.8.A44A-.A44Z Dioceses, archdioceses, and ecclesiastical provinces, A-Z
5720.8.A45A-.A45Z Cities, A-Z
Oceanian
Covers general, and period before self-governing units were established
5721 Periodicals. Serials
5722 Societies
Conferences, etc.
5723 General
5724.A-Z Local, A-Z
5725 Directories
Documents
5726 Collections
5727 Special. By date
5728 Collected works
5729 Study and teaching
For individual seminaries see BV4160.A+
History
5730 General works
5731.A-Z By country, A-Z
Hawaiian Islands see BX5917.H3
5732.A-Z By ecclesiastical province, diocese, etc., A-Z
5733.A-Z By city, etc., A-Z
5734 General works
Sermons. Tracts. Addresses. Essays
5735.A1 Collections
5735.A2-Z Individual authors. By author and title, A-Z
5736 Liturgy and ritual
5736.2 Government and discipline
Religious communities. Conventual life
5736.4 General works
Men
5736.5 General works
5736.6.A-Z Individual communities, A-Z
Women
5736.7 General works

Church of England
Church of England outside of Great Britain
Oceanian
Religious communities. Conventual life
Women -- Continued
5736.8.A-Z Individual communities, A-Z
5737.A-Z Individual churches. By place, A-Z, or by name if nonurban
5738.A-Z Relations with other churches, A-Z
Biography
5739 Collective
5740.A-Z Individual, A-Z
Episcopal Church. Protestant Episcopal Church in the United States of America
Including Church of England in Colonial period
5800 Periodicals
5810 Societies. Guilds
Conventions, congresses, etc.
5820 General
5823 Confederate States
5825 Local
Individual dioceses see BX5918.A+
Dictionaries and encyclopedias see BX5007
5830 Directories
Documents
5833 Collections
5835 Individual. By date
Includes Pastoral letters from House of Bishops
5837.A-Z Pastoral letters, charges, etc. By individual bishops, A-Z
Collected works
5840 Several authors
5845 Individual authors
Study and teaching
5850 General works
Individual seminaries see BV4070.A+
Sunday schools (Church schools)
5869 Societies, conventions, etc.
5870 General works. Organization, etc.
5873 Service books
Textbooks
5874 Series
5875 Single works
5876.A-Z Individual Sunday schools. By place, A-Z
History
5879 Collections
For Colonial period see BX5881
5880 General works

Episcopal Church. Protestant Episcopal Church in the United States of America
History -- Continued
By period
5881 17th-18th centuries. Church of England in the colonies
5882 19th-20th centuries
5883 General special
Including historical pageants
By region
5885 New England
5890 North
5895 South
5900 Central
5915 Western
5917.A-.W By state, A-W
5917.H3 Hawaii
5917.5.A-.W By ecclesiastical province, A-Z
5918.A-Z By diocese and missionary district, A-Z
For Constitutions, canons, etc. see BX5957.A+
5919.A-Z By city, A-Z
For individual churches see BX5980
5925 Movements and parties
Including High, Low, Ritualistic, etc.
Episcopal Church and other churches
Including the problem of Christian union, reunion, etc.
5926.A1 Periodicals. Serials
5926.A2 Societies
5926.A3 Conferences, congresses, etc.
5926.A5-.Z5 General works. History, etc.
5926.Z6 Attitude toward the ecumenical movement
5926.Z7 Special aspects (not A-Z)
5927 Relations with the Orthodox Eastern Church (Greek and Russian)
5927.5 Relations with the Oriental churches
5927.8 Relations with the Church of England
5928 Relations with the Roman Catholic Church
5928.5.A-Z Relations with other churches, A-Z
5928.5.P65 Presbyterian Church
General works. Doctrines, etc.
5929 Early through 1800
5930 1801-1950
5930.2 1951-2000
5930.3 2001-
5933 Other
5935 Pamphlets, addresses, essays, etc.
5936 Controversial works, satire, etc.
Cf. BX5135 Works against the Church of England

Episcopal Church. Protestant Episcopal Church in the United States of America -- Continued

Sermons. Tracts. Addresses. Essays

Sermons on special topics may be classified with the subject, especially biography and history

For sermons for children, young people, etc. see BV4310+

For addresses, essays, etc. on general doctrines or polity see BX5935

Cf. BX5840+ Collected works

Several authors

Homilies of the church

5937.A1A3 Texts. By date

5937.A1A33-.A1A39 Criticism

5937.A1A4-.A1Z Other

5937.A3-Z Individual authors. By author and title, A-Z

5938 Articles of religion

5939 Creeds and catechisms

Cf. BX5139 Church of England

Liturgy and ritual. Church service

Cf. BV30+ Church year

Cf. BX5140.5+ Church of England

5940 General works

Book of Common Prayer

Texts

5943.A1 English editions. By date

5943.A3 English editions (undated)

5943.A4 Adaptations. By editor or date

5943.A5 Adaptations for children. By editor or date

5943.A6-Z Translations. By language, A-Z

5944.A-Z Special parts, A-Z

e.g.

5944.C7 Collects

5944.C75 Communion service

5944.D2 Daily service

5944.E9 Evening prayer

5944.L5 Litany

5944.O4 Offices of instruction

5945 History. Commentary, etc.

5945.A3 Additions and changes. By date

Psalter, canticles, etc.

Cf. BX5146 Church of England

Cf. M2169+ Church music (scores)

5946.A1 English editions. By date

5946.A3 Additions and changes. By date

5946.A4A-.A4Z Translations. By language, A-Z

5946.A7-Z History, commentary, etc.

Episcopal Church. Protestant Episcopal Church in the United States of America
Liturgy and ritual. Church service -- Continued
5947.A-Z Other special, A-Z
e.g.
5947.B5 Ceremonial of bishops
5947.B7 Books of hours
5947.B8 Books of offices
5947.B9 Burial service
5947.C4 Children's services
5947.C5 Christian healing services
5947.C55 Church dedication services
5947.C6 Consecration services
5947.D4 Dead (Prayers for)
Family worship see BV255+
5947.F7 Fourth of July services
5947.H5 Holy Week services
Homilies see BX5937.A1A3+
Inclusive language liturgical prayers see BX5947.N64
5947.I5 Introits
5947.I6 Office of Institution of ministers
5947.L4 Lessons. Lectionaries. Gospels and Epistles
5947.L6 Lord's supper (Nonofficial services)
5947.M5 Missals
5947.N64 Nonsexist language liturgical prayers
5947.R5 Rector's manuals
5947.S8 Stations of the Cross
5947.T4 Office of Tenebrae
5947.Z9 Other. By date
e.g. May 10, 1910. Order of service in memory of King Edward VII
5948 Other
e.g. Altar servers' manual
Hymns in English see BV372
Hymns in languages other than English see BV470+
5949 Sacraments, etc.
Including theology, liturgy and rite
5949.A1 General works
5949.B2 Baptism
5949.C5 Communion
5949.C6 Confession
5949.C7 Confirmation
5949.M3 Marriage
5949.O7 Ordination
Government. Organization. Discipline
Including constitutional history
5950 General works

Episcopal Church. Protestant Episcopal Church in the United States of America
Government. Organization. Discipline -- Continued
5952 Episcopal Synod of America
Law. Constitution, canons, courts, etc.
5955 General works
5956 Confederate States of America
5957.A-Z By diocese, A-Z
Trials
5959 General works. Procedure, etc.
5960.A-Z Special, A-Z
Finance
5961 General works
Clerical relief, pensions, etc. see BX5965.5
5962 Parish accounts, records, forms, etc.
5963 The cathedral
Clergy
Cf. BX5837.A+ Pastoral letters, charges, etc.
5965 General works
5965.3 Women clergy
5965.5 Clerical relief, pensions, etc.
5966 Bishops
5967 African American clergy
5967.5 Other church officers (Clerical and lay)
e.g. Archdeacons, deacons, lay readers, church wardens
5968 Laity
5968.5 Women
Cf. BX5965.3 Women clergy
5969 Parish missions. Evangelistic work
Religious orders. Conventual life
Cf. BX5183+ Religious communities (Church of England)
5970 General works
Men
Cf. BX5184.A+ Church of England
5971.A1 General works
5971.A6-Z Individual orders
e.g.
5971.C6 Congregation of the Companions of the Holy Savior
Biography
5972.A1 Collective
5972.A6-Z Individual
Prefer BX5995
Women. Sisterhoods
Cf. BX5185.A+ Church of England
5973.A1 General works
5973.A6-BZ5973.Z Individual orders
e.g.

Episcopal Church. Protestant Episcopal Church in the United States of America
Religious orders. Conventual life
Women. Sisterhoods
Individual orders -- Continued
5973.O8 Order of Saint Anne
5973.S5 Sisterhood of the Holy Nativity
5973.S65 Society of Saint Margaret
Biography
5974.A1 Collective
5974.A6-Z Individual
e.g.
5974.B65 Bowie, Susannah Frances
5974.E8 Eva Mary, Mother
5974.H3 Hall, Louise Gardiner
5975 Church societies, guilds, etc.
Class here general works, manuals, etc.
Cf. BX5810 Publications of societies, guilds
5978 Benevolent work. Welfare work
5979 African Americans and the Episcopal Church
5979.5.A-Z Other special topics, A-Z
5979.5.H65 Homosexuality
5979.5.P4 Peace
5979.5.P73 Preaching
5979.5.R32 Race relations
Individual churches
Subarranged by place or by name if nonurban
5980 United States
5983 Other
e.g.
5983.A1 Collective
5983.R6 Rome (City)
Biography
5990 Collective
5995.A-Z Individual, A-Z
e.g.
5995.B38 Bass, Edward, Bp.
Bowie, Susannah Frances see BX5974.B65
5995.B68 Bray, Thomas
5995.B7 Breck, James Lloyd
5995.B8 Brooks, Phillips, Bp.
Eva Mary, Mother see BX5974.E8
Hall, Louise Gardiner see BX5974.H3
5995.H6 Hobart, John Henry, Bp.
5995.H75 Huntington, Frederic Dan, Bp.
5995.M8 Muhlenberg, William Augustus
5995.P7 Potter, Henry Codman, Bp.

Episcopal Church. Protestant Episcopal Church in the United States of America
Biography
Individual, A-Z -- Continued
5995.S3 Seabury, Samuel, Bp.
5995.S7 Spalding, Franklin Spencer, Bp.
5995.W5 White, William, Bp.
Episcopal Church outside the United States
By region or country
Latin America
5996 General works (Table BX3)
5997 Brazil (Table BX3)
5999 Central America (Table BX3)
West Indies
5999.3 Cuba (Table BX3)
5999.5 Haiti (Table BX3)
Including the Orthodox Apostolic Church in Haiti (Église Orthodox Apostolique Haïtienne)
Mexico
6001 Periodicals. Serials
6002 Societies
Conferences, etc.
6003 General
6004.A-Z Local, A-Z
6005 Directories
Documents
6006 Collections
6007 Special. By date
6008 Collected works
6009 Study and teaching
For individual institutions see BV4160.A+
History
6010 General works
6011.A-Z By civil province, etc., A-Z
6012.A-Z By ecclesiastical province, diocese, etc., A-Z
6013.A-Z By city, etc., A-Z
6014 General works
Sermons. Tracts. Addresses. Essays
6015.A1 Collections
6015.A2-Z Individual authors. By author and title, A-Z
6016 Liturgy and ritual
6016.2 Government and discipline
Religious communities. Conventual life
6016.4 General works
Men
6016.5 General works
6016.6.A-Z Individual communities, A-Z

Episcopal Church outside the United States
By region or country
Latin America
Mexico
Religious communities. Conventual life -- Continued
Women
6016.7 General works
6016.8.A-Z Individual communities, A-Z
6017.A-Z Individual churches. By place, A-Z, or by name if nonurban
6018.A-Z Relations with other churches, A-Z
Biography
6019 Collective
6020.A-Z Individual, A-Z
Other regions or countries
6022 Europe (Table BX3)
Asia
6026 Philippine Islands (Table BX3)
Africa
6030 Liberia (Table BX3)
Oceania
Hawaiian Islands see BX5917.H3
6040 Anglican Catholic Church (Table BX3)
Reformed Episcopal Church
6051 Periodicals. Serials
6053 Societies
6055 Conferences
6057 Directories
6059 Collected works
Study and teaching
6061 General works
Individual seminaries see BV4070.A+
Sunday schools (Church schools)
6062 General works. Organization, etc.
6063 Service books
6064 Textbooks, etc.
6064.5.A-Z Individual Sunday schools. By place, A-Z
History
6065 General works
By region or country
United States
6066 General works
6067.A-.W By state, A-W
6068.A-Z By city, A-Z
Cf. BX6081+ Individual churches
6069.A-Z Other regions or countries, A-Z
e.g.

Reformed Episcopal Church
History
By region or country
Other regions or countries, A-Z -- Continued
6069.G7 Great Britain
"Free Church of England, otherwise called the Reformed Episcopal Church in the United Kingdom of Great Britain and Ireland"
6071 General works. Theology, doctrines, etc.
6072 Addresses, essays, lectures
6073 Controversial works against the Reformed Episcopal Church
6074 Creeds and catechisms
6075 Liturgy and ritual. Service books
Hymns in English see BV373
Hymns in languages other than English see BV470+
6076 Government and discipline. Clergy and church officers
Sermons. Tracts
Sermons on special topics may be classified with the subject, especially biography and history
For sermons for children, young people, etc. see BV4310+
Cf. BX6059 Collections, collected works
6077.A1 Several authors
6077.A3-Z Individual authors, A-Z
Individual churches
Subarranged by place or by name if nonurban
6081 United States
6083 Other
Biography
6091 Collective
6093.A-Z Individual, A-Z
e.g.
6093.C78 Cummins, George David, Bp.
6093.F3 Fallows, Samuel, Bp.
Other Protestant denominations
Arranged alphabetically
Adventists. "Millerites"
6101 Periodicals
6103 Societies
6105 Conferences
6109 Directories
6111 Collected works
6113 Study and teaching
History
6115 General works
6117 Juvenile works
6121 General works. Doctrine

Other Protestant denominations
Adventists. "Millerites" -- Continued
6122 Addresses, essays, lectures
Hymns in English see BV375
Hymns in languages other than English see BV470+
6123 Sermons. Tracts
6124 Controversial works against the Adventists
Ordinances. Sacraments
6124.3 General works
6124.6 Lord's Supper
6126 Churches of God, Seventh Day
For individual branches see BX6131+
Individual branches of Adventists
6131-6134 Evangelical Adventists. American Millennial Association (Table BX22)
6135-6138 Church of God, Seventh Day (Salem, W. Va.) (Table BX22)
6141-6144 Advent Christian Church (Table BX22)
6151-6154 Seventh-Day Adventists (Table BX22)
Cf. RA975.S49 Seventh-Day Adventist health facilities
6155 Study and teaching. Textbooks
6156-6159 Seventh-Day Adventist Reform Movement (Table BX22)
6160 General Association of Davidian Seventh-Day Adventists
6161-6164 Church of God (Seventh Day), Denver, Colo. (Table BX22)
6171-6174 Life and Advent Union (Table BX22)
6175-6178 Worldwide Church of God (Herbert W. Armstrong) (Table BX22)
WCG secessionist or derivative bodies
6178.1 General works
6178.2 Congregation of God Seventh Day Association
6178.4 Church of God, International
6178.6 Foundation for Biblical Research
6181-6184 Church of God (Abrahamic Faith) (Table BX22)
Formerly Churches of God in Jesus Christ. Headquarters, Oregon, Ill.
6184.5 House of David (Table BX3)
6185.A-Z Individual churches. By place, A-Z, or by name if nonurban
Converts
6189.A1 Collective
6189.A3-Z Individual, A-Z
Biography
6191 Collective
6193.A-Z Individual, A-Z
e.g.
6193.M5 Miller, William

Other Protestant denominations
Adventists. "Millerites"
Biography
Individual, A-Z -- Continued
6193.W5 White, Ellen Gould (Harmon)
Adventists - Arminians
6194.A35 Africa Inland Church
6194.A36-.A368 African Church (Table BX4)
6194.A38 African Independent Pentecostal Church of Africa
6194.A4 African Orthodox Church
6194.A43 African Orthodox Church of New York
6194.A45 African Universal Church
6194.A46-.A468 African American Spiritual churches (Table BX4)
Aladura Church of the Lord see BX7068.5
6194.A5 American Rescue Workers
6194.A55 Antonians (Anton Unternahrer)
6194.A6 Apostolic Christian Church (S. H. Fröhlich)
6194.A63 Apostolic Church of John Maranke
Apostolic Faith (Charles F. Parham) see BX8766
6194.A7 Apostolic Faith Mission
6194.A8 Apostolic Overcoming Holy Church of God
6194.A86 Apostolosk kirke i Danmark
Armenian Evangelical Church see BX7990.H48
6194.A9-.A98 Armenian Evangelical Union (Table BX4)
Arminians. Remonstrants. Remonstrantsche Broederschap
Including works for and against Arminianism
Cf. BT809+ Predestination and Free will
Cf. BX9470+ Reformed Church of Holland
6195.A1 Collected works
6195.A2-.A5 Documents
General works. Histories
6195.A6-.A69 By Arminius
6195.A7-Z By other authors
6195.15 Collegiants
6195.2.A-Z Individual churches. By place and name, A-Z, or by name, A-Z, if nonurban
Biography
6196 Arminius
6197.A-Z Other, A-Z
e.g.
6197.C3 Camphuysen, Dirk Rafaelszoon
6197.E6 Episcopius, Simon
6198 Arminians - Baptists
Assemblies of God (Springfield, Mo.) see BX8765.5

Baptists
Class here comprehensive treatises dealing with all Baptist groups and especially with "regular" or "missionary" Baptists
See also other "Baptist" bodies, e.g. Anabaptists, German Baptist Brethren, etc.
For Baptist groups neither "regular" nor "missionary" see BX6349+
For African American Baptists see BX6440+
6201 Periodicals
6205 Societies
Class here worid-wide and general American societies
For national societies in other countries and all local and historical societies, see the country divisions
6206 Congresses
Conventions. Conferences see BX6349+
State conventions and state associations see BX6349+
Associations of churches see BX6349+
6211 Dictionaries. Encyclopedias
6213 Directories
Collected works
6215 Several authors
6217 Individual authors
Study and teaching
6219 General works
Individual seminaries see BV4070.A+
Sunday schools (Church schools)
6222 Societies. Conventions, etc.
6222.A1 General works on Baptist Sunday-school associations, etc.
6223 General works. Organization, etc.
6224 Service books
6225 Textbooks, etc.
6227.A-Z Individual Sunday schools. By place, A-Z
History
Cf. BV803+ Baptism
Cf. BX4929+ Anabaptists
6231 General works
6232 Addresses, essays, lectures
By region or country
America. North America
6233 General works
United States
6235 General works
By period
6236 17th-18th centuries
6237 19th-20th centuries
By region

Baptists
History
By region or country
America. North America
United States
By region -- Continued
6239 New England
6241 South
6243 Central
6245 West
6247.A-Z By nationality or race, A-Z
For Black Baptists see BX6440+
6248.A-.W By state, A-W
6249.A-Z By city, A-Z
Individual churches see BX6480+
Canada
6251 General works
6252.A-Z By region, province, etc., A-Z
6253.A-Z By city, A-Z
Latin America
6254 General works
Mexico
6255 General works
6256.A-Z By region, state, etc., A-Z
6257.A-Z By city, A-Z
Central America
6260 General works
6261.A-Z By region or country, A-Z
6262.A-Z By city, A-Z
West Indies
For Spiritual or Shouter Baptists see BX9798.S65+
6265 General works
6266.A-Z By region or country, A-Z
6267.A-Z By city, A-Z
South America
6271 General works
6272.A-Z By country, A-Z
6273.A-Z By city, A-Z
Europe
6275 General works
Great Britain. England
6276.A1 Periodicals. Collections, etc.
6276.A3-Z General works
6277.A-Z By county, etc. (England), A-Z
6278.A-Z By city (England), A-Z
Ireland
6281.A1 Periodicals. Collections, etc.

Baptists
History
By region or country
Europe
Great Britain. England
Ireland -- Continued
6281.A3-Z General works
6282.A-Z By county, etc., A-Z
6283.A-Z By city, A-Z
Scotland
6285.A1 Periodicals. Collections, etc.
6285.A3-Z General works
6286.A-Z By region, etc., A-Z
6287.A-Z By city, A-Z
Wales
6291.A1 Periodicals. Collections, etc.
6291.A3-Z General works
6292.A-Z By county, etc., A-Z
6293.A-Z By city, A-Z
France
6295.A1 Periodicals. Collections, etc.
6295.A3-Z General works
6296.A-Z By region, department, etc., A-Z
6297.A-Z By city, A-Z
Germany
6301.A1 Periodicals. Collections, etc.
6301.A3-Z General works
6302.A-Z By state, etc., A-Z
6303.A-Z By city, A-Z
Italy
6305.A1 Periodicals. Collections, etc.
6305.A3-Z General works
6306.A-Z By region, province, etc., A-Z
6307.A-Z By city, A-Z
6310.A-Z Other European regions or countries, A-Z
Asia
6315 General works
6316.A-Z By region or country, A-Z
e.g.
6316.J3 Japan
Africa
6320 General works
6321 South Africa
6322.A-Z Other, A-Z
e.g.
6322.L5 Liberia
Australia

Baptists
History
By region or country
Australia -- Continued
6325 General works
6326.A-Z Local, A-Z
New Zealand
6326.2 General works
6326.3.A-Z Local, A-Z
Oceania
6327 General works
6328.A-Z Local, A-Z
6329.A-Z Relations with other churches, A-Z
6329.A1 General works
6329.R6 Roman Catholic Church
General works. Doctrine, etc.
6330 Early through 1800
6331 1801-1950
6331.2 1951-2000
6331.3 2001-
6332 Addresses, essays, lectures
For Sunday-school textbooks see BX6225
Sermons. Tracts
Sermons on special topics may be classified with the subject, especially biography and history
For sermons for children, young people, etc. see BV4310+
6333.A1 Several authors
6333.A3-Z Individual authors. By author and title, A-Z
6334 Controversial works against the Baptists
6335 Creeds. Confessions, etc.
6336 Catechisms
6337 Service. Ritual. Liturgy
Hymns in English see BV380+
Hymns in languages other than English see BV470+
Sacraments
Including sacramental theology, liturgy and rites
6338 General works
6339.A-Z Special, A-Z
e.g.
Baptism (except for liturgical forms) see BV803+
6339.C5 Communion
Government and discipline
Prefer individual branches
6340 General works
Trial
6342 General. Procedure, etc.

Baptists
Government and discipline
Trial -- Continued
6343.A-Z Special, A-Z
Clergy
6345 General works
6345.5 Clerical relief, pensions, etc.
6346 Other church officers. Deacons, etc.
6346.3 Laity
6346.5 Finance. Stewardship
Benevolent work. Welfare work, etc.
6347 General works
6348 Methods. Manuals for societies
Individual branches, conventions, associations, etc.
Including world-wide and national conventions, state and regional conventions and associations, individual branches, etc.
6349.5-.58 American Baptist Association (Table BX25)
6350-6358 Baptist Church of Christ (Table BX23)
6359.3-.38 Baptist General Conference (Table BX25)
6359.385-.3858 Baptist Missionary Association of America (Table BX25)
6359.388-.3888 Baptist State Convention of North Carolina (Table BX25)
6359.4-.48 Baptized Church of Christ, Friends to Humanity (Table BX25)
6359.493-.4938 Clear Creek Baptist Association (Ill.) (Table BX25)
6359.494-.4948 Coffee County Baptist Association (Ala.) (Table BX25)
6359.5-.58 Conservative Baptist Association of America (Table BX25)
6359.6-.68 Cullman Baptist Association (Ala.) (Table BX25)
6359.7-.78 Dover Baptist Association (Va.) (Table BX25)
6359.79-.798 Elkhorn Baptist Association (Table BX25)
6359.8-.88 Enon Baptist Association (Okla.) (Table BX25)
6359.91-.918 Fayette County Baptist Association (Ala.) (Table BX25)
6359.93-.938 First South Florida Missionary Baptist Association (Table BX25)
Freewill Baptists
6360-6368 Original Freewill Baptists (Table BX23)
Limited to Baptists using the word "Original"
6370-6378 Freewill Baptists or Free Baptists (Table BX23)
Including Freewill Baptists founded in New Hampshire; Freewill Baptists founded in North Carolina; National Association of Free Will Baptists; etc.
6378.6-.68 Gasper River Association (Table BX25)
6379.3-.38 General Baptists (Table BX25)
Cf. BX6276+ General Baptists (Great Britain)
6379.394-.3948 Georgia Baptist Association (Table BX25)
6379.397-.3978 Goshen Baptist Association of Virginia (Table BX25)
6379.398-.3988 Grand Canyon Baptist Association (Table BX25)

Baptists
Individual branches, conventions, associations, etc. -- Continued

6379.4-.48 Greenbriar Baptist Association (Ark.) (Table BX25)
6379.49-.498 Gulf Stream Baptist Association (Table BX25)
6379.5-.58 Holiness Baptists (Table BX25)
6379.595-.5958 Middle District Baptist Association (Va.) (Table BX25)
6379.598-.5988 Murray County Baptist Association (Georgia) (Table BX25)
6379.6-.68 New Bethel Baptist Association of Texas (Table BX25)
6379.7-.78 Northern Kentucky Baptist Association (Table BX25)
6379.785-.7858 Northwest Baptist Convention (Table BX25)
6379.8-.88 Old Line Baptists (Table BX25)
Missionary, not anti-missionary Baptists
6380-6388 Old School, Old Order, or Primitive Baptists. "Hardshell Baptists" (Table BX23)
6388.5-.58 Philadelphia Baptist Association (Table BX25)
6389.2-.28 Pilot Mountain Baptist Association (N.C.) (Table BX25)
6389.285-.2858 Providence Anti-Slavery Baptist Association (Table BX25)
6389.29-.298 Reformed Baptists (Table BX25)
6389.3-.38 Regular Baptists (Table BX25)
6389.39-.398 Old Regular Baptists (Table BX25)
6389.5-.58 Salem Association of Baptists (Kentucky) (Table BX25)
6389.6-.68 Separate Baptists (Table BX25)
6390-6398 Seventh Day Baptists (Table BX23)
6400-6408 German Seventh Day Baptists (Table BX23)
6410-6418 General Six Principle Baptists (Table BX23)
6419.6-.68 Strict Baptists (Great Britain) (Table BX25)
6420-6428 Two Seed in the Spirit Baptists (Table BX23)
6430-6438 United Baptists (Table BX23)
6439.5-.58 Walker Baptist Association (Alabama) (Table BX25)
6440-6448 African American Baptists (Table BX23)
6450 Sunday schools (General)
For individual Sunday schools see BX6480+
6452 Sermons. Addresses. Essays
Biography
6453 Collective
6455.A-Z Individual, A-Z
6456-6456.8 National Baptist Convention of the United States of America (Table BX24)
6457-6457.8 National Baptist Convention of America (Table BX24)
6460-6460.8 National Primitive Baptist Convention of the U.S.A. (Table BX24)
Formerly Colored Primitive Baptists
6460.9.A-Z Other organizations. By name, A-Z
Subarrange by author

Baptists
Individual branches, conventions, associations, etc. -- Continued
6461-6461.8 American Baptist Churches in the U.S.A. (Table BX24)
Formerly Northern Baptist Convention; American Baptist Convention
6462-6462.8 Southern Baptist Convention (Table BX24)
6470.A-Z Other. By name, A-Z
Subarrange by author
e. g.
6470.B38 Baptist General Convention of Texas
Baptist camp meetings, summer camps, summer conferences, retreats, etc.
6475 General works
6476.A-Z Individual, A-Z
Individual Baptist churches
Subarrange by place or by name if nonurban
6480 United States
6490 Other
Biography
Cf. BX6453+ African American Baptists
6493 Collective
6495.A-Z Individual, A-Z
e.g.
Bunyan, John see PR3331
6495.C56 Clifford, John
6495.C6 Conwell, Russell Herman
6495.F75 Fuller, Andrew
6495.H26 Hall, Robert
6495.R3 Rauschenbusch, Walter
6495.S7 Spurgeon, Charles Haddon
6495.W55 Williams, Roger
For Williams as an historical figure see F82
Baptists - Catholic Apostolic Church
6510.B3 Battle-axes
6510.B44 Bethel Evangelical Church
6510.B48 Bible Christian Church
6510.B55 Bible Christians
6510.B58 Bible Fellowship Church
Withdrew from United Missionary Church (formerly Mennonite Brethren in Christ) in 1952. Adopted above name in 1959
6510.B62-.B628 Bible Mission (Andhra Pradesh, India) (Table BX4)
6510.B65-.B658 Bible Protestant Church (Table BX4)
6510.B665 Bible Standard Churches
6510.B67 Bible Way Churches of Our Lord Jesus Christ World Wide
6510.B75-.B758 Bond van Vrije Evangelische Gemeenten in Nederland (Table BX4)

	Baptists - Catholic Apostolic Church -- Continued
	Bourignonists
6510.B8A2-.B8A5	Works by Antoinette Bourignon
6510.B8A6-.B8Z	General works
6510.B82	Biography
6510.B83	Bremische Evangelische Kirche
	Brethren (Church of the Brethren) see BX7801+
	Brethren (German Baptist) see BX7801+
	Brethren (Plymouth Brethren) see BX8799+
	Brethren, United see BX8551+
	Brethren Church (Progressive Dunkers) see BX7829.B6+
	Brethren in Christ see BX9675
	Brothers of Christ see BX6651+
6510.B9	Buchanites
	Bund der Evangelischen Kirchen in der DDR see BX4844.82
6510.C35-.C358	Calvary Chapel movement (Table BX4)
	Camisards see BX7593
	Revolt of the Camisards see DC127.C3
	Campbellites see BX7301+
6551-6593	Catholic Apostolic Church. Irvingites (Table BX1 modified)
	Biography
6591	Collective
6593.A-Z	Individual biography, A-Z
	e.g.
6593.A6	Andrews, William Watson
6593.I7	Irving, Edward
	Catholic Apostolic Church - Christadelphians
6600.C35-.C358	Celestial Church of Christ (Table BX4)
6600.C37-.C378	Cherubim and Seraphim (Society) (Table BX4)
6600.C38-.C388	Cherubim and Seraphim Church Movement (Table BX4)
6600.C4-.C48	Chiesa evangelia italiana (Table BX4)
6600.C49-.C498	Chiesa universale giurisdavidica della Santissima Trinita (Table BX4)
6600.C4995-.C49958	Children of Peace (Table BX4)
6600.C52-.C528	Christ Apostolic Church (Table BX4)
6600.C57-.C578	Christ Brotherhood (Table BX4)
6651-6693	Christadelphians. Brothers of Christ (Table BX1 modified)
	Biography
6691	Collective
6693.A-Z	Individual biography, A-Z
	e.g.
6693.T4	Thomas, John
	Christadelphians - Christian Church
6700	Christian and Missionary Alliance (Table BX3)
6710	Christian Brethren Assemblies

6751-6793 Christian Church (General Convention of the Christian Church) (Table BX1 modified)
Merged with the National Council of the Congregational Churches of the United States in 1931 to form the General Council of the Congregational and Christian Churches of the United States
Includes the Christian Connection, Christian Church South, American Convention, etc.
For Disciples of Christ, Campbellites see BX7301+
Biography
6791 Collective
6793.A-Z Individual, A-Z
e.g.
6793.O4 O'Kelly, James
6793.P8 Purviance, David
6793.S6 Smith, Elias
Stone, Barton Warren see BX7343.S8
6793.S8 Summerbell, Joseph James
Christian Church - Christian Reformed Church
6799.C2-.C28 Christian Churches and Churches of Christ (Table BX4)
6799.C3 Christian Congregation
Christian Conventions see BX9798.T85+
6799.C5 Christian Israelite Church
Christian Methodist Episcopal Church see BX8460+
6801-6843 Christian Reformed Church (Table BX1)
Offshoot of Dutch Reformed Church
Christian Science
6901 Periodicals. Serials
6903 Societies
Conventions
6905 General
6907 Local
6911 Directories
Collected works
6913 Several authors
6915 Individual authors
For Mrs. Eddy's works see BX6941.A+
6916 Bible selections and adaptations by Christian Science authors
6917 Study and teaching
History
6931 General and the United States
United States
6933.A-.W By state, A-W
6934.A-Z By city, A-Z
6935.A-Z Other countries, A-Z
General works

	Christian Science
	General works -- Continued
6941.A-Z	By Mary (Baker) Eddy. By title, A-Z
6943	By others
6945	Addresses, essays, lectures
6947	Other
6950	Christian Science healing
	Christian Science and the law see class K
6955	Controversial works against Christian Science
6958	Church organization. Manuals, etc.
6960	Service. Ritual. Liturgy
	Hymns in English see BV390
	Hymns in languages other than English see BV470+
	Individual churches. By place
6980	United States
6985	Other countries
	Biography
6990	Collective
	Individual
6995	Eddy, Mary Baker
6996.A-Z	Other, A-Z
	e.g.
6996.S7	Stetson, Augusta Emma (Simmons)
6997	Modifications of Christian Science
6997.A2	Periodicals
	Christian Science Parent Church see BX7577.F4+
	Church of Integration see BX7065
	Divine Science Church see BX7351
	Fellowship of the Universal Design see BX7577.F4+
7001	Christian Science - Christian Union
	Christian Spiritual Church see BX9798.S7
7003	Christian Union (Table BX3)
	Church of America, Liberal see BX7990.L4+
7008	Church of America, which is the Church of God (Table BX3)
7009	Church of American Science (Table BX3)
7012	Church of Christ (Holiness) (Table BX3)
	Church of Christ (Jones) see BX7012
	Church of Christ (Remnant Group) see BX8680.R3+
	Church of Christ (Temple Lot) see BX8680.T4+
	Church of Christ, Scientist see BX6901+
7013	Church of Christ in Africa (Table BX3)
7014	Church of Christ in China
7016	Church of Christ in Nigeria (Table BX3)
7018	Church of Daniel's Band (Table BX3)

7020 Church of God (Table BX3)
Class here general works on the bodies using Church of God in their name and also works not identifiable with any particular body
Church of God, International see BX6175+
Church of God (A. J. Tomlinson) see BX7050
Church of God (Abrahamic Faith) see BX6181+
7025-7027 Church of God (Anderson, Ind.) (Table BX2)
7029 Church of God (Apostolic) (Table BX3)
Church of God (Atlanta - Quarterman) see BX7042
Church of God (Atlanta - Holiness) see BX7080
Church of God (Belleville, Va.) see BX7052
Church of God (Chattanooga, Tenn.) see BX8750.O7+
7032-7034 Church of God (Cleveland, Tenn.) (Table BX2)
Church of God (Crowdy) see BX7052
Church of God (Dunkers) see BX7829.C4+
Church of God (General Assembly) see BX7032+
Church of God (Holdeman) see BX8129.C4
7038 Church of God (Holiness) (Table BX3)
Church of God (Homer A. Tomlinson) see BX7045
Church of God (Independent Holiness People) see BX7038
Church of God (Memphis, Tenn.) see BX7056
Church of God (Mennonite) see BX7054
Church of God (Mennonite -- Holdeman) see BX8129.C4
Church of God (Oregon, Ill.) see BX6181+
Church of God (Original) see BX8750.O7+
7042 Church of God (Quarterman) (Table BX3)
7045 Church of God (Queens Village, N.Y.) (Table BX3)
Church of God (Salem, W. Va.) see BX6135+
Church of God (Seventh Day), Denver, Colo. see BX6161+
Church of God (Seventh Day), Salem, W. Va. see BX6135+
Church of God (Spurling) see BX8750.O7+
Church of God (Stanberry, Mo.) see BX6161+
7050 Church of God (Tomlinson), 1923-1943 (Table BX3)
Church of God (Tomlinson), 1943-1952 see BX7058+
Church of God (Wakarusa, Ind.) see BX7054
Church of God (Winebrenner) see BX7095
7052 Church of God and Saints of Christ (Table BX3)
7054 Church of God as Organized by Christ (Table BX3)
7056 Church of God in Christ (Table BX3)
Church of God in Christ (Holdeman) see BX8129.C4
Church of God in Christ (Mason) see BX7056
Church of God in Christ (Mennonite) see BX8129.C4
Church of God in the Spirit see BX7097.C4
7058-7060 Church of God of Prophecy (Table BX2)
7061 Church of God of the Mountain Assembly (Table BX3)
7063 Church of Illumination (Table BX3)

7065 Church of Integration (Table BX3)
7065.5 Church of Jericho (Swaziland) (Table BX3)
Church of Jesus Christ see BX8680.C4+
Church of Jesus Christ (Bickertonites) see BX8680.B5+
Church of Jesus Christ (Cutlerites) see BX8680.C8+
Church of Jesus Christ (Strangites) see BX8680.S8+
Church of Jesus Christ of Latter-Day Saints see BX8601+
7066 Church of Nigeria (Table BX3)
7066.3 Church of North India (Table BX3)
7066.4 Church of Our Lord Jesus Christ of the Apostolic Faith (Table BX3)
7066.5 Church of South India (Table BX3)
Church of the Brethren see BX7801+
7067 Church of the Eternal Son (Table BX3)
7067.5 Church of the First Born (Table BX3)
7068 Church of the Living God, Christian Workers for Fellowship (Table BX3)
Church of the Living God, "The Pillar and Ground of Truth" see BX7990.H8+
7068.5 Church of the Lord (Aladura) (Table BX3)
Church of the Nazarene see BX8699.N3+
7068.7 Church of the Nazarites (Table BX3)
Church of the New Jerusalem see BX8701+
7069 Church of the New Name (Table BX3)
Church of the New Thought see BF638+
7071 Church of the Prophetess Nontetha (Table BX3)
Church of the Transforming Covenant see BX7577.F4+
Church of the United Brethren in Christ (New Constitution) see BX9875+
Church of the United Brethren in Christ (Old Constitution) see BX9877.1
Church of the Universal Design see BX7577.F4+
7075-7077 Churches of Christ (Table BX2)
7078 Churches of Christ in Christian Union (Table BX3)
7079 Churches of God, General Conference (Table BX3)
7080 Churches of God, Holiness (Table BX3)
Churches of God in Christ Jesus see BX6181+
7095 Churches of God in North America (Table BX3)
Churches of God in North America - Congregationalism
7097.C4 Congregation of God in the Spirit
7097.C6 Congregational Holiness Church
Congregationalism
Cf. BX9301+ Puritanism
Cf. BX9884+ United Church of Christ
7101 Periodicals. Serials
7105 Societies
Class historical societies with individual countries

Congregationalism -- Continued
Conventions. Conferences
Cf. BX7108.A+ Associations
7106 International
United States
7107 General
7108.A-Z Conferences and associations, A-Z
7109 Other countries
7111 Dictionaries. Encyclopedias
7113 Directories
Collected works
7115 Several authors
7117 Individual authors
Study and teaching
7119 General works
Individual seminaries see BV4070.A+
Sunday Schools (Church schools)
7121 Societies, conventions, etc.
7122 History
7123 General works. Organization
7124 Service books
7125 Textbooks, etc.
7127.A-Z Individual Sunday schools. By place, A-Z
History
7131 General works
7132 Addresses, essays, lectures
By region or country
America. North America
7133 General works
United States
7135 General works
By period
7136 17th-18th centuries
7137 19th-20th centuries
By region
7139 New England
For 17th-18th centuries see BX7136
7141 South
7143 Central
7145 West
7147.A-Z By nationality or race, A-Z
7148.A-.W By state, A-W
For associations see BX7108.A+
7149.A-Z By city, A-Z
Individual churches see BX7255

Congregationalism
History
By region or country
America. North America
United States -- Continued

7150 National Council of the Congregational Churches of the United States (1861-1931) (Table BX3)
Merged with the Christian Church in 1931 to form the General Council of the Congregational and Christian Churches of the United States

7150.4 General Council of the Congregational and Christian Churches of the United States (1931-1957) (Table BX3)
In 1940 the word "and" between the words Congregational and Christian was dropped
Merged with the Evangelical and Reformed Church in 1957 to form the United Church of Christ

7150.6 National Association of the Congregational Christian Churches (1955-) (Table BX3)
Formed in 1955 by Congregational churches not wanting to join in the formation of the United Church of Christ

Canada
7151 General works
7152.A-Z By region, province, etc., A-Z
7153.A-Z By city, A-Z

Mexico
7155 General works
7156.A-Z By region, state, etc., A-Z
7157.A-Z By city, A-Z

Central America
7160 General works
7161.A-Z By region or country, A-Z
7162.A-Z By city, A-Z

West Indies
7165 General works
7166.A-Z By region or country, A-Z
7167.A-Z By city, A-Z

South America
7171 General works
7172.A-Z By country, A-Z
7173.A-Z By city, A-Z

Europe
7175 General works
Great Britain. England
7176.A1 Societies. Collections, etc.
7176.A3-Z General works

Congregationalism
History
By region or country
Europe
Great Britain. England -- Continued
7177.A-Z By county, etc. (England), A-Z
7178.A-Z By city (England), A-Z
Ireland
7181.A1 Societies. Collections, etc.
7181.A3-Z General works
7182.A-Z By county, etc., A-Z
7183.A-Z By city, A-Z
Scotland
7185.A1 Societies. Collections, etc.
7185.A3-Z General works
7186.A-Z By region, etc., A-Z
7187.A-Z By city, A-Z
Wales
7191.A1 Societies. Collections, etc.
7191.A3-Z General works
7192.A-Z By county, etc., A-Z
7193.A-Z By city, A-Z
France
7195.A1 Societies. Collections, etc.
7195.A3-Z General works
7196.A-Z By region, department, etc., A-Z
7197.A-Z By city, A-Z
Germany
7201.A1 Societies. Collections, etc.
7201.A3-Z General works
7202.A-Z By state, etc., A-Z
7203.A-Z By city, A-Z
Italy
7205.A1 Societies. Collections, etc.
7205.A3-Z General works
7206.A-Z By region, province, etc., A-Z
7207.A-Z By city, A-Z
7210.A-Z Other European regions or countries, A-Z
Asia
7215 General works
7216.A-Z By region or country, A-Z
e.g.
7216.P5 Philippines
Africa
7220 General works
7221 South Africa
7222.A-Z Other, A-Z

Congregationalism
History
By region or country -- Continued
Australia
7225 General works
7226.A-Z Local, A-Z
e.g.
7226.N4 New South Wales
Oceania
7227 General works
7228.A-Z Local, A-Z
General works. Doctrines, etc.
7230 Early through 1800
7231 1801-1950
7231.2 1951-2000
7231.3 2001-
7232 Addresses, essays, lectures
Sermons. Tracts
Class sermons on special topics with the subject, especially biography and history
For sermons for children, young people, etc. see BV4310+
Cf. BX7115+ Collected works
7233.A1 Several authors
7233.A3-Z Individual authors. By author and title, A-Z
7234 Controversial works against Congregationalists
Creeds, confessions, covenants, catechisms, etc.
7235 Early through 1800
7236 1801-1950
7236.2 1951-2000
7236.3 2001-
7237 Service. Ritual. Liturgy
Hymns in English see BV395
Hymns in languages other than English see BV470+
Sacraments
Including theology, liturgy, rite
7238 General works
7239.A-Z Special sacraments, A-Z
7239.L6 Lord's Supper
Government and discipline
7240 General works
Trials
7242 General works. Procedure, etc.
7243.A-Z Special, A-Z
Clergy
7245 General works
7245.5 Salaries, pensions, etc.

Congregationalism
Government and discipline -- Continued
7246 Other church officers
7247 Benevolent work. Social work, welfare work, etc.
Special schools of doctrine
7250 The New England theology
7251 Hopkinsianism
7252.A-Z Other, A-Z
e.g.
7252.N5 New Haven theology (Taylorism)
7252.S4 Separates or Strict Congregationalists
Individual churches
Subarrange by place or by name if nonurban
7255 United States
7256 Great Britain
7257 Other countries
Biography
7259 Collective
7260.A-Z Individual, A-Z
e.g.
7260.B3 Beecher, Henry Ward
7260.B31 Beecher-Tilton case
7260.B33 Beecher, Lyman
7260.B9 Bushnell, Horace
7260.C79 Cotton, John
7260.E3 Edwards, Jonathan, 1703-1758
7260.E4 Edwards, Jonathan, 1745-1801
7260.F47 Finney, Charles Grandison
7260.F583 Forsyth, Peter Taylor
7260.G45 Gladden, Washington
7260.H6 Hopkins, Samuel
(7260.M3) Mather, Cotton
see F67
(7260.M4) Mather, Increase
see F67
7260.M555 Morgan, George Campbell
7260.M57 Morse, Jedidiah
7260.P3 Parker, Joseph
7260.S53 Shepard, Thomas
7283 Deutsche Evangelische Kirche in Chile (Table BX3)
Deutsche Evangelische Kirche von Rio Grande do Sul
7287.A1 Periodicals. Serials
(7287.A15-.A2) Yearbooks
see BX7287.A1
Conferences
7287.A3-.A39 General
7287.A4A-.A4Z Special. By name, A-Z

	Deutsche Evangelische Kirche von Rio Grande do Sul -- Continued
7287.A5	Other documents: Constitution, discipline, etc. By date
7287.A6-Z	General works. History, doctrine, liturgy
7287.A6-.A69	Official works
7287.32-.5	By region or country
	United States
	General works see BX7287+
7287.4.A-.W	By state, A-W
7287.5.A-Z	Other regions or countries, A-Z
7288	Sermons. Tracts. Addresses. Essays
	Individual churches. By place
7288.8	United States
7288.9	Other regions or countries
	Biography
7289.A1	Collective
7289.A3-Z	Individual, A-Z
	e.g.
7289.R6	Rotermund, Wilhelm
	Deutsche Evangelische Synode von Nordamerika see BX7901+
7301-7343	Disciples of Christ. Campbellites. Christians (Table BX1 modified)
	Cf. BX6751+ Christian Church
	Biography
7341	Collective
7343.A-Z	Individual, A-Z
	e.g.
7343.C2	Campbell, Alexander
7343.S8	Stone, Barton Warren
7350	Divine, Father (the man and his following) (Table BX3)
	Founder of the Peace Mission Movement
7351	Divine Science Church (Table BX3)
	Doukhobors see BX7433
	Dowieism. Christian Catholic Church
7401	Periodicals. Societies
7405	Conferences, etc.
7409	Collected works
7415	General works. History
7420	Liturgy and ritual
7425.A-Z	Individual churches. By place, A-Z, or by name if nonurban
7430.A-Z	Biography, A-Z
	e.g.
7430.A1	Collective
7430.D7	Dowie, John Alexander
7433	Dukhobors
7435	Dukhobors - Evangelical and Reformed Church

Dukhobars - Evangelical and Reformed Church -- Continued
Dunkards see BX7801+
7435.E44 Église de Jésus-Christ sur la terre par le prophète Simon Kimbangu
7435.E443 Église du Christ au Zaïre
7435.E45-.E458 Église évangélique du Cameroun
7435.E459 Église évangélique du Gabon
7435.E4593 Église néo-apostolique du Zaïre
Église Orthodox Apostolique Haïtienne see BX5999.5
7435.E4595 Église protestante unie de Belgique (Verenigde Protestantse Kerk in België)
7435.E46 Églises réformées évangéliques indépendantes
7435.E5-.E58 Elim Foursquare Gospel Alliance (Great Britain) (Table BX4)
Cf. BX7990.I6+ International Church of the Foursquare Gospel
7435.E77 Eternal Sacred Order of the Morning Star and St. Michael Star Fountain of Life, Mount Zion
Ethiopian Church Mekane Yesus see BX8063.E85
Evangelical Alliance, Ukrainian see BX9798.U6
7451-7493 Evangelical and Reformed Church (Table BX1 modified)
Founded by the union in 1934 of the Reformed Church in the United States (German Reformed) and the Evangelical Synod of North America. Merged in 1957 with General Council of the Congregational Christian Churches to form the United Church of Christ
Cf. BX9884+ United Church of Christ
7455 Documents. Conferences, etc.
Synods
7470.A2 General works
7470.A4-Z Individual synods
Classes
7470.5.A2 General works
7470.5.A4-Z Individual classes
7501-7543 Evangelical Association of North America. Evangelical Church (Table BX1 modified)
Founded by Jacob Albright. The Evangelical Church was formed in 1923 by the reunion of the Association and the United Evangelical Church. In 1946 merged with the Church of the United Brethren in Christ (New Constitution) to form the Evangelical United Brethren Church
Cf. BX7556 Evangelical United Brethren Church
7523.4 Relations with other churches
Evangelical Church Mekane Yesus see BX8063.E85
7545.E65-.E658 Evangelical Church of England (Table BX4)
Evangelical Church of Italy see BX6600.C4+

7545.E8	Evangelical Congregational Church Composed of congregations of the United Evangelical Church that rejected the reunion of that body with the Evangelical Association of North America
7546	Evangelical Church of North America (Table BX3)
7546.6	Evangelical Convention Church (Table BX3)
7547	Evangelical Covenant Church of America. Svenska evangeliska missionsförbundet i Amerika (Table BX3)
7547.4	Evangelical Covenant Church of Canada (Table BX3)
7547.8	Evangelical Free Church Association (Table BX3) Formerly Norwegian and Danish Evangelical Free Church Association of North America. In 1950 merged into Evangelical Free Church of America
7548	Evangelical Free Church of America (Table BX3)
	Evangelical Mission Covenant Church of America see BX7547
	Evangelical Protestant Church see BX7850
	Evangelical Synod of North America see BX7901+
	Evangelical Synod of the West see BX7901+
7555.E5-.E58	Evangelical Union (Table BX4) Founded by James Morison of Scotland
7555.E58A-.E58Z	Biography, A-Z e.g.
7555.E58A1-.E58A5	Collective
7555.E58M6	Morison, James
7556	Evangelical United Brethren Church (Table BX3) On April 23, 1968, the Evangelical United Brethren Church was united with the Methodist Church (United States) to form the United Methodist Church (United States)
	Evangelische Gemeinschaft see BX7501+
7561	Evangelische Kirche Berlin-Brandenburg-Schlesische Oberlausitz (Table BX3)
7563	Evangelische Kirche der altpreussischen Union (Table BX3)
	Evangelische Kirche der Kirchenprovinz Sachsen
7563.84	General works
	Biography
7563.88.A1-.A5	Collective
7563.88.A6-Z	Individual, A-Z
7564	Evangelische Kirche der Union (EKU)
7566	Evangelische Kirche des Gorlitzer Kirchengebietes (Evangelische Kirche von Schlesien)
7567	Evangelische Kirche im Rheinland (Table BX3)
7568	Evangelische Kirche in Berlin-Brandenburg
	Evangelische Kirche in Berlin-Brandenburg (Berlin-West)
7568.5	General works
	Biography
7568.58.A1-.A5	Collective
7568.58.A6-Z	Individual, A-Z

Evangelische Kirche in Deutschland see BX4844.6
7568.7 Evangelische Kirche in Hessen und Nassau
7569 Evangelische Kirche von Kurhessen-Waldeck
7569.7 Evangelische Kirche von Westfalen (Table BX3)
7570 Evangelische (Landes) Kirche in Baden (Table BX3)
Including Vereinigte Evangelisch-Protestantische Landeskirche Badens
7570.6 Evangelische Landeskirche Anhalts (Table BX3)
7571 Evangelische Landeskirche Greifswald (Pommersche Evangelische Kirche)
7571.7 Evangelische Landeskirche in Württemberg
7575 Familists. Family of Love
Hendrick Niclaes, John Etherington, etc.
Cf. BX7990.G8 Grindletonians
Familists - Free Congregations
7577.F3 Fareinistes
7577.F4-.F48 Fellowship of the Universal Design of Life (Table BX4)
Christian Science Parent Church, Church of the Universal Design. Founded by Annie C. Bill
7577.F485 Fiangonan'i Jesoa Kristy Madagasikara
7577.F5-.F58 Fire-Baptized Holiness Association of America
7577.F6 Free Christian Zion Church of Christ
Free Church of England see BX6069.G7
7577.F67 Free Church of Finland (Suomen Vapaakirkko)
7577.F7 Free Church of God in Christ
Free Congregations (Germany). Freie Gemeinden
7580 General works. History
7582 Sunday schools (Church schools)
Including textbooks
7583.A-Z Biography, A-Z
e.g.
7583.U5 Ulich, Leberecht
Free Magyar Reformed Church in America see BX9499.3
(7590) Free Religious Association
see BR21.F8+
7593 French Prophets
Including Lacy's prophesies
Cf. DC127.C3 Camisards
French Protestant Church (England) see BX9458.G7
French Protestant Church (England) - Friends
7597.F83 Fria missionen (Finland)
Friends. Society of Friends. Quakers
7601 Periodicals. Serials
7605 Associations (General)
For historical associations, societies, etc., prefer BX7635.A1, BX7676.A1, etc.
7606 Almanacs

Friends. Society of Friends. Quakers -- Continued
Conferences, yearly meetings, etc.
7606.5 International
American
7607.A1-.A2 General
7607.A3-.A39 "Orthodox"
7607.A4-.A5 "Hicksite"
7607.A6-Z Local
Under each:
(1) Orthodox
Including united meetings resulting from the merger of Orthodox and Hicksite groups
(2) Hicksite
e.g.
Philadelphia yearly meeting (Orthodox) and Philadelphia yearly meeting (established 1955)
7607.P4A3 Minutes. By date
7607.P4A4 Discipline. By date
7607.P4A7-.P4Z History
Philadelphia monthly meeting (Orthodox) and Philadelphia monthly meeting (established 1955)
7607.P45A3 Minutes. By date
7607.P45A4 Discipline. By date
7607.P45A7-.P45Z History
Philadelphia yearly meeting (Hicksite)
7607.P5A3 Minutes. By date
7607.P5A4 Discipline. By date
7607.P5A7-.P5Z History
Philadelphia monthly meeting (Hicksite)
7607.P55A3 Minutes. By date
7607.P55A4 Discipline. By date
7607.P55A7-.P55Z History
7608 Other regions or countries
7611 Dictionaries. Encyclopedias
7613 Directories
Collected works
7615 Several authors
7617.A-Z Individual authors. By author and title, A-Z
Including religious works of William Penn and George Fox
For Penn's Treatises of oaths see BX7748.O2
Study and teaching
7619 General works
Individual seminaries see BV4070.A+
First-day schools
7621 Periodicals. Societies. Congresses
7623 General works. Organization, etc.

Friends. Society of Friends. Quakers
Study and teaching
First-day schools -- Continued
7625 Textbooks, etc.
7627.A-Z Individual First-day schools. By place, A-Z
History
General works
7630 Early through 1800
7631 1801-1950
7631.2 1951-2000
7631.3 2001-
7632 Addresses, essays, lectures
By region or country
7633 America. North America
United States
7635.A1 Periodicals. Societies
7635.A3-Z General works
By period
7636 17th-18th centuries
7637 19th-20th centuries
By region
7639 New England
7641 South
7642 Central
7645 West
7648.A-.W By state, A-W
7649.A-.W By city, district, etc., A-Z
Individual meeting houses see BX7780
Canada
7650 General works
7652.A-Z By division, province, etc., A-Z
7653.A-Z By city, A-Z
Mexico
7655 General works
7656.A-Z By division, state, etc., A-Z
7657.A-Z By city, A-Z
Central America
7660 General works
7661.A-Z By division, country, etc., A-Z
7662.A-Z By city, A-Z
West Indies
7665 General works
7666.A-Z By division, country, etc., A-Z
7667.A-Z By city, A-Z
South America
7671 General works
7672.A-Z By country, A-Z

Friends. Society of Friends. Quakers
History
By region or country
America. North America
South America -- Continued
7673.A-Z By city, A-Z
Europe
7675 General works
Great Britain. England
7676.A1 Periodicals. Societies
General works
7676.A2 Early through 1800
7676.A3-Z 1801-1950
7676.2 1951-2000
7676.3 2001-
7677.A-Z By region, county, etc. (England), A-Z
7678.A-Z By city, district, etc. (England), A-Z
Ireland
7681.A1 Periodicals. Societies
General works
7681.A2 Early through 1800
7681.A3-Z 1801-1950
7681.2 1951-2000
7681.3 2001-
7682.A-Z By region, county, etc., A-Z
7683.A-Z By city, district, etc., A-Z
Scotland
7685.A1 Periodicals. Societies
General works
7685.A2 Early through 1800
7685.A3-Z 1801-1950
7685.2 1951-2000
7685.3 2001-
7686.A-Z By region, county, etc., A-Z
7687.A-Z By city, district, etc., A-Z
Wales
7691.A1 Periodicals. Societies
General works
7691.A2 Early through 1800
7691.A3-Z 1801-1950
7691.2 1951-2000
7691.3 2001-
7692.A-Z By region, county, etc., A-Z
7693.A-Z By city, district, etc., A-Z
France
7695.A1 Periodicals. Societies
General works

Friends. Society of Friends. Quakers
History
By region or country
Europe
France
General works -- Continued
7695.A2 Early through 1800
7695.A3-Z 1801-1950
7695.2 1951-2000
7695.3 2001-
7696.A-Z By region, department, etc., A-Z
7697.A-Z By city, district, etc., A-Z
Germany
7701.A1 Periodicals. Societies
General works
7701.A2 Early through 1800
7701.A3-Z 1801-1950
7701.2 1951-2000
7701.3 2001-
7702.A-Z By region, state, etc., A-Z
7703.A-Z By city, district, etc., A-Z
Italy
7705.A1 Periodicals. Societies
General works
7705.A2 Early through 1800
7705.A3-Z 1801-1950
7705.2 1951-2000
7705.3 2001-
7706.A-Z By region, province, etc., A-Z
7707.A-Z By city, district, etc., A-Z
7710.A-Z Other European regions or countries, A-Z
Asia
7715 General works
7716.A-Z By region or country, A-Z
e.g.
7716.P5 Philippines
Africa
7720 General works
7721 South Africa
7723.A-Z Other, A-Z
Australia
7725 General works
7726.A-Z Local, A-Z
New Zealand
7726.5 General works
7726.6.A-Z Local, A-Z
Oceania

Friends. Society of Friends. Quakers
History
By region or country
Oceania -- Continued
7727 General works
7728.A-Z Local, A-Z
General works. Doctrine, etc.
7730 Early through 1800
7731 1801-1950
7731.2 1951-2000
7731.3 2001-
7732 Addresses, essays, lectures
Sermons. Tracts
Class sermons on special topics with the subject, especially biography and history
For sermons for children, young people, etc. see BV4310+
Cf. BX7615+ Collected works
7733.A1 Several authors
7733.A3-Z Individual authors. By author and title, A-Z
Controversial works against the Friends
7734.A2 Early through 1800
7734.A3-Z 1801-1950
7735 1951-2000
7735.3 2001-
7737 Service. Ritual. Liturgy
Hymns in English see BV400
Hymns in languages other than English see BV470+
7738 Spiritual life
Government and discipline
Prefer individual branches
For individual yearly meetings see BX7606.5+
7740 General works
7743.A-Z Proceedings against individual persons, A-Z
e.g.
7743.K4 Keith, George
Ministry
7745 General works
7746 Women
7747 Benevolent work. Social work, public welfare, etc.
7748.A-Z Other special topics, A-Z
7748.A77 Art
7748.B2 Baptism
7748.B8 Business
7748.C45 Children
7748.C5 Civil government
Conscientious objectors see UB341+

Friends. Society of Friends. Quakers
Other special topics, A-Z -- Continued
Consensus see BX7748.D43

7748.C7 Costume
7748.C8 Creeds
7748.D43 Decision-making
Including consensus and sense of the meeting
7748.D73 Dreams
7748.E35 Economics
Cf. BX7748.B8 Business
7748.E4 Education
Cf. LC570+ Friends' schools
7748.E97 Experience (Religion)
7748.G39 Gay marriage
7748.H2 Hat customs
7748.I5 Inner light
7748.I64 Integrity
7748.I65 International activities
Cf. BV2535 Missions
7748.L3 Language
7748.L37 Liberty
7748.L4 Literary work of Friends
7748.L5 Literature, Attitudes toward
7748.M5 Miracles
7748.M8 Music and singing, Attitudes toward
7748.M9 Mysticism
7748.N37 Nature
7748.O2 Oaths
7748.P43 Peace
7748.P76 Prophecy
7748.R3 Race problems
Religious experience see BX7748.E97
7748.S2 Sacredness of human life
7748.S4 Self-defense
Sense of the meeting see BX7748.D43
7748.S5 Silence
Slavery in the United States see E441
Social problems see HN37.F9
7748.T2 Taxation
7748.T5 Temperance
7748.T54 Testimony
7748.U5 Unemployment, Attitude toward
7748.W2 War
7748.W64 Women

Individual branches of Friends
For Society of Friends (Orthodox) see BX7601+

Friends. Society of Friends. Quakers
Individual branches of Friends -- Continued
Hicksite. Liberal
For conferences, yearly meetings, etc. see BX7607.A4+
7752 History and other general
Progressive
7761 Conferences, etc.
7762 History and other general
Conservative. Wilburites
7765 Conferences, etc.
7766 History and other general
Primitive Friends
7771 Conferences, etc.
7772 History and other general
7775.A-Z Other, A-Z
e.g.
7775.A6 Anti-Slavery Friends (Indiana)
Individual meeting houses. By place
7780 United States
7783 Other countries
Biography
Collective
7790 Series
7791 General works
7793 Women
7795.A-Z Individual, A-Z
e.g.
7795.A6 Allen, William
Bunyan, John see PR3331
7795.F7 Fox, George
7795.G7 Grellet, Stephen
7795.G85 Gurney, Joseph John
7795.H5 Hicks, Elias
7795.J55 Jones, Rufus Matthew
7795.K3 Keith, George
Cf. BX7743.K4 The case of George Keith
Penn, William see F152.2
7795.W5 Wilbur, John
7795.W7 Woolman, John
Friends - German Baptist Brethren
7800.F35-.F358 Fukuin Dendō Kyōdan (Table BX4)

Friends - German Baptist Brethren -- Continued

7800.F86-.F868 Fundamentalist churches (Table BX4)

Class here general works on Fundamentalist churches and works on Fundamentalist churches not identifiable with any particular body

For Fundamentalist theology and movement in general see BT82.2

7800.G425 Geredja Kalimantan Evangelis

7800.G428 Geredja Kristen Indonesia Indramaju

7800.G429 Geredja Kristen Protestan Simalungun

7800.G43 Geredja Masehi Indjili Minahasa

7800.G44 Geredja Masehi Indjili Sangihe dan Talaud

7800.G447 Gereja Kemah Injil Indonesia

7800.G45 Gereja Kristen Indonesia

7800.G455 Gereja Kristen Jawa

7800.G46 Gereja Kristen Jawa Jakarta

7800.G463 Gereja Kristen Jawa Nehemia

7800.G467 Gereja Kristen Muria Indonesia

7800.G47 Gereja Kristen Protestan di Bali

7800.G473 Gereja Kristen Sulawesi Tengah

7800.G475 Gereja Kristen Sumba

7800.G476 Gereja Masehi Injili di Timor

7800.G477 Gereja Methodist Indonesia

7800.G48 Gereja Pantekosta Di Indonesia

7800.G488 Gereja Protestan di Bagian Barat

7800.G49 Gereja Protestan Maluku

7800.G65 Gereja Toraja

7801-7843 German Baptist Brethren. Church of the Brethren. "Dunkards" or "Dunkers" (Table BX1 modified)

7829.A-Z Individual branches, A-Z

7829.B5-.B58 Brethren Church (Ashland, Ohio) (Table BX4)

7829.B6-.B68 The Brethren Church (Progressive Dunkers) (Table BX4)

7829.C4-.C48 Church of God (New Dunkers) (Table BX4)

7829.N3-.N38 National Fellowship of Brethren Churches. Fellowship of Grace Brethren Churches (Table BX4)

7829.O4-.O48 Old German Baptist Brethren (Table BX4)

7850 German Evangelical Protestant Church of North America. Evangelical Protestant Church of North America

7860.A-Z Individual churches. By city, A-Z

Biography

7865.A1 Collective

7865.A3-Z Individual

7901-7943 German Evangelical Synod of North America. Evangelical Synod of North America (Table BX1)

German Reformed Church see BX9551+

German Reformed Church - Lutheran churches

7990.G6 God's Christian Church

German Reformed Church - Lutheran churches -- Continued

7990.G65	Gortonites (Samuel Gorton)
7990.G67	Gospel of God Church
	Gospel Trumpet work see BX7025+
7990.G8	Grindletonians
7990.H4	Hahnische Gemeinschaft. Michelhahnites (Johann Michael Hahn
7990.H46	Han'guk Kurisudo ui Kyohoe
	Harmonists see HX656.H2
7990.H47-.H478	Harris Church (Côte d'Ivoire) (Table BX4)
	Biography
7990.H478A6-.H478Z	Individual, A-Z e.g.
7990.H478H37	Harris, William Wade
7990.H48	Hay Awetaranakan Ekeghets'i
7990.H5	Hephzibah Faith Missionary Association
	Holiness churches Class here general works on the Holiness movement and works not identifiable with any particular body Cf. BX8762+ Pentecostal churches
7990.H6A1-.H6A5	Periodicals. Societies, etc.
7990.H6A6-.H6Z	General works. History, doctrine, polity. Sermons
7990.H615	African American Holiness
7990.H62	Biography
	Special branches
	Church of Christ (Holiness) see BX7012
	Church of God (Holiness) see BX7038
	Church of the Nazarene see BX8699.N3+
	Churches of Christ in Christian Union see BX7078
	Churches of God, Holiness (Georgia) see BX7080
	Congregational Holiness Church see BX7097.C6
	Fire-Baptised Holiness Association of America see BX7577.F5+
7990.H65-.H658	Holiness Christian Church (Table BX4)
7990.H67-.H678	Holiness Church (Table BX4)
7990.H69	Korea Christian Holiness Church
	Pilgrim Holiness Church see BX8795.P45+
	Holy Spirit Association for the Unification of World Christianity see BX9750.S4+
7990.H73	Hōrinesu Kyōkai (Japan)
(7990.H75)	House of David see BX6184.5
7990.H8-.H88	House of God, which is the Church of the Living God, the Pillar and Ground of Truth, Inc. (Table BX4)
7990.H95	Huria Kristen Batak Protestan
	Hutterian Brethren (Rifton, N.Y.) see BX8129.B6+
	Hutterite Brethren see BX8129.H8

German Reformed Church - Lutheran churches -- Continued
7990.I37-.I378 Iesu Fukuin Kyōdan (Table BX4)
7990.I4 Iglesia Apostólica de la Fe en Cristo Jesús
7990.I42 Iglesia Christiana Evangélica
7990.I43 Iglesia Española Reformada Episcopal
7990.I45 Iglesia Evangélica Española
7990.I48 Iglesia ni Cristo (Philippines)
7990.I53-.I538 Independent Fundamental Churches of America (Table BX4)
7990.I55 Independent Greek Church (Canada)
7990.I57-.I578 Indian Shaker Church (Table BX4)
7990.I6-.I68 International Church of the Foursquare Gospel (Table BX4)
Cf. BX7435.E5+ Elim Foursquare Gospel Alliance
7990.I68 Biography
e.g.
7990.I68M3 McPherson, Aimee Semple
7990.I685 International Churches of Christ. Boston Movement
7990.I69 International Commission of Charismatic Churches
7990.I75 International Council of Community Churches
7990.I85 Israel of God's Church White Horse Army
7990.J3 Jansonists (Erik Jansson)
Cf. F549.B6 Bishop Hill Colony (Collective settlements)
Jehovah's Witnesses see BX8525+
7990.J5 Jezreelites (James Joershom Jezreel)
7990.K25 al-Kanīsah al Injīlīyah (Egypt)
7990.K3 Katharist (George Bessonet)
7990.K47 Khritsačhak Phra Phọnchai (Church of Christ in Thailand)
7990.K53-.K538 Kidokkyo Taehan Pogŭm Kyohoe (Table BX4)
7990.K57 Kirisuto Dōshinkai
7990.K58 Kirisutokyō Dōjin Shadan
7990.K6 Kodesh Church of Immanuel
7990.K67 Kościół Ewangelicko-Unijny w Polsce
7990.L2 Labadists (Jean de Labadie)
7990.L4-.L48 Liberal Church of America (Table BX4)
7990.L5 Liberal Reformed Catholic American Church of America
7990.L63 Local Church
Lutheran churches
8001 Periodicals
8003 Societies
8004 Congresses
e.g.
8004.L8 Lutheran World Convention
8004.L9 Lutheran World Federation
8005 Documents
Prefer the country divisions
8007 Dictionaries. Encyclopedias
8009 Directories. Yearbooks. Almanacs. Calendars
Collected works

Lutheran churches
Collected works -- Continued
8011.A1 Several authors
8011.A3-Z Individual authors
8011.5 Radio programs. Motion picture and television presentations
Study and teaching
8012 General works
Individual seminaries see BV4070.A+
Sunday schools (Church schools)
Including religious work of the Christian day school
8013 General works. Organization, etc.
8013.A1 Societies, conventions, etc.
8014 Service books
8015 Textbooks, etc.
8016.A-Z Individual Sunday schools. By place, A-Z
History
Cf. BR300+ Reformation
8018 General works
By region or country
Germany
Including Vereinigte Evangelisch-Lutherische Kirche Deutschlands
For United (uniert) Churches, see the Church in Class BX
For Evangelische Kirche in Deutschlands see BX4844.6
For Reformed Churches see BX9460+
8020 General works
8022.A-Z Individual branches, territorial churches, etc. By place, A-Z
e.g.
8022.B74 Bremen
East Prussia see BX7563
Hamburg (City and state) see BX8023.H28
8022.H3 Hanover
Hesse see BX7568.7; BX7569
Prussia see BX7563
8022.S3 Saxony
For Evangelische Kirche der Kirchenprovinz Sachsen see BX7563.8+
West Prussia see BX7563
Westphalia see BX7563; BX7569.7
8022.W7 Württemberg
8023.A-Z By city, A-Z
e.g.
Bremen see BX8022.B74
8023.H28 Hamburg
Hanover see BX8022.H3

Lutheran churches
History
By region or country -- Continued
8025 Austria
8025.2 Czech Republic
8025.3 Hungary
Poland
8025.5 General works
8025.6.A-Z Individual branches, synods, etc., of Lutherans, A-Z
8025.7 Romania
Russia. Soviet Union. Former Soviet republics
8027 General works
8027.5.A-Z Local, A-Z
e.g.
8027.5.E87 Estonia
Finland
8029 General works
8030.A-Z Local, A-Z
Scandinavia
8031 General works
Denmark. Danske Folkekirke
8033 General works
8034.A-Z Local, A-Z
Iceland. Tjodkirkja Íslands
8035 General works
8036.A-Z Local, A-Z
Norway. Norske Kirke
8037 General works
8038.A-Z Local, A-Z
8038.5.A-Z Other branches, synods, etc., of Lutherans, A-Z
8038.5.N67 Norske evangelisk-lutherske frikirke
Sweden. Svenska kyrkan
8039 General works
8040.A-Z Local, A-Z
8040.5.A-Z Other branches, synods, etc., of Lutherans, A-Z
8040.5.E85 Evangelisk-lutherska kyrkan i Sverige
America. United States
For other countries see BX8063.A+
8041.A1-.A5 General conferences, documents, etc.
8041.A6-Z General works
United States
8042.A-Z By region or state, A-Z
8043.A-Z By city, A-Z
For individual churches see BX8076

Lutheran churches
History
By region or country
America. United States
United States -- Continued
Individual branches, synods, etc., of Lutherans
For regional jurisdictions of branches located entirely outside of the United States prefer classification with country
8043.5 Mergers. Federations
Unless specified, all subsidiary synods are in BX8048.4+
8044 General Synod of the Evangelical Lutheran Church in the United States of America
8045 United Synod of the Evangelical Lutheran Church in the South
8046 General Council of the Evangelical Lutheran Church in North America
Evangelical Lutheran Church of America see BX8054
8047 Evangelical Lutheran Synodical Conference of North America
American Lutheran Church (1930-1960)
8047.2 General works
8047.3.A-Z Districts, A-Z
8047.5 American Lutheran Conference
American Lutheran Church (1961-1987)
8047.7 General works
8047.8.A-Z Districts, A-Z
8048 United Lutheran Church in America (1918-1963)
Merged with the Lutheran Church in America in 1963
For local synods see BX8061.A+
8048.2 Lutheran Church in America (1963-1987)
For local synods see BX8061.A+
8048.3 Evangelical Lutheran Church in America (1987-)
For local synods see BX8061.A+
Synods on a linguistic basis other than German
Scandinavian Lutherans
Swedes
8048.4 General works
8048.5 Early history (Delaware and Pennsylvania)
Augustana Evangelical Lutheran Church
8049 General works
8049.1.A-Z Individual conferences, A-Z
e.g.
8049.1.M6 Minnesota Conference

Lutheran churches
History
By region or country
America. United States
United States
Individual branches, synods, etc., of Lutherans
Mergers. Federations
Synods on a linguistic basis other than German
Scandinavian Lutherans -- Continued
Norwegians
8050 General works
8051 Hauge's Norwegian Evangelical Lutheran Synod
8052 Synod for the Norwegian Evangelical Lutheran Church in America
8053 United Norwegian Lutheran Church of America
8054 Evangelical Lutheran Church of America
Formerly Norwegian Lutheran Church of America
8055.A-Z Other Norwegian branches, A-Z
8055.E9 Evangelical Lutheran Synod
Formerly Norwegian Synod of the American Evangelical Lutheran Church
8055.L8 Lutheran Free Church
Formerly Norwegian Lutheran Free Church
Norwegian Synod of the American Evangelical Lutheran Church see BX8055.E9
Danes
8056 General works
8057 Danish Evangelical Lutheran Church in North America
8058 United Evangelical Lutheran Church in America
Formerly United Danish Evangelical Lutheran Church in America
8059 Icelanders
8060.A-Z Other national or racial groups, A-Z
e.g.
African Americans see BX8060.N5
Blacks see BX8060.N5
8060.D8 Dutch
8060.E7 Estonians
8060.F5 Finns

	Lutheran churches
	History
	By region or country
	America. United States
	United States
	Individual branches, synods, etc., of Lutherans
	Mergers. Federations
	Synods on a linguistic basis other than German
	Other national or racial groups, A-Z -- Continued
8060.L5	Letts
8060.N5	Negroes. Blacks. African Americans
8060.S55	Slovaks
8061.A-Z	Other synods, A-Z Preferably by state
8061.A85	Association of Free Lutheran Congregations (U.S.)
8061.C4	Evangelical Lutheran Synod in the Central States
8061.C5	Chicago Synod of the Evangelical Lutheran Church
8061.F55	Florida Synod of the United Lutheran Church in America
8061.G4	Georgia-Alabama Synod of the United Lutheran Church in America
8061.I67	Olive Branch Evangelical Lutheran Synod of Indiana
8061.I8	Evangelical Lutheran Synod of Iowa and other States
8061.I8A1-.I8A5	Proceedings. Documents, etc.
8061.I8A6-.I8A7	General works
8061.I82-.I89	Districts (alphabetically) e.g.
8061.I85	Northern
8061.M67	Lutheran Church in America. Minnesota Synod
8061.M7	Lutheran Church--Missouri Synod Formerly Evangelical Lutheran Synod of Missouri, Ohio, and other States
8061.M7A1-.M7A5	Proceedings. Documents, etc.
8061.M7A6-.M7Z	General works
	Districts
8061.M72	Central
8061.M723	Eastern
8061.M7235	Northwest
8061.M7236	Northwestern
8061.M724	Southeastern
8061.M725	Southern

Lutheran churches
History
By region or country
America. United States
United States
Individual branches, synods, etc., of Lutherans
Mergers. Federations
Other synods, A-Z
Lutheran Church--Missouri Synod
Districts -- Continued

8061.M73 Western
8061.M735 Atlantic
8061.M74 California and Nevada
8061.M745 Colorado
8061.M75 English
Illinois
8061.M76 General works
8061.M762 Central Illinois
8061.M763 Northern Illinois
8061.M764 Southern Illinois
8061.M765 Iowa
8061.M77 Kansas
8061.M773 Michigan
8061.M777 Minnesota
8061.M778 Nebraska
8061.M78 North Dakota and Montana
8061.M7815 Oklahoma
8061.M782 Ontario
8061.M783 South Dakota
8061.M785 Texas
8061.M788 North Wisconsin
8061.M79 South Wisconsin
8061.M8 English Evangelical Lutheran Synod of Missouri and other states
8061.N2 Nebraska Synod of the Lutheran Church in America
8061.N78 United Lutheran Synod of New York and New England
Formerly Evangelical Lutheran Ministerium of the State of New York and Adjacent States and Countries
8061.N8 Evangelical Lutheran Synod of North Carolina
Evangelical Lutheran Synod of Ohio and other States
8061.O312A2-.O312A35 Proceedings. Documents, etc.
8061.O312A5-.O312Z General works

BX

Lutheran churches
History
By region or country
America. United States
United States
Individual branches, synods, etc., of Lutherans
Mergers. Federations
Other synods, A-Z
Evangelical Lutheran Synod of Ohio and other States -- Continued

8061.O314-.O39 Districts
e.g.
8061.O314 Eastern
8061.O315 Northern
8061.O317 Western
8061.P2 Pacific Synod of the Evangelical Lutheran Church
8061.P22 Lutheran Church in America. Pacific Northwest Synod
8061.P38 Central Pennsylvania Synod of the Lutheran Church in America
8061.P4 Evangelical Lutheran Ministerium of Pennsylvania and Adjacent States
8061.P52 Eastern Pennsylvania Synod of the Lutheran Church in America
8061.P54 Southeastern Pennsylvania Synod
8061.S6 South Carolina Synod
8061.S63 South Dakota Synod
8061.S65 Southeastern Synod of the Lutheran Church in America
8061.T5 Evangelical Lutheran Tennessee Synod
8061.T55 Lutheran Church in America. Texas-Louisiana Synod
8061.W6 Wisconsin Evangelical Lutheran Synod. Minnesota District
Formerly Evangelical Lutheran Joint Synod of Wisconsin and Other States
8063.A-Z Lutheran Church in other regions or countries, A-Z
Including national and ethnic groups
e.g.
8063.B77 Brazil
Estonia see BX8027.5.E87
8063.E85 Ethiopia
8063.L48 Liberia
Poland see BX8025.5+
8063.P6 Portugal
8063.S7 South Africa

Lutheran churches
History
By region or country
Lutheran Church in other regions or countries, A-Z -- Continued
8063.Y8 Yugoslavia
8063.5.A-Z By national and ethnic groups outside their native countries, A-Z
e.g.
8063.5.L5 Letts
8063.7.A-Z Relations with other churches, A-Z
8063.7.A1 General works
8063.7.C3 Catholic Church
8063.7.C5 Church of England
Cf. BX5004.4 Relations with the Anglican Communion
8063.7.O78 Orthodox Eastern Church
(8063.7.P7) Presbyterian Church
see BX9171.L8
8063.7.R4 Reformed Church
General works on Lutheranism. Doctrine, church government, etc.
8064 Early to 1800
8065 1801-1950
8065.2 1951-2000
8065.3 2001-
8065.5 Charismatic movement
Sermons. Tracts. Addresses. Essays
Class sermons on special topics with the subject, especially biography and history
For Luther's sermons see BR332.S3+
For sermons for children, young people, etc. see BV4310+
For sermons on the Catechism see BX8070.L8
Cf. BX8011.A+ Collected works
8066.A1 Several authors
8066.A3-Z Individual authors. By author and title, A-Z
Liturgy and ritual
8067.A1 General works. History, treatises, etc.
General service books
8067.A2 German
8067.A3 English
8067.A4 Norwegian
8067.A45 Swedish
8067.A5A-.A5Z Other languages, A-Z
8067.A6-Z Other special, A-Z
8067.A7 Advent services
8067.A77 Altar guild manuals

Lutheran churches
Liturgy and ritual
Other special, A-Z -- Continued
8067.C6 Collects
8067.C7 Order of confession
8067.D3 Daily office book
8067.E7 Epistles
For sermons and other lessons on these see BX8066.A+
8067.F3 Family service books
8067.G45 General intercessions. Prayer of the Faithful
8067.G67 Good Friday service
8067.G7 Gospels
For sermons and other lessons on these see BX8066.A+
8067.L4 Lectionary
8067.M5 Minister's manuals
8067.O33 Occasional services
8067.O7 Orisons
8067.P69 Prayer books for seminarians
Prayer of the Faithful see BX8067.G45
8067.P7 Prayers
8067.P8 Psalter
Worship planning
8067.2 General works
8067.3 Church year worship planning
Hymns in English see BV410
Hymns in languages other than English see BV470+
Catechisms, creeds, etc.
8068.A1 General works
Texts
Book of Concord
8068.A2 German editions. By date
8068.A3 English editions. By date
8068.A5A-.A5Z Other languages. By language, A-Z, and date
8068.A7-Z History and criticism
Augsburg Confession
8069.A2 Texts. By date
8069.A3-Z General works
8069.3 Saxon Confession, 1551
8069.4 Formula of Concord
8070.A-Z Other special, A-Z
e.g.
Luther's catechisms
Texts of the Larger and Smaller Catechisms published together
8070.L52 English

	Lutheran churches
	Catechisms, creeds, etc.
	Other special, A-Z
	Luther's catechisms
	Larger catechisms
	German editions
8070.L6A2	Before 1800. By date
8070.L6A3	1801-1950. By date
8070.L6A4	1951- . By date
8070.L6A5-.L6Z	By editor or publisher
	English editions
8070.L62A2	Before 1800. By date
8070.L62A3	1801-1950. By date
8070.L62A4	1951- . By date
8070.L62A5-.L62Z	By editor or publisher
	Scandinavian editions
	Norwegian editions
8070.L65A2	Before 1800. By date
8070.L65A3	1801-1950. By date
8070.L65A4	1951- . By date
8070.L65A5-.L65Z	By editor or publisher
	Swedish editions
8070.L66A2	Before 1800. By date
8070.L66A3	1801-1950. By date
8070.L66A4	1951- . By date
8070.L66A5-.L66Z	By editor or publisher
8070.L67	Other languages (not A-Z)
	Smaller catechisms
	German editions
8070.L7A2	Before 1800. By date
8070.L7A3	1801-1950. By date
8070.L7A4	1951- . By date
8070.L7A5-.L7Z	By editor or publisher
	English editions
8070.L72A2	Before 1800. By date
8070.L72A3	1801-1950. By date
8070.L72A4	1951- . By date
8070.L72A5-.L72Z	By editor or publisher
	Scandinavian editions
	Norwegian editions
8070.L75A2	Before 1800. By date
8070.L75A3	1801-1950. By date
8070.L75A4	1951- . By date
8070.L75A5-.L75Z	By editor or publisher
	Swedish editions
8070.L76A2	Before 1800. By date
8070.L76A3	1801-1950. By date

Lutheran churches
Catechisms, creeds, etc.
Other special, A-Z
Luther's catechisms
Smaller catechisms
Scandinavian editions
Swedish editions -- Continued
8070.L76A4 1951- . By date
8070.L76A5-.L76Z By editor or publisher
8070.L77 Other languages (not A-Z)
8070.L8 History and criticism of the catechisms, including catechetics and sermons on the catechism
Schmalkaldischen Artikel
8070.S3 German editions
8070.S32 English editions
Scandinavian editions
8070.S35 Norwegian editions
8070.S36 Swedish editions
8070.S37 Other languages (not A-Z)
8070.S4 History and criticism of the articles
Including sermons on the articles
Clergy. Church officers
8071 General works
8071.2 Women clergy
8071.5 Religious communities. Conventual life
8071.7 Laity
Sacraments
Including theology, liturgy, and rite
8072 General works
8073 Lord's supper. Real presence, etc.
8073.5 Baptism
8074.A-Z Other special, A-Z
8074.B4 Benevolent work. Social work, welfare work, etc.
8074.C6 Confession. Penance. Reconciliation of penitents
8074.C7 Confirmation
8074.H42 Health. Medicine
8074.H65 Homosexuality
8074.H85 Human ecology
8074.H87 Human rights
8074.I55 Initiation of adults
8074.M3 Marriage
Medicine see BX8074.H42
8074.P4 Peace
Penance see BX8074.C6
8074.P73 Preaching
Reconciliation of penitents see BX8074.C6
8074.S35 Saints and martyrs

Lutheran churches
Other special, A-Z -- Continued
8074.W65 Women
8074.Y68 Youth
Individual churches
Subarranged by place and name
8075 Germany
8076 United States
8077.A-Z Other countries, A-Z
Subarrange each country by city, A-Z
e.g.
8077.D4C6 Copenhagen. Nikolaj Kirke
Biography
8079 Collective
8080.A-Z Individual, A-Z
e.g.
8080.B62 Bodelschwingh, Friedrich von
8080.E4 Eielsen, Elling
8080.G76 Grundtvig, Nikolai Frederik Severin
8080.H27 Hasselquist, Tufve Nilsson
8080.H3 Hauge, Hans Nielsen
8080.K68 Krauth, Charles Porterfield
8080.L6 Löscher, Valentin Ernst
Luther, Martin see BR325
8080.M9 Mühlenberg, Henry Melchior
Munk, Kaj Harold Leininger see PT8175.M84
8080.N48 Niemöller, Martin
8080.R4 Reuterdahl, Henrik, Abp.
8080.R66 Rosenius. Carl Olof
8080.S6 Söderblom, Nathan, Abp.
8080.S7 Spaeth, Adolph
8080.S738 Stoecker, Adolf
8080.W3 Walther, Carl Ferdinand Wilhelm
Mar Thoma Syrian Church see BX160+
8090 Maranatavàckelsen (Table BX3)
8095 Masowe weChishanu Church
Mennonites
8101 Periodicals. Serials
8103 Societies
8105 Conferences, etc.
8106 Dictionaries. Encyclopedias
8107 Directories
8109 Collected works
Menno Simons' works
Collected works
Dutch
8109.M3 General

Mennonites
Collected works
Menno Simons' works
Collected works
Dutch -- Continued

8109.M31	Selections
8109.M32-.M33	English
8109.M34-.M35	French
8109.M36-.M37	German
8109.M4A-.M4Z	Other languages, A-Z
	Individual works
	Dat fundamentum
8109.M5	Dutch
8109.M52	English
8109.M55	German
	Study and teaching
8111	General works
	Individual seminaries see BV4070.A+
	Sunday schools (Church schools)
8112	General works. Organization, etc.
8112.A1	Societies. Conventions, etc.
8113	Service books
8114	Textbooks, etc.
8114.5.A-Z	Individual Sunday schools. By place, A-Z
	History
8115	General works
	By region or country
	United States
8116	General works
8116.3.A-Z	By nationality or race, A-Z
8116.3.A37	African Americans
	By region
8116.4	New England
8116.42	Middle Atlantic
8116.43	South
8116.44	Central
8116.45	West
8116.46	Pacific States
8117.A-.W	By state, A-W
8118.A-Z	By city, A-Z
	Canada
8118.5	General works
8118.6.A-Z	By region, province, etc., A-Z
8118.7.A-Z	By city, A-Z
8119.A-Z	Other regions or countries, A-Z
	General works

Mennonites
General works -- Continued
8120 Early through 1800
Cf. BX8109.M3+ Works of Menno Simons
8121 1801-1950
8121.2 1951-2000
8121.3 2001-
8122 Addresses, essays, lectures
8123 Controversial works against the Mennonites
The Mennonites and other churches
8123.4.A1 Periodicals. Serials
8123.4.A2 Societies
8123.4.A3 Conferences, congresses, etc.
8123.4.A5-.Z5 General works. History, etc.
8123.4.Z6 Attitude toward the ecumenical movement
8123.4.Z7 Special aspects (not A-Z)
8124 Catechisms and creeds
8125 Liturgy and ritual. Service books
Hymns in English see BV412
Hymns in languages other than English see BV470+
8126 Government and discipline. Clergy and church officers
Sermons. Tracts
Class sermons on special topics with the subject, especially biography and history
For sermons for children, young people, etc. see BV4310+
Cf. BX8109 Collected works
8127.A1 Several authors
8127.A3-Z Individual authors, A-Z
8128.A-Z Special topics, A-Z
8128.C34 Camps
8128.C47 Charismatic movement
8128.C49 The Church
Including the nature, the meaning, or the mission of the church
8128.C6 Colonization
8128.C7 Costume
8128.E36 Economics
8128.H56 Hispanic Americans
8128.H67 Homosexuality
8128.P4 Peace
8128.T44 Telephone
8128.W4 Welfare work. Benevolent work, relief work, etc.
8128.W64 Women
8129.A-Z Individual branches of Mennonites
For Old Mennonites see BX8120+
8129.A1 Collective

Mennonites
Individual branches of Mennonites -- Continued
Amish Mennonites
8129.A5 General works
8129.A6 Old Order Amish
8129.B47 Bergthaler Mennonite Church of Manitoba
8129.B48 Bergthaler Mennonite Church of Saskatchewan
8129.B6-.B68 Bruderhof Communities (Arnold). Hutterian Society of Brothers. Hutterian Brethren (Rifton, N.Y.) (Table BX4)
(8129.B7) Breuder-Gemeinde (Schellenberger)
see BX8129.M37
8129.C3 Central Conference Mennonite Church
Church of God as Organized by Christ see BX7054
8129.C4 Church of God in Christ (Holdeman)
8129.C66 Conference of Mennonites in Canada
8129.C69 Conservative Mennonite Conference
8129.D4 Defenseless Mennonites. Evangelical Mennonite Brethren Church. Fellowship of Evangelical Bible Churches
8129.E82 Evangelical Mennonite Conference. Klein Gemeinde
8129.E85 Evangelical Mennonite Society of East Pennsylvania
8129.G4 General Conference Mennonite Church
General Conference of Mennonite Brethren Churches see BX8129.M37+
Hutterian Brethren (Rifton, N.Y.) see BX8129.B6+
Hutterian Society of Brothers see BX8129.B6+
8129.H8 Hutterite Brethren
8129.I69 Iowa-Nebraska Conference
Klein Gemeinde see BX8129.E82
Mennonite Brethren Church of North America see BX8129.M37+
8129.M37-.M378 Mennonite Brethren Church. Mennoniten Bruedergemeinde. General Conference of Mennonite Brethren Churches. Mennonite Brethren Church of North America (Table BX4)
8129.M4 Mennonite Brethren in Christ
After 1947, see BX9889 United Missionary Church; BX8129.M42 Mennonite Brethren in Christ Church of Pennsylvania, Incorporated
8129.M42-.M428 Mennonite Brethren in Christ Church of Pennsylvania, Incorporated (Table BX4)
Continuing the Pennsylvania District of the Mennonite Brethren in Christ
8129.M5 Mennonite Church
Mennoniten Bruedergemeinde see BX8129.M37+
8129.O4 Old Colony Mennonites
Old Order Amish see BX8129.A6

Mennonites
Individual branches of Mennonites -- Continued
8129.O43 Old Order Mennonites
Including Wisler, Wenger, "Black Bumper," and Reidenback groups
8129.R4 Reformed Mennonite Church. Herrites
Wisler Mennonites. Old Order Mennonite Church see BX8129.O43
Individual churches
8131.A-Z United States. By city, A-Z
8132.A-Z Other countries. By country and city, A-Z
Assign the first Cutter for country; second Cutter for city
Biography
8141 Collective
8143.A-Z Individual, A-Z
e.g.
8143.M5 Menno Simons
Methodism
8201 Periodicals. Serials
8203 Associations. Societies
For local (state, county, city, etc.), see the country divisions
8205 Epworth League
8207 Conferences. Societies
Prefer the special locality or church division, e.g.
For Methodist Episcopal Church see BX8381
8207.A1 General works
8211 Dictionaries. Encyclopedias
8213 Directories
Collected works
8215 Several authors
8217 Individual authors
e.g.
Works of John Wesley
8217.W5 Collected works. By date
8217.W54A-.W54Z Selected works. By editor, A-Z
Study and teaching
8219 General works
Individual seminaries see BV4070.A+; BV4160.A+
Sunday schools (Church schools)
8222 Societies. Conventions, etc.
8223 General works. Organization
8224 Service books
Textbooks
8225.A1 Periodicals
8225.A2-Z General works
8227.A-Z Individual Sunday schools. By place, A-Z
History

Methodism
History -- Continued
8231 General works
8232 Sermons, pageants, etc.
By region or country
America. North America
8233 General works
United States
8235 General works
By period
8236 18th century
8237 19-20th centuries
By region
8239 New England
8241 South
8243 Central
8245 West
8247.A-Z By nationality or race, A-Z
8248.A-.W By state, A-W
8249.A-Z By city, A-Z
By church see BX8481
Black Methodists see BX8435+
Canada
8251 General works
8252.A-Z By division, province, etc., A-Z
8253.A-Z By city, A-Z
Latin America
8254 General works
Mexico
8255 General works
8256.A-Z By division, state, etc., A-Z
8257.A-Z By city, A-Z
Central America
8260 General works
8261.A-Z By country, A-Z
8262.A-Z By city, A-Z
West Indies
8265 General works
8266.A-Z By country, A-Z
8267.A-Z By city, A-Z
South America
8271 General works
8272.A-Z By country, A-Z
8273.A-Z By city, A-Z
Europe
8275 General works
Great Britain. England

Methodism
History
By region or country
Europe
Great Britain. England -- Continued
8276 General works
By conference see BX8350+
8277.A-Z By division, county, etc. (England), A-Z
8278.A-Z By city (England), A-Z
Ireland
8281 General works
8282.A-Z By division, county, etc., A-Z
Including conferences
8283.A-Z By city, A-Z
Scotland
8285 General works
8286.A-Z By division, region, etc., A-Z
Including conferences
8287.A-Z By city, A-Z
Wales
8291 General works
8292.A-Z By division, county, etc., A-Z
Including conferences
8293.A-Z By city, A-Z
France
8295 General works
8296.A-Z By division, department, etc., A-Z
Including conferences
8297.A-Z By city, A-Z
Germany
8301 General works
8302.A-Z By division, state, etc., A-Z
Including conferences
8303.A-Z By city, A-Z
Italy
8305 General works
8306.A-Z By division, region, etc., A-Z
Including conferences
8307.A-Z By city, A-Z
8310.A-Z Other regions or countries of Europe, A-Z
e.g.
8310.S87 Sweden
8310.S9 Switzerland
Asia
8315 General works
8316.A-Z By country, A-Z
e.g.

Methodism
History
By region or country
Asia
By country, A-Z -- Continued
8316.C5 China
8316.I4 India
8316.J3 Japan
8316.P5 Philippines
Africa
8320 General works
8321 South Africa
8322.A-Z Other, A-Z
Australia and New Zealand
8325 General works
8326.A-Z Local, A-Z
Oceania
8327 General works
8328.A-Z Local, A-Z
8329.A-Z Relations with other churches, A-Z
8329.A1 General works
8329.C3 Catholic Church
Church of England see BX5129.8.M4
Evangelical Church see BX7523.4
8329.E9 Evangelical United Brethren Church
Orthodox Eastern Church see BX324.53
8329.P8 Puritans
General works. Doctrine, etc.
8330 Early through 1800
8331 1801-1950
8331.2 1951-2000
8331.3 2001-
8332 Addresses, essays, lectures
Sermons. Tracts
Class sermons on special topics with the subject, especially biography and history
For sermons for children, young people, etc. see BV4310+
Cf. BX8215+ Collected works
8333.A1 Several authors
8333.A3-Z Individual authors. By author and title, A-Z
8334 Controversial works against the Methodists
8335 Creeds and catechisms
8336 Forms of worship (not A-Z)
Including children's day service, Christmas service, mid-week service, etc.
8337 Services. Ritual. Liturgy

Methodism -- Continued
Hymns in English see BV415+
Hymns in languages other than English see BV470+
Sacraments
Including theology, ritual, rite
8338.A1 General works
8338.A3-Z Special
8339 Finance. Stewardship
Government and discipline. Judiciary. Law
Prefer individual branches
8340 General works
8342 Church membership. Probation, etc.
8343 Trials
8345 Church officers. Bishops, clergy, etc.
8345.3 Clerical relief: pensions, etc.
8345.5 Laymen
8345.7 Women
8346 Class meetings, leaders, etc.
8347 Benevolent work. Social work, welfare work, etc.
8348 Methodism and amusements
8349.A-Z Other special topics, A-Z
8349.C58 Church growth
8349.C64 Conversation
8349.C73 Creative ability
8349.H4 Health. Medicine
8349.H64 Holiness
8349.H66 Homosexuality
8349.I56 International affairs
8349.L43 Leadership
8349.M35 Marriage
Medicine see BX8349.H4
8349.N38 Nature
8349.P43 Peace
8349.P46 Pentecostalism
8349.S65 Sociology, Christian
8349.S67 Spiritual direction
8349.S68 Spirituality
Individual branches of Methodists
For branches limited to one country other than the United States and England, see the country
Methodist Church (England). Wesleyan Methodist Church
In 1932 the Wesleyan Methodist Church was merged with the United Methodist and Primitive Methodist churches to form the Methodist Church (England)
Periodicals see BX8201
8351 Conferences
History see BX8276+

Methodism
Individual branches of Methodists
Methodist Church (England). Wesleyan Methodist Church
General works (Doctrine, etc.) see BX8330+
Hymns in English
see BV416
Hymns in languages other than English
see BV470+
Government and discipline see BX8340+
8359.A-Z Individual biography, A-Z
Wesleyan Methodist Connection (or Church) of America
see BX8431.W4
(8360-8369) Calvinistic Methodist Church
For the American church of this name see BX8999.C3
For the Welsh church of this name see BX9100+
8370-8379 Primitive Methodist Church (Table BX26)
United Methodist Church (United States). Methodist Church (United States). Methodist Episcopal Church
On May 10, 1939, the Methodist Episcopal Church, the Methodist Episcopal Church South, and the Methodist Protestant Church were united to form the Methodist Church (United States). On April 23, 1968, the Methodist Church (United States) and the Evangelical United Brethren Church were united to form the United Methodist Church (United States)
Periodicals see BX8201
8380 Societies. Yearbooks, etc.
Conferences
Conferences that continue the prior-to-1939 numbering should also continue the classification used before the merger
For all Black conferences that are part of these bodies see BX8435+
8381 Methodist Episcopal Church
Including all Methodist Conferences in the United States before 1844
Methodist Church (United States)
8382.A13A-.A13Z Annual Conference
8382.A15A-.A15Z Uniting Conference
8382.A25A-.A25Z General Conference
8382.A4-Z Jurisdictional Conference. By name, A-Z
8382.2 United Methodist Church (United States)
(8383) History
see BX8235+
Biography see BX8491+
8385.A-Z Special topics, A-Z
8385.C65 Confirmation

	Methodism
	Individual branches of Methodists
	United Methodist Church (United States). Methodist Church (United States). Methodist Episcopal Church
	Special topics, A-Z -- Continued
8385.H65	Homosexuality
8385.L39	Lay ministry
8385.M4	Methodist Book Concern
8385.R33	Race relations
8385.W34	Walk to Emmaus movement
8387	General works Prefer BX8331+
	Government and discipline. Judiciary. Law Cf. BX8340+ Methodist polity (General)
8388	General works
8389	Trials
8389.5	Church officers. Bishops, clergy, etc.
	Methodist Episcopal Church, South On May 10, 1939, was merged in the Methodist Church (United States) BX8380+ Conferences that continue the prior-to-1939 numbering should also continue the classification used before the merger
	Periodicals see BX8201
8391	Conferences
	History see BX8235+
	Biography see BX8491+
8397	General works
	Hymns in English see BV416
	Hymns in languages other than English see BV470+
8398	Government and discipline
8400-8409	Methodist Protestant Church (Table BX26) On May 10, 1939, was merged in the Methodist Church (United States), BX8380+ Conferences that continue the prior-to-1939 numbering should also continue the classification used before the merger
8410-8419	Free Methodist Church of North America (Table BX26)
8431.A-Z	Other branches, except Black, A-Z
8431.A82	Association of Independent Methodists. Mississippi Association of Methodist Ministers and Laymen
8431.C7	Congregational Methodist Church
8431.E88	Evangelical Methodist Church
8431.E98	Evangelical Wesleyan Church of North America

Methodism
Individual branches of Methodists
Other branches, except Black, A-Z -- Continued

8431.M5 Methodist New Connexion
Formed by secession from Wesleyan Methodist Church; merged into United Methodist Church in 1907
Mississippi Association of Methodist Ministers and Laymen see BX8431.A82
8431.S7 Stilwellites
8431.U56 Union Methodist Episcopal Church
8431.W4 Wesleyan Methodist Connection (or Church) of America
Black Methodists
8435 General works
8436.A-.W By state, A-W
8440-8449 African Methodist Episcopal Church (Table BX26)
8450-8459 African Methodist Episcopal Zion Church (Table BX26)
8460-8469 Christian Methodist Episcopal Church (Table BX26)
8471.A-Z Other branches, A-Z
e.g.
8471.A4 African Union Methodist Protestant Church
8472 Sermons. Tracts
Biography
8473.A1 Collective
8473.A3-Z Individual
Prefer special branch if known
e.g.
8473.L3 Lane, Isaac
Methodist camp meetings
8475 General works
8475.5.A-.W By state, A-Z
8476.A-Z Individual, A-Z
e.g.
8476.O2 Ocean Grove Camp Meeting Association of the Methodist Episcopal Church
Individual Methodist churches. By place
8481 United States
8483 Other countries
Biography
Cf. BX8473.A+ Black Methodists
Collective
Cf. BX8213 Directories
8491 General works
8493 Women
8495.A-Z Individual, A-Z
e.g.
8495.A8 Asbury, Francis
8495.B884 Bunting, Jabez

Methodism
Biography
Individual, A-Z -- Continued
8495.C245 Cannon, James
8495.C57 Clarke, Adam
8495.C6 Coke, Thomas
8495.E4 Embury, Philip
8495.F6 Fletcher, John William
8495.L4 Lee, Jesse
8495.M24 McKendree, William
8495.M33 Marvin, Enoch Mather
8495.O93 Oxnam, Garfield Bromley
8495.R53 Roberts, Robert Richford
8495.S55 Simpson, Matthew, Bp.
8495.T3 Taylor, William
8495.W323 Watson, Richard
Wesley family
8495.W35 General works
8495.W4 Wesley, Charles
8495.W5 Wesley, John
8495.W55 Wesley, Susanna (Annesley)
Whitefield, George see BX9225.W4
Methodism - Millennial Dawnists
8500.M3 Metropolitan Church Association
Metropolitan Community Church see BX9896
Michelhahnites see BX7990.H4
Millennial Dawnists. Jehovah's Witnesses
Russellites, International Bible Students Association, Watch Tower Bible and Tract Society
Cf. D804.5.J44 Jehovah's Witnesses in the Holocaust
8525 Periodicals. Serials
Collected works
8525.5 Several authors
8525.55 Individual authors
History
8525.7 General, and United States
8525.8.A-Z Other regions or countries, A-Z
8526 General works
8526.5 Controversial works against Jehovah's Witnesses
Biography
8527.A1 Collective
8527.A2-Z Individual
e.g.
8527.R8 Russell, Charles Taze
8527.R85 Rutherford, Joseph Franklin
8528.A-Z Individual branches, A-Z
8528.D3-.D38 Dawn Bible Students Association (Table BX4)

Millennial Dawnists - Moravian Church
8530.M4 Missionary Bands of the World
8530.M5 Missionary Church
Formerly Missionary Church Association
8530.M6 Molokans (Molakans)
8530.M7 Monarch Church
Moravian Church. United Brethren. Unitas Fratrum. Herrnhuters
8551 Periodicals. Serials
8553 Societies
8555 Conferences, etc.
8557 Directories
8559 Collected works
8560 Pictorial works
Study and teaching
8561 General works
Individual seminaries see BV4070.A+
Sunday schools (Church schools)
8562.A1 Societies. Conventions, etc.
8562.A2-Z General works. Organization, etc.
8563 Service books
8564 Textbooks, etc.
8564.5.A-Z Individual Sunday schools. By place, A-Z
History
8565 General works
By region or country
United States (and Canada)
8566 General works
8567.A-.W By state, A-W
8568.A-Z By city, A-Z
Cf. BX8581+ Individual churches
8569.A-Z Other regions or countries, A-Z
General works. Theology. Doctrine, etc.
8570 Early through 1800
8571 1801-1950
8571.2 1951-2000
8571.3 2001-
8572 Addresses, essays, lectures
8573 Controversial works against the Moravians
8573.7 Forms of worship. Moravian practice
8574 Liturgy and ritual. Service books
Hymns in English see BV417
Hymns in languages other than English see BV470+
8575.A-Z Devotional works
e.g.
Losungen (Loosungen)
German

Moravian Church. United Bretheren. Unitas Fratrum. Herrnhuters
Devotional works
Losungen (Loosungen)
German -- Continued
8575.L6 Collections
8575.L64 Bethlehem, Pa., edition
8575.L65 Gnadau edition
8575.L653 For Swiss use
English
8575.L66 Bethlehem, Pa., edition
8575.L663 For the Armed Services
8576 Government and discipline. Clergy and church officers
Sermons. Tracts
Class sermons on special topics with the subject, especially biography and history
For sermons for children, young people, etc. see BV4310+
Cf. BX8559 Collected works
8577.A1 Several authors
8577.A3-Z Individual authors. By author and title, A-Z
8578 Creeds and catechisms
Individual branches or sects of Moravians or Unity
8579 Unity of the Brethren (Texas)
Camp meetings
8580 General works
8580.5.A-Z Individual, A-Z
8580.5.M68 Mount Lebanon, Pa.
Individual churches. By place
8581 United States
8583 Other countries
Biography
8591 Collective
8593.A-Z Individual, A-Z
e.g.
8593.Z6 Zinzendorf, Nicolaus Ludwig, graf von
Mormons. Church of Jesus Christ of Latter-Day Saints
For general works on Utah and the Mormons see F821+
8601 Periodicals. Serials
8603 Societies
8605 Conferences
8605.5 Dictionaries. Encyclopedias
8606 Directories
Documents
8607.A1 Collections
Special
8607.A2-.A5 Mormon Church

Mormons. Church of Jesus Christ of Latter-Day Saints
Documents
Special -- Continued
8607.A6-Z Other, A-Z
e.g. United States
Collected works
8608 Several authors
8608.5 Minor collections. Quotations, maxims, etc.
8609 Individual authors
Study and teaching
Including Sunday schools and their catechisms
8610.A1 Periodicals. Serials
8610.A3-Z General works
History
Cf. BX8645+ Controversial works against the Mormons
8611 General works
By region or country
United States
History see BX8611
8615.A-Z By region or state, except Utah, A-Z
8617.A-Z Other regions or countries, A-Z
Sources of Mormonism. The Sacred Books (Teachings of Joseph Smith)
8621 General works
8622 History, criticism, concordances, etc.
Book of Mormon
8623 Texts (English). By date
8624 In characters of the Deseret alphabet
8625.A-Z Translations. By language, A-Z
8627.A1 Concordances. Dictionaries. Encyclopedias
8627.A2 Adaptations. Paraphrases
8627.A3-Z History and criticism
Including works on the Mormon theory of the origin of the Indians, the Jaredites, Nephites, Lamanites
Cf. BX8645+ Controversial works against the Mormons
Biography. Characters of the Book of Mormon
8627.3 Collective
8627.4.A-Z Individual, A-Z
8627.5 A Book of Commandments
8627.5.A2 Texts. By date
8628 Book of Doctrine and Covenants
Texts
8628.A3 Orthodox editions. By date
8628.A35A-.A35Z Translations. By language, A-Z
8628.A4 Reorganized church editions. By date
8628.A5A-.A5Z Adaptations. Paraphrases

Mormons. Church of Jesus Christ of Latter-Day Saints
Sources of Mormonism. The Sacred Books (Teachings of Joseph Smith)
Book of Doctrine and Covenants -- Continued
8628.A6-Z History, criticism, concordances, etc.
8629.A-Z Other special books. By title, A-Z
Under each:
.x Texts. By date
.x3A-.x3Z Criticism
8629.P5-.P53 The Pearl of Great Price
8629.W6-.W63 Word of Wisdom
Bible versions
Joseph Smith's version
English
8630.A2 All texts. By date
Including whole Bibles. Old Testament texts, New Testament texts, texts of individual books, selections, etc.
8630.A2A-.A2Z Translations. By language and date
8630.A3-Z History, commentaries, Bible stories, etc.
8630.2 Other Mormon versions. By translator or editor
8631 Biblical sources. Topical indexes, etc.
General treatises. Doctrines, etc.
8635 Early through 1950
8635.2 1951-2000
8635.3 2001-
8635.5 Apologetics
8637 Addresses, essays, lectures
8638 Other
Including pictorial works, etc.
Sermons. Tracts
Class sermons on special topics with the subject, especially biography and history
Cf. BX8607.A+ Collected works
8639.A1 Several authors
8639.A3-Z Individual authors. By author and title, A-Z
Special topics
8641 Polygamy. Women in Mormonism. Marriage
Cf. HQ994+ Polygamy (Social problem)
8643.A-Z Other, A-Z
8643.A25 Abraham (Biblical patriarch)
8643.A3 Adam (Biblical figure)
8643.A35 African Americans
Apostasy, Great see BX8643.G74
8643.A74 Asian Americans
8643.A85 Atonement
Cf. BX8643.J4 Jesus Christ

Mormons. Church of Jesus Christ of Latter-Day Saints
Special topics
Other , A-Z

	Baptism. Baptism for the dead see BX8655.3
	Blacks in Mormonism see BX8643.A35
8643.B6	Blood atonement
8643.C24	Camps
8643.C5	Celestial marriage
8643.C55	Child sexual abuse
8643.C56	Children
	Church camps see BX8643.C24
	Church leadership see BX8643.L4
8643.C66	Communication
8643.C67	Consolation
8643.C68	Cosmology
8643.C7	Counseling
8643.C75	Creation
	Covenants see BX8657
8643.C84	Cultural assimilation
8643.D4	Death
8643.D44	Depression, Mental
	Determinism see BX8643.F69
8643.D5	Diet
8643.D58	Divorce
8643.E34	Egypt
8643.E54	Enoch
8643.E83	Eschatology
8643.E85	Ethnic relations
8643.E92	Eve (Biblical figure)
8643.E94	Evolution
8643.F3	The family
8643.F69	Free will and determinism
8643.F87	Future life
	Genealogy see class CS
8643.G63	God
8643.G74	Great Apostasy
8643.H35	Happiness
8643.H57	Hispanic Americans
8643.H63	Holy Ghost. Holy Spirit
8643.H65	Homosexuality
8643.H67	Hope
8643.H8	Hygiene
8643.I53	Indians
	Israel see BX8643.J84
	Jaredites see BX8627.A3+

Mormons. Church of Jesus Christ of Latter-Day Saints
Special topics
Other, A-Z -- Continued

8643.J4 Jesus Christ
Cf. BX8643.A85 Atonement
8643.J67 Joseph (Biblical patriarch)
8643.J84 Judaism. Jews. Israel
Lamanites see BX8627.A3+
8643.L4 Leadership
8643.L5 Legal status of Mormons
8643.L55 Lesbianism
8643.L66 Lost tribes of Israel
8643.M35 Man
8643.M37 Mary, Blessed Virgin, Saint
8643.M4 Medicine
8643.M45 Mental health
8643.M54 Millennialism
8643.M67 Moroni (Ancient prophet)
8643.N6 Noah (Biblical figure)
8643.O25 Occult sciences
8643.O44 Olive
8643.O73 Order
8643.P36 Patriarchal blessings. Patriarchs
8643.P43 Peace
8643.P47 Perfection
8643.P6 Politics. Church and state
8643.P64 Pornography
8643.P67 Preexistence
8643.P7 Prophets
8643.R36 Regeneration
8643.R39 Religion and science
8643.R4 Revelation
8643.S2 Sabbath
8643.S25 Salvation
8643.S43 Second Advent
8643.S49 Sex
8643.S55 Single people
Social problems see HN37.M6
8643.S93 Suffering
8643.S95 Suicide
8643.T4 Temples
8643.T45 Testimony. Witness bearing
8643.T5 Tithes
8643.T72 Translation to heaven
8643.W3 War
8643.W37 Wealth
8643.W4 Welfare work

Mormons. Church of Jesus Christ of Latter-Day Saints
Special topics
Other, A-Z -- Continued
Witness bearing see BX8643.T45
8643.Y6 Youth
8643.Z55 Zion
Controversial works against the Mormons
Cf. BX8627.A3+ History and criticism of the Book of Mormon
Cf. BX8641 Polygamy
8645 General works
8645.5 History and criticism
8647 Relation to other churches
8648 Church records. Forms, etc.
8649 Creeds and catechisms
8651 Liturgy and ritual
Hymns in English see BV420
Hymns in languages other than English see BV470+
Sacraments
8655 General works
8655.2 Lord's Supper
8655.3 Baptism. Baptism for the dead
8656 Christian life. Spiritual life
8657 Government and discipline
Priesthood
8659 General works
8659.5 Aaronic Priesthood
8659.6 Melchizedek Priesthood
8661 Missions
Individual branches or sects of Mormons
Community of Christ. Reorganized Church of Jesus Christ of Latter-Day Saints
8670 Periodicals. Serials
Official documents, governing boards, conferences
8671.A1-.A5 General
8671.A6-Z Local, A-Z
Study and teaching. Sunday schools
8672 General works
8672.2.A-Z Individual schools. By city, A-Z
History
8673 General and United States
8673.2.A-Z By ecclesiastical jurisdiction, A-Z
8673.3.A-.W By state, A-W
8673.4.A-Z By city, A-Z
8673.5.A-Z Other countries, A-Z

Mormons. Church of Jesus Christ of Latter-Day Saints
Individual branches or sects of Mormons
Reorganized Church of Jesus Christ of Latter-Day Saints -- Continued

8674 General works
Including collections, collected works, dictionaries, encyclopedias
8675 Doctrines, creeds, catechisms, liturgy, rituals, sacraments, government, discipline, membership
Hymns see BV437.R56
8676 Sermons. Tracts
8677.A-Z Special churches. By place, A-Z, or by name if nonurban
Biography
8678.A1-.A5 Collective
8678.A6-Z Individual, A-Z
8680.A-Z Other, A-Z
8680.A2-.A28 Aaronic order (Table BX4)
8680.B5-.B58 Church of Jesus Christ (Bickertonites) (Table BX4)
8680.C4-.C48 Church of Jesus Christ (Table BX4)
8680.C8-.C88 Church of Jesus Christ (Cutlerites) (Table BX4)
8680.L4-.L48 Church of the Firstborn of the Fulness of Times (Le Baronism) (Table BX4)
8680.M5-.M58 Mormon fundamentalism (groups around J. Musser, J. Taylor, Rulon Allred) (Table BX4)
8680.M6-.M68 Morrisites (Table BX4)
8680.R3-.R38 Church of Christ (Remnant Group). Revelation of Otto Fetting (Table BX4)
8680.S8-.S88 Church of Jesus Christ (Strangites) (Table BX4 modified)
Biography
8680.S88A1-.S88A5 Collective
8680.S88A6-.S88Z Individual
e.g.
8680.S88S8 Strang, James Jesse
8680.T4-.T48 Church of Christ (Temple Lot) (Table BX4)
Individual temples, etc. By place
8685 United States
8687 Other countries
Biography
8693 Collective
8695.A-Z Individual, A-Z
e.g.
8695.K5 Kimball, Heber Chase
8695.P7 Pratt, Parley Parker
8695.R58 Roberts, Brigham Henry
8695.S6 Smith, Joseph
8695.S63 Smith, Joseph Fielding
Smoot, Reed see E664.S68

Mormons. Church of Jesus Christ of Latter-Day Saints
Biography
Individual, A-Z -- Continued
Strang, James Jesse see BX8680.S88S8
8695.Y7 Young, Brigham
8697 Muckers (Ebelians)
8698 Muggletonians
Muggletonians - New Jerusalem Church
8699.M8 Mukyokaishugi Shūkai. "Non-Churchism Assembly"
8699.N27-.N278 National Council of Community Churches (U.S.) (Table BX4)
8699.N3-.N38 Church of the Nazarene. Pentecostal Church of the Nazarene (Table BX4)
8699.N4 Nazarenes (Wirz)
Church of the Nazarites see BX7068.7
8699.N5 New Apostolic Church
Pentecostal Church of the Nazarene see BX8699.N3+
New Jerusalem Church. New Church. Swedenborgianism
Classification does not differentiate between the General Convention, the General Church, and other bodies
8701 Periodicals. Serials
8703 Societies
8705 Conferences
8707 Directories
Collected works
8709 Several authors
Individual authors
Swedenborg
8711 Collected works
8711.A1 Latin. By date
8711.A2 English. By date
8711.A3 French. By date
8711.A4 German. By date
8711.A5A-.A5Z Other languages, A-Z. By date
8711.A7A-.A7Z Selections. Compendiums. Memorabilia. Dictionaries. By editor, A-Z
8711.A8-Z Criticism of Swedenborg's works
For individual works see BX8712.A+
8712.A-Z Individual works, A-Z
8712.A3-.A4 Apocalypse explained (Apocalypsis explicata) (Table BX27)
8712.A3 Texts in Latin. By date
8712.A3A-.A3Z5 Excerpts in Latin. By English name of excerpt
8712.A3A8 Athanasian creed (De fide Athanasiana)
Cf. BX8712.P825 De Athanasii symbolo
8712.A5-.A6 Apocalypse revealed (Apocalypsis revelata) (Table BX27)
8712.A7-.A8 Arcana coelestia (Heavenly arcana) (Table BX27)

New Jerusalem Church. New Church. Swedenborgianism
Collected works
Individual authors
Swedenborg
Individual works, A-Z -- Continued
Canones seu integra theologica Novae Ecclesiae see BX8712.P82

8712.C7-.C8 Conjugal love (Delitiae sapientiae de amore conjugiali) (Table BX27)

8712.D3-.D4 Divine love and wisdom (Sapientia angelica de divino amore) (Table BX27)

8712.D5-.D6 Divine providence (Sapientia angelica de divina providentia) (Table BX27)

8712.D7-.D8 Four leading doctrines of the New Church (Quatuor doctrinae) (Table BX27)

8712.D91-.D92 Doctrine concerning the Lord (Doctrina Novae Hierosolymae de Domino) (Table BX27)

8712.D93-.D94 Doctrine concerning the Sacred Scriptures (Doctrina Novae Hierosolymae de Scriptura Sacra) (Table BX27)

8712.D95-.D96 Doctrine concerning life (Doctrina vitae pro Nova Hierosolyma) (Table BX27)

8712.D97-.D98 Doctrine concerning faith (Doctrina Novae Hierosolymae de fide) (Table BX27)

8712.D993-.D994 Dreams (Drömmar) (Table BX27)

8712.E2-.E3 Earths in the universe (De telluribus in mundo nostro solari) (Table BX27)

8712.H4-.H5 Heaven and hell (De coelo et ejus mirabilibus) (Table BX27)

8712.H6-.H7 Heavenly doctrine of the New Jerusalem. The New Jerusalem and its heavenly doctrine (De nova Hierosolyma et ejus doctrina coelesti) (Table BX27)

8712.I5-.I6 Intercourse between soul and body. Nature of influx (De commercio animae et corporis) (Table BX27)

8712.L3-.L4 Last Judgment (De ultimo judicio et Babylona destructa) (Table BX27)

8712.P6-.P7 Posthumous tracts (Table BX27)

8712.P8-.P89 Special

Tracts are arranged by Latin names

Use same Cutter numbers for originals and translations; subarrange by date

8712.P82 Canones, seu integra theologia

Use same Cutter numbers for originals and translations; subarrange by date

New Jerusalem Church. New Church. Swedenborgianism
Collected works
Individual authors
Swedenborg
Individual works, A-Z
Posthumous tracts
Special -- Continued
8712.P825 De Athanasii symbolo
Use same Cutter numbers for originals and translations; subarrange by date
8712.P833 De charitate
Use same Cutter numbers for originals and translations; subarrange by date
8712.P84 De Domino
Use same Cutter numbers for originals and translations; subarrange by date
8712.P87 Dicta probantia Veteris et Novi Testamenti
Use same Cutter numbers for originals and translations; subarrange by date
8712.S6-.S7 Spiritual diary (Diarium spirituale) (Table BX27)
8712.T7-.T8 True Christian religion (Vera Christiana religio) (Table BX27)
8712.W4-.W5 White horse mentioned in Revelation (De equo albo) (Table BX27)
8712.W6-.W7 Worship and love of God (De cultus et amore Dei) (Table BX27)
Works in science and philosophy
see classes Q and R
8713.A-Z Other authors, A-Z
Study and teaching
8714.A1 General works
Individual seminaries see BV4070.A+
Sunday schools (Church schools)
8714.A15 Societies. Conventions, etc.
8714.A2 General works. Organization, etc.
8714.A3 Service books
8714.A5-Z Textbooks
History
8715 General works
By region or country
United States
8716 General works
8717.A-.W By state, A-W
8718.A-Z By city, A-Z
8719.A-Z Other regions or countries, A-Z
General works. Theology
8721 Early through 1950

New Jerusalem Church. New Church. Swedenborgianism
General works. Theology -- Continued
8721.2 1951-2000
8721.3 2001-
8723 Addresses, essays, lectures
Sermons. Tracts
Class sermons on special topics with the subject, especially biography and history
Cf. BX8709+ Collected works
8724.A1 Several authors
8724.A3-Z Individual authors. By author and title, A-Z
Special topics
8726 New Church interpretation of the Bible
8727 Doctrine of correspondences
8729.A-Z Other, A-Z
Bible see BX8726
8729.C5 The Church
8729.C7 Creation
8729.D4 Doctrine of Degrees
8729.E7 Eschatology
8729.E83 Evangelistic work
8729.F8 Future life
8729.H4 Heaven
8729.H5 Hell
8729.L3 Last judgment
8729.R37 Reality
8729.R4 Regeneration
8729.S6 Spiritualism
8731 Controversial works against Swedenborgianism
8733 Creeds and catechisms
8735 Liturgy and ritual
Including prayer books, devotions, etc.
Hymns in English see BV425
Hymns in languages other than English see BV470+
Sacraments
Including theology, liturgy, rite
8736.A1 General works
8736.A3-Z Special
8737 Government and discipline
Individual churches. By place
8741 United States
8743 Other regions or countries
Biography
8747 Collective
Individual

New Jerusalem Church. New Church. Swedenborgianism
Biography
Individual -- Continued
8748 Swedenborg, Emanuel
For Swedenborg as a philosopher see B4468.S8+
For Swedenborg as a scientist see Q143.S8
8749.A-Z Other, A-Z
New Jerusalem Church - Pentecostal churches
8750.N45-.N458 Nihon Fukuin Kirisuto Kyodan (Table BX4)
8750.N46-.N468 Nihon Iesu Kirisuto Kyodan (Table BX4)
8750.N48-.N488 Nihon Kirisuto Kaikakuha Kyokai (Table BX4)
8750.N5-.N58 Nihon Kirisuto Kyodan Japanese Christian Church (Table BX4)
8750.N62-.N628 Nihon Kirisuto Kyokai (Table BX4)
8750.N64-.N648 Nihon Kumiai Kirisuto Kyōkai (Table BX4)
8750.O7-.O78 (Original) Church of God (Table BX4)
Orthodox Apostolic Church in Haiti see BX5999.5
Peace Mission Movement see BX7350
8750.P43 Peculiar people. Union of Evangelical Churches
Pentecostal churches
Class here general works on Pentecostal churches and works not identifiable with any particular body
For Pentecostal or Charismatic movements in specific denominations, see the denomination, e.g. BX2350.57 Catholic Church; BX8065.5 Lutheran churches
For general works on Pentecostalism or the Charismatic Movement see BR1644+
8762 General works (Table BX3)
8762.5 African American Pentecostal Churches (Table BX3)
8763 Oneness Pentecostal Churches
Class here also works on Jesus-Only, Apostolic, or Non-Trinitarian Pentecostal churches treated collectively
Relations with other denominations
8764 General works
8764.2 Catholic Church
Orthodox Eastern Church see BX324.54
Individual branches
8764.5 Apostolic Church (Great Britain) (Table BX3)
8765 Apostolic Church of Pentecost of Canada (Table BX3)
8765.5 Assemblies of God (Table BX3)
8765.7 Assemblies of God in Great Britain and Ireland (Table BX3)
8766 Apostolic Faith (Charles F. Parham) (Table BX3)
8766.5 Apostolic Faith Churches of God (Table BX3)
8766.6 Apostolic Faith Mission in Malawi (Table BX3)
8766.7 Apostolic Faith Mission of South Africa (Table BX3)
8768 Finnish Pentecostal Churches in America (Table BX3)
8768.5 Gereja Bethel Indonesia (Table BX3)

	Pentecostal churches
	Individual branches -- Continued
8768.6	Iglesia Evangelica Filadelfia (Table BX3)
8768.7	Igreja Universal do Reino de Deus (Table BX3)
	International Church of the Foursquare Gospel see BX7990.I6+
8769	Liberty Fellowship of Churches and Ministers (Table BX3)
8770	Mt. Calvary Holy Church of America (Table BX3)
8770.3	New Life Churches of New Zealand (Table BX3)
8770.5	Open Bible Standard Churches (Table BX3)
8770.7	Original United Holy Church International (Table BX3)
8771	Pentecostal Assemblies of Jesus Christ (Table BX3)
8772	Pentecostal Assemblies of the World (Table BX3)
8773	Pentecostal Church, Inc. (Table BX3)
	Pentecostal Church of the Nazarene see BX8699.N3+
8773.15	Pentecostal Church of God of America (Table BX3)
8773.2	Pentecostal Church of Zaire (Table BX3)
8773.5	Pentecostal Churches of the Apostolic Faith Ass'n. (Table BX3)
8773.7	Pentecostal Fire-Baptised Holiness Church (U.S.) (Table BX3)
8774-8776	Pentecostal Holiness Church. International Pentecostal Holiness Church (Table BX2)
	Pentecostal Union see BX8795.P5
	Pilgrim Holiness Church see BX8795.P45+
8776.5	Redeemed Christian Church of God (Table BX3)
8777	Rock Church Fellowship (Table BX3)
8777.3	United Christian Ministerial Association (Table BX3)
8777.5	United Holy Church of America (Table BX3)
8777.6	United House of Prayer for All People (Table BX3)
8778-8780	United Pentecostal Church. United Pentecostal Church International (Table BX2)
8785	Vineyard Christian Fellowship. Association of Vineyard Churches (Table BX3)
8787	YaʼItyopyā qāla ḥeywat béta kerestiyān (Table BX3)
	Pentecostal churches - Plymouth Brethren
8795.P4	Perfectionists (John Humphrey Noyes) Cf. HX656.O5 Oneida Community, N.Y.
8795.P43	Philadelphia Society
	Pietism see BR1650+
8795.P45-.P458	Pilgrim Holiness Church (Table BX4)
8795.P5	Pillar of Fire (Alma White)
	Plymouth Brethren. Darbyites
8799	Periodicals. Societies. Serials
8800	General works
	Biography
8808	Collective

Plymouth Brethren. Darbyites
Biography -- Continued
8809.A-Z Individual, A-Z
e.g.
8809.D3 Darby, John Nelson
8809.G7 Groves, Anthony Norris
Presbyterianism. Calvinistic Methodism
8901 Periodicals. Serials
8905 Associations. Societies
For local (State, county, city, etc.), see the country divisions
8907 Conventions. Conferences (General)
Prefer the special denominations
8909 Dictionaries. Encyclopedias
8911 Directories
Prefer special country or sect
Collected works
8913 Several authors
8915 Individual authors
Study and teaching
8917 General works
Individual seminaries see BV4070.A+
Sunday schools (Church schools)
8920 Societies. Conventions, etc.
8921 General works. Organization, etc.
8922 Service books
8923 Textbooks, etc.
8925.A-Z Individual Sunday schools. By place, A-Z
History
General works
8930 Early through 1800
8931 1801-1950
8931.2 1951-2000
8931.3 2001-
8932 Addresses, essays, lectures
By region or country
America. North America
8933 General works
United States
8935 General works
By period
8936 17th-18th centuries
8937 19th-20th centuries
By region
8939 New England
8941 South
8943 Central
8945 West

Presbyterianism. Calvinistic Methodism
History
By region or country
America. North America
United States -- Continued
8946.A-Z By nationality or race, A-Z
e.g.
8946.A35 African Americans
8946.G4 Germans
8946.H8 Hungarians
8946.I8 Italians
8947.A-.W By state, A-W
8949.A-.W By city, A-Z
Individual branches of Presbyterians
Presbyterian Church in the United States of America. United Presbyterian Church in the United States of America
On May 28, 1958, the Presbyterian Church in the United States of America merged with the United Presbyterian Church of North America to form the United Presbyterian Church in the United States of America
8950 Periodicals. Yearbooks. Directories
8951 Conferences. Assemblies, etc.
History see BX8935+
Biography see BX9220+
8956 Government and discipline
For trials, see BX9192+
8957.A-Z Synods, A-Z
8958.A-Z Presbyteries, A-Z
Churches
see BX9211
8959.A2-.A28 Presbyterian Church of America (1936-1938). Orthodox Presbyterian Church (1939-) (Table BX29)
8959.A3-.A38 Reformed Presbyterian Church, Evangelical Synod. Evangelical Presbyterian Church (1961-1965). Bible Presbyterian Church (Table BX29)
For the merger with the Presbyterian Church in America in 1982 see BX8968.5+
8959.A4-.A48 Bible Presbyterian Church, Collingwood Synod (1955-). Followers of Carl McIntire (Table BX29)
For the split from the Bible Presbyterian Church see BX8959.A3+
8959.A5-.A58 Evangelical Presbyterian Church (1981-) (Table BX29)

Presbyterianism. Calvinistic Methodism
History
By region or country
America. North America
United States
Individual branches of Presbyterians -- Continued
Presbyterian Church in the United States (Southern Presbyterian Church), 1861-1983
For the split in 1973 from this church by the Presbyterian Church in America see BX8968.5+
8960 Periodicals. Yearbooks. Directories
8961 Conferences. Assemblies, etc.
Biography see BX9220+
History by state see BX8947.A+
History by city see BX8949.A+
8966 Government and discipline
For trials, see BX9192+
8967.A-Z Synods, A-Z
8968.A-Z Presbyteries, A-Z
Churches
see BX9211
Presbyterian Church in America
Formed in 1973 by congregations seceding from the Presbyterian Church in the United States. In 1982 the Reformed Presbyterian Church, Evangelical Synod merged with this church
8968.5 Periodicals. Yearbooks. Directories
8968.51 Conferences. Assemblies, etc.
History
8968.52 General works
Including collective biography
8968.53.A-.W By state, A-W
8968.54.A-Z By city, A-Z
8968.55 Doctrines, creeds, catechisms, liturgy
8968.56 Government and discipline
Trials see BX9192+
8968.57.A-Z Synods, A-Z
8968.58.A-Z Presbyteries, A-Z
Individual churches see BX9211+
Presbyterian Church (U.S.A.), 1983-
On June 10, 1983 the United Presbyterian Church in the United States of America merged with the Presbyterian Church in the United States to form the Presbyterian Church (U.S.A)
8969 Periodicals. Yearbooks. Directories
8969.1 Conferences. Assemblies, etc.

Presbyterianism. Calvinistic Methodism
History
By region or country
America. North America
United States
Individual branches of Presbyterians
Presbyterian Church (U.S.A.), 1983- -- Continued
History

8969.2 General works
8969.3.A-Z By region or state, A-Z
8969.4.A-Z By city, A-Z
8969.5 Doctrines, creeds, catechisms, liturgy
Hymns in English see BV430+
Hymns in languages other than English see BV470+
Government and discipline
8969.6 General works
Trials see BX9192+
8969.7.A-Z Synods, A-Z
8969.8.A-Z Presbyteries, A-Z
Individual churches see BX9211+
Biography see BX9220+
8970-8978 Cumberland Presbyterian Church (Table BX28)
Biography see BX9220+
8980-8988 United Presbyterian Church of North America (Table BX28)
For merger with Presbyterian Church in the United States of America see BX8950+
Biography see BX9220+
Reformed Presbyterian churches
8990.A1 Periodicals of all churches
Individual churches see BX9211+
Individual biography see BX9223+
Individual Reformed Presbyterian churches
Reformed Presbytery in America (1774-1782)
8990.A2 Documents, proceedings, etc.
8990.A3 General works. History, etc.

Presbyterianism. Calvinistic Methodism
History
By region or country
America. North America
United States
Individual branches of Presbyterians
Reformed Presbyterian churches
Individual Reformed Presbyterian churches -- Continued
Reformed Presbyterian Church of North America. Reformed Presbyterian Church. Reformed Presbytery of America
In 1969 the Associate Presbyterian Church of North America merged with this group
For the split in 1840 from this group by the Reformed Presbytery (Steelites) see BX8998.1+
For the split in 1833 from this church by the Reformed Presbyterian Church in North America, General Synod (New Light) see BX8998.2+

8990.A8-Z Periodicals. Yearbooks. Directories
8991 Conferences. Assemblies, etc.
History
8992 General works
Including collective biography
8993.A-.W By state, A-W
8994.A-Z By city, A-Z
8995 Doctrines, creeds, catechisms, liturgy
8996 Government and discipline
Trials see BX9192+
8997.A-Z Synods, A-Z
8998.A-Z Presbyteries, A-Z
Individual churches see BX9211+
Reformed Presbytery (Steelites) (1840-)
8998.1 Periodicals. Yearbooks. Directories
8998.11 Conferences. Assemblies, etc.
History
8998.12 General works
Including collective biography
8998.13.A-.W By state, A-W
8998.14.A-.W By city, A-Z
8998.15 Doctrines, creeds, catechisms, liturgy
8998.16 Government and discipline
Trials see BX9192+
8998.17.A-Z Synods, A-Z
8998.18.A-Z Presbyteries, A-Z

Presbyterianism. Calvinistic Methodism
History
By region or country
America. North America
United States
Individual branches of Presbyterians
Reformed Presbyterian churches
Individual Reformed Presbyterian churches
Reformed Presbytery (Steelites) (1840-) -- Continued
Individual churches see BX9211+
Reformed Presbyterian Church in North America, General Synod (New Light) (1833-1965)
For the merger with the Evangelical Presbyterian Church in 1965 to form the Reformed Presbyterian Church, Evangelical Synod see BX8959.A3+
8998.2 Periodicals. Yearbooks. Directories
8998.21 Conferences. Assemblies, etc.
History
8998.22 General works
Including collective biography
8998.23.A-.W By state, A-W
8998.24.A-Z By city, A-Z
8998.25 Doctrines, creeds, catechisms, liturgy
8998.26 Government and discipline
Trials see BX9192+
8998.27.A-Z Synods, A-Z
8998.28.A-Z Presbyteries, A-Z
Individual churches see BX9211+
Associate Presbyterian churches. Associate Reformed Presbyterian churches
8999.A6-.A67 Periodicals for all churches
Individual churches see BX9211+
Biography see BX9211+
Individual Associate Presbyterian churches
Associate Presbytery of Pennsylvania (1754-1782)
8999.A68 Documents, proceedings, etc.
8999.A682 General works. History, etc.
Associate Presbytery of New York (1776-1780)
8999.A685 Documents, proceedings, etc.
8999.A686 General works. History, etc.
Associate Presbytery of Pennsylvania (1782-1801)
8999.A69 Documents, proceedings, etc.

BX

Presbyterianism. Calvinistic Methodism
History
By region or country
America. North America
United States
Individual branches of Presbyterians
Associate Presbyterian churches. Associate Reformed Presbyterian churches
Individual Associate Presbyterian churches
Associate Presbytery of Pennsylvania (1782-1801) -- Continued

8999.A692 General works. History, etc.

Associate Presbytery of Kentucky (1798-1801)

8999.A695 Documents, proceedings, etc.

8999.A696 General works. History, etc.

Associate Synod of North America (1801-1858)

8999.A7 Periodicals. Yearbooks. Directories

8999.A701 Conferences. Assemblies, etc.

History

8999.A702 General works

Including collective biography

8999.A703A-.A703W By state, A-W

8999.A704A-.A704Z By city, A-Z

8999.A705 Doctrines, creeds, catechisms, liturgy

8999.A706 Government and discipline

Trials see BX9192+

8999.A707A-.A707Z Synods, A-Z

8999.A708A-.A708Z Presbyteries, A-Z

8999.A708C2 Cambridge

8999.A708C4 Chartiers

8999.A708K4 Kentucky

8999.A708P5 Philadelphia

Merged in 1858 into the United Presbyterian Church of North America. A minority continued the denomination

Individual churches see BX9211+

Associate Synod of North America (1859-1969). Associate Presbyterian Church of North America

For the merger in 1969 into the Synod of the Reformed Presbyterian Church of North America see BX8990.A8+

8999.A709 Periodicals. Yearbooks. Directories

8999.A71 Conferences. Assemblies, etc.

History

8999.A72 General works

Including collective biography

Presbyterianism. Calvinistic Methodism
History
By region or country
America. North America
United States
Individual branches of Presbyterians
Associate Presbyterian churches. Associate Reformed Presbyterian churches
Individual Associate Presbyterian churches
Associate Synod of North America (1859-1969). Associate Presbyterian Church of North America
History -- Continued

8999.A73A-.A73W	By state, A-W
8999.A74A-.A74Z	By city, A-W
8999.A75	Doctrines, creeds, catechisms, liturgy
8999.A76	Government and discipline
	Trials see BX9192+
8999.A77A-.A77Z	Synods, A-Z
8999.A78A-.A78Z	Presbyteries, A-Z
	Individual churches see BX9211+
	Associate Reformed Presbyterian churches
	Associate Reformed Synod. Associate Reformed Church. Associate Reformed Church in North America (1782-1855)
8999.A8	Periodicals. Yearbooks. Directories
8999.A801	Conferences. Assemblies, etc.
	History
8999.A802	General works
	Including collective biography
8999.A803A-.A803W	By state, A-W
8999.A804A-.A804Z	By city, A-Z
8999.A805	Doctrines, creeds, catechisms, liturgy
8999.A806	Government and discipline
	Trials see BX9192+
8999.A807A-.A807Z	Synods, A-Z
8999.A807C2	Carolinas (1804-1822)
	Independent in 1822 and continued as Associate Reformed Synod of the South
8999.A807N5	New York (1804-1822)
	The only surviving synod in 1822, it called itself the Associate Reformed Church in North America
8999.A807P5	Pennsylvania (1804-1822)
	Merged in 1822 into the Presbyterian Church in the U.S.A.

BX

Presbyterianism. Calvinistic Methodism
History
By region or country
America. North America
United States
Individual branches of Presbyterians
Associate Presbyterian churches. Associate Reformed Presbyterian churches
Associate Reformed Presbyterian churches
Associate Reformed Synod. Associate Reformed Church. Associate Reformed Church in North America (1782-1855)
Synods, A-Z -- Continued

8999.A807S3 Scioto (1804-1820)
Independent in 1820 and continued as Associate Reformed Synod of the West
8999.A808A-.A808Z Presbyteries, A-Z
Individual churches see BX9211+
Associate Reformed Synod of the South. General Synod of the Associate Reformed Presbyterian Church. Associate Reformed Presbyterian Church (1822-)
8999.A809 Periodicals. Yearbooks. Directories
8999.A81 Conferences. Assemblies, etc.
History
8999.A82 General works
Including collective biography
8999.A83A-.A83W By state, A-W
8999.A84A-.A84Z By city, A-Z
8999.A85 Doctrines, creeds, catechisms, liturgy
8999.A86 Government and discipline
Trials see BX9192+
8999.A87A-.A87Z Synods, A-Z
8999.A88A-.A88Z Presbyteries, A-Z
Individual churches see BX9211+
8999.A882 Associate Reformed Synod of the West (1820-1841)
8999.A883 Second Associate Reformed Synod of the West (1839-1841)
8999.A884 Associate Reformed Synod of Illinois (-1852)
8999.A885-.A8858 Associate Reformed Church of the West (1841-1855) (Table BX29)
Merged with the Associate Reformed Church in North America in 1855 to form the General Synod of the Associate Reformed Church

Presbyterianism. Calvinistic Methodism
History
By region or country
America. North America
United States
Individual branches of Presbyterians
Associate Presbyterian churches. Associate Reformed Presbyterian churches
Associate Reformed Presbyterian churches -- Continued

8999.A886-.A8868 General Synod of the Associate Reformed Church (Table BX29)
Merged in 1858 with the Associate Synod of North America to form the United Presbyterian Church of North America

8999.A9-.Z8 Other Presbyterian churches
Bible Presbyterian Church see BX8959.A3+

8999.C3 Calvinistic Methodist Church in the U.S.A.
Merged with the Presbyterian Church in the U.S.A. in 1920

Orthodox Presbyterian Church see BX8959.A2+

8999.R4 Reformed Cumberland Presbyterian Church

8999.U54 United Synod of the South

Canada. British America

9001 General works

9002.A-Z By province, A-Z

9003.A-Z By city, A-Z

Mexico

9011 General works

9012.A-Z By state, A-Z

9013.A-Z By city, A-Z

Central America

9021 General works

9022.A-Z By country, A-Z

9023.A-Z By city, A-Z

West Indies

9031 General works

9032.A-Z By country, A-Z

9033.A-Z By city, A-Z

South America

9041 General works

9042.A-Z By country, A-Z

9043.A-Z By city, A-Z

Europe

9050 General works

Great Britain. England

9052 Directories

Presbyterianism. Calvinistic Methodism
History
By region or country
Europe
Great Britain. England -- Continued
Conventions, assemblies, etc.
9053 Westminster Assembly of Divines
9054.A-Z Other, A-Z
9055 General works. Histories
9056 Other
9057.A-Z By county (England), A-Z
9058.A-Z By city (England), A-Z
Ireland
9060 General works
9061.A-Z By county, A-Z
9062.A-Z By city, A-Z
Scotland
9070 General works
By period
9071 Early to 1800
9072 19th-20th centuries
9073.A-Z By county, A-Z
9074.A-Z By city, A-Z
Individual branches of Presbyterians
Church of Scotland
9075.A1 Periodicals (Historical)
9075.A2 Societies
9075.A3 Collections
Including Wodrow Society publications
Documents. Acts. Proceedings, etc.
9075.A4-.A49 Collections
9075.A5 Special. By date
9076 Directories
General works, histories see BX9070+
9078 Government and discipline
For doctrine, confessions, etc. see BX9174+
9079 Clergy. Patronage, etc.
9081 Covenanters, 1638-1688
9082 Covenanters (or Cameronians), 1712
9083 Secession Church, Burghers, etc., 1733-
Free Church of Scotland, 1843-
Including all the works of the Disruption of 1843
9084.A1 Periodicals
9084.A3-Z General works. Histories
9087 United Presbyterian Church, 1847-1900

Presbyterianism. Calvinistic Methodism
History
By region or country
Europe
Great Britain. England
Scotland
Individual branches of Presbyterians -- Continued
9089 United Free Church of Scotland, 1900-
Including Free Church union case and reports of government commissions
Formed in 1900 by the union of a majority of the Free Church of Scotland and the United Presbyterian Church. In 1929 a majority united with the Church of Scotland
9092 Reformed Church of Scotland
9095.A-Z Other, A-Z
e.g.
9095.R4 Relief Church of Scotland
9099 Biography (Collective)
Wales
9100 General works
9101.A-Z By county, A-Z
9102.A-Z By city, A-Z
9105 British colonies (General)
France
9110 General works
9111.A-Z By province, department, etc., A-Z
9112.A-Z By city, A-Z
Netherlands (Holland)
9120 General works
9121.A-Z By province, A-Z
9122.A-Z By city, A-Z
Switzerland
9130 General works
9131.A-Z By canton, A-Z
9132.A-Z By city, A-Z
9140.A-Z Other European countries, A-Z
e.g.
9140.I8 Italy
Asia
9150 General works
9151.A-Z By Asian regions or countries, A-Z
e.g.
9151.K8 Korea
Africa
9160 General works
9161 South Africa

Presbyterianism. Calvinistic Methodism
History
By region or country
Africa -- Continued
9162.A-Z Other African regions or countries, A-Z
Australia and New Zealand
9165 General works
9166.A-Z Local, A-Z
Oceania
9168 General works
9169.A-Z Local, A-Z
Relations with other denominations
9171.A1 General works
9171.A3-Z Special
9171.C38 Catholic Church
9171.L8 Lutheran Church
Episcopal Church. Protestant Episcopal Church in the United States of America see BX5928.5.P65
General works. Doctrine, government, etc.
9174 Early through 1800
9175 1801-1950
9175.2 1951-2000
9175.3 2001-
9177 Addresses, essays, lectures
Sermons. Tracts
Class sermons on special topics with the subject, especially biography and history
For sermons for children, young people, etc. see BV4310+
Cf. BX8913+ Collected works
9178.A1 Several authors
9178.A3-Z Individual authors. By author and title, A-Z
9180 Controversial literature against Presbyterianism
9183 Creeds, confessions, covenants, etc. Westminster confession
Catechisms
Larger catechism
9184.A2 Texts. By date
9184.A3A-.A3Z Explanations. By author or title, A-Z
Shorter catechism
9184.A4 Texts. By date
9184.A5A-.A5Z Explanations. By author or title, A-Z
9184.A6-Z Other catechisms
Service. Ritual and liturgy
9185 General
9187 Other
Including use of instrumental music in churches

Presbyterianism. Calvinistic Methodism -- Continued
Hymns in English see BV430+
Hymns in languages other than English see BV470+
Sacraments
Including theology, liturgy, rite
9188 General works
9189.A-Z Special, A-Z
9189.B3 Baptism
9189.C5 Communion. Lord's supper
9189.C7 Confirmation
9189.M3 Marriage service
9189.O7 Ordination
9189.5 Finance. Stewardship
Government and discipline
For early works see BX9174+
9190 General works
Law
see class K
Trials
Cf. Trials, Class K
9192 General works. Procedure, etc.
9193.A-Z Special, A-Z
9195 Clergy, elders, deacons, etc.
9199.A-Z Special topics, A-Z
9199.S62 Sociology. Social ethics
Individual churches
Subarrange by place or by name if nonurban
9211 United States
9215 Other regions or countries
Biography
9220 Collective
Individual
9223 John Knox
9225.A-Z Other, A-Z
e.g.
9225.B5 Beecher, Lyman
9225.C29 Campbell, John McLeod
9225.C4 Chalmers, Thomas
9225.D33 Davies, Samuel
9225.D8 Drummond, Henry
9225.G826 Griffin, Edward Dorr
9225.H6 Hodge, Charles
9225.M258 MacLeod, Norman
9225.M352 Marshall, Peter
9225.M4 Melville, Andrew
9225.P3 Parkhurst, Charles Henry
9225.T3 Talmadge, Thomas DeWitt

Presbyterianism. Calvinistic Methodism
Biography
Individual
Other, A-Z -- Continued
9225.T4 Tennent, William
9225.W4 Whitefield, George
9250 Protestant Reformed Churches of America (Table BX3)
Offshoot of Christian Reformed Church
Puritanism
Prefer Classes D, E, and F for historical works
9301 Periodicals. Serials
9303 Societies
Collected works
9313 Several authors
9315 Individual authors
9316.A-Z Relations with other churches, A-Z
9316.A1 General works
Methodist churches see BX8329.P8
General works. History. Puritan doctrine, government, etc.
9318 Early works through 1800
9321 1801-1950
9322 1951-2000
9323 2001-
9327 Addresses, essays, lectures
9329 Controversial works against the Puritans
By region or country
Great Britain. England
9331 Documents
General works. History
9333 Early works through 1800
9334 1801-1950
9334.2 1951-2000
9334.3 2001-
9335.A-Z Local, A-Z
e.g.
9335.L7 London
Biography
9338 Collective
9339.A-Z Individual, A-Z
9340.A-Z Other special, A-Z
e.g.
9340.I7 Ireland
9340.W34 Wales
9340.W65 Women
9341 Netherlands (Holland)
America
Cf. BX7133+ Congregationalism

Puritanism
By region or country
America -- Continued
9351 Documents
General works. History
9353 Early works through 1800
9354 1801-1950
9354.2 1951-2000
9354.3 2001-
9355.A-Z Local, A-Z
Biography
9358 Collective
9359.A-Z Individual, A-Z
Puritanism - Qu
9365.P8 Pythagorean Christians
Quietism and Quietists see BV5099
Qu - Reformed churches
9375.R3 Ranters
9375.R43-.R438 Redeemed Church in Uganda (Table BX4)
Reformed Church in Spain see BX9798.S6
Reformed or Calvinistic churches
9401 Periodicals. Serials
9403 Societies
9405 Documents. Conferences, etc.
Prefer local history except for general documents
9406 Dictionaries. Encyclopedias
9407 Directories
Collected works
9409 Several authors
9410 Individual authors
Cf. BX9420.A+ Calvin
9412 Study and teaching
For individual seminaries see BV4070.A+
9413 Textbooks
9415 History
Biography
Cf. BX9439.A+ Biography in individual countries
9417 Collective
Individual
9418 Calvin
Including his theology
For Calvinistic theology by country see BX9424.5.A+
9419.A-Z Other, A-Z
e.g.
9419.B4 Bèze (Beza), Théodore de
9419.C3 Capito, Wolfgang Fabricius
9419.D4 Desmarets, Samuel

Reformed or Calvinistic churches
Biography
Individual
Other, A-Z -- Continued

9419.J8 Juda, Leo
9419.O3 OEcolampadius, Joannes
9419.O4 Olevianus, Kaspar
9419.U7 Ursinus, Zacharias
9419.5.A-Z Relations with other churches, A-Z
9419.5.A1 General works
Lutheran Church see BX8063.7.R4
General works on Reformed doctrine. Calvinism
Early through 1800
By Calvin
9420.A2 Collected works. By date
9420.A22-.A29 Translations. By language and translator, A-Z
9420.A3A-.A3Z Selections. By editor, A-Z
9420.A32-.A39 Translations. By language and translator, A-Z
9420.A4-Z Individual works, A-Z
9421.A-Z By others, A-Z
9422 1801-1950
9422.2 1951-2000
9422.3 2001-
9422.5 Addresses, essays, lectures
9423.A-Z Special topics, A-Z
9423.A77 Art
9423.B45 Benevolent work. Social work, welfare work, etc.
9423.C3 Capitalism
9423.C43 Church unity
9423.C46 Civil rights
9423.C5 Communion. Eucharist
9423.C73 Confession
9423.D45 Democracy
9423.H43 Health. Medicine
9423.H66 Homosexuality
9423.L3 Law
9423.M37 Marriage
Medicine see BX9423.H43
9423.S33 Sacraments
9423.S36 Science
Social work see BX9423.B45
9423.S63 Sociology. Social ethics
Welfare work see BX9423.B45
9423.Y68 Youth
Controversial works against Calvinism
Cf. BX6195+ Arminians
9424.A2 Early through 1800

Reformed or Calvinistic churches
Controversial works against Calvinism -- Continued
9424.A3-Z 1801-1950
9424.2 1951-2000
9424.3 2001-
9424.5.A-Z Calvinistic theology. By region or country, A-Z
9425 Church government and organization
Sermons. Tracts
Class sermons on special topics with the subject, especially biography and history
Prefer church divisions, BX9435+
For sermons for children, young people, etc. see BV4310+
Cf. BX9409+ Collected works
9426.A1 Several authors
9426.A2-Z Individual authors. By author and title, A-Z
Liturgy and ritual
For Dutch Reformed churches in the United States see BX9523+
For German Reformed churches in the United States see BX9573+
9427 General works
9427.5.A-Z Special, A-Z
9427.5.B36 Baptism
9427.5.C6 Confessions
9427.5.P7 Prayer
9427.5.P74 Psalters
Hymns in English see BV433+
Hymns in languages other than English see BV470+
Catechisms, creeds, etc.
9428.A1 General works. History, etc.
Heidelberg catechism
By language
9428.A2 German. By date
9428.A3 English. By date
9428.A4A-.A4Z Other, A-Z
9428.A5-Z Works about the Heidelberg catechism
9429.A-Z Other catechisms and creeds, A-Z
9429.B4 Belgic confession
9429.C27 Calvin's catechism
9429.C34 Catehismul calvin
9429.G4 Geneva catechism
9429.H38 Hellenbroek's catechism
Helvetic confessions
9429.H4 First, 1536
9429.H43 Second, 1566
9429.P3 Paris, 1559

Reformed or Calvinistic churches
Catechisms, creeds, etc.
Other catechisms and creeds, A-Z -- Continued
9429.R43 Reina's Confession of faith
Individual churches
see BX9437+
Biography
see BX9417+ and individual countries
By country
9430-9439 Reformed Church of Switzerland (Geneva) (Table BX30 modified)
9436.A-Z Cantons, A-Z
Biography
9439.A1 Collective
9439.A3-Z Individual, A-Z
e.g.
9439.G63 Goltz, Hermann, freiherr von der
9440-9449 Reformed Church of Hungary (Table BX30)
9450-9459 Reformed Church of France. Huguenots (Table BX30 modified)
Including churches in other countries
For Edict of Nantes and Revocation see BR845
Cf. DC111+ Huguenot wars
9458.A-Z Huguenots in other countries, A-Z
e.g.
For Huguenots in relation to the history of specific countries or as an element of the population of specific countries see the country in classes D-F.
9458.G3 Germany
9458.G7 Great Britain
9458.I7 Ireland
9458.U5 United States
Biography
9459.A1 Collective
9459.A3-Z Individual
e.g.
9459.C4 Châteillon (Castellion), Sébastien
9459.M7 Monod, Adolphe
9459.R3 Rabaut, Paul
9460-9469 Reformed Church of Germany (Table BX30)
9470-9479 Reformed Church of the Netherlands (Table BX30 modified)
All bodies differentiated only by subject
Cf. BX6195+ Arminians
9478 Synod of Dort, 1618-1619
Biography
9479.A1 Collective

Reformed or Calvinistic churches
By country
Reformed Church of the Netherlands
Biography -- Continued

9479.A3-Z Individual, A-Z
e.g.
9479.G8 Gunning, Johannes Hermanus
9479.K8 Kuyper, Abraham
9480.A-Z Other European countries, A-Z
Under each (unless otherwise specified):

.x	*General works. History*
.x2A-.x2Z	*Local, A-Z*
	Biography
.x3A1	*Collective*
.x3A3-.x3Z	*Individual, A-Z*

e.g.
Belgium. Flanders
9480.B4 General works. History
9480.B5A-.B5Z Local, A-Z
Biography
9480.B6A1 Collective
9480.B6A3-.B6Z Individual, A-Z
9480.P7-.P73 Poland
United States
9495 General works. History
9496.A-.W By state, A-W
9497.A-Z By city, A-Z
9498.A-Z By nationality or race, A-Z
e.g.
9498.H8 Hungarians
9499 Hungarian Reformed Church
Became part of the Reformed Church in the United States in 1922 except for a minority that continued as the Free Magyar Reformed Church in America
9499.3 Hungarian Reformed Church in America
Prior to 1958 was the Free Magyar Reformed Church in America
9499.6 Lithuanian Evangelical Reformed Church. Lietuviu̕ Evangeliku̕ Reformatu̕ Bažničia-JAV
Reformed Church in America (Dutch Reformed)
For Christian Reformed Church see BX6801+
9501 Periodicals. Serials
9503 Societies
9505 Conferences, etc.
9507 Directories
9509 Collected works
Study and teaching

Reformed or Calvinistic churches
By country
United States
Reformed Church in America (Dutch Reformed)
Study and teaching -- Continued
9511 General works
Individual seminaries see BV4070.A+
Sunday schools (Church schools)
9513.A1 Societies. Conventions, etc.
9513.A3-Z General works
History (United States)
9515 General works
9516.A-.W By state, A-W
9517.A-Z By city, A-Z
Synods
9518.A1-.A5 General works
9518.A6-Z Other
9519.A-Z Classes, A-Z
e.g.
9519.M7 Montgomery
9519.N4 Newark
9519.P3 Paramus
9520.A-Z Other organizations, A-Z
9521 General works. Organization, doctrine, etc.
9522 Government and discipline. Clergy and church officers
Liturgy and ritual
9523 General works
9525.A-Z Special, A-Z
e.g.
9525.C7 Confirmation
Hymns in English see BV434
Hymns in languages other than English see BV470+
Sermons. Tracts
Class sermons on special topics with the subject, especially biography and history
For sermons for children, young people, etc. see BV4310+
For addresses, essays, etc., on general doctrines or polity see BX9521
Cf. BX9509 Collected works
9527.A1 Several authors
9527.A3-Z Individual authors
9529 Individual branches of the Reformed Church in America
True Reformed Dutch Church see BX9798.T7
Individual churches. By place and name or by name if nonurban
9531 United States

Reformed or Calvinistic churches
By country
United States
Reformed Church in America (Dutch Reformed)
Individual churches. By place and name or by name if nonurban -- Continued

9533 Other countries
Biography
9541 Collective
9543.A-Z Individual, A-Z
e.g.
9543.D45 De Witt, Thomas
9543.L55 Livingston, John Henry
9543.P4 Peale, Norman Vincent
Reformed Church in the United States (German Reformed)
In 1934 merged with the Evangelical Synod of North America to form the Evangelical and Reformed Church
For the Evangelical and Reformed Church see BX7451+
9551 Periodicals. Serials
9553 Societies
9555 Conferences
9557 Directories
9559 Collected works
Study and teaching
9561 General works
Individual seminaries see BV4070.A+
Sunday schools
9563.A1 Societies. Conventions, etc.
9563.A3-Z General works
History (United States)
9565 General works
9566.A-.W By state, A-W
9567.A-Z By city, A-Z
Synods
9568.A1-.A5 General works
9568.A6-Z Other
e.g.
9568.C5 Central
9568.E2 Eastern
9568.I6 Interior
9568.M5 Midwest
9568.N7 Northwest
9568.O3 Ohio
9568.P7 Potomac
9568.S7 Southwest

Reformed or Calvinistic churches
By country
United States
Reformed Church in the United States (German Reformed) -- Continued

9569.A-Z Classes, A-Z
e.g.
9569.A6 Allegheny
9569.G4 Gettysburg
9569.I6 Indiana
9569.J8 Juniata
9569.L5 Lebanon, Pa.
9569.M3 Maryland
9569.O3 Eastern Ohio
9569.S5 Sheboygan
9569.W6 Westmoreland
9569.Z7 Zion's
9570 Other organizations
9571 General works. Organization, doctrine, etc.
Mercersburg theology
Creeds, catechisms, etc. see BX9428+
9572 Government and discipline. Clergy and church officers
Liturgy and ritual
9573 General works
9575.A-Z Special, A-Z
e.g.
9575.C7 Confirmation
Hymns in English see BV435
Hymns in languages other than English see BV470+
Sermons. Tracts, Addresses. Essays
Cf. BX9559 Collected works
9577.A1 Several authors
9577.A3-Z Individual authors
9579 Individual branches of the Reformed Church in the United States
Individual churches. By place
9581 United States
9583 Other countries
Biography
9591 Collective
9593.A-Z Individual, A-Z
e.g.
9593.B6 Boehm, John Philip
9593.N4 Nevin, John Williamson
9593.S3 Schlatter, Michael
Canada
9596 General works. History

Reformed or Calvinistic churches
By country
Canada -- Continued
9598 Canadian Reformed Churches (Table BX3)
West Indies
9610 General works
9611 Gereformeerde Kerk te Curaçao
Asia
9615 General works
9616.A-Z By region or country, A-Z
Africa
9618 General works
9619 Angola
9619.5 Namibia
South Africa
9620 General works. History
9620.5 Afrikaanse Protestantse Kerk (Table BX3)
9621 Gereformeerde Kerk in Suid-Afrika (Table BX3)
9622 Nederduitse Gereformeerde Kerk (Table BX3)
9623 Nederduitse Gereformeerde Sendingkerk in Suid-Afrika (Table BX3)
9624 Nederduitse Hervormde Kerk (Table BX3)
Zambia
9640 Reformed Church in Zambia (Table BX3)
9645 Australia
9650 New Zealand
9655 Oceania
Reformed Episcopal Church see BX6051+
Reformed Episcopal Church - River Brethren
Reformed Spanish Church see BX9798.S6
9670.R27 Reformed Zion Union Apostolic Churches of America
9670.R3 Religion Deima
Founded by Bagui Honoyo
Remonstrants, Remonstrantsche Broederschap see BX6195+
9670.R5-.R58 Ringatu Church (Table BX4)
9675 River Brethren. Brethren in Christ (Table BX3)
River Brethren - Salvation Army
Rock Church Fellowship see BX8777
Russellism see BX8525+
9680.S3 Sabbatarians
9701-9743 Salvation Army (Table BX1 modified)
Biography
9741 Collective
9743.A-Z Individual, A-Z
e.g.
9743.B6 Booth, Mrs. Catherine (Mumford)

Salvation Army
Biography
Individual, A-Z -- Continued
9743.B7 Booth, William
9743.B8 Booth-Clibborn, Mrs. Catherine
9747 Sandemanians (Glassites or Glasites)
Sandemanians - Schwenckfelder Church
9748.S4 Schweinfurth Sect
Founded by George Jacob Schweinfurth
9749 Schwenckfelder Church. Schwenckfeldians
Schwenckfelder Church - Shakers
9750.S4-.S48 Segye Kidokkyo T'ongil Sillyŏng Hyŏphoe (Sun Myung Moon). Unification Church (Table BX4)
For relations with Orthodox Eastern Church see BX324.6
Shakers. United Society of Believers. Millennial Church
9751 Periodicals. Serials
9755 Conventions. Conferences
9757 Directories. Registers. Yearbooks
9759 Collected works
Study and teaching
9761 General works
9764 Textbooks, etc.
History
9765 General works
Including early history in England, persecutions, travels, decadence, etc.
By region or country
United States
Cf. HX653+ Communistic settlements in the United States
9766 General works
9767.A-.W By state, A-W
9768.A-Z By society. By place, A-Z
Under each:
.xA1-.xA7 *Documents*
.xA8-.xZ *Other works*
Spiritual names are set within quotation marks
9768.A6 Alfred, Me. "Holy Land"
9768.B8 Busro or West Union, Ind. (Eagle and Straight Creek)
9768.C3 Canterbury, N.H. (Shaker village) "Holy Ground"
9768.E6 Enfield, Conn. "City of Union"
9768.E7 Enfield, N.H. "Chosen Valley"
9768.G7 Groveland, N.Y. "Union Branch"
9768.H2 Hancock and West Pittsfield, Mass. "City of Peace"
9768.H3 Harvard, Mass. (South Groton) "Lovely Vineyard"
9768.K5 Kissimmee, Fla. "Olive Branch"
9768.N5 New Lebanon, N.Y. (Canaan) "Holy Mount of God"

Shakers. United Society of Believers. Millennial Church
History
By region or country
United States
By society. By place, A-Z -- Continued

9768.N7 North Union, Ohio. "Valley of God's Pleasure"
9768.P6 Pleasant Hill, Ky. "Holy Sinai Plains"
9768.S2 Sabbathday Lake, New Gloucester, Me. "Chosen Land"
9768.S5 Shirley, Mass. "Pleasant Garden"
9768.S7 Sodus, N.Y. (Moved to Groveland)
9768.T9 Tyringham, Mass. "City of Love"
9768.U6 Union Village, Ohio. "Wisdom's Paradise"
9768.W2 Watervliet, N.Y. "Wisdom's Valley"
Earlier, Niskayuna or Nisqueunia, N.Y.
9768.W3 Watervliet, Ohio
Earlier, Beaver Creek, Beulah, Mad River
9768.W4 Whitewater, Ohio. "Lonely Plain of Tribulation"
9769.A-Z Other regions or countries, A-Z
9771 General works. Theology, etc.
9772 Addresses, essays, lectures
9773 Controversial works against the Shakers
9774 Catechisms, etc.
9775 Service books
Hymns in English see BV442
Hymns in languages other than English see BV470+
9776 Government and discipline
Sermons. Tracts
Class sermons on special topics with the subject, especially biography and history
Cf. BX9759 Collected works
9777.A1 Several authors
9777.A3-Z Individual authors
9778.A-Z Special doctrines, A-Z
9778.C4 Christianity
9778.C8 Confession
9778.D7 Dreams and visions
9778.G7 God
9778.I5 Inspiration
9778.J8 Judgment day
9778.P8 Prophecy
9778.R4 Resurrection
9778.R5 Revelation
9778.S4 Second coming
9778.S7 Spiritualism
9778.S8 Sunday
9778.T5 Testimony

Shakers. United Society of Believers. Millennial Church -- Continued

Missions

9779 General works

9780.A-Z By region or country, A-Z

9781 Religious life

Including Shaker dancing, singing, Sunday observance, etc.

9783 Benevolent work. Social work, welfare work, etc.

Economic life

9784 General works

9785.A-Z Special industries, A-Z

Agriculture. Farm products

9785.A4 General works

9785.A5 Catalogs

9785.C4 Chairs

9785.C6 Cloaks

9785.F8 Furniture

Horticulture. Plants. Flowers

9785.H6 General works

9785.H7 Catalogs

Seeds see BX9785.S4

Medicines. Roots, herbs, etc.

9785.M4 General works

9785.M5 Catalogs

9785.S4 Seeds

9785.W3 Washing machines

9786 Shakers as authors

Including diaries, letters, inspirational writings, etc.

Shakers and the law. Legal status, etc.

see class K

9789.A-Z Other topics, A-Z

9789.A6 Amusements

9789.C4 Celibacy

9789.C5 Children in Shakerism

9789.C7 Community life

9789.C8 Costume

9789.E8 Ethics

9789.H8 Hygiene

9789.L7 Love

9789.M3 Marriage

9789.P7 Politics and government

Sabbath see BX9781

9789.S3 Schools

9789.S7 Social conditions

9789.T3 Taxation

9789.V4 Vegetarianism

9789.W2 War and peace. Militia, etc.

Shakers. United Society of Believers. Millennial Church
Other topics, A-Z -- Continued
9789.W7 Women in Shakerism
Biography
9791 Collective
9793.A-Z Individual, A-Z
e.g.
9793.E8 Evans, Frederick William
9793.L4 Lee, Ann
Shakers - Unitarianism
Shouter Baptists see BX9798.S65+
9798.S47 Skoptsy
9798.S48 Smith's Friends
9798.S5 Social Brethren
Society of Christian Israelites see BX6799.C5
Society of Life (Church of Integration) see BX7065
9798.S6 Spanish Reformed Church (Iglesia Española Reformada)
9798.S65-.S658 Spiritual Baptists. Shouter Baptists (Table BX4)
9798.S7 Spiritualists
As a religious sect (All bodies)
Cf. B841.A+ Modern philosophy
Cf. BD331 Metaphysics
Cf. BF1228 Parapsychology
9798.S8 Stundists
9798.S82 Svenska alliansmissionen
9798.S83 Svenska missionsförbundet
Swedish Evangelical churches see BX7547
9798.T39 Tempel Gesellschaft
9798.T4 Temple Society in America
9798.T42 Tenshin Ōmikamikyō
9798.T45 Thearch Society
9798.T56 Tinker Tailor
9798.T7 True Reformed Dutch Church
9798.T85-.T858 Two-by-Two's. Christian Conventions (Table BX4)
9798.U6 Ukrainian Evangelical Alliance
Unierte evangelische Kirche in Polen see BX8025.6.A+
Unierte evangelische Kirchen (of Germany) see BX8020+
Unification Church see BX9750.S4+
Union of Evangelical Churches (Great Britain) see BX8750.P43
Unitarianism
Including the merger in 1961 of the Unitarian Universalist Association
9801 Periodicals. Serials
9803 Associations. Societies
Conventions
9805 General works

Unitarianism
Conventions -- Continued
9807.A-Z Local, A-Z
9809 Dictionaries. Encyclopedias
9811 Directories
Collected works
9813 Several authors
9815.A-Z Individual authors, A-Z
e.g.
9815.C4 Channing, William Ellery
9815.C6 Clarke, James F.
9815.D3 Davies, A. Powell
9815.M28 Martineau, James
9815.P3 Parker, Theodore
9815.P68 Priestley, Joseph
Study and teaching
9817 General works
Individual seminaries see BV4070.A+
Sunday schools (Church schools)
9818 Societies. Conventions
9819 General works. Organization, etc.
9820 Service books
9821 Textbooks
9823.A-Z Individual Sunday schools. By place, A-Z
History
9831 General works
Including centennial services
By region or country
United States
9833 General works
By region
9833.4 New England
9833.42 Middle Atlantic
9833.43 South
9833.44 Central
9833.45 West
9833.46 Pacific States
9833.48.A-Z By nationality or race, A-Z
9833.48.A47 African Americans
9833.5.A-.W By state, A-W
9833.6.A-Z By city, A-Z
9834 Great Britain
9835.A-Z Other regions or countries, A-Z
General works. Principles. Beliefs
Cf. BT115 Anti-Trinitarian works
9840 Early through 1800
1801-1950

Unitarianism
General works. Principles. Beliefs
1801-1950 -- Continued
9841.A1 Several authors
9841.A3-Z Individual authors
9841.2 1951-2000
9841.3 2001-
9842 Addresses, essays, lectures
Sermons. Tracts
Class sermons on special topics with the subject, especially biography and history
For sermons for children, young people, etc. see BV4310+
Cf. BX9813+ Collected works
9843.A1 Several authors
9843.A3-Z Individual authors. By author and title, A-Z
9847 Controversial literature against Unitarianism
9848 Joint debates and discussions on Unitarianism
9850 Government and discipline. Clergy and church officers
9853 Services
Hymns in English see BV445
Hymns in languages other than English see BV470+
Sacraments
9854.A1 General works
9854.A3-Z Special
9854.C5 Communion
9855 Christian life. Spiritual life
9856 Benevolent work. Social work, welfare work, etc.
Individual churches
Subarrange by place or by name if nonurban
9861 United States
9863 Other regions or countries
Biography
9867 Collective
9869.A-Z Individual, A-Z
e.g.
9869.B3 Barrows, Samuel June
9869.B75 Bradlee, Caleb Davis
9869.C4 Channing, William Ellery
9869.C6 Clarke, James Freeman
9869.C7 Collyer, Robert
9869.C8 Conway, Moncure Daniel
9869.F6 Follen, Charles Theodore Christian
9869.F83 Frothingham, Octavius Brooks
9869.H3 Hale, Edward Everett
9869.H535 Holmes, John Haynes
9869.K5 King, Thomas Starr

	Unitarianism
	Biography
	Individual, A-Z -- Continued
9869.M4	Martineau, James
9869.M45	Mayhew, Jonathan
9869.P3	Parker, Theodore
9869.P75	Price, Richard
9869.P8	Priestley, Joseph
9869.S4	Servetus, Michael
9869.W3	Ware, Henry
9873	Unitarianism - United Brethren
	United Brethren see BX8551+
	United Brethren in Christ. Church of the United Brethren in Christ (New Constitution)
	Merged with the Evangelical Church to form the Evangelical United Brethren Church
	For Church of the United Brethren in Christ (Old Constitution) see BX9877.1
	Cf. BX7556 Evangelical United Brethren Church
9875.A1	Periodicals. Serials
(9875.A15-.A2)	Yearbooks
	see BX9875.A1
	Conferences
9875.A3-.A39	General
9875.A4A-.A4Z	Special. By name, A-Z
	e.g.
9875.A4A8	Auglaize
9875.A4E2	East Pennsylvania
9875.A4V5	Virginia
9875.A4W5	White River
9875.A5	Other documents: Constitution, discipline, etc. By date
9875.A6-Z	General works. History, doctrine, liturgy
9875.A6-.A69	Official works
	By region or country
	United States
	General works see BX9875+
9875.4.A-.W	By state, A-W
9875.5A-.5Z	Other regions or countries, A-Z
9876	Sermons. Tracts. Addresses. Essays
	Individual churches. By place
9876.8	United States
9876.9	Other regions or countries
9877.A-Z	Biography, A-Z
	e.g.
9877.A1	Collective
9877.N4	Newcomer, Christian
9877.O8	Otterbein, Philip William

9877.1 United Brethren in Christ. Church of the United Brethren in Christ (Old Constitution) (Table BX3)

9879 United Christian Church

United Christian Ministerial Association see BX8777.3

9880 United Church in Papua, New Guinea, and the Solomon Islands

United Church of Canada

Organized in 1925 by merger of the Presbyterian, Methodist, and Congregational churches of Canada

9881.A1 Periodicals. Serials

(9881.A15-.A2) Yearbooks

see BX9881.A1

Conferences

9881.A3-.A39 General

9881.A4A-.A4Z Special. By name

9881.A5 Other documents: Constitution, discipline, etc. By date

9881.A6-Z General works. History, doctrine, liturgy

9881.A6-.A69 Official works

By region or country

Canada

General works see BX9881+

9881.4.A-Z By province, A-Z

9881.5.A-Z Other regions or countries, A-Z

9882 Sermons. Tracts. Addresses. Essays

Individual churches. By place

9882.8 Canada

9882.9 Other countries

9882.95.A-Z Relations with other churches, A-Z

Anglican Church of Canada see BX5618.U5

9883.A-Z Biography, A-Z

9884-9886 United Church of Christ (Table BX2)

A union in 1957 of the Evangelical and Reformed Church and the General Council of the Congregational Christian Churches

9886.5 United Church of Christ in the Philippines (Table BX3)

9886.9 United Church of Zambia (Table BX3)

9887 United Evangelical Church (Table BX3)

Organized in 1894 after separation from the Evangelical Association of North America. Reunited to form the Evangelical Church in 1923. Congregations that rejected the reunion took the name Evangelical Congregational Church

9887.5 United Evangelical Church of the Philippines (Table BX3)

United Holy Church of America see BX8777.5

United House of Prayer for All People see BX8777.6

9889 United Missionary Church (Table BX3)

Prior to 1947 was the Mennonite Brethren in Christ

Cf. BX8129.M4 Mennonite Brethren in Christ

United Missionary Church - Universal

United Missionary Church - Universal -- Continued
9890.U23-.U238 United Protestant Church in Curaçao (Table BX4)
9890.U25-.U258 United Reformed Church (Table BX4)
9890.U34-.U348 Uniting Church in Australia (Table BX4)
Unity of the Brethren (Texas) see BX8579
9890.U48 Unity-Progressive Council
9890.U5-.U58 Unity School of Christianity (Table BX4)
9895 Universal Apostolic Church of Life (Table BX3)
9896 Universal Fellowship of Metropolitan Community Churches (Table BX3)
Universalism. Universalists
9901 Periodicals. Serials
9903 Associations. Societies
Conventions
9905 General
9907.A-Z Local, A-Z
9909 Dictionaries. Encyclopedias
9911 Directories
Collected works
9913 Several authors
9915 Individual authors
Study and teaching
9917 General works
Individual serminaries see BV4070.A+
Sunday schools (Church schools)
9918 Societies. Conventions, etc.
9919 General works. Organization, etc.
9920 Service books
9921 Textbooks
9923.A-Z Individual Sunday schools. By place, A-Z
History
9931 General works
Including centennial services
By region or country
United States
9933 General works
9933.5.A-.W By state, A-W
9934 Great Britain
9935.A-Z Other regions or countries, A-Z
General works. Principles. Beliefs
Including works of writers of other denominations on universal salvation
9940 Early through 1800
1801-1950
9941.A1 Several authors
9941.A3-Z Individual authors
9941.2 1951-2000

Universalism. Universalists
General works. Principles. Beliefs -- Continued
9941.3 2001-
9942 Addresses, essays, lectures
Sermons. Tracts
Class sermons on special topics with the subject, especially with biography and history
For sermons for children, young people, etc. see BV4310+
Cf. BX9913+ Collected works
9943.A1 Several authors
9943.A3-Z Individual authors
9946 Joint debates and discussions on Universalism
9947 Controversial literature against Universalism
9950 Government and discipline. Clergy and church officers
9953 Services
Hymns in English see BV450
Hymns in languages other than English see BV470+
Sacraments
9954.A1 General works
9954.A2-Z Individual
9954.C5 Communion
Individual churches
Subarrange by place or by name if nonurban
9961 United States
9962 Other regions or countries
Biography
9967 Collective
9969.A-Z Individual, A-Z
e.g.
9969.B3 Ballou, Hosea
9969.M8 Murray, John
9969.W7 Winchester, Elhanan
9970 Vereinigte Protestantisch-Evangelische Kirche der Pfalz (Table BX3)
Formerly Vereinigte Protestantisch-Evangelisch-Christliche Kirche der Pfalz
9972 Vereinigte Protestantse Gemeente van Curaçao
Volunteers of America
9975.A1 Periodicals. Serials
9975.A3-Z General works
Biography
9976 Collective
9977.A-Z Individual, A-Z
9980 Walloon Church
9995 Walloon Church - Z

Walloon Church - Z -- Continued

9995.W37 Way, Inc. (The Way)

Founded by V. P. Wierwille

9995.W4-.W48 Wesleyan Church (Table BX4)

Worldwide Church of God (Herbert W. Armstrong) see BX6175+

9995.Y35 Ya 'Ityop̣yā wangélawit béta kerestiyān

9995.Z45 Zionist Churches (Africa)

9995.Z5 Zioniterne

9995.Z54 Zjednocsony Kościół Ewangeliczny w Polskiej Rzeczypospolitej Ludowej

9995.Z6 Society of Separatists of Zoar

9995.Z8 Zwijndrechtsche Nieuwlichters

9998 Other beliefs and movements akin to Christianity

e.g. Thomas Lake Harris

Cf. BF1995+ Other beliefs and movements occult in nature

Cf. BP600+ Other beliefs and movements including cults oriental in origin

9999.A-Z Independent churches, parishes, societies, etc. By city, A-Z

e.g.

9999.B6 Boston. Community Church

9999.F6 Fleetwood, Pa. St. Paul's Union Church

9999.P3 Paris. American Church

9999.P5 Philadelphia. First Independent Church

9999.V3 Van Hornesville, N.Y. Otsquago Valley, Larger Parish

(9999.V5) Virginia Beach, Va. Association for Research and Enlightenment

see BP605.A77

	Collected works
.x date	Greek or Latin. By date
.xA-.xZ	Other languages. By language and date
	Selected works
	For selections from an individual work see BR1 .x3A+
.x2	Greek or Latin. By date
.x2A-.x2Z	Other languages. By language and date
.x3A-.x3Z	Separate works. By title
	Including selections and translations of selections from an individual work
.x4A-.x4Z	Spurious and doubtful works. By title
.x55	Dictionaries, indexes, etc.
.x6	Criticism

TABLES

0	Periodicals. Societies. Collections, etc.
1	Directories
2	General works
3	Other
	By period
4	Early and medieval to Reformation
5	16th-18th centuries
6	1801-1945
6.3	1945-
7.A-Z	By region, counties, states, etc., A-Z
8.A-Z	By city, town, etc., A-Z
9	Biography (Collective)

.x	Latin. By date
.xA-.xZ	Other languages. By language and date
.x2	Criticism

1	Latin. By date
1A-1Z	Other languages. By language and date
2	Criticism

1	Texts. By date
2	History and criticism, etc.

.x date	Texts. By date
.x2	History and criticism Subarrange by main entry

1 Texts. By date

2 History of individual printings, editions, translations, etc.

For history of all translations of the Bible in any one language see BS460.A+

	Texts
.x	Bible as a whole. By date
.x1	Selections. Liturgical lessons. By date
.x2	Old Testament. By date
	Selections see BS4 .x1
.x22	Historical books. By date
.x23	Pentateuch. By date
.x27	Prophets. By date
.x3A-.x3Z	Individual books or parts. By name, A-Z, and date
.x5	New Testament. By date
.x6	Selections. Liturgical lessons. Liturgical Epistles and Gospels. By date
.x7A-.x7Z	Individual books or parts. By name, A-Z, and date
.x8	Paraphrases. Bible stories. By date
.x82-.x89	Dialects
	Subarrange alphabetically by name or place of dialect
.x9	History and criticism of texts and versions
	For general criticism, commentaries, etc., see BS410+

.x date — Texts. By date

Including whole Bibles, Old Testament texts, New Testament texts, texts of individual books, selections, etc.

.xA-.xZ — History and criticism of texts and versions

Including paraphrases, stories, etc.

For general criticism, commentaries, etc., see BS410+

	Texts
	Including selections
.A1	Polyglot. By date
	Hebrew (Old Testament). Greek (New Testament)
	For Greek Old Testament texts or Hebrew New Testament texts see BS6 .A4A+
.A2A-.A2Z	Printed texts. By editor, A-Z, or date
	Manuscripts
.A22	General works
	Individual manuscripts
.A23A-.A23Z	By name, A-Z
.A24	By number
	Latin
.A25A-.A25Z	Printed texts. By version, translator or editor, A-Z, or date
	Manuscripts
.A252	General works
	Individual manuscripts
.A253A-.A253Z	By name, A-Z
.A254	By number
	English
.A3A-.A3Z	Printed texts. By version, translator or editor, A-Z, or date
	Manuscripts
.A32	General works
	Individual manuscripts
.A33A-.A33Z	By name, A-Z
.A34	By number
.A4A-.A4Z	Other early languages and modern European languages, A-Z
	Subarrange by date
	Including Greek Old Testament texts and Hebrew New Testament texts
	Modern non-European languages
	see BS315+
.A5-.Z7	Criticism, commentaries, etc.
	For works on specific manuscripts or versions see BS6 .A1+

	Texts
	Including selections
<.A1>	Polyglot. By date
	Hebrew (Old Testament). Greek (New Testament)
	For Greek Old Testament texts or Hebrew New Testament texts see BS6a .A4A+
<.A2A-.A2Z>	Printed texts. By editor, A-Z, or date
	Manuscripts
<.A22>	General works
	Individual manuscripts
<.A23A-.A23Z>	By name, A-Z
<.A24>	By number
	Latin
<.A25A-.A25Z>	Printed texts. By version, translator or editor, A-Z, or date
	Manuscripts
<.A252>	General works
	Individual manuscripts
<.A253A-.A253Z>	By name, A-Z
<.A254>	By number
	English
<.A3A-.A3Z>	Printed texts. By version, translator or editor, A-Z, or date
	Manuscripts
<.A32>	General works
	Individual manuscripts
<.A33A-.A33Z>	By name, A-Z
<.A34>	By number
<.A4A-.A4Z>	Other early languages and modern European languages, A-Z
	Subarrange by date
	Including Greek Old Testament texts and Hebrew New Testament texts
	Modern non-European languages
	see BS315+
<.A5-.Z7>	Criticism, commentaries, etc.
	For works on specific manuscripts or versions, see the language in BS6a .A2+

	Texts
	Including selections
1	Polyglot. By date
	Hebrew
2.A-Z	Printed texts. By editor, A-Z, or date
	Manuscripts
2.3	General works
	Individual manuscripts
2.5.A-Z	By name, A-Z
2.7	By number
	English
3.A-Z	Printed texts. By version, translator or editor, A-Z, or date
	Manuscripts
3.3	General works
	Individual manuscripts
3.5.A-Z	By name, A-Z
3.7	By number
4.A-Z	Other early languages and modern European languages, A-Z
	Subarrange each language by version, translator, or editor, A-Z e.g.
4.G7	Greek versions
	Septuagint
4.G7S4	Texts. By date
	Including selections
4.G7S41-.G7S49	Criticism
	Modern non-European languages
	see BS315+
	Criticism, commentaries, etc.
5	Early through 1950
	1951-2000
5.2	Criticism
5.3	Commentaries
5.4	Sermons. Meditations. Devotions
5.5	Other
	2001-
5.52	Criticism
5.53	Commentaries
5.54	Sermons. Meditations. Devotions
5.55	Other
5.6.A-Z	Special topics, A-Z
	For list of Cutter numbers see BS1199.A+

Each apocryphal book to which this table applies has been assigned two Cutter numbers. To use the table, substitute the first Cutter number for "x1" and the second Cutter number for "x2".

	Texts
.x1A1	Polyglot. By date
.x1A3	English. By date
.x1A5-.x1Z	Other languages, A-Z Subarrange each language by date
.x2	History, criticism etc. Including works on manuscripts

	Texts
1A1	Polyglot. By date
1A3	English. By date
1A5-1Z	Other languages, A-Z Subarrange each language by date
2	History, criticism etc. Including works on manuscripts

	Texts
	Including selections
0	Polyglot. By date
	Greek
1.A-Z	Printed texts. By editor, A-Z, or date
	Manuscripts
1.3	General works
	Individual manuscripts
1.5.A-Z	By name, A-Z
1.7	By number
	Latin
2.A-Z	Printed texts. By version, translator, or editor, A-Z, or date
	Manuscripts
2.3	General works
	Individual manuscripts
2.5.A-Z	By name, A-Z
2.7	By number
	English
3.A-Z	Printed texts. By version, translator or editor, A-Z, or date
	Manuscripts
3.3	General works
	Individual manuscripts
3.5.A-Z	By name, A-Z
3.7	By number
4.A-Z	Other early languages and modern European languages, A-Z
	Modern non-European languages
	see BS315+
	Criticism, commentaries, etc.
5	Early through 1950
	1951-2000
5.2	Criticism
5.3	Commentaries
5.4	Sermons. Meditations. Devotions
5.5	Other
	2001-
5.52	Criticism
5.53	Commentaries
5.54	Sermons. Meditations. Devotions
5.55	Other
5.6.A-Z	Special topics, A-Z
	For list of Cutter numbers see BS2545.A+

	Each language to include its dialects unless otherwise provided for
199	A-Basque
	Afrikaans see BS10 225.5
199.A5	Albanian (Tosk, Gheg)
200-201	Basque (Labourdin, etc.) (Table BS3)
	Bohemian see BS10 220.C9
206-207	Breton (Table BS3)
209-210	Bulgarian (Table BS3)
212-213	Catalan (Table BS3)
	Church Slavic
	see BS110+
215-216	Cornish (Table BS3)
	Creole
	see BS350.A+
	Croatian see BS10 290+
220.C9	Czech
221-222	Dano-Norwegian (Danish, Norwegian) (Table BS3)
	For Old Norwegian, Old Norse see BS10 268
224-225	Dutch and Flemish (Table BS3)
225.5	Afrikaans (South African Dutch)
226	Dutch-Finnish
	Dutch Creole
	see BS350.D8+
226.E8	Estonian
226.F37	Faroese
227	Finnish
	French
228	Old French
	Modern French
229	Parallel versions
230	Other versions. By date
231	History and criticism, etc.
232	French-German
232.F7	Frisian
232.G3	Gaelic
234	Gagauz
	German
235	Parallel versions
	Early German to 1500
	Including High and Low German forms
	Cf. PT1505 Middle High German
236	Texts. By date
236.5	History and criticism, etc.
	Low German see BS10 269+
237-238	Catholic (Table BS3)
239-240	Protestant (Table BS3)

German -- Continued
241 Jewish
Gothic
see BS105+
242-243 Greek (Modern) (Table BS3)
245-246 Hungarian (Table BS3)
248-249 Icelandic (Table BS3)
For Old Icelandic, Old Norse see BS10 268
251-252 Irish (Table BS3)
254-255 Italian (Table BS3)
256 Ladino
257-258 Lapp (Table BS3)
260-261 Latvian (Table BS3)
263-264 Lithuanian (Table BS3)
Macedonian
265 Texts. By date
265.2 History of individual printings, editions, translations, etc.
For history of all translations of the Bible in Macedonian see BS460.A+
266-267 Manx (Table BS3)
Norwegian see BS10 221+
268 Old Norse (Old Norwegian, Old Icelandic)
269-270 Plattdeutsch (Low German) (Table BS3)
272-273 Polish (Table BS3)
275-276 Portugeuse (Table BS3)
276.3.A-Z Portuguese dialects, A-Z
277 Portugeuse-Romansch
277.P8 Provençal
278-279 Romansch (Raeto-Romance) (Table BS3)
280 Romany
281-282 Rumanian (Table BS3)
284-285 Russian (Table BS3)
287-288 Ruthenian (Ukrainian) (Table BS3)
288.5 Scandinavian languages
For individual languages, see BS10 221+ ; BS10 248+ ; BS10 268 ; BS10 302+
289 Scots
290-291 Serbo-Croatian (Table BS3)
293-294 Slovak (Table BS3)
296-297 Slovenian (Table BS3)
Sorbian (Upper and Lower) see BS10 311+
Spanish
298 Old Spanish
299-300 Modern Spanish (Table BS3)
301 Spanish-Swedish

Spanish-Swedish -- Continued
  Spanish Creole (Creolese)
    see BS350.S7+

302-303 Swedish (Table BS3)

305-306 Turkish (Table BS3)

Udmurt

307 Texts. By date

307.5 History of individual printings, editions, translations, etc.
  For history of all translations of the Bible in Udmurt see BS460.A+

Ukrainian see BS10 287+

308-309 Welsh (Cymric) (Table BS3)

311-312 Wendic. Sorbian (Upper and Lower) (Table BS3)

313 Yiddish

.x date	Collected works. By date
.x3	History and criticism (General)
.x4A-.x4Z	Individual hymns. By title, A-Z

0	General works. History and criticism
1.A-Z	By denomination, A-Z Use successive Cutter numbers for history and texts Including hymnbooks of individual churches
2	Nondenominational hymnbooks
3.A-Z	By country, A-Z Use successive Cutter numbers for history and texts For hymns of a specific denomination see BV2 1.A+
4.A-Z	Hymns of individual authors and individual hymns of unknown authors, A-Z Subarrange each author by Table BV1

.A1	Periodicals
.A2A-.A2Z	Societies, A-Z
.A5A-.A5Z	Conventions, A-Z
.A6-.Z	General works

.x1	General works
	Biography
.x2A1-.x2A19	Collective
.x2A2-.x2Z	Individual, A-Z

.x1	General works Including collective biography unless otherwise provided for
.x2A-.x2Z	Individual biography, A-Z

	Do not use except for institutions already established with this table in the Library of Congress shelflist
.x1-.x14	Periodicals
	Devoted to the work of the institution
.x15	Charters, laws, etc. By date
.x2-.x29	Catalogs, announcements, etc.
	Administrative reports
.x3-.x34	Annual, etc.
.x35	Special. By date
.x4-.x49	Alumni lists, general catalogs, necrologies, etc.
.x5	Societies
.x55	Classes. By year
	Biography
.x59A2	Collective
.x59A3-.x59Z	Individual, A-Z
	History
.x6	General works
.x65	Anniversary celebrations. By date
	Historical material only
	Cf. BV6 .x35 Special reports
.x66-.x69	Special events
.x7	Descriptive works
.x8	Other works
.x89	Minor printed matter

	Official publications
.xA1-.xA39	Serial publications
.xA4-.xA59	Monographs
.xA6-.xZ	Other. By author, A-Z

.A1	Periodicals. Societies. Collections, etc.
.A3	Documents. Rules, constitutions, etc.
.A4-.Z4	General works
.Z5A-.Z5Z	By region or country, A-Z
	Biography
.Z7	Collective
	Individual see BR1725, BX4827, or by denomination in BX5620, BX8080, BX9419, etc.

.xA1-.xA29	History and criticism
.xA3	Official compilations
.xA5-.xZ	Other collections. By compiler, A-Z

1 Periodicals. Serials
3 Societies
Publishers and publishing
see BV2360+ Z116+
5 Conferences, etc.
7 Directories
9 Collected works
9.5 Minor collections. Quotations, maxims, etc.
Study and teaching
11 General works
Individual seminaries
see BV4070
Sunday schools (Church schools)
12 General works. Organization, etc.
12.A1 Societies. Conventions, etc.
13 Service books
14 Textbooks, etc.
14.5.A-Z Individual Sunday schools. By place, A-Z
History
15 General works
By region or country
United States (and Canada)
16 General works
17.A-.W By state, A-W
18.A-Z By city, A-Z
Cf. BX1 31+ Individual churches
18.5.A-Z By nationality, race, ethnic group, etc., A-Z
19.A-Z Other regions or countries, A-Z
20.A-Z By administrative unit (district, synod, etc.), A-Z
20.5.A-Z By subordinate administrative unit, A-Z
e.g. Classes composing a synod
General works. Theology. Doctrine, etc.
21 Early through 1950
21.2 1951-2000
21.3 2001-
22 Addresses, essays, lectures
23 Controversial works against the denomination
23.4 Relation to other churches
24 Creeds and catechisms
25 Liturgy and ritual. Service books
Hymns
see subclass BV
25.5.A-Z Sacraments, A-Z
Including theology, liturgy, rite
25.5.A1 General works
26 Government and discipline. Clergy and officers. Membership

	Sermons. Tracts
	Class sermons on special topics with the subject, especially biography and history
	For sermons for children, young people, etc., see BV4310+
	Cf. BX1 9 Collected works
27.A1	Several authors
27.A3-Z	Individual authors. By author and title, A-Z
27.3	Benevolent work. Social work, welfare work, etc.
29.A-Z	Individual branches, A-Z
	Camp meetings. Summer camps. Summer conferences, retreats, etc.
30.A1	General works
30.A3-Z	Individual
	Individual churches
	Subarrange by place or by name if nonurban
31	United States
35	Other regions or countries
	Biography
41	Collective
43.A-Z	Individual, A-Z

1.A1	Periodicals, societies, directories, yearbooks
	Official documents, governing boards, conferences
1.A2A1-.A2A5	General
1.A2A6-.A2Z	Local
	Study and teaching. Sunday schools
1.A3	General works
1.A32A-.A32Z	Individual schools. By city, A-Z
	History
1.A4-.Z3	General and country of origin
1.Z4A-.Z4Z	By ecclesiastical jurisdiction, A-Z e.g. Dioceses
1.Z5A-.Z5Z	By state, province, department, etc., A-Z
1.Z6A-.Z6Z	By city, A-Z
1.Z7A-.Z7Z	Other countries, A-Z
	General works. Collections, collected works, dictionaries, encyclopedias
2.A1-.A5	Several authors
2.A6-Z	Individual authors
3.A-.Z5	Doctrines, creeds, catechisms, liturgy, ritual, sacraments, government, discipline, membership
	Hymns see subclass BV
	Sermons. Tracts. Addresses. Essays
3.Z6A1-.Z6A5	Several authors
3.Z6A6-.Z6Z	Individual authors, A-Z
3.Z7A-.Z7Z	Special churches. By place, A-Z, or by name if nonurban
	Biography
3.Z8A1-.Z8A5	Collective
3.Z8A6-.Z8Z	Individual

	Use only for churches and denominations where indicated
.A1	Periodicals, societies, directories, yearbooks
	Official documents, governing boards, conferences
.A2A1-.A2A5	General
.A2A6-.A2Z	Local
	Study and teaching. Sunday schools
.A3	General works
.A32A-.A32Z	Individual schools. By city, A-Z
	History
.A4	General and country of origin
.A42A-.A42Z	By ecclesiastical jurisdiction, A-Z e.g. Dioceses
.A43A-.A43Z	By state, province, department, etc., A-Z
.A44A-.A44Z	By city, A-Z
.A45A-.A45Z	Other countries, A-Z
.A5-.Z4	General works. Collections, collected works, dictionaries, encyclopedias
.Z5	Doctrines, creeds, catechisms, liturgy, ritual, sacraments, government, discipline, membership
	Hymns see subclass BV
	Sermons. Tracts. Addresses. Essays
.Z6A1-.Z6A5	Several authors
.Z6A6-.Z6Z	Individual authors, A-Z
.Z7A-.Z7Z	Special churches. By place, A-Z, or by name if nonurban
	Biography
.Z8A1-.Z8A5	Collective
.Z8A6-.Z8Z	Individual, A-Z

TABLES

	Use only for churches and denominations where indicated
.x	Periodicals, societies, directories, yearbooks
	Official documents, governing boards, conferences
.x1A1-.x1A5	General
.x1A6-.x1Z	Local, A-Z
	Study and teaching. Sunday schools
.x2	General works
.x22A-.x22Z	Individual schools. By city, A-Z
	History
.x3	General and country of origin
.x32A-.x32Z	By ecclesiastical jurisdiction, A-Z e.g. Dioceses
.x33A-.x33Z	By state, province, department, etc., A-Z
.x34A-.x34Z	By city, A-Z
.x35A-.x35Z	Other countries, A-Z
	General works. Collections, collected works, dictionaries, encyclopedias
.x4A1-.x4A5	Several authors
.x4A6-.x4Z	Individual authors
.x5	Doctrines, creeds, catechisms, liturgy, ritual, sacraments, government, discipline, membership
	Hymns see subclass BV
	Sermons. Tracts. Addresses. Essays
.x6A1-.x6A5	Several authors
.x6A6-.x6Z	Individual authors, A-Z
.x7A-.x7Z	Special churches. By place, A-Z, or by name if nonurban
	Biography
.x8A1-.x8A5	Collective
.x8A6-.x8Z	Individual, A-Z

	Texts
.xA15	Polyglot. By date
.xA2	Greek. By date
.xA3	Latin. By date
.xA35	Syriac. By date
.xA4	Church Slavic. By date
.xA45	English. By date
.xA5-.xA59	Other languages Arrange alphabetically by language and date
.xA6-.xZ	General works

TABLES

0	Periodicals. Societies
1	Directories. Yearbooks
2	Documents
	Study and teaching
2.5	General works
	Education of the clergy and of religious men and women
2.6	General works
2.7.A-Z	By country, A-Z
2.8.A-Z	Seminaries, colleges, etc. By place, A-Z
	History
3	General works
4.A-Z	Local, A-Z
	Including individual dioceses, monasteries, and churches
5.A1-.A5	Collected works
5.A6-Z	General works
	Including catechisms
6	Sermons. Tracts. Addresses. Essays
	For collections see BX6 5.A1+
(7)	Ritual and liturgy
	see BX350.A1+
8	Other topics (not A-Z)
	Biography
9.A1	Collective
9.A3-Z	Individual, A-Z

.x	Periodicals. Societies
.x1	Directories. Yearbooks
.x2	Documents
	Study and teaching
.x25	General works
	Education of the clergy and of religious men and women
.x26	General works
.x27A-.x27Z	By country, A-Z
.x28A-.x28Z	Seminaries, colleges, etc. By place, A-Z
	History
.x3	General works
.x4A-.x4Z	Local, A-Z
	Including individual dioceses, monasteries, and churches
.x5A1-.x5A5	Collected works
.x5A6-.x5Z	General works
	Including catechisms
.x6	Sermons. Tracts. Addresses. Essays
	For collections see BX7 .x5A1+
(.x7)	Ritual and liturgy
	see BX350.A1+
.x8	Other topics (not A-Z)
	Biography
.x9A1	Collective
.x9A3-.x9Z	Individual, A-Z

TABLES

	Acts, etc.
.A2	Latin. By date
	Translations
.A3A-.A3Z	English. By translator, A-Z
.A4A-.A4Z	Other. By language, A-Z, and date
.A45A-.A45Z	Special documents. By first significant word of Latin title, A-Z
.A48	Indexes
.A49	Directories
.A5-.Z	Histories, etc.

	General
1.A1	Periodicals. Societies. Serials
1.A15	Congresses
1.A2	Collections
	Documents
1.A3	Collections
1.A35	Special. By date.
1.A4	Directories
	General works
1.A5	Early through 1800
1.A6-Z	1801-1950
1.2	1951-2000
1.3	2001-
2.A-Z	Local. By place, A-Z Including individual monasteries by city, A-Z, or by name if nonurban

.A1	Periodicals. Yearbooks. Congresses
	Documents
.A2	Collections
.A25	Special. By date
.A3	Directories
.A5-.Z	General works

1	General
1.A1	Periodicals. Yearbooks. Congresses
	Documents
1.A2	Collections
1.A25	Special. By date
1.A3	Directories
1.A5-Z	General works
2.A-Z	Country divisions, A-Z Including ecclesiastical jurisdictions, by place, A-Z
3.A-Z	Cities, A-Z Including individual monasteries and abbeys by city, A-Z, or by name if nonurban

.xA1	Collections. By date
.xA2-.xZ5	Special liturgical books. By date For the Ordo divini officii recitandi of each order, see BX1999
.xZ6-.xZ99	History and criticism

.A1	Polyglot texts
	Greek texts (Early to 4th century)
	see BV185
.A2	Latin texts. By date
.A3	Latin texts. By name and date
.A35	Manuscripts in facsimile. By name
	Translations
.A4A-.A4Z	English. By translator, A-Z, or date
.A5A-.A5Z	Other languages. By language, A-Z, and date
.A55	Adaptations for children
.A6-.Z	General works

	Texts
.x date	Latin. By date
.x2-.x29	Other languages. By language and date
.x3A-.x3Z	Criticism

.x date	Texts. By date
.x2-.x29	Translations, adaptations, etc.
.x3-.x39	Criticism, concordances, etc.

1	Periodicals. Societies. Serials
1.3	Collected works (nonserial)
1.5	Congresses
2.A1	Dictionaries. Encyclopedias
2.A15	Directories
	General works
2.A2	Early through 1800
2.A3-Z	1801-1950
2.2	1951-2000
2.3	2001-
3	Monastic life. Vows. Discipline, etc.
3.3	Lay brothers
	Rules. Instructions. Constitution, etc.
4.A2	Latin texts. By date
4.A4-.Z4	Other languages. By language, A-Z, and date
4.Z5	Commentaries
	Liturgy and ritual
	see BX2049
	Prayer books and devotions
	see BX2050
	Government and administration
4.4	General works
4.42	General chapters. Visitations
4.44	Local government
4.5	Relations with Rome, bishops, etc.
4.6	Superiors
	Controversial works against the order
5.A2	Early through 1800
5.A3-Z	1801-1950
5.2	1951-2000
5.3	2001-
	Missions
	see BV2245+
	History
	For individual monasteries, abbeys, etc., see BX2525.A+ BX2529.A+ etc.
	General works
6.A2	Early through 1800
6.A3-Z	1801-1950
6.2	1951-2000
6.3	2001-
	By region or country
	America. North America
7	General works
	United States
8	General works

History
By region or country
America. North America
United States -- Continued
9.A-.W By state, A-W
10.A-Z By city, etc., A-Z
Canada
11.A1 General works
11.A5-Z Local, A-Z
Mexico
12.A1 General works
12.A5-Z Local, A-Z
Central America
12.4 General works
12.5A-.5Z By country, A-Z
West Indies
12.6 General works
12.7A-.7Z By country, A-Z
13.5 Latin America
South America
14.A1 General works
14.A5-Z By country, A-Z
Europe
15 General works
Great Britain. England
16 General works
17.A-Z By English county, A-Z
18.A-Z By city, A-Z
By monastery
see BX2595.A+
Ireland
19 General works
20.A-Z By Irish county, A-Z
21.A-Z By city, A-Z
By monastery
see BX2602.A+
Scotland
22 General works
23.A-Z By Scottish region, A-Z
24.A-Z By city, A-Z
By monastery
see BX2599.A+
Wales
25 General works
26.A-Z By Welsh county, A-Z
27.A-Z By city, A-Z

History
By region or country
Europe
Scotland
By monastery
see BX2605.A+
Austria
28 General works
29.A-Z By country division, A-Z
For Bohemia, see BX16 45.C9
For the Czech Republic, see BX16 45.C9
30.A-Z By city, A-Z
France
31 General works
32.A-Z By country division, A-Z
33.A-Z By city, A-Z
Germany
34 General works
35.A-Z By country division, A-Z
36.A-Z By city, A-Z
Italy
37 General works
38.A-Z By country division, A-Z
39.A-Z By city, A-Z
Netherlands (Low countries). Holland
40.A1 General works
40.A5-Z Local, A-Z
Belgium
41.A1 General works
41.A5-Z Local, A-Z
Portugal
42.A1 General works
42.A5-Z Local, A-Z
Scandinavia
43.A1 General works
By country
Denmark
43.D4 General works
43.D5A-.D5Z Local, A-Z
Iceland
43.I2 General works
43.I3A-.I3Z Local, A-Z
Norway
43.N8 General works
43.N9A-.N9Z Local, A-Z
Sweden

	History
	By region or country
	Europe
	Scandinavia
	By country
	Sweden -- Continued
43.S8	General works
43.S9A-.S9Z	Local, A-Z
	Spain
44.A1	General works
44.A5-Z	Local, A-Z
45.A-Z	Other European regions or countries, A-Z
45.C9	Czech Republic. Bohemia
45.L5	Lithuania
45.P6	Poland
45.R8	Russia. Soviet Union
45.S9	Switzerland
	Asia
46.A1	General works
46.A5-Z	By country, A-Z
	Africa
47.A1	General works
47.A5-Z	By country, A-Z
	Australia and New Zealand
48.A1	General works
48.A5-Z	By country, A-Z
	Oceania
49.A1	General works
49.A5-Z	By island or group of islands, A-Z
49.5	Developing countries
50.A-Z	By congregation or province, A-Z
	Tertiaries. Third Order
51	General works
52.A-Z	Rules. Manuals and guides. By language, A-Z, and date
53.A-Z	By region or country, A-Z
54.A-Z	Other branches (not otherwise provided for), A-Z
	By region or country see BX16 7+
	Biography
55	Collective
(56)	Individual see BX4700+

TABLES

1	Periodicals. Societies. Collections, etc.
1.4	Directories
1.5	Documents. By date
	Including rules, constitutions, manuals, etc.
	For prayer books, see BX2060
2	General works
2.2	Government and administration
	Missions
	see BV2245+
3.A-Z	By region or country, A-Z
3.6.A-Z	By congregation, province, etc., A-Z
	Biography
3.7	Collective
	Individual
3.8	Foundresses (except saints) (not A-Z)
	Other
	see BX4700+
4.A-Z	Individual houses of women. By city, A-Z, or by name if nonurban
	Including convents, abbeys, priories, etc.

.A1 Periodicals. Societies. Collections, etc.
.A2 Directories
.A3 Documents. By date
Including rules, constitutions, manuals, etc.
For prayer books, see BX2050
.A4-.Z4 General works
Including history, purpose, vows, discipline, etc.
.Z45 Government and administration
Missions
see BV2245+
.Z5A-.Z5Z By region or country, A-Z
.Z6A-.Z6Z By congregation, province, A-Z
Biography
.Z7 Collective
Individual
.Z8 Foundresses (except saints) (not A-Z)
For founders of religious orders for men see BX4700+
Other individual
see BX4700+
.Z9A-.Z9Z Individual houses of women. By city, A-Z, or by name if nonurban
Including convents, abbeys, priories, etc.
For monasteries, abbeys, etc., for men see BX2525+

TABLES

.A1 General works. Collections

.A3-.Z Individual cities or churches. By city, A-Z, or by name of church if nonurban

Under each city, use A2 and date for general works and collections

.x	General works. Collections
.x2A-.x2Z	By city, A-Z Including individual churches, by city, A-Z, or by name if nonurban

.x1	Periodicals. Societies
.x12	Congresses. Councils. Synods
.x125	Directories
.x13	Documents
	Collections
.x14	Several authors
.x15	Individual authors
	History
.x2	General works
	By period
.x22	To 1917
.x23	1918-
.x25	Outside of native area
	General works. Doctrine. Government
.x32	Early to 1800
.x33	1801-1950
.x34	1951-2000
.x35	2001-
.x4.A-Z	Ecclesiastical jurisdictions; patriarchates, ex-archates, dioceses, etc., A-Z
	Canon law
.x52	Documents
.x55	Treatises
	Liturgy and ritual
.x62	General collections
.x63	History and criticism
.x65.A-Z	Special books. By title, A-Z *Under each:* *.x* — *Texts. By date* *.x3A-.x3Z* — *Criticism*
.x67	Lay folk's books
.x68	Hagiography. Icons (not A-Z)
	Sermons
.x69	Several authors
.x692.A-Z	Individual authors. By author and title, A-Z
	Christian life. Spiritual life
.x7	General works
.x72	Devotional literature
	Monasticism
.x74	General works
.x75	Collections
.x76	Orders Whenever established for Eastern monasticism
.x77	Orders of the Roman Church adapted to the East. Inter-ritual orders

.x8.A-Z	Individual churches, monasteries, etc., A-Z. By place or by name if nonurban
	Biography
	Saints
.x9	Collective
.x92.A-Z	Individual, A-Z
	Other
.x94	Collective
.x95.A-Z	Individual, A-Z

	Conferences
1	General
2.A-Z	Local, A-Z
	History
3	General works
	By region or country
	United States
3.2	General works
3.3.A-Z	By region or state, A-Z
3.4.A-Z	Other regions or countries, A-Z
4	General works. Doctrine. Government and discipline

0	Periodicals. Societies. Yearbooks
1	Congresses
3	History. General and the United States
	United States
4.A-.W	By state, A-W
5.A-Z	By city, A-Z
6.A-Z	Other countries, A-Z
7	General works. Doctrine, etc.
	Hymns
	see BV380+
8	Government and discipline
	Biography
	see BX6453+ BX6493+

TABLES

0	Periodicals. Societies. Yearbooks
0.1	Congresses
0.3	History. General and the United States
	United States
0.4.A-.W	By state, A-W
0.5.A-Z	By city, A-Z
0.6.A-Z	Other countries, A-Z
0.7	General works. Doctrine, etc.
	Hymns
	see BV380+
0.8	Government and discipline
	Biography
	see BX6453+ BX6493+

.x	Periodicals. Societies. Yearbooks
.x1	Congresses
.x3	History. General and the United States
	United States
.x4.A-.W	By state, A-W
.x5.A-Z	By city, A-Z
.x6.A-Z	Other countries, A-Z
.x7	General works. Doctrine, etc.
	Hymns
	see BV380+
.x8	Government and discipline
	Biography
	see BX6453+ BX6493+

TABLES

0	Periodicals. Societies. Yearbooks, etc.
1	Conferences
	History
	Including collective biography
3	General, and the United States
	United States
	General works see BX26 3
4.A-.W	By state, A-W
5.A-Z	By city, A-Z
6.A-Z	Other countries, A-Z
7	General works. Doctrine, etc.
	Hymns in English
	see BV416
	Hymns in languages other than English
	see BV470+
8	Government and discipline
9.A-Z	Individual biography, A-Z

.x1	Texts in Latin. By date
.x1A-.x1Z5	Excerpts in Latin. By English name of excerpt
.x1Z7-.x1Z8	Miscellaneous selections in Latin
.x2	Texts in English. By date
.x2A-.x2Z5	Excerpts in English. By English name of excerpt
.x2Z7-.x2Z8	Miscellaneous selections in English
.x21-.x28	Texts in other languages (alphabetically)
.x29	Criticism

0	Periodicals Yearbooks. Directories
1	Conferences. Assemblies, etc.
	History
2	General works
3.A-.W	By state, A-W
4.A-Z	By city, A-Z
5	Doctrines, creeds, catechisms, liturgy
6	Government and discipline
	For trials, see BX9192+
7.A-Z	Synods, A-Z
8.A-Z	Presbyteries, A-Z
	Churches
	see BX9211

.x	Periodicals Yearbooks. Directories
.x1	Conferences. Assemblies, etc.
	History
.x2	General works
	Including collective biography
.x3.A-.W	By state, A-W
.x4.A-Z	By city, A-Z
.x5	Doctrines, creeds, catechisms, liturgy
.x6	Government and discipline
	For trials, see BX9192+
.x7.A-Z	Synods, A-Z
.x8.A-Z	Presbyteries, A-Z
	Churches
	see BX9211

TABLES

0	Periodicals. Societies. Movements
1	Collections
2	Documents
	General works. History, doctrine, government
3	Early through 1800 (except sermons)
4	1801-1950
4.2	1951-2000
4.3	2001-
	Liturgy and ritual see BX9427
	Hymns in English see BV433
	Hymns in languages other than English see BV470+
5	Sermons. Tracts. Addresses. Essays
6.A-Z	By country division, A-Z
7.A-Z	By city, A-Z
	Biography
9.A1	Collective
9.A3-Z	Individual, A-Z

0	Periodicals. Societies
0.5	Dictionaries. Encyclopedias
1	Documents. Councils, etc.
	History
	General works
2	Early through 1800
3	1801-1950
3.2	1951-2000
3.3	2001-
4.A-Z	By country, A-Z
4.5.A-Z	By city, town, etc., A-Z
	e.g.
4.5.J4	Jerusalem
	General works. Doctrine, etc.
5	Early through 1800
6	1801-1950
6.2	1951-2000
6.3	2001-
6.6	Sermons
	Liturgy and ritual
7.A1	Polyglot. By date
7.A2	Original language. By date
7.A3	English. By date
7.A5A-.A5Z	Other languages, A-Z
7.A6-Z	History, treatises, etc.
	Church year
7.13	General works
7.14	Fasts and feasts
7.15	Christian life. Spiritual life
7.2	Monasticism
7.3	Monasticism for women
8.A-Z	Individual churches, monasteries, etc. By place and name, A-Z, or by name, A-Z
	Biography
9.A1	Collective
9.A3-Z	Individual, A-Z

1	General (Table BX10)
	By period
	Pre-Reformation period
	see BR745+
2	Reformation to Catholic Emancipation Act, 1517-1829. Protestant persecution of Catholics
3	1801-1945
3.2	1945-
	Local
4.A-Z	Counties, etc., A-Z
5.A-Z	Ecclesiastical jurisdictions. By place, A-Z
6.A-Z	Cities, A-Z

1	General (Table BX10)
	Local
2.A-Z	Country divisions, A-Z
	Including ecclesiastical jurisdictions, by place, A-Z
3.A-Z	Cities, A-Z

	Texts
.A1	Polyglot
.A2	Greek
.A3A-.A3Z	Other ancient texts. By language, A-Z, and date e.g.
.A3L3	Latin
.A3S8	Syriac
.A4	Russian. By date
.A5	English. By translator (or editor), A-Z, and date
.A6A-.A6Z	Other languages, A-Z, and date e.g.
.A6C45	Church Slavic
.A6G4	German
.A7-.Z	History, treatises, etc.

A

INDEX

INDEX

D

INDEX

INDEX

INDEX

INDEX

O

Q

R

INDEX

INDEX

W

GPO U.S. GOVERNMENT PRINTING OFFICE: 2008–340–014/60027